Friendship and the Novel

Friendship *and the* Novel

Edited by
Allan Hepburn

McGill-Queen's University Press
Montreal & Kingston • London • Chicago

ISBN 978-0-2280-2006-6 (cloth)
ISBN 978-0-2280-2037-0 (paper)
ISBN 978-0-2280-2007-3 (ePDF)
ISBN 978-0-2280-2008-0 (ePUB)

Legal deposit first quarter 2024
Bibliothèque nationale du Québec

Printed in Canada on acid-free paper that is 100% ancient forest free (100% post-consumer recycled), processed chlorine free

Funded by the Government of Canada | Financé par le gouvernement du Canada | Canada

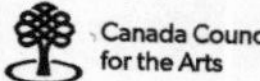

We acknowledge the support of the Canada Council for the Arts.
Nous remercions le Conseil des arts du Canada de son soutien.

McGill-Queen's University Press in Montreal is on land which long served as a site of meeting and exchange amongst Indigenous Peoples, including the Haudenosaunee and Anishinabeg nations. In Kingston it is situated on the territory of the Haudenosaunee and Anishinaabek. We acknowledge and thank the diverse Indigenous Peoples whose footsteps have marked these territories on which peoples of the world now gather.

Library and Archives Canada Cataloguing in Publication

Title: Friendship and the novel / edited by Allan Hepburn.
Names: Hepburn, Allan, editor.
Description: Includes bibliographical references and index.
Identifiers: Canadiana (print) 20230524672 | Canadiana (ebook) 20230524702 | ISBN 9780228020066 (cloth) | ISBN 9780228020370 (paper) | ISBN 9780228020080 (EPUB) | ISBN 9780228020073 (ePDF)
Subjects: LCSH: English fiction—19th century—History and criticism. | LCSH: English fiction—20th century—History and criticism. | LCSH: Friendship in literature.
Classification: LCC PR868.F75 F75 2024 | DDC 823/.809353—dc23

For Maria DiBattista
whose friendship is a blessing

Contents

Part Three: Modern Instances

Part Four: Contemporary Friendships

Acknowledgments

On 5–6 May 2022, thirteen scholars met in Montreal for a colloquium on the subject of "Friendship and the Novel." At that event, presentations probed the patterns, singularities, and complexities of novelistic friendships; those presentations form the basis of the chapters in this collection. That colloquium was generously funded by a research grant from the Fonds de recherche du Québec – Société et culture (FRQSC). Other funds were provided by the James McGill Chair in Twentieth-Century Literature at McGill University. I owe a particular debt of thanks to Isabelle Daunais, principal investigator of "Travaux sur les arts du roman" and a wizard at writing grant applications. Over the years, Xander Manshel and Tabitha Sparks have generously offered insights into the art, ends, and techniques of the novel, as well as excellent tips on what to read. Robert Lecker has provided inspiration and conversation in equal measure. I am grateful to Lindsay Holmgren for logistical advice. For technical support, I owe thanks to Pascale Théorêt-Groulx.

Two anonymous readers gave insightful and helpful feedback on this collection of essays. Their comments have made this book better than it was. Jonathan Crago has been a resourceful and supportive proponent of this project from its early stages through its completion. I would be remiss if I did not make special mention of Philip Cercone, with whom I have worked for many years at McGill-Queen's University Press, not only on this book but also on many others.

Several friends have died in the past few years, and I miss each of them more than I can say. Thirty years ago, Douglas Chambers put in a good word on my behalf at the University of Toronto, where I started my university teaching career, and to him I owe sincere thanks for his mentorship and wisdom. David Blewett and Arthur Sheps had a tremendous gift for friendship, "like sparks among the stubble," that brought people into their house and their ambit, and I am happy to count myself among them. Over many years in Montreal, Ken Woodman and Ted Phillips never failed in their hospitality or good humour: their laughter filled rooms. Michael Ciciretto, who died suddenly at sixty-one, knew the value of old friends – their shared experience, their irreplaceability – and I cherish his memory. In some ways, this book aims not just to account for friendships that grow over time but also to reckon with the legacies that friends bequeath in their passing.

Friendship and the Novel

Introduction

Friendship and the Novel: Plot, Feeling, Form

ALLAN HEPBURN

Why do so many novels feature friends – old friends, best friends, childhood friends, friends in need, frenemies, friends in high places, friends who become lovers, lovers who want to remain friends after a breakup, family friends, late-life friends? Is the novel even conceivable without the familiar figure of the friend? In their various guises, friends inhabit the zones of affection and intimacy that comprise private life. Fictional characters, like their counterparts in reality, turn to friends to talk over existential and emotional conundrums. Henry James, theorizing one kind of novelistic friendship, calls a protagonist's confidant a *ficelle*, who, through conversation, fully engages with the perplexities that a principal character faces and helps surmount those problems, as Maria Gostrey does for Lambert Strether in *The Ambassadors*. In some instances, friends establish the possibilities of the *Bildungsroman* by suggesting to protagonists options about how to think, act, or feel in given situations. Whatever else it entails, friendship is a form of trust. It allows for shared experience without constraining the freedom of either party. Friends may respond to an event in different ways, and the discrepancies between their responses nourish the friendship rather than limit it. In its ideal form, friendship is intimate yet selfless, disinterested yet sympathetic, fulfilling yet liable to end at any moment.

Friendship has a decisive bearing on plot, character, feeling, and novelistic form. Many novels publicize the interactions and experiences of friendship in their titles, such as Elizabeth Sandham's *Friendship*, Charles Dickens's *Our*

Mutual Friend, Anatole France's *Le livre de mon ami*, Elizabeth Bowen's *Friends and Relations*, Anita Brookner's *Family and Friends*, Maeve Binchy's *Circle of Friends*, Paek Nam-nyong's *The Friend*, Hervé Guibert's autofictional *To the Friend Who Did Not Save My Life*, John le Carré's *Absolute Friends*, Lisa Wingate's *The Book of Lost Friends*, Kamila Shamsie's *Best of Friends*, Sigrid Nunez's *The Friend*, Sally Rooney's *Conversations with Friends*, and Elena Ferrante's immensely popular *L'amica geniale*, translated into English as *My Brilliant Friend*. Some novels dwell on the intensity and magnitude of friendship, while others concern inappropriate or bad friends who actively undermine relationships. The end of friendship sets the parameters for the plot of some novels, while others focus on reconciliation and forgiveness between estranged friends. No matter how it is represented, friendship has a natural affinity with the novel in terms of plot trajectories and structures of feeling.

Defining friendship is notoriously difficult. More often than not, attempts lead to character analysis and illustrative stories, if not rhapsodies and euphemisms. According to the OED, a friend is a close acquaintance, an ally, a sympathizer, a supporter, a helper, a kinsman, a kindred spirit, a patron, or "a person with whom one has developed a close and informal relationship of mutual trust and intimacy."[1] When friendship crosses languages, its meanings necessarily shift. In Garth Greenwell's *What Belongs to You*, an American teacher of English in Sofia has sex with a male prostitute named Mitko, who uses the word *priyateli*, the Bulgarian word for "friends," to refer variously to clients, lovers, online contacts, or fellows from whom he can cadge money, as if friendship had too many nuances to settle into a single meaning.[2] Befriending someone who speaks a different language, as happens in Greenwell's novel, can lead to misunderstandings about motives and degrees of feeling, and those misunderstandings compromise the sincerity of the friendship.

Patterns of friendship change from one culture to another and from one epoch to another. In Victorian fiction, siblings often provide a template for friendship: what one learns from brothers or sisters translates into behaviour outside the family. Nineteenth-century orphans – Becky Sharp, Oliver Twist, Jane Eyre, Tom Sawyer – have to prove their reliability as friends without having had the advantage of an upbringing among siblings. In modern fiction, friends tend to be less anchored in family and more subject to social contingencies brought about by mobility, urban anonymity, and work. In *To the Lighthouse*, William Bankes and Lily Briscoe feel affinities for each other, even though they seldom meet; however, they do not feel that they must marry in order to solidify their friendship, despite Mrs Ramsay's fervent wishes that they do so. In this regard, friendship exists outside marriage and provides a respite from domestic routine. Many contemporary novels instrumentalize friendship, insofar as close friends turn out to be rivals in disguise. Friendship in contemporary fiction therefore tends toward betrayal and disillusionment, like the on-again, off-again relationship between Frances and Bobbi in *Conversations with Friends*.

Regardless of the era in which a novel is written, friends create a narrative structure – the friendship plot, I will call it – in which characters help each other and promote intellectual and emotional growth. The friendship plot establishes limits, patterns, and possibilities for interaction – a way of being that is singular to each friendship. The friendship plot may apply to people from the same social milieu or from diverse backgrounds, which allows novels to investigate whether friendship equalizes differences between parties or re-inscribes those differences as unbridgeable obstacles. Friends may be same-sex or opposite sex, and eroticism may or may not be encoded in friendship, according to the degree of affection or attraction between parties. This structure has stages and unfolds over time, which explains why the novel, as a temporal genre, naturally favours the representation of friendship. The duration of the plot is not fixed in advance, because the duration of a friendship is never predictable. In the friendship plot, the most common sequence of events is a meeting of friends, followed by interruption or falling out, then reunion.

Not all plots, of course, are so straightforward. Some friendships fizzle out because of changing circumstances, the intrusion of spouses, or indifference; others end catastrophically with harsh words, tantrums, violence, and recriminations. Regardless of its configuration, the friendship plot offers lessons about how to relate to other people, how to discern friends from enemies, and how to belong to the world through friendship.

Thinking Friendship

Literary criticism about friendship is surprisingly thin, and, more often than not, it dwells on female friendships. As she charts five kinds of novelistic friendship – sentimental, erotic, manipulative, political, and social – Janet

Todd notes that in "female friendship the heroine can momentarily forget the feminine image she must create for a man and relax from the strenuous demands of romantic love."[3] Second-wave feminism enriches the vocabulary for female friendships, often with reference to lesbian couples. After discussing the long history of same-sex friendships and sexual liaisons between women, Lillian Faderman concludes that "love between women, coupled with their emerging freedom, might conceivably bring about the overthrow of heterosexuality."[4] In the same vein, Martha Vicinus observes that women in the long nineteenth century "constructed same-sex intimacy as a narrative of romantic or spiritual discovery."[5] In *Between Women*, Sharon Marcus disputes the opposition between heterosexual and queer relations in nineteenth-century studies: "Family life incorporated friendship between women; consumer culture was saturated with female homoeroticism; and multiple social networks included women in marital relationships with other women."[6]

Whereas Faderman, Vicinus, and Marcus dwell on female friendships, other critics, notably Eve Kosofsky Sedgwick in *Between Men* and Tom Roach in *Friendship as a Way of Life*, focus on male friendships, either in terms of homosociality or solidarity in the face of the AIDS crisis. Sedgwick, who is manifestly more intrigued by erotic desire than by friendship, hypothesizes "the potential unbrokenness of a continuum between homosocial and homosexual."[7] Although desire may animate some male-male relations, it does not animate all of them, nor does homosociality capture the shape or dimensions of every male friendship.

As against literary criticism, philosophy has a rich tradition of discussing friendship. In *Nicomachean Ethics*, Aristotle claims that friendship enhances life in its spiritual and affective dimensions rather than its material ones: "without friends no one would choose to live, though he had all other goods."[8] In Cicero's *De Amicitia*, which has been translated rather cheerfully into English under the title *How to Be a Friend* – as if it were an advice manual along the lines of Dale Carnegie's *How To Win Friends and Influence People* – the Roman statesman and thinker praises friends as "the finest and most beautiful adornment of life."[9] Yet there is no friendship without risk, as both Aristotle and Cicero note. The greater the friendship, states Aristotle, "the more exposed it is to risk."[10] At the same time, the greater the risk of friendship, the more intense its satisfactions may be, for risk has the advantage of heightening as well as diminishing returns. "When someone does a great service or takes a great risk for a friend," writes Cicero, "who doesn't shower that person with the highest praise?"[11] By the logic of this rhetorical question, the risk itself is a proof of friendship.

Whether expressed through risk, sympathy, sacrifice, or other indicators, friendship is a form of selflessness. Genuine friendship, as Aristotle and Cicero both claim, is its own end: it seeks nothing beyond itself, neither pleasure nor advantage, although those benefits may accrue to friendship collaterally. As Cicero states, "friendship doesn't result from advantage, but advantage results from friendship."[12] Friends add lustre to existence by enhancing the intellectual and emotional dividends of experience. To share an experience with a friend is to refract it through a second point of view and thus multiply its pleasure and interest. A genuine friend, a friend whose goodwill, judgment, trustworthiness, and generosity remain beyond all doubt, is, as Cicero claims, "quite simply, another self."[13]

Time and familiarity are required for trust to develop. Those people who offer their friendship too readily may have hidden motives. "Like wine," Cicero states in a metaphor that makes a virtue of maturity, "an old friend grows more delightful with time."[14] In this sense, friendship has a temporality – long or short – as well as an intensity and a style. Certainly, not all friendships survive. Some acquaintanceships fail because one of the friends falls into bad company or unacceptable habits. Cicero makes the point that friendships of utility, in which one party gains an advantage from the other, "will end when that person has nothing left to give us."[15] Friendships that no longer generate emotional satisfaction are also apt to end. In this regard, the duration of the friendship cannot be known from the outset, but it informs the friendship plot as it moves through acquaintance, flourishing, trust, and mutual pleasure, before declining into suspicion, treachery, animosity, and anger, and finally being extinguished by bitterness or disaffection.

Old friends are not inevitably the best friends, but they have withstood the test of time and have proven their steadfastness and integrity to whatever degree they are capable. In *Robinson Crusoe*, a friendship plot endures for decades despite long interruptions. Before he sets sail for Guinea, where he intends to buy slaves, Crusoe entrusts his property to several plantation owners and writes a will leaving his estate to a Portuguese sea captain who had previously saved his life. When he returns years later, after shipwreck and survival on a desert island, Crusoe discovers that his wealth has grown considerably under the stewardship of the plantation owners. For a reckoning of his affairs, he calls upon the sea captain, whom he refers to as "my old Friend."[16] Although the captain has had his own reversals of fortune, he has watched over Crusoe's business interests conscientiously while awaiting his return. Crusoe is touched by the captain's fidelity, which he understands as a sign of friendship: "remembring what he had done for me, how he had taken me up at Sea, and how generously he had used me on all Occasions, and particularly, how sincere a Friend he was now to me, I could hardly refrain [from] Weeping."[17] If the sea captain's selfless behaviour can be used as a guide, a sincere friend appears at timely intervals and intervenes in one's destiny. A sincere friend never loses hope that his absent friend will return; meanwhile, he looks after every aspect of the absentee's commercial and personal affairs. This true friend acts from reasonable motives and gives an honest account of his actions. The temporality of the friendship knows no bounds: it withstands adversity and stretches indefinitely into the future.

The Portuguese captain exemplifies the virtues of friendship set forth in Plato's *Lysis*, Aristotle's *Nicomachean Ethics*, Cicero's *How to Be a Friend*, and Montaigne's "Of Friendship" – a roster of texts that name the pursuit of virtue as the chief glory of friendship. According to Aristotle, "Perfect friendship is the friendship of men who are good, and alike in virtue; for these wish well alike to each other *qua* good, and they are good in themselves."[18] As Aristotle acknowledges, certain friendships exist for utility or pleasure, but they are inferior to friendship pursued for its own sake. From Plato onward, almost every classical commentary on friendship dwells on goodness as the chief end of friendship. Aristotle defines the superior kind of friendship in terms of virtue: "the good man in becoming a friend becomes a good to his friend."[19] In antiquity, this sort of friendship is usually found between two male athletes, warriors, or citizens; rare though these good men may be, when they meet, they recognize their shared virtue and willingness to sacrifice all they have for the other person. As Cicero states with regard to this ideal, "Nothing is more appealing in another person than virtue, for nothing draws us more to love and admire someone."[20]

Like Plato and Aristotle, Cicero believes that "friendship is not possible except between good people."[21] He concedes that a pair of rogues may league together, but he does not believe that their alliance constitutes true friendship. The possibilities for betrayal are too great. A rogue will always be a rogue; because he is deceitful by nature, he cannot be trusted, certainly not as a friend. Ideally, friendship draws out, enhances, and ennobles the goodness of each person. In this sense, friendship is an ethical commitment – as the Portuguese captain demonstrates with regard to Crusoe's estate during his long absence – and that commitment can survive the death of one of the friends. In *Lysis*, Socrates argues that good people love what is good in others and, by emulating that goodness, make it increase. Friends thus set moral standards against which others measure themselves.

Yet Socrates also wonders about the self-sufficiency of good people. If they are good in themselves, why do they need friends to identify and extol their goodness? One possible answer to this conundrum pertains to the perfectibility of people. Socrates argues that "there's one thing, alone, to which one thing, alone, becomes friend: the neither good nor bad becomes friend to the good."[22] In this ambiguous statement, he appears to mean that people who are not purely good or purely bad take the opportunity to befriend someone who is better than they are themselves. Through friendship, they improve their own quota of goodness. In such a model, friendship does not have to occur between people with the same proportion of good and bad, nor does friendship provide a perfectly reciprocal exchange between people at the same level of goodness or badness. Every person is perfectible, and friendship helps along that human perfectibility.

Philosophers tend to define friendship as a relationship outside age, class, race, religion, gender, age, or other differences. In this regard, friendship erases differences and establishes similitudes, even self-identification. When Montaigne declares that perfect friendship "has no other model than itself, and can be compared only with itself,"[23] he deliberately echoes Cicero's idea of the friend as another self. "The power of friendship," Cicero remarks, "is that it makes, as it were, several souls into one."[24] If two or more friends' souls blend into one, inequalities disappear under the levelling forces of love, selflessness, and solidarity. According to Aristotle, who more realistically understands that individuals remain themselves despite the equalizing power of friendship, love should be proportional to each party. Between friends who are unlike in any way whatsoever, proportion "equalizes the parties and preserves the friendship."[25]

Reciprocity reconciles differences without dissolving them, which leads to the possibility that friendship survives because of differences, not in spite of them. Even before he makes this remark about proportion, Aristotle qualifies it: "the better [person] should be more loved than he loves, and so should the more useful."[26] He means that the party possessing greater stature, whether in terms of prestige or power, should have the magnanimity to bestow upon his friend whatever gifts are within his power. He should spend his wealth if that expenditure allows his friend to gain more.[27] Selfless gestures, according to Aristotle's logic, dignify both friends.

Friendship plots in novels test the dignity of individuals over and against differences in social stature, race, class, and other factors, although the results are not always quite what Aristotle and Cicero imagine. In Jane Austen's *Emma*, Emma Woodhouse befriends Harriet Smith, although the two young women are very different in station, Emma being wealthy and Harriet being of obscure parentage. In short, Harriet is "not the superior young woman which Emma's friend ought to be."[28] When Emma tries to match Harriet with Mr Elton, the local vicar, she hoists her friend above her social rank and seriously misjudges Harriet's abilities. Emma champions Harriet instead of showing true friendship, in which the just assessment of character has to play its part.

By contrast, in Charles Dickens' *Hard Times*, Sissy Jupe, despite being the daughter of a lowly circus performer, proves a true friend to Louisa Bounderby, unhappy wife of a bombastic industrialist. Sissy's capacity for compassion reduces the differences between her and Louisa. Sissy loves Louisa for her qualities of character, even when they are obscured by misjudgments and temptations: "I have always loved you, and have always wished that you should know it. But you changed to me a little, shortly before you left home. Not that I wondered at it. You knew so much, and I knew so little, and it was so natural in many ways, going as you were among other friends, that I had nothing to complain of, and was not at all hurt."[29] In the friendship plot, the genuine friend wishes her friend every success and rejoices in her happiness, even if she knows that her friend's choices are misguided.

Friendships, by their very nature, are affectionate, and affection sometimes tips over into sexual intimacy. In *Lysis*, Socrates dispenses advice to Hippothales, who is in love with a young man named Lysis. He recommends that Hippothales not overpraise Lysis until he is sure of his love, "out of fear for how the future will turn out."[30] If Lysis scorns him, Hippothales can at least retrieve his dignity. Plato's dialogue turns on the difference between lovers and friends without satisfactorily distinguishing one from the other, nor does the dialogue fully separate physical love from charitable feeling or friendship per se. *Eros* shares a lot of terrain with *agape* and *philia*, no matter how carefully the terms are parsed. For his part, Montaigne distinguishes the "fickle flame" of sexual ardour from the "constant and settled warmth" of friendship.[31] Whereas erotic desire has fleshly ends and can be temporarily satiated, friendship has spiritual ends and grows in proportion to its being nourished. Although Montaigne dismisses "licentious Greek love," he often sees the spectre of eroticism, even homoeroticism, between friends, as when he urges that, in true friendships, "each one [should] give himself so wholly to his friend that he has nothing left to distribute elsewhere."[32]

Sex complicates – or on occasion fulfills – the friendship plot. In Mary Renault's historical novel, *The Last of the Wine*, set in ancient Athens at the time of the Theban invasion, a runner named Alexias falls in love with beautiful and slightly older wrestler named Lysis. (Renault deliberately alludes to Plato's dialogue.) Once they overcome their shyness and exchange vows of fidelity, Alexias and Lysis share everything: travels, sorrows, kisses, Olympic glory, boar hunts, and military campaigns. Sexual intimacy is an attribute of their friendship. Their fellow soldiers are, in Alexias' words, "kind to our friendship. The usual jokes were made, but without any malice."[33] Humbled by Lysis' love, Alexias invokes worth as the constitutive element of their relationship, along the lines set forth by Aristotle and Cicero: "he was too good for me. Often it has seemed to me that it was only he who made me a man."[34] When Lysis dies in a battle that frees Athens from Theban tyranny, Alexias describes the posterity of their friendship not in terms of lasting virtue but in terms of alienation: "I was as a stranger to the earth, and to my own soul."[35] Lysis' friendship, as long as it lasts, makes Alexias feel at home in the world and makes him a friend to himself. With the death of Lysis, he loses the integral part of living that accommodated him in the world.

Alexias and Lysis bond as lovers and as Athenian citizens. As *The Last of the Wine* implies, friendships are, by their very nature, political, in that they provide a basis for social relations. Aristotle draws an explicit connection between kinship and democracy: citizens behave toward each other as brothers do. In democracies, founded on fraternity, "the ideal is for the citizens to be equal and fair."[36] Citizens are not actually brothers; instead, they behave as brothers, and that fraternity forms the basis of democracy – an assembly of friends. By further analogous reasoning, the identification of the good in individuals can be extrapolated to the identification and pursuit of the common good. Within tyrannies, by contrast, there are no friends, nor justice either. A perfect or perfectible political system would expand the mutual respect and reliance that friends show each other to impersonal respect and reliance, which is to say that, in a democracy, all strangers should be treated as friends. In *The Politics of Friendship*, Jacques Derrida refers to the "responsibility" within friendship and more particularly to "responsible friendship *before* reason, when reason makes the Idea of equality an obligation."[37] The gist of this responsibility is to recognize strangers not as enemies but as equals and potential friends, and to do so spontaneously, irrespective of legal requirements to treat strangers as equals.

The Friendship Plot

The friendship plot has a general arc with infinite variations: people meet; they warm to each other; they share experiences; they consolidate their mutual respect and affinity by staying in touch; they lose sight of each other, or they decide to end the friendship altogether. Depending on which aspects of this arc are included in the narrative – not all novels dwell on every element in the trajectory – the friendship plot may move into the genres of comedy, tragedy, melodrama, or romance. In some cases, a sidekick turns out to be a friend, as Sancho Panza becomes for Don Quixote. In other novels, friendship, even the most incipient kind, devolves into outright hostility, as when Razumov betrays Haldin to the police for no particular reason in *Under Western Eyes*. Tragedy, it might be said, is the result of repudiated friendship or denial of those who seek a helping hand. Whether comic or tragic, the friendship plot runs alongside and intersects with other novelistic possibilities, such as plots that revolve around marriage, seduction, murder, war, or the rise from rags to riches.

In many friendship plots, a pair of friends function as protagonists, although there may be some jostling for priority between them. In Alain-Fournier's *Le Grand Meaulnes*, Augustin Meaulnes – a tall, charismatic seventeen-year-old – is a natural leader who gives everything he does a touch of the "extraordinary."[38] He vivifies life with his risk-taking and adventures, certainly in the eyes of François Seurel, the fifteen-year-old schoolboy who narrates the story. Sometimes friends are lesser or minor characters who assist, soothe, teach, or admire the protagonist, much as Herbert Pocket does with Pip in *Great Expectations*. These supporting characters facilitate their friends' growth by drawing lessons from experience. In contradistinction to novels that feature duos, some novels concentrate on clusters of friends. Mary McCarthy's *The Group*, Muriel Spark's *The Girls of Slender Means*, and Hanya Yanagihara's *A Little Life*, for example, explore the dynamics of people united by mutual interests or shared experience.

Even if the roster of characters is limited, and the possibilities of friendship are therefore circumscribed, it is virtually impossible to think of a novel that does not include friends. Beckett's novels – *Murphy*, *Molloy*, *Watt*, *Malone Dies*, *The Unnamable* – have very few characters and even fewer friendships. Existentialist fiction has a special line in friendlessness. In Jean-Paul Sartre's *Nausea*, Antoine Roquentin makes fun of an autodidact who professes his love for humanity: "At heart he is as lonely as I am: no one cares about him. Only he doesn't realize his solitude."[39]

Anti-heroes are, by definition, loners; their flaws set them apart. In Albert Camus's *The Outsider*, Meursault, a friendless type if ever there was one, has a manipulative neighbour named Raymond Sintès who inveigles him into writing a letter to a girlfriend, a gesture that gives Meursault a glimpse into the murkier corners of another man's intimacies. "You're a real pal," Sintès tells him after he writes the letter, which causes Meursault to think, without saying aloud, "I didn't care one way or another about being pals."[40] Sintès subsequently invites Meursault to the beach for a weekend with the ulterior motive of having an extra person around to fend off the angry brothers of his girlfriend, an Arab woman whom he has beaten up more than once. Meursault takes this gesture for what it is, a *quid pro quo*, even though he implicates himself in several criminal acts by helping Sintès. "Was he your friend?"[41] the judge asks Sintès at Meursault's trial for murder, then repeats the question to Meursault. Both admit their friendship with understandable reluctance. In Camus' novel, claiming to be someone's friend is tantamount to being an accomplice in a crime. *Nausea* and *The Outsider* both promote the idea that friends inhibit existential freedom: they create complications instead of solutions. Nonetheless, neither novel dispenses with friendly figures, tawdry and manipulative though they may be.

Irrespective of the number of friends who figure in a novel, the friendship plot regularly offers tips on how to be a good friend, either by example or by principle. In this regard, novels continue the line of inquiry about friendship developed by Plato, Aristotle, Cicero, and Montaigne. "True friends should give faithful advice to each other,"[42] Cicero aphorizes in *How to Be a Friend*. Among the "chief duties of friendship," Montaigne states in "Of Friendship," are "admonitions and corrections."[43] In the friendship plot, friends talk over their reactions to situations and possible ways of proceeding; they advise each other. Yet this advisory role comes with a caveat: the friend's advice should be free of ulterior motives. To give bad advice intentionally is a betrayal of the duties, as well as the spirit, of friendship. Beyond counsel, the friend has to have the honesty to identify errors of behaviour, reasoning, or judgment and reprove a friend.

By virtue of their advisory function, friendship plots promote social integration. In Elizabeth Sandham's *Friendship*, a cautionary tale "designed for young people," the family is the prototype for tolerance and friendship. Two sisters, Charlotte and Maria Darford, exhibit no "rivalship."[44] Instead, they praise each other's virtues, correct each other's faults, read books for edification, and uplift all those who have the good fortune to belong among their circle of friends. The friendship between sisters extends to outsiders, who are treated with the same consideration and firm moral standards as family members. The sisters exude goodwill toward everyone regardless of status, age, or achievements. In a characteristic utterance, Charlotte claims, "it always gives me pleasure to see others pleased."[45]

Friendship offers no end of sensible advice about how to discern genuine friends from hypocrites. Before falling under the tutelage of Maria and Charlotte, spoiled and fashionable Arabella Campbell thinks that friendship consists of "expecting others to conform to her will, and exert themselves in her service."[46] Arabella's mother having died, her wealthy father marries an indolent second wife, who lavishes more attention on her fat, waddling dog than on her infant son. She is openly hostile to her stepdaughter and refuses to receive her, except once, and then only briefly. Cast out of her biological family,

Arabella lives upon the hospitality of various acquaintances. Arrogant and foolish, she learns the hard way to recognize "a sincere friend,"[47] like elderly Mrs Mortimer, who watches out for her interests and courteously leaves her a tidy fortune. Friendship, it turns out, is more durable than family ties, at least for Arabella, the visitor and outsider. Whereas family members are expected to demonstrate generosity to kith and kin, friends have no obligation to do so. According to Cicero, friendship is stronger than kinship because goodwill can be absent from bloodlines without affecting the relation – a cousin remains a cousin whether you like her or not – but goodwill cannot be removed from friendship without ending the relationship.[48]

In *Friendship*, amiability frames social comportment and good manners. The word "amiable," with its etymological link to both lovable and friendly traits of character, figures frequently in Sandham's novel and establishes the conditions for social integration. Amiability has two subject positions. In an obsolete usage, amiability means being worthy of love; an amiable person deserves and receives others' affection. In current usage, the word refers to friendliness, affability, and pleasantness; it is an affective position directed toward others. In the early nineteenth century, "playing the amiable"[49] meant engaging in polite conversation with a hint of acting and insincerity. In Sandham's *Friendship*, which declares its literary debts to Jane Austen quite openly – the Darfords are not unlike the Dashwood sisters – amiability suppresses all artifice, which makes it the opposite of fashionableness. "*Amiable!*" exclaims Arabella before she learns the value of true friendship, "you don't suppose that to be fashionable – we must become otherwise than *amiable*?"[50] Too much of a poser to grasp her own irony, Arabella presumes that fashionableness includes amiability, in the sense of social pretense, but wiser characters, Maria and Charlotte among them, know that genuine amiability excludes those beholden to changeable fashion.

Amiability has a national dimension as well. While Charlotte and Maria improve Arabella by slow degrees, their father, Captain Darford, wins several naval victories. As a leader, he epitomizes amiability. When his men die in battle or afterwards from their wounds, he attends their funerals and feels "the tie of affection which bound him to his crew draw him closer towards those who were left."[51] His amiability fortifies the nation and spurs it on to victory. For his successes in battle, he is promoted in quick succession to commodore, then admiral, before he retires with a handsome pension and a baronetcy. The novel ends by "leaving all of whom it relates happy and amiable."[52] In *Friendship*, amiability – a propensity for goodwill and congeniality – is objective. It extends to those who have defects of character as readily as those who display moderation, courage, or other virtues. As a disposition, amiability underlies the friendship plot. Whether they are widows, admirals, or young women, friends quietly but firmly promote good sense and sensibility in those around them. By extension, friendship integrates characters into a community or social group, especially characters who feel, or are, marginal.

Paek Nam-nyong's *The Friend* offers very different conclusions about the integrative force of friendship. Published in North Korea in 1988, the novel contributed to the Hidden Hero campaign of the 1980s, a state-sponsored program that recognized "the extraordinary achievements of otherwise ordinary citizens."[53] In this novel, the ultimate friend, trustworthy and absolute in judgment, is the state itself. A judge named Jeong Jin Wu handles various legal dossiers, but he has a particular interest in divorces because of challenges in his own marriage. When Chae Sun Hee, a temperamental opera singer, petitions to divorce her husband, Lee Seok Chun, who works in a factory and uses his spare time to invent lathes, the judge decides that he has a duty to restore harmony to the family: "If he could prevent a divorce and regenerate the couple's lost love, then going out of his way for them was no trouble."[54] To accomplish his goal, he takes measures that exceed his role as a judge, such as carrying the couple's son home in a downpour and slipping into an ice-cold river to dig up chunks of sand that might help Lee Seok Chun with his inventions.

Interceding as a friend, not as an official, Jeong Jin Wu advises the unhappy couple that a change of heart rather than a divorce is in everyone's best interest: the son's for his development, the husband's for his inventions, the wife's for her singing, and the nation's for its productivity. "A family may be small," the judge counsels, "but it's connected to one's world."[55] He means that families and friends are microcosmic units of the state. It is everyone's duty to advance in social position for the sake of the state – "*true* national duty,"[56] not some phony assertion of personal unhappiness as a reason for divorce. The state, represented by Jeong Jin Wu, is a reliable, conscientious, and sage friend who behaves more like a marriage counsellor than an arbiter of the law. Astonishingly, the couple heed the judge's advice, for they realize that the damage of a divorce outweighs any benefits it might bring. The couple promise to mend their ways, respect each other, and put others' interests ahead of their own. The state is a friend, and the friend, when he embodies as much wisdom as Jeong Jin Wu does, cannot be wrong. In *The Friend*, personal unhappiness yields to national achievement through the integrative power of the friendship plot.

Whereas Sandham's *Friendship* and Paek's *The Friend* demonstrate the integrative force of friendship, whether to individuals or the state, Sally Rooney's *Conversations with Friends* focuses on the fluidity of friendship, its blending of affection with sexual intimacy, and its transformation by social media. In this novel, characters communicate via texts or emails as readily as they talk on the telephone or meet face to face. The immediacy of communication shapes their friendships, yet that immediacy does not create greater honesty. "I wasn't betraying anyone's loyalties by being Bobbi's girl-friend," confides Frances, a twenty-one-year-old student and the unreliable narrator of Rooney's novel: "I didn't have close friends … I was lonely and felt unworthy of real friendship."[57] After the two women separate, Frances does not tell Bobbi that she is sleeping with Nick, a married actor. Bobbi sends Frances an email that draws a fine line between friendship and sex: "it's really devaluing to our friendship to make out like i'm competing with a man for your attention."[58]

Conversations with Friends tests and retests the definition of friendship, particularly in the way it encompasses everyone from casual acquaintances to former lovers. "We're all friends here,"[59] says a straight-talking publisher named Valerie, with a menacing candour that is designed to allow frank disclosures about everyone's personal lives. In Rooney's novel, calling someone a friend licenses a broad spectrum of bad behaviour, including flagrant deceit, meanness, bullying, manipulation, advantage-seeking, revenge, and ghosting former lovers. For Rooney, friends have a use-value, and that use-value is transactional. Friends promote one's fame. Friends provide shelter and boost one's ego, as needed. Friends are indistinguishable from social networks and contacts that enhance one's celebrity rather than enhancing personal goodness.

Lessons drawn from *Friendship*, *The Friend*, and *Conversations with Friends* do not provide a unified or complete definition of friendship. Do friends increase happiness? If having friends is good, is it better to have hundreds rather than just a handful? Why do some friends habitually cause crises, like the godmother in Anatole France's *Le livre de mon ami*, who "put into her friendships an extraordinary ardour and a touch of madness"?[60] Are bad friends ultimately useful, in the sense that those who are motivated by self-interest or wicked intentions demonstrate ways of behaving, if only by negative example? The fictional friendship plot, which has an infinite number of variations, is not archetypal; rather, it provides a mould for answering questions about the shape and meaning of friendship.

Betrayal and Forgiveness

With its emphasis on advice and development, the friendship plot often merges with the *Bildungsroman*. Abiding by the general principles of this genre – growth is predicated on unprecedented experiences – the hero's development occurs because of disillusionment, which is another way of saying that novels of experience depend on the hero's ability to distinguish between false and true friends.

The *Bildungsroman* takes different forms according to gender. In novels about male development, a youth filled with great expectations goes up to town, faces trials and tribulations, loses his illusions or some of them, but gains in knowledge as recompense. In novels about female development, solidarity between girls or women often provides a form of resistance to inappropriate marriage prospects or outdated social values, although the experiential growth of the female protagonist can also be measured by her divergence from old friends. Female solidarity, however, should not occlude the countless novels about women who betray their younger female charges: Madame de la Rougierre conspiring against Maud in *Uncle Silas* or Anna Quayne abandoning Portia to a merciless social set in *The Death of the Heart*.

To lose illusions and to acquire wisdom, the protagonist of the *Bildungsroman* experiences betrayal, usually by guardians, protectors, or friends. In this sense, the *Bildungsroman* questions the value and validity of friendship. In Rufi Thorpe's *The Girls from Corona del Mar*, a young woman named Mia, who narrates her story in the first person, dismisses female friendships as sentimental: "Normally friendships between girls are stowed away in boxes of postcards and ticket stubs, but whatever was between me and Lorrie Ann was not so easy to set aside."[61] Mia and Lorrie Ann are childhood friends who grow apart over time. Mia attends Yale, then graduate school in Michigan, where she develops an expertise in reading cuneiform. She marries the man she loves, has a perfect son, and lands a job as a professor in San Diego. On a very different career trajectory, Lorrie Ann has a child with cerebral palsy, loses her husband during the war in Afghanistan, and develops a drug addiction. Childhood friendship imprisons the two women instead of creating a solid basis for ongoing interaction. In a heated exchange, Mia yells at Lorrie Ann: "The fact that I thought we were friends was delusional. I don't understand you. I can't make peace with your decisions. I can't make you my friend again just by telling you a secret, okay?"[62] Childhood friendship may evolve around secret sharing, but that model does not translate into responsible, adult relationships. As Mia acknowledges, a broken friendship cannot resume just because a new secret is added to past secrets. Friendship requires mutual understanding and reciprocity, whether that reciprocity is founded on lived experiences, compassion, or like-mindedness.

By tracing the development of two women whose lives converge in childhood before widely diverging in adulthood, *The Girls of Corona del Mar* offers a lesson about the inequalities inherent in the *Bildungsroman*. Mia's growth as an individual is measured against her erstwhile friend – not favourably, it has to be said. The divergences between Lorrie Ann and Mia cannot be reversed unless one or the other renounces her world view, and neither is even remotely tempted to do so. The narration of the novel from Mia's point of view exaggerates the impossibility of turning back the clock on friendship to a time of carefree innocence. "We really were friends,"[63] Lorrie Ann writes in a note to Mia, when she leaves in the middle of the night after shooting up in the bathroom. The past tense in Lorrie Ann's note is not lost on Mia. As she reflects on the phrase, she arrives at an impasse in her definition of friendship: "What was most alarming, in the end, was the vertiginous sense that I did not know Lorrie Ann, and, in fact, had never known her."[64] If friendship requires some degree of mutual understanding or sympathy, it dissolves when that reciprocity disappears, and it causes the past to disintegrate too. Ultimately, the *Bildungsroman*, at least in this instance, depends on shedding friends as much as it depends on making friends.

If someone betrays a friend on moral grounds – the friend has committed some act or spoken a word so reprehensible that the only solution is extirpation of the friendship – the betrayal may feel like a release. With reference to espionage fiction, in which characters are not reliable even when they swear that their intentions are amicable, Eva Horn argues that "betrayal is an ambivalent gesture, an act of enmity based on friendship, but maybe also a form of friendship in disguise, an act of moral self-mutilation."[65] Friends always bear the potential of becoming enemies, so ending a friendship pre-empts the inevitability of betrayal. Magnus Pym's friend Axel in *A Perfect Spy* and Ted Mundy's friend Sasha in *Absolute Friends* prove the pertinence of this observation, although all of John le Carré's novels teem with traitors who play upon personal emotions for political advantage. Confidants pivot into antagonists, all the more powerful for knowing the ex-friend's secrets. The logic of moral self-mutilation would have it that, in political situations, a betrayal allows both parties to preserve their convictions instead of imposing them on the other person – or even killing the other person to score an ideological point. In dire straits, betrayal is a better alternative than death.

Betrayal converts the idea of friendship into an abstraction: if someone who was once a friend can betray trust, everyone becomes potentially an enemy, instead of being a potential friend. A novelistic example might best illustrate the complexities of betrayal within the friendship plot. Hanya Yanagihara's *A Little Life* is explicitly about American-style male friendship, with queer and straight variations. "Friendship, companionship," the all-knowing narrator ruminates, "it so often defied logic, so often eluded the deserving."[66] In interviews, Yanagihara often mentions her quasi-anthropological interest in male friendship and its taboos: "Men are discouraged from talking about shame and vulnerability and fear. So it's a great gift as a writer to explore friendships among people who are limited fundamentally by society in what they're allowed to feel and say."[67]

A Little Life circles around the lives of four men who meet at college: Jude, Willem, Malcolm, and JB. The foursome have different takes on friendship. Willem, easygoing and good-looking, does not "seek to be everyone's friend," but he takes pleasure in those friendships that matter to him.[68] JB, a painter with a streak of cruelty, wants his friends to be in thrall to him.[69] Jude, with more hang-ups and traumas than anyone can count, is described as a "weird friend."[70] Malcolm remains friends with everybody while establishing a career as a high-flying architect. The four friends have much in common, not least ambition and talent. "Everyone thought they would be friends for decades, forever,"[71] but this sentimental fantasy proves untrue because of various betrayals within the group. In a moment of drug-befuddled spite, JB imitates

Jude's leg-dragging gait and slack-mouthed demeanour. After this unpardonable breach of goodwill, neither Jude nor Willem speaks to JB for years. In a further betrayal, JB invades his friends' privacy by painting pictures of them in unguarded moments. When the Whitney Museum of American Art hosts a retrospective of JB's work, Jude visits the show and JB kisses him – a Judas-kiss that asserts an intimacy that does not exist and violates Jude's rueful privacy.

Betrayal in the novel bears on the duties of friendship that one owes to oneself and to other people. In *A Little Life*, Jude acquires friends, but he never trusts them fully, except, perhaps, Willem. At first, Willem calls Jude "one of his dearest friends."[72] That affection broadens into a same-sex relationship, of the all-encompassing kind familiar from *Lysis* and *The Last of the Wine*. The narrator waxes philosophical about friendship, with the inference that friendship lays the foundation for happy, intimate couples. A successful relationship is "one in which both people had recognized the best of what the other person had to offer and had chosen to value as well."[73] Jude becomes a ferociously gifted lawyer, and Willem becomes an internationally celebrated movie star. Despite their respective fame and fortune, Willem and Jude recognize the best in each other – loyalty, gentleness, willingness to tolerate crises and miseries – and choose to cherish those attributes with a pact of friendship. Willem, against his instinct to condemn Jude for regularly cutting his arms with a razor to stave off disgust and despair, learns to accept that Jude is someone who mutilates himself. "Friendship," as a *ne plus ultra* of human compassion, is the apt word for Jude and Willem's relationship: "wasn't friendship its own miracle, the finding of another person who made the entire lonely world seem somehow less lonely?"[74] The sentimentality of this summing up does not necessarily disqualify it from being true. The novel compensates for these slips into mawkishness by showing the transformative effects of friendship. That Willem sticks by his friend despite his incommunicativeness and unhappiness, his lies and his self-blame, changes Jude by degrees into someone who knows that he deserves love and happiness.

Although the novel frames male friendships in terms of longevity and varying kinds of intimacy, it also frames friendship as adjacent to and aligned with legal obligations. Harold Stein, a law professor who adopts Jude as his son, gives a lecture about the "obligations we have to one another as members of society, and how far society can go in enforcing those obligations."[75] Even if friendship is not a legally binding relationship, a betrayal of friendship is more morally damaging than betrayal of the social contract. The only possibility for repairing a broken friendship is to pardon the breach of bad manners or betrayal. In other words, the friendship plot, after a breakdown between parties, can culminate in reconciliation and forgiveness. When JB starts a detox program to overcome his crystal meth habit, Jude falls asleep at his bedside. In a Dickensian touch, JB whispers to his sleeping friend, "*Forgive me, Jude.*"[76] In a philosophical assessment of forgiveness, Charles Griswold points out that reconciliation implies a narrative "in which the two parties begin as friends, become estranged, and become friends again – the basic pattern being one of unity, division, and reunification."[77] Like friendship, forgiveness requires reciprocity. Pardoning another person may alleviate the effects of betrayal. It may even strengthen a friendship over time, if the act of forgiveness is complete and sincere.

Of course, no one is ever obliged to extend the olive branch of forgiveness to an alienated friend. Nineteenth-century plots, however, favour reconciliation over alienation. *Hard Times* concludes with the boastful punished and the true of heart rewarded. In contemporary fiction, betrayal haunts the friendship plot and takes precedence over forgiveness. *The Girls from Corona del Mar* excludes the possibility of a reunion to heal the rift between friends. Instead of forgiveness, the friendship plot disintegrates because of accumulated betrayals or manipulation for personal gain. At the end of *Conversations with Friends*, Frances and Nick resume their sexual liaison without any regard for the unhappiness that they have inflicted on friends and partners. With her betrayed friend Bobbi in mind, Frances asks Nick, "It's always going to be fucked up like this, isn't it?"[78] The future of friendship, at least as Frances foresees it, lies somewhere across a zone of emotional wreckage. In Rooney's novel, conversations with so-called friends may be ongoing, but they do not inspire confidence in the sincerity of friendship.

No matter how friendships are represented, they provoke questions about privacy, intimacy, affection, shared beliefs and experience, even happiness. In *Nicomachean Ethics*, Aristotle summarizes the meaning and effects of friendship at length before concluding with observations about happiness: "everything that we choose we choose for the sake of something else – except happiness, which is an end."[79] If, as the adage goes, people choose their friends but not their family or neighbours, they choose those friends for the sake of happiness, if Aristotle's reasoning holds true. Friends augment happiness, which Aristotle understands as an end in itself, perhaps the ultimate end, quite apart from advantage or pleasure. In such a world view, friendship, regardless of its configuration and outcome, increases happiness while it lasts. It is a means to happiness, in which loyalty, honesty, reciprocal care, shared beliefs and aspirations – all the attributes of friendship – find their proper and fullest expression.

NOTES

1 "friend," n. and adj., OED, www.oed.com.
2 Garth Greenwell, *What Belongs to You* (New York: Picador, 2016), 13, 20, 25, 111.
3 Janet Todd, *Women's Friendship in Literature* (New York: Columbia University Press, 1980), 2.
4 Lillian Faderman, *Surpassing the Love of Men: Romantic Friendship and Love between Women from the Renaissance to the Present* (New York: William Morrow, 1981), 411.
5 Martha Vicinus, *Intimate Friends: Women Who Loved Women, 1778–1928* (Chicago: University of Chicago Press, 2004), 233.
6 Sharon Marcus, *Between Women: Friendship, Desire and Marriage in Victorian England* (Princeton: Princeton University Press, 2007), 259.
7 Eve Kosofsky Sedgwick, *Between Men: English Literature and Male Homosocial Desire* (New York: Columbia University Press, 1985), 1.
8 Aristotle, *Nicomachean Ethics*, ed. Lesley Brown (Oxford: Oxford University Press, 2009), 142.
9 Marcus Tullius Cicero, *How to Be a Friend*, trans. Philip Freeman (Princeton: Princeton University Press, 2018), 101.
10 Aristotle, *Nicomachean*, 142.
11 Cicero, *Friend*, 49.
12 Ibid., 97.
13 Ibid., 139.
14 Ibid., 121.
15 Ibid., 65.
16 Daniel Defoe, *Robinson Crusoe* (1719; Oxford: World's Classics, 1972), 279.

17 Ibid., 282.
18 Aristotle, *Nicomachean*, 145.
19 Ibid., 148.
20 Cicero, *Friend*, 57.
21 Ibid., 35.
22 Plato, *Lysis*, trans. and ed. Terry Penner and Christopher Rowe (Cambridge: Cambridge University Press, 2005), 342.
23 Montaigne, "Of Friendship," in *The Complete Essays of Montaigne*, trans. Donald M. Frame (Stanford: Stanford University Press, 1965), 139.
24 Cicero, *Friend*, 157.
25 Aristotle, *Nicomachean*, 162.
26 Ibid., 150.
27 Ibid., 175.
28 Jane Austen, *Emma* (1816; New York: Norton, 2001), 22.
29 Charles Dickens, *Hard Times* (1854; New York: Norton, 2001), 169–70.
30 Plato, *Lysis*, 328.
31 Montaigne, "Of Friendship," 137.
32 Ibid., 138, 141.
33 Mary Renault, *The Last of the Wine* (London: Longmans, 1956), 123.
34 Ibid., 243.
35 Ibid., 369.
36 Aristotle, *Nicomachean*, 156.
37 Jacques Derrida, *Politics of Friendship*, trans. George Collins (London: Verso, 1997), 68, 276.
38 Alain-Fournier, *Le Grand Meaulnes* (1913; Paris: Librairie Générale Française, 2008), 202.
39 Jean-Paul Sartre, *Nausea*, trans. Lloyd Alexander (1938; New York: New Directions, 1964), 121.
40 Albert Camus, *L'Étranger* (1942; Paris: Gallimard / Folio, 1957), 55. My translation: "Cela m'était égal d'être son copain."
41 Ibid., 147.
42 Cicero, *Friend*, 85.
43 Montaigne, "Of Friendship," 136.
44 Elizabeth Sandham, *Friendship: A Tale* (London: Bowdery and Kerby, 1820), 243, 57.
45 Ibid., 193.

46 Ibid., 221–2.
47 Ibid., 227.
48 Ibid., 39.
49 "amiable," n. OED.
50 Sandham, *Friendship*, 163.
51 Ibid., 218.
52 Ibid., 307.
53 Immanuel Kim, "Afterword" to *The Friend*, by Paek Nam-nyong, trans. Immanuel Kim (New York: Columbia University Press, 2020), 223.
54 Paek Nam-nyong, *The Friend: A Novel from North Korea*, trans. Immanuel Kim (New York: Columbia University Press, 2020), 157.
55 Ibid., 175.
56 Ibid., 126.
57 Sally Rooney, *Conversations with Friends* (London: Hogarth, 2017), 7–8.
58 Ibid., 79.
59 Ibid., 145.
60 Anatole France, *Le livre de mon ami* (1885; Paris: Calmann-Lévy, 1928), 49. My translation: "Marcelle, qui mettait dans ses amitiés une ardeur extraordinaire et une sorte de folie."
61 Rufi Thorpe, *The Girls from Corona Del Mar* (New York: Vintage, 2014), 6.
62 Ibid., 201.
63 Ibid., 219.
64 Ibid., 228.
65 Eva Horn, *The Secret War: Treason, Espionage, and Modern Fiction*, trans. Geoffrey Winthrop-Young (Evanston: Northwestern University Press, 2013), 35.
66 Hanya Yanagihara, *A Little Life* (New York: Doubleday, 2015), 91–2.
67 Jennifer Dam, "Hanya Yanagihara on Male Intimacy" *New Zealand Herald*, 23 April 2016.
68 Yanagihara, *Little Life*, 44, 225.
69 Ibid., 265.
70 Ibid., 201.
71 Ibid., 567.
72 Ibid., 21.
73 Ibid., 568.
74 Ibid., 597, 573.
75 Ibid., 117.

76 Ibid., 281.

77 Charles Griswold, *Forgiveness: A Philosophical Exploration* (Cambridge: Cambridge University Press, 2007), xxv.

78 Rooney, *Conversations*, 306.

79 Aristotle, *Nicomachean*, 193.

Part One
Patterns

1

Between Women and Men: George Eliot's Friendships

DEBORAH EPSTEIN NORD

As *Middlemarch* winds to its conclusion, Dorothea Brooke expresses confidence in the integrity of Tertius Lydgate and offers some of her widow's fortune to fund his plans for a new hospital. At this announcement, the young, ambitious but dejected doctor registers a novel sensation: "It was the first assurance of belief in him that had fallen on Lydgate's ears … it was something very new and strange in his life that these few words of trust from a woman should mean so much to him." Lydgate is struck not only by the fact that a woman offers such encouragement – Rosamond, his wife, cannot – but that this gesture, coming from a woman, should touch him so greatly. As Lydgate leaves Dorothea, he recognizes what lies at the heart of this encounter: "She seems to have what I never saw in any woman before," he thinks, "a fountain of friendship towards men – a man can make a friend of her."[1] It has taken Lydgate hundreds of pages and decades of a lifetime to understand that friendships between men and women are possible and consequential and that some women depart from the models of femininity to which he had always, disastrously, been drawn; yet it is precisely Lydgate's evolving understanding of women that Eliot wishes to trace in the novel. She does so in part by constructing a narrative in which she can bring him together with Dorothea Brooke, weaving their lives together, offering them as parallel cases, and staging crucial episodes like this one, when their stories dramatically intersect.

Dorothea and Lydgate are but one pair in Eliot's oeuvre that afforded the novelist the opportunity to represent sustained relationships between men and women that could not ultimately be understood as romantic ones, did not fit neatly into the courtship plot as Eliot inherited it, and accorded with her acute interest in the complex variety of elements that constitute relations between the sexes. Dinah Morris and Seth Bede come to mind, as do, more importantly, Maggie Tulliver and Philip Wakem, and, most complicated of all, Gwendolen Harleth and Daniel Deronda. Eliot's investment in what I am calling "friendships" between men and women is inseparable from her desire to experiment with the structure and purpose of the novel form. Readers and critics have long noticed the permutations of male-female relations in her fiction that defy more conventional and chaste categories and ally her with strains of the continental novel: flirtation, for example, and adultery. Eliot's own circumstances as the long-time partner of a man not divorced from his legal wife doubtless underlay some of her unconventional views about marriage, even marriage in the novel. Hers was a friendship that was a marriage, a marriage that was a friendship, a marriage that was not one in the eyes of the law.

As Rosemarie Bodenheimer suggests, Eliot's interest in the early 1850s in the lives and writing of European women gave her a certain intellectual energy and enabled her to "redefine 'woman' in more generous terms than Victorian England allowed."[2] Loosened possibilities for novelistic relations between men and women meant that Eliot could not only entertain justifications for adultery but could also investigate intimate but anomalous or eccentric male-female bonds. In this way, she sought to reconfigure fictional narratives while investigating what makes for both a good friendship and, ultimately, a good marriage. She directly acknowledged and weighed the importance of sexual attraction and the lack of it, and she consistently imagined relationships of all kinds between men and women as deeply tied to familial bonds, most particularly to the sibling ties of childhood. In this essay, I consider the psychological and narrative complexities of these friendships, as well as their iconography in Eliot's works, and end with a brief comment about the relationship between friendship and Eliot's ethical credo as a novelist.

Remaking the Novel

By elaborating the intricacies and durability of friendships between men and women in her novels, Eliot deepened elements of her characters' psychological complexity and ambivalence. These friendships are inseparable from the triangular courtship plots of her most favoured predecessors. Scott, whom she worshipped "devoutly," appears in *The Mill on the Floss* as the author of romantic plots in which the dark-haired heroines could never claim victory over their blond-haired rivals.[3] Maggie Tulliver, of the dark-haired lineage, tells Philip Wakem that she cannot bear to finish Madame de Staël's *Corinne* because she sees this pattern about to be repeated.[4] Austen and the Brontës made ample use of the paradigm of triangular love plots, though with Scott's genders of two women and a man reversed, and Dickens employed it in both *David Copperfield* and, in a minor way, *Our Mutual Friend*. What, then, did Eliot add, and how do her versions of romantic triangles allow for an expanded exploration of male-female relations?

In Austen's novels, the heroine's choice between suitors involves a process of moral education. Elizabeth Bennet must learn to judge a man's character and to avoid letting her pride get in the way of genuine feelings of affection. Not Wickham but Darcy. Anne Elliot, older and wiser than Elizabeth, must learn to have faith in her own judgment – not to be "persuaded" – and mistrust the superficial affability of William Elliot. Not Mr Elliot but Wentworth. In both of these cases one of the suitors is clearly the wrong one, a man with dubious motives and little real love in his heart. In *Jane Eyre*, St John Rivers is not a bad man, but Brontë signals clearly that he is the wrong man, despite his priestly character, and that Rochester, despite his bigamous intent and sordid past, is the right one. David Copperfield's heart must be *educated* into knowing that Agnes is the better mate for him, and in the end there is no real contest between the upwardly striving Bradley Headstone and the once predatory but reformed Eugene Wrayburn. Eliot, by contrast, preferred an element of ambiguity about correct choices.

It is Brontë's *Villette*, then, that stands as the truest template for Eliot's fiction. She admired Brontë's final novel above all her others and found "something almost preternatural in its power."[5] Bodenheimer suggests that M. Paul Emanuel, the "forbidden soul mate" of Lucy Snowe, might indeed have seemed to Eliot an uncanny prefiguration of her own partner, George Henry

Lewes, but there seems another, perhaps related, reason for Eliot's ardent response.[6] John Bretton, though he shares part of St John Rivers' name, is a more sustained and complicated character than his namesake, and Lucy appears to remain attached to him and perhaps even expectant of his returned affection long into the novel. By the same token, M. Paul's flawed and often unreadable character and Lucy's open rebellion against his tyrannical nature continue to make him a quixotic choice. Lucy's preferences seem to vacillate, her neurotic fondness for Dr John seems unshakable, and the precise moment at which she transfers her affection from the doctor to the irascible teacher is impossible to identify.

The emotional murkiness, narrative ambiguity, and near impenetrability of characterization in *Villette* find their way into Eliot's novels in her creation of male-female relations. She makes room for competing and coexisting desires and for choices that confound the reader. Brontë, giving us in M. Paul a saturnine, scolding schoolmaster who leaves cigar-scented books in his colleague's desk, inspires Eliot to imagine love affairs that are, sometimes uneasily, also friendships and to explore the challenges of blending erotic and intellectual attraction.

This ambiguity of relations between male and female characters allowed Eliot to engage readers in imagining what Barbara Hardy long ago called "alternative destinies" and "unacted possibilities."[7] Is it possible, some may wonder, for Dorothea and Lydgate to fall in love, for her to be the one who changes the doctor's mind about women and thereby redeems him? Could Maggie Tulliver choose Philip Wakem and leave St Oggs for London, where an anomalous woman and a neurasthenic with an injured spine might find happiness? Or would Stephen Guest's elopement with Maggie culminate in some form of passionate coupling? Most compelling of all as an invitation to readers' speculation is the possibility of a Gwendolen-Daniel match. After all, Eliot begins *Daniel Deronda* with their charged encounter and threads through the entire novel a complex, gripping, and wholly original relationship.

These relationships, which end in continued friendship rather than matrimony, are integral to the structure of double plotting Eliot forged for her two most formally ambitious novels, *Middlemarch* and *Daniel Deronda*. The bonds between Dorothea and Lydgate on the one hand and Gwendolen and

Daniel on the other are not merely affective but also structural: they tie together the sprawl of *Middlemarch* and what have usually been regarded as the two halves of *Deronda*. Encounters between the two characters in each pair, such as the one involving Lydgate and Dorothea with which I began, create hinges between plots and, beyond that, suggest parallelisms that unite strands of the novels in both theme and structure. Both Dorothea and Lydgate are reformers and idealists bent on bringing the recalcitrant society of Middlemarch into the future. They aspire to noble vocations and each, in turn, is thwarted. Both enter into misguided marriages that undermine their aspirations. "You know what sort of bond marriage is," Lydgate tells her, "[y]ou will understand everything" (765). Their different fates are underscored by their parallel paths. Unlike Lydgate, Dorothea, as a woman, is denied even the beginning of a vocation but, also unlike Lydgate, she is allowed a second chance at wedlock and finds happiness, albeit "absorbed into the life of another" (836). What might be called Eliot's sociological sensibility finds one of its keenest expressions in this link between Dorothea and Lydgate, two "kindred natures," as Lydgate reflects, moving in the "same embroiled medium" (290).

Gwendolen and Daniel are even more starkly representative of their novel's two strands than Dorothea and Lydgate, so much so that critics and readers have long referred to the Gwendolen half and the Deronda half (or, more frequently, the Jewish half). Some, like Henry James and F.R. Leavis, have even seen the two as eminently separable and the Jewish half as expendable, or at least regrettable. (Leavis designated the Jewish plot of the novel as the "weak and bad side of *Daniel Deronda*.")[8] Though the tendency to see Gwendolen's and Daniel's stories as dissonant persists, careful readers of the novel have understood that the relationship between Gwendolen and Daniel provides many of the themes and variation that bind the novel together.[9] Not only do their encounters and the reader's likely expectation of their love affair accomplish this, but so too do at least two central motifs in the novel: abandoned womanhood and the need for rootedness in what Eliot calls "some spot of native land."[10] The spectre of a mother ruined, disinherited, or stranded haunts and unites them. After Gwendolen comes to know Daniel, he and his phantom mother are associated in her mind with Lydia Glasher, Grandcourt's discarded mistress, and her disinherited son, whom Gwendolen feels she has betrayed. This apprehension on Gwendolen's part contributes to her moral education and to the gradual, if limited, widening of her world. The associations multiply as Daniel speculates that Mirah Cohen may also be a woman like his mother, and so the textual web of the novel is woven. Less remarked, and perhaps even more vital to Eliot's grand plan, is the connection between Gwendolen's rootlessness, her lack of a "homestead ... in which affection can take root," and, in the "Jewish half," Daniel's ultimate discovery of a people and a homeland (22).

Intellectual Sympathy and Desire: The Mill on the Floss

In the various versions of male-female relationship across her novels, Eliot represented with unusual deliberateness and power the pull of sexual attraction, celebrated the importance of the kind of "intellectual sympathy" that she shared with Lewes, and explored the precise connection between romantic love and the affection between brother and sister that she had keenly felt in her own youth.[11] In *The Mill on the Floss*, these strands of ideal love appear as identifiable and discrete elements and prove impossible for Maggie Tulliver to resolve. Their irreconcilability is ultimately fatal, which illustrates, perhaps, how nearly out of reach such a synthesis of affective ties might be, especially for an idiosyncratic woman.

When contemporary readers of *The Mill on the Floss* complained about both Maggie's attachment to Philip Wakem and her attraction to Stephen Guest, they intuited that neither was the proper mate for her but could not comprehend what Eliot was up to. John Blackwood, her publisher, wished for "a more goodly lover" than Wakem for "noble Maggie" as he read Eliot's drafts but consoled himself with the idea that Maggie did not "seem really in love" with Philip.[12] Predictably, though, most correspondents and critics expressed dismay at Maggie's near-elopement with Stephen. To one such, Bulwer-Lytton, who had reprimanded Eliot for an "error," a misstep at odds with Maggie's previously "heroic" character, Eliot replied sharply: "it is too vital a part of my whole conception and purpose for me to be converted to the condemnation of it. If the ethics of art do not admit the truthful presentation of a character essentially noble but liable to great error ... the ethics of art are too narrow, and must be widened to correspond to a widening psychology."[13]

Neither of these readers grasped that Eliot wished to represent the salience of both friendship – the kind of intellectual comradeship that would prompt Maggie not just to befriend Philp but to become engaged to him – and sexual attraction – the overriding impulse that draws her to Stephen and allows her to drift with him down the river. Nor did they understand the complexity of character and desire – the "widening psychology" – that she sought to explore in her fiction.

Barbara Hardy refers to Maggie and Stephen's flirtation as "perhaps George Eliot's only real portrayal of sexual tension."[14] Hardy exaggerates, for Eliot often portrays something like sexual frisson between undeclared lovers. Dinah Morris blushes a "deep rose-colour" and betrays "suppressed agitation" when walking with Adam Bede, and Eliot registers Will Ladislaw and Dorothea Brooke's attraction to one another in a variety of ways.[15] But the explicit and extended account of Maggie and Stephen's mutual attraction demonstrates Eliot's concerted effort to render palpable and undeniable the natural course of desire, whether sanctioned or transgressive.

The narrative in "The Great Temptation," the penultimate book of the novel, focuses explicitly on Stephen's attraction to Maggie, perhaps because Eliot wished to displace the burden of desire onto the exigent male and to make Maggie the passive and less purposeful partner. He is "thrown into a fever by her" and his eyes "devour" her (422). He, along with the narrator, feels the sensuous beauty of her arm – "the dimpled elbow ... the gently-lessening curves down to the delicate wrist, with its tiniest, almost imperceptible nicks in the firm softness" – and he kisses that arm impulsively (559–61). Though shaken by Stephen's and her own longing and even affronted by this kiss, Maggie succumbs to the "influence" of his presence, and Eliot conveys this agitation through the mediating agent of music. As Philip plays the piano and Stephen sings, Maggie fears being overcome and tries to resist the music's effects by sticking to her needlework. Soon she throws down her stitching, "her intentions ... lost in the vague state of emotion produced by the duet – emotion that seemed to make her at once strong and weak; strong for all enjoyment, weak for all resistance. When the strain passed into the minor, she half-started from her seat with the sudden thrill of that change." She exhibits "the slightest perceptible quiver through her whole frame as she leaned a little forward, clasping her hands as if to steady herself; while her eyes dilated and brightened" (532). Music proves the medium that best arouses and, indeed, conveys what the text calls a "vague" feeling, likely erotic but nonetheless inchoate and outside of verbal expression.

When Philip sings in his "pleading tenor," Maggie is "touched, not thrilled," but his song does arouse memory, one of the hallmarks of their bond of friendship. He had sung this song when they were younger, in the Red Deeps, the place of their growing intimacy and attachment, when he gave her books to read, admired her emerging beauty, and warned her against stupefying self-denial (533). The problem for Maggie – the conundrum that engages Eliot in this novel – is that this friendship and courtship lack the element of attraction, while the sexual tension between Maggie and Stephen exists in isolation from the elements of friendship that Eliot and her characters most prize: intellectual companionship, common purpose, and, above all, loyalty to the past.

Wholeness, an integrated sensibility of judgment and desire, eludes Maggie, as does the opportunity to escape the familial economy in which she is trapped. Philip's tenor voice, crippled spine, love of literature and art, and tendency to tilt his head to the side "like a girl" all paint him as an implausible lover. Before Maggie agrees to marry him, she avers that his "mind is a sort of world" to her but that it is "quite impossible that we should ever be more than friends – brother and sister in secret, as we have been" (437). Still, after she stoops to kiss his "pale face … full of pleading, timid love – like a woman's," she is moved to "real happiness" at the thought that, "if there were sacrifices in this love, it was all the richer and more satisfying" (438). This tendency toward self-sacrifice and pity, which Philip himself warned against, signals a danger in the realm of male-female relations that returns as a leitmotif in *Daniel Deronda*. Yet Philip maintains what Stephen threatens to sunder when he runs off with Maggie and betrays both Lucy and Philip – that which connects them to the past, what Maggie calls "the most sacred ties that can ever be formed on earth" (601). Philip, though anathema to Tom Tulliver, roots Maggie in their shared past and, as she tells him more than once, he is her brother, a better brother than Tom.

Sororal Love

Maggie ends her short life with neither Philip nor Stephen but with Tom Tulliver, the brother who bullies and tries to rein her in but who also signifies her indelible earliest memories of love and attachment. "The first thing I ever remember in my life," she tells Philp, "is standing with Tom by the side of the Floss, while he held my hand: everything before that is dark to me" (402–3). Eliot was haunted by familial and especially sororal-fraternal bonds. The idyll of sibling unity both shapes and cripples Maggie Tulliver's choices, even as it forms a template for Eliot's vision of male-female friendship in her life and fiction. Responding to an 1873 letter from John Blackwood in which he had described a picnic with his son and daughter, Eliot wrote:

> [Very] pretty, and a good enough subject for a poem. I hope that the brother and sister love each other very dearly: life might be so enriched if that relation were made the most of, as one of the highest forms of friendship. A good while ago I made a poem … on the childhood of a brother and sister – little bits on the mutual influences of their small lives. This was always one of my best loved subjects.[16]

Eliot refers to "Brother and Sister" (1869), an elegiac sonnet sequence in which the poet memorializes the closeness of siblings, calling it, in the Wordsworthian language she often used to evoke childhood, "my root of piety."[17] As in the rendering of young Maggie and Tom, the poem evokes a physical intimacy between brother and sister that is embedded in paradisiacal nature: "our two lives grew like two buds that kissed / At lightest thrill from the bee's swinging chime."[18]

The image of a brother and sister holding hands figures elsewhere in Eliot's oeuvre, most memorably in the "Prelude" to *Middlemarch*, when the narrator describes the young Saint Theresa as "a little girl walking forth one morning hand-in-hand with her still smaller brother, to go and seek martyrdom in the land of the moors" (3). In her autobiography, St Teresa recounts that the brother she "loved most" was an older sibling, as was Eliot's brother Isaac.[19] The ages are reversed in *Middlemarch* – the sister is the elder – though Eliot mainly gives the impression of comradeship in this "child-pilgrimage," an image reminiscent of Maggie and Tom and of the brother and sister of Eliot's poem. Hand-holding, as a repeated iconographic detail in Eliot's fiction, signals the sibling relationship, as well as the bond of friendship between man and woman. It suggests a strong similarity between these two kinds of relations – siblings and friends – as Eliot's letter to Blackwood implies, while hinting at Eliot's insistence on the needful aura of innocence within romantic love.

Maggie and Philip hold hands repeatedly throughout the final three books of the novel. From the time of their meetings in the Red Deeps, through Philip's proposal of marriage, their betrothal, their subsequent encounters, and up until Maggie's disappearance with Stephen, this gesture is the tic or the tell of their relationship: it echoes the hand-in-hand clasp of Maggie and Tom in her earliest memories, roots this attachment in both a childhood and sibling bond, and hints at the chaste, asexual core of their friendship. After Tom has forbidden Maggie to see Philip and she breaks her engagement to him, the two lean toward each other, their "hands ... clasped again, with a look of sad contentment like that of friends who meet in the memory of recent sorrow" (527). They have sustained their friendship even as they have been forced to separate, sad but somehow content.

Somewhat later, after Stephen impulsively lunges at Maggie and showers kisses on her arm, she encounters Philip and "a keen remembrance and keen pity impelled [her] to put her hand in [his]. They had so often walked hand-in-hand!" (563). We are reminded frequently that Maggie towers over the stunted Philip and invited to contrast Stephen's spontaneous, lusty kiss of her arm with Maggie's stooping to kiss Philip's pleading face. Maggie's frustrating, stymied story ends with the incorporation of romantic love into a consummation of fraternal love in the moment of Maggie and Tom's death, when they drown "in an embrace ... living through again in one supreme moment the days when they had clasped their little hands in love, and roamed the daisied fields together" (655).

Love and Friendship: Middlemarch

From the bifurcated and unreconciled longings of Maggie Tulliver, Eliot moved on to imagine what the loves of less divided selves might look like. Both *Middlemarch* and *Daniel Deronda* continue to represent scenes of flirtation (Rosamond Lydgate and Will Ladislaw) and the spectre of adultery

(Will and Dorothea Casaubon, Deronda and Gwendolen Grandcourt). These novels also reach for some vision of synthesis of desire, friendship, and, ultimately, a common commitment to some larger force, "some Stronger something," as Deronda puts it, passionately if vaguely (663).

I have talked about how the principal structuring friendship between a man and a woman in *Middlemarch* draws the novel together by placing Lydgate and Dorothea in parallel and intersecting narratives. Yet there is another crucial male-female friendship in the novel, the one between Dorothea and Will Ladislaw, a relationship that moves in fits and starts toward consummation for most of the novel, involves intellectual comradeship as well as attraction, and gives the novelist scope to work out the seemingly elusive balance between the two. As Stephen Guest is a forbidden lover, so too is Will. The tabooed nature of their possible respective unions with Maggie and Dorothea accentuates the risks and limitations of desire, however indispensable – the need for it to be resisted, sanctified, or augmented by some aspiration beyond the self. At the same time, Will is heir to Philip Wakem's heterodox masculinity. With artistic sensibilities, the gifts of a receptive and sometimes teacherly interlocutor, and an inclination to interpret and warn against Dorothea's "fanaticism of sympathy," Will reproduces qualities that made Philip an unusual but indispensable friend. Unlike Lydgate, a man who avoids intimate conversation, Will loves to converse. "I wanted to talk about things," he tells Dorothea before she becomes a widow. "Each looked at each other," the narrator observes, "as if they had been two flowers which had opened then and there ... [I]t seemed fresh water at [Dorothea's] lips to speak without fear to the one person she had found receptive" (362–3). If music with its wordless power conveys erotic feeling in *The Mill on the Floss*, in *Middlemarch* conversation establishes the grounds for friendship.

Will's unconventional masculinity takes other forms as well. In him, Philip's distorted, wounded body is transmuted into a bohemian and exotic form. Philip's girlishness, associated with his bodily weakness and supplicating affection, is replaced in Will by delicacy of features and "bushy light-brown curls" (79). His femininity is that of a Romantic youth, a Shelleyan poet, a student dreamily in search of his place in the world, a wanderer with a tinge of foreignness and more than a tinge of Wertherism. In Rome and in Middlemarch he rambles among the poor; in Middlemarch he displays a "fondness, half artistic, half affectionate, for little children" (463). He leads them pied-piper-like out to the woods at nutting time, and his radicalism, bohemian lineage, and uncertain social status unnerve Middlemarchers. They refer to him with a series of epithets: he has "dangerously mixed blood," he is a Gypsy, an Italian with white mice, a Corsican, a Jew (463). Though older than Dorothea, he seems younger, possessed of a boyishness, even an immaturity, that at once vivifies her and inspires her protectiveness. When she discovers Will at the home of Rosamond and suspects them of a romantic entanglement, her heart feels torn in two, "as if it had been the heart of a mother who seems to see her child divided by the sword, and presses one bleeding half to her breast while her gaze goes forth in agony towards the half which is carried away by the lying woman who has never known the mother's pang" (486). This strange evocation of the story of Solomon's child points to the difference between Dorothea's authentic, apparently selfless attachment and Rosamond's duplicitous and superficial interest; at the same time, it hints at a grief born of maternal as well as romantic despair.

Will's youthfulness, exoticism, and artist's spirit do not disqualify him as a lover; on the contrary, these qualities make him a magnetic one. Dorothea, a woman who had once believed it would be delightful to marry someone who was like a father, a scholar whose amanuensis she could be, a man "above [her] in judgment and in all knowledge," undergoes a marital education in the novel and accordingly learns that she prefers a Shelley to a Milton, a youth to a patriarch (40). Eliot strives for metaphors to convey Dorothea's and Will's attraction to one another, even as she does in the case of Maggie and Stephen in *The Mill on the Floss*. The difference in *Middlemarch* is that a bond of sympathy and companionship – of friendship – has already been established between Dorothea and Will. When he learns Dorothea is about to enter the library where he sits waiting, he "start[s] up as if from an electric shock, and felt a tingling at his finger-ends" (388). After Casaubon's death and a period of separation, Dorothea herself registers a "deep blush ... with painful suddenness" when she sees Will walking toward her (541). For the moment "proudly resistant" to those who wish to separate them, "the same electric shock" passes through the two of them (545).

Burdened by the prohibitions set by Casaubon, stories about Will's birth that circulate in Middlemarch, his likely poverty, and the residue of Dorothea's discovery of Will with Rosamond, the pair believe they must part for good.

In the scene that most readers of the novel find either thrilling or melodramatic (or both), Eliot introduces the most theatrical metaphor yet for their mutual passion: a thunderstorm. Will has just declared that he will go away and that she must think of him as "on the brink of the grave":

> While [Will] was speaking there came a vivid flash of lightning which lit each of them up for the other ... Dorothea darted instantaneously from the window; Will followed her, seizing her hand with a spasmodic movement; and so they stood, with their hands clasped, like two children, looking out on the storm while the thunder gave a tremendous crack and roll above them, and the rain began to pour down. Then they turned their faces towards each other, with the memory of his last words in them, and they did not loose each other's hands. (810)

In the midst of this climactic moment, as their intense feeling for one another is conveyed in a spectacular "electric" flash and their love is about to be consummated in a "trembling" kiss, they are, at the same time, "like two children," made innocent, chaste, newly born – or reborn. The words sanctify and absolve the guilt of their passion by returning them to a state of childhood purity. The haunting history of Dorothea's first marriage is here expunged: Dorothea will cease to be a widow and again become a bride. The taint of suspected adultery and of Will's bohemian sexuality, with its casual disregard for the boundaries of marriage, will also ostensibly be erased in this return to innocence.

The iconography of holding hands that marks both Maggie's sororal relation to Tom and her sibling-like affection for Philip is transposed when Dorothea and Will clasp hands while standing side by side. In the union of Dorothea and Will, Eliot imagines a synthesis of love and friendship that incorporates elements of sibling affection, passionate attraction, intellectual companionship, and dedication to that "[s]tronger something." The wider purpose that Dorothea herself had sought emerges in the end as Will's political mission and dedication to reform, with Dorothea lending "wifely help" to the cause (836). She also leaves everyone wondering – author and readers alike – what else is in Dorothea's power to do.

Between Men: Daniel Deronda

In *Daniel Deronda* Eliot returns to the scheme of the love triangle that she had deployed in *The Mill on the Floss* and combines it with the double plot of *Middlemarch.* Daniel and Gwendolen anchor the two intertwined stories of the novel and also form two sides of one of its triangles, would-be lovers whose match is dangled before the reader from the first chapter and continues until surprisingly late in the novel as a temptation to Daniel and a growing desire for Gwendolen. It is an oversimplification to call the relationship between Daniel and Gwendolen a friendship, and yet it persists in some inchoate form, not a romance and not even a mutual attraction, until almost the last page. Indeed, the relationship intensifies in the later section of the novel as Gwendolen suffers in her marriage, and it becomes even more charged after Grandcourt's death. Though Daniel anchors the so-called "Jewish half" of *Deronda*, he plays a leading role in Gwendolen's story as well. She thinks of him variously as her "superior" (rather than her "admirer"), her conscience, her educator, her confessor, her counsellor, and her priest (415). The nature of their friendship must be understood in relation to his intense bond with Mordecai; his anomalous identity as a man without known parentage; his discovery of his mother and his Jewishness; and his love for Mirah, the third side of the second of two interlocking triangles.

From the outset Gwendolen experiences Daniel as supercilious, a man who appears out of nowhere to slap her on the wrist for reckless gambling, which, as the narrator subsequently discloses, she had reason to undertake. He even presumes to redeem the jewellery that she pawns and returns it to her. Though she ultimately comes to crave his moral guidance, it acts initially as an impediment to romance and even to flirtation. More serious an obstacle than his priggishness, however, is the fact that he is ineligible as a husband for Gwendolen because his past and therefore his future are uncertain. Though a determined rescuer of women and intrigued by her potential need for his salutary influence, he practices a certain restraint with regard to her, as he does with Mirah, simply because he does not know who he is.

For Mirah, he would need to be a Jew; for Gwendolen, an Englishman of position and wealth. He is loath to take advantage of Mirah, a woman who had been exploited by her father, and has good reason to believe that his questionable birth would disqualify him as a lover in Gwendolen's eyes. This uncertain identity keeps him aloof from all potential matches and in the equivocal category of rescuer and adviser – in other words, a friend. For Gwendolen's part, the novel signals early on that her coldness, indifference to marriage, dislike of wooing and being touched, and fierce virginity – she is a Diana figure – make her unlikely to fall in love with any man, including Daniel Deronda. Their relationship lacks the erotic pull between Maggie Tulliver and Stephen Guest, and Daniel's interest in Gwendolen remains one of solicitude, pity, almost a novelist's interest in her drama, her "hidden wound and ... self-dread," and a keen but detached fascination with this "fair creature in silk and gems" (564).

Nevertheless, in book 7 of the novel, just before Daniel is to meet his mother in Genoa, his mind wanders to the Spanish Jews driven from their homeland during the Inquisition, who rested briefly in this Italian port city as poor, ill, and hungry refugees. Mordecai's "dreamy construction of [his] possible ancestry" is much on his mind as he faces the discovery of its truth or falsity (532). He desires it to be true. Nonetheless, he feels a gnawing anxiety about Gwendolen, an anxiety connected to the sense that she has presented him with a need he cannot fulfill. Then we read this insistently oblique, abstracted passage:

> In the wonderful mixtures of our nature there is a feeling distinct from that exclusive passionate love of which some men and women (by no means all) are capable, *which yet is not the same with friendship*, nor with a merely benevolent regard, whether admiring or compassionate: a man, say – for it is a man who is here concerned – hardly represents to himself this shade of feeling toward a woman more nearly than in the words, "I should have loved her, if –": the "if" covering some prior growth in the inclinations, or else some circumstances which have made an inward prohibitory law as a stay against the emotions ready to quiver out of balance. The "if" in Deronda's case carried reasons of both kinds; yet he had never throughout his relation with Gwendolen been free from the nervous consciousness that there was something to guard against not only on her account but on his own – some precipitancy in the manifestation of impulsive feeling – some ruinous inroad of what is but momentary on the permanent chosen treasure of the heart. (621; emphasis added)

What he feels for Gwendolen, at least in this moment, is neither passionate love nor, exactly, friendship but rather an awareness that he might have loved her had he not been in love with someone else or had he not held the belief that he was out of bounds as a lover. He also harbours a nervousness that some impulse, some inclination toward Gwendolen, might escape his control and ruin the love he has chosen: for Mirah, whom he loves as much for being a Jew and Mordecai's sister as for her beauty, grace, and goodness.

This lingering nervousness discomfits Daniel until his mother confirms his Jewish birth and Grandcourt drowns. These threads of the narrative are tightly interwoven in the Genoa chapters of book 7 in order simultaneously to secure Daniel's future as Mirah's husband and Mordecai's spiritual heir and to stifle the "impetuous determining impulse" he had felt toward Gwendolen – the impulse to "carry out to the last the rescue he had begun in the monitory redemption of the necklace" (765). Daniel hears Gwendolen's confession, her conviction that she had caused her husband's death by willing it and is consequently tormented, wracked with guilt. He counsels, comforts, and tends to her, tries to give her hope that she might become a better woman for this repentance and baring of her soul, but a gulf has opened between them that she cannot grasp. Daniel's consciousness that he is now irrevocably separate from her because of his Jewishness and the fact of her inchoate but palpable guilt (her "murderous will") and need for spiritual and moral renovation interrupt all possibility of attachment (699).

Just as Eliot wrote a reversion to childhood into the dénouement of the stories of Maggie and Tom Tulliver and, in quite a different way, Dorothea and Will, she does so again in *Daniel Deronda* by signalling a shift in the nature of Daniel's relation to Gwendolen: "He took one of her hands, and clasped it as if they were going to walk together like two children" (690). As Lydgate had never experienced an expression of trust from any woman until Dorothea extended it to him, so Gwendolen had "never before had from any man a sign of tenderness which her own being needed" (691). Even more desperately dependent on him, she "cried as the child cries whose little feet have fallen backward – cried to be taken by the hand, lest she should lose herself" (771). As in Maggie's regard for Philip, Daniel's predominant sentiment toward Gwendolen is now pity, a feeling Eliot makes clear might be a basis for friendship but not for love.

For Daniel, however, the fraternal-sororal attachment suggested in the childlike holding of hands does not bring him back to innocence or childhood or a precious familial relationship. For that he turns to the bond, ordained by a common heritage, of intense friendship with Mordecai; a union with Mirah, the Esther to her brother's Mordecai; and the idea of a home rooted in ancient memory. Maggie Tulliver's insistence that she not sever ties to her past resonates with Daniel's choices, albeit on a different scale. One of the most direct musings on the nature of friendship in all of Eliot's works appears as an epigraph to chapter 46 of *Daniel Deronda*. As a commentary on Daniel and Mordecai's friendship, Eliot quotes Montaigne's essay "Of Friendship": "If anyone should importune me to give a reason why I loved him, I feel it could no otherwise be expressed than by making answer, 'Because it was he; because it was I.' There is, beyond what I am able to say, I know not what inexplicable and inevitable power that brought on this union" (566).[20]

The mystical aspects of Mordecai's character, among these that he has been looking for his "second soul," the right Jewish man to carry out his vision of return, and discovers him, miraculously, on Blackfriar's Bridge in an Englishman, a probable bastard with a well-bred air, have perplexed, even annoyed many a reader of the novel. Eliot's use of these lines from Montaigne suggest a context well beyond the Kabbalah: an idea of friendship that is brought on by some "inexplicable" power, a kind of love at first sight that knows no rational explication or prefatory exchange. Indeed, some critics have insisted that the bond between Mordecai and Daniel is more a homoerotic love than a friendship. After just a brief acquaintance, the two share an "intense consciousness as if they had been two undeclared lovers" (495). Yet it seems more in keeping with what the novel tells us that Mordecai, a dying man, is not only friend and guide but also brother and parent to Daniel, a man without a family whose mother has given him up. In place of children, Mordecai chooses a hardy Englishman to whom he can transmit his learning and his dreams, a surrogate who might enter the Promised Land after his own death. In place of a family, Daniel adopts a maternal, consumptive prophet and his sister as his past and future.

In giving him a family, Mordecai also gives him a mission, a "larger duty," a "social captainship," to blend with "a complete personal love" (623). The creation of a Jewish polity in the Levant, a return to Zion to "revive the organic centre" of his people, will restore their nobility and help purge their benighted European co-religionists of superstition and coarseness (532). Reunified Italy is Mordecai's model and inspiration, the "*patria mia*" of which Mirah sings: "when Italy sat like a disconsolate mother in chains" (559). For the parentless, whether Deronda, Mirah, or any other Jew who has lost a family, the past, a people, and a homeland will fill the void. For Mordecai, orphaned and childless, as he declares his position in a debate about assimilation versus the need for a homeland, "the past becomes my parent, and the future stretches towards me the appealing arms of children" (528).

It is exactly what Gwendolen lacks and Daniel urges on her, an awareness of the world and people beyond her, a widening of horizons and commitment to "the higher life ... in which the affections are clad with knowledge," that the Jewish past and kinship will provide (451). The service to "an ideal task," to something larger than the self that Gwendolen can barely even imagine and that Dorothea Brooke aspired to but only found as an adjunct to her husband, will not be denied Deronda. He will find it in "some spot of a native land," that human requirement the narrator tells us very early on that Gwendolen lacked (22).

And what of Mirah? If Gwendolen tempts and intrigues Daniel but seems neither the object of his desire nor a companion who shares his vision of the world, what in Mirah draws him to her? For him she represents a "beloved type," an ideal of gentle, giving, and needy femininity, a woman to be rescued and restored, an artist who shuns egotistic display – the opposite of his cold mother (744). But Mirah's ethereal nature is belied and her desire for him betrayed when she proves jealous of Gwendolen and feels an attendant pain "as definite as pincers on her flesh." The narrator, in a nod to Brontë's *Villette*, cautions readers not to think that such fervid emotions "require the bulk of a Cleopatra" (734). As Gwendolen regresses to a childlike state, Mirah changes from a girl whose "infantine feet" inspire protectiveness in Daniel to a "dark-tipped yet delicate ivory-tinted flower" (808). Central to Daniel's love for her is, of course, that she is Mordecai's sister. His loves for sister and brother are of a piece, part of the familial homecoming that binds him to his Jewishness.

Structurally, too, their marriage is foreordained. As the Biblical Mordecai sent his niece, Esther, to offer herself as bride to the Persian king, Ahasuerus, so that he would not destroy their people, so does Eliot's Mordecai unite his sister to the assimilated Jew, lately just an Englishman, who will restore their people to a vibrant and rooted existence. Eliot reinforces this familial tie and generational transmission of purpose and affiliation with another Biblical allusion. Mordecai's last words to Daniel echo those that Ruth, the prototypical convert to Judaism, utters to her beloved Hebrew mother-in-law, Naomi, as she is about to go back to her homeland: "Where thou goest, Daniel, I shall go ... Have I not breathed my life into you?" (811). Mordecai, the life-giving parent, about to die, will nonetheless accompany his chosen offspring across the sea and to a homeland that is as yet only an idea.

Between Eliot and Us

Finally, I want to suggest that the essence of Eliot's male-female friendships mimics the author's relationship to her own characters as well as her ethical guidance to readers. Eliot offers these friendships as a template for human relations in general. The protagonists Eliot typically casts as the principal side of her romantic triangles are women or, as one of the books of *Daniel Deronda* is ironically titled, "maidens choosing." In this, her final novel, she places a man in the central position, the position of chooser, a fact that allows her both to grant him the heroic vocation denied to Maggie Tulliver and Dorothea Brooke and to give him a role often occupied by female characters. "In some mysterious way," the narrator remarks, Daniel was becoming "a part of [Gwendolen's] conscience, as one woman whose nature is an object of reverential belief may become a new conscience to a man" (415).

In this way Daniel is not only a man who is like a woman, or like women in novels often are, but he also resembles some of Eliot's own heroines and Eliot herself. He is one of her most compelling avatars, a being capable of world-altering, even epic, action, as well as a moral guide who offers compassionate, sustained friendship toward the complicated character of Gwendolen Harleth. Like the novelist who created him, Daniel trains a generous eye on the deeply flawed and unlovable, including the Princess, the mother who gave him up. Before he parts from her for good, he puts his arms around her and presses her head "tenderly" beneath his. Moved by her agitation, "deep, deep compassion" stifles his words (664–7). Much recent critical discussion of the Princess focuses on how she is to be judged, but little attention has been paid to the extraordinary way that Deronda responds to her. Like the narrator of *Middlemarch*, who asks us to shift our gaze from Dorothea and look again at Casaubon; or Dorothea, who extends her trust and succour to the flailing Lydgate; or Philip Wakem, who tries to comprehend the reasons for Maggie Tulliver's self-destructive inclinations even as they benefit him, Daniel enacts Eliot's novelistic credo of what in *Adam Bede* she simply calls "deep human sympathy" (180). Eliot implants in her fictional friendships the acts of sympathy and disposition of fruitful detachment that she performs as a novelist and, in so doing, expands the meaning of friendship for her readers. Her most favoured avatars, among them Dorothea and Daniel, offer not only understanding and love but also forgiveness.

NOTES

1 George Eliot, *Middlemarch* (New York: Penguin, 1994), 762. Subsequent references to this novel appear parenthetically in the text.

2 Rosemarie Bodenheimer, *The Real Life of Mary Ann Evans: George Eliot, Her Letters and Fiction* (Ithaca and London: Cornell University Press, 1994), 88.

3 George Eliot to Mrs Charles Bray, 25 July 1871, in *The George Eliot Letters*, ed. Gordon S. Haight, 9 vols (New Haven and London: Yale University Press, 1954–74), 5:170.

4 George Eliot, *The Mill on the Floss* (New York: Penguin, 1979), 432–3.

5 George Eliot to Mrs Charles Bray, 15 February 1853, in *The George Eliot Letters*, 2:87.

6 Bodenheimer, *Real Life*, 96.

7 Barbara Hardy, *The Novels of George Eliot* (London: University of London Press, 1963), 135, 148.

8 F.R. Leavis, *The Great Tradition* (Harmondsworth: Penguin, 1962), 100. "There is nothing to do but cut it away," Leavis says of the "bad part" of *Deronda* (137). For James, see "Daniel Deronda: A Conversation," which Leavis published as an appendix to *The Great Tradition* (275–95).

9 Though Leavis's radical rejection of what he saw as the "weak and bad side" of *Deronda* has largely been discredited, its echoes can be heard in criticism of recent decades. See Amanda Anderson's *The Powers of Distance* (Princeton: Princeton University Press, 2001) for a survey of critiques of *Daniel Deronda* that revolve around seeing fissures between the realist story of Gwendolen, which depicts the "unstable conditions of modernity," and the idealist and

utopian strains of the Mordecai-Daniel story (119–20). These critiques, as Anderson points out, are also consistent with certain ideological readings that see an implicit defence of nationalism and colonialism in the novel.

10 George Eliot, *Daniel Deronda* (New York: Penguin, 1995), 22. Subsequent references to this novel appear parenthetically in the text.

11 Bodenheimer, *Real Life*, 88.

12 John Blackwood to George Eliot, 20 February 1860, in *The George Eliot Letters*, 3:264.

13 George Eliot to John Blackwood, 9 July 1860, in *The George Eliot Letters*, 3:317–18. Bulwer-Lytton sent the letter to Blackwood, who in turn sent it to Eliot (*Eliot Letters*, 318n585).

14 Hardy, *Novels of George Eliot*, 56.

15 George Eliot, *Adam Bede* (New York: Penguin, 1985), 485.

16 George Eliot to John Blackwood, 21 April 1873, in *The George Eliot Letters*, 5:403.

17 George Eliot, "Brother and Sister," in *The Victorians: An Anthology of Poetry and Poetics*, ed. Valentine Cunningham (Oxford: Blackwell, 2000), 502.

18 Ibid., 500.

19 *The Life of St Teresa of Jesus, Written by Herself*, trans. David Lewis (London: Thomas Baker, 1904), 5.

20 Michel de Montaigne, "Of Friendship," in *The Complete Essays of Montaigne*, trans. Donald M. Frame (Stanford: Stanford University Press, 1957), 138. "We sought each other before we met," Montaigne continues, a statement with which Mordecai would no doubt concur.

2

Faux Amis *in Charlotte Brontë's* Villette

LISA STERNLIEB

In perhaps the most famous passage of *Jane Eyre* (1847), the eponymous heroine stands on the roof of Thornfield and longs "for a power of vision which might overpass that limit; which might reach the busy world, towns, regions full of life I had heard of but never seen: that then I desired more of practical experience than I possessed; more of intercourse with my kind, of acquaintance with variety of character, than was here within my reach."[1] Over the next twenty-six chapters Jane interacts with very few other people; her story confines itself to several rural areas. Six years later, Brontë sent another of her heroines, Lucy Snowe, to a city modelled on Brussels. There Lucy encounters a large number of characters in scenes set at theatres, museums, and festivals. The first readers of *Villette* (1853) were captivated by its minor characters – Miss Marchmont, Paulina, Ginevra Fanshawe – and spent as much time focused on them as on Lucy herself.[2] Yet *Villette*, not *Jane Eyre*, is a novel about profound and desperate friendlessness. How can we account for this paradox?[3]

In this essay I argue that in writing *Villette* Brontë works through the pain caused by a scathing review of *Jane Eyre*. In her review, Elizabeth Rigby, posing as a male critic, writes authoritatively about the definition of friendship. Never content to disparage the novel that she is reviewing, she casts aspersions on Currer Bell as well. Not only has Bell failed as a novelist, she is, if a woman, an unworthy friend who has "long forfeited the society of her own sex."[4] Jane Eyre is a poor role model who, suspiciously, has never managed to make a friend. Governesses, who Rigby believes deserve a strong champion, will not find such a friend in Jane Eyre or in the pages of *Jane Eyre*. Rigby's review up-ended Brontë's sense of her readers. Whereas Jane, even in her solitude, believes she can create an ideal reader as friend, Lucy Snowe knows better. *Villette* bears the wounds that Elizabeth Rigby inflicted. From Rigby, Brontë learned to her shock and horror that she could not construct an ideal reader. The reader of *Jane Eyre* is one consistent figure throughout, a woman who may doubt Jane at times only to be seduced back into a position of trust. But the reader of *Villette* must contend with a cruel narrator, a false friend. Rather than inviting a friend in, rather than commiserating with a cherished companion, Lucy constructs a narrative in which she is well defended against the falsest of friends. Instead of one ideal reader, she imagines a variety of readers all hostile to Lucy's narrative: "Religious reader, you will preach to me a long sermon about what I have just written, and so will you, moralist; and you, stern sage: you, stoic, will frown; you, cynic, sneer; you, epicure, laugh."[5]

Unfriendly Readers

Rigby's double review of both *Jane Eyre* (1847) and *Vanity Fair* (1847–48) ran in the *Quarterly Review* in December 1848. The lengthy essay begins by insisting that the English have no gift for friendship:

> A remarkable novel is a great event for English society. It is a kind of *common friend*, about whom people can speak the truth without fear of being compromised, and confess their emotions without being ashamed. We are a particularly shy and reserved people, and set about nothing so awkwardly as the simple art of getting really acquainted with each other. We meet over and over again in what is conventionally called "easy society," with the tacit understanding to go so far and no farther; to be as polite as we ought to be, and as intellectual as we can; but mutually and honourably to forbear lifting those veils which each spreads over his inner sentiments and sympathies. For this purpose a host of devices have been contrived by which all the forms of friendship may be gone through, without committing ourselves to one spark of the spirit ... We invite our neighbour to a walk with the deliberate and malicious intent

> of getting thoroughly acquainted with him. We ask no impertinent questions – we proffer no indiscreet confidences – we do not even sound him, ever so delicately, as to his opinion of a *common friend*, for he would be sure not to say, lest we should go and tell; but we simply discuss Becky Sharp, or Jane Eyre, and our object is answered at once.[6]

In English society, Rigby notes, we do not ask "one friend" about a "common friend," lest the "friend" suspect that his opinions be shared with that "common friend." We English, Rigby suggests in her anthropological observation, cannot trust each other with confidences. And why should we? A mere invitation to a walk is inspired by "malicious intent." A "remarkable novel," however, provides the ideal "common friend." Two "friends" will readily gossip about *Jane Eyre* or Jane Eyre. There is no danger that one friend will betray the other to Jane Eyre. The beauty of this "common friend" is that she has no voice, no ability to participate in this common friendship. With an actual, flesh and blood "common friend," one risks being hurt. But, as Rigby makes clear, the purpose of friendship is to inflict, not to receive pain. We cultivate friendship in order to express the malice hiding just beneath our carefully arranged "veils," not to hear what others have to say about *us*.

Indeed, Rigby did not fear Currer Bell's response, for she published the review safely veiled by anonymity. Like Charlotte Brontë, Elizabeth Rigby was a spinster in her thirties, but while she took pains to conceal her own identity, she spends much of the review trying to expose Bell's. Throughout her review, Rigby shows that the mutuality of friendship terrifies her. She is free to declare Jane Eyre a "pre-eminently anti-Christian composition"[7] while nastily unleashing her own deeply anti-Christian sentiments amidst large doses of hypocrisy. After associating English friendship with deception and contrivance, after assuring us of the impossibility of genuine English friendship, Rigby attacks Jane for lacking friends:

> She flees from Mr. Rochester, and has not a being to turn to. Why was this? The excellence of the present institution at Casterton, which succeeded that of Cowan Bridge near Kirkby Lonsdale – these being distinctly, as we hear, the original and the reformed Lowoods of the book – is pretty generally known. Jane had lived there for eight years with 110 girls and fifteen teachers. Why had she formed no friendships among

them? Other orphans have left the same and similar institutions, furnished with friends for life, and puzzled with homes to choose from. How comes it that Jane had acquired neither?[8]

We might be tempted to laugh at Rigby's ridiculous review (what serious criticism bashes a fictional character for failing to make friends?) were it not for the fact that contemporary critics routinely blame the failure of other female characters on the success of *Jane Eyre*: "The actual deaths of other women, particularly of Helen Burns and Bertha Mason Rochester, are presented in the novel as crucial to Jane's education ... Jane's extraordinary narrative authority becomes insidious ... [her] voice can be empowered only through the silencing of other women's voices."[9] This criticism fails to notice that, far from sacrificing other women, Jane Eyre consciously and deliberately invokes them throughout her "autobiography."

Through thirty-five direct addresses to her female reader, Jane constructs an unbreakable friendship between herself and what she has imagined as the ideal reader of her narrative. She strategically cultivates a relationship in which her reader cannot fail to trust her. She confides her shortcomings and affections as if to an intimate friend: "I had not intended to love him: the reader knows I had wrought hard to extirpate from my soul the germs of love there detected."[10] The reader as confidant is required to acknowledge Jane's flaws and excuse them; in this regard, Jane, prompted of course by Brontë, crafts a double portrait of herself and her confidential reader. Jane draws attention to her affective state not just as a form of intimacy but as a form of educating, apprising, and shaping the reader: "Perhaps you think I had forgotten Mr Rochester, reader, amidst these changes of place and fortune. Not for a moment."[11] Jane does not forget, nor should the reader, which is the reason for calling the reader to order with these sharp rebukes.

At every stage of her life Jane shares with her reader what she cannot tell those with whom she lives. In fact, her "gentle reader" knows Jane far better than Rochester does. Her reader learns of Jane's love for Rochester long before her master does. After Jane leaves Rochester, she bravely soldiers on, hiding her despair from others while working as a teacher at a school in Morton, but her reader is told the truth: she dreams nightly of passionate encounters with Rochester. She returns to Rochester, as she tells her reader but not him, because she has heard him calling out to her from many miles away.

Jane seduces her female reader as Rochester has seduced her. Jane's reader is a friend, a friend she cultivates through inclusion: "stay till he comes reader and you shall share the confidence."[12] But Rigby's "common friend" is specifically excluded from confidences. In Brontë's and Jane's model, the reader is a friend, loyal and devoted to the writer and her heroine. In Rigby's model, however, Brontë and Jane are incidental to the friendship created between readers. The book, its author, and its characters live outside the boundaries of participation. They exist in order to be excluded from the friendship that their existence has enabled. For Rigby a book is instrumental in the formation of English friendships, but the book itself may lack any friends. Perhaps Brontë had naively hoped that reviewers would see themselves as friends to books, but in Rigby's view books are desirable friends precisely because we owe them nothing, least of all friendship. Reeling from Rigby's review, Brontë grieved for her creation, her defenceless friend. Yet, like Rigby, Jane does not necessarily value the reciprocity of friendship. Jane's seduction does not permit her reader much latitude. She is free to doubt Jane, but only momentarily. Crucially, her seduction is one-sided. She expects loyalty, but does not necessarily offer loyalty in return. She requires devotion but does not necessarily deal fairly or honestly with her reader.[13] Brontë's narrator often uses treachery, but Brontë was wholly unprepared to encounter treachery in her readers.

We know how deeply Rigby's review wounded Brontë because she wrote a response to it as the preface to *Shirley* (1849). The publishers were dismayed by its contents and refused to publish it; in turn, Brontë refused to submit a different preface. After so carefully constructing and designing her ideal reader, Brontë was shocked to find that an actual reader could be so cruel. Although Brontë never met Rigby and indeed did not know the name of the anonymous reviewer, she uses Rigby's emphasis on friendship against her and treats her as an actual friend who has betrayed her. She begins the preface by informing every other reader of *Shirley* to ignore its contents. It is meant to be read by only one person: "The Public is respectfully informed that with this Preface it has no manner of concern, the same being a private and confidential letter to a friend, and what is more, a 'lady friend.'"[14] Brontë begins her preface by using Rigby's own ruse against her. Rigby had consulted "a lady friend" to prove that Currer Bell is obviously a man, for no woman could be so ignorant of feminine affairs:

> No woman – a lady friend, whom we are always happy to consult, assures – makes mistakes in her own métier – no woman trusses game and garnishes dessert-dishes with the same hands, or talks of so doing in the same breath. Above all, no woman attires another in such fancy dresses as Jane's ladies assume … Even granting that these incongruities were purposely assumed, for the sake of disguising the female pen, there is nothing gained; for if we ascribe the book to a woman at all, we have no alternative but to ascribe it to one who has, for some sufficient reason, long forfeited the society of her own sex.[15]

Brontë's disclaimer is odd in every way. Why include a private and confidential letter in a book she hopes to have thousands of people read? Brontë's relation to her friendly and unfriendly readers changes utterly between *Jane Eyre* and *Shirley*. In the former, the carefully designed reader ideally perceives Jane's autobiography as written privately and confidentially to her one true friend. When that one true friend opens *Shirley*, she is to be told that she is excluded from the author's private confidences. This extraordinary gesture epitomizes a rhetorical tactic that Brontë takes to greater lengths in *Villette*. Brontë, like Lucy, expresses unbearable grief by longing for companionship and aggressively pushing it away.

In the preface to *Shirley*, Currer Bell returns to the theme of gender identity by assuring Rigby that he is a man whom "you should see assisting at a tea table" and that he is sure he has dressed Blanche Ingram appropriately because he "has just taken a train to Ingram Park to ask [her] maid about the material of her morning dress."[16] Bell also dispels Rigby's suggestion that the author of *Jane Eyre* is actually the governess to Thackeray's children: "What other 'romantic rumours' have been current in Mayfair? … Who manufactures fictions to supply their cravings? I need not ask who vends them: you, Madam, are an active sales-woman."[17] Although Brontë did not know Rigby's identity at the time that she wrote the preface, she was certain that the man who wrote the *Quarterly Review* piece was a woman: "What a nice, pleasant gossip you and I have had together, Madam. How agreeable it is to twaddle at one's ease, unmolested by a too fastidious public. Hoping to meet you again one day and offering you such platonic homage as it becomes an old bachelor to pay."[18] By guessing at the gender of the reviewer who takes cover behind anonymity, accurately as it happens, Brontë tries to beat Rigby at her own game. If Rigby can masquerade as a man, so can Brontë. If Rigby can seek the advice of fictional female friends, so can Brontë. But Brontë's preface shows none of Rigby's practised viciousness. Instead, Brontë reveals her own vulnerability, her own capacity to go on hurting long after the publication of Rigby's review.

Rigby was certainly not the only treacherous reader of *Jane Eyre*. George Henry Lewes had written to Brontë as a friend, then went on to expose her sex to the general public. Brontë wrote to Lewes in November 1849: "I wish you did not think me a woman: I wish all reviewers believed Currer Bell to be a man – they would be more just to him. You will – I know – keep measuring me by some standard of what you deem becoming to my sex."[19] Two months later Lewes reviewed *Shirley* in the *Edinburgh Review*. Cruelly, from Brontë's perspective, he revealed Currer Bell to be a woman and reviewed her book on exactly the terms she had claimed would condemn her: "We take Currer Bell to be one of the most remarkable of female writers; and believe it is now scarcely a secret that Currer Bell is the pseudonyme [*sic*] of a woman ... Currer Bell ... must learn ... to sacrifice a little of her Yorkshire roughness to the demands of good taste: neither saturating her writings with such rudeness and offensive harshness, nor suffering her style to wander into such vulgarities as would be inexcusable – even in a man."[20] Affronted by this unwanted exposure, Brontë took Lewes to task:

> After I had said earnestly that I wished critics would judge me as an AUTHOR not as a woman, you so roughly – I even thought – so cruelly handled the question of sex. I daresay you meant no harm, and perhaps you will not now be able to understand why I was so grieved at, what you will probably deem such a trifle; but grieved I was, and indignant too. There was a passage or two which you did quite wrong to write ... You know much and discover much, but you are in such a hurry to tell it all, you never give yourself time to think how your reckless eloquence may affect others, and, what is more, if you knew how it did affect them you would not much care ... I still feel angry and think I do well to be angry.[21]

In an influential essay Ivan Kreilkamp argues that, in *Jane Eyre* and *Villette*, "Brontë resists the equation of novel-writing with speech in order to develop a more effective means by which women writers might participate in the public print sphere and attain the 'full reward' of professional success in its terms … this authorship self-consciously addresses a mass readership, a readership imaginable only as a necessarily abstract collection of readers dispersed throughout an expansive public sphere."[22] By the time Brontë wrote *Villette* she could not convince herself of any "abstract collection of readers." The voices, the faces, and the personalities of the stoic, the sage, the traitor, and the shrew fully occupy her imagination. Certainly, Brontë craves anonymity. Yet even as she laments Lewes's betrayal, she knows, as she has known since the publication of *Jane Eyre*, that her work will always be judged "by some standard of what [is deemed] becoming to [her] sex."

Lewes's words uncannily echo Rigby's: "without entering into the question whether the power of the writing be above her, or the vulgarity below her, there are, we believe, minutiae of circumstantial evidence which at once acquit the feminine hand."[23] They also echo a review in the *Christian Remembrancer*: "a book more unfeminine, both in its excellences and defects, it would be hard to find in the annals of female authorship. Throughout there is masculine power, breadth and shrewdness, combined with masculine hardness, coarseness, and freedom of expression."[24] In mid-nineteenth-century England, Brontë can dream of being read as an author but has to settle for being judged as a woman hiding behind a masculine mask or a man ventriloquizing women.[25] Lucy Snowe's cramped, embittered narrative testifies to the fact that she cannot trust a reader to be unintrusive. She writes with a relentless awareness of "reckless," overly curious readers.

False Friends

Readers of *Jane Eyre* grow accustomed to Jane's touching vulnerability, with its friendly overtures and intimacies: "gentle reader, may you never feel what I then felt." In *Villette*, by contrast, Lucy Snowe snubs amiable interest and shared confidences. In this regard, she clearly embodies Brontë's reaction to rude, intrusive readers such as Rigby and Lewes. Lucy's impossible silences frustrate critics inclined to believe they know her.

As Jane transitions from Lowood to Thornfield she tells her reader that she will "now pass a space of eight years almost in silence."[26] The odd syntax suggests Jane stopped talking for eight years, almost as if she had taken a vow.

More probably, she means that nothing terribly important happened between the death of Helen Burns and Jane's arrival at Thornfield. Her time at Lowood was without incident. A similar passage in *Villette* suggests that large gaps of time are not just unpleasant but possibly catastrophic:

> On quitting Bretton, which I did a few weeks after Paulina's departure – little thinking then I was never again to visit it: never more to tread its calm old streets – I betook myself home, having been absent six months. It will be conjectured that I was of course glad to return to the bosom of my kindred. Well! The amiable conjecture does no harm, and may therefore be safely left uncontradicted. Far from saying nay, indeed, I will permit the reader to picture me, for the next eight years, as a bark slumbering through halcyon weather, in a harbour still as glass. Picture me then idle, basking, plump, and happy, stretched on a cushioned deck, warmed with constant sunshine, rocked by breezes indolently soft. However, it cannot be concealed that, in that case, I must somehow have fallen over-board, or that there must have been wreck at last ... In fine, the ship was lost, the crew perished. As far as I recollect, I complained to no one about these troubles. Indeed, to whom could I complain? Of Mrs. Bretton I had long lost sight.[27]

Lucy says nothing about what has befallen her. When she is reunited with the Brettons many chapters later, she is forced to "recur to gone-by troubles, to explain causes of seeming estrangement, to touch on single-handed conflict with Life, with Death, with Grief, with Fate."[28] She allows the reader an "amiable conjecture" about being warmly received by her family, but her irony undercuts that conjecture. Instead of complaining to the friendly reader, who has no first-hand knowledge of these unhappy circumstances, whatever they may be, Lucy deliberately excludes readers from her confidences. She does not allow access to her conversations with old friends either. She has suffered much, but she refuses to divulge the reasons for that suffering. Betrayed by her readers, Brontë creates in Lucy Snowe the loneliest figure in Victorian fiction.

Just as she began to write *Villette*, Brontë wrote to Lewes: "I can be on my guard against my enemies, but God deliver me from my friends!"[29] Lucy

Snowe analyzes the word relentlessly, but has any literary character been more reluctant to utter the word "friend"? In conversation with M. Paul, she distinguishes between "friend" and "*ami*." The distinction does not bear on the nature of friendship, which requires the test of time, but on the nature of linguistic differences. Her future fiancé proclaims, "I will have no monsieur: speak the other word, or I shall not believe you sincere: another effort – *mon ami*, or else in English, – my friend!"[30] Before she commits to calling him "my friend," Lucy mulls over the distinction between the French and English words for undisclosed possibilities of affection and love. She does this silently, then narrates her decision, not in dialogue, but in the past tense as if it were an incident to pass over lightly: "Now, 'my friend' had rather another sound and significancy than '*mon ami*,' it did not breathe the same sense of domestic and intimate affection: '*mon ami*' I could not say to M. Paul; 'my friend,' I could, and did say without difficulty. This distinction existed not for him, however, and he was quite satisfied with the English phrase. He smiled. You should have seen him smile, reader."[31] Oddly, M. Paul sees no distinction between the French and English words for friend, but Lucy discerns intimate affection in French that she either does not feel or cannot express. Yet the whole situation triangulates with the reader, who has a glimpse into Lucy's thoughts and the reaction that her friendly utterance provokes, but is told about this minor drama after the fact. That triangulation raises questions about degrees of friendship, whether measured by intimacy, proximity, or shared stories.

Lucy's reluctance to express her friendship with M. Paul in French may have something to do with the gradations of meaning between *un ami* (a friend) and *mon ami* (my friend), with the possessive hinting at a possible amorous bond. In French, *un petit ami*, or its feminine equivalent, *une petite amie*, more usually refers to a boyfriend or girlfriend, although this usage arises only in the twentieth century. Certainly, *ami* in French has as many nuances as friend does in English – *un ami cher* (a cherished friend), *des grands amis* (great friends), *ami commun* (a mutual friend), and so on. About Lucy's hesitation to call M. Paul *un ami*, William Cohen writes: "If the word in question were not in fact 'ami,' one might cite this as a case of what the French call *faux amis* between brethren languages: false friends, where what appears to be a cognate term has in actuality a different meaning in the two languages – sometimes a risibly different one, whereby *faux amis* lead to faux pas."[32]

In fact, the term "*faux amis*" was coined in 1928 by two French translators and refers to homophones in different languages which can lead to embarrassing situations. If, for example, a French man says "*je suis embarrassé*" to a Spanish woman, she may wonder how he has managed to get himself *embarazada*, or pregnant. Although Cohen rejects the term *faux ami* because it is too easy a pun to describe the situation in *Villette*, the example he cites is not in fact a false friend. Brontë, of course, would not have known the current meaning of the term since it arose after her time. For her, *une fausse amie* would have connoted a treacherous, untrustworthy, or deceitful friend, and that false friend may be incarnated in the reader. Brontë's conspicuous use of French in *Villette* exemplifies her vexed relationship with a reader for whom she often shows contempt.[33]

This scene between Lucy and M. Paul is confusing on many different levels. M. Paul is happy to hear the English word "friend" because he does not appear to understand the meaning of a simple word in his own language – "*ami*." More surprising still, M. Paul knows the English word "friend," despite his limited command of the language. He examines all the students at Madame Beck's pensionnat in every subject but one – English. When Lucy tells him that she does not want to examine the girls in English and would prefer that he do the examination himself, they argue until he admits that he knows only three phrases and a few words in English: "de sonn, de mone, de stare est-ce bien dit?"[34] He does not bother to wait for Lucy's response before he abruptly becomes conciliatory: "Come we will not be rivals. We will be friends ... After all you are solitary and a stranger and have your way to make and your bread to earn – it may be well that you should become known. We will be friends. Do you agree?" Lucy agrees, and while doing so, she compares the equalities available in friendship with the triumphant feeling that a vaudeville performance inspired in her: "I am glad of a friend. I like that better than a triumph."[35] The intimacies of friendship, she thinks, are preferable to having an audience at her feet.

This exchange, one of the rare long speeches out of M. Paul's mouth, is transcribed in English. After the brief list of badly pronounced, monosyllabic words that precedes this friendly speech, it has to be assumed that he is speaking to Lucy in French. In other words, some two hundred pages before Lucy agrees to call M. Paul "friend," she has already happily called him "*ami*." Or at least that must be what the reader assumes, for why, after M. Paul displays his non-existent English, would she immediately speak to him in English? Over and over Brontë puts the reader in a deliberately confusing position. Indeed, she explicitly wants to confuse her reader. Writing to her publisher about *Shirley*, she asked, "Will they print all the French phrases in Italics? I hope not; it makes them look somehow obtrusively conspicuous."[36] Although her publisher asked for footnotes for the French in *Villette*, Brontë refused to provide translations. Her inconsistent, often burdensome, use of French is one way in which she proves herself a false friend to her reader. If Rigby and other reviewers believed that they could unmask Currer Bell and her narrator, *Villette* proves that the motives of an author and her narrator remain unknowable. Rather than the reader being a false friend, Lucy goes out of her way to mislead, if not betray, her reader.

In some ways, the experience of reading *Villette* replicates Lucy's own confusion when she arrives in Labassecour. She speaks nary a word of French. When Madame Beck asks her to teach the English class, Lucy is terrified because she has by then learned only rudimentary French and wonders how she will manage:

> Could I but have spoken in my own tongue, I felt as if I might have gained a hearing; for, in the first place, though I knew I looked a poor creature, and in many respects actually was so, yet nature had given me a voice that could make itself heard, if lifted in excitement or deepened by emotion. In the second place, while I had no flow, only a hesitating trickle of language, in ordinary circumstances, yet under stimulus such as was now rife through the mutinous mass – I could in English have rolled out readily phrases stigmatizing their proceedings as such proceedings deserved to be stigmatized … One might possibly get command over this wild herd and bring them into training, at last.[37]

Should she speak English? Should she speak French? Instead of either, Lucy speaks no language at all. After ripping up one student's lesson, she locks another student in a closet without a word. Her reaction is not simply a difference between nineteenth- and twenty-first-century pedagogy. If Brontë's use of untranslated French seems intended deliberately to aggravate her reader, it is also used to demonstrate her cruelty to her own narrator. On her first day of teaching, Lucy calls her sixty nasty pupils a "wild herd." Who but a false friend would have sent her clueless narrator to a primitive country named "Labassecour," French for "barnyard"?

Despite the excessive amount of French, *Villette* is still overwhelmingly spoken in Lucy's own tongue. This does not, however, clarify her meaning. Throughout the novel she is at pains to define the word "friend." In the chapter entitled "Auld Lang Syne," Lucy is reunited with her godmother Mrs Bretton and her godmother's son, Graham Bretton. Lucy learns that her godmother is living in Labassecour, but she has known for many months that Dr John is Graham Bretton. She has never bothered to reintroduce herself to him, and he has had no idea of her identity. Nor has she ever bothered to let her reader know that the Dr John she mentions so often is the same character who appears in the first chapter. "Auld Lang Syne" is a happy enough reunion, but Lucy concludes with reflections on friends: "When I had said my prayers, and when I was undressed and laid down, I felt that I still had friends. Friends, not professing vehement attachment, not offering the tender solace of well-matched and congenial relationship; on whom, therefore, but moderate demand of affection was to be made, of whom but moderate expectation formed; but towards whom, my heart softened instinctively and yearned with an importunate gratitude, which I entreated Reason betimes to check."[38]

Lucy cannot use the word "friend" without attempting to define, classify, or qualify its meaning. When Graham refers to Ginevra as her friend, Lucy thinks: "Friend, Forsooth, but it would not do to contradict; he must have his own way; I must own the soft impeachment, friend let it be."[39] Lucy quotes Mrs Malaprop who mixes up "impeachment" with "appellation" or "name" in Sheridan's *The Rivals* (1775). Once again in Lucy's finicky thinking, "friend" is a *faux ami*, a malapropism, a word in English which may resemble but not mean the same as another word in English. The passage from "Auld Lang Syne" should remind the reader of the opening paragraph of Rigby's review. For the English, acquaintance entails awkwardness. We go so far and no further. All the forms of friendship may be gone through without committing ourselves to one spark of the spirit. Each time Lucy takes a step toward embracing her old friends anew, she forcibly pushes herself back. In the elaborate dance that Rigby performs, an Englishman first craves the chance to speak the truth to his friend, then sashays away from him for fear of being lied to. Lucy's choreography lacks a partner. She plays out the whole course of an amiable, tempestuous, unexceptional, extraordinary friendship with these two people in her head in the lonely minutes before falling asleep.

Hiding from Friends

The woman who wrote *Villette* was more desperately lonely than one can possibly imagine. She had published *Jane Eyre* in October 1847 and begun work on her next novel, *Shirley*. In September 1848 she buried her brother Branwell. In December she lost her sister Emily, and the following May she lost her sister Anne. She, Emily, and Anne had written their novels together at their father's dining-room table. When it came to writing *Villette*, she longed for friendly advice. In the absence of all her siblings, on whose counsel she once depended, she wrote to her publisher, George Smith:

> You must notify me honestly what you think of *Villette* when you have read it. I can hardly tell you how much I hunger to have some opinion besides my own, and how I have sometimes desponded and almost despaired because there was no one to whom to read a line – or of whom to ask a counsel. *Jane Eyre* was not written under such circumstances, nor were two thirds of *Shirley*. I got so miserable about it, I could bear no allusion to the book. It is not finished yet – but now – I hope.[40]

That terribly lonely young woman had become famous. She had dined with Thackeray and become friends with Harriet Martineau and Elizabeth Gaskell. Yet after lamenting her profound solitude, she begged George Smith to publish her novel anonymously. "As to the anonymous publication … I should be most thankful for the sheltering shadow of an incognito. I seem to dread the advertisements – the large lettered 'Currer Bell's New Novel' or 'New Work by the Author of '*Jane Eyre*.'"[41] Not only did she dread being known as Charlotte Brontë, but also she could no longer bear the limited privacy of her pseudonym either. This tug of war between privacy and publicity underlies many of her letters in this period. She first expresses her loneliness, then begs to be left in solitude and obscurity.

This contradictory pull also informs the characterization of Lucy Snowe. At Madame Beck's pensionnat, she actively refuses companionship on moral grounds:

> I might have had companions, and I chose solitude. Each of the teachers in turn made me overtures of special intimacy; I tried them all. One I found to be an honest woman, but a narrow thinker, a coarse feeler, and an egotist. The second was a Parisienne, externally refined – at heart, corrupt – without a creed, without a principle, without an affection: having penetrated the outward crust of decorum in this character, you found a slough beneath. She had a wonderful passion for presents; and, in this point, the third teacher – a person otherwise characterless and insignificant – closely resembled her. This last-named had also one other distinctive property – that of avarice. In her reigned the love of money for its own sake. The sight of a piece of gold would bring into her eyes a green glisten, singular to witness. She once, as a mark of high favour, took me upstairs, and opening a secret drawer, showed me a hoard – a mass of coarse, large coin – about fifteen guineas, in five-franc pieces. She loved this hoard as a bird loves its eggs.[42]

In the funniest moment of "Bartleby, the Scrivener," published the same year as *Villette*, Melville's narrator tries to find a different form of employment for Bartleby: "How then would going as a companion to Europe, to entertain some young gentleman with your conversation, – how would that suit you?"[43] In Melville's story the joke is at the expense of the narrator; no reader would entertain the possibility of Bartleby as a travel companion. But when Lucy is offered the position of companion to Paulina at three times the amount that she is paid at Madame Beck's, with the prospect of being released from her dreary job and the dismal interactions with women she detests, she turns it down. The offer comes soon after her desperate loneliness has led to a complete breakdown: "I declined. I think I should have declined had I been poorer than I was, and with … more stinted narrowness of future prospect … I would deliberately have taken a house-maid's place, bought a strong pair of gloves, swept bed-rooms and staircases, and cleaned stoves and locks, in peace and independence. Rather than be a companion, I would have made shirts and starved."[44] Lucy insists that she will remain with Madame Beck because "I was not her companion, nor her children's governess; she left me free."[45] In this chapter, Lucy tries to persuade us that she craves liberty more than anything else. But chapters earlier, as a *companion* to Miss Marchmont, Lucy tells us that "two hot, close rooms thus became my world; and a crippled woman, my mistress, my friend, my all ... I forgot that there were fields, woods, rivers, seas ... I was almost content to forget it ... I would have crawled on with her for twenty years [but] ... my little morsel of human affection, which I prized as if it were a solid pearl, must melt in my fingers and slip thence like a dissolving hailstone."[46]

Are we meant to believe that Lucy prefers the company of an elderly cripple trapped in two small rooms to that of a young, beautiful girl with whom she could travel the world? Are we meant to understand that Lucy had no desire for liberty in England but craves nothing more in Labassecour? Is it accurate to suggest that "Lucy tries to persuade us" of anything? Would not such persuasion require a desire for some kind of intimacy with her reader? Reasons and yearnings are meant to be shared with friends; Lucy reminds us in this unaccountable passage that we are excluded from her confidences and can only speculate as to her motives.

Many readers of *Villette,* however, do speculate. Most agree that Lucy shuns companionship because she is morally superior to the native population. Many critics read both Lucy and Brontë as profoundly committed to honesty. Some have read *Villette* as a conflict between Protestantism and Catholicism and have viewed Brontë's novel as an example of the anti-Catholic novel so popular in mid-century England. Whereas novels by Anthony Trollope, Charles Kingsley, and others show priests to be diabolical figures eager to kidnap and convert unsuspecting English girls, Brontë's is the only one set in a Catholic country, Labassecour, her version of Belgium. Catholicism, in their reading of Brontë, is a breeding ground for lies. These critics use as evidence the famous scene in which a desperate Lucy enters a Catholic church and confesses to a priest. The scene originates in an incident Charlotte wrote to Emily about in 1843:

> An odd whim came into my head. In a solitary part of the Cathedral six or seven people still remained kneeling by the confessionals. In two confessionals I saw a priest. I felt as if I did not care what I did, provided it was not absolutely wrong, and that it served to vary my life and yield a moment's interest. I took a fancy to change myself into a Catholic and go and make a real confession to see what it was like. Knowing me as you do, you will think this odd, but when people are by themselves they have singular fancies. A penitent was occupied in confessing … I commenced with saying I was a foreigner and had been brought up a Protestant. The priest asked if I was a Protestant then. I somehow could not tell a lie, and said "yes." He replied that in that case I could "jouir du bonheur de confesse" [*sic*] but I was determined to confess, and at last he said he would allow me because it might be the first step towards returning to the true church. I actually did confess – a real confession. When I had done he told me his address, and said that every morning I was to go to the rue du Parc – to his house – and he would reason with me and try to convince me of the error and enormity of being a Protestant!!! I promised faithfully to go. Of course, however, the adventure stops there, and I hope I shall never see the priest again. I think you had better not tell papa of this. He will not understand that it was only a freak, and will perhaps think I am going to turn Catholic.[47]

Nine years later, Brontë repurposed this experience in *Villette*. Lucy recounts a similar confession to a Roman Catholic priest, although she addresses the reader rather than a sister. When she enters the confessional, she immediately declares that she is a Protestant and the priest therefore asks why she has come:

> I said I was perishing for a word of advice or an accent of comfort … as well as I could I showed him the mere outline of my experience … 'Confession, like other things, [he said,] is apt to become formal and trivial with habit. You have come and poured your heart out; a thing seldom done … I see you are ill, and this church is too cold; you must come to my house … Be there tomorrow morning at ten.' In reply to this appointment, I only bowed, and pulling down my veil and gathering round me my cloak, I glided away.

> Did I, do you suppose, reader, contemplate venturing again within that worthy priest's reach? As soon should I have thought of walking into a Babylonish furnace.[48]

According to Rosemary Clark-Beattie this scene focuses on surveillance and conscience. For Madame Beck, "virtue consists not in inner rectitude but in outward propriety. Providing her students act as they should, their actual propensities are of no concern; discipline is a simple matter of exerting external control. From the perspective of the Protestant, surveillance and the ecclesiastical practice on which it is based, namely confession, are ways not only of failing to cure error, but of actively nurturing vice."[49] The schoolgirls' mechanical monthly confessions aside, does Lucy's conscience rebuke her? Are Lucy and Brontë as invested in honesty as critics claim? Both women openly lie to the priest. Lucy has no intention of seeing him again. How is this different from or better than the pupils who confess to the priest that they tell lies? Whereas the little girls ask to be forgiven for the lies they have told, Lucy does not ask for forgiveness. She asks for friendship, friendship she then immediately rejects.[50]

Clark-Beattie's focus on severe Protestantism ignores the obvious delight that Brontë takes in game playing. I read *Jane Eyre* as an elaborate confidence game in which Rochester takes Jane into his confidence in order to lie to her, and Jane takes her friend – the reader – into her confidence to lie to her as well. (Brontë loves to deceive her reader, but demands absolute loyalty in return.) Rigby ends her review of *Jane Eyre* by regretting loathsome Jane Eyre's advocacy of governesses since they are in desperate need of "earnest and judicious befriending."[51] After the death of Helen Burns, neither of Brontë's narrator heroines associates friendship with earnestness. Lucy lies about her friendship with Dr John and lies to him about her relationship with Ginevra. She lies to a kindly priest as her author did before her. Does Jane Eyre record her last meeting with Mrs Reed because she *earnestly* longs for her aunt's forgiveness or because she needs her reader to appreciate her aunt's unregenerate nastiness? When Madame Beck calls Lucy "bonne amie," Lucy diagnoses her earnestness as deceit: "the unction, the suavity of her behaviour offered, for one who knew her, a sure token that suspicion of some kind was busy in her brain."[52] Brontë's devious sense of humour may not be to everyone's taste, but surely the funniest moment in *Villette* is when Miss Marchmont admits that she has led a selfish life and that "small is [her] chance of salvation." She vows to repent "tomorrow ... by trying to make [Lucy] happy. I will endeavour to do something for you, Lucy: something that will benefit you when I am dead,"[53] and then promptly dies, leaving Lucy alone and penniless.

Rigby's review continued to enrage those readers who love *Jane Eyre*. Algernon Charles Swinburne, three decades after the publication, wrote that the *Quarterly* reviewer, whom he believed to be a man, "deserved to be strung up like a polecat."[54] Although Rigby's review deeply influenced the composition of *Villette*, I wonder if Brontë still carried a grudge after the novel's publication. *Villette* is a deeply depressing novel written by a novelist in unimaginable pain, but by the time she sent it off into the unpredictable world of readers, Charlotte Brontë appears to have decided not to take it too seriously. Rigby had the power to wound Brontë because she was earnestly attached to her friend Jane Eyre and ached for her unloved heroine. Brontë steeled herself against further pain by forming no such earnest attachments to the readers of *Villette*, but more crucially by eschewing an earnest attachment to her own creation. Who cares what happens to Lucy Snowe? Apparently not Charlotte Brontë. When anxious readers wrote to her and her publisher wondering if M. Paul made it back to Labassecour to marry Lucy or had drowned at sea, Brontë wrote to her publisher:

> With regard to that momentous point – M. Paul's fate – in case anyone in future should request to be enlightened thereon – they may be told that it was designed that every reader should settle the catastrophe for himself, according to the quality of his disposition, the tender or remorseless impulse of his nature – Drowning and matrimony are the fearful alternatives. The merciful ... will of course choose the former and milder doom – drown him to put him out of his pain. The cruel-hearted will on the contrary pitilessly impale him on the second horn of the dilemma – marrying him without ruth or compunction to that person – that – that individual – "Lucy Snowe."[55]

The reader of Jane Eyre had been given no such liberties. If she questioned Jane's loyalties – "and reader do you think I feared him in his blind ferocity" – she was promptly chastised – "if you do you little know me."[56] That reader was meticulously "designed" to be a sympathetic, loving friend who rejoices when she reaches the final chapter's opening words: "Reader, I married him."[57] But the less-than-ideal reader of *Villette* has never been and will never be a friend. She is as amorphous and unpredictable as its narrator. Perhaps she sympathizes with Lucy; perhaps she detests her. By the time the public was reading *Villette*, Brontë no longer needed to battle with the demonic readers of her imagination and seems, from the evidence of this letter, to be ready to take on flesh and blood members of the human race. Brontë's brief years in the spotlight had taught her that Rigby was right. English society in the mid-nineteenth century did not reveal a plethora of sympathetic readers, but this was never Brontë's fault. She need not doubt herself if Elizabeth Rigby or another "remorseless" critic cast aspersions on this "common friend." Instead of regretting the quality of her own writing, she could blame the quality of her reader's "disposition."

NOTES

1 Charlotte Brontë, *Jane Eyre* (1847; Oxford: Clarendon Press, 1969), 93.

2 See Anna Clark, "*Villette* and the Ends of Interpretation," *Victorian Review* 42, no. 2 (2016): 361–75.

3 Linda C. Hunt contends that Lucy cannot be friends with such characters as Mrs Bretton, Paulina, Ginevra, and Madame Beck because of the vast differences in their life experiences. Hunt ignores the fact that Lucy offers almost no narrative of her life experiences to support this claim. Linda C. Hunt, "Sustenance and Balm: The Question of Female Friendship in *Shirley* and *Villette*," *Tulsa Studies in Women's Literature* 1, no. 1 (1982): 55–66.

4 Elizabeth Rigby, "*Vanity Fair* – and *Jane Eyre*," *Quarterly Review* 84, no. 167 (December 1848): 176. The review was published anonymously.

5 Charlotte Brontë, *Villette* (1853; Oxford: Oxford University Press, 2000), 157.

6 Rigby "*Vanity*," 153–4 (emphasis added). See Julie Sheldon's fascinating discussion of Rigby's review, "'In Her Own Metier': The *Quarterly Review* of *Jane Eyre*." *Women's History Review* 18, no. 5 (2009): 835–47.

7 Rigby, "*Vanity*," 173.

8 Ibid.

9 Kelly A. Marsh discusses the views of Elisabeth Bronfen and Susan Sniader Lanser in "Jane Eyre and the Pursuit of the Mother's Pleasure," *South Atlantic Review* 69, no. 3/4 (2004): 81.

10 Brontë, *Jane Eyre*, 218–19.
11 Ibid., 509.
12 Ibid., 348.
13 See Lisa Sternlieb, "*Jane Eyre*: Hazarding Confidences," *Nineteenth-Century Literature* 53, no. 4 (1999): 452–79. For a very different approach to Brontë's first-person narratives, see Anna Gibson, "Charlotte Brontë's First Person," *Narrative* 25, no. 2 (2017): 203–26. Gibson challenges the common reading of Lucy's and Jane's narratives as displays of self-definition and authority.
14 Charlotte Brontë, "A Word to the *Quarterly*, Charlotte Brontë's Rejected Preface to *Shirley*," *Brontë Society Transactions: The Journal of Brontë Studies* 16, no. 5 (1975): 329.
15 Rigby, "*Vanity*," 175.
16 Brontë, "A Word to the Quarterly," 330.
17 Ibid., 331.
18 Ibid., 332.
19 Charlotte Brontë to George Henry Lewes, 1 November 1849, in Juliet Barker, ed., *The Brontes: A Life in Letters* (London: Penguin Books, 1997), 248.
20 George Henry Lewes, review of *Shirley*, by Currer Bell, *Edinburgh Review*, January 1850, quoted in Barker, *The Brontës*, 260–1.
21 Charlotte Brontë to George Henry Lewes, 19 January 1850, quoted in Barker, *The Brontës*, 262.
22 Ivan Kreilkamp, "Unuttered: Withheld Speech and Female Authorship in *Jane Eyre* and *Villette*," *Novel: A Forum on Fiction* 32, no. 3 (1999): 331–2.
23 Rigby, "*Vanity*," 175.
24 Review of *Jane Eyre*, by Currer Bell, *Christian Remembrancer* (1848). The review was published anonymously.
25 Thackeray's response to *Jane Eyre* is a rare and important exception. Thackeray assumed that Currer Bell was female and asked her publisher to thank the woman "whose novel is the first English one … that I've been able to read for many a day." See William Makepeace Thackeray to William Smith Williams, 23 October 1847, quoted in Barker, *The Brontës*, 171. Brontë was thrilled: "I hardly ever felt delight equal to that which cheered me when I received your letter containing an extract from a note by Mr Thackeray in which he expressed himself gratified with the perusal of 'Jane Eyre.'" See Charlotte Brontë to William Smith Williams, 11 December 1847, quoted in Barker, *The Brontës*, 172.

26 Brontë, *Jane Eyre*, 326.

27 Ibid., 98.

28 Brontë, *Villette*, 35.

29 Charlotte Brontë to George Henry Lewes, January 1850, quoted in Barker, *The Brontës*, 262.

30 Brontë, *Villette*, 320.

31 Ibid., 320–1.

32 William Cohen, "Why Is There So Much French in *Villette*?" *ELH* 84, no. 1 (2017): 190.

33 Kate Lawson and Lynn Shakinovsky focus not on Brontë's, but on Lucy's use of French. They find Lucy "sloughing off … the chains of narrow national identification." "That Lucy writes significant portions of the text in French, the language M. Paul taught her, reflects his capacity to encourage her to speak and to think differently, to extend her identification beyond the narrowly national and pedagogical one to which she clings initially in Labassecour." Kate Lawson and Lynn Shakinovsky, "Fantasies of National Identification in *Villette*," *Studies in English Literature 1500–1900* 49, no. 4 (2009): 939–41.

34 Brontë, *Villette*, 155.

35 Ibid., 155–6.

36 Charlotte Brontë to W.S. Williams, 17 September 1849, quoted in Barker, *The Brontës*, 244.

37 Brontë, *Villette*, 80.

38 Ibid., 178.

39 Ibid., 188.

40 Charlotte Brontë to George Smith, 30 October 1852, quoted in Barker, *The Brontës*, 353.

41 Ibid.

42 Brontë, *Villette*, 126.

43 Herman Melville, "Bartleby, the Scrivener," in *Melville: Short Novels*, ed. Dan McCall (New York: Norton, 2004), 3–34; 30.

44 Brontë, *Villette*, 298.

45 Ibid.

46 Ibid., 37–8.

47 Charlotte Brontë to Emily Brontë, 2 September 1843, quoted in Barker, *The Brontës*, 117.

48 Brontë, *Villette*, 161.

49 Rosemary Clark-Beattie, "Fables of Rebellion: Anti-Catholicism and the Structure of *Villette*," *ELH* 53, no. 4 (1986): 824. Most critics have read *Villette* as anti-Catholic. For an alternative perspective see Micael M. Clarke, "Charlotte Brontë's *Villette*, Mid-Victorian Anti-Catholicism, and the Turn to Secularism," *ELH* 78, no. 4 (2011): 967–89.

50 This much-discussed scene continues to divide critics. Ivan Kreilkamp reads it as evidence of Brontë's and Lucy's privileging of the written over the spoken word. Helen Groth, however, maintains that the scene privileges the ear over the eye. See Groth, "Charlotte Brontë and the Listening Reader," in *The Brontës and the Idea of the Human: Science, Ethics, and the Victorian Imagination*, ed. Alexandra Lewis (Cambridge: Cambridge University Press, 2019), 107–24.

51 Rigby, "*Vanity*," 176.

52 Brontë, *Villette*, 115.

53 Ibid., 42.

54 Algernon Charles Swinburne, *A Note on Charlotte Brontë* (London: Chatto and Windus, 1877), 88–90.

55 Charlotte Brontë to George Smith, 26 March 1853, quoted in Barker, *The Brontës*, 368.

56 Brontë, *Jane Eyre*, 436.

57 Ibid., 574.

3

Friendship, Liberalism, and the Novel: A Passage to India

JONATHAN GREENBERG

Friendship, liberalism, and the novel: all three terms have become objects of scrutiny and even skepticism in recent years, either as relics of a value system no longer relevant to the present, or, worse, as falsely valorized objects that never merited the esteem in which they were held. The technology industry has repurposed the word "friend" as a verb ("to friend someone"), and our easy adoption of this usage suggests that friendship itself has been compromised by the logic of social media, which allows market forces to reach ever more deeply into our private lives. This phenomenon is, however, merely an intensification of a transformation already lamented by Theodor Adorno in 1944, when he observed that personal relationships were being contaminated by the need to forge professional connections: "The private lives of countless people are becoming those of agents and go-betweens; indeed the entire private domain is being engulfed by a mysterious activity that bears all the features of commercial life without there being actually any business to transact … [People] believe that only by empathy, assiduity, serviceability, arts and dodges, by tradesmen's qualities, can they ingratiate themselves with the executive they imagine omnipresent, and soon there is no relationship that is not seen as a 'connection.'"[1] Self-advancement is regarded as honesty, while private friendship is eyed with suspicion: "Today it is seen as arrogant, alien and improper to engage in private activity without any ulterior motive."[2] Thus, aspiring professionals are told that they have no choice but to be on social media. Indeed, younger readers may be silently correcting me right now, noting that Facebook has been supplanted by newer platforms, and that the term "friend" has given way to the more ominous "follower" – a transformation whose implications Adorno surely would have discerned.

Liberalism, meanwhile, has long been a target for those on both ends of the political spectrum, but only lately has liberalism as a political system appeared on the defensive. Francis Fukuyama provides a global context: "It is clear that liberalism has been in retreat in recent years. According to [the nonprofit organization] Freedom House, political rights and civil liberties around the globe rose during the three and a half decades between 1974 and the early 2000s, but have been falling for 15 straight years prior to 2021 in what has been labeled a democratic recession or even depression."[3] During these years, elected leaders in Hungary, Poland, Brazil, Turkey, and the US "have used their electoral mandates to attack liberal institutions … [including] the courts and justice system, nonpartisan state bureaucracies, independent media, and other bodies limiting executive power under a system of checks and balances."[4]

The attacks come from both political extremes. On the right, conservatives may regard so-called classical economic liberalism as a beneficent force, but they view the accompanying rise of cultural and political liberalism – the centuries-long expansion of individual autonomy, equal rights, and personal freedoms – as corrosive of valued traditions and hierarchies. Meanwhile, the academic left invokes the word "liberalism" with a slightly different valence, associating it with humanism, Enlightenment, and sometimes capitalism. They decry liberalism as a false universalism masking the operations of power, or a philosophical framework that fails to offer sufficiently systematic analysis, so that, as Amanda Anderson points out, "there remains … a widespread default use of 'liberal' to signal benighted, ideological, or normative elements of thought or art."[5]

The novel, lastly, has survived the rise of movies and television, of the new journalism and the memoir, yet it is once again being laid out and toe-tagged in the morgue of cultural forms. The writer Will Self declares the death of the novel even as he carves out exceptions for various popular genres. Self, writing during the ascendance of *Harry Potter* and *Fifty Shades of Grey*, laments not merely the novel's diminished prestige but its diminished relevance to the intellectual life of a society:

> I do not mean narrative prose fiction *tout court* is dying – the kidult boywizardsroman and the soft sadomasochistic porn fantasy are clearly

> in rude good health. And nor do I mean that serious novels will either cease to be written or read. But what is already no longer the case is the situation that obtained when I was a young man. In the early 1980s, and I would argue throughout the second half of the last century, the literary novel was perceived to be the prince of art forms, the cultural capstone and the apogee of creative endeavour.[6]

The culprit for Self is, once more, the digital universe, which erodes our ability to enjoy extended private reading with offers of limitless screen time, gaming, and binge-watching. If Walter Benjamin is right that "the birthplace of the novel is the solitary individual,"[7] then its final resting place must be the social media influencer.[8]

Having laid out these narratives of decline, I do not intend either to affirm or to refute them. I have no special ability to prognosticate, particularly when it comes to such vast, uncertain subjects as the fate of social relations in a technologized world, the future of political systems, or the forms and media that will become the dominant modes of expression of the human imagination. But, in turning to E.M. Forster's *A Passage to India*, I do want to suggest that our attachments to all three of the ideas in my title are related, and that liberalism might constitute an unspoken third term in the framing of this volume on friendship and the novel. For each of these concepts in its own discrete sphere – the social, the political, the aesthetic – relies on a valorization of the individual, the pluralistic, and the contingent. Thus, we value a friend precisely for those gifts that lie outside or beyond the professional realm, resistant to the medium of exchange. Liberalism, with its commitment to the individual over the nation or the tribe, may seem ineffectual, but its ideals look very much like the ideals of friendship writ large. And while the novel, at least for Foucaultians, has been understood as a technology of ideological discipline, such disparate thinkers as Mikhail Bakhtin, Milan Kundera, and Lionel Trilling have affirmed its ability to honour that which is overlooked, denigrated, or expunged by totalizing ideologies – the peculiarities, eccentricities, and necessary flaws of human beings and human life.

Forster famously declared, "I belong to the fag-end of Victorian liberalism,"[9] and early critical studies by Trilling, Frederick Crews, and others situated liberal values firmly at the centre of his work. Trilling argues that "Forster's novels are politically and morally tendentious and always in the liberal direction";

he counts among Forster's liberal ideals "spontaneity of feeling," "the virtues of sexual fulfillment," and "the values of intelligence."[10] Crews, meanwhile, identifies the inner tensions of liberal political philosophy in late nineteenth-century Britain and positions Forster in the intellectual traditions descending from Paine, Bentham, and Mill.[11] Yet with the rise of poststructuralist theory and its offshoots, liberalism (along with its cousin humanism) becomes a term of derogation, even among readers who ultimately commend Forster's work for adumbrating alternative political or philosophical value systems. For example, in an essay focused on friendship, David Ayers sees *A Passage to India* as "anticipat[ing] current demands in postmodern philosophy" precisely because it supersedes the "classic liberal pose" represented by the character of Cyril Fielding.[12] Benita Parry similarly praises Forster by rejecting the label of liberal: "When Forster is relegated as a bloodless liberal, whose understanding of and opposition to empire was circumscribed, or whose affection for the East is suspect ... his considerable distance from the prevalent ideological positions of his day is occluded."[13] Even Paul Armstrong, who does defend the idea of Forster as a liberal, suggests that he might be read for a "postmodern hermeneutic sensibility."[14] Taken together, these essays affirm Anderson's judgment that "the dominant forms of literary scholarship in recent decades have not only kept their distance from liberalism, but also constituted liberalism as an assumed stable target of critique."[15]

To be sure, the reader can easily find expressions of liberal sentiment in *A Passage to India*. Fielding is introduced as a man "happiest in the give-and-take of a private conversation," who believes the world "a globe of men who are trying to reach one another and can best do so by the help of good will plus culture and intelligence" and who lacks "racial feeling."[16] He says to Aziz, "I believe in teaching people to be individuals, and to understand other individuals. It's the only thing I do believe in" (131). For his part, Aziz tells Fielding that what India requires is "[k]indness, more kindness, and even after that more kindness" (126), while Mrs Moore tells Ronny that what is needed is "[g]ood will and more good will and more good will" (53). Of course, it is always a challenge in reading Forster to gauge the level or quality of his irony; if these statements hint at a naïveté in the liberal world view, do we ascribe that naïveté to the limitations of the characters or to the novel as a whole? Moreover, *A Passage to India* is a novel that from the first pages insists on a multiplicity of viewpoints, warning the reader repeatedly against mistaking a "spurious unity" for something "durable" (94), and so taking a character's passing thought as an authorial dictum looms as a special risk.[17]

Still, admitting the novel's complexities, we can safely affirm that Forster's major political statements show him to be a liberal and, moreover, to articulate a connection between liberalism and friendship. In his essay "What I Believe," Forster declares himself "an individualist and a liberal" as he famously offers up his "two cheers for Democracy" as a system "less hateful than other contemporary forms of government."[18] (Even when affirming his creed, Forster can sound anxiously aware of its weak spots.) Forster begins his essay with a paradox, "I do not believe in Belief"; however, writing in 1939, he feels compelled to declare belief in something and that something is "personal relationships" (67). This phrase, of course, is familiar to the reader of *Howards End*, where it serves almost as a refrain; Forster in 1939 sounds a lot like Helen Schlegel of 1910, for whom "personal relations are the real life, for ever and ever."[19] But Forster, again, is attuned to his internal interlocutors, and so even as it valorizes personal relations, *Howards End* also tells us that "nomadic civilization," or modernity more broadly, "is altering human nature … profoundly, and throws upon personal relations a stress greater than they have ever borne before."[20] Similarly, some twenty years later, Forster concedes in "What I Believe" that the self upon which any personal relationship depends is unstable; his defence of liberalism begins with the psychoanalytic insight that the so-called liberal subject has been "shattered" (68).

The lesson that Forster draws from the shattered state of the subject is not to dispense with personal relations, but to redouble his commitment to them, by aspiring to "be as reliable as possible" (68). And reliability, he declares, "is not a matter of contract – that is the main difference between the world of personal relationships and the world of business relationships. It is a matter for the heart, which signs no documents" (68). Invoking the tradition of Renaissance humanism, Forster declares his law-givers to be not Moses and Paul but Erasmus and Montaigne. On this prompt we might recall Montaigne on friendship, the true form of which is never transactional: "the union of such [true] friends, being truly perfect, makes them lose the sense of such duties, and hate and banish from between them these words of separation and distinction: benefit, obligation, gratitude, request, thanks, and the like."[21] Consistent with Montaigne's understanding of friendship as beyond relations of exchange, Forster cordons off personal relations from the world of business and contracts, anticipating the fear that Adorno voices – that friendship, by definition lacking in instrumental value, might be swallowed up by forces of rationalization or commodification.

Indeed, in Forster's view, both the business class and the class-conscious left are wary of friendship: "Personal relations are despised today. They are regarded as bourgeois luxuries, as products of a time of fair weather which is now past, and we are urged to get rid of them, and to dedicate ourselves to some movement or cause instead. I hate the idea of causes, and if I had to choose between betraying my country and betraying my friend I hope I should have the guts to betray my country" (68). In this passage, the most famous in the essay, Forster explicitly opposes friendship to nationalism or group identification. This opposition, again, is familiar to readers of his fiction, since both *Howards End* and *A Passage to India* test the ability of characters to forge friendships – to connect – across barriers of group identity: education, class, and gender in the earlier novel; nation, race, and religion in the later. *A Passage to India*, in fact, even organizes its plot in order to dramatize exactly the hypothetical choice that Forster the essayist imagines: when Aziz is accused of sexual assault, Fielding is forced to choose between betraying his friend or his countrymen. Even outside of this central crisis, Forster urges us to think about the potential tension between friendship and nation; the novel both opens and closes by asking whether friendship is even possible between an Indian and an Englishman.[22]

In the novel's first full scene, Aziz joins some Indian friends for dinner as they consider the question "whether or no it is possible to be friends with an Englishman" (6–7). The topic provokes lively discussion, but no anger: "Mahmoud Ali argued that it was not, Hamidullah disagreed, but with so many reservations that there was no friction between them" (7). Forster, in other words, not only discusses but also dramatizes friendship, so that the conversation offers a loose model of liberal deliberative debate as an effort among friends to reach consensus. At the same time, the provocative conversation-starter allows a rehearsal of various indignities suffered at the hands of the British that binds the discussants in a shared validation of their otherwise shameful experiences. The opening thus puts the (English) reader on their heels, privileges the perspective of Indians, and allows insight into the injustices of British rule.

The question of English-Indian friendship arises even before the opening scene. Forster apparently does consider such a bond possible, since he dedicates the book "to Syed Ross Masood and to the seventeen years of our friendship." Masood, the prototype for Aziz, came from a prominent family of Muslim intellectuals; he arrived in England at age seventeen and Forster tutored him for his Oxford entrance exams. According to Wendy Moffat, Forster fell in love with the tall, handsome Masood (ten years his junior), but Masood was not gay and the relationship remained platonic.[23] Still, Forster "romanticized his new friend," writing in his diary in 1906, "Masood gives up duties for friends – which is civilisation."[24] Visiting Masood was the reason for Forster's first journey to India in 1912, and the Englishman saw his Indian friend again on his 1921–22 trip during which, according to Moffat, he "was happy to see [Masood] married, and they seamlessly renewed their friendship."[25] When he finished writing the novel, Forster saluted his friend as "the only person to whom I can open my heart and feel occasionally that I am understood."[26] In dedicating the book to Masood, then, Forster idealizes not only his friend but the very idea of friendship.

Even as he idealizes friendship, however, Forster is attuned to the weakness of its bonds in the face of nationalism or identity politics. For this reason, he uses his introduction of the English characters to draw a sharp opposition between private and public modes of feeling. When the English gather at the Chandrapore Club for an amateur theatrical production, we see how their rituals shore up their group identity:

> the performance ended, and the amateur orchestra played the National Anthem. Conversation and billiards stopped, faces stiffened. It was the Anthem of the Army of Occupation. It reminded every member of the club that he or she was British and in exile. It produced a little sentiment and a useful accession of willpower. The meagre tune, the curt series of demands on Jehovah, fused into a prayer unknown in England, and though they perceived neither Royalty nor Deity they did perceive something, they were strengthened to resist another day. (24)

The passage offers a sly analysis of nationalist feeling. The grammatical description of "God Save the King" as a "curt series of demands on Jehovah," combined with the dismissal of the melody as a "meagre tune," defamiliarizes the anthem, while satirically recasting it as an anthropological oddity. The reflexive change of behaviour and the stiffening of faces illustrate the action of ideology on the body itself, how politics inheres in manners. The ritual as a whole strengthens the British resolve "to resist another day" – even though what the British are resisting is nothing but resistance to their own imperium. Thus, while the anthem enforces a sense of group identity, the bonds that it forges are clearly not the bonds of friendship. They are the bonds of nation.

To a critic of liberalism, however, such stirrings of national sentiment are not a target for dry satire; they are ennobling. Consider the anti-liberal theorist Carl Schmitt. As Forster's almost perfect contemporary, Schmitt confronted the same far-reaching questions about national identity, empire, war, liberalism, democracy, human rights, global order, and the rule of law that Forster did, and though he generally rejected all that Forster stood for, the points of overlap and contrast are illuminating.[27] Most notably, Schmitt insists on the importance of the concept of the friend to political life: "The specific political distinction to which political actions and motives can be reduced is that between friend and enemy."[28] But this concept of the friend does not belong in any idealized Forsterian realm of personal relations. On the contrary, Schmitt's concepts of friend and enemy are emphatically not to be understood "in a private-individualistic sense," but rather in a public one, determined under pressure of life-or-death struggle: "An enemy exists only when, at least potentially, one fighting collectivity confronts a similar collectivity. The enemy is solely the public enemy, because everything that has a relationship to such a collectivity of men, particularly to a whole nation, becomes public by virtue of such a relationship" (28). Whereas Mrs Moore tells Ronny that "God has put us on earth to love our neighbors" (53), Schmitt argues, on the contrary, that the Christian injunction to "[l]ove your enemies" has no bearing on politics: "Never in the thousand-year struggle between Christians and Moslems did it occur to a Christian to surrender rather than defend Europe out of love for the Saracen or the Turk" (29).

For Schmitt, then, a national identity is forged among friends in opposition to enemies, and it is in recognizing friends and enemies that we recognize the fundamental purpose of existence: "Each participant [in a war or political struggle] is in a position to judge whether the adversary intends to negate his opponent's way of life and therefore must be repulsed or fought off in order to preserve one's own form of existence" (27). True political struggle forces a decision on whether one's "form of existence" is worth dying for. One of the problems with liberalism, in Schmitt's view, is that it weakens this nationalist identification, depriving a people of the collective identity that furnishes their existential raison d'être. Although for Forster such sentiment is, as shown by the anthem scene, utterly factitious or superficial, for Schmitt it is the essence of authenticity: "The high points of politics are simultaneously the moments in which the enemy is, in concrete clarity, recognized as the enemy" (67). While it is a short distance from Schmitt's position to an outright fascist celebration of violence, his is nonetheless a position that Forster must take seriously.[29] Ironically, the character who articulates this Schmittian perspective is the liberal Fielding. Musing on Aziz's request for kindness, he thinks, "yes, that he might supply, but was that really all that the queer nation needed? Did it not also demand an occasional intoxication of the blood?" (127).

Alongside his analysis of national sentiment, however, Forster examines the bonds of transcultural friendship. A key scene in this regard is the first meeting between Aziz and Fielding. Fielding accidentally steps on a collar stud while dressing; Aziz offers his own while falsely claiming it is a spare. Sara Suleri (among others) notes the Freudian imagery of homoerotic encounter in which Aziz inserts his stud into the "back hole" of Fielding's collar, but she ultimately sees the scene as an instance of failed interracial intimacy.[30] Yet even if this exchange represents a sublimated erotic bond between friends, it is still influenced by the differences of power that stem from the fact of British rule. Aziz's gift of the stud prompts a discussion of why collars are worn at all; for the modern-minded, cosmopolitan Fielding, they are merely an outmoded feature of style, but for Aziz, they are protection against racial profiling: "If I'm biking in English dress – starch collar, hat with ditch – they [the police] take no notice. When I wear a fez, they cry, 'Your lamp's out!'" (69). The critique of British injustice here advances the prevailing anti-imperial argument, while also affording Fielding an understanding of Aziz's experience of daily humiliation. At the same time, Aziz's unprovoked generosity expresses an incipient friendship; he undertakes the gesture, in the spirit of Montaigne, with no transactional purpose. Indeed, it is Aziz who, later in the novel, rebukes Fielding with perhaps the most Montaignian account of friendship that the book offers: "If you are right, there is no point in any friendship; it all comes down to give and take, or give and return, which is disgusting" (283).

Ultimately, in spite of the budding good feeling, Aziz's excessive deference renders the friendship something just short of a relation between equals. Aziz knows to conceal the fact that he takes the stud from his own collar, and his little silent prayer that his own collar "would not spring up at the back during tea" (68) reveals misgivings about his sacrifice. What taints this otherwise pure gesture of friendship, then, is the racial-national hierarchy of power whose dictates Aziz has unconsciously absorbed. Moreover, Forster refers to the scene some twenty pages later, when Ronny interprets the missing stud as characteristic of "the Indian," an example of "the fundamental slackness that reveals the race" (87). This particular instance of Ronny's offhand racism, significantly, is an insult that Aziz will never hear or have the opportunity to correct. Since neither Adela nor Mrs Moore corrects it, the reader must fill the vacuum. We are prompted to experience the outrage that Aziz cannot and to become his silent defenders. The dramatic irony makes the insult all the more cruel; this slur comes in response to an act of generosity from Aziz, one that he knew made him vulnerable and performed nonetheless. Even Aziz's seemingly ideal gesture of friendship, then, is entangled in a wider political context.

It is the putative assault in the Marabar Caves, however, that pushes to the fore the question raised in "What I Believe," whether to betray one's friend or one's country. However one interprets the incident in the cave itself,[31] the evidently false accusation against Aziz forces Fielding to make exactly such a choice. And while the instinctively apolitical Fielding "regret[s] taking sides" (193), he does choose friend over nation. In forcing this choice, the trial constitutes precisely one of those "high points of politics" that Schmitt celebrates as "moments in which the enemy is, in concrete clarity, recognized as the enemy" (67). Such a sentiment is expressed repeatedly. Major Callendar says, "You can't run with the hare and hunt with the hounds, at least not in this country" (208). McBryde, the police superintendent, tells Fielding, "at a time like this there's not room for – well – personal views. The man who doesn't toe the line is lost" (190). Even Hamidullah greets Fielding's decision with skepticism by asking him, "you are actually on our side against your own people?" (193). The Schmittian moment of decision thus confirms Ronny's earlier comments that "Nothing's private in India" (32), and that "one's always facing the footlights" (50). The private is subsumed into the political. Predictably, then, an "exalted emotion" (199), akin to the patriotic sentiments stirred by the anthem, takes hold of the whole community: "Each felt that all he loved best in the world was at stake, demanded revenge, and was filled with a not unpleasing glow" (203). The responses of the English, indeed, confirm Schmitt's claim that moments of determining the enemy are what imbue a collectivity with purpose.

Again, the contrast between Forster and Schmitt can illustrate how liberalism and anti-liberalism respond to a similar moment. In "What I Believe," Forster recognizes that there are times when politics demands participation in the collective decision of the nation, but his instinct is to resist the will of the collective as coercive and potentially authoritarian: "Love and loyalty to an individual can run counter to the claims of the State. When they do – down with the State" (69). Schmitt, for his part, recognizes that in moments of political crisis or decision, "a part of the population" – the part made up of free-thinkers like Fielding – sometimes "declares that it no longer recognizes enemies." But in that case, he maintains, the dissenting individual either "joins their side and aids them" or "place[s] himself outside the political community to which he belongs and continue[s] to live as a private individual only" (51). Therefore, when Ronny enters the club, the English "in instinctive homage, [rise] to their feet." Fielding, precisely because he recognizes the decisive force of Schmitt's friend-enemy distinction, understands that "while honouring him they condemned Aziz and India" and so refuses to rise (208). We sympathize with Fielding's choice, but he is operating within the political logic that Schmitt describes.

In *A Passage to India*, then, it is not only the characters' decontextualized statements of belief that valorize both friendship and liberalism. The narrative tone and the dramatic unfolding of scenes and sequences offer liberal indictments of the arrogance and racism of British rule, while dignifying Aziz by valuing his perspective on events and implicitly commending Fielding's guts in choosing friendship over country. Indeed, when Adela recants her accusation, Aziz is vindicated, and with him Fielding; both friendship and liberalism seem to have their day. Adherence to a liberal institutional process – what McBryde, with bitter sarcasm, calls "the fruits of democracy" (217) – has compelled Adela to testify and allowed her the opportunity to recant. Even here justice is achieved more by the vagaries of Adela's conscience, perhaps influenced by the supernatural "telepathy" (293) of the deceased Mrs Moore, than through the healthy operation of a functional liberal court system. Mahmoud Ali is convincing when he shouts, during the trial, "this is English justice, here is your British Raj ... I am not defending a case, nor are you trying one. We are both of us slaves" (249). From the Indian perspective, the court system is not a truly liberal institution, but a sham that supports the imperial power.

Although Forster surely means for his reader to admire Fielding's loyalty to Aziz and to celebrate Aziz's acquittal, critics such as Ayers are not wrong to note that liberal values such as "liberal, rational interchange" are nonetheless challenged in *A Passage to India*.[32] Even Trilling, the great champion of Forster's "liberal imagination," insists that although Forster is "tendentious" in a "liberal direction," "he is deeply at odds with the liberal mind," adding that "while liberal readers can go a long way with Forster, they can seldom go all the way."[33] As we have seen, Forster never ignored what Trilling calls the "weaknesses and complacencies" of liberalism.[34] The trajectories of two characters in particular, Mrs Moore and Aziz, hint at some of his doubts.

Mrs Moore is, like Fielding, in many ways a liberal herself, even if her sentimental Christianity stands in contrast to Fielding's "blank, frank" atheism (284). Her first meeting with Aziz in the mosque, like Aziz's collar stud exchange with Fielding, presents an ideal of friendship arising spontaneously through understanding and humour. Despite an initial misunderstanding, Aziz and Mrs Moore can joke about all that they share, while remaining aware of their differences of age, gender, nation, and religion:

> "Mrs Moore, this is all extremely strange, because like yourself I have also two sons and a daughter. Is not this the same box with a vengeance?"
>
> "What are their names? Not also Ronny, Ralph, and Stella, surely?"
>
> The suggestion delighted him. "No, indeed. How funny it sounds!" (20)

Both have lost their spouses, both have two sons and a daughter, and so they are in "the same box." Yet they can still laugh at the cultural gulf between them, which is given comic form in the suggestion that Aziz's Indian children would have English names. As widow and widower fall silent, both are "thinking of their respective families" (20), sharing an even deeper transcultural bond. And this bond proves durable: Mrs Moore, like Fielding, also refuses to aid in Aziz's persecution, telling Ronny, "I will not help you torture him for what he never did" (228). During the trial itself, Mahmoud Ali invokes her presence as the "poor Indians' friend" who "would have proved [Aziz's] innocence" (249). She then becomes transmuted into what Kenneth Burke calls a "tutelary deity" whose "expression of disbelief" in Aziz's guilt "had been the exact thing needed to help awaken Adela from her trance."[35] In other words, her spectral presence, either literally or figuratively, seems to secure Aziz's acquittal.

Although Mrs Moore proves a true friend in death, she also, while in India, begins to question the value she has always placed on personal relations: "She had brought Ronny and Adela together by their mutual wish, but really she could not advise them further. She felt increasingly (vision or nightmare?) that, though people are important, the relations between them are not, and that in particular too much fuss has been made over marriage; centuries of carnal embracement, yet man is no nearer to understanding man" (149). While these doubts are part of Forster's more general skepticism about marriage – skepticism that can be linked to queer or feminist perspectives – they also extend to his humanism.

Mrs Moore's experience in the caves, as traumatic in its own way as Adela's, prompts a rejection of what she calls "poor little talkative Christianity" (166) in favour of the terrifying nihilistic insight that "Everything exists, nothing has value" (165). Hers, then, is not a political critique of liberalism but a philosophical one, a critique that so dramatically alters our perspective on human existence that value itself dissipates. This view aligns with both Forster's invocation of the antiquity of the Indian landscape and his mischievous observations about the obliviousness of animal life ("the majority of living beings" [123]) to the political situation of the country. Nor must this perspective be granted the stamp of authorial approval; Parry argues that Mrs Moore "(mis)recognizes" the echo of the caves as sign of "nullity," and that their significance can be better understood as an expression of a Jain "cosmology incommensurable with positivism, humanism, or theism."[36] Whether we take Mrs Moore's changed world view as the misrecognition of an Englishwoman with a limited frame of reference or the insight of an aging widow gaining wisdom about personal relationships, her crisis casts a shadow over the rest of the novel, placing human existence in the context of a meaningless cosmos.

In contrast to this quasi-mystical alternative to liberalism, the trajectory of Aziz offers a different critique, that of an invigorated nationalism. Aziz too is a liberal in outlook, and he too begins the novel seeking cross-cultural friendships that escape the demands of politics. During the outing to the caves, he sounds resolutely apolitical as he laughs with Fielding about the burden of British rule: "Kick you out? Why should I trouble over that dirty job? Leave it to the politicians ... This picnic is nothing to do with English or Indian; it is an expedition of friends" (177–8). After his acquittal, various events and misunderstandings estrange him from his friend and defender.[37] When, in "Temple," Fielding returns to India after two years, the ties of friendship have been broken, or at least frayed. The intervening years have strengthened Aziz's sense of injury and national feeling, while for his part Fielding wonders "at his own past heroism" and thinks, "Would he to-day defy all his own people for the sake of a stray Indian?" (358).

The change in Aziz may in part reflect changes in Forster's larger vision of the novel, which he put aside in 1913 to write *Maurice* and did not resume until after his second trip to India in 1921–22. Back in England, he wrote to Masood: "When I began the book I thought of it as a little bridge of sympathy between East and West, but this conception has had to go ... I think that most Indians, like most English people, are shits, and I am not interested in whether they sympathize with one another or not."[38] No doubt the causes of this new attitude were many, including the death of his lover Mohommed el Adl,[39] but the political situation in India had altered considerably between his two trips. In particular, the brutal Amritsar Massacre of 1919, in which the British brigadier general Reginald Dyer slaughtered hundreds of peaceful nationalists protesting the extension of wartime emergency measures, provoked a joint Hindu-Muslim non-cooperation movement – alluded to in *A Passage to India* as a "Hindu-Moslem entente" (296) – that "claimed complete social equality between the British and Indians."[40] Forster, never friendly to imperialism, was sympathetic to the new nationalism, and his second sojourn in India may have strained his confidence in a politics that relied too heavily on goodwill, the quality that Mrs Moore, early in the novel, calls for in abundance.

Whatever we make of the changes in Forster's attitudes, Aziz's awakened political consciousness seems a direct consequence of his trial. There is a telling sequence early in the novel, when, after a combative exchange with Panna Lal, Aziz begins to worry that he has offended the district collector, Turton: "The complexion of his mind turned from human to political. He thought no longer, 'Can I get on with people?' but 'Are they stronger than I?'" (62). This shift "from human to political" thinking suggests a sudden awareness of group conflicts – both Hindu-Muslim conflict and Indian-English – that had been suspended during Aziz's spontaneous round of polo with an unnamed British soldier, with its "fire of good fellowship" (60). It is a shift to the kind of political consciousness that Schmitt values, in which each participant in a struggle "must judge whether the adversary intends to negate his opponent's way of life and therefore must be repulsed or fought off" (27). The shift here is momentary, but it foreshadows the later shift in Aziz's attitude that appears more entrenched.

The novel's final scene therefore presents the problem of forging friendship across socio-political divides as considerably more difficult than what is suggested by the collar-stud scene with Fielding or the mosque scene with Mrs Moore. As Aziz and Fielding ride together on horseback in the state of Mau, they argue the future of the Raj. In an about-face, Fielding defends the British presence as a necessary evil, while Aziz voices a full-throated nationalism: "India shall be a nation! No foreigners of any sort! Down with the English anyhow. That's certain. Clear out, you fellows, double quick, I say. We may hate one another, but we hate you most. If I don't make you go, Ahmed will, Karim will, if it's fifty-five hundred years we shall get rid of you, yes" (361). Even allowing for some playful irony in Aziz's tone, the contrast with his words at the picnic, where he leaves the job of expelling the British to "the politicians," could not be starker.

For Fielding, however, this nationalist fervour is hard to take seriously. "India a nation!" he declares. "What an apotheosis! Last comer to the drab nineteenth-century sisterhood! Waddling in at this hour of the world to take her seat! She, whose only peer was the Holy Roman Empire, she shall rank with Guatemala and Belgium perhaps!" (361). On the one hand, for the cosmopolitan Fielding, nationalist aspirations belong to the century gone by, and are something to be overcome, not celebrated. On the other hand, for Aziz, nationhood is the only route to dignity. "[India] must imitate Japan," he tells himself. "Not until she is a nation will her sons be treated with respect" (298). It now appears that the choice between friend and countryman, which seems straightforward to the Forster of "What I Believe" and even the Fielding of Aziz's trial, is not so simple. National identification creates a positive barrier to forming a friendship in the first place.

Of course, in spite of the political differences, Aziz qualifies his anger, and though he promises to "drive every blasted Englishman into the sea" (361), he also rides right up against Fielding and, "half kissing him" (362), tells him that after the British are expelled, the two men can be friends. Fielding reciprocates the physical warmth, "holding him affectionately" (362). "Why can't we be friends now?" he asks. He then adds, "It's what I want. It's what you want" (362). The personal affection is as strong as ever, but the notion that friendship can obtain under political conditions of oppression appears dubious. The injustice of British rule is represented as a force of nature pulling the friends apart: "But the horses didn't want it – they swerved apart; the earth didn't want it, sending up rocks through which riders must pass single file; the temples, the tank, the jail, the palace, the birds, the carrion, the Guest House, that came into view as they issued from the gap and saw Mau beneath: they didn't want it, they said in their hundred voices, 'No, not yet,' and the sky said, 'No, not there'" (362). The non-human world of animals and landscape not only serves as a metaphor for political forces obstructing friendship but also seemingly collaborates in enforcing a physical distance between the two men. The relationship has taken a Schmittian turn from the human to the political, in apparent defiance of the Forsterian desire to choose friend over nation.

The mysticism of Mrs Moore and the nationalism of Aziz clearly complicate any effort to derive a unitary, simple politics from *A Passage to India*. The presence of these troubling alternatives, these incompatible perspectives, is a testament both to the form of the novel that accommodates them and to the political system that allows for the existence of difference. That system is assuredly not one that insists, à la Schmitt, on an intoxication of the blood. Rather, as Trilling would say, what is needed is a capacious liberalism, "a large tendency rather than a concise body of doctrine," one that remains receptive to critique and recognizes the pressures that social and political forces place on human relations.[41] A novel that expresses such an outlook will disallow any gratifying reconciliation based on wish fulfillment.

The capaciousness and flexibility of the novel form, its ability to represent and dramatize an ongoing negotiation among competing values and world views, proves superior to more monological kinds of discourse in accommodating these antagonisms. In other words, literature in general and the novel in particular are congenial to Forster because they promote, through the directed use of our imaginative faculties, a capacity to recognize simultaneously the abiding affection between Fielding and Aziz and the intransigent claims of the political. Forster's liberalism, realized in the imaginative construction that is *A Passage to India*, ultimately consists not simply in a valorization of friendship in a protected private sphere outside of politics, nor merely in the espousal of a progressive political cause, but in the novelistic perspective that can represent both of these goods without falsely reconciling them.

Ultimately, a political thinker far more sympathetic to Forster than Schmitt is Isaiah Berlin, for whom the clash of different value systems is not a rousing call to arms that gives life meaning but a sometimes tragic consequence of the variety of human cultures and values. Nonetheless, Berlin adheres to liberalism in a way that aligns closely with the values embodied in Forster's novel. In his famous essay "Two Concepts of Liberty," he upholds the idea of pluralism, which, rooted in "negative liberty," offers "a truer and more humane ideal" than that of "'positive' self-mastery by classes, or peoples, or the whole of mankind." It is truer because it recognizes a plurality of often incommensurate "human goals," more humane because it allows the individual and not the collective to determine their own values. Thus Berlin insists on the importance of standing for one's values "without claiming eternal validity for them" – a recognition of both their contingency and their legitimacy. Indeed, Forster's readers of various theoretical persuasions generally agree on the capacity of *A Passage to India* to accommodate multiple perspectives and interpretations, even incompatible ones. As Aziz says to Adela on their ill-fated picnic, "Nothing embraces the whole of India, nothing, nothing" (160).

NOTES

1 Theodor W. Adorno, *Minima Moralia: Reflections from Damaged Life*, trans. E.F.N. Jephcott (London: Verso, 1978), 23.

2 Ibid., 23.

3 Francis Fukuyama, *Liberalism and Its Discontents* (New York: Farrar, Strauss, and Giroux, 2021), viii.

4 Ibid. With the rise of Narendra Modi, we can add India to this list.

5 Amanda Anderson, *Bleak Liberalism* (Chicago: University of Chicago Press, 2016), 47.

6 Will Self, "The Novel Is Dead (This Time It's for Real)," *Guardian*, 2 May 2014, www.theguardian.com/books/2014/may/02/will-self-novel-dead-literary-fiction.

7 Walter Benjamin, "The Storyteller: Reflections on the Works of Nikolai Leskov,"

in *Illuminations: Essays and Reflections*, trans. Harry Zohn (New York: Schocken, 1968), 87.

8 Behind the success of the digital universe stands another villain – neoliberalism. Under neoliberalism, writes Daniel Rodgers, "Politics, deliberation, and public action dissolve under the relentless pressure for leveraging one's self into a position of greater human capital and competitive advantage. The state remodels itself as a firm, the university as a factory, and the self as an object with a price tag." It is thus essential to disentangle neoliberalism from liberalism proper, as Anderson and Fukuyama have done; to use the older vocabulary of Frederick Crews, the economic liberalism of utilitarianism needs to be distinguished from the moral liberalism of the Enlightenment. Rogers, "The Uses and Abuses of Neoliberalism," *Dissent* 65, no. 1 (2018): 84–5. Crews, *E.M. Forster: The Perils of Humanism* (Princeton: Princeton University Press, 1962), 25.

9 E.M. Forster, "The Challenge of Our Time," in *Two Cheers for Democracy* (New York: Harcourt, Brace, and World, 1951), 56.

10 Lionel Trilling, *E.M. Forster: A Study* (London: Hogarth Press, 1944), 14.

11 See Crews, *E.M. Forster*, especially chapter 2. Michael Levenson argues that Forster was always dubious about the compatibility of an "old" liberalism that emphasized personal freedoms and a "new" Benthamite liberalism that emphasized the collective good. Michael Levenson, *Modernism and the Fate of Individuality* (Cambridge: Cambridge University Press, 1991), 86–8.

12 David Ayers, "The Politics of Friendship in *A Passage to India*," in *English Literature of the 1920s* (Edinburgh: Edinburgh University Press, 1999), 215, 217.

13 Benita Parry, "Materiality and Mystification in *A Passage to India*," *Novel: A Forum on Fiction* 31, no. 2 (1998): 190.

14 Paul B. Armstrong, "Reading India: E.M. Forster and the Politics of Interpretation," *Twentieth Century Literature* 38, no. 4 (1992): 366. Armstrong, mounting the strongest defence of liberalism, draws upon Richard Rorty and Jürgen Habermas to make a case for Forster as a liberal ironist and pragmatist.

15 Anderson, *Bleak Liberalism*, 4.

16 E.M. Forster, *A Passage to India* (New York: Harcourt Brace, 1984), 65. Further references appear parenthetically in the essay.

17 Armstrong details some of the ways in which partial knowledge in the novel "result[s] in disastrous misreadings." "Reading India," 371.

18 E.M. Forster, "What I Believe," 76, 70. Further references appear parenthetically in the essay.

19 E.M. Forster, *Howards End: A Norton Critical Edition*, ed. Paul B. Armstrong (1910; New York: Norton, 1998), 22.

20 Ibid., 186.

21 Michel de Montaigne, "Of Friendship," in *The Complete Essays of Montaigne*, trans. Donald M. Frame (Stanford: Stanford University Press, 1958), 141.

22 Forster's short story, "The Other Boat," completed in 1957–58 and published posthumously in a version reconstructed by Oliver Stallybrass, depicts a love affair between an Englishman, Lionel March, and Cocoanut, a mixed-race businessman "influential in shipping circles." Lionel's attraction to Cocoanut seems bound up with the transgressive nature of an interracial love. Ultimately, however, the fear of exposure induces homosexual panic in Lionel, leading him to murder Cocoanut and then kill himself. In this instance, a childhood friendship develops into adult sexual love, and because the characters indulge their homosexual desires, the friendship must die. E.M. Forster, "The Other Boat," in *The Life to Come and Other Short Stories*, ed. Oliver Stallybrass (New York: Norton, 1972), 171.

23 One can only speculate on the degree to which the renunciation of physical desire stemming from a difference in sexual orientation was displaced into Forster's representation of the unfulfilled friendship between Fielding and Aziz on the basis of racial and national difference, or as Ayers says, that the friendship "denied in the novel by the history which divides their respective nations … [derives from] Masood's unresponsiveness to Forster's love." Ayers, "Politics," 217. Suleri adds that "Aziz is … both a tribute to Syed Ross Masood and a memorial to Forster's Egyptian lover Mohommed ed Edl." This is not to say that racial or national concerns are merely displaced representations of sexual ones, but rather that the emotions deriving from Forster's cross-cultural friendships, sexual and platonic, informed his representation of the relationship between Fielding and Aziz. Suleri, *The Rhetoric of English India* (Chicago: University of Chicago Press, 1992), 136.

24 Wendy Moffat, *A Great Unrecorded History: A New Life of E.M. Forster* (New York: Picador, 2010), 90.

25 Ibid., 187.

26 Ibid., 190.

27 Michael Lind writes, "If Schmitt were merely one of many German conservatives of the Weimar era who disgraced themselves by collaborating with the Nazis, he would be of interest only to historians. Instead, Schmitt's reputation

as a major thinker endures, sometimes in surprising quarters. American law professors wrestle with Schmitt's theories about constitutionalism and power, while the Western Left is impressed by his denunciation of liberal globalism as a mask for Anglo-American and capitalist imperialism." Michael Lind, "About Schmitt," review of *Carl Schmitt: A Biography*, by Reinhard Mehring, *National Interest* 137 (May/June 2015): 81.

28 Carl Schmitt, *The Concept of the Political: Expanded Edition*, trans. George Schwab (Chicago: University of Chicago Press, 1996), 26. Further references appear parenthetically. For Schmitt it is axiomatic that the political is autonomous, distinct from moral, economic, aesthetic, or other aspects of life; just as "good" and "evil" are the defining terms of morality, so "friend" and "enemy" are the defining terms of politics.

29 Richard Wolin offers a blistering critique of Schmitt's rejection of liberal democracy and embrace of fascist dictatorships: "Schmitt's account of politics wished to replace a rational world of norms and rules with a pre-rational order of visceral ruthlessness in which tolerance was inimical to survival and war was eternal." Richard Wolin, "The Cult of Carl Schmitt," *Liberties: A Quarterly Journal of Culture and Politics* 3, no. 2 (2023): 115.

30 Cf. Suleri, *The Rhetoric of English India*, 138–9. In Suleri's tortuous formulation, Forster "attempts to reconfigurate colonial sexuality into a homoeroticization of race" (135), but she more felicitously concludes that the failed intimacy of the collar-stud scene "suggests the prevailing cultural sadness that inhabits utopian narratives … of friendship across cultures" (139).

31 The incident in the caves is of course both central to the text and famously unresolved. Space prohibits a full analysis, but I tend to credit the view that the assault is Adela's projection of an unconscious fantasy: not attracted to her fiancé, wary of married life in British India, she is drawn instead to the Indian doctor whom she has just imagined to be a sexually vigorous polygamist.

32 Ayers, "Politics," 213. Ayers argues for a conception of friendship operating in the novel that "goes beyond … the pragmatics of politics," a Derridean *aimance*, a friendship like that of Aziz and Mrs Moore "based precisely on loving/liking before knowing" that lies outside "the rigidity" of the British Raj (219–20).

33 Trilling, *E.M. Forster*, 14.

34 Lionel Trilling, *The Liberal Imagination: Essays on Society and Literature* (New York: Harcourt Brace Jovanovich, 1979), ii.

35 Kenneth Burke, "Social and Cosmic Mystery: *A Passage to India*," in *Language as Symbolic Action: Essays on Life, Literature, and Method* (Berkeley: University of California Press, 1966), 229.

36 Parry, "Materiality," 185.

37 Armstrong argues that "After unequivocally affirming the possibility of finding a legitimate agreement about truth and right at Aziz's trial, Forster throws open the question of justice and consensus again in the debate about compensation which ultimately drives Fielding and Aziz apart." Armstrong, "Reading," 376.

38 Moffat, *Great Unrecorded History*, 190.

39 Ibid., 189.

40 G.K. Das, "*A Passage to India*: A Socio-Historical Study" in *A Passage to India: Essays in Interpretation*, ed. John Beer (Totowa: Barnes and Noble, 1985), 2. Das shows how Forster threads through his novel multiple references to recent outrages of British rule, and maintains that he viewed the non-cooperation movement with "sincere interest and sympathy" (4).

41 Trilling, *The Liberal Imagination*, xii. As Anderson argues, "Properly assessed, liberalism can be seen to encompass, and not simply occasionally to disclose, the psychological, social, and economic barriers to its moral and political ideals." Anderson, *Bleak Liberalism*, 2.

Part Two
American Examples

4

Henry James's Ficelles *as Friends*

BRIAN GINGRICH

What are the relationships that really define Henry James?

What if they are not those he cultivated in society, or those he kept in private, or those he created with his great heroines or heroes, but those he resisted in crafting the lesser characters of his fiction?

What if one were to read James's famous preface to *The Portrait of a Lady* and look past his remarks on life in Venice, past his description of rooms on the Riva Schiavoni, and past his vision of Isabel Archer? What if one were to focus instead on the point where his thoughts converge, at the end of the preface, on the figures of Henrietta Stackpole (of *The Portrait of a Lady*) and Maria Gostrey (of *The Ambassadors*), and what if one were to ask why James compares these characters to mere postilions, even fishwives, maybe nothing more than wheels of a carriage that enable the more interesting dramas of their respective novels to play out?

> [N]either belongs to the body of that vehicle, or is for a moment accommodated with a seat inside. There the subject alone is ensconced, in the form of its "hero and heroine," and of the privileged high officials, say, who ride with the king and queen … Maria Gostrey and Miss Stackpole then are cases, each, of the light *ficelle*, not of the true agent; they may run beside the coach "for all they are worth," they may cling to it till they are out of breath (as poor Miss Stackpole all so visibly does), but neither, all the while, so much as gets her foot on the step, neither ceases for a

> moment to tread the dusty road. Put it even that they are like the fish-wives who helped to bring back to Paris from Versailles, on that most ominous day of the first half of the French Revolution, the carriage of the royal family.[1]

Take this as an allegory for how James views character relationships across his fiction. The royal family is headed back to Paris from Versailles.[2] Their destination is, ultimately, the guillotine. They represent for James the good heroes and heroines of his works – the Isabel Archers, Milly Theales, Lambert Strethers, Maggie Ververs, and so on. Those waiting for them at the scaffold would be the deceivers or, in some cases, the villains: Gilbert Osmond; Kate Croy; Chad Newsome and Mme de Vionnet; Charlotte Stant and the Prince. Versailles seems a kind of Eden; in James's imagination, it is an innocent America as well. Paris is Europe, or the world. Knowledge is what the heroes will have gained at the gallows.

James does not mention the carriage-driver in this scenario, and the fact that he does not is characteristic of his craft. The driver must, after all, be the author himself, or his narrator, the one most likely to be held responsible for the whole journey, but also the one whose role, if made too conspicuous, would distract from the drama staged between the heroes (in the carriage) and the villains (at the guillotine). So James makes a peculiar choice. Ignoring the driver, he places responsibility for the movement of the carriage on several odd figures running alongside it – poor women who know the way. They guide the carriage forward, giving directions, until they, having themselves been offered no seat or step, are left in the dust. These seem pathetic figures, quickly put out of use. In James's analogy, they are "fishwives." In the terms of his craft, he calls them *ficelles*.

These *ficelles* are familiar to dedicated readers of James. They are side characters who, first, guide central characters into the drama of his narratives and, typically, serve as companions in conversation with those centres.[3] The typical examples are Henrietta Stackpole in *The Portrait of a Lady*, Maria Gostrey in *The Ambassadors*, Susan Stringham in *The Wings of the Dove*, and Fanny Assingham in *The Golden Bowl*. (Male *ficelles*, such as Waymarsh in *The Ambassadors* or Colonel Assingham in *The Golden Bowl*, are more peripheral. The pronouns in what follows are therefore typically feminine.) It is above all in his prefaces to *The Portrait of a Lady* and *The Ambassadors* that James, speaking of Henrietta and Maria, describes such a character's role. He borrows the term *ficelles* from the language of French theatre. It means literally "strings" or "threads" but refers to the tricks or devices of dramatic technique. And it is for the purpose of narrative drama or scenic presentation that James employs *ficelle* characters. He means to present a work of fiction in which the narrator may step aside or fade into the background, a work in which the role of narration is largely displaced onto the thoughts and perceptions of central characters. Narration, likewise, is displaced onto scenes played out between those characters and functional partners. The functional partners are ready-made in his works as directors, guides, knowers, *ficelles*, or, as he insists on figuring them, fishwives.

Several points may be made about James's *ficelles* from the start.

The first is that James describes Maria Gostrey, and implicitly all *ficelle* characters, as "the reader's friend."[4] And, as far as casual reader responses go, that seems to be true. Readers tend to like Maria, respect her, and wish her well.

The second is that James seems determined to devalue this friendship between reader and character. In the preface to *The Ambassadors* he insists that a *ficelle* like Maria is really *only* the reader's friend: she "acts in that capacity, and *really* in that capacity alone, with exemplary devotion, from the beginning to end of the book." And then he adds, in a gesture of rather cruel exposure, "She is in fine, to tear off her mask, the most unmitigated and abandoned of *ficelles*."[5]

The third point is that this is a bald disavowal. James cares about Maria, and he is, in the very act of writing her, on the verge of "liking" – in his terms, "befriending" – her very meaningfully. The same goes, more or less, for her companions in other novels. In general, James tends to befriend his *ficelles*.

That tendency matters for writerly craft as well as literary history. It marks an extraordinary possibility: to take the thing that one conceives of as the most crafted element of one's work, something whose functionality one in fact regards with embarrassment, and to shape it in such a way that one cannot but give it a humanity that warrants friendship. Then, it marks a suggestive limit: the impossibility of acknowledging such craft as friendly or human. What is remarkable in James's works, in addition to being revelatory for the history of the novel, is the extent to which the conflict between that possibility and that limit in his fiction marks a breaking point for traditions of nineteenth-century craft. In the twentieth century, those possibilities and limits are inverted. "Modern fiction" will no longer be a craft that, incidentally, gives the impression of human character; it will be an expression of human character that relies, incidentally, on craft.[6] So says, at least, Virginia Woolf.

Woolf, too, uses the figure of a "carriage" – in her case, a modern train car – to describe the role of character in fiction. Whereas James's carriage is a figure for a craft that, in conveying "royal" protagonists, must abandon "fishwife" *ficelles*, Woolf's is a figure for a literary history that has long conveyed fishwives and now must acknowledge them. Conveyed in Woolf's carriage is a "clean, threadbare old" Mrs Brown: she travels "from one age of English literature to the next," and, although writers in recent eras have not "so much as looked at" her, this modern fishwife goes by the name of "human nature."[7] Woolf distrusts craft as a means to express such humanity just as James distrusts humanity unexpectedly expressed by it. Yet the conflict in James's novels is, as the end point of an established craft-based tradition, the catalyst of a humanist-modernist one. To question his possibilities and limits is to outline a turning point in the history of how novelists relate to their characters. To question the possibilities, one may ask how he befriends his *ficelles*. To question the limits, one asks why he disavows them.

"Friendship," in this case, is defined in a more or less classical sense. It is what Aristotle calls virtuous *philia*: a loving relation to another person that ignores their use or utility and embraces them for their own good.[8] Yet, more specifically, friendship in James's fiction is exceptional in that it is extended to someone who was created for use. From the perspective of craft, friendship is what occurs when an author, creating a character as a mere plot function, finds the character transcending that function itself. From the perspective of a reader, it is what happens when one becomes allied with the needs of a character born of necessity. From both perspectives, friendship is what happens when one dismisses the function that another character may have in one's own plot or action and allows them a freedom that seems human. To this extent, James is an odd sort of Pygmalion. Odd, perhaps, because his creation is not in itself erotic; odd, furthermore, because he refuses to recognize humanity in it. In the end, he regards his creation with shame and denial. He hastens to "tear off the mask" of his all-too-human *ficelle*, denouncing its artifice and unconjuring it back into sculpture. James plays the role of a Pygmalion affronted.

How does James humanize or befriend his *ficelles*? One may do justice to him by using his own critical terminology: the terms of "picture" (or description, or telling) versus "drama" (or action, or some sort of showing).

First, picture. How much does James's affection for *ficelle* characters arise, in the course of his narratives, through his mere acts of telling, of describing such characters at length? It is in fact a result of James's artistic concerns that his *ficelles*, in contrast to his heroes, heroines, focalizers, or reflectors, are more likely to be described from the start. Since, ideally for James, the central characters of his novels are meant to be observers whose appearance takes shape belatedly, through the observations of surrounding characters – above all, *ficelles* – then one is less likely to "see" those heroes than to witness what they or an unconcerned narrator see of other characters like *ficelles*. The point is that we do get remarkable descriptions of *ficelle* characters; and it is possible that James, in the process of writing his way into those descriptions, finds himself meeting those characters with affection. The results are, however, unconvincing. Fanny Assingham appears as an actress, a Southerner, an Easterner, recumbent on divans and in hammocks, sharing sugared fruit with a pet gazelle. Henrietta Stackpole is introduced as "a bunch of brown ringlets" and a "peculiarly open, surprised-looking eye" (her voice "not rich, but loud").[9]

What is comical in these portrayals is, though not cruel, certainly wanting in affection. When affection does seem to appear in James's treatment of a *ficelle* character, it is at a late stage in a narrative, when a *ficelle* has already transformed from a describable object into a describer. By a quarter of the way through *The Golden Bowl*, it is Fanny, rather than the narrator, who applies touches to the portrait of Maggie Verver. It is Susan Stringham, at the end of *The Wings of the Dove*, who knows everything. With fear or awe, Merton Densher and Kate Croy realize that "she's a person who does see."[10] The irony, of course, is that the reader hardly sees anything the *ficelle* sees at this point: the *ficelle*'s clairvoyance is alluded to, but the sights are left almost wholly up to the imagination. Still, the point, for our purposes, is clear: the *ficelles* tend to be pictured in their early comic stages as functions; by the time they attract friendship, they are less pictures than lenses.

"Picturing" *ficelles* can, nevertheless, be considered a significant act in James's character relations. It is true that the term "picture" provides little insight into the *ficelle* character's transition from a lesser stage of Aristotelian social relations to a higher one – from a relation of use to a relation of virtuous *philia*. The former stage is one that James refuses to describe seriously, and the latter he describes hardly at all. But picture may provide more insight if one considers those Aristotelian social relations in a manner that is more, say, Marxian. There is an intermediate stage between utility and transcendent *philia* – something more like *eros* or imagining a *ficelle*'s use-value as approaching the status of a commodity fetish – that is registered more readily in Jamesian description. If the *ficelle* herself, in her early narrative stage of use-value, does not draw attraction pictorially, certain objects associated with her labour certainly do. They are objects that, in fact, stand out as mysterious products of her work in mediating social relations.

Consider the drift of Strether's gaze as he regards James's most exemplary *ficelle* character early in *The Ambassadors*. He has so far, in his first encounter with Maria Gostrey, recognized little more than a lady with features "not freshly young, not markedly fine, but on happy terms with each other."[11] At the beginning of Book Second, he sees something associated with her that produces desire. He dines with Maria, among "pink lights" and "vague sweetness," and he fixes his attention on a "broad red velvet band" worn round her throat. Her dress is "cut down"; the band stands out intimidatingly; and the Jamesian narrator, rather than taking this as a cue to describe all her features, allows us simply to share in Strether's bewildered perception. The broad band serves "to carry on and complicate … his vision."

> It would have been absurd of [Strether] to trace into ramifications the effect of the ribbon from which Miss Gostrey's trinket depended, had he not for the hour, at the best, been so given over to uncontrolled perceptions. What was it but an uncontrolled perception that his friend's velvet band somehow added, in her appearance, to the value of every other item – to that of her smile and of the way she carried her head, to that of her complexion, of her lips, her teeth, her eyes, her hair?[12]

The "friend's velvet band" – a friendly string or *ficelle* – is not simply, for my purposes, an occasion for wordplay. In place of a conventional description of Miss Gostrey – a specification of complexion, lips, teeth, eyes, and hair – we get a small object that adds to the value of all else in her that we do not directly see. James must be aware that this object is, to some extent, a crude narrative device, a substitute for description and a shortcut to character development that launches the reader into the realm of European desire. Yet the object is also a perfect figure for what is produced by the *ficelle*. Following one line of thought, it is fetish: a signifier that stands out as a surplus of all that Maria is otherwise; an addition to her appearance, reduced from her social being, that provides mystery to what her appearance or being may be. Still in another way, it is utility: not a surplus but an equivalent of its bearer, a *ficelle* as James conceives Maria herself to be, a device for spurring the central character's drama. What makes the band also, ultimately, an object of friendship is not simply that Strether and the reader interpret it as something that belongs to a friend ("his friend's velvet band"), but also that James himself, in his efforts to dissimulate the function of the band and its wearer, gives them "natural" or "human" value.

It is part of the realism of James's craft that he feels compelled to "motivate" his *ficelle* devices, disguising their functionality by making them seem natural outgrowths of their storyworlds. But it is something beyond realism that drives James to dissimulate and motivate so far that a *ficelle* character gains freedom from function. It is certainly something beyond realism that drives him to unmask them as functions. The Maria that he presents in the preface to *The Ambassadors* is stripped of the charms of dissimulation: she stands "[in a] draughty wing with her shawl and her smelling salts."[13] This portrayal is James's reaction to what begins in the velvet band and what ultimately defines his *ficelle* characters: having been essential, as devices, they become excessive, in their lingering appearance.

The *ficelle* character in James is a device motivated – her functionality strategically disguised and dissimulated by him, her presence displaced onto minor scenes, side rooms, and curios – in such a way that she attracts surplus value. If that value eventually becomes – for an affronted James outside the storyworld – one of friendship or *philia*, it may be an extension of the fact that the *ficelle* should produce functionally in the story, for characters and readers, excess *eros*. Maria through her velvet band clearly communicates something erotic; so does, say, the no doubt non-erotic shopkeeper of *The Golden Bowl*, whose collection of objects bears an aura of secrecy and desire fuelling the central drama of the novel's romances.

The best *ficelle* figure of conflict between *eros* and functionality in James is the girl who operates the telegraph in *In the Cage*.[14] The strands of paper-tape telegrams that she handles – messages exchanged, through her, between lovers

– are her own velvet bands. She uses them to insert herself into others' romances, asserting her influence over the messages, creating an excess of signs, and seeking an excess of meaning. In the first paragraph of that story we learn that she, dealing with customers sending telegrams, seeks out anyone "who could add something to the poor identity of her function."[15] And so with Jamesian relations: it is not simply that erotic or romantic dialogue is mediated by a poor *ficelle*, but that *ficelle*, ultimately left out of the romance, is configured (and perhaps desperate) to draw from that dialogue human value – a social "identity" from a narrative "function." That is the ideal arc of the *ficelle* as portrayed through "picture" in James: to emerge, out of a social conflict between, on the one side, mere utility or use-value, and on the other, a commodity-value tending toward *eros*, with a freedom of seeing, describing, or on her own part, picturing.

So much for picture or description. Scenic drama, the other side of Jamesian craft, seems to register variations in James's treatment of *ficelle* characters above all in variations of dialogue. (Hence the aspiration of the girl "in the cage": to find, in others' dialogue, her social value.) At this point one can turn back from figurative mediators (bearers of velvet bands, bowls, and telegrams) toward characters featured throughout whole novels. Admittedly, certain challenges become clear. How does one find "the" scene in which James makes friendly contact with a *ficelle*? How does one identify the moment of dialogue where he allows her to speak freely and without function? The answers are speculative but still worth suggesting.

In chapter 44 of *The Portrait of a Lady*, Henrietta Stackpole shows up in Florence. She is concerned about Isabel Archer, now unfortunately married to Gilbert Osmond. Yet she first visits not Isabel but a character who is peripheral like herself: Osmond's sister, the Countess Gemini. The encounter is meaningfully funny – a comic mismatch between the uptight and opinionated "free" American and the droll yet despairing and encumbered cosmopolitan. Their dialogue across two or three pages is something like a sparring of moods. One character speaks optimistically, the other responds with pessimism, and then that character's turn toward optimism is met pessimistically. Questions and responses follow a comic pattern of slight misunderstandings based on cultural cues. But, at a certain point, a moment of compromise emerges. Henrietta says that she has come to Italy because she has "wanted to look after" Isabel. The Countess responds:

"Ah, that's very pretty – *c'est bien gentil*! Isn't it what they call friendship?"

"I don't know what they call it. I thought I had better come."

"She's very happy – she's very fortunate," the Countess went on. "She has others besides." And then she broke out passionately. "She's more fortunate than I! I'm as unhappy as she – I've a very bad husband; he's a great deal worse than Osmond. And I've no friends. I thought I had, but they're gone. No one, man or woman, would do for me what you've done for her."

Henrietta was touched; there was nature in this bitter effusion. She gazed at her companion a moment, and then: "Look here, Countess, I'll do anything for you that you like. I'll wait over and travel with you."

"Never mind," the Countess answered with a quick change of tone: "only describe me in the newspaper!"[16]

Forget whatever self-pity or self-righteousness may be at play in this dialogue. The author who arranged this situation finds something touching in these comically adrift characters' connection. Henrietta and the Countess are unnecessarily generous to one another; and James, allowing them freedom apart from the plot, is unnecessarily generous as well. The two characters' friendship is charmingly incidental – their expressions of alternating optimism and pessimism end in abrupt compromise whereby the Countess's envy (of others' friendship) is met by spontaneous pity (and friendship) – and James's interest in the scene, too, has an incidental or happened-upon quality. Even the definition of friendship that surfaces reveals a certain collaboration between characters and author. Henrietta describes it, the Countess names it, and James, suggesting that Henrietta's dismissal of it is uncharacteristically modest, seems to endorse it. The definition is worth considering across James's work. Friendship is "looking after" another.

One struggles to learn much more from looking at dialogue. It is one of the most elusive objects of narrative analysis. Yet there is still something to be gained in considering the subtle ways in which the author presents it. Consider the mere "tags" that James uses to give rhythm to a conversation – the "he saids" and "she saids" that accompany speeches. "The Countess went on … she broke out passionately … Henrietta was touched … she gazed … The Countess answered with a quick change of tone …" Such phrases may reveal turns of affection in the person writing the character's speeches. For James to describe Henrietta as "touched" and "gaz[ing]" is indeed an event. The phrase "she gazed at her companion" is a beat in the rhythm of what constitutes narrative friendship.

But that rhythm can be tracked better in tags accompanying a *ficelle*'s dialogue with a true centre of a novel. Consider a passage chosen, more or less randomly, from *The Ambassadors*. In Book Eleventh, chapter 2, Strether is discussing with Maria his unfortunate attempt to approach the sister of Chad Newsome (the rich wayward son of the novel) and convince her that Chad is "all right." Maria begins by asking Strether how Chad's sister has affected him:

> "Do you mean that she has shocked you as you've shocked her?"
>
> Strether weighed it. "I'm probably not so shockable. But on the other hand I've gone much further to meet her. She, on her side, hasn't budged an inch."
>
> "So that you're now at last" – Maria pointed the moral – "in the sad stage of recriminations."
>
> "No – it's only to you I speak. I've been like a lamb to Sarah. I've only put my back to the wall. It's to that one naturally staggers when one has been violently pushed there."
>
> She watched him a moment. "Thrown over?"
>
> "Well, as I feel I've landed somewhere I think I must have been thrown."
>
> She turned it over, but as hoping to clarify much rather than to harmonise. "The thing is that I suppose you've been disappointing –"
>
> "Quite from the very first of my arrival? I dare say. I admit I was surprising even to myself."
>
> "And then of course," Maria went on, "I had much to do with it."
>
> "With my being surprising – ?"
>
> "That will do," she laughed, "if you're too delicate to call it my being! Naturally," she added, "you came over more or less for surprises."
>
> "Naturally!" – he valued the reminder.[17]

The value of this passage – as a chance at identifying something of a James-*ficelle* friendship – is, first, that it is unremarkable. There is something unessential and even unnecessary in it that violates James's principles of economy. Yet there is, nevertheless, something informative. For the first two-thirds of

The Ambassadors, Maria's speeches have been tagged with words like "explained," "added," "returned," "confirmed," and, always assertively, "said." Even the "saids" are less frequent in the third part; certainly there are fewer "addeds" or "explaineds." It matters that in Book Eleventh Maria no longer "echoes" or "harmonises" in her dialogues with Strether. The tags tend toward verbs such as "pursues," "keeps up," and "clarifies." Having once guided the hero, she strains to find clarity. The rhythm of the above dialogue itself is determined by her attempts at clarification and Strether's resistance: he says "no" to her "moral"; she can provide little else, until her final statement, than half-formed suggestions or questions. The same transformation – from knowing to naive *ficelle*-dialogue – can be seen (for example) in *The Golden Bowl*: the once confident Fanny Assingham curiously shifts, around chapter 30, into phrases tagged not just with "pursued" and "kept up" but also "wondered" and, with unusual frequency, "quavered."

Jamesian *ficelle* characters, considered as speakers in scenes, transform in two ways in the course of their narratives: first, by finding themselves bewildered and excluded; second, by gaining freedom. The very exclusion that they are portrayed as experiencing in their storyworlds strikes their portrayer as a narrative excess that, ultimately, frees them from function. The very fact that Henrietta speaks on the periphery with Countess Gemini, that Maria, speaking with Strether, finds herself increasingly peripheral, and that other *ficelle* characters find their speech acts disregarded or weak – above all, the fact that they are all still allowed to remain in the narrative frame – is a triumph. A perverse one. It is, of course, a freedom that the characters in their storyworlds will never "know" (they know mainly exclusion), and it is a freedom that James will glimpse and eventually reject.

Perverse, as well, may be the fact that the *ficelles*, in becoming non-functional, partly take on new functions. Henrietta and Maria, though no longer guides, serve as "interrogators," sounding boards, or echoes to a central character's narcissism.[18] What distinguishes their new functionality is, first, that it is more tenuous and less aligned with an author figure; more crucial, however, is that it is a functionality the author seems not to have foreseen. They speak briefly, ineffectively, or inordinately, with little to say; they pose questions to Millie, Maggie, or Lambert that those heroes could have asked to themselves; they drive circumlocutions around what the plot leaves unknown. They keep talking. The lecture that James delivered more than any other in his lifetime ends with a warning about dialogue in fiction. "Dialogue," he says, is "essentially the fluid element"; it tends toward excess – all too often, toward "large, loose, facile flood of talked movement."[19] *Ficelle* characters precisely seem to lead James to such excess. He lets them keep talking, and allows them a presence he had not unaccounted for. And he, in many ways, keeps talking about them. The preface to *The Portrait* ends not with Isabel but with Henrietta. It ends, in fact, with an acknowledgment and some embarrassment of her surplus: "Henrietta … exemplifies, I fear, in her superabundance, not an element of my plan, but only an excess of my zeal." He continues this theme of excess: "Henrietta must have been at that time a part of my wonderful notion of the lively." Isabel Archer at this point has not been mentioned for more than a page, and she will not be mentioned further. It is with the thought of Henrietta that James concludes his preface: "There is really too much to say."[20] Much to say about the periphery, far less about the centre.

How does James befriend his *ficelles*? One can phrase it better: how does he write them into a relation of friendship? Maybe it is, to some extent, through pictorial description (letting them be seen by others); more likely, it is through scenic drama (letting them speak over others). Yet the most decisive factor is the most elusive one: it is through regarding them in a state of having returned. The ultimate surplus value of the *ficelle* character is a result of her temporarily leaving the narrative – being exiled from it, gaining independence from it – and returning with a difference. Maria, Henrietta, Susan Stringham, and Fanny Assingham are absent for a hundred or so pages in the third quarters of their respective novels. They return without fanfare and, as they themselves acknowledge, without function. The most revealing phrase that Maria speaks to Strether in that conversation in Book Eleventh, chapter 2 addresses this lack of function: "I seem to have ceased to serve you."[21] No longer a figure of the author (displaced, as a fishwife guiding the carriage) or a figure of the reader (implied, as a spectator of the carriage's movement) – no longer guide or prognosticator, no longer essential device – she returns from her absence with little consequence. There is a reason why that chapter in Book Eleventh is placed elsewhere in some editions of *The Ambassadors* and entirely omitted from others. It does not clearly matter. And so, one may assume, the *ficelle* character's state of having returned, if it does appeal to James, is a state of not mattering.

But that is not exactly the case. It seems, in fact, that a state of not mattering for plot corresponds to a new state of mattering for the plotter. James himself seems to acknowledge such a correspondence in his portrayal of "plotting" characters – characters who, tending to use others as functions, are less friends than, say, foes. These, in fact, are the characters most concerned with the *ficelles*' absences once they have departed their narratives. Chad Newsome twice presses the question to Strether, "Has Miss Gostrey come back?"[22] Kate Croy presses Milly Theale not to rely on Susan Stringham: "You shouldn't take your people from *her*."[23] Charlotte Stant-Verver suddenly seems to become, despite the *ficelle*-couple's absence, "restrictive about the Assinghams."[24] Henrietta haunts Gilbert Osmond: "She strikes me as a kind of monster."[25] What is comical, particularly in that last example, is also meaningful. The fact that the profound plotters are suddenly vexed by seemingly less-than-profound *ficelle* characters – the fact that the *ficelles* suddenly matter to them – seems precisely to do with the fact that the *ficelles* are on the verge of not mattering to the plot. The new or non-functionality of the having returned *ficelle* is opposed to plot in such a way that seems to provoke in a plotter some obsession. It is an excess that draws curious attention – above all, from the ultimate plotter who caused it.

If James becomes attentive to *ficelles* who, having returned, no longer matter, he expresses it less through telling (picture) or showing (scene) than through something that strikes the reader as curious watching. Watching is, essentially, the central act of Jamesian fiction and of James himself. It is an ambiguous act, performed as much by guides, compatriots, and friends as by deceivers, manipulators, and foes. Still, when James defines watching as the central act of the novelist in the preface to *The Portrait of a Lady* – describing "the posted presence of the watcher" in "the house of fiction" as "the consciousness of the artist" – he means it for the most part benevolently, as what one does to take care of a central character, an Isabel Archer. If one follows the arc of James's discussion in this passage, his attention to central characters like Isabel veers steadily toward characters who are *ficelles*, in particular, Henrietta and Maria. There he finds himself admitting that, despite his intentions, "[these] smaller female fry … insist on mattering." And he oddly goes further, quoting George Eliot: "Through these frail vessels is borne onward through the ages the treasure of human affection."[26]

The transition is striking: from a posted presence watching over a hero to a pursuit of a frail, now-human *ficelle*-vessel. James, adopting Eliot's moral as craft, slightly adjusts the task of the novelist. It is, no doubt, to watch one's central subject, to allow it its freedom or humanity, but it is also to watch further as frail figures on the periphery become present, draw one's attention, and maybe even more significantly than the centres themselves, draw human affection. Henrietta Stackpole's idea of friendship – "looking after" another – seems to be taken seriously. The artist looks from the centre to the *ficelle*, who in turn looks after the centre. The *ficelle*, far from a lagging fishwife, moves in the company of the artist. She looks after a friend, and James looks after her.

It is in a state of having returned – of surprisingly still being there – that the *ficelle* character most attracts James's friendship. This state is, much more than any that one may call simply pictorial or dramatic, hard to characterize. But one might find it nevertheless manifested in the middle of chapter 44 of *The Portrait of a Lady*, just after the conversation between Henrietta and the Countess Gemini cited above.

Henrietta becomes an observer whose gaze comes into alignment with James's own. She leaves the Countess, walks through Florence, and prepares to meet with Caspar Goodwood, Isabel's American suitor, in a scene that will be functional (if minorly so) for the narrative. In the meantime, her walk through Florence gains a degree of attention from the narrator that makes its, and her, specific function unclear. It is a rare event for James to track a character on a path through a city, much less a minor character. Still, he follows a lone Henrietta through streets and squares, across bridges, narrating her movements with remarkable precision. Eventually, he arrives with Henrietta at the Uffizi, where she seeks out her favourite painting, the so-called Correggio of the Tribune:

> she ascended the high staircase which leads to the upper chambers. The long corridor, glazed on one side and decorated with antique busts, which gives admission to these apartments, presented an empty vista in which the bright winter light twinkled upon the marble floor. The gallery is very cold and during the midwinter weeks but scantily visited. Miss Stackpole may appear more ardent in her quest of artistic beauty than she has hitherto struck us as being, but she had after all her preferences and admirations. One of the latter was the little Correggio of the Tribune – the Virgin kneeling down before the sacred infant, who lies in a litter of straw, and clapping her hands to him while he delightedly laughs and

crows. Henrietta had a special devotion to this intimate scene – she thought it the most beautiful picture in the world.[27]

Henrietta is impressively alone in this situation. She seems to see in the Virgin a portrait of Isabel – Henrietta's own portrait, defined by her own devotion to and idealization of her friend – that matches James's devotion and idealization remarkably.[28] James has so far allowed Isabel to be viewed as a portrait only twice in *The Portrait of a Lady*, both instances having been set in the gallery at her uncle's estate at Gardencourt. Fifty pages into the novel, her ailing cousin looks at her among a number of paintings and sees her as "thin, and light, and middling tall … hair dark, even to blackness … light grey eyes."[29] Eighty pages later, in the same gallery, Lord Warburton sees an Isabel with a light figure, white neck, dark braids, and strange eyes.[30]

Yet Henrietta's view of a more allegorical Isabel seems to be privileged. James tells us, in fact, that "it is our privilege to look over [Henrietta's] shoulder." He offers her to us as a viewer, centre, focalizer, and he allows her a brief moment to freeze our attention. Those present-tense verbs ("the gallery is very cold") are not merely tics of James as a travel writer; they are signs of his taking a character's gaze seriously. A few lines later James attributes to Henrietta "a great sense of beauty in all ways" – and, although his judgment is not without irony, what may be comic in it is not unaffectionate.[31] Henrietta, as a *ficelle*, does have a sense of beauty. We feel this not because we have seen what she sees and agree with her, but because we have been left alone with her and seen that she sees freely enough. One is compelled to see her freedom and solitude, in the story, as effects of her having existed outside the narrative. Henrietta, having returned, is suddenly worth watching with a sincerity that her initial characterization never suggested. And her act of watching, allowing us to see an idealized portrait of Isabel, appears to be more aligned with James's attempt at painterly portrayal than any other moment of the novel.

Henrietta both aligns herself with James's gaze and is suggestively observed by a character who seems to manifest it. Ralph Touchett, the ailing cousin of Isabel Archer in *The Portrait of a Lady*, wavers somewhere between a figurative reader and author of the novel. He watches at times passively, at times somewhat schemingly. There is an outstanding moment when Isabel walks in on him and finds him with his, up until now, apparent foe: Henrietta. Ralph casually explains: "Oh yes, we are intimate enemies." The narrator clarifies:

"in reality they became excellent friends."[32] So it seems that Ralph may be an ideal figure for an author, who, having been prepared to leave his *ficelle* character in the dust of his narrative, ends up conveying her with some affection.

But Ralph dies soon after that scene. Milly Theale dies, abandoning Susan Stringham. Maggie Verver learns how to use and dismiss Fanny Assingham. Strether, of course, rejects Maria. The typical fate of the *ficelle* character is not, ultimately, affection. It is an abandonment by other characters, arranged by the author, and reflective of his own impulse to deny them.

Consider the progression in *The Portrait of a Lady* and *The Ambassadors* of the way James versus his heroes (Isabel, Strether) relates to his *ficelle* characters (Henrietta, Maria). In the early and mid-late moments of both novels, James and the heroes relate to the *ficelles* inversely. James uses Henrietta and Maria as *ficelles*, then befriends them in a way that allows them their freedom, while Isabel and Strether are first amused by those *ficelles* – listening to them, assuming their freedom – only to surpass them as they themselves gain knowledge, freedom, and authority. The third and last stage of this movement, however, leaves both the author and the heroes in a direct or parallel relation to one another. James disavows his *ficelles* as mere artifice, and the heroes disappoint them by declining their offers. Isabel declines Henrietta's proposal of Goodwood; Strether declines Maria's implicit offer. The heroes do, in fact, offer friendship in place of some other affection, but friendship, in these instances, is expressed as denial.

There is something unnecessary in these turns of disappointment and abandonment. When James was first developing *The Ambassadors*, he sketched out a plan that included an explanation of why Strether must ultimately refuse a romantic relationship with Maria. He said that such a relationship would have been, first, "vulgar" and, second, lacking "the mark of the real." These justifications are, like most writers' explanations of their craft, both weak and revelatory. In place of a "vulgar" romance between Strether and Maria, James claims to offer his audience their friendship: "we don't do anything so vulgar as make him 'take up,' save for a friendship that he quite sincerely hopes may last with poor, convenient, amusing, unforgettable, impossible Gostrey." One notes that this friendship is expressed in the manner described above – namely, through denial. It occurs not between James and any given character but rather between a central character and a *ficelle* whose value James dismisses. Meanwhile, in place of what is not "real" in Maria and Strether's romance, James says that he would like to offer the "vivid and concrete and interesting." But then he slightly corrects himself and seems to prefer another term: "verisimilitude."[33]

Verisimilitude, to the extent that it is opposed to the not "real," and friendship, to the extent that it is opposed to "vulgar" romance, are the categories by which James limits a *ficelle* character's freedom. Given the discussion so far, these terms are hard to accept. Friendship, after all, has been defined as what grants a *ficelle* freedom; realism has been implied as what should release her from mere function. But the confusion is mainly a matter of what James imagines in his storyworld versus what he performs as an author.

Yes, mere friendship within a story, offered unconvincingly by a central character to a Maria or a Susan or a Fanny, tends to restrict a *ficelle*'s freedom. But that restriction, imposed by James as a purported defence against vulgarity, is in many ways a reflex of what he has, with regret, already granted the *ficelle* as friendship and decency. A final friendship in the story is his final revocation of their freedom.

Verisimilitude, meanwhile, is a category opposed not just to the not-real but also to realism.[34] As an already guaranteed mark of the real in a character, it removes the need for that character's realization. The characters that James considers inherently real are, of course, his centres or heroes. "The mark of the real never ceases to show in [Strether]," he states, then immediately adds, "with the real only the real – of verisimilitude, of consistency – consorts."[35] The division is clear. On the one side stand the central characters whose presence costs the narrative nothing, since they are granted from the start verisimilitude. On the other side stand the *ficelle* characters who cost significantly, in that they must be rigorously dissimulated, motivated, and realized. Maria Gostrey is, as James puts it, "pre-engaged at a high salary"; both her use and her dissimulation must be paid for. James certainly does give her credit in his preface to *The Ambassadors* for making a quick profit. The moment she does so is a familiar one. "By the time she has dined with Strether in London and gone to a play with him," he says, "her intervention as a *ficelle* is, I hold, expertly justified." Her inevitability and her invisibility go without saying: "Her function speaks at once for itself."[36]

Nevertheless, as we have seen, a *ficelle* like Maria develops beyond terms of use, cost, profit, and economy altogether. This is something that a central, already "real" character could never do. Only a *ficelle* could affect an author with such extraordinary surplus because only a *ficelle* is expected by an author to function with such ordinary use. One is then left to ask why a *ficelle* like Maria, having reached such an extraordinary state, having been paid for by James, and having exceeded whatever returns he expected, does not deserve the minor cost that would motivate her final romance. Why does she receive a friendship (with a character) that seems to dismiss her value, rather than a friendship (with her author) that appreciates her surplus?

Call it, on James's part, strange pride. His need to unmask Maria is that of a proud conjurer who, having found his act of dissimulation successful, cannot but reveal the trick, as he does in his preface to *The Ambassadors*. Or, on the other side of pride, call it embarrassment – that he himself was taken in by his trick, befriending mere *ficelles* and needing to deny it. Call it ethics. James revokes those *ficelles*' friendliness or freedom because it would be artistic dishonesty to pass off a function as a free soul. Above all, one may call James's disavowal of Maria an attempt to elevate theory over practice. The James who wrote the prefaces to the New York Edition of his works in the early twentieth century was willing to sacrifice the seeming humanity of his intermediate characters in order to develop a "theory" or "art" of fiction, a study of "types" and "functions" of characters in the name of a new era of "craft."

When Theodora Bosanquet, James's amanuensis and friend in his later years, reflected on his social life, she said that "the cultivation of friendships may be said to have been his sole recreation." She quickly added that his capacity for maintaining friendly "relations" had "definite limits." James "loved his friends, but he was condemned by the law of his being to keep clear of any really entangling net of human affection and exaction."[37] The letters and personal accounts left in his wake return to this contradiction. James was a masterful socialite who remained socially distant. He accepted over a hundred dinner invitations in a "season" while claiming to have no "talent for making friends."[38] He had both a great interest in and a great anxiety about friendships. That tendency holds for his fiction as well as for his social life. He developed his fiction, of course, out of his social encounters. He found "germs" of anecdotes in dinner conversations, adapted lonely figures into heroines. James knew that he used people. If he used them as most authors do, he seems still to have used them more and with such a consciousness of craft that he was driven relentlessly to consider that use. Indeed, anxiety over such use tainted James's idea of friendship. Nonetheless, in his life as in his fiction, he continued to offer friendship to others and thrived on social interactions. In his fiction, he continued to perceive in functional characters – *ficelles*, fishwives – something that could be developed as near-real, near-human, and free. Then, inevitably, he would renounce that development and revoke that freedom.

James knew, maybe better than anyone, how to see beyond the use of others and how to transform use into friendship. But he knew just as well, and was haunted by the fact, that friendships might always originate in, and remain bound to, considerations of use. James let "decent" friendships go – as he also let go, for several reasons, "vulgar" romances. What one is left wondering is not so much whether he should have sought further to offer someone humanity or freedom – he went as far as any author could – but whether he should have allowed himself the pleasure of their use. Use is, of course, not the true bond of friendship, but at least it is binding. Friendship is a granting of freedom as well as a bond. If James struggled to accept this compromise, it is because he knew both sides of it too well. He knew friendship as what could transform another person's use into their freedom, and he knew use as what reduces friendship to functionality and craft. He seems reluctant to have known that he could, all at once, relate to someone as a function and allow them freedom, and acknowledge both of those impulses as linked, however vulgarly, to his own need.

NOTES

1 Henry James, preface to the New York Edition of *The Portrait of a Lady* (1908), in *The Portrait of a Lady* (1881; New York: Penguin, 2011), 638.

2 In fact, the royal family was brought from Varennes, not Versailles.

3 See Christopher Nash, "Henry James, Puppetmaster: The Narrative Status of Maria Gostrey, Susan Stringham, and Fanny Assingham as *Ficelles*," *Studies in the Novel* 9, no. 3 (1977): 297–310.

4 Henry James, *The Ambassadors* (1903; New York: Norton, 1994), 12.

5 Ibid.

6 See Virginia Woolf, "Character in Fiction," in *Selected Essays* (Oxford: Oxford University Press, 2008), 42.

7 Ibid., 47.

8 Aristotle, *Nicomachean Ethics*, trans. C.D.C. Reeve (Indianapolis: Hackett, 2014), 136–55.

9 Henry James, *The Golden Bowl* (1905; Oxford: Oxford University Press, 1983), 26–7; James, *Portrait*, 87.

10 Henry James, *The Wings of the Dove* (1902; New York: Penguin, 2008), 479.

11 James, *The Ambassadors*, 18.

12 Ibid., 42.

13 Ibid., 12.

14 Robert Caserio suggested the importance of the shopkeeper and the girl in the cage to me.

15 Henry James, *In the Cage*, in *Tales of Henry James*, ed. Christof Wegelin and Henry B. Wonham (1898; New York: Norton, 2003), 229.

16 James, *Portrait*, 479.

17 James, *Ambassadors*, 299.

18 Nash, "Henry James, Puppetmaster," 300.

19 Henry James, "The Lesson of Balzac" (1905), in *Literary Criticism: French Writers, Other European Writers, The Prefaces to the New York Edition*, ed. Leon Edel (New York: Library of America, 1984), 138.

20 James, "Preface," in *Portrait*, 640.

21 James, *Ambassadors*, 294.

22 Ibid., 187.

23 James, *The Wings of the Dove*, 225.

24 James, *Golden Bowl*, 376.

25 James, *Portrait*, 516.

26 James, "Preface," in *Portrait*, 632–4.

27 James, *Portrait*, 480.

28 Gerald Eager sees Isabel's image in the Correggio painting as "an ingenuous American heroine whose unspoiled originality shines forth in the dusky disenchantment of the European milieu." Gerald Eager, "A Portrait of Isabel Archer: Correggio's *Virgin Adoring the Christ Child* in Henry James's *The Portrait of a Lady*," CEA *Critic* 47, no. 4 (1985): 39–50.

29 James, *Portrait*, 47.

30 Ibid., 138.

31 Ibid., 481.

32 Ibid., 521.

33 Henry James, "Project of Novel by Henry James" (1900), in *The Ambassadors*, 403.

34 What follows is a discussion of narrative functionality, dissimulation, realization, and verisimilitude that, drawn from the terms of James's own writings, belongs to a later tradition of formalist-structuralist theory. See for example Gérard Genette, "Vraisemblance et motivation," in *Figures II* (Paris: Editions de Seuil, 1969), 71–9.

35 James, "Project of Novel," 403.

36 James, *The Ambassadors*, 12–13.

37 Theodora Bosanquet, *Henry James at Work* (1924; Ann Arbor: University of Michigan Press, 2006), 48.

38 Henry James to Mary Walsh James, 31 January 1879, in *The Complete Letters of Henry James, 1878–1890*, ed. Pierre A. Walker and Greg W. Zacharias (Lincoln: University of Nebraska Press, 2014), 104.

5

Willa Cather and the Posterity of Friendship

ALLAN HEPBURN

In Willa Cather's novels, friendship provides an alternative to marriage and kinship. "Only solitary men know the full joys of friendship," Cather writes in *Shadows on the Rock*: "Others have their family; but to a solitary and an exile his friends are everything."[1] In *The Professor's House*, Godfrey St Peter's friendship with Tom Outland liberates his writing style and frees him from the pettiness of his marriage. When Tom dies in the First World War, Godfrey feels that his capacity for affection toward other people expires with his young friend. Nowhere is friendliness more sublime, yet sublimated, than in *Death Comes for the Archbishop*. On the morning that Jean Marie Latour and Joseph Vaillant depart from their village in the Auvergne for training at a missionary college in Paris, Vaillant vacillates. He does not want to leave his father, and he does not want to break his vow to God. In that moment of hesitation, Latour "had not known how to comfort his friend."[2] Yet Latour's unswerving support of Vaillant sustains him through the long years that he spends expanding the mission of the church in North America. The moment during which Vaillant wavers and Latour reassures sets the course for their lifelong dependence on each other despite differences in rank and personality. In Cather's novels, friends diversify existence. They fortify each other. They make living bearable, even when they are no longer present.

Cather herself had a gift for making and keeping friends. According to Edith Lewis, with whom she lived for thirty-nine years, Cather took "great pleasure in friendship."[3] Friendships formed during her youth in Nebraska lasted throughout her life.[4] She happily counted men and women among her closest friends – Isabelle McClung, Louis Brandeis, Olive Fremstad, Yehudi Menuhin – yet she rarely represents "intimate, lifelong bonds between women in her fiction."[5] Instead, the permutations of male friendship catch her attention and inform her narratives. In addition to gender, friendship holds other mysteries for Cather. Her novels are filled with friends who have been cast aside. Through these discarded friends, Cather speculates on the magnitude of friendship and the genre that best captures that magnitude – short story, novel, or epic.

In Cather's handling, friendship varies in its temporality from one situation to the next. Can friendship endure after a friend dies, as happens in *The Professor's House*, or does it become something else altogether? In *How to Be a Friend*, Cicero sums up the permanence of friendship beyond the grave: "so powerful and real are the memories of true friends, so great and tender is the longing for them, that even in death they are a blessing and live in us."[6] Not just restricted to the here and now, friendship has an afterlife, subject to remembrance and the lasting influence that friends have upon each other. Cather, whose knowledge of Greek and Latin texts was formidable, often thinks about friendship in terms of transformation, along the lines laid down by Cicero: friendship improves individuals who strive to match each other in goodwill, generosity, and selflessness. In this sense, the temporality of friendship is always slightly in the future, for friendship is always perfectible without ever being quite perfect.

Novel and Epic

In 1931, Cather wrote a story called "Two Friends," in which an unnamed narrator reflects on the breaking up of a great friendship between two businessmen, R.E. Dillon and J.H. Trueman. The men are opposites in every way. Dillon is a Democrat of Irish extraction who has crisp articulation and a "wide-awake voice";[7] Trueman is a Republican, an old-time American who is laconic to the point of inarticulateness. Dillon is a family man who despises gambling; Trueman is a widower who hosts a nightly poker game in his back office. Despite their differences, the two men sit on the sidewalk when the weather is fine and talk about this, that, and the other. When Dillon decides to back William Jennings Bryan in the 1896 presidential election, Trueman withdraws his money from Dillon's bank and has nothing further to do with him. After Dillon dies suddenly of pneumonia, Trueman orders flowers for the funeral and leaves town on the first possible train. He returns briefly to sell his businesses and property before settling in San Francisco.

Trueman's strange actions, a mixture of respect and indifference, could be construed as a form of mourning, but the narrator, who looks back on these events from an unspecified time in the future, neither confirms nor denies that interpretation. The rapid collapse of the friendship, the vanishing of the surviving friend, all the unanswered questions about Trueman's behaviour become the property of the narrator, who speculates on the uneasy posterity of friendship: "the feeling of something broken that could so easily have been mended; of something delightful that was senselessly wasted, of a truth that was accidentally distorted – one of the truths we want to keep."[8] In "Two Friends," friendship is unfathomable, enlivening, and pleasurable, until it is no longer any of those things. In this regard, friendship acquires a temporality, even a permanence, when it ceases to exist.

In Cather's novels, discarded friends tend to disappear from view. In *A Lost Lady*, after Captain Daniel Forrester dies, his widow renounces her old friends and invites a cadre of younger men to her house. Niel Herbert, who idolizes Captain Forrester for his integrity and admires Marian Forrester for her charm, finds her behaviour as a widow intolerable. Once Niel decides that he wants nothing more to do with Mrs Forrester, he leaves town without saying goodbye and never sees her again. Years later, Niel hears about the surprising reversal of fortune of Mrs Forrester, cast now as his "old friend,"[9] who remarries and moves to Buenos Aires. Old in the sense of being long-standing but not constant, Mrs Forrester never develops a close relationship with Niel. While still a young man, he fetches her mail and fills out her dinner table when necessary. Yet their acquaintance goes nowhere. He admires her too much to allow her any freedom, certainly not the sexual freedom that she pursues with Frank Ellinger and Ivy Peters.

In some of Cather's novels, close friends loiter in the margins of the story, as if they are not significant enough to move to the centre of attention, or as if the nature of their friendship is too mysterious to yield to explanation. In *O Pioneers!*, Alexandra regrets Carl Linstrum's move to St Louis, which effectively deprives her of her sole friend. "We've never either of us had any other close friend," she says to Carl on the eve of his departure, "and now I must remember that you are going where you will have many friends, and will find the work you were meant to do."[10] As a friend, Alexandra sees that Carl has to confront his destiny by going forth into the world. When Carl returns years later, he and Alexandra decide to marry despite the objections of her brothers. "I think when friends marry, they are safe,"[11] she says to Carl, by which she means that friendship strengthens marriage and forestalls suffering.

In *My Ántonia* and *One of Ours*, sensitive young men seek friendships without really knowing what will satisfy their longing. They have artistic natures, yet they expect other people, usually musicians or scholars, to interpret their personalities for them. In *One of Ours*, Claude Wheeler bears a hope that amounts to a conviction "that there was something splendid about life, if he could but find it."[12] He thinks friendship would heighten that splendour, because the right friend will explain what he is missing. Blighting his own potential, he constantly turns "his back on old pleasures and old friends"[13] because he distrusts the fineness of his feelings and his ability to measure up to those who extend friendship toward him.

In *My Ántonia*, a frame narrative represents friendships between men while foreclosing on friendships between the sexes. An anonymous, first-person male narrator meets Jim Burden on a train. "He and I are old friends,"[14] the narrator explains, without elaborating on the connection. The two men begin talking about Ántonia Shimerda, whom they both knew in Nebraska. When the narrator challenges Jim to set down his recollections of Ántonia, Jim produces a long manuscript, on the cover of which he writes "Ántonia," then adds "my" as an afterthought.[15] Jim speaks of Ántonia as a part of himself: "It's through myself that I knew and felt her, and I've had no practice in any other form or presentation."[16] This statement resonates with Cicero's observation that "a friend is, quite simply, another self."[17] Montaigne, who quotes Cicero liberally in his essay "On Friendship," defines true friends as those "who mingle and blend with each other so completely that they efface the seam that joined them, and cannot find it again."[18] The possessive adjective in Cather's title signifies plurality: Jim's version of Ántonia magnifies her uniqueness instead of commandeering or belittling it. "My Ántonia" does not exclude other versions, least of all her own. Nor do Jim's recollections control Ántonia so much as celebrate her good sense and pioneering spirit.

In *My Ántonia*, the path to idealized friendship is long and rocky. When Jim and Ántonia arrive in Black Hawk, Nebraska, on the same train, he eyes her from a distance while refusing to speak to her. He, an orphan uprooted from Virginia and sent to live with his grandparents, and she, a Bohemian who speaks no English, have a neighbourly rather than a friendly footing. As Jim notes, the Shimerdas are the Burdens' "nearest neighbours."[19] Whereas neighbours have a relationship of proximity, friends choose each other, as Jim and Ántonia eventually do. In *My Ántonia*, neighbours lend each other equipment and pitch in at harvest time, but such reciprocity does not preclude wariness or suspicion. When a misunderstanding about a borrowed horse collar causes friction between the Burdens and Shimerdas, neighbourliness reasserts itself. "No friends any more,"[20] Ántonia says to Jim in her imperfect English – a language, incidentally, that he has taught her. In an echo of this neighbourly resentment, Jim announces, "I'll never be friends with them again."[21] The novel thus distinguishes between friends and neighbours as categories of sociability, with allowances for the chance that neighbours can convert into friends or fall back into being neighbours as circumstances dictate. "Our neighbours seemed glad to make peace with us,"[22] Jim observes when an act of forgiveness clears up the misunderstanding between families.

Throughout *My Ántonia*, men pair off as couples, much as the anonymous narrator pairs off with Jim in the train. When the Burdens lease their farm and move to town, their two hired hands, Otto and Jake, light out for the territories in search of gold and adventure; they send back one letter to say how they are faring, then fall silent. The novel does not track the fate of these friends. Numerous are the men who strike up similar companionships. A handsome Czech named Anton Jelinek "batches"[23] with a compatriot named Jan Bouska. At university, Jim develops a friendship with his classics professor, Gaston Cleric, who sometimes stops by Jim's rooms at night to talk about Virgil and smoke his cigarettes. Two Russian men, Peter and Pavel, live together on a homestead but are preyed upon by bad luck. When Pavel falls ill, he watches Peter "with a contemptuous unfriendly expression,"[24] no doubt because he fears, in his hallucinatory state, that Pavel will sacrifice him, just as, years earlier, they tossed a bride to a pack of wolves in Ukraine, an event that instigates all their troubles. In Cather's reckoning, no friendship is free of suspicion or the potential for unravelling. Nevertheless, some same-sex friendships create a network of support. Tiny and Lena, two women from Black Hawk who make their fortunes in, respectively, gold mining and dressmaking, do not live together but help each other when they both settle in San Francisco.

In *My Ántonia*, same-sex friendships offer consolations that are unavailable to male-female friends. Lena Lingard flirts with men, but keeps them at a distance. "Come and see me sometimes when you're lonesome," she whispers in Jim's ear. "But maybe you have all the friends you want. Have you?"[25] Without saying so, she is probing the nature of Jim's friendship with Gaston Cleric, while signalling the possibility of a friendship that transcends such minor concerns as sex. In truth, she is indifferent to Jim as a sexual partner. Men, she teases, always mistake friendship for love. Worse, marriage pre-empts or ends friendships between men and women. As Lena tells Jim in a moment of commendable frankness, "Men are all right as friends, but as soon as you marry them they turn into cranky old fathers, even the wild ones."[26] By this reckoning, friends are infinitely preferable to spouses or kin.

The friendship between Jim and Ántonia is inscribed in a rhetoric of impossibility. Jim consents to the prohibition of friendship between men and women when he lays out the roles that Ántonia might have fulfilled for him: "I'd have liked to have you for a sweetheart, or a wife, or my mother or my sister – anything that a woman can be to a man."[27] In this roster of possible relationships, with its alarming movement between extra-familial love and intra-familial incest, Jim neglects to mention "friend," as if the only possible exclusion between a man and woman were friendship. By contrast, when Ántonia writes to Jim, she signs the letter as "your old friend."[28] When Jim finally returns to Nebraska to see Ántonia twenty years on, her countless children greet him as "an old friend of the family"[29] because they have heard stories about him and seen his photograph. Despite this reunion, the novel is neither a comedy nor a romance. Jim and Ántonia reunite not to revive the discarded possibility of marriage; after all, both are married to other people – Ántonia happily, Jim unhappily. Instead, Jim comes around to seeing Ántonia as a viable friend: "Whatever we had missed, we possessed together the precious, the incommunicable past."[30] In this sense, friendship is neither a future anterior nor a present perfect phenomenon, but a pluperfect segment of a life sealed off from romantic continuation.

Possessing an incommunicable past locates Jim and Ántonia's friendship in the realm of the mythic. Throughout the 1920s, Cather gradually shifted her thinking about friendship from the novelistic to the epic. *One of Ours*, *A Lost Lady*, *The Professor's House*, and *Death Comes for the Archbishop* all contain elements of the epic, each with an increasing investment in the grandeur of friendship. *A Lost Lady* begins with a proem that turns to a mythic past to measure the decline between then and now: "Thirty or forty years ago, in one of those grey towns along the Burlington railroad, which are so much greyer today than they were then, there was a house."[31] The nine chapters in part 2 of *A Lost Lady* mimic and parody the nine chapters in part 1, in demonstration of the sentiment that the pioneering and railroad-building generation has truly disappeared from the West: "This was the very end of the road-making West … It was already gone, that age; nothing could ever bring it back."[32] In addition to being glamorous, the past is a source of inspiration. Pining for company, Niel Herbert reads Ovid, Byron, Goethe, and Montaigne as if these authors were not just literary antecedents but his friends and guides to an ethical and imaginative life.[33]

For Cather as for Niel Herbert and Jim Burden, the classics vivify human relations, especially friendships. In *My Ántonia*, while Ántonia plows fields and harvests wheat, Jim swots up his trigonometry and Virgil in order to matriculate at the university. From sheer enchantment with Latin poetry, he memorizes long passages of the *Aeneid*.[34] While an undergraduate, he reads the *Georgics* and discusses Dante's veneration of Virgil with Gaston Cleric. In particular, these works enrich Jim's understanding of himself and his friendships: "whenever my consciousness was quickened, all those early friends were quickened within it, and in some strange way they accompanied me through all my new experiences. They were so much alive in me that I scarcely stopped to wonder whether they were alive anywhere else, or how."[35] Friendships live beyond the pages of books, even as they acquire meaning from literary precedents. In other words, the posterity of friendship, in which life has been animated and clarified by one or a few people, is literature itself.

As an adolescent in Red Cloud, Willa Cather learned Greek and Latin from an eccentric scholar named William Ducker. Under his tutelage, she read "Virgil, Ovid, the *Iliad*, some of the odes of Anacreon."[36] Overcome by a *malaise* one day, Ducker died on his living-room couch with "a copy of the *Iliad* lying open on the floor beside him."[37] At the University of Nebraska, Cather studied both classics and English, although she missed being instructed by George Edward Woodberry, an inspired professor who left Lincoln before Cather arrived. In his critical biography of Cather, E.K. Brown notes that Woodberry's course on the epic "was exactly what Willa Cather longed for, and indeed required – a study of ideas, personalities, and forms conducted by a man to whom all three were living realities."[38]

As Cather would have known from her intensive training in classic Greek and Latin literature, one of the abiding topics of the epic is friendship, whether Aeneas' friendship with Pallas in the *Aeneid* or Gilgamesh's affection for Enkidu in *The Epic of Gilgamesh*. The epic expresses the magnitude of friendship differently, if not better, than the novel does. In its length and in its invocations of the interplay between human and divine realms, the epic measures out the full meanings of loyalty, integrity, endurance, and selflessness within friendship.

In *One of Ours*, Cather demonstrates the epic versus the novelistic dimensions of friendship. Claude Wheeler accidentally starts out in a *Bildungsroman* and finds his proper place only when he moves into the more spacious dimensions of the epic. The first three books of *One of Ours* have the classic contours of a *Bildungsroman*. Claude makes friends with the same ease as Pip does in *Great Expectations* and sloughs them off as easily as Stephen Dedalus does in *A Portrait of the Artist as a Young Man*. Claude has a gift for friendship, but he does not know how to use it. After a football game, the cultured Erlich boys take Claude home to meet their artistic mother, and the whole family become his "good friends."[39] When his father orders him to stop attending university and take over the family farm, Claude ceases all communication with the Erlichs; he feels ill at ease about keeping up such distinguished and citified connections. Broken friendships are a pattern for him. In his youth, he and Ernest Havel are "chums."[40] Obstinate, teetotalling Enid breaks up this friendship because she considers Ernest too radical. "I never, you know, liked Ernest Havel," she tells Claude.[41] Even when Enid leaves for China – her going provokes immense relief all around, not least for Claude who has misguidedly married her – Ernest figures it would be "indelicate to renew their former intimacy."[42]

In fact, the novel sheds characters as it proceeds: Mrs Erlich, Bayliss Wheeler, Nat Wheeler, Enid, Ernest, a flying ace named Victor Morse, Mademoiselle de Courcy who works for the Red Cross. All sink below the surface of friendship and disappear from representation without so much as a word about their afterlife. They are important only insofar as they fulfill Claude's need for friendship, even if they do not become his enduring friends. Having friends is crucial to the *Bildungsroman*, but as Cather indicates in *One of Ours*, shedding friends is just as important to individual growth or the refusal to grow from experience.

The last two books of *One of Ours* veer away from the developmental plot to a sea voyage and trench warfare in an epic register. The fourth book, entitled "The Voyage of the Anchises," flags this generic shift. Anchises, elderly father of Aeneas, appears throughout the *Aeneid*. Cather appropriates his name for the decrepit ship that transports soldiers from New York to Europe during the First World War. The war creates opportunities for Claude to have new experiences and to make new friends. At the front, he meets an accomplished violinist named David Gerhardt, who has abandoned his concert career to become a soldier. Described as Claude's "best friend,"[43] David combines sensibility with courage. Epic friendship, in this instance, is a contingency of war, namely "the common interests that make men friends."[44] Their camaraderie recalls the friendship of Achilles and Patroclus in the *Iliad*, although Achilles' fury on the battlefield does not quite find its equivalent in the gentle conversations about art that David and Claude have during their leaves together. By denying his talent – David consents to play the violin only once, because family friends persuade him to do so – he offers a parallel to Claude's incompleteness. Denial of ambition, talent, and fineness of feeling brings the two men together. Indeed, during the war Claude finally has the "feeling of being completely understood, of being no longer a stranger."[45]

H.L. Mencken despised *One of Ours* because of its two unequal parts. "There is a lyrical nonsensicality in it that often glows half pathetic; it is precious near the war of the standard model of lady novelist," Mencken sneered in a review.[46] Yet Cather's representation of the war is inspired by the *Iliad* and the *Aeneid* more than dispatches from the trenches or John Dos Passos' *Three Soldiers*, to which Mencken compares *One of Ours*. The novel thrives on a rhetoric of expectations. "What do you expect?" Ernest asks Claude in his youth, apropos of the daily round of work and pleasure.[47] Expectations can be individual or national, great or small, but they are always oriented to the future. David Gerhardt conjectures that the war bears importantly on the future, although he cannot predict how: "Nothing we expect, but something unforeseen."[48] He imagines the unforeseen in terms of mythology and Olympian efforts to bring some new idea into the world, as when "the sons of the gods were born, [and] the mother always died in agony."[49] That new idea may be epic friendship, something surpassing the common run of novelistic friendship, something monumental in scale and scope, something too large or too close to apprehend.

The Posterity of Friendship

In autumn 1946, E.K. Brown published an appreciation of Willa Cather's fiction in the *Yale Review*. In this overview, Brown praises Cather's craftsmanship for its "alien definiteness and firmness of beauty."[50] He especially likes *A Lost Lady* for being "wholly uncluttered," and he singles out *Death Comes for the Archbishop* as "her great book" because of its technical accomplishment.[51] Brown's article caught Cather's eye. Rather uncharacteristically, she wrote to Brown to second his opinions about *O Pioneers!* ("I was very much disappointed") and *Death Comes for the Archbishop* ("my best book").[52] A correspondence sprang up between Cather and Brown, but it did not last long: Cather died in April 1947, mere months after they were first in touch.

Aware of this "epistolary friendship," Edith Lewis asked Brown to write an authorized biography of Cather.[53] As Cather's literary executrix, Lewis kept alive the flame of her friend's genius, while respecting as best she could Cather's fierce desire for privacy. Cather expressly forbid the publication of any of her correspondence, in whole or in part, after her death, which considerably complicated investigations into her past, her friendships, and her personal life. In the circumstances, the only way to proceed with a biography was with Lewis's permission. Once Lewis gave her consent, Brown contacted friends and members of Cather's family. His research was painstaking. He established once and for all that Cather was born in 1873, not 1874 or 1875 as she sometimes gave out. He travelled to Pittsburgh to research Cather's years there. "It was a bit too early in the year for ideal results in seeing the old friends of Willa C.," Brown wrote to his friend, Leon Edel, on 30 March 1949; "[s]ome were still in Florida."[54] In the same letter, he asked Edel to track down letters between Sarah Orne Jewitt and Cather if he was in Boston.

It would have been difficult for Edith Lewis to find a more congenial, diplomatic, and authoritative critic than Brown to sum up Cather's literary achievement. Born in 1905, Brown took a BA at the University of Toronto, and he returned to teach there even before he had completed his doctorate at the

Sorbonne.[55] For his statesmanlike ability, he was recruited successively to chair English departments at the University of Manitoba, Cornell University, and the University of Chicago. A master of his discipline, Brown published on all manner of subjects: a critical study of Matthew Arnold; essays on Edith Wharton, Algernon Swinburne, Thornton Wilder, and other writers; a foundational work called *On Canadian Poetry*; an enterprising overview of genre called *Rhythm in the Novel*; a translation of Balzac's *Père Goriot*; an edition of *David Copperfield*; and dozens of book reviews, columns, and *causeries*. Among his papers when he died was a series of essays on transformations in the British novel from George Eliot and Thomas Hardy through Elizabeth Bowen and Henry Green.[56]

While still in his twenties, Brown was instrumental in reviving the *University of Toronto Quarterly*, which he co-edited from 1932 until 1941, and for which he wrote annual roundup reviews of Canadian poetry. In 1942, Brown took a six-month leave from his duties at Cornell to move to Ottawa and write speeches for William Lyon Mackenzie King; he subsequently wrote a profile of the Canadian prime minister for *Harper's* that was designed to make him seem less like a mystical oddball than he actually was. Interspersed with these duties, Brown kept up a cheerful stream of letters to Edel and wrote letters of recommendation on his friend's behalf for various jobs and awards.

Before he could finish the biography of Cather, E.K. Brown died suddenly of brain cancer in April 1951, at the age of forty-five. Upon hearing of Brown's death, Lewis wrote to his widow, Peggy, to offer condolences: "One felt so immediately his great integrity, his good will and friendliness, and his sensitive, penetrating understanding of people and life. How many friends he must have had! For even the few people to whom I introduced him in the course of his work on the Biography spoke with such warmth and admiration of him."[57]

After some kerfuffle about who should complete Brown's biography of Cather – Lewis herself thought about taking up the task, various academics were consulted, and Alfred Knopf meddled – Leon Edel took over the project. By his own estimation, Edel had roughly a third of the book left to write. If the choice of Brown as a biographer was canny, so was the choice of Edel as the appropriate person to bring the book to completion. Edel and Brown had been contemporaries and friends at the Sorbonne and had parallel careers. Born in Pittsburgh in 1907, Edel was raised in Saskatchewan and took his undergraduate degree at McGill University. In the 1930s, he interviewed Edith

Wharton and laid the foundations for his massive biography of Henry James by collecting correspondence and editing volume after volume of James's works. When he picked up the threads of the Cather biography, Edel had the doubly difficult task of courting Edith Lewis and respecting the wishes of Brown's widow, Peggy, with whom he was on friendly terms. Lewis wanted to protect Cather's literary reputation; Peggy Brown wanted to protect her husband's scholarly legacy. Having signed a contract to complete the work in January 1952, Edel dedicated himself to the task. He expanded chapters, changed titles, sutured in material from Brown's essay in the *Yale Review*, wrote two chapters about Cather's years in Pittsburgh, added a conclusion, and harmonized the whole manuscript.

Meanwhile, he coaxed letters by or about Cather from Lewis's personal collection. She dealt out information reluctantly, not to say parsimoniously. On 22 April 1952, Edel informed Peggy Brown, "Miss L., with whom I'm having an active correspondence, produced a letter of Edward's in which he spoke of wanting to elaborate that chapter [on *Death Comes for the Archbishop*]."[58] On 3 May, he wrote again with an update: "I spent 3½ hours with Miss Lewis and read all his letters to her – they did clarify a number of things, among others that he intended to re-name his chapters which now in reality have only tentative labels. I will have to think that one out carefully. Miss L. was more friendlier [*sic*] than hitherto; I think a thaw is setting in. She actually gave me some notes for the last chapter to take home and study."[59] Two weeks later, Edel reported, "This morning (at the crack of dawn) I completed the book."[60] Despite this confident announcement, he anticipated further revisions after discussion with Lewis.

Edel was not kidding about Lewis's frostiness. In a letter dated 22 April 1952, she takes issue with Brown's "misapprehension" about the religious content in Cather's later novels: "I can't help feeling that Mr Brown's stress on [Cardinal] Newman falsifies a little her religious attitude. In fact, I think his theory about it (her religious attitude) throughout goes a little aside from the reality."[61] In the same letter, she asserts, not without the authority of domestic routine, that Cather kept *The Pilgrim's Progress* on her night table and read it tirelessly. In May and June 1952, Lewis perused Edel's manuscript and sent back notes for revision. Some suggestions pertained to facts, others sniffed at word choices or sags in the narrative momentum. The account of the genesis of *O Pioneers!* was not altogether accurate, she lamented, nor was the story about Cather's move from Houghton Mifflin to Knopf. Edel's revisions ultimately satisfied her, for she extolled "the Biography," always with an upper case *B*, as "magnificent in every way."[62] In particular, she approved of the way that Brown and Edel captured Cather's character. "I am glad that we seem to have overcome the myth that Miss Cather was a cold, grim recluse," Lewis wrote to Edel on 17 March 1953. "Where *do* people get such ideas?"[63]

In March 1953, *Willa Cather: A Critical Biography* was published alongside Edith Lewis's memoir, *Willa Cather Living*. At E.K. Brown's request, Lewis had written up her recollections of Cather; in fact, Brown and Edel quote amply from Lewis's notes in the biography. When Alfred Knopf read Lewis's remarks, he agreed to publish them separately as a memoir. "I have not tried in these pages to set down more than the memories and impressions that came to me spontaneously out of my long friendship with Willa Cather," Lewis writes in the foreword to her book.[64] By Melissa Homestead's reckoning, theirs was a "creative partnership,"[65] not a hierarchy of literary celebrity to amanuensis, as had long been assumed. From *The Song of the Lark* on, Lewis acknowledges, "we read the copy and proofs of all her books."[66] Lewis had worked for years as an editor and had a firm grasp of syntax and style. Her suggestions to Edel and her insistence on accuracy with regard to facts derived from professional editorial insight, not just personal fussiness. She recalls that Cather "always said it was what she left out that counted."[67] Certainly, omission is a guiding principle in *Willa Cather Living*. Absenting herself as much as possible from an account of her day-in, day-out relationship with Cather, Lewis refers merely to "our long friendship and association, which lasted until her death."[68]

Robert Thacker interprets the unusual details about the writing and publication of *Willa Cather: A Critical Biography* in terms of what happens when a celebrated writer becomes the property of admirers and researchers.[69] As domestic partner, Lewis did not intend to relinquish control over Cather's reputation easily. The title of her memoir, *Willa Cather Living*, has a Dantean quality about it: the flame of the famous author flickers still, and Lewis guards that flame as long as she can in honour of their friendship and its posterity. As Cather's literary trustee, Lewis understood her role to be that of sentry, rectifier of mistakes, and editor of the past. "She had a gift for immediately creating a personal relationship of some kind with anyone she met," Lewis writes about Cather. "It was something more than good manners, or even charm."[70] In particular, Lewis wanted to capture and commemorate Cather's gift for friendship. When Lewis extols their "long friendship and association," the queer resonances of the statement are self-evident. Yet Lewis also means, surely, that friends, whether construed as creative partners or domestic companions, are owed the duty of remembrance.

Time

Especially in *The Professor's House* and *Death Comes for the Archbishop*, Cather ponders the temporality of friendship. Both novels position significant friendships recessively – late in the narrative sequence but at an early point in the chronology of events – a strategy that amplifies the consequences of friendship over time. Whereas the central complication of *The Professor's House* is a broken friendship, the central virtue of *Death Comes for the Archbishop* is a pact of friendship that sustains characters across a lifetime.

In *The Professor's House*, Cather dwells on the friendship between Tom Outland and Godfrey St Peter as a correction of, or recompense for, the broken friendship between Tom Outland and Roddy Blake. Despite a ten-year difference in age, Tom and Roddy become "fast friends,"[71] on the pattern of an older and younger brother. Roddy, a working man, has been double-crossed by his fiancée and cheated out of money by men pretending to be his friends. After so many bad experiences, Roddy feels he can "unbend"[72] with Tom in a way that he cannot with anyone else. As a gesture of friendship, Roddy gives up his job on the railway to stay with Tom. When Roddy is the worse for drink, Tom sits vigil over him. A bond of trust unites them. Together, they excavate an Indigenous city built atop a mesa. In an effort to interest the US government in protecting the cliff city and its artifacts, Tom wastes several months in Washington in hopes of catching the ear of congressmen and directors at the Smithsonian. No sooner does he return to the Southwest than he hears that Roddy has sold everything from the excavation – the artifacts having been rudely demoted to "curios" or "pots and pans" – for four thousand dollars.[73] Tom cannot condone Roddy's crass commercialization of aesthetic and historical artifacts. Nor can he forgive Roddy for selling goods that belonged "to all the people,"[74] not Tom, not Roddy, not anyone.

While berating Roddy, Tom summons up the spectre of friendship as something that transcends money or other social relations: "If it was my money you'd lost gambling, or my girl you'd made free with, we could fight it out, and maybe be friends again. But this is different."[75] In Tom's mind, the end of the friendship is a *fait accompli*: nothing can repair the harm that Roddy has inflicted. When Roddy finally understands that Tom's anger is implacable, he leaves. In a parting shot, Roddy delivers a version of forgiveness disguised in an insult: "I'm glad it's you that's doing this to me, Tom; not me that's doing it to you."[76] He means that Tom's bruising treatment is not something he would wish even on Tom; as a true friend, he would spare him that hurt. Yet he also means that Tom will have to carry the burden of this hurt forever after, and that burden will be harder to bear when forgiveness is no longer a possibility. Roddy disappears for good. Tom's subsequent efforts to find him come to nothing. With their fading echo of Montaigne's statement about the tautological reciprocity of friendship and its inalienable specificity – because it was he; because it was I – Roddy's last words convey not only that friendship is entangled with forgiveness, but also that forgiveness, once withdrawn, is the end of friendship.

A friend is someone whom you forgive, many times in succession if need be, and someone who forgives you in turn, until such time as some unforgivable act terminates the friendship, as happens in *The Professor's House*. "In a world of harm," writes Sarah Beckwith, "the act of forgiveness allows a way of going on to new futures."[77] In this regard, friendship unfolds around futurity, insofar as friends are allies, comrades-in-arms, defenders, interlocutors, and helpmeets for an indefinite duration. In friendship, forgiveness need not always be articulated, because it is understood as a foregone sympathy and blessing. In this sense, forgiveness signifies leniency in judging the other person for wrongs committed. Forgiveness, argues Richard Gibson, has the power to free offenders from the consequences of their misdeeds.[78] It also has the power to sustain friendship through a mutual recognition of shortcomings. As an interpersonal relation, forgiveness creates a nuclear unit of at least two, although it may extend to cells of friends and create a community of the like-minded – a group of friends.

As Roddy predicts in his parting salvo, Tom continues to pay the emotional cost of breaking with his friend. With recourse to a metaphor of debt, Tom states, "Anyone who requites faith and friendship as I did, will have to pay for it."[79] In a manner of speaking, Tom compensates for his bad behaviour toward Roddy by befriending Godfrey. Godfrey is something of a surrogate for Roddy.

(The connection between the two friendships is never explicit, but their names – Roddy, Godfrey – sound alike in terms of assonance and trochaic meter, and both friendships feature an older and a younger man.) Godfrey cherishes his friendship with Tom because it returns him to the past: Godfrey's forgotten boyhood in Kansas, from which he feels separated by success, his not entirely happy marriage with status-oriented Lillian, and his sense of having come to the end of an intellectual experience when he completes his multi-volume history of the Spanish conquistadores.

When Tom is killed in the war, Godfrey begins a "new friendship,"[80] as he calls it, with himself. As a genuine friend, Tom makes Godfrey know himself better. They liberate something in each other that can be activated by no one else. Speaking about Tom, Godfrey expresses the reciprocity of friendship as a paradox: "he owed me no more than I owed him."[81] In Scott Herring's words, Tom gives the professor the "princely gift of unnameable friendship,"[82] which is to say that the posterity of Tom's friendship is Godfrey's reconciliation with his solitude, his ambitions, and his accomplishments.

Friendship is a gift in that it strives to break away from the language of debt and commerce, at least as Tom and Godfrey understand it. When Tom gives turquoises to Rosie and Kitty, he does not disclose that they were given to him by Roddy: "I'd never sell them. They were given to me by a friend. I have a lot, they're no use to me, but they'll make pretty playthings for little girls."[83] Tom's speech hints at more meanings than he actually states. The stones are a gift that can only be passed along to someone else, not repaid to the original friend. Metaphorically, Tom has more stones than he knows what to do with, which is to say that he has an immense capacity for friendship that others seldom meet. The genius of youth, Cather implies, is the wantonness with which one makes and loses friends, without knowing their true value until later. The girls cannot know what gift they have been given, nor what the turquoises mean as a token of an obsolete friendship. The consequences of friendship thus spread outward: Godfrey befriends Tom to redress his past and to fulfill his life at the same time; Tom bequeaths turquoises on Rosie and Kitty as a reparation for the harm inflicted on Roddy. Friendship supports the central design of *The Professor's House* insofar as friendship exists in time and has consequences through time.

So, too, the hidden meanings of friendship structure the narrative in *Death Comes for the Archbishop*. Joseph Vaillant is initially identified as Jean Marie

Latour's "boyhood friend."[84] From different social milieux, the boys meet at the seminary in Montferrand, France. From the instant he sets eyes on Vaillant, Latour resolves to "take this new boy under his protection."[85] Akin to love at first sight, this pattern of immediate and absolute friendship underlies Latour's other relationships. When he meets Kit Carson, for example, Latour instantly senses the American's "standards, loyalties, a code which is not easily put into words."[86] Inevitably, they become fast friends. These male friendships have spiritual connotations, whether within the Roman Catholic Church or between white settlers and Indigenous people. During a long, dignified pause, Eusabio, who is Navajo, clasps Latour's hand, then greets him solemnly as "my friend."[87] Jacinto, an Indigenous guide from the Pecos pueblo, respects Latour for his sincerity; reciprocally, Latour feels that he has "gone a good way toward gaining his guide's friendship, though he did not know how."[88] In each of these friendships, integrity irons out differences. As is the case with Eusabio, friendly gestures summon up "welcome, confidence, appreciation"[89] – qualities that garner trust and instigate friendship.

The spiritual dimension of friendship reconciles the considerable differences in temperament between Latour and Vaillant. Latour is scholarly and cultivated, yet given to occasional doubts about his faith. By contrast, Vaillant is exuberant, hardworking, and utterly convinced of his purpose. Latour possesses a few fine books and a pair of silver candlesticks; Vaillant possesses nothing at all and begs for money and vestments from parishioners, much to Latour's embarrassment. Whereas Vaillant is quick to make friends, Latour is hesitant to "form new ties."[90] As a friend and a spiritual guide, Latour tests the limits of Vaillant's faith. He coaxes him into leaving Montferrand for Paris, Paris for Sandusky, and Sandusky for Santa Fé. When Latour imposes new tests, Vaillant tries to dig in: "This is far enough. Do not drag me any farther."[91] Friendship, defined as moral and spiritual enhancement, has ethical limits. How far can you provoke your friend with new challenges and still remain friends? In *Death Comes for the Archbishop*, Latour ponders this ethical dilemma: "Why, the Bishop was asking himself, had he ever brought his friend to this life of hardship and danger?"[92] Durability in the face of hardship and danger tests the limits of friendship by threatening its extinction. What are friends for if not to provide solace and inspiration over the course of time? What is friendship if it has no possible ending?

To prove this point about the rigours of time on friendship, the novel does not follow a linear sequence. Anecdotes, legends, trials, character sketches, meetings, incidents – all are tossed together as stories, some narrated first-hand by the priests, some told by a narrator from no particular temporal location, like an epic poet recounting a mythic past. Throughout the novel, precise dates have little to do with the grandeur of legend, in which Indigenous history blends with tales about white settlement, miracles that happen to early Franciscan missionaries, and the Colorado gold rush. Book 1 begins with an unambiguous temporal marker – "One afternoon in the autumn of 1851"[93] – then moves backward to a year earlier in Cincinnati, followed by a shipwreck in Galveston, a caravan across Texas, the obstinacy of Father Martínez, who refuses to recognize the new bishop's authority, and Latour's losing his way amidst red hills somewhere in the uncharted expanses of New Mexico. The narration proceeds not chronologically but anecdotally to demonstrate the historical and epic contours of friendship. Friendship, in all its magnitude, triumphs over time; it enters into legendary status. At the end of his life, Latour has done with "calendared time."[94] Days and months simply cease to matter, which explains in part the unusual organization of the novel into nine separate books, with subsections and a prologue, as if this were an epic along the lines of the *Aeneid* or the *Iliad*.

Within this diffuse temporality, the friendship between Latour and Vaillant endures. As Jonathan Goldberg points out, the two friends "chose each other above every other relationship, even possibly their relationship to God."[95] The two priests wear matching cloaks and ride matching white donkeys. As if their friendship were something entirely outside time, they bless each other "for the past – for the future."[96] The dash that connects the past and future stands for the present, the temporality in which friendship is most at home but least articulate.

In *Death Comes for the Archbishop*, the crucial event in Vaillant and Latour's friendship appears late in the narrative yet early in their lives. The two young seminarians, having taken a vow to become missionaries, decide to leave Montferrand secretly for Paris. In effect, Vaillant and Latour elope. The scene bears all the hallmarks of a young man assuring a young woman to defy family wishes and start a new life together in a big city, except that the principal roles are taken by two men. For Vaillant, whose mother is dead and whose father he does not wish to cross, the decision requires Latour's reassurance and determination: "That parting was not a parting, but an escape – a running away, a betrayal of family trust for the sake of a higher trust."[97] Ever after, Vaillant swears to stand by Latour and "share his hardships," as if they were a married couple, because Latour had previously stood by him: "I will be to him now what he was to me that day when we stood by the road-side, waiting for the diligence to Paris, and my purpose broke, and, – he saved me."[98]

When the scene returns, it is narrated more fully as an elopement. The young men wear civilian clothes to disguise their purpose, "as if they were criminals, escaping by stealth from their homes."[99] They meet by agreement "at dawn in a certain field," a field described as "tip-tilted by reason of its steepness."[100] Latour bucks up Vaillant's resolve so thoroughly that the two men never leave each other, except when their missionary duty requires that they separate to propagate the faith. On his deathbed, Latour remembers this scene – the "tip-tilted green field," the consolation, the diligence rumbling down the mountain gorge[101] – with its persistence in his memory being the sign of its centrality to his existence. The vow of friendship, for that is what the moment of saving Vaillant amounts to, remains with Latour until the hour of his death. He twirls Vaillant's signet ring on his finger as a reminder of that vow. Indeed, the elopement is never not in the men's minds. Years earlier, while sharing a Christmas meal in Santa Fé, they jointly remember the "tilted cobble street"[102] in their French village, with the word "tilted" activating the scene of elopement without mentioning it outright. Shared experience is the secret that binds them to each other, the secret, it might be said, of their friendship itself.

Death Comes for the Archbishop advances the hypothesis that, whatever its benefits, whatever its scale, whatever its intensity and purpose, friendship may have no posterity. Vaillant wonders whether Latour's fine personality will leave a trace in years to come, "some ideal, or memory, or legend."[103] In general, the fineness of a personality is felt in the present or in such tangible by-products as a cathedral, a carved wooden saint, or a painting of St Francis, among other material artifacts that appear in the novel. The posterity of friendship is far less evident. As the narrator keeps observing, everything has its day. Father Martínez belongs to an old order: "his day was over."[104] Latour understands that everything comes to fruition in due course – "Time brings things to pass, certainly"[105] – and everything dies away too in its time. There is, therefore, a reason for allowing events to take their course, including the course of friendship.

NOTES

1 Willa Cather, *Shadows on the Rock* (New York: Knopf, 1931), 146.
2 Willa Cather, *Death Comes for the Archbishop* (1927; New York: Vintage, 1990), 283.
3 Edith Lewis, *Willa Cather Living: A Personal Record* (1953; Lincoln: University of Nebraska Press, 1976), 177.
4 Ibid., 14.
5 Melissa J. Homestead, *The Only Wonderful Things: The Creative Partnership of Willa Cather and Edith Lewis* (Oxford: Oxford University Press, 2021), 14.
6 Marcus Tullius Cicero, *How to Be a Friend*, trans. Philip Freeman (Princeton: Princeton University Press, 2018), 47.
7 Willa Cather, *Obscure Destinies* (New York: Knopf, 1932), 205.
8 Ibid., 230.
9 Willa Cather, *A Lost Lady* (1923; New York: Vintage, 1990), 148.
10 Willa Cather, *O Pioneers!*, ed. Marilee Lindemann (1913; Oxford: World's Classics, 1999), 33.
11 Ibid., 170.
12 Willa Cather, *One of Ours* (1922; New York: Vintage, 1991), 86.
13 Ibid., 176.
14 Willa Cather, *My Ántonia* (1918; New York: Penguin, 1994), 3.
15 Ibid., 6.
16 Ibid., 5.
17 Cicero, *Friend*, 139.
18 Michel de Montaigne, "Of Friendship" in *The Complete Essays of Montaigne*, trans. Donald M. Frame (Stanford: Stanford University Press, 1965), 139.
19 Cather, *My Ántonia*, 16.
20 Ibid., 103.
21 Ibid.
22 Ibid., 105.
23 Ibid., 86.
24 Ibid., 46.
25 Ibid., 203.

26 Ibid., 217.
27 Ibid., 240.
28 Ibid., 245.
29 Ibid., 256.
30 Ibid., 273.
31 Cather, *A Lost Lady*, 1.
32 Ibid., 133.
33 Ibid., 66–8.
34 As many critics have noticed, Virgil saturates Cather's imagination. The epigraph to *My Ántonia*, "Optima dies … prima fugit," is a compressed version of *Georgics*, book 3, lines 56–7. In *The Professor's House*, Tom memorizes passages from Virgil's *Aeneid* while camping on the blue mesa. Cristina Giorcelli compares Cather's representation of friendship with Virgil's in terms of "unselfishness" and "limitless generosity," as against the limitations of heterosexual marriage. Cristina Giorcelli, "Latin Perspectives and Special Friendships in the *Aeneid* and *The Professor's House*." *Willa Cather Newsletter and Review* 58, no. 2 (2015): 27.
35 Cather, *My Ántonia*, 198.
36 Lewis, *Willa Cather Living*, 21–2.
37 Ibid., 23.
38 E.K. Brown, *Willa Cather: A Critical Biography*, completed by Leon Edel (New York: Knopf, 1953), 54.
39 Cather, *One of Ours*, 34.
40 Ibid., 167.
41 Ibid., 106.
42 Ibid., 186.
43 Ibid., 363.
44 Ibid., 332.
45 Ibid., 316.
46 H.L. Mencken, review of *One of Ours*, by Willa Cather, reprinted in *Willa Cather and Her Critics*, ed. James Schroeter (Ithaca: Cornell University Press, 1967), 12.
47 Cather, *One of Ours*, 46.
48 Ibid., 330.
49 Ibid.
50 E.K. Brown, "Willa Cather," *Willa Cather and Her Critics*, ed. James Schroeter

(Ithaca: Cornell University Press, 1967), 85. When first published, this article bore the title "Homage to Willa Cather," *Yale Review* 36, no. 1 (1946): 77–92.

51 Ibid., 76, 80.

52 Willa Cather to E.K. Brown, typed transcript of letter [original at Yale University], undated [January 1947]. Leon Edel Collection, MSG 993, McGill University, box 72, file 13 "Brown-Cather." The files in the Edel papers are alphabetical; some bear pencilled numbers, but not all. For this reason, file titles, when used, are given in this and subsequent notes.

53 Brown, *Willa Cather*, v.

54 E.K. Brown to Leon Edel, typed letter initialled, dated 30 March 1949. Leon Edel Collection, box 72, file 12 "E.K. Brown."

55 Biographical details about Brown appear in Laura Smyth Groening, *E.K. Brown: A Study in Conflict* (Toronto: University of Toronto Press, 1993). A concise account appears in David Staines, "Introduction," *E.K. Brown Responses and Evaluations: Essays on Canada* (Toronto: New Canadian Library, 1977), vii–xvi.

56 A copy of this unpublished manuscript is located in the Leon Edel Collection, box 72, file 16, "E.K. Brown (4)."

57 Edith Lewis to Peggy Brown, autograph letter signed, undated [April 1951]. Leon Edel Collection, box 72, file "Mrs Brown (5)."

58 Leon Edel to Petty Brown, typed letter, unsigned carbon, 22 April 1952. Leon Edel Collection, box 72, file 28, "LE to Mrs E.K. Brown The Cather Project."

59 Leon Edel to Peggy Brown, typed letter, unsigned carbon, 3 May 1952. Leon Edel Collection, box 72, file 28, "LE to Mrs E.K. Brown The Cather Project."

60 Leon Edel to Peggy Brown, typed letter, unsigned carbon, 15 May 1952. Leon Edel Collection, box 72, file 28, "LE to Mrs E.K. Brown The Cather Project."

61 Edith Lewis to Leon Edel, autograph letter signed, 22 April 1952. Leon Edel Collection, box 8, file "Edith Lewis."

62 Edith Lewis to Leon Edel, autograph letter signed, 21 February 1953. Leon Edel Collection, box 8, file "Edith Lewis."

63 Edith Lewis to Leon Edel, autograph letter signed, 17 March 1953. Leon Edel Collection, box 8, file "Edith Lewis."

64 Lewis, *Willa Cather Living*, v.

65 Homestead, *The Only Wonderful Things*, 11.

66 Lewis, *Willa Cather Living*, xviii.

67 Ibid., 183.

68 Ibid., xiii.

69 Robert Thacker, "'A Critic Who Was Worthy of Her': *The Writing of Willa Cather: A Critical Biography*," *Cather Studies* 7 (2007), https://cather.unl.edu/scholarship/catherstudies/7.

70 Lewis, *Willa Cather Living*, 135.

71 Willa Cather, *The Professor's House* (New York: Vintage, 1990), 164.

72 Ibid., 165.

73 Ibid., 214, 219.

74 Ibid., 219.

75 Ibid., 222.

76 Ibid., 224.

77 Sarah Beckwith, *Shakespeare and the Grammar of Forgiveness* (Ithaca: Cornell University Press, 2011), 8.

78 Richard Hughes Gibson, *Forgiveness in Victorian Literature: Grammar, Narrative, and Community* (London: Bloomsbury, 2015), 28, 11.

79 Cather, *Professor's House*, 229.

80 Ibid., 239.

81 Ibid., 50.

82 Scott Herring, "Catherian Friendship; or, How Not to Do the History of Homosexuality," *Modern Fiction Studies* 52, no. 1 (2006): 81.

83 Cather, *Professor's House*, 103.

84 Cather, *Death Comes*, 22.

85 Ibid., 225.

86 Ibid., 75.

87 Ibid., 220.

88 Ibid., 93.

89 Ibid., 220.

90 Ibid., 251.

91 Ibid., 40.

92 Ibid., 119.

93 Ibid., 19.

94 Ibid., 288.

95 Jonathan Goldberg, *Willa Cather and Others* (Durham: Duke University Press, 2011), 177.

96 Cather, *Death Comes*, 280.

97 Ibid., 204.

98 Ibid.
99 Ibid., 283.
100 Ibid., 282–3.
101 Ibid., 297.
102 Ibid., 41.
103 Ibid., 252.
104 Ibid., 153.
105 Ibid., 242.

Part Three

Modern Instances

6

The Friendship of Joseph Conrad and André Gide: From Admiration to Disillusion and Back

EMILY O. WITTMAN

> [Y]our friendship … is quite the greatest treasure that I have won at the point of my pen.[1]
>
> – Conrad to Gide, 1916

> I only keep asking myself what I have done to earn this affectionate friendship, which is surely the "great prize" of my literary life. But what's the point. It is a gift from the gods.[2]
>
> – Conrad to Gide, 1918

> I felt I had neglected him. I went a long time without seeing or writing to him. Was I ever able to communicate all the affection, admiration, and veneration that persisted, despite the absences and silences? Of my elders, I only knew, only loved him.[3]
>
> – Gide on Conrad's death, 1924

The friendship between French Nobel Prize laureate André Gide and Polish-English writer Joseph Conrad is one of the great literary friendships of the twentieth century. It was a mid- to late-life and primarily epistolary affair that began in 1911, when Gide, in his early forties, met Conrad, in his mid-fifties, at the latter's home in England, and once again in 1912, before corresponding until Conrad's death in 1924. What can two brief encounters and over fifty letters, only forty of them extant, allow for? A lot, as we will see. We have a great deal to learn from their friendship: what it meant to each of them and what evolved from it. Their example can help us understand much about their work and about mid- to late-life friendship.

Two monographs have detailed the influence of Conrad's work on Gide's writing: Walter Putnam's *L'aventure littéraire de Joseph Conrad et André Gide* (1990) and Russell West's *Conrad and Gide: Translation, Transference, and Intertextuality* (1996). I concentrate on the details and character of their friendship as they lived it together in person and through letters. Conrad typically threw away his correspondence; for this reason, there are twenty-five letters from Conrad but only fifteen from Gide. I also cover Gide's correspondence with friends *about* Conrad, as well as his four-page contribution to *La Nouvelle revue française* (NRF) memorial edition published in 1924, from which I drew the above epigraph from Gide. All the extant letters are in French, a language Conrad knew quite well, having lived in Marseille for four years in his youth.

Conrad and Gide's relationship originated in 1911, when Gide undertook a pilgrimage to Conrad's Capel House in Kent, in the company of Valery Larbaud and the American Agnes Tobin, who introduced the French writers to Conrad. Gide was elated to meet Conrad, whose work he read with his English tutor, and he quickly became interested in aiding Conrad in his perennial attempts to find French translators. According to biographers and critics, understanding a Conradian friendship requires an understanding of his poverty and bad health, as well as his need for help, occasionally attended with ire and irked pride. Understanding a Conradian friendship also involves acknowledging that true friendship was very rare in his life as in his oeuvre, which, to a large extent, features solitudinous characters. In this regard, his life mirrored his work.

Whatever happened at Capel House that made them feel such affinity and, in the case of Gide, enormous generosity? The greatest account comes after Conrad's death in 1924 with the NRF memorial edition. Gide's impression of Conrad is worth examining: "Nothing was more congenial, more pure, and more virile than his laugh, his gaze, and his voice. But, like the sea and its currents, I felt him capable of violent passions, of tempests."[4] Gide is writing in hindsight, a misunderstanding with Conrad still in mind, and focusing on his virility, which Conrad insisted upon during his lifetime, at one point in opposition to Gide. Another sentence can help us understand Gide's fellow feeling: "However great his curiosity about the shadowy intricacies of the human spirit, he despised anything sly, sleazy, or vile."[5] As the three epigraphs to this essay strongly suggest, Conrad and Gide felt real affinity for each other. Unfortunately, Gide gives only a cursory account of the visit to Capel House. He recalls that Conrad did not want to talk about the sea and changed the subject when Gide broached it. Later in the evening, at a group dinner, they had an amusing discussion that left Conrad uncharacteristically laughing "like a child."[6] The tenor of the gathering appears to have been celebratory.

At Capel House, Gide offered to pressure translators who were ostensibly working on Conrad's novels. This tactic did not work. So, in 1915, he campaigned for the NRF Gallimard imprint to bring out the collected works of Conrad – the first foreign writer in the series – which Gide himself promised to oversee. Ultimately, Gide served as a promoter, translator, and general manager in introducing Conrad to French readers. During the First World War, and until 1919, Gide was not only Conrad's friend, but also the most important person associated with Conrad's translation and consecration in France. He assigned translators and oversaw their translations, completing one himself, and aspiring to publish two translated works per year. Conrad understood that Gide's intervention was unusual for a writer of his stature and indeed saw it as a sign of friendship. Such efforts and signs of friendship were ultimately one-sided.

Why did such a busy and prolific writer as Gide do so much for Conrad? In the first place, labouring on behalf of Conrad coincided with Gide's contemporaneous pursuits, which included an *engouement* for England, English writers, and the English language. Gide was looking not only for affinity but also for inspiration, in the belief that Conrad could renew his own work and, more generally, French literature overall. Gide had long been expanding his search for powerful writing beyond national and linguistic borders and thought it his duty to translate and support writers with whom he felt a rapport. He was excited to meet and promote international authors, although he did not generally befriend them. Conrad was an exception; in Gide's desire to help Conrad so exhaustively, we must see the ripples of Gide's powerful fellow feeling.

Gide, with passion and industry, became the main actor in Conrad's French reception. Conrad saw in Gide an entrance to the world republic of letters during an unproductive period. Their private and professional relationship, built upon mutual esteem, proved fruitful. It also led to a pivotal and instructive, although brief, disagreement over Gide's decision to hire a female translator for Conrad's 1919 novel *The Arrow of Gold*. Despite this contretemps, they quickly regained their friendship. Conrad died as a great friend of Gide, and there is a Conradian afterlife in Gide's writing.

Both Putnam and West have offered accounts of the details of their connection, especially Conrad's influence on Gide, both as a novelist and as a political *engagé*. At the time of his visit, Gide had already read quite a bit of Conrad's writing, with particular interest in his early work; *Lord Jim* (1900) was and remained his favourite among Conrad's novels. Although, as far as we know, Conrad only read one Gide novel, *The Immoralist* (1902), his letters are full of empathy and enthusiasm for whatever Gide was writing during the thirteen years of their friendship. As Frederick Karl notes, "Conrad felt no inclination to reciprocate by plunging into Gide's work, commenting on it no more than politely, or, possibly, not even reading what Gide sent him."[7] Karl sees this as part of a pattern: "Conrad sat back and received admiration; and Gide was simply one of many substitute 'sons' ... who gathered at his feet in the second decade of the century and offered homage."[8] Conrad felt no need to intervene in Gide's English reception and consecration. Friendship with Conrad seemed, at times, in the case of Gide, to lead to a kind of one-sided worship.

Conrad liked to flatter fellow writers, but he rarely deigned to read contemporary writing. This disdain notwithstanding, I choose to believe Conrad's claim that he read and enjoyed *The Immoralist*. In a letter to Gide in 1911, not long after his visit, he wrote: "I admit then that I read and admired *The Immoralist* all of two years ago. Davray [a would-be French translator of Conrad] gave it to me."[9] If this statement is true, Conrad would have read Gide's novel in French, as the English translation did not appear until 1930. In my view, Conrad found in *The Immoralist* a similar perspective to his own, an alignment that validates his comments. As I show below, this shared perspective is best understood by examining *The Immoralist* through a Nietzschean lens.

Four readings follow: an interpretation of *The Immoralist*, in which I use Nietzsche to illuminate Conrad's sense of affinity with Gide; a study of Gide's translation of Conrad's 1902 novella *Typhoon*; an analysis of their one-sided fight over the translation of Conrad's 1919 novel *The Arrow of Gold*; and a brief discussion of the ways in which Gide, in later life, took inspiration from Conrad's objections to colonialism and emulated Conrad's point of view about gender and translation.

~

At the end of 1911, Conrad wrote to his friend Henri Ghéon (to whom *The Immoralist* is dedicated) with some "one of us" words: "I beg you to tell Gide – who is a friend of yours, no? – that I am going to turn up at his door one of these days in a nightshirt, barefoot, with a rope around my neck. He will understand."[10] Conrad is making a declaration of fellowship in craft but also one of neurodivergence and self-destruction. This observation can help us envision Conrad's feelings of affinity with Gide, even if he did not embrace Gide's wider oeuvre.

As mentioned, Conrad read *The Immoralist* two years before Gide's first visit. Gide wrote the novel during his early thirties, and it features, like so many of Conrad's works, a white man going wrong far from home but in sight of Indigenous people, who are in some way involved in the situation, always repressed, often harmed. Although neither writer has always aged well, Edward Said reminds us that Conrad is a writer consistently open to new interpretations and understandings and can always be plugged productively into contemporary debates, especially those around race, colonialism, and the politics of travel. The same is true of Gide. Certainly, these tropes are relevant to Gide's protagonist Michel in French Algeria, just as much of Conrad's work is engaged with colonial systems and their abuses.

According to his biographer Alan Sheridan, Gide had difficulty writing *The Immoralist*; he was fallow for stretches. But he did not forsake his suffering. As he said to Francis Jammes in 1901, "I get through books like one gets through illnesses. Nowadays I only like books that nearly killed off their authors."[11] In this regard, he is in the spirit of Conrad and aligned with the way in which Conrad wrote books. Conrad, like Gide, exhausted himself during his prolific writing to the point of illness. When they met, Conrad suffered from gout, pleurisy, and wretched moods.

In *The Immoralist*, the young narrator Michel relates his story of self-discovery from sickness to convalescence and beyond, to an audience of two friends, who have been summoned to a small town in French Algeria for that purpose. *The Immoralist* is thus framed by a homosocial setting where the gathered friends, as in Conrad's early frame novels, are of the same social class as the protagonist, with similar privileges, needs, and even pursuits.

The Immoralist was and remains controversial. After its publication in France in 1902, critics alternately sanctioned or approved its erotic content and its Nietzschean re-evaluation of morals and mores. One of the major differences between Conrad's early work and *The Immoralist* is that there is, in my view, little *eros* in Conrad's early nautical works, whereas a grotesque and deeply unfortunate *eros* shades *The Immoralist* and Michel's encounters with young Arab and Kabylie boys, as well as young women in French Algeria. In Conrad's early works, women, even seen briefly, are powerful and symbolic, but *eros* is absent.

To understand their affinity better, I turn to Friedrich Nietzsche. In many ways, Nietzsche shapes the narrative of *The Immoralist* and gives it its animating force. Gide began reading Nietzsche in his teens at the Lycée Henri IV. Sheridan maintains that reading Nietzsche was "the decisive philosophical encounter of his life."[12] In 1898, near the time when he began *The Immoralist*, Gide penned a thirty-six-page essay on Nietzsche.

Of the greatest importance to *The Immoralist* is Nietzsche's lengthy preface to the second edition of *The Gay Science* (1887), in which his philosophical project is likened to an epiphanic convalescence: "Gratitude pours forth continually, as if the unexpected had just happened – the gratitude of a convalescent – for *convalescence* was unexpected ... [The] saturnalia of a spirit who has patiently, severely, coldly, without submitting, but also without hope – and who is now all at once attacked by hope, the hope for health, and the *intoxication* of convalescence."[13] Michel is Nietzschean insofar as he has an epiphanic convalescence after a deadly sickness and rethinks his values and beliefs. He is less so when it comes to the liberty and omniscience that he permits himself in Algeria. Rejuvenation of older people by means of various forms of contact with younger people is not an unknown theme, but Gide takes it to a scopophilic outcome with impoverished children, as well as two sexual encounters with Indigenous women. He plants the seeds for this behaviour early in the book when he notices that an Arab boy is naked underneath his *bernous*.

Conrad would have responded favourably to most of the Nietzschean elements of the book. Michael John DiSanto, in *Under Conrad's Eyes*, gives us a warrant to say that Conrad read Nietzsche with interest and responded to him in his books, *Victory* and *The Secret Agent* in particular. He notes that Conrad refers to Nietzsche in his correspondence and proposes that Conrad "struggles with his sympathy and antipathy toward Nietzsche's ideas, some of which are uncomfortably close to Conrad's own convictions."[14]

Given the chronology under consideration in this chapter, we should take particular note of Conrad's attention to his friend Edward Garnett's celebrated article about Nietzsche, which appeared in the journal *Outlook* on 8 July 1899. Garnett gives an overview of Nietzsche's thought writ large: "Poet, philosopher, classicist, scientific critic all in one, Nietzsche is undoubtedly the deepest, though most biased, psychologist of human institutions that our century has seen."[15] Conrad mentions this publication twice in his letters. In the first letter, from 28 October 1899, he refers to an epistolary exchange about the article, and notes having "letters from all sorts of people."[16] On 9 November of the same year, he wrote again to Garnett, this time identifying some of his interlocutors, illustrating that the conversation about Nietzsche was ongoing. Elsewhere, he mentions Nietzsche's "mad individualism."[17] In a letter to Ford Madox Ford in 1901, he alludes to Nietzsche's "overman."[18]

As George Butte suggests, "Conrad's responses to Nietzsche were contradictory, and included unwilling sympathy and hostility, imitation and parody, as Conrad seems to argue with Nietzsche about the best human response to knowing the worst of our condition."[19] From this we can infer that, however favourably Conrad might have responded to the Nietzschean elements of *The Immoralist*, the issue of permission, of throwing away all mores, might, following Butte, have given him pause, as it is the kind of permission – not to mention the sort of narrative – that is strongly informed by colonialism and the Orientalist gaze. It is a gaze that at once objectifies and eroticizes a relation based upon hugely unequal social, economic, and political power. Conrad was wise to these inequities, which Gide, inspired by Conrad, would only become aware of after the latter's death.

Conrad, however, likely felt affinity with Gide's upending of European values, something that links the book to *Heart of Darkness* (1899) and in particular with the episode of the "intended," the young woman who is supposed to marry Kurtz. Conrad also counts the gains from a coming-out-of-sickness, for instance with respect to Razumov's delirium in *Under Western Eyes* or Marlow's disorientation in *Heart of Darkness*. The gains, however, are different for

Conrad. In his early novels and stories, especially "Youth," we can also read danger for sickness, but in Conrad the gains of convalescence after danger are maturity and perspective. In contrast, for Gide, convalescence leads to a profoundly problematic liberation for Michel, and a justification of the behaviour he describes to his pact-bound friends, who learn that he is no longer the puritan of his youth.

The French word *faible* ("weak") or derivatives thereof appear twenty-one times in Gide's short novel. Michel's convalescence involves an inevitable mirage of health but still marks him with the attendant benefits; he comes back to health with new vitality. During his convalescence, a tidal urge toward life definitively separates his present from his past: "What matters is that merely being alive became quite amazing for me, and that the daylight acquired an unhoped for radiance. Till now, I would think, I never realized that I was alive. Now I would make the thrilling discovery of life."[20] Michel seemingly finds health through the vitality of the young children whom his wife Marceline brings to their *pension*. He expresses the belief that different cultures have different epistemic codes and different relationships to life.

Conrad and Gide are united by the notion of self-study and recovery of oneself in a colonial setting. In *Heart of Darkness*, Indigenous people worship Kurtz; the devastating workings of colonialism are exposed in all their nefariousness. Colonialism in Gide's novel, by contrast, is an enabling force; it allows him to travel and live however he chooses. The Indigenous Algerians do not worship Michel in the least, but the children crowd around him, curious, watching the spectacle of the ailing white colonial, even as he spies, through the reflection of a glass fireplace door, on a child who steals a pair of scissors, an act that provides a thrill for the newly immoral Michel: "My heart pounded a moment, but the most prudent rationalization could not produce in me the slightest feeling of disgust. Quite the contrary, I could not manage to convince myself that the feeling that filled me at that moment was anything but amusement, but delight."[21] In Michel's response, we can see the casual masochism of the powerful, who thrill to a small mistreatment while remaining the most powerful person in the room, with every advantage available to French citizens in colonial Algeria.

At times, Gide pushes Nietzschean thought to the limits, as when Michel reflects favourably on his convalescence and its surprising outcome: "This was more than a convalescence – this was an increase, a recrudescence of life, the afflux of a richer, hotter blood which would touch my thoughts one by one, penetrating everywhere, stirring, coloring the most remote, delicate and secret fibers of my being."[22] Michel suggests that his convalescence leads to psychic expansion; it leaves him with more avenues, more tools than he had before, albeit with murky ethics. Likewise, he is augmented by his Nietzschean friend Ménalque, who performs the function of keeping him Nietzschean even when he is back in Europe, doing scholarship, and far away from the crowd of children who made his convalescence meaningful and transformative.

When Marceline dies – whether due to Michel's inattentiveness or lack of concern is not clear – *The Immoralist* becomes a homosocial book. There is no doubt that Michel is free in his way, ready to be recast and reborn, along the lines that Zarathustra, who advocates for the *Übermensch*, takes and rejoices without concern for morals or fairness or any notion of transgression, creating life's worth himself. Yet it is worth emphasizing that Michel and Ménalque, however much they echo Nietzsche, never become true *Übermenschen*, neither does any Conrad character, nor do Gide and Conrad themselves.

The clearest affinity in this aspect is between *The Immoralist* and "Youth." In "Youth," victory is born of enthusiasm; Marlow overcomes setbacks through vitality and gaiety, orienting him so that, despite whatever misfortune besets him, he faces and believes in the future. "Youth" is also a story of coming to life; it is concerned with maturity, but in the end, like Michel, like Ménalque, youth, or at least a kind of staying-young, turns out to be the key to survival and the recipe for ensuing joy. In the end, both Marlow and Michel seem to study at the school of Ménalque, who claims: "People are afraid to find themselves alone, and don't find themselves at all."[23] Perhaps the most Nietzschean quality that binds Gide to Conrad is the interest in solitude and the power of solitude, often a kind of ludic solitude. Like Michel, the protagonists of Conrad's early nautical novels, as well as *The Secret Agent*, are solitary, often friendless.

Finally, we can connect *The Immoralist* and Conrad's early work by thinking of the role of settings. Problems and misadventures abroad cause places to be a defining feature in both writers' work, whether protagonists face the brutality of colonialism in the Belgian Congo or colonial power and eroticism in French Algeria. Self-knowledge and knowledge of the other come by means of travel to poorer, colonized, and, typically, warm or hot spaces; this displacement into colonial settings forcefully unites Conrad and Gide. Indeed, at the end of his narrative in *The Immoralist*, Michel points to North Africa as not only the place but also the *cause* of his transformation: "But this climate, I believe, is what's responsible for the change. Nothing discourages thought so much as this perpetual blue sky."[24] Their works cohere as semi-autobiographical travel literature and can be read as such, however problematically. In whatever way we decide to register Gide or Conrad after reading these books, their literary affinity is clear.

~

Such affinity led to the duties of friendship for Gide. The translation project that he undertook for Conrad was enormous. As he mused in his journal, "Conrad himself will never know, or even suspect, the trouble I have taken simply through affection for him … and for the 'well-done job.'"[25] The greatest gesture of friendship – one that Gide very much enjoyed – was translating Conrad's novella *Typhoon* (1902), and making sure that it was the first work to be published by NRF Gallimard. We thus have the imprimatur of Gide, a *littérateur* of high standing on the one hand, and Conrad, a cult author in France (small though the circle was at that time), on the other. This generosity, even if one-sided, marked the high point of their friendship.

In letters written subsequent to their two meetings, among many declarations of mutual admiration, Gide first proposed translating "Youth" and *Heart of Darkness*. Conrad, delighted and grateful, understood this proposal as an act of friendship, as he acknowledged in a 1916 letter: "I don't know how to thank you for your letter. Your promise to translate 'Youth' and 'H. of D.' absolutely 'in your way' is an immeasurable honour before the world and makes me feel an inward joy over a very precious proof of your friendship."[26] After several years of hesitation, Gide ultimately chose to translate *Typhoon* instead of "Youth" or *Heart of Darkness*. Although a shorter work, its intricate maritime vocabulary confronted Gide with specific linguistic challenges. He knew its difficulties in advance not only from having read it but also from having overseen the previous, unfinished translation of it by Marie-Thérèse Müller (whom he did not acknowledge in the eventual publication).

Gide and Conrad shared a philosophy of translation. Gide wanted to translate books that he believed he might have written himself if he was in another place or another time. Conrad wanted his books translated in a similar fashion. Gide laboured assiduously over *Typhoon* because he was eager to please Conrad. Their shared philosophy of translation is best articulated in a 1928 open letter to a student that Gide published in the NRF. Gide outlines his general theory: "If I were Napoleon, I would begin a project for writers. Each of them – I'm speaking of the ones who merit this honor – would be obligated to enrich French literature by translating a work with which his talent or genius offers an affinity."[27] With *Typhoon*, Gide undertook just such a task. He notes that a paraphrastic as opposed to a literal approach is the only way, and that some of the translations of Conrad failed because of their literal word-for-word, non-idiomatic approach: "Having spent, a few years ago, much time working on the translation of Conrad's work, I occasionally dealt with translations that were so conscientious and so exact that they had to be rewritten in their entirety – because of this literal approach that made the French incomprehensible or, at least, lose all its quality."[28]

According to Gide, a good translator must know the nuances of both the translated language and the target language. Of the translating language, the writer should "know about the subtleties, the suppleness, the hidden resources."[29] Moreover, the translator should "penetrate the spirit and the sensibility of the author whose work he is translating, to the point of identifying with him."[30] Gide conceptualized his translation of *Typhoon* in this manner, and he counselled others to do the same.

Conrad also advised a paraphrastic approach for his translators. Idioms, he suggested, should be replaced by similar idioms in the translating language. As he once advised Gide: "my style is almost always completely idiomatic. One can therefore translate me faithfully by seeking the equivalent French idioms … [T]he most simple, most energetic idiom is always preferable. As for the literal translation … it seems to me impossible."[31] We are perhaps in the domain of what Eugene Nida refers to as "dynamic equivalence," a translation practice that allows for extreme liberties in a paraphrastic translation in the interest of a "receptor response" rather than a "source message."[32]

Conrad was eager to have the translations continue and expressed exuberance about Gide's generous friendship in 1918: "Your idea of a small edition of *Typhoon* gives me great, very great pleasure, as you can imagine. In truth, you spoil me. It is extremely pleasant to be spoiled by a friend like you."[33] The translation of *Typhoon* was a particular gift to a cherished friend and perceived as such by Conrad. If we look at Gide and Conrad's friendship, this moment is no doubt the apex, with Gide's superlative gesture and Conrad's attendant gratitude. Suffering physically, Conrad also saw this moment as late-life recognition: "It is a great blessing to befall me toward the end of my life – for now I am a sexagenarian – a useless man!"[34] Gide, for his part, felt some sense of ownership of *Typhoon*, given their shared philosophy of translation. In his words, it was "my own work, freely chosen, and I shall gladly sign it."[35]

As it happened, Gide's translation of *Typhoon* was his only translation of Conrad's prose. Alert to the difficulties that Conrad's work created for the translator by translating what Conrad considered one of his most difficult books, Gide had waded deep into maritime vocabulary. He even enlisted two experts to advise him. To Gide's disappointment, his serialized translation of *Typhoon* was not initially well received due to what were, he reported to Paul Valéry, "very unfortunate flaws"; he had to rework the translation for the volume publication and it now stands as a notable translation in French literary history.[36] Although Gide's translation of *Typhoon* is often incorrect, Conrad approved it and felt that the translation succeeded in conveying the spirit of the book. Gide would always consider it his own work and an important gesture of friendship that brought him and his idolized friend together in the same book.

~

In *The Arrow of Gold*, Conrad recognizes the unlikeliness of his late-life novel resonating with a reader: "The response of a reader depends on the mood of the moment, so much so that a book may seem interesting when read late at night, but might appear merely a lot of vapid verbiage in the morning."[37] More than that, Conrad, in late life, wondered about the suitability of some readers – or more particularly translators – for specific works. Gide's choice of a female translator for *The Arrow of Gold: A Story between Two Notes* (1919) was the *casus belli* for the one-sided fight that nearly ended his cherished friendship with Conrad.

In November 1919, Conrad wrote to his friend, translator, and future biographer Georges Jean-Aubry, "I am afraid that I have quarreled with Gide for good."[38] Indeed, Conrad was prepared to lose Gide as a friend, as well as the overseer of the translation of his entire work into French, over the issue of the translation of one novel. It is hard to believe that Conrad would do something so reckless. If we are to understand their friendship, we must understand why this concern erupted specifically over *The Arrow of Gold*, as a number of women had translated Conrad's texts prior to the fight, and he was happy with their translations. As he said of Isabelle Rivière's translation of *Victory*, a project that caused Gide much chagrin, "I couldn't be more satisfied."[39] His request for a male translator was not general; it applied to *The Arrow of Gold* in particular.

Critics are nearly unanimous in designating *The Arrow of Gold* as Conrad's worst novel. Daphna Erdinast-Vulcan castigates "its inflated rhetoric, the failure to dramatize characters and emotions, the apparent lack of narrative control and the ineffectiveness of its symbolism."[40] Elizabeth Campbell notes that "Conrad gave vent to long repressed emotions about a cold blunt truth, but in misplacing the emotions onto the wrong objects, he becomes the victim of his own exaggeration."[41] Zdzisław Najder declares *The Arrow of Gold* Conrad's "weakest novel."[42] Jocelyn Baines refers to its "failure of imagination."[43]

But *The Arrow of Gold* is also a rare Conrad work insofar as there is a strong female character, Doña Rita, and, to a lesser extent, her forceful but sabotaging sister, Theresa, who speaks a lot and plays a key role in the action. The novel is set in Marseille in the 1870s. A Carlist plot connects the main characters with M. George, Conrad's youthful avatar, who is involved in gun-running for the cause. Conrad claimed that the story was autobiographical. How much of Conrad's claim is true, no one knows for certain. That Conrad aided Carlist causes and got shot in the chest (although by himself, not by duel as in *The Arrow of Gold*) is well known. It is curious that critics deem it an epistolary romance, rather than a *Bildungsroman*, as M. George goes from drifting and gambling to his first love, and then to his métier at sea. In fact, the amatory autobiographical content might explain some of Conrad's sensitivity about the novel and its translation by a woman.

The one-sided fight with Gide came about in the summer of 1919. When *The Arrow of Gold* was published, Conrad talked to Jean-Aubry about translating it. He then wrote to Gide with a request: "Aubry is very eager to translate this volume. What do you think ... I promised him that I would mention it to you."[44] This request raised complications. Conrad's publisher, T. Fisher Unwin, had already sent a copy to Gide, which he had assigned to Madeleine Octave Maus, who was already underway with a translation. In a letter now lost, Gide wrote to Conrad to explain the situation. Conrad's resulting ire was clear from a letter to Jean-Aubry: "I have just now had a letter from Gide in which he says that a woman just got hold of *The Arrow* for translation. I am going to protest with all my might. He throws me as bait to a gaggle of women."[45] For the first time in their correspondence, there is conflict and, for the first time, misogyny surfaces. Gide simply could not understand the fuss.

Conrad's reasons seemed obvious to him. As he put the matter on 4 November 1919, "If my writings have a pronounced character it is their virility – of spirit, inclination, style ... Very well, I want to be interpreted by masculine intelligences."[46] In this outbreak of misogyny, we can wonder if Conrad is also nastily hinting at supposed effeminacy related to Gide's homosexuality, although I tend to think not. Putnam speaks rather of "Conrad's stormy and demanding character."[47] If Gide was wounded by the affair of *The Arrow of Gold*, he was not alone. Three days later, Conrad wrote again to Jean-Aubry for support: "The answer [Gide] sent to my request to let you translate A. of G. is not the sort of answer you send to a man whom you take seriously ... I need to tell you in all this I tried to appear more hurt than angry. The truth of the matter however is that the more I thought [about] the letter during this fortnight the more angry I felt myself to be ... After all, my very severe annoyance is quite justifiable."[48]

Gide's swift response shows how alarmed he was by Conrad's anger. On 10 November, he sent Conrad a measured reply:

> I read your letter, stupefied, and could not fully understand what I did to deserve this wrath. My dear Conrad, you must know that, above all, I'm looking to satisfy you. It is only my profound fellow feeling and my admiration for you that make me oversee the translation of your work; I have only friendly interests and it has already taken quite a lot of time ... [I] who remain your very affectionate and profoundly devotee. Your letter is too painful to me – please take it back. I can't keep it.[49]

The Arrow of Gold controversy was hard on Gide, who suffered from a lack of confidence in friendship overall. In full depression, three years before *The Arrow of Gold* fight, he mused in his diary: "I get to the point of being unable to understand, at times, to what I owe the friendship that certain people bear me."[50] Conrad violently probed Gide's sense of insecurity about his friends, an insecurity made worse by their professional entanglement.

In a conciliatory letter to Conrad, now lost, Gide conceded defeat and offered to turn the translation of *The Arrow of Gold* over to Jean-Aubry. Nonetheless, Maus refused to give up the contract, which provoked a further small crisis. On 21 November, Gide wrote to tell Conrad that the translation was already under contract, and he could not dissolve it. He asked a question that was bound to annoy Conrad: "Are you so sure as all that that a masculine translation would necessarily be better than a feminine one?"[51] Conrad, however, had already sent a familiar and conciliatory letter himself, so he clearly had not received Gide's second letter before he replied on 5 November. Feeling that his demands are being met, Conrad is contrite but firm:

> So my dear fellow, I confess that I should be infinitely grateful if you could give the *Arrow* to Aubry. I shall have him here, under my hand. True I don't know French, but I understand it and even have the feel of it quite well. And perhaps I can give him a better idea of the nuances of my thinking *viva voce*. I hold this book of my sixtieth year very close to my heart. Perhaps you can forgive me this weakness … Here I end abruptly with the assurance of my great affection for you.[52]

In Conrad's next letter to Gide, some two weeks later, he does not mention *The Arrow of Gold* and finishes with a nod to his poor health, and an affirmation of friendship: "Excuse this horrible scrawl. I have a gouty wrist. What a bother this gout is! – I do not know how to thank you for your indulgence and your patient friendship."[53] They continued to correspond but with much less frequency. They never met again. One year before his death, in 1923, Conrad did try to visit Gide and his wife at their estate, Cuverville, but Gide was in Tunisia. The fight, having worn both of them out, exposed possibilities that were painful for both writers to think about. Jean-Aubry's translation of *The Arrow of Gold* was published five years after Conrad died, and there had been no co-translation.

Why did this dispute centre on *The Arrow of Gold* specifically, the book of Conrad's "sixtieth year"? Putnam argues that it meant a lot symbolically since Conrad was less productive than usual and both he and his wife were ill. Loss of *eros* is one aspect of late style, and it explains some of the oddity of *The Arrow of Gold*. I believe this is the key to the book. Young Doña Rita, the goat herder turned muse and wealthy Carlist, is chaste and unkempt. M. George and Doña Rita fall into passionate conversation and love but they do not fall into lust. The only potential *eros* in the book is Doña Rita's hairpiece, an arrow of gold with a jewelled shaft that eventually gets lost at sea by M. George. But we do better to see the arrow of gold as virginal Artemis's weapon than any kind of phallic metaphor. The ultimate flight by M. George and Doña Rita to the Maritime Alps appears chaste even as it tarnishes Doña Rita's reputation and necessitates M. George's departure.

There is no record of Gide ever reading *The Arrow of Gold*. In correspondence between the two writers toward the end of Conrad's life, Conrad expressed his gratitude to Gide: "What consoles me is the success (moderate, I admit) of the French translations. And this consolation I owe to you."[54] This wistful letter, the final one he sent to Gide, ends with a request: "Think of me as your loyal admirer and friend."[55]

~

After learning about Conrad's death, Gide wrote to Jacques Rivière, fellow writer and editor at the NRF: "This news moves me as much as can be believed, because I had, for Conrad, more than just my admiration. I had a true affection for him and I was extremely appreciative that he felt the same for me."[56]

The afterlife of their friendship is also remarkable. In 1927, just three years after Conrad's death, Gide travelled to the Congo and Chad as if following on the heels of Conrad, consulting *Heart of Darkness* as a kind of manual, turning his interests in literature into an exposé of the atrocities of colonialism, and dedicating one of the ensuing books to Conrad – *Voyage au Congo*.

In later years, Gide tested the notion of male friendship and sorted through various idioms. Conrad, perhaps surprisingly, influenced Gide's view of translation and the relationship of his own writing to his gender identity. Indeed, he reproduced the one-sided argument with Conrad when he told his principal translator Dorothy Bussy (née Strachey), who was in love with him, that his late-life novella, *Thésée* (1946), which reworked a Greek myth, could not be translated by a woman, whose "vocal chords were inappropriate for so deep a voice."[57] No doubt this affair brought Gide's lamented friend to mind.

Gide would continue to read Conrad's work long after his friend's death, in no particular order, with mixed assessments, but with an undying love for *Lord Jim* and a remodelled affection for its author. Conrad and Gide went from admiration, even idolization on Gide's part, to disillusion and back. They parted as great friends.

NOTES

1 Joseph Conrad, *Collected Letters of Conrad*, ed. Frederick R. Karl, Laurence Davies, et al., 9 vols (Cambridge: Cambridge University Press, 1983–2008), 5:590–1. "Votre amitié qui est bien le plus grand trésor que j'aie conquis à la pointe de ma plume."

2 Ibid., 6:207–8. "Je me demande seulement ce que j'ai pu faire pour gagner cette affectueuse amitié qui est certainment le 'Grand Prix' de ma vie littéraire. Mais à quoi bon. C'est un cadeau des dieux."

3 André Gide, "Joseph Conrad," *La nouvelle revue française*: *Hommage à Conrad* 135 (Dec. 1924): 17. "Je me sentais en retard envers lui. J'étais resté longtemps sans le revoir, sans lui écrire. Avais-je jamais su lui dire, ce que je lui écrivis aussitôt, toute l'affection, l'admiration, la vénération, que, malgré tant d'absence et de silence, je n'avais cessé de lui vouer? De mes aînés, je n'aimais, ne connsaissais que lui."

4 Ibid., 20. "Rien n'était plus cordial, plus pur et plus viril, que son rire, que son regard et que sa voix. Mais, comme la mer et ses bonaces, on le sentait capable de passions violents, de tempêtes."

5 Ibid., 20. "Si grand que fût sa curiosité pour les replis ténébreux de l'âme humaine, il détestait tout ce que l'homme pouvait présenter de sournois, de louche ou de vil."

6 Ibid., 19. "Comme un enfant."

7 Frederick Karl, "Conrad and Gide: A Relationship and a Correspondence," *Comparative Literature* 29, no. 2 (1977): 161.

8 Ibid., 169.

9 Conrad, *Collected Letters*, 4:527–8. "Je vous avoue enfin que j'ai lu et admiré l'Immoraliste il y a bien deux ans de ça. C'est Davray qui me l'a donné."

10 Ibid., 4:509–10. "Dites – je vous prie à Gide – qui est bien de vos amis, n'est-ce pas? – que je vais me présenter à sa porte un des ces jours, en chemise de nuit, pieds nu et la corde au cou. Il comprendra."

11 Quoted in Alan Sheridan, *André Gide: A Life in the Present* (London: Hamish Hamilton, 1998), 182.

12 Ibid., 51.

13 Friedrich Nietzsche, *The Gay Science* (New York: Random House, 1974), 32.

14 Michael John DiSanto, *Under Conrad's Eyes: The Novel as Criticism* (Montreal and Kingston: McGill-Queen's University Press, 2009), 192.

15 Edward Garnett, "Views and Reviews: Nietzsche," *Outlook*, 8 July 1899, 746–8, 747.

16 Conrad, *Collected Letters*, 2:209.

17 Ibid., 2:188.

18 Ibid., 2:344.

19 Georges Butte, "What Silenus Knew: Conrad's Uneasy Debt to Conrad," *Comparative Literature* 41 no. 2 (1989): 155–69, 155.

20 André Gide, *The Immoralist* (New York: Vintage International, 1996), 31. "L'important c'était que la mort m'eût touché, comme l'on dit, de son aile. L'important, c'est qu'il devînt pour moi très étonnant que je vécusse, c'est que le jour devînt pour moi d'une lumière inespérée. Avant, pensais-je, je ne comprenais pas que je vivais. Je devais faire de la vie la palpitante découverte." André Gide, *L'immoraliste* (Paris: Mercure de France, 1902), 31.

21 Gide, *Immoralist*, 52. "Mon Coeur battit avec force un instant, mais les plus sages raisonnements ne purent faire aboutir en moi le moindre sentiment de révolte. Bien plus! je ne parvins pas à me prouver que le sentiment qui m'émplit alors fût autre chose que de la joie." Gide, *L'immoraliste*, 55.

22 Gide, *Immoralist*, 59. "Il y avait ici plus qu'une convalescence. Il y avait une augmentation, une recrudescence de vie, l'afflux d'un sang plus riche et plus chaud qui devait toucher mes pensées, les toucher une à une, pénétrer tout, émouvoir, colorer les plus lointaines, délicates et secrètes fibres de mon être." Gide, *L'immoraliste*, 63.

23 Gide, *Immoralist*, 107. "Lois de l'imitation; je les appelle: lois de la peur. On a peur de se trouver seul; et l'on ne se trouve pas du tout." Gide, *L'immoraliste*, 117.

24 Gide, *Immoralist*, 165. "Mais ce climat, je crois, en est cause. Rien ne décourage autant la pensée que cette persistance de l'azur." Gide, *L'immoraliste*, 180.

25 André Gide, *The Journals of André Gide* vol. 2: 1914–1927 (New York: Knopf, 1948), 193. "Jamais Conrad lui-même ne connaîtra sans doute, ni jamais n'ira soupçonner, le mal que je me donne ici par unique amour de lui . . . et de la 'besogne bien faite.'" André Gide, *Journal* 1 (Paris: Gallimard, 1996), 1018.

26 Conrad, *Collected Letters*, 5:590–1. "Je ne sais pas comment vous remercier pour Votre letter. Votre promesse de traduire *Youth* et *H. of D.* tout-à-fait 'a votre

façon' m'a fait un honneur infini devant le monde et me procure un sentiment de joie intime comme prevue bien précieuse de Votre amitié."

27 André Gide, "Lettre ouverte à André Thérive," *La nouvelle revue française* 31 (Sept. 1928): 312. "Je serais Napoléon; chacun d'eux (littératures), je parle du moins de ceux qui mériteraient cet honneur, se verrait imposer cette tâche d'enrichir la littérature française du reflet de quelque oeuvre avec laquelle son talent ou son génie présenterait quelque affinité."

28 Ibid. "Ayant eu beaucoup à m'occuper, il y a quelques années de la traduction des oeuvres de Conrad j'eus affaire parfois à certaines traductions si consciencieuses et si exactes, qu'elles étaient à récrire complètement; – en raison de cette littéralité même, le français devenait incompréhensible, ou tout au moins perdait toutes ses qualités propres."

29 Ibid., "en connaître les subtilités, les souplesses, les ressources cachées."

30 Ibid., 313: "pénétrer l'esprit et la sensibilité de l'auteur qu'il enterprend de traduire, jusqu'à s'identifier à lui."

31 Conrad, *Collected Letters*, 5:590–2. "[M]on style est presque constamment tout à fait idiomatique. On peut donc me traduire fidèlement en cherchant les idioms équivalents français ... c'est toujours l'idiome le plus simple, les plus énergique [*sic*] qui es préférable. Quant à la traduction littérale ... elle me parait impossible."

32 Eugene Nida, "Principles of Correspondence," ed. Lawrence Venuti, *The Translation Studies Reader*, 3rd ed. (New York: Routledge, 2012), 141–55, 150.

33 Conrad, *Collected Letters*, 6:207–8. "Votre idée d'une petite édition du Typhon me fait un très grand plaisir. Vous pensez bien. En verité vous me gatez. C'est très agréable d'être gaté par un ami tel que Vous." All French spelling errors are Conrad's.

34 Ibid. "C'est un grand bonheur qui m'arrive vers la fin de la vie – car me voilà sexagénaire – un homme inutile!"

35 Gide, *Journals*, vol. 2, 193. "[O]euvre mienne, à mon gré, et que je signerai joyeusement." Gide, *Journals*, vol. 1, 1018.

36 André Gide and Paul Valéry, *Correspondance 1890–1942* (Paris: Gallimard, 1955), 465. "Mon *Typhon* paraît dans La revue de Paris avec des fautes assez désobligeant. Tant pis."

37 Joseph Conrad, *The Arrow of Gold* (New York: Norton, 1968), 337.

38 Conrad, *Collected Letters*, 6:517.

39 Conrad, *Collected Letters*, 5:649. "Je suis on ne peut plus satisfait."

40 Daphna Erdinast-Vulcan, *Joseph Conrad and the Modern Temper* (Oxford: Clarendon Press, 1991), 186.

41 Elizabeth Campbell, "Auto-Mythology in *The Arrow of Gold*," *Conradiana: A Journal of Conrad Studies* 25, no. 2 (1993): 140.

42 Zdzisław Najder, *Joseph Conrad: A Chronicle* (New Brunswick: Rutgers University Press, 1983), 48.

43 Jocelyn Baines, *Conrad: A Critical Biography* (London: Weidenfeld and Nicolson, 1960), 411.

44 Conrad, *Collected Letters*, 6:469–70. "Aubry a grande envie de traduire ce volume. Qu'en dites-Vous? … J'ai lui ai promis de Vous en parler."

45 Ibid., 6:502–3. "Je viens de recevoir une lettre de Gide ou il me dit qu'une femme vient de s'emparer de *Arrow* pour le traduire. Je vais protester de toutes mes forces. Il me jette en pature [*sic*] a un tas des femmes."

46 Ibid., 6:515–16. "Si mes écritures ont un caractère prononcé c'est leur virilité – esprit, allure, expression … Eh bien, j'ai le désir d'être interprété par des esprits masculins."

47 Walter Putnam, *L'aventure littéraire de Joseph Conrad et d'André Gide* (Saratoga: Anma Libri, 1990), 13. "caractère ombrageux et exigéant de Conrad."

48 Conrad, *Collected Letters*, 6:517.

49 Gabrijela Vidan and Ivo Vidan, "Further Correspondence between Joseph Conrad and André Gide," *Studia Romanica et Anglica* 29–32 (1970–71): 528–9. "Je lis votre lettre avec stupeur et ne comprends vraiment pas ce qui peut me valoir votre courroux … Mon cher Conrad, persuadez-vous que je cherche avant tout à vous satisfaire. C'est uniquement ma profonde sympathie et mon admiration pour vous qui m'ont fait surveiller la traduction de vos oeuvres; je n'y ai d' intérêt que tout amicable et cela m'a déjà pris un temps considérable … [Je] reste votre très affectueusement et profondément dévoué. Votre lettre m'est décidément trop pénible; reprenez-la. Je ne puis la garder."

50 Gide, *Journals*, vol. 2, 141. "J'en arrive à ne plus comprendre même, parfois, d'où peut me venir l'amitié que certains me portent." Gide, *Journal*, 947.

51 Vidan and Vidan, "Further Correspondence," 530. "Êtes vous si sûr que cela qu'une traduction masculine sera forcément meilleure qu'une féminine?"

52 Conrad, *Collected Letters*, 6:535–36. "Mon cher Gide … [J]e confesse que je Vous serai infiniment reconnaissant si Vous pouviez donner le *Arrow* à Aubry. Je ne connais pas le français il est vrai, mais je le comprends et même je le sens assez

bien. Et peut-être pourrai je lui faire comprendre mieux de vive voix les nuances de ma pensée. Ce livre de ma 60ième année me tient fort au Coeur Vous qui comprenez tant de choses … Je termine brusquement ici avec l'assurance de ma grande affection pour Vous."

53 Ibid., 6:543–44. "Pardonnez moi cet atroce gribouillage. J'ai le poignet goutteux. Quelle scie cette goutte! – Je ne sais pas comment Vous remercier de Votre indulgence et de ta patiente amitié."

54 Conrad, *Collected Letters*, 8:369. "Ce qui me console c'est le succès (modéré j'en conviens) des traductions françaises. Et cette consolation c'est a Vous que je la dois."

55 Ibid., 369–70. "Pensez a [*sic*] moi comme Votre fidèle admirateur et ami."

56 André Gide and Jacques Rivière, *Correspondance 1909–1925* (Paris: Gallimard, 1998), 757–8. "Cette nouvelle m'affecte autant que tu peux croire, car j'avais pour Conrad, en plus de mon admiration, une affection véritable et j'étais extrêmement sensible à celle qu'il me témoignait."

57 André Gide, *Selected Letters of André Gide and Dorothy Bussy*, ed. Richard Tedeschi (Oxford: Oxford University Press, 1985), 249.

7

The Elusive Figure of Friendship in Virginia Woolf's Novels

ERWIN ROSINBERG

Virginia Woolf has often been characterized as the modernist writer most deeply and consistently interested in the vicissitudes of individual being. Her novels pulse with intersubjective contact, but they also distinctively demonstrate how forms of relationality can never entirely dissolve the self into categories of social belonging and connection. The "discovery" she made while composing the novel that would become *Mrs Dalloway* suggests how, for Woolf, the truth of subjectivity must inform any sense of shared reality: "I dig out beautiful caves behind my characters: I think that gives exactly what I want; humanity, humor, depth. The idea is that the caves shall connect and each come to daylight at the present moment."[1] The process of linking the individual "caves" and "com[ing] to daylight" – through which interpenetrated but essentially isolated consciousnesses inhabit a shared plane of being on the day of Clarissa's party – gains its credibility through the thorough differentiation of interiorities that lie behind each character's supposedly visible personality. In *Mrs Dalloway*, as in so much of Woolf's work, technique and theme alike point to the particular nature of her genius: an ability to render in lyrical language the emergent, inchoate, and isolated self.

Moments in which Woolf's characters most fully experience themselves as individuals often come with a sense of heady disorientation, communicating at once an elevated or heightened significance and a cosmic powerlessness, an anonymity that threatens to undo the usual boundaries of the self. One can think in this regard of young Nancy in *To the Lighthouse*, standing in a tide pool at the beach as she lifts her hand to block the sun, momentarily plunging the assorted sea creatures into darkness. "[S]he became with all that power sweeping savagely in and inevitably withdrawing, hypnotized," Woolf writes, but the hypnotic rush soon reverses so that Nancy is herself cast in the metaphorical tide pool, a realization that carries "an intensity of feelings which reduced her own body, her own life, and the lives of all the people in the world, for ever, into nothingness."[2] To feel that one makes the world, to feel caught in a world never of one's own making: how common this duality of sensation and experience must be, and yet, as the "intensity" of Nancy's feelings implies, how little shared or discussed. The pool of water in which she stands underscores the solitariness not only of Nancy but also of her oceanic feelings of connection and dissolution. The sensation that joins her to humanity – "her own life" to "the lives of all the people in the world" – is precisely what reminds her that she is alone.

Yet to stop with this insight, to say alongside *To the Lighthouse*'s Mr Ramsay in his anxious and repetitive quoting of William Cowper, "*We perish'd, each alone*,"[3] would be to downplay another essential feature of Woolf's work, namely the value placed on a kind of friendship that does not seek to dislodge or deny the fundamental solitude of being but rather recognizes, and even thrives upon, that which cannot be known about the other. Recent scholarly work has highlighted some of the ways that Woolf's own mutable friendships informed her writing. While noting that friendships fluctuated "in intensity and intimacy" throughout Woolf's life, Kathryn Simpson draws upon the rich body of scholarship about the Bloomsbury ethos to posit friendship as a category that Woolf used "to satisfy her complicated, unconventional, and sometimes contradictory needs and desires" and to "sustain the creative act."[4] Natania Rosenfeld characterizes the marriage of Virginia and Leonard Woolf as a kind of friendship in which the pair are defined less by the conventions of the marital institution and more by an ongoing and mutual negotiation of their respective forms of marginalization, in their lives as well as in their writing.[5] These studies show how Woolf, as a matter of both policy and instinct, pursued relationships that placed her at odds with social, cultural, and political norms. This essay focuses exclusively on Woolf's fictional art in order to reveal her understanding of friendship as the form of relationality that not only bristles against inherited structures and labels designed to support the centrality of heterosexual marriage and family life but also remains compatible with the essential isolation of subjective experience.

The question of how, or whether, one can enter into a relationship while remaining – as one must – essentially oneself is a question about friendship, and it underlies Woolf's novelistic career. Friendship can, of course, overlap with other forms of relationship, including sexual and conjugal relations, as it does in Woolf's life and in her work. It is nevertheless made distinguishable by its inherently elective nature and its elusiveness of description, both of which contribute to the ethical force of friendship in Woolf's novels. In *Mrs Dalloway*, Woolf touches repeatedly upon Clarissa's distanced admiration for the life of a woman who is known to her only from peering out of her window, a form of relationship that – since they never meet – obviously strains most conventional understandings of what constitutes a friendship. The motif still serves as a useful reminder that Woolf, like Clarissa, appears to be in search of a form of human connection that preserves what the novel calls "the privacy of the soul."[6] The portion of the novel dealing with Septimus Smith plays out the grave danger inherent in the assumption that shared spaces of human existence bring shared understandings of reality; thus, by contrast, Clarissa's respectful regard for the woman's domestic routine serves as a kind of theoretical model for friendship's potentiality. Other, darker readings of Clarissa's fascination remain plausible. Perry Meisel, for example, has read the scene in which Clarissa contemplates the woman following news of Septimus's suicide as a dissolution of the boundaries that have marked Clarissa's sense of a subjective self, akin to Nancy in the tide pool: "What Clarissa sees in the window is the continuity between everything around her, living, dead, and about to die … In the very act of exalting subjectivity to its presumably most decisive moment in the history of literature, subjectivity is in point of fact disassembled."[7] Where Meisel sees a form of self-erasure or even death in Clarissa's sympathetic gaze, I interpret the duality of Clarissa's affectionate observation – which deconstructs the usual binary of intimacy and distance – as the symbol of an idealized form of companionship: a way of being with others that also lets others be.

In what follows, I show how this ideal animates friendships in Woolf's novels that are more actual than theoretical. Moving from *Night and Day*, a novel in which the primary characters struggle against the social and narrative pressure to convert their instinctual and idiosyncratic friendship into the more recognizable and classifiable form of a marriage, to *The Waves*, in which friendship emerges as the ineffable reality through which all six characters understand both self and other, we can see Woolf making the case for friendship as a structure that shapes life itself. Two main claims emerge in my pairing of these novels: one, that friendship is the closest any form of relationality can come to resolving the tension between the need for companionship and "the privacy of the soul," precisely because of its resistance to any claims or expectations other than those activated by the heart; and two, that friendship is conveyed primarily through figurative language in Woolf, through elusive or mutable symbols used to convey an ongoing closeness of interpersonal being that need not be made subservient to existing categories of description or to the teleological drive of storytelling.

Night and Day: *"Yes, the world looks something like that to me, too"*

Woolf's early novel *Night and Day*, first published in 1919, may not initially seem to place friendship at the centre of its concerns, as it both reprises and re-examines the courtship and marriage plots of its Victorian forebears. The appearance of a reprise has led some readers, then and now, to regard it as a retrograde work. Such was the assessment of Katherine Mansfield, who wrote, "We had thought that this world was vanished for ever, that it was impossible to find on the great ocean of literature a ship that was unaware of what has been happening; yet there is *Night and Day*, new, exquisite – a novel in the tradition of the English novel. In the midst of our admiration it makes us feel old and chill."[8] Both in its occasional reliance on a descriptive realism that Woolf would later repudiate and in its ultimate concession to a matrimonial conclusion as the apparent answer to its protagonists' anxieties about authentic relations, the novel can indeed seem a backward-looking text, particularly in the aftermath of the social and cultural upheaval of the First World War. Jane de Gay and Steve Ellis, among others, have offered more recuperative readings that characterize the novel as the literary site through which Woolf most explicitly and self-consciously works through her relationship to a Victorian literary and historical past that is, after all, her own.[9] In both form and thematic substance, the reversion to tradition can be seen as an attempt to inhabit inherited structures – novelistic and sociocultural – in order to discover what potential for the new might be housed within them. In this way, the novel does still manage to suggest "that the proper stuff of fiction is a little other than custom would have us believe it," as Woolf advocates in "Modern Fiction," even if its experiments are less visible on the surface than in *The Voyage Out* or in Woolf's later work.[10]

The moments in which the novel most urgently articulates its modernity – and its resistance to a default continuation of what Woolf disapprovingly calls the "love interest ... in the accepted style"[11] – are those in which its central characters attempt to pry apart their feelings of deep and instinctual friendship from the marriage plot in which they are enmeshed. Though Katharine Hilbery and Ralph Denham seem marked for matrimony from their initial, tense meeting in the Hilberys' drawing room, they are hindered in the completion of this destiny not only by differences in expectation and social status but also by their shared sense that the institution of marriage cannot possibly contain their burgeoning friendship. "Why, after all, isn't it perfectly possible to live together without being married?" Katharine asks her mother.[12] Her plaintive question speaks at once to the force of inherited conventions and to her desire to honour a relationship that she has come to value precisely because of its improvisational and uncategorizable qualities. Throughout the novel, Katharine seems to understand marriage as a story that she is expected to see to its predictable and scripted conclusion, one that would smoothly bridge past and future by establishing the continuity of the family's position and legacy.

Class and gender fix Katharine's sense of life possibilities in a way that renders friendship with Ralph both unthinkable and irresistible to her. Listening to Ralph talk as the pair stroll in Kew Gardens, she considers his botanical discourse – with its attention to "living things endowed with sex" that both highlights and displaces the tension between them – and comes to regard everything beyond the ambiguous and charged space that they share as a symbol of the world's inhospitable disposition to authentic relations: "The very trees and green merging into the blue distance became symbols of the vast external world which recks so little of the happiness, of the marriages and deaths of individuals."[13] Ralph's reaction to Katharine's increasingly abstracted look encapsulates why, when the pair are considered apart from matrimonial emplotment, they are best understood as friends. His romantic instinct to close the gap between them – or, for that matter, his masculinist instinct to possess her, with which Ralph periodically struggles throughout the novel – is pushed aside in favour of a companionate silence: "he looked at her taking in one strange shape after another with the contemplated, considering gaze of a person who sees not exactly what is before him, but gropes in regions that lie beyond it … And for him too, perhaps, it was best to keep aloof, only to know that she existed, to preserve what he already had – perfect, remote, and unbroken."[14]

The Kew Gardens scene touches upon the possibility that one can be with another while still preserving "the privacy of the soul," and it brings together some of the images and motifs, trees and silence, through which the novel manages to register friendship's persistent presence amidst the marriage plot it almost begrudgingly seems to adopt. Knowing that she is expected to marry – that the story impressed upon her is one of marriage – Katharine's best hope is for a marriage that affords her some measure of privacy, which could be enabled by a relationship disinterested enough to allow her the time and space to continue her pursuit of mathematics. Katharine's interest in working on her mathematical problems in isolation is one indication of her inclination toward solitude, or at least toward relationships that would neither tax her nor fix her identity. Another comes in the form of an ongoing reverie about traversing a landscape of "leaf-hung forests" that symbolizes her desire to inhabit a world and a story different than the one in which she seems to be living. Just as she is about to conclude that she must give in to marrying William Rodney, a man who arouses only tepid feeling in her, she feels herself transported into this "dream state, in which she became another person, and the whole world seemed changed … If she had tried to analyze her impressions, she would have said that there dwelt the realities of the appearances which figure in our world; so direct, powerful, and unimpeded were her sensations there, compared with those called forth in actual life. There dwelt the things one might have felt, had there been cause; the perfect happiness of which here we taste the fragment; the beauty seen here in flying glimpses only."[15]

As she moves from abstraction to analysis, Katharine finds her dream state to be utterly incompatible with reality, since her reality is defined largely by patriarchal impositions that she has internalized to an extent that almost disguises the imposition. At the same time, though, these visions are more real to her than reality itself, and they are not solely dreams of solitude. There is no story in this alternative world of Katharine's, only fragments; these fragments contain abstract hints of a companion who could enable adventure rather than continuity with past traditions, and they also include some imagery that recurs in Woolf's later novels: "But there certainly she loved some magnanimous hero, and as they swept together among the leaf-hung trees of an unknown world, they shared the feelings which came fresh and fast as the waves on shore."[16] Although the dream of the "magnanimous hero" is charged with romantic feeling in a way that blurs the usual distinction between lover and friend, when considered in relation to the actuality of the novel's social world this figure remains aligned with the realm of friendship, a domain of potential improvisational freedom that is positioned in opposition to the prospect of matrimony.

Though Ralph's visions and dreams are different from Katharine's – populated more specifically by a version of Katharine herself – the two characters share a similar dilemma: within the sphere of their lived experience, all of their desire becomes attached to a person who seems more appropriately consigned to the role of friend than spouse. In their pursuit of friendship, too, they are left somewhat adrift, having inherited few significant models or stories of how friendship between the sexes is supposed to proceed, and not knowing, for that matter, whether friendship has a story built into it, a destination toward which it should tend. As in the Kew Gardens scene, Woolf regularly distinguishes their bond from the story-driven imperative to marry in part by illustrating how much of their relationship is built through moments of shared and silent intuition. Sometimes these silences are awkwardly long, unnerving both Katharine and Ralph, but nevertheless silence becomes symbolic of a counter-normative – and counter-narrative – impulse that they share.

In the first chapter, an old Victorian novelist named Mr Fortescue holds forth at a tea party hosted by Katharine's mother, and his "rounded structures of words" strike both Katharine and her unexpected guest, Ralph, as performative bluster.[17] Their shared silence amidst the din of the social gathering indicates the potential for an ongoing, largely unspoken form of sparring between the two. Katharine finds herself silenced by a "malicious determination not to help this young man … by any of the usual feminine amenities," while Ralph silently controls "his desire to say something abrupt and explosive, which should shock her into life."[18] Silence also signals their mutual resistance to outmoded conversational niceties: "Being much about the same age and both under thirty, they were prohibited from the use of a great many convenient phrases which launch conversation into smooth waters."[19] The contrast between Fortescue's rote story-making and their tense but communicative silence sets in motion a pattern than runs throughout the novel, in which nonverbal communication through gesture or image becomes prized as a sign of the authentic and the modern – and as a sign, too, of friendship.

The narrator first remarks upon Katharine's habitual silence as a way of indicating potential unappreciated in her by the older generations in her family: "Silence being, thus, both natural to her and imposed upon her, the only other remark that her mother's friends were in the habit of making about it was that it was neither a stupid silence nor an indifferent silence. But to what quality it owed its character, since some sort of character it had, no one troubled themselves to inquire."[20] Later, when Katharine begins to realize that Ralph could be a more surprising, more complicated, and more meaningful presence in her life than she first surmised, she silently ruminates about him in a way that suggests the revision of a story once thought settled. Her silence in this instance signals renewed and potentially subversive thought, rather than repression: "Perhaps, then, he was the sort of person she might take an interest in, if she came to know him better, and as she had placed him among those she would never want to know better, this was enough to make her silent. She hastily recalled her first view of him ... and ran a bar through half her impressions, as one cancels a badly written sentence, having found the right one."[21] For much of the novel, the relationship proceeds according to this model of vision and revision. They silently share moments of understanding, attempt to abandon their projections and presuppositions of one another, and loop back over familiar emotional territory, deflecting the marriage plot onto their relationships with others as they pursue a less constrictive and more mutable friendship with one another.

In the continuation of their conversation at Kew Gardens, amidst entanglements and marital engagements (both failed and accepted) with other people, Katharine and Ralph try to inscribe the relationship they have formulated more specifically with the language of friendship. At first, they toy with the notion that there must be some kind of relation in which "people live together, if you like, where each is free, where there's no obligation upon either side," but they cannot get past thinking such an arrangement purely theoretical;

"obligations always grow up," Katharine says, feeling that this not-marriage would eventually fall subject to the expectations – emotional if not legal – of marriage itself. Following this exchange, Ralph endeavours "to lay down terms for a friendship which should be perfectly sincere and perfectly straightforward." In near-contractual terms, he attempts to lend structure and rules to a type of bond that, by nature, wants to escape such definitional specificity: "'In the first place, such a friendship must be unemotional,' he laid it down emphatically. 'At least, on both sides it must be understood that if either chooses to fall in love, he or she does so entirely at his own risk. Neither is under any obligation to the other. They must be at liberty to break or to alter at any moment. They must be able to say whatever they wish to say. All this must be understood.'"[22] Katharine is intrigued by the freedom and the promise of his proposal, but in trying to pin the elusiveness of friendship to contractual language, the scene ultimately plays out as yet another attempt to resist matrimonial emplotment.

Eventually, they do give in to the marriage plot, eased in their anxieties by Katharine's mother, who assures them that each previous generation has suffered similar worry about getting caught in a too-predictable story, and that marriage might be practised in a way that honours the uniqueness of their bond as friends. The climax of the novel, however, comes not at the altar but in an earlier moment of inscrutable, shared, and symbolic silence. Ralph struggles to convey his feelings to Katharine in a poem, and his writer's block leads him to ruminate, via image and abstraction, on the limitations of language itself. He tries to tell her of

> a world such as he had a glimpse of the other evening when together they seemed to be sharing something, creating something, an ideal – a vision flung out in advance of our actual circumstances. If this golden rim were quenched, if life were no longer circled by an illusion (but was it an illusion after all?), then it would be too dismal an affair to carry to an end; so he wrote with a sudden spurt of conviction which made clear way for a space and left at least one sentence standing whole.[23]

Soon, though, all language feels inadequate to his meaning, and he finds himself drawing a doodle on the side of the page, which, to his embarrassment, draws Katharine's eye:

"I like your little dot with the flames round it," she said meditatively.

Ralph nearly tore the page from her hand in shame and despair when he saw her actually contemplating the idiotic symbol of his most confused and emotional moments.

He was convinced that it could mean nothing to another, although somehow to him it conveyed not only Katharine herself but all those states of mind which had clustered around her since he first saw her pouring out tea on a Sunday afternoon. It represented by its circumference of smudges surrounding a central blot all that encircling glow which for him surrounded, inexplicably, so many of the objects of life, softening their sharp outline, so that he could see certain streets, books, and situations wearing a halo almost imperceptible to the physical eye. Did she smile? Did she put the paper down wearily, condemning it not only for its inadequacy but for its falsity? Was she going to protest once more that he only loved the vision of her? But it did not occur to her that this diagram had anything to do with her. She said simply, and in the same tone of reflection:

"Yes, the world looks something like that to me too."[24]

Ralph is mystified that his "idiotic symbol" conveys more to Katharine than his words do, but at this point in the novel, Woolf's readers should not share his surprise. Katharine's response – "Yes, the world looks something like that to me too" – serves as the culmination of the story of their friendship, insofar as friendship needs any kind of culmination. The comic energy that concludes the marriage plot works as a cover story through which the more elusive and untamed energy of their friendship can find some form of continuance, since they are expected, after all, to centre their lives around marriage and family, rather than friendship. Katharine's recognition of the "little dot with the flames round it" indicates the overlap, although not exactly the merging, of some of their most abstract, private, and silent visions; the signification of this symbol, the conjoined understanding of the world that it suggests, is limited in part to those characters who have participated in its construction.

There are, of course, more conventional friendships in *Night and Day*, and one of the most complicated of these is the friendship between Katharine and a potential rival for Ralph's affections, Mary Datchet. Although Katharine and Mary often find themselves assessing one another in relation to their status with Ralph, they share scenes of mutual understanding and sympathy, too. Mary's pining for Ralph exists in tandem with her pursuit and enjoyment of a life, and a room, of her own, and when Ralph drifts more definitively toward Katharine, the two women for a time become confidants who begin to share their worries and visions about the lives they are still working to shape. In the end, though, Katharine and Ralph decline to visit Mary, a sign that the marriage plot has indeed crowded out other forms of friendship – in particular, friendship between women – from view.

Settled with Ralph, feeling more assured that the intensity of her friendship with him can be accommodated within marital tradition, Katharine feels that "she held in her hands for one brief moment the globe which we spend our lives in trying to shape, round, whole, and entire from the confusion of chaos. To see Mary was to risk the destruction of this globe."[25] The globe image recalls Ralph's doodle, the dot with flames around it, and casts Mary, who continues to work on behalf of women's suffrage and on a political treatise, as a threat to its stability. This summative retreat from the possibility of multiple friendships is revised in such later texts as *To the Lighthouse*, in which the impassioned friendship of Mrs Ramsay and Lily Briscoe exists alongside the Ramsay marriage and crucially upholds the narrative and philosophical design of the novel. In *The Waves*, Woolf's formal innovation allows her to convey not only the possibility of multiple, overlapping friendships within a life but also the multiplicity of friendship itself.

The Waves: *The Six-Sided Flower*

The Waves, which traces the interlocking lives of six friends from childhood to adulthood, is an audaciously experimental novel. Only twelve years separate its date of publication in 1931 from that of *Night and Day*, but in many ways – style, form, and theme – it feels like the production of an entirely different literary era. In *Night and Day*, Woolf's investment in the elusive category of friendship and the figurative language that she uses to explore it creates eddies and stoppages in the momentum of a more conventional marriage plot. In *The Waves*, these eddies comprise the entirety of the novel. The novel is not exactly about what happens in its six characters' lives; rather, it is about what happens in their minds as life happens to them. And what happens to them as individuals is inseparable from what happens to them as a collective or coterie, a point put most directly by Bernard in the novel's final section that he alone narrates: "Our friends, how seldom visited, how little known – it is true; and yet, when I meet an unknown person, and try to break off, here at this table, what I call 'my life,' it is not one life that I look back upon; I am not one person; I am many people; I do not altogether know who I am – Jinny, Susan, Neville, Rhoda, or Louis: or how to distinguish my life from theirs."[26] Bernard suggests that there is no "I" without a "them" to which it attaches; the subjective self may be formed in part through differentiation within a group (in this case, a group of childhood friends who keep in touch or at least keep track of one another's lives over the years), but the ongoing importance of the group suggests that one's awareness of self as an individual is perpetually dependent upon an ever-shifting network of relations.

The novel in both form and content thus disintegrates any perceived dichotomy between solitude and friendship. Since their identification as individuals is so porous and intermingled, Bernard, Jinny, Susan, Neville, Rhoda, and Louis are never truly alone, always enmeshed in the story of their collective lives. At the same time, even in parts of the novel that gather all six characters together, they are never entirely relieved of their sense of solitary being. The foregrounding of friend relations tells a story not of aloneness alleviated by togetherness, but rather of aloneness and togetherness as inescapable – and simultaneously experienced – facts of life.

The Waves alternates between two kinds of writing, both distinctively Woolfian. Prefatory interludes describing the shifting light of day as the sea interacts with the shore and sky introduce each section of what one could call the novel proper; these passages of meditative natural description suggest, among other things, the passage of life itself, but they do so without human presence. Thus the experience of time passing for the six friends is juxtaposed with nonhuman scales of time in order to suggest the ephemeral nature of all life experience: the experience of aloneness and the experience of togetherness alike. The bulk of the novel is comprised of the voices of the six friends (with a seventh, the doomed Percival, appearing frequently in their ruminations but never speaking himself). These voices may seem a version of the introspective passages of stream-of-consciousness narration one finds in *Mrs Dalloway* or *To the Lighthouse*, but the fact that these monologues are marked as a kind of speech creates an entirely different effect. That each new passage comes with a speaker's tag – "said Bernard," "said Jinny," "said Susan," and so on – suggests a silent or subliminal conversation among the friends as they move through life. Their reactions to life events, their inchoate memories, sensations, and impressions, are uniquely their own, and yet imagery and ideas frequently flow across the soliloquies, indicating the continuing impact of their group identity even in times when they are divided.

Early in the novel's first section, in which the characters are young children, Bernard offers one model for what friends can do for one another when he uses his story-making skills to provide Susan with a needed imaginative escape. When Susan sees Jinny kissing Louis behind the hedge, she is shaken to the core, and her reaction suggests something more complicated than mere jealousy: "'I saw her kiss him,' said Susan. 'I looked between the leaves and I saw her. She danced in flecked with diamonds light as dust. And I am squat, Bernard, I am short. I have eyes that look close to the ground and see insects in the grass. The yellow warmth in my side turned to stone when I saw Jinny kiss Louis. I shall eat grass and die in a ditch in the brown water where leaves have rotted.'"[27] Susan's self-consciousness about her body, which contrasts with Jinny's bodily confidence, is linked to the vulnerability of her emergent sense of self; witnessing this kiss, she seems to foreclose the possibility of any such romantic adventure in her life and dramatically envisions her own ignored death, her body returning ignominiously to nature.

Bernard senses Susan's distress and uses his facility with language to enlist her in the construction of a fabular site of play and escape – the mythical Elvedon – out of the very natural materials that she has just associated with death and disintegration. The temporary intimacy that emerges is both palpable and indescribable: "'When we sit together, close,' said Bernard, 'we melt into each other with phrases. We are edged with mist. We make an unsubstantial territory.'"[28] The word "unsubstantial" signifies in multiple ways, perhaps suggesting, at least in part, the vagueness of their shared imaginative enterprise and its seeming irrelevance to their developmental narratives. Alternatively, "unsubstantial" may indicate not insignificance but rather a deeper and stranger kind of significance; it might point to Elvedon as a site that can be seen, understood, and appreciated only by the friends who made it, a territory as elusive and unclassifiable as friendship itself. This vision of two childhood friends whose words and bodies are "edged with mist" also brings to mind the "circumference of smudges" surrounding Ralph's doodle in *Night and Day*, in each case suggesting the creation of a private, interpersonal world that is both within and apart from the larger, so-called "real" world that surrounds it.

Elvedon is recalled repeatedly throughout the novel as the characters grow into adults, acting as a symbol or index of the childhood imagination in which friendship is so often first forged. It is also a site associated with the generation of stories, as Bernard's further invocation in the first chapter details: "'Let us now crawl,' said Bernard, 'under the canopy of the currant leaves, and tell stories. Let us inhabit the underworld. Let us take possession of our secret territory.'"[29] This enthusiasm for storytelling or phrase-making becomes one of the leitmotifs of Bernard's character, so it is remarkable to see how by the end of the book he has come to regard storytelling not as an escape that protects the generative potential of friendship, but rather as a form that inherently falsifies life experience – too orderly, too obligatory, too caught up with people's ideas of what life is and ought to be:

> in order to make you understand, to give you my life, I must tell you a story – and there are so many, and so many – stories of childhood, stories of school, love, marriage, death and so on; and none of them are true. Yet like children we tell each other stories, and to decorate them we make up these ridiculous, flamboyant, beautiful phrases. How tired I am of stories, how tired I am of phrases that come down beautifully with all their feet on the ground! Also, how I distrust neat designs of life that are drawn upon half-sheets of note-paper. I begin to long for some little language such as lovers use, broken words, inarticulate words, like the shuffling of feet on the pavement. I begin to seek some design more in accordance with those moments of humiliation and triumph that come now and then undeniably. Lying in a ditch on a stormy day, when it has been raining, then enormous clouds come marching over the sky, tattered clouds, wisps of cloud. What delights me then is the confusion, the height, the indifference and the fury. Great clouds always changing, and movement; something sulphurous and sinister, bowled up, helter-skelter; towering, trailing, broken off, lost, and I forgotten, minute, in a ditch. Of story, of design, I do not see a trace then.[30]

This passage reframes and reassesses Bernard's understanding of himself as the group's storyteller (though not its most successful published writer, who is Neville). In its broadest application, it offers a justification for the fragmentation and abstraction of the novel as a whole, characterized in this case as a kind of fidelity to life's mutability and unpredictability.

Some readers have viewed Bernard as oppressive in his dedication to storytelling and his pursuit of authorship. David Bradshaw, for example, links his observational tendencies to the descriptive realism Woolf lambastes in "Mr Bennett and Mrs Brown" and notes the frequency of his use of the first person, the "I" that signals the unyielding male ego in *A Room of One's Own*.[31] In this moment, though, Woolf brings Bernard's affinity for story to a crisis point that leaves him longing for intangible figures and symbols, much as Katharine longs to replace the expected "story" of marriage with a nonspecific "magnanimous hero" and "leaf-hung forests" in *Night and Day*. Moreover, in projecting himself into a ditch where he watches a stormy sky unleash its fury, Bernard obliquely recalls Susan's dejected reaction to the childhood kiss that precipitated the creation of Elvedon. Recalling the origin point of the storytelling instinct in childhood friendship, he laments its development into narratives that are more conventional – "stories of childhood, stories of school, love, marriage, death and so on" that people tell themselves in order to make sense of ephemerality and unpredictability – and instead "delights" in confusion, indifference, and lack of design, as well as an immersive relationship with the whims of the nature. His struggle is for a language that does not bring with it the falsification of an end-driven plot; therefore, his meditation can be seen as an attempt to restore to primacy the "unsubstantial territory" of the network of childhood friendships that is already in place from the inception of the novel.

Certainly, the six friends live through events that carry storytelling potential: Percival's death in India casts a long shadow over all of their lives, and the members of the group marry and start families, have love affairs, and make and unmake careers. Yet even when a significant story event, such as the news of Rhoda's suicide, rises to the surface of Bernard's speech in this final section, the novel wants to resist the very idea of closure. It is the structure of the six, with Percival as the absent and silent centre, that continues to matter over and above the particularities and the chronology of their life stories.

The language that Bernard comes to value most highly, then, is the figurative and the symbolic, which have factored into Woolf's own narrative design all along. For the most part, the symbolic register of the novel does not provide symbols of friendship itself; rather, it supplies imagistic content that quells our readerly impulse to be caught up in individual plot lines and refocuses our attention on the existential questions of aloneness and togetherness that are at the centre of its investigation of group friendship. In a diary entry dated 7 February 1931, Woolf explains the symbolic intentions of her just-completed novel:

> What interests me in the last stage was the freedom and boldness with which my imagination picked up, used and tossed aside all the images, symbols which I had prepared. I am sure that this is the right way of using them – not in set pieces, as I had tried at first, coherently, but simply as images, never making them work out; only suggest. Thus I hope to have kept the sound of the sea and the birds, dawn and garden subconsciously present, doing their work under ground.[32]

Offering potential symbols but "never making them work out," letting them "only suggest," Woolf brings her readers closer to the coterie of six friends in her novel, who themselves often puzzle over tantalizing suggestions of meaning. One such recurring image is that of "a fin in a waste of waters," which, as Christine Froula has shown, recalls language in Woolf's diary that attests to the novel's genesis and to Woolf's feeling, upon completing the manuscript, that she had "netted" a long-gestating intuition. Froula reads the fin as one sign that the novel is an act of diffracted self-portraiture that "ventriloquizes a woman's vision through six lyric voices that tell a 'life of anybody'" and thereby "seeks women's freedom from identity and its politics."[33] The fin, in its suggestive inscrutability and its inseparability from the waste of waters that contain it, also seems linked to the inseparability of aloneness and togetherness in the novel, and thus to the larger structure of group friendship from which the novel's subjectivities emerge.

In one moving passage, the fin indicates a temporary break in the companionate silence that can accompany the shared reading practices of friends. As he sits with Neville, Bernard reflects:

> Now and then I break off a lump, Shakespeare it may be, it may be some old woman called Peck; and say to myself, smoking a cigarette in bed, 'That's Shakespeare. That's Peck'– with a certainty of recognition and a shock of knowledge which is endlessly delightful, though not to be imparted. So we shared our Pecks, our Shakespeares; compared each other's versions; allowed each other's insight to set our own Peck or Shakespeare in a better light; and then sank into one of those silences which are now and again broken by a few words, as if a fin rose in the wastes of silence; and then the fin, the thought, sinks back into the depths, spreading round it a little ripple of satisfaction, content.[34]

The "ripple of satisfaction" that the thought leaves behind remains linked to the silence that precedes and follows it, which leads into the unspoken fact of their friendship. Notably, the mood changes as Neville awaits the arrival of a lover – he "poked the fire and began to live by that other clock which marks the approach of a particular person"[35] – which suggests the fin symbol is attached to the underlying structure of friendship and not to the more story-driven element of awaiting a "love interest." The fin, or rather its absence, also arises when Bernard tries to account for the impact of Percival's death: "I cried then with a sudden conviction of complete desertion. Now there is nothing. No fin breaks the waste of this immeasurable sea."[36] The image in this case attests to the psychic damage that the six friends experience in the wake of losing Percival, the centre of fascination around which their lives seem to revolve. In another instance, the fin appears in one of the prefatory chapters about the waves: "*Through all the flowers the same wave of light passed in a sudden flaunt and flash as if a fin cut the green grass of a lake.*"[37] Tracking these transmutations, Maria DiBattista suggests that "[t]he fin becomes a symbol that comments on its own symbolic nature as a medium in which the mutable constantly transforms itself into ever finer emblems of permanence."[38]

Scrutinizing the fin in its various appearances for such emblems of permanence, one begins to see that only change, loss, and friendship form the common waters from which meaning can occasionally be netted. The symbolic register associated with friendship in *The Waves* thus bears an affinity with some of Woolf's more famous pronouncements about friendship in her novels, in which she calls attention to a permanent structure of relations that underlies unpredictable patterns of disappearance and reappearance. One thinks of William Bankes's observation in *To the Lighthouse* that "friendships, even the best of them, are frail things" – sometimes surfacing again only as a way of honouring former affections, but nevertheless radiating throughout a lifespan – and also of Peter Walsh's acknowledgment in *Mrs Dalloway* that his periodic meetings with Clarissa, "brief, broken, and often painful," have nevertheless had an "immeasurable" impact on his life.[39]

In *The Waves*, one further mutable symbolic presence is Percival himself, if we follow Woolf's definition of the symbolic as that which is "subconsciously present, doing [its] work under ground." Percival is, of course, a person in these characters' lives, and his death at age twenty-five – which mirrors the death of Woolf's brother Thoby at the same age – is a deeply felt loss that punctuates all six voices in the novel. At the same time, he acts as a centre for the group of friends; his allure and his loss are equally indescribable, experienced distinctly by all six and yet shared. Prior to Percival's death, the six await his arrival at a restaurant, each of them anxiously eyeing the doorway that will be transformed by his passing through. What is it about Percival that so beguiles all of them? He is hale and seems comparatively untroubled by the existential questions that, in different ways, can be found in the soliloquies of Bernard, Susan, Jinny, Neville, Louis, and Rhoda. That he appears as such to the reader may well be a function of the fact that we only hear about him through the appreciative and desiring voices of those who loved him.

Neville's language about Percival has the most piercing intensity, since its expression is compounded by the coded nature of same-sex desire; at the restaurant, Neville muses, "If he should not come I could not bear it. I should go. Yet somebody must be seeing him now. He must be in some cab; he must be passing some shop. And every moment he seems to pump into this room this prickly light, this intensity of being, so that things have lost their normal uses – this knife-blade is only a flash of light, not a thing to cut with. The normal is abolished."[40] The quivering desire in this passage is particular to Neville, but the sense that Percival transforms the normal – in part by seeming so blissfully normal himself – is shared among the group. The specifics about why and how they came to share this impression remain, beyond these suppositions, unanswerable. Just as Katharine looks at Ralph's doodle in *Night and Day* and thinks, "Yes, the world looks something like that to me too," the six friends look at Percival – or at the void he leaves behind – and feel their world transformed in similar ways. Their mutual fascination with him, or attraction to him, and their mutual sense of loss after his death are a part of what give them a shared identity over time, but the precise "meaning" of Percival to them is allowed to remain suggestive or elusive, like the images and symbols to which Woolf refers in her diary.

In a later section of the novel, all six characters, now adults, reunite at a dinner. The absent Percival is still on their minds, as ever, but he becomes a more general emblem of mortality. Bernard recalls their earlier dinner at Hampton Court and in doing so creates an image that functions as a symbol of friendship in the novel: "'The flower,' said Bernard, 'the red carnation that stood in the vase on the table of the restaurant when we dined together with Percival, is become a six-sided flower; made of six lives.'"[41] Bound together in the image of the cut flower that is both a specific site of memory as well as a memento mori, the six friends are cast in a symbolic structure that renders them part of a single organic whole even as they retain their solitary individuality. Woolf thus shows that not only is it possible to be with others while retaining "the privacy of the soul," but also it is nature's design, necessary and true. In *The Waves*, and indeed across her fiction, she reveals friendship as a foundational structure undergirding life itself.

NOTES

1 Virginia Woolf, *A Writer's Diary* (New York: Harcourt Brace Jovanovich, 1953), 59.

2 Virginia Woolf, *To the Lighthouse* (1927; New York: Houghton Mifflin Harcourt, 1981), 75–6.

3 Ibid., 165. Mr. Ramsay's ruminations on the poem are delivered in fragmentary fashion: "'We perished,' and then again, 'each alone.'"

4 Kathryn Simpson, "Friends and Lovers" in *The Oxford Handbook to Virginia Woolf*, ed. Anne Fernald (Oxford: Oxford University Press, 2021), 27, 41. Simpson details how Woolf's friendships were often premised on the possibility of mutual provocation (or criticism) as well as reassurance, and how her rhetoric about friendship as well as her lived experience of friendship blurs categories: "What she sought and gained from her friendships was varied and complex, sometimes platonic, sometimes erotic or sexual, and sometimes a precarious mixture of both" (28).

5 Natania Rosenfeld, *Outsiders Together: Virginia and Leonard Woolf* (Princeton:

Princeton University Press, 2000). In making her case that the Woolfs – "she privileged by her background, but excluded from centers by her gender, he privileged by gender and marginalized through background" – constitute a "chiasmic alliance" that "forces social borderlines into relief," Rosenfeld characterizes their marriage itself as a kind of interstitial space, thriving upon a "between-ness" more associated with the unregulated category of friendship (4).

6 Virginia Woolf, *Mrs Dalloway* (1925; New York: Harcourt, 1981), 126. The phrase appears as Clarissa expresses reservations about "love and religion" and their potential alliance with the forces of conversion that she associates with Miss Kilman. She turns to the woman looking out the window as an emblem of the "privacy of the soul" that she wishes to protect.

7 Perry Meisel, *Criticism after Theory from Shakespeare to Virginia Woolf* (New York: Routledge, 2022), 67.

8 Katherine Mansfield, review in *Athenaeum*, 21 November 1919, reprinted in *Virginia Woolf: The Critical Heritage*, ed. Robin Majumdar and Allen McLaurin (London: Routledge, 1975), 82.

9 See Jane de Gay, *Virginia Woolf's Novels and the Literary Past* (Edinburgh: Edinburgh University Press, 2006), 44–66; and Steve Ellis, *Virginia Woolf and the Victorians* (Cambridge: Cambridge University Press, 2007), 12–42.

10 Virginia Woolf, "Modern Fiction," in *The Common Reader: First Series* (New York: Harcourt, 1953), 154.

11 Ibid.

12 Virginia Woolf, *Night and Day* (1919; London: Penguin, 2019), 411.

13 Ibid., 281–2.

14 Ibid., 282.

15 Ibid., 116.

16 Ibid.

17 Ibid., 6.

18 Ibid., 7.

19 Ibid.

20 Ibid., 33.

21 Ibid., 77.

22 Ibid., 286–7.

23 Ibid., 414–15.

24 Ibid., 419–20.

25 Ibid., 428.

26 Virginia Woolf, *The Waves* (1931; Oxford: Oxford University Press, 2015), 165.
27 Ibid., 7.
28 Ibid., 8.
29 Ibid., 12.
30 Ibid., 143.
31 David Bradshaw, introduction in *The Waves*, by Virginia Woolf (Oxford: Oxford University Press, 2015), xxxv–xxxvi.
32 Woolf, *A Writer's Diary*, 165.
33 Christine Froula, *Virginia Woolf and the Bloomsbury Avant-Garde* (New York: Columbia University Press, 2005), 177.
34 Woolf, *The Waves*, 163.
35 Ibid., 163–4.
36 Ibid., 170.
37 Ibid., 107.
38 Maria DiBattista, *Virginia Woolf's Major Novels: The Fables of Anon* (New Haven: Yale University Press, 1980), 156.
39 Woolf, *To the Lighthouse*, 89; and Woolf, *Mrs Dalloway*, 153.
40 Woolf, *The Waves*, 69.
41 Ibid., 136. The flower image that represents the underlying structural bond between the six friends again calls to mind Peter Walsh's reflection on the impact of his occasional reunions with Clarissa in *Mrs Dalloway*. Though the "actual meeting" is "horribly painful as often as not," its after-effect unfolds in the mind in a way that suggests he finds himself through the ongoing connection: "in absence, in the most unlikely places, it would flower out, open, shed its scent, let you touch, taste, look about you, get the whole feel of it and understanding, after years of lying lost … She had influenced him more than any person he had ever known." Woolf, *Mrs Dalloway*, 153.

8

Charles Ryder's Sentimental Education: The Lessons of Friendship in Brideshead Revisited

JAY DICKSON

Brideshead Revisited is Evelyn Waugh's best known and bestselling novel, and it brought him worldwide acclaim for the first time in his writing career. In many ways, however, it is the least characteristic of his novels. Certainly, it retains the waggish humour of his earlier works, and also details, as the others do, the trials and misadventures of the upper classes. Yet its prose does not follow the satirical style of his previous novels, with their staccato, dialogue-heavy texture. Waugh initially thought this was a promising new direction for his writing when he composed and published the novel at the end of his wartime service. In letters to his wife Laura, he referred to the work as his "magnum opus" or his "Mag. Op.," and he confidently told John Betjeman that he thought the finished novel "splendid."[1] When the novel was castigated by Edmund Wilson in the *New Yorker*, Waugh defended it in *Life* by characterizing it as his "best book."[2]

Yet Waugh's experimentation with the florid style of *Brideshead Revisited* later embarrassed him. In a letter to Graham Greene on 27 March 1950, he noted that rereading *Brideshead* at some distance from the strained circumstances of its wartime creation left him appalled: "I can find many excuses – that it was the product … of spam, Nissen huts, black-out, but it won't do for peace-time."[3] When he brought out a new edition of the novel in 1959, Waugh discovered he could not do much to remove the style without completely altering the message of the book, although he was able to pare down its "purple passages,"[4] about which Cyril Connolly had complained to Nancy Mitford. In his preface to the new edition, Waugh confessed his unhappiness with the form of the novel, "whose more glaring defects may be blamed on the circumstances in which it was written," at a time that he describes as "the period of soya beans and Basic English – and in consequence the book is infused with a kind of gluttony, for food and wine, for the splendours of the recent past, and for rhetorical and ornamental language, which now with a fuller stomach I find distasteful."[5] Second-guessing his achievement, he only touched up the prose somewhat: "I have modified the grosser passages but have not obliterated them because they are an essential part of the book" (ix).

This ineradicable centrality of style to Waugh's project for the book becomes all the more puzzling in light of the fact that this was exactly the type of novel he once implied he would *never* write. In an article called "Why Glorify Youth?" published in *Women's Journal* in 1932, Waugh mocks "the Glorious Youth Legend," which he claims was "invented by the elderly and middle aged,"[6] rather than by Bright Young Things, of whom he was one. In the article, he explicitly parodies the florid styles of two other British writers close to his own age, Rosamond Lehmann and John Van Druten, in their recent respective bestsellers, *Dusty Answer* (1927) and *Young Woodley* (1929). "Oh, lovely youths and maidens," Waugh writes in imitation of Lehmann's and Van Druten's ecstatic styles, "Oh bodies of classic grace and splendour! Rapturous calf love! Important doubts and disillusionments! Oh grand apotheosis of pimply adolescence!"[7] Thirteen years later, Waugh praises youth in exactly the same extravagant terms in *Brideshead Revisited*, and even surpasses his predecessors' exclamatory raptures:

> The languor of Youth – how unique and quintessential it is! How quickly, how irrevocably lost! The zest, the generous affections, the illusions, the despair, all the traditional attributes of Youth – all save this – come and go with us through life. These things are a part of life itself; but languor – the relaxation of yet unwearied sinews, the mind sequestered and self-regarding – that belongs to youth alone and dies with it. Perhaps in the mansions of Limbo the heroes alone enjoy some such compensation for their loss of the Beatific Vision; perhaps the Beatific Vision itself has some remote kindship with this lowly experience; I, at any rate, believed myself very near heaven, during those languid days at Brideshead. (72)

The juxtaposition of the two passages is quite striking. At twenty-four, Waugh finds the excessive praise of youth by Lehmann and Van Druten to be cynically and fraudulently manufactured for their elders' pleasure, with the repetition of "oh" marking a pointedly factitious exclamation. *Brideshead Revisited*, written when Waugh was in middle age, attempts to evoke that sense of emotion – particularly its "languor" – by the length of the sentences themselves, which are fitted out with dashes and semi-colons, and capped with exclamation marks. These sentences acknowledge that languorous youth can never be recaptured fully in any way. Charles describes that past as akin to the Beatific Vision of God that, for Aquinas, marks the end of the soul's journey to heaven. The languid language of youth can never be produced innocently, then, but must always be evoked through a debased rhetoric that can only point toward its former glory. The whole of *Brideshead Revisited* stages this dynamic.

Despite his mockery of Lehmann's and Van Druten's books, Waugh in fact wrote *Brideshead* according to the conventions of their shared novelistic sub-genre, that is, the varsity novel, which rehearses the story of a young English protagonist attending one of the Oxbridge colleges. This sub-genre is unlike classic *Bildungsromane* insofar as protagonists undergo their development more or less at a leisured remove from economic hardship, protected as they are by the wealth and privilege of their university surroundings. Education is not set in the hardscrabble "real world," but at enough of a distance to make development primarily *sentimental.* In other words, these novels document the education of the sentiments: of sensory pleasures, to be sure, such as taste and touch and sight, but also of aesthetic experience. More important, the varsity novel also offers instruction in the ways of higher feelings such as love.

In this regard, works in this sub-genre take their pattern from Gustave Flaubert's *L'éducation sentimentale* (1869), which is not a varsity novel per se, since its hero Frédéric Moreau does not start off wealthy, and the novel begins after his formal schooling in law has finished. Nonetheless, it provides a blueprint for the process of sensory and sensual edifications. Sentimental educations in the varsity novels written after Flaubert's great *Bildungsroman* usually begin with the love of friends – what the ancient Greeks called *philia*. Just as the passage about "the Langour of Youth" in *Brideshead Revisited* potentially affords a foretaste of the Beatific Vision, so does *philia* or affectionate friendship – expressed through Charles's love for Lord Sebastian Flyte and then Sebastian's entire aristocratic family – lead him through a process of sentimental education toward the promise and hope of a more perfected love. Friendship offers lessons in love, as well as lessons in affection, fidelity, and respect. The failure of his *philia* for Sebastian results in Charles's inability to attain the full grace available to youth, and the style of his retrospective narration, which aims to recapture that grace, ultimately fails to attain it.

Despite Waugh's mockery of Lehmann's and Van Druten's works, varsity novels excited him as a young adult. Although he had not been much of a fan of fiction during his secondary schooling, before he started at Oxford in January 1922, he not only read poems by Matthew Arnold, Arthur Quiller-Couch, and Hilaire Belloc that were set in the ancient university city but also absorbed some of the varsity novels set there, including Max Beerbohm's *Zuleika Dobson* (1911) and Compton Mackenzie's controversial and bestselling *Sinister Street* (1913–14).[8] Mackenzie's novel was especially popular among Waugh's circle. Cyril Connolly could quote it by the page, and kept a copy of it hidden by his bed, which Eric Blair (later George Orwell) once stole. In fact, Orwell remembered the schoolmasters beating Connolly for owning the book.[9]

Contemporary readers considered *Sinister Street* racy because its protagonist, Michael Fane, has an erotic obsession with a prostitute and discovers that he is the illegitimate son of an earl. What apparently fascinated its adolescent readership most, however, and assured its status as the quintessential varsity novel of the early twentieth century, was its glamorous depictions of the university that Fane attends and its surrounding city. Andro Linklater, in his biography of Mackenzie, notes that *Sinister Street* portrayed "the Oxford of mist-covered streets, of bonfires in the quads, of rags, aesthetes, and hearties – a standing wave of youth in the river of time."[10] The novel is written in an excessively florid and languorous style, which Linklater calls "luxuriant … decorated with epithets of excessive abstruseness, such as *fulminating, desquamating, feculent, tintamar,* and *fum.*"[11] Mackenzie's work, more than others, pre-determined Waugh's perceptions of university life by offering a map for his collegiate career, and more specifically for enlarging aesthetic experience and forming bonds of friendship. In *Brideshead Revisited* Charles Ryder places a copy of *Sinister Street* on the shelves of his Oxford rooms (23).

The varsity novel began as a Victorian genre, just as Oxford was beginning to undergo significant reforms in its educational processes during the 1850s.

Prior to this cultural moment, the British universities had not necessarily formed an image of glamour in the national literary imagination. As the university's commissioners concluded in 1852, "The education imparted at Oxford was not such as to conduce to the advancement in life for many persons, except those intended for the ministry."[12] During the later nineteenth century, the university became famous for its defence of humane ideals in a materialistic era. It also developed a reputation for the leisured and intense social experience that it provided for undergraduates, many of whom were from wealthy and aristocratic families.

In response to this shift in perceptions of the universities, a tradition of popular fiction emerged around undergraduate life – the varsity novel. Mortimer Proctor estimates that 85 percent of these novels, up to the middle of the twentieth century, centred upon Oxford, with the rest set at Cambridge.[13] The early books in this sub-genre – such as Edward Bradley's *The Adventures of Verdant Green* (1854), Thomas Hughes's *Tom Brown at Oxford* (1859), or the opening chapters of William Makepeace Thackeray's *Pendennis* (1848–50) – emphasize the rough-and-tumble escapades of undergraduate men courting women or getting into scrapes in town. As the sub-genre extended and developed, what became far more important to their writers and readerships were evocations of the lasting friendships made at university. "Among the many deficiencies attending a university education," states Sir Spencer Walpole, he observed one benefit, "and that was the education which the undergraduates gave themselves. It was impossible to collect some thousand or twelve hundred of the best young men in England, to give them the opportunity of making acquaintance with one another, and full liberty to live their lives in their own way, without evolving in the best among them, some admirable qualities of loyalty, independence, and self-control."[14] If the ostensible schooling offered by the dons was not adequate preparation for life, one would instead learn from being near the best and the brightest – as well as the richest and the best born – the importance of the homosocial bonds that sustained the Empire.

Even more important than the development of comradeship was the cultivation of especially dear friends at university. Part of the pleasures described in these works are the forging of close intimacies with classmates, sometimes remaining chastely convivial (like the Duke of Dover and his friends in the Junta club in Max Beerbohm's *Zuleika Dobson*), and sometimes blossoming into full erotic intimacy (as happens between Judith Earle and her fellow student Jennifer in *Dusty Answer*). But university-forged *philia* is no light business, even in Beerbohm's comic novel. All the men of Oxford in that work feel honour-bound to follow the example of their comrade the Duke of Dover and drown themselves over their disappointed love for the eponymous heroine.

George E. Haggerty has noted the special importance of what he calls Platonic friendship in the Oxbridge novels of the late nineteenth and early twentieth centuries, following the model of friendship applied from the works of Plato and Aristotle newly and evocatively translated by Benjamin Jowett.[15] The frequent flowering of these friendships into fuller erotic love only intensified the ways in which *philia* became a gateway in these plots to other kinds of education of the senses. From friends, protagonists in varsity novels learn to appreciate fine wines, good food, tasteful clothes, and the pleasures to be felt from the arts.[16] In male-focused novels such as Mackenzie's *Sinister Street*, the elaborate and expensive banquets among the students at his college's High Table afford Michael Fane some of his most joyful university experiences. Learning to appreciate beauty from friends – first through the senses, then through an applied study of the fine arts – is an important benefit of *philia* in the varsity novel. *L'éducation sentimentale* establishes this pattern of intimacy as refinement: Frédéric Moreau's same-sex friendships, which often involve his sampling of exquisite foods and wines, as well as new ideas about art, are as formative as his great and endlessly frustrated love affair with Madame Arnoux.

In *Brideshead Revisited*, which David Lodge once termed "perhaps the 'swan song' of the varsity novel tradition,"[17] Charles Ryder's initiation into a full sentimental education begins with the forging of his friendship with Lord Sebastian Flyte. He dates his Oxford life from this meeting, even though it does not take place until his third term at the university. The centrality of this friendship to Charles's emotional growth is brought into perspective by his own "lonely childhood" (39). His mother died in Bosnia while serving with the Red Cross during the First World War, and his eccentric father became more removed and ironical toward his only child after his wife's death. In a chapter of an unfinished prequel to *Brideshead Revisited* called "Charles Ryder's Schooldays," written in 1945 but not published until 1981, Charles's only "friendships" before Oxford at public school were highly competitive, filled with resentment, and loveless.

The affiliation with Sebastian is completely different from these childhood acquaintances and marks for Charles the most important part of his time spent at Oxford. When his cousin Jasper remonstrates with him for associating with "the *very worst set in the university*" (36), Charles, who ignores Jasper's advice to pursue "friendships of utility" that might advance his career, reflects that his cousin cannot know what he has gained from his feelings of *philia* for Sebastian (which Waugh clearly suggests shades into *eros*).[18] Charles favourably compares the amorous education that he receives from Sebastian to the exams for which he had to cram at Oxford. "I remember no syllable of [the books I had to read] now," he reminisces, "but the other, more ancient lore which I acquired in that term will be with me in one shape or another to my last hour" (39). In retrospect, Charles wonders whether he could have elucidated at the time the pedagogical aspect of his love for Sebastian, namely that "to know and love one other human being is the root of all wisdom" (39).

Waugh renders Charles's friendship with Sebastian in educational terms. After their first friendly meeting over a splendid lunch, Sebastian takes Charles to see the many varieties of ivy at the Botanical Gardens, which Charles says he has never visited before. "Oh, Charles, what a lot you have to learn!" Sebastian tells his friend (28). Beyond botanical specimens, Sebastian educates Charles in many sensory delights – plovers' eggs, fine wines with strawberries, dashes into the countryside, and even a sudden trip to Italy. Charles learns not simply to widen his sensuous appreciation but also to change his aesthetic, especially after Sebastian drunkenly vomits into his suite of rooms on the quad, which Charles had decorated according to the reigning Bloomsbury sensibility of the day, with a reproduction of Van Gogh's *Sunflowers* and a Roger Fry screen from the Omega Workshops.[19]

After his first lunch in Sebastian's rooms, Charles detects in his own décor "a jejune air that had not irked me before" (28). By having his scout remove the offending items, Charles effectively abandons the Bloomsbury aesthetic, which might, as Jennie-Rebecca Falcetta notes, be what causes Sebastian to vomit.[20] With its newer, *outré*, and excessive appurtenances – a Lalique decanter and glasses, along with a human skull acquired from the School of Medicine – his redecorated rooms approximate the excessive aesthetic of

Sebastian's rooms, which feature a Gothic-cased harmonium, large Sèvres vases, and an elephant's-foot wastepaper basket: "my room had cast its austere winter garments," Charles states, "and, by not very slow stages, assumed a richer wardrobe" (36).

According to Plato, the best instances of *eros* born of *philia* ultimately result in an appreciation of the beautiful, or at least that is Diotima's instruction in the *Symposium*. As Marc Redfield has shown, *Bildungsromane* often incorporate the tutelage of the beautiful into their subject matter insofar as the works themselves "thematize and enact the very motion of aesthetic education."[21] The alteration in Charles Ryder's aesthetic sense learned from Sebastian allows him to understand not just how to see art differently but also how to find a language for this enhanced appreciation. During their idyllic first summer together at Brideshead, Sebastian encourages both men's budding oenophilia by sampling with Charles the contents of Lord Marchmain's cellars. After Sebastian discovers a book on wine-tasting, the two young men follow its instructions closely; they candle their glasses, swirl wine in their mouths, and nibble Bath Oliver biscuits. Under the influence of this private study, their language becomes more and more exotic:

> "It is a little shy wine, like a gazelle."
> "Like a leprechaun."
> "Dappled, in a tapestry meadow."
> "Like a flute by still water."
> "And this is a wise old wine."
> "A prophet in a cave."
> "... And this is a necklace of pearls on a white neck."
> "Like a swan."
> "Like the last unicorn." (75–6)

As their metaphorical language increases in extravagance, the two young men build upon each other's observations, as if they learn not just how to isolate and clarify sensuous pleasures jointly but also how to find an appropriate figurative language with which to do so.

Critics have often observed this novel follows the pattern of a *Künstlerroman*, with Charles learning his vocation as an artist through the Flytes.[22] At Brideshead, the family's country estate, he completes his first architectural drawing, a rendition of the Italian fountain on the grounds, and then on a whim paints the interior of the house's office. As a result of these forays into art, Bridey gives Charles his first significant commission: four small paintings of the Flytes' doomed London residence. Although the novel documents Charles's discovery of his métier as a painter, it also details the process that makes him into a writer, whose "sacred and profane memoirs" provide the content of *Brideshead Revisited*. The excessive and luxurious language that Charles employs as a writer is encouraged by and shared with Sebastian during his formative period.

The move from Oxford to Brideshead Castle is necessary for the completion of Charles's education. Already by the 1920s, the preponderance of wealthy aristocrats at Oxford and the importation into undergraduate life of their manners caused "fictional Oxford [to have] all the atmosphere of an institutional country house."[23] Cousin Jasper even tells Charles as much when he arrives on campus, "Dress as you do in a country house" (21). The relocation to Brideshead Castle is explicitly cast in terms of furthering Charles's "aesthetic education," in part because of its architectural variety, from the "Soanesque library" to the "Chinese drawing room" and the "Pompeian parlour" (72).

Most important of all for Charles's education is the style of architecture in which the majority of the house was built. "This was my conversion to the Baroque," he remembers (73), and the house seems most clearly to partake of the British version of that style, championed by Sir John Vanbrugh and Nicholas Hawksmoor in the late seventeenth and early eighteenth centuries. In recent books on Waugh's friendly relations with the aristocratic Lygon family, both Paula Byrne and Jane Mulvagh argue for the similarities of the Lygons' family estate of Madresfield Court in Worcestershire, with its art nouveau chapel, as the original for Brideshead Castle. Nonetheless, it is hard to dispute that the primary architectural influence for the Flytes' home is Vanbrugh and Hawksmoor's joint endeavour, Castle Howard in Yorkshire, which Waugh visited just before his second marriage to Laura Herbert.[24] Not only is it an architectural masterpiece of the baroque, but also it is the only domed large country house in that style in the whole of the United Kingdom.[25] For this reason, both of the filmed adaptations of the novel, Charles Sturridge's 1981 miniseries for Granada Television and the Julian Jarrold–directed 2008 motion picture, employed Castle Howard as the stand-in for Brideshead Castle in exterior shots and some interior ones as well.

The excessive ornamentation at Castle Howard finds an echo in Charles's prose:

> Here under that high and insolent dome, under those coffered ceilings: here as I passed through those arches and broken pediments to the pillared shade beyond and sat, hour by hour, before the fountain, probing its shadows, tracing its lingering echoes, rejoicing in all its clustered feats of daring and invention, I felt a whole new system of nerves alive within me, as though the water that spurted and bubbled among its stone, was indeed a life-giving spring. (73–4)

As Alexandra Harris notes, the main architectural style of Brideshead Castle mirrors the baroque style of the narrative, as if the protagonist-narrator were trying to recreate the house in prose.[26] Waugh's favourite metaphor for writing was architecture.[27] Given his oft-professed love for the country houses of Vanbrugh and Hawksmoor,[28] it is perhaps inevitable that he tried to recapture their style in the baroqueness of his prose.

This inevitability was no doubt given urgency by the distressed physical state of Castle Howard when the book was written in 1944 and 1945. Requisitioned for schoolgirls during the early years of the war, the castle suffered extreme damage on 9 November 1940 from a fire supposedly started by accident in a fireplace in the Great Hall. Although no one died in the conflagration, the great Vanbrugh-designed domed leaden lantern – decorated, by a stroke of cosmic irony, with Giovanni Antonio Pellegrini's mural *The Fall of Phaeton* – melted into slag and ran into the Great Hall. Bereft of its crowning architectural marvel, Castle Howard was thus a remnant of its former glory when *Brideshead Revisited* was published in 1945. The dome was rebuilt some years later, but even today the interior of the south-east portion of the house remains severely damaged by the fire. After his paintings of Marchmain House establish his reputation as an architectural painter, Charles ruefully recalls, "I was called to all parts of the country to make portraits of houses that were deserted or debased; indeed, my arrival seemed often to be only a few paces ahead of the auctioneer's, a presage of doom" (212). Just as Charles's paintings recreate lost houses, so too does Waugh's novel reconstruct Castle Howard, if only in part and only in language.

Friendship prompts Charles's first sojourn to Brideshead Castle. Sebastian insists on visiting his family's house "[t]o see a friend … name of Hawkins" (19). His former nanny resides in – and never seems to leave – rooms that are inside the false dome of Brideshead, such that she becomes, as Allan Hepburn notes, in large part the *genius loci* of the house.[29] Charles quickly becomes friends with Nanny Hawkins; in fact, hers is his most lasting friendship in the book, since she is the only person still living in the house when Charles returns during the Second World War. On their initial visit together, Sebastian worries that Charles might make friends with the rest of the family if he stays too long. Although he can abide the notion of Charles befriending Nanny Hawkins, he wants to keep him away from his siblings and parents. About his kin, Sebastian warns Charles, "If they once got hold of you with their charm, they'd make you their friend, not mine, and I won't let them" (32). Of course, this hypothesis comes true: in due time, Charles extends his *philia* with Sebastian to the rest of his family, such that he feels at ease describing the entire aristocratic family as "friends of mine" (325).

As Anthony Blanche tells Charles, all the Flytes strongly resemble one another, with the exception of Teresa, the Marchioness of Marchmain, who marries into the family (47). Just so, each of the Flytes becomes friends with Charles to one degree or another. Bridey banters convivially when Charles visits the house with Julia in the 1930s; Cordelia has a true-blue affection for him; Lady Marchmain makes affable attempts to convert him to her point of view regarding Sebastian's drinking problem. With Lady Julia, who most resembles Sebastian physically (67), the friendly relationship that begins in mutual contempt during Charles's first summer at Brideshead veers ultimately into *eros* when the two consummate their love during a transatlantic voyage. As Lord Marchmain says of Charles to his daughter, Julia, "He has a penchant for my children" (260). Although these new friendships offer Charles the possibility of learning more fully the varieties of love that he first knew under Sebastian's tutelage, he ultimately fails to complete his sentimental education to its highest potential, given his own inadequacies as a friend.

As Sebastian predicts, all these friendships with the Flyte family alienate Charles from Sebastian, who finds truer friendship apart from Charles. When he moves abroad, Sebastian lives for a time with "his *new* friend" Kurt, whom Anthony Blanche describes as "a great clod of a German" (191). Although the two men clearly share a homosexual living arrangement in Morocco, all the characters in the novel refer to Kurt pointedly as Sebastian's "friend," as if to compare the men's more supportive friendship to Sebastian's aborted relationship with Charles, who could not meet his aristocratic friend's emotional needs. As Sebastian says of his relationship with Kurt, "You know Charles . . .

it's rather a pleasant change when all your life you've had people looking after you, to have someone to look after yourself" (202). Even this more blatantly erotic friendship fails, however, after Kurt abandons Sebastian to join the Nazis, who send him to a concentration camp, presumably as a degenerate, where he hangs himself.[30] Ultimately, Sebastian finds fuller and more lasting all-male fellowship at a monastery near his home in Morocco. According to Cordelia, he acts as "a sort of under-porter" (285) for the monks. She says approvingly of the monastery, "They loved him there" (285).

Cordelia's narrative of Sebastian's path toward finding true friendship highlights Charles's comparative failure in continuing to love his former friend. With reference to Julia and Sebastian, Cordelia says, "She never loved him, you know, as we do" (289). For Charles, this statement is painful. "*Do*," he thinks: "The word reproached me; there was no past tense in Cordelia's verb 'to love'" (289). Indeed, Charles has all but forgotten Sebastian. Twice, once while crossing the Atlantic and again while staying at Brideshead, he tells Julia that Sebastian was "the forerunner" of his love for her (240, 284).

Although Charles clearly sees the change in his beloved from Sebastian to Julia as a mark of maturation and progress, the novel suggests that his sentimental education ends in failure because he treats one form of love as exclusive of the other. Nonetheless, Charles's friendships are perhaps not quite so utilitarian as are those of his superficial wife Lady Celia, who acts as if all on board the transatlantic voyage are her friends, even though they gossip behind her back about her husband's affair with Julia. Nor are they as transactional as those of Rex Mottram, who dismisses university experience as a liability. "No, I was never here," he tells Charles at Oxford. "It just means you start life three years behind the other fellow" (101).

Rex's only constant friends seem to be his political lackeys, whom Mr Samgrass calls aggregately "the 'Brideshead set'" (248), and who gather at Rex's wife's castle to parrot one another's opinions in rapid-fire conversations about the abdication crisis and the coming conflict with Hitler:

> "All that's wanted is a good strong line."
> "A line from Rex."
> "And a line from me."
> "We'll give Europe a good strong line. Europe is waiting for a speech from Rex."

"And a speech from me."
"And a speech from me." (275)

As if in parody of Charles's and Sebastian's stimulating dialogue of aesthetic appreciation, Rex's cronies endlessly reiterate their self-importance, with one interlocutor after another drowning out the others instead of building dialogue into a meaningful conversation.

Even so, Charles's own inability to extend and sustain his *philia* with the rest of the Flytes recurs throughout the final portion of the novel, paralleling his failure to do so with Sebastian. Charles views Bridey's failed attempts to have a Catholic priest administer the last rites to Lord Marchmain almost as if he were exulting in the defeat of a rival, rather than sharing the disappointment of his potential brother-in-law. "It's great sucks to Bridey," he tells Julia, while resorting to the language of schoolyard rivalries (268). By the end of his relationship with Julia, Charles seems incapable of giving her the emotional support she needs as her father declines, as he did even earlier when she is upset by Bridey's rejection of her marital woes. As Charles notes, "I was failing her in sympathy" (268).

Charles's petty failures in love contrast with Cordelia's example of selflessness and generosity of spirit. Despite her appearance of having been "thwarted" in her childhood promise, she lives up to the promise of the highest of loves signalled by her name and has potentially the most to teach Charles about friendship and love as forms of cordiality. She understands the promise of the final type of love that Charles has yet to learn during his sentimental education, namely the Aquinian notion of *caritas*, or friendship of man for God that extends to a love of all mankind. "I've seen so much suffering in the last few years; there's so much coming for everybody soon," Cordelia tells Charles regarding her work with international war relief efforts. Then she adds an unexpected afterthought: "It's the spring of love" (290–1). The promise of a godly love for all, redeeming the world's wartime sacrifices, is something Charles still does not understand when he sets down his memoirs. He complains that his love for the men in his army company has "died" (1). He even compares this failure in camaraderie to a failed marriage, as if the lessons of his sentimental education have been for nothing, not only in terms of his inability to feel affection consistently for his friends but also by dint of his incompetence at expressing his feelings clearly.

Charles's incapacity to retain the lessons of his education recall his aesthetic inadequacies, of which Anthony Blanche had warned him years earlier at Oxford. Anthony is the other great friend whom Charles makes at university, yet Charles's inability to love his friends fully and simultaneously prevents him from entirely absorbing Anthony's lessons. Both Martin Green and Michael Gorra see Anthony as important a mentor for Charles as any other figure in the novel.[31] This includes Sebastian, who, when Anthony flatteringly compares Charles to "a young Ingres," trivializes Charles's abilities by saying of his teddy bear and pretend friend, "Yes, Aloysius draws very prettily, too, but of course he's rather more modern" (46). Anthony tries to point Charles toward a more rigorous education, as if to fulfill the role of a proper friend more completely than does the intellectually languid Sebastian, who would make Charles a mere rival to his teddy bear.

Christopher Perricone has argued that the Aristotelean notion of the ideal friend, derived from the *Nicomachean Ethics*, is fully comparable to that of an artist's relationship to a wise aesthetic appreciator and guide. Charles, however, is unwilling to heed Anthony's wise words: "And then Anthony spoke of the proper experiences of an artist, of the appreciation and criticism and stimulus he should expect from his friends, of the hazards he should expect from his friends, of the hazards he should take in the pursuit of emotion, of one thing and another while I fell drowsy and let my mind wander" (49). Distracted by his love for his other friend, Charles fails to heed the words of the friend who has most fully his aesthetic education in mind.

For his indifference, Charles pays a price: his art suffers. His first exhibition is a success, and Anthony recognizes its promise at the time. "I found it – charming," he tells Charles: "There was an interior of Marchmain House, very English, very correct, but quite delicious. 'Charles has done something,' I said; 'not all he will do, not all he can do, but something'" (253). When he hears that Charles has tried to move beyond English subject matter for the paintings that comprise *Ryder's Latin America*, Anthony hurries to view the exhibition; he wants to see if Charles has found a new style for his new subject matter, a style presumably less English, less correct, less like "a young Ingres" (254). Anthony is not impressed by what he sees: "What did I find? I found, my dear, a very naughty and very successful practical joke. It reminded me of dear Sebastian when he liked so much to dress up in false whiskers. It was charm again, my dear, simple, creamy, English charm, playing tigers" (254–5).

Anthony Blanche, who proudly proclaims his non-English status by referring to himself as "a degenerate old d-d-dago" (254), thinks that Charles cannot move beyond his limited English sensibility. In Anthony's view, the insularity of the English inhibits their artistic development. For example, to a nation that did not embrace Counter-Reformation ideals, the importation of the baroque around the Age of Anne was met with suspicion. The baroque, as Mario Praz points out, found a foothold in the United Kingdom during this period almost solely in its architecture.[32] For Charles to embrace a lurid style for *Ryder's Latin America* is perhaps as doomed a venture as his employing the overwrought writing style in recounting his narrative.

Severo Sarduy describes the baroque as an attempt always to say more via ornamentation and superabundance: "In contrast to language that is communicative, economic, austere, and reduced to its function as a vehicle for information, Baroque language delights in surplus, in excess, and in the partial loss of its object."[33] The whole enterprise becomes bankrupt, however, if genuine conviction and feeling do not stand behind the stylistic extravagance. Just as Charles's paintings become, according to Anthony's superior judgment, like a child's game of wearing false whiskers, so too does the novel's elaborate narrative style fail to point a way forward for modernism at the war's end and instead regresses into the florid rhetorical ornamentation of Mackenzie's *Sinister Street*. In that light, *Brideshead Revisited* becomes not a revivification of the baroque, but remains, like the house itself, a ruin. For this reason, Waugh speaks dismissively of the text in his 1959 preface to the novel as a "souvenir" of the past (x). If Charles's education had previously seemed "sentimental" – that is, as partaking of the sentiments in the eighteenth-century sense of the term – the book's style might reveal it as "sentimental" in the meaning it accrued much later into Waugh's time and beyond as manufactured, overwrought, and false.

As Eve Kosofsky Sedgwick argues, sentimentality is always a relational structure, such that a style that appears as an expression of genuine feeling can seem, from another perspective, factitious.[34] We are reminded of this in the lessons Charles learns in aesthetic appreciation from Cordelia, who as a child passionately defends the house's art nouveau chapel, which Charles clearly finds aesthetically wanting. "I think it's *beautiful*," she says with tears in her eyes (83). When the chapel is deconsecrated after her mother's death, Cordelia's opinion changes: "suddenly, there wasn't any chapel there any more, just an oddly decorated room" (206). For Cordelia, the possessor of the truest heart of anyone in the novel, the elaborate decoration is beautiful only with the infusion of proper feeling – in this case, the religious sentiment that the deconsecration disallows for her. Such might be said, too, for other styles, which are always dependent on time and perspective for deciding their merit. As Charles himself says when assessing the chapel's aesthetic worth, "Probably in eighty years it will be greatly admired." When Bridey replies that its aesthetic value must be inherent – "But surely it can't be good twenty years ago and good in eighty years, and not good now?" – Charles responds, "Well, it may be *good* now. All I mean is that I don't happen to like it much" (83).

Is there finally a difference between liking a thing and thinking it good, as Bridey then responds to Charles? The novel hesitates over definitively endorsing any style transhistorically, just as Waugh himself changed his opinions on the worth of his luxuriant style in *Brideshead Revisited*. Charles sees an unbridgeable difference between his position and Bridey's: "I knew that this disagreement was not a matter of words only, but expressed a deep and impassable division between us; neither had any understanding, nor ever could" (83). But Charles's own conversion to Catholicism – and his witnessing the chapel's purpose renewed after its reconsecration during wartime occupation – seems to suggest an alternative way of looking at the matter:

> The builders did not know the uses to which their work would descend; they made a new house with the stones of the old castle; year by year, generation after generation, they enriched and extended it; year by year the great harvest of timber in the park grew to ripeness; until, in a sudden frost, came the age of Hooper; the place was desolate and the work was all brought to nothing. *Quomodo sedet solca civitas*. Vanity of vanities, all is vanity.
>
> "And yet," I thought, stepping out more briskly, towards the camp, where the bugles after a pause had taken up the second call … and yet that is not the last word; it is not even an apt word; it is a dead word from ten years back. (325–6)

As Charles makes his final review of the house, his syntax and sentiment recall the encouraging aesthetic judgment that Anthony Blanche made of his interior of Marchmain House: "Charles has done something … not all he will do, not all he can do, but something" (253). Charles has come to learn that the importance of artistic reconstruction – the making of a new house, even in an amalgam of styles – depends on effort. This effort must be sustained even when the project seems desolate, superannuated, or abandoned. In his apparent conversion to Catholicism, Charles learns to infuse such works as the chapel with superabundance of feeling in the baroque manner. Waugh's own ability to re-employ the extravagant style of Compton Mackenzie's exemplary varsity novel can seem, to appreciative eyes, an attempt to recreate a new house out of the stones of an old one. Yet the success of this can only occur if the appreciator can imbue the flamboyant flourishes with the proper feeling. Charles believes the flame lit by the original "builders and tragedians" might still burn within the old wreck of the castle, and he returns to his second-in-command looking "unusually cheerful" (326).[35] If this optimism is itself to falter after the circumstances of its composition – as the judgment wrought after a period of "soya beans and basic English" – then this style can wait for another time, like Brideshead Castle, for its sentimental re-incandescence. Such, Charles has learned, are the lessons of friendship.

NOTES

1 Nancy Mitford and Evelyn Waugh, *The Letters of Nancy Mitford and Evelyn Waugh*, ed. Charlotte Mosley (London: Hodder and Stoughton, 1996), 202, 205, 238.

2 Evelyn Waugh, "Fan-Fare," in *A Little Order: Selected Journalism*, ed. Donat Gallagher (London: Penguin, 2019), 33.

3 Mitford and Waugh, *Letters*, 368.

4 Ibid., 16.

5 Evelyn Waugh, *Brideshead Revisited* (1945; London: Penguin, 2000), x. Further references to the novel, including the preface, appear parenthetically in the text.

6 Waugh, "Why Glorify Youth?" in *A Little Order*, 23.

7 Ibid.

8 Humphrey Carpenter, *The Brideshead Generation: Evelyn Waugh and His Friends* (Boston: Houghton Mifflin, 1990), 61.

9 Andro Linklater, *Compton Mackenzie: A Life* (London: Chatto and Windus, 1987), 128.

10 Ibid., 131.

11 Ibid.
12 Quoted in Sir Spencer Walpole, *History of Twenty Five Years*, vol. 4 (London: Longmans, Green, 1908), 136–7.
13 Mortimer Proctor, *The English University Novel* (Berkeley: University of California Press, 1957), 4.
14 Walpole, *History*, 40.
15 George E. Haggerty, *Queer Friendship: Male Intimacy in the English Literary Tradition* (Cambridge: Cambridge University Press, 2018), 120.
16 The fineness of the meals enjoyed by the male students at Oxbridge prompted bitter reflections on the inadequacies of similar fare at the women's colleges by Virginia Woolf in *A Room of One's Own*. Woolf nevertheless praised the conviviality forged among undergraduates by food and drink.
17 David Lodge, "The Campus Novel," *The W.H. Book Review* 6 (1982): 4. Postwar novels about university life often centre upon faculty protagonists, such as C.P. Snow's *The Masters* (1951) and Kingsley Amis's *Lucky Jim* (1954). Novels featuring undergraduate life continue in Tom Sharpe's *Porterhouse Blue* (1974) and Frederic Raphael's *The Glittering Prizes* (1976), although varsity novels are now less common than campus novels.
18 Critics debate whether Charles and Sebastian's love is merely Platonic or physically consummated. Charles claims that his relationship with Sebastian included "naughtiness high in the catalogue of grave sins" (39). It therefore seems ridiculous to assert, as Tison Pugh does, that Charles's and Sebastian's relationship is only "a romantic friendship." Most critics agree that the relationship has a clearly carnal side. As Allan Hepburn claims, "Charles' love for Sebastian is explicit and clearly homosexual." See Tison Pugh, "Romantic Friendship, Homosexuality, and Evelyn Waugh's *Brideshead Revisited*," *English Language Notes* 38, no. 4 (2001): 65. Allan Hepburn, "Good Graces: Inheritance and Social Climbing in *Brideshead Revisited*," *Troubled Legacies: Narrative and Inheritance*, ed. Allan Hepburn (Toronto: University of Toronto Press, 2007), 261n2.
19 The detailings of the décor of Oxbridge rooms are always a hallmark of varsity novels. In *Jacob's Room*, Virginia Woolf parodies this descriptive trait when she catalogues the contents of Jacob Flanders' rooms at Cambridge. Virginia Woolf, *Jacob's Room* (1922; Oxford: Oxford University Press, 2008), 48–9.
20 Jennie-Rebecca Falcetta, "Brideshead Illustrated: The Sacred and Profane Aesthetics of Captain Charles Ryder," *Religion and Literature* 46, no. 1 (2014): 60.

21 Marc Redfield, *Phantom Formations: Aesthetic Ideology and the Bildungsroman* (Ithaca: Cornell University Press, 1996), 55.

22 See Robert Murray Davis, *Brideshead Revisited: The Past Redeemed* (Boston: Twayne, 1990), 36–7; Frederick L. Beaty, *The Ironic World of Evelyn Waugh: A Study of Eight Novels* (DeKalb: Northern Illinois University Press, 1992), 145.

23 John Dougill, *Oxford in English Literature: The Making, and Undoing, of "The English Athens"* (1998; Milton Keynes: AuthorHouse, 2010), 113.

24 Evelyn Waugh, *The Diaries of Evelyn Waugh*, ed. Michael Davie (1976; London: Phoenix, 2009), 441.

25 Jeffrey Manley points out that Castle Howard and Brideshead Castle are not completely co-extensive: the chapel of the former is not in the art nouveau style, and the real-life castle has a true dome rather than the false one described in Waugh's novel. Nevertheless, Manley concludes, "Any reasonable person comparing Castle Howard to other baroque residences in England fitting Waugh's description of Brideshead Castle would have to agree that it probably comes closest to the novel." Jeffrey Manley, "Anthony Powell, Brideshead and Castle Howard Revisited," in *Anthony Powell, Shakespeare and Other Literary Influences: Proceedings of the 2016 Anthony Powell Society Conference*, ed. John Roe and Keith C. Marshall (Greenford: The Anthony Powell Society, 2017), 188.

26 Alexandra Harris, *Romantic Moderns: English Writers, Artists, and the Imagination from Virginia Woolf to John Piper* (New York: Thames and Hudson, 2010), 273.

27 In a review of Cyril Connolly's *Enemies of Promise*, Waugh states: "'Creative' is an invidious term too often used at the expense of the critic. A better word, except that it would always involve explanation, would be 'architectural.' I believe that what makes a writer, as distinct from a clever and cultured man who can write, is an added energy and breadth of vision which enables him to conceive and complete a structure." Waugh, *A Little Order*, 124.

28 In an article first published without a title in *John Bull* in 1932, Waugh notes, "[Sir John] Vanbrugh gave up writing plays to build the most lovely homes in England." In his 1938 article "A Call to the Orders," Waugh enthuses over "that superb succession of masterpieces from Vanbrugh to Soane." Waugh, *A Little Order*, 29, 62.

29 Hepburn, "Good Graces," 252–3.

30 Sebastian's erotic friendship with Kurt has its happiest moment in Greece, the

classical origin of male erotic friendship. As Cordelia notes to Charles, "You know how Germans sometimes seem to discover a sense of decency when they get to a classical country. It seems to have worked with Kurt. Sebastian says he became quite human in Athens" (287). Notwithstanding his outburst of humanity, Kurt ends up in prison and is deported back to Germany, where he joins the Nazis.

31 Martin Green, *Transatlantic Patterns: Cultural Comparisons of English with America* (New York: Basic Books, 1977), 155–7; Michael Gorra, *The English Novel at Mid-Century: From the Leaning Tower* (Houndmills: Macmillan, 1990), 185.

32 Mario Praz, "Baroque in England," in *Baroque New Worlds: Representation, Transculturation, Counterconquest*, ed. Lois Parkinson Zamora and Monika Kaup (Durham: Duke University Press, 2010), 133. Praz finds baroque elements in the poems of Richard Crashaw, John Milton, and John Dryden, but he claims that a baroque aesthetic is otherwise absent from British art during the era in question.

33 Severo Sarduy, "The Baroque and the Neo Baroque," in Zamora and Kaup, *Baroque New Worlds*, 287.

34 Eve Kosofsky Sedgwick, *Epistemology of the Closet* (Berkeley: University of California Press, 1990), 150–1.

35 Given its aesthetic valences, the "small red flame" that Charles finds "burning anew among the old stones" inevitably suggests the "hard, gem-like flame" in the conclusion to Pater's *Studies in the History of the Renaissance.* Just as Waugh saw Oxford-educated Max Beerbohm as a mentor, so did Beerbohm see his own aesthetic father in Oscar Wilde, who undertook significant instruction at Oxford from Pater. The flame was thus passed down generation by generation. Walter Pater, *Studies in the History of the Renaissance* (1873), ed. Matthew Beaumont (Oxford: Oxford University Press, 2010), 120.

9

Muriel Spark's Ensembles

JACQUELINE SHIN

The absence of sentiment renders Muriel Spark's novels chilling, thrilling, and devastating. An epistemological author whose chief weapons are subversion and ridicule, she sees the purpose of art as providing pleasure by sharpening our wits, refining our intellects, teaching us to know ourselves better and to appraise life in all its absurdity.[1] In her 1970 essay, "The Desegregation of Art," she articulates her desire to see "less emotion and more intelligence" in literature.[2] In the face of the enormous problems of the second half of the twentieth century, which produced an atmosphere of the oppressively absurd, she wanted less "impulsive generosity" and fewer indignant representations of social justice; instead, she desired "a more deliberate cunning, a more derisive undermining of what is wrong."[3] She is successful in achieving this aim in her own fiction, where she reserves her fiercest indignation for stupidity and her greatest ridicule for those who provide false comfort in the guise of wise counsel.

Ian Rankin calls Spark "peerless, sparkling, inventive and intelligent," and, in a nod to her most famous work, *The Prime of Miss Jean Brodie*, "the crème de la crème" – the "greatest Scottish novelist of modern times."[4] She was, as many critics, readers, and fans agree, a genius. Michiko Kakutani refers to Muriel Spark as the "master of malice and mayhem."[5] Her "complex and spare" novels are elegant mash-ups, delighting readers with their unexpected juxtapositions.[6] Many of her admirers remark on the dark humour and stylistic deftness in her works. Graham Greene describes *Memento Mori* as "funny and macabre."[7] John Updike calls the prose in *The Abbess of Crewe* "stylized, sinister, and soothing."[8] John Lanchester contrasts the "near-jaunty tone" with the "jet-black content" of *The Driver's Seat*; in most novels, these two qualities would be at odds, but in "Spark-world, they go together, like murderer and victim."[9] Critics have a tendency to compare Spark's mind and work to the keenness of knives, dirks, blades, or shards of ice. Able and eager to write about sex, surveillance, and murder, she often adopts a whodunit plot to investigate human relationships between siblings, married couples, teachers and students, or friends. Friendship, as an intimate relationship of mutual trust and care, is, in addition to romantic love, quietly eviscerated in Spark's fiction.

In twenty-two novels, ranging from her first, *The Comforters*, through her last, *The Finishing School*, Spark foregrounds narrative control while exploring the dynamics of authority and submission.[10] She often sets up a parallel between, on the one hand, the vertical relationship that connects narrators or author figures to readers, and, on the other hand, the hierarchical relationships that obtain within the narratives themselves, with her own narrative authority ironically undermining the fictional ones. The authoritarian narrative structures of her novels render privacy, and thus friendship, unlikely if not impossible. In general, authoritarianism prohibits friendship by creating inequalities that cannot be surmounted.

Spark depicts relationships that *look* like friendships but really are not, especially in what I am calling her "ensemble novels" – works that centre on a group of girls or women who form a tight-knit community. The notion of an ensemble suggests individuals working together as a coordinated whole, as in an orchestra; Spark's ensembles, rather than fostering connection or amity, as might be expected, become microcosms of division. They have rigid hierarchies within which the stupidest characters are singled out for ridicule from both the group and the narrator. Female characters are not friendly toward each other, nor is Spark especially friendly toward those characters. Maintaining one's position in the hierarchy can license almost any amount of cruelty or manipulation.[11] Without the ability to speak privately – because someone may overhear a conversation or tape it for the purposes of blackmail – trust cannot be built, and without trust, friendship lacks a foundation.

Rather than friends, Spark populates these novels with an ensemble of characters held together by a force that ultimately proves weaker than the force that pulls them apart. In *The Comforters*, the ensemble is comprised of characters who encroach on each other's privacy. In *The Prime of Miss Jean Brodie*, the ensemble is a group of schoolgirls described as fellow fascisti. In *The Girls of Slender Means* and *The Abbess of Crewe*, the ensembles are, respectively, women in a hostel who become fellow survivors and nuns who are essentially cross-dressers. In these works, Spark sets the structural and narrative conditions of possibility for friendship while denying its likelihood.

Characters in a Novel: The Comforters

Throughout her career, Spark was fascinated by the Biblical story of Job. In 1955, she wrote an essay on "The Mystery of Job's Suffering" and repeatedly returned to what she called this "dramatic poem" in her fiction.[12] She named her first novel after Job's comforters. Outside the Biblical context, the word "comforters" evokes positive sentiments – the kind of warm feelings that friends might provoke. Yet the title is intentionally ironic. The term "comforters" actually refers to Job's "tormentors," who, according to Spark, form a "conspiracy of mediocrity" in their insistence that Job's suffering must be deserved, for God does not punish the innocent.[13] As Spark observes, Job's tribulations are horrible enough on their own, but they are made even worse by the zealous individuals, called "friends" in the Book of Job, who commiserate with his circumstances and offer their advice, all of it wrong.[14] These comforters attempt to interfere with a divine plot to test Job's faith. In the process of interfering, they expose their own ignorance. For Spark, the narrative of Job presents a situation that epitomizes both stupidity on the part of the so-called comforters and general human incomprehension; it marks the point where human reason fails in its understanding of the divine.[15] What passes for comfort is, in Spark's estimation, a form of foolishness that distracts Job's friends from surrendering to divine will or accepting suffering as a necessity. Spark's tongue-in-cheek first novel thus refuses to provide the conditions within which novelistic friendships can flourish.

In *The Comforters*, Spark places Caroline Rose, the protagonist, in a situation that defies reason and realism. Caroline is seemingly thinking her own thoughts in the privacy of her mind when she hears the sound of a typewriter, then a voice or a chorus of voices "chanting in unison," rather like a "concurrent series of echoes."[16] The tapping of the typewriter seems to come through the wall, as if slightly dislocated from where Caroline is. The voices exactly repeat her thoughts, already phrased in omniscient third-person narration: "On the whole she did not think there would be any difficulty with Helena."[17] Caroline searches outside her door and inside her apartment; finding nothing or no one, she fears that she is going mad. She is afterwards plagued by this typewriter sound and responds by transcribing in shorthand whatever narration she hears, even trying, unsuccessfully, to capture the sounds through a recording device to prove that it or they are more than just noises in her head.

She turns to a series of "comforters," including Willi Stock, a quasi-friend whose existence she had "half-forgotten"; Father Jerome, her spiritual adviser; and Laurence Manders, the man she was going to marry and from whom she separated for religious reasons.[18] These three men conclude that she is ill, perhaps suffering from a mental breakdown; they refuse to take seriously her theory, more a conviction really, that the voices must spring from an author who exists on another plane of existence. That author, she speculates, is writing a novel about Caroline and her circle. Laurence presses her on this idea:

> Was the author disembodied? – She didn't know. If so, how could he use a typewriter? How could she overhear him? How could one author chant in a chorus? – That she didn't know, that she didn't know. Was the author human or a spirit, and if so –
>
> "How can I answer these questions? [Caroline replies.] I've only begun to ask them myself. The author obviously exists in a different dimension from ours. That will make investigation difficult."[19]

There is something hilarious about this metaphysical and metafictional mystery, even as the reader can empathize with Caroline's initial fear, as well as Laurence's skepticism. Caroline is the natural "receiver" of these sounds, as she is writing a book on *Form in the Modern Novel*, although, as she tells Willi without a trace of irony, she is "having difficulty with the chapter on realism."[20] If the realist novel gives Caroline trouble, it also gives Spark pause. Realism may afford certain kinds of relationship to flourish, such as friendships, but it forbids, by its insistence on some correspondence between representation and reality, other kinds of relationship, such as the rapport between human beings and the divine. Caroline has no way of ascertaining whether these voices are friendly or, like the comforters' advice in the Book of Job, ostensibly comforting but actually misguided.

As the novel unfolds, Caroline develops a relationship with this author figure, whom she comes to call, rather dismissively, "The Typing Ghost." The two become locked in an intense power struggle. At one point Caroline announces that she is on the alert and says to the air, "if anyone's listening, let them take note!" The narrator both amusingly and menacingly responds, "Well, well!"[21] The author sees and knows everything that is happening inside the fictional world. This vertical arrangement renders friendship structurally untenable in the novel. According to Allan Hepburn, intrusion and interference operate as "assertions of authority" in the novel.[22] With every authorial intrusion, the characters are rendered more and more patently fictional. In other words, Caroline's friends are not really friends because they are just other characters in a made-up novel.

Increasingly, the narrator intrudes upon Caroline's privacy and freedom, while Caroline in turn intrudes upon the narrator. Rather than transcribing what has already been thought or has already happened, the authorial voice begins to narrate future events. In one instance, the Typing Ghost predicts that Caroline will travel by car, so she decides to travel by train instead. In the end, this plan is foiled and she travels by car, a change of plan that proves the narrator right. While in the car, Caroline is involved in an accident and winds up in the hospital, as if the narrator plans to get rid of her but cannot quite manage to do so. Toward Caroline, the narrator takes a diagnostic and dismissive tone:

> It is not easy to dispense with Caroline Rose. At this point in the tale she is confined in a hospital bed, and no experience of hers ought to be allowed to intrude. Unfortunately she slept restlessly. She never sleeps well. And during the hours of the night, rather than ring for the nurse and a sedative, she preferred to savor her private wakefulness, a luxury heightened by the profound sleeping of seven other women in the public ward. When her leg was not too distracting, Caroline among the sleepers turned her mind to the art of the novel, wondering and cogitating, those long hours, and exerting an undue, unreckoned, influence on the narrative from which she is supposed to be absent for a time.

Tap-tick-click. Caroline among the sleepers turned her mind to the art of the novel …[23]

In this instance, the italicized voice appears to emanate from Caroline in a feedback loop that addresses the narrator's dispassionate assessment of her as a fitful patient.

Caroline's relationship with the Typing Ghost becomes increasingly antagonistic and interactive, based on an indirect, back-and-forth dialogue. In the hospital, Caroline comments to Laurence: "'The Typing Ghost has not recorded any lively details about this hospital ward. The reason is that the author doesn't know how to describe a hospital ward. This interlude in my life is not part of the book in consequence.' It was by making exasperating comments like this that Caroline Rose continued to interfere with the book."[24] Although framed in the passive voice, the exasperation clearly pertains to the Typing Ghost, who resents Caroline's interference with the book. The relationship, which might be defined as the give-and-take between author and inspiration, is decidedly unfriendly.

The narrator offers a detailed description of the hospital ward, with rather gratuitous details, as if the narrator is bent on proving Caroline wrong through superior knowledge. In another instance, the narrator makes observations about the large breasts of one character – the oppressive and despicable villain of the novel, Mrs Hogg. Caroline then critiques the passage, saying it is in "bad taste," noting how Mrs Hogg is merely a "gargoyle" – meaning she is one-dimensional and not well written.[25] It is as if the narrator takes this critique of one-dimensionality to heart and pushes it even further in defiance: "However, as soon as Mrs Hogg stepped into her room she disappeared, she simply disappeared. She had no private life whatsoever. God knows where she went in her privacy."[26] When Mrs Hogg drowns, almost dragging Caroline down with her to a watery death, the narrator is similarly dismissive: "God knows where she went."[27] Some events remain outside the narrator's ken and those zones of knowledge that do not matter to the plot are dismissed as unimportant. Indeed, the narrator assumes a touchy, even hostile, tone toward the reader, like the tone taken toward Caroline.

In fact, none of the characters in *The Comforters* has a truly private life. Either the narrator or author is "listening in" and typing out their thoughts, or else the Typing Ghost is so uninterested in the psychological dimensions of characters, as with Mrs Hogg, that their private life is simply a blank. Spark is clearly not interested in realism, character depth, or interiority; in this sense, she diverges from Jane Austen or other authors writing within the realist tradition. Under the narrative meta-conditions of *The Comforters*, friendship – certainly any friendship that goes beyond a superficial level – cannot take root. Friendship requires that certain thoughts *not* be shared; it demands respect for each person's privacy. The protagonist Fleur in *Loitering with Intent* says, "Complete frankness is always a mistake among friends," a very Wildean but also Austenian aphorism.[28] Friendship is a mutual recognition of privacy. "Privacy is the foundation of individuality," Hepburn states.[29] Privacy, we might add, is also the foundation of friendship.

For friendship to exist in a novelistic milieu, there needs to be some suspension of disbelief, an agreement that the characters are "real." Caroline ends up writing the novel that we are reading, a novel that she claims is self-referentially about "characters in a novel."[30] In a way, it is her ultimate victory; she jots down what the Typing Ghost says and she uses these notes for her own ends. She "maintains her own freedom" by accepting "omniscience as an operative principle," even participating "in omniscience, insofar as she is humanly capable."[31] She takes over the role of author and narrator, however, only by keeping to this prewritten script. Instead of a triumph for either the narrator or Caroline, they reach a stalemate. Spark's first novel sets a pattern of narrative authoritarianism that continues to play out in her ensemble novels, establishing a vertical dynamic rooted in judgment that overshadows the more or less equal and horizontal give-and-take structure of friendships.

Spark's Ensembles: The Prime of Miss Jean Brodie

The Prime of Miss Jean Brodie, The Girls of Slender Means, and *The Abbess of Crewe* are set at, respectively, a girl's school in Edinburgh in the 1930s; a women's hostel in London at the end of the Second World War; and a Benedictine convent in Crewe, England, during the 1950s. As John Updike observes, "Groups of females have always been a congenial subject for [Spark]."[32] We might expect these ensemble pieces to explore communal structures that enable friendships to develop, as in Virginia Woolf's choral novel *The Waves*. Many readers associate Spark with her most famous novel, *The Prime of Miss*

Jean Brodie, which had stage and film adaptations after it appeared in print.[33] More particularly, people remember this novel for its representation of girlhood friendship. Yet this remembrance is largely erroneous, even sentimental. Instead of congenial schoolgirl solidarity, *The Prime of Miss Jean Brodie* dwells on hierarchies and narrative control that severely inhibit friendships. Rather than forming bonds rooted in similarity or in a shared position of vulnerability against the larger world, each Spark character is self-interested and acutely aware of her place in a pyramidal structure. At the same time, Spark wields her own authority in order to undermine authoritarianism and expose this ensemble as a fascist model in miniature.

The narrator of *The Prime of Miss Jean Brodie* controls what we know and when we know it. Several scholars have noted Spark's use of prolepsis, as well as repetition. Matthew Wickman, for example, refers to Spark's "[f]amous 'flash forward' technique."[34] In *The Prime of Miss Jean Brodie*, the narrative jumps back and forth in time, although the novel is mainly set at the Marcia Blaine School for Girls in Edinburgh in the 1930s. A group of schoolgirls spend a great deal of time together, both inside and outside school hours, but they are not communal in any sense. They are called Miss Brodie's "set," and they are almost exclusively held together in their relation to their "leader," Miss Brodie. Each girl is differentiated for some talent or attribute: Monica Douglas is famous for math and her anger; Rose Stanley becomes famous for sex; Eunice Gardiner is famous for her "spritely gymnastics and glamorous swimming"; Sandy Stranger is "notorious merely for her small, almost non-existent eyes" and for her vowel sounds; Jenny Gray, Sandy's "best friend," is famous for her prettiness and gracefulness.[35] Lastly, Mary Macgregor's fame "rested on her being a silent lump, a nobody whom everybody could blame."[36] An unredeemable character, Mary has "merely two eyes, a nose and a mouth like a snowman," and is "later famous for being stupid and always to blame and who, at the age of twenty-three, lost her life in a hotel fire."[37] The narrator's cutting summations of each girl's fame echo the perspective of Miss Brodie, who tries to pigeonhole each girl. Yet Miss Brodie herself is also viewed from this cruel and unforgiving perspective, and she ends up demonstrating a stupidity that rivals Mary Macgregor's.

Apart from Sandy and Jenny, the Brodie set are not friends. Miss Brodie selects them as the *crème de la crème*, which sounds privileged, but really means that they serve her own purposes:

> Miss Brodie had already selected her favorites, or rather those whom she could trust; or rather those whose parents she could trust not to lodge complaints about the more advanced and seditious aspects of her educational policy ... Miss Brodie's special girls were taken home to tea and bidden not to tell the others, they were taken into her confidence, they understood her private life and her feud with the headmistress and the allies of the headmistress.[38]

This enlisting of the girls in the Brodie set demolishes each girl's special status. Miss Brodie praises their qualities only to harness each girl's devotion to her narrow cult of personality. She demands the girls' time and loyalty with the assurance that their parents will not complain. Whenever she senses a plot to oust her from her position at the school, she consults her set. She is imperious and ultimately obtuse about her own egotism. Sandy Stranger, with her tiny eyes, is the most clear-eyed about Miss Brodie's faults, and she is the one who betrays her in the end.

It is Sandy who discerns the parallels between the Brodie set and Mussolini's fascisti. One day as the group is walking through the historical centre of Edinburgh, kept in line by Miss Brodie, she is reminded of a photograph that Miss Brodie showed them in class. Mussolini and his followers "were dark as anything and all marching in the straightest of files, with their hands raised at the same angle, while Mussolini stood on a platform like a gym teacher or a Guides mistress and watched them."[39] The comparison is certainly a putdown, in at least two ways. Mussolini's prestige shrinks to that of a gym teacher's or Girl Guide leader's. At the same time, it raises Miss Brodie's prestige to a level of Il Duce's, which is, at best, a dubious distinction:

> It occurred to Sandy, there at the end of the Middle Meadow Walk, that the Brodie set was Miss Brodie's fascisti, not to the naked eye, marching along, but all knit together for her need and in another way, marching along. That was all right, but it seemed, too, that Miss Brodie's disapproval of the Girl Guides had jealousy in it, there was an inconsistency, a fault. Perhaps the Guides were too much of a rival fascisti, and Miss Brodie could not bear it. Sandy thought she might see about joining the Brownies. Then the group-fright seized her again, and it was necessary to put the idea aside, because she loved Miss Brodie. (29–30)

Never one to resist a treacherous impulse, Sandy thinks that joining the Brownies would loosen Miss Brodie's authority and show up the flaws in her cult of personality. What bothers Sandy is not the fact that the Brodie set behaves like Mussolini's fascisti, but rather that Miss Brodie is threatened by the Girl Guides and thus reveals a kind of pettiness that does not align with confident leadership. Sandy's seditious feelings, such as they are, are kept in check by her "group-fright" and the obedience that it elicits, both of which, over time, fray.

As with the fascists, group-fright licenses cruel behaviour. Everyone in the Brodie set, including Jean Brodie, picks on Mary Macgregor. Feeling a sudden charitable impulse, Sandy is about to show some small kindness to Mary when she hears "Miss Brodie's presence" and stops.[40] Sandy grasps that by being kind to Mary she would "separate herself, and be lonely, and blameable in a more dreadful way than Mary who, although officially the faulty one, was at least inside Miss Brodie's category of heroines in the making."[41] Rather than being kind, Sandy says something cruel and persecutes Mary until she begins to cry. For this wanton cruelty, Sandy loathes herself. She understands that her companions form a "body with Miss Brodie for the head"; they are held together "in unified compliance to the destiny of Miss Brodie, as if God had willed them to birth for that purpose." An authoritarian structure such as this does not allow for an ethics of care, nor does it allow for friendship. The weakest, instead of being shown mercy, are ridiculed, then eliminated. Mary is admitted into the Brodie set because she can be blamed for everything; she is a scapegoat for the group's inhumane impulses. Remaining in the group and maintaining one's standing in the hierarchy is of the utmost importance, and the only way out of that predicament imposed by group mentality is to take down the leader. Group mentality squashes the potential for friendship; it encourages cruelty in the name of fellowship. Sandy is mean to Mary for "good fellowship's sake" – not fellowship with Mary, but with the group.[42]

As with *The Comforters*, an authoritarian dynamic in *The Prime of Miss Jean Brodie* is comprehended and actively resisted by Sandy, as well as by the structure of narration itself. In this regard, Spark's narrator operates like an "arranger" figure in James Joyce's texts: "something between a persona and a function, somewhere between the narrator and the implied author."[43] Something of a control freak, the arranger is responsible for "the suppression of information and action."[44] Spark's "arrangers" or "arranging personae" crosscut between different timelines, juxtapose different voices and perspectives, create harmony and more usually antiphony, a call and response.[45] By exerting authority, Spark's arrangers subvert authority and at the same time create fictional worlds where friendship simply fails to take root, let alone thrive.

In *The Prime of Miss Jean Brodie*, the arranger carefully sets Miss Brodie's controlling statements against Sandy's subversive thoughts, just as the arranger sets examples of Miss Brodie's power during her prime against images of her after she loses her position at the Marcia Blaine School for teaching fascism to her pupils. Miss Brodie remains unrepentant; she mildly chastises Hitler as "quite naughty" for ravaging Europe with a needless war.[46] Marilyn Reizbaum describes "an ongoing wrestling for control" in this novel between Sandy and Miss Brodie.[47] I would qualify this assessment by suggesting that the battle is between the arranger persona and Miss Brodie, with the arranger derisively highlighting Miss Brodie's stupidity – primarily, her failure to predict her betrayal and to recognize her betrayer, but also her gross misreading of Mussolini and Hitler, and her reckless encouragement of an impressionable girl to go fight in the Spanish Civil War, where she ends up being killed.[48]

One of the episodes that underscores Miss Brodie's blindness and moral vacuity is her attempt to groom one of the girls, Rose, to have sex with the art teacher, with whom Miss Brodie herself is in love, and to have Sandy report back to her about all the details of this orchestrated liaison. Even the outlines of this scenario reveal the extent to which privacy is intruded upon in this narrative world. Instead of following Miss Brodie's plan, Sandy ends up having sex with the art teacher when she is eighteen, and Rose reports this news back to Miss Brodie. While Miss Brodie speaks of herself as the man's muse, Sandy castigates her for her overweening authoritarianism: "She thinks she is Providence … she thinks she is the God of Calvin, she sees the beginning and the end." She decides that "the woman is an unconscious lesbian," and then the narrative jumps forward to when Sandy is a nun, known as Sister Helena of the Transfiguration.[49] Miss Brodie is triply undermined: for her self-delusion, for her blindness to Sandy's true feelings, and for her diminished importance from a future perspective. The prolepsis elongates the time-scale of the narrative in order to show Miss Brodie's pettiness and errors of judgment.

Even when Miss Brodie contemplates who betrayed her, she never suspects Sandy. She cannot even recognize that her former student feels "bored and afflicted" in her presence. The arranger juxtaposes narrative present with narrative future, Miss Brodie's words with Sandy's thoughts, Miss Brodie's words with contemptuous narrative observation. In this novel, the narrator sees that treachery underlies allegiances. Viewed retrospectively from the flattening perspective of the future, the characters in *The Prime of Miss Jean Brodie* seem less fully realized individuals than victims or traitors.

Regarding this novel, Paddy Lyons observes that "at no point does the narration ever render the thoughts or feelings of its magnetic central figure, Jean Brodie, whose vivid utterances are given, as if in a Compton-Burnett dialogue, without a commentary attributing to her any subjective elements." Jean Brodie is "purely dramatic, a performance artist," while the other characters in the novel are given "an inner world of contemplation [and] speculation," wherein "the authorship and authority [that] Miss Brodie takes for granted comes under scrutiny."[50] Although I agree with Lyons in general, I do not think any of the characters have "inner worlds of contemplation," just more or less convincing bits of interiority that are arranged in relation to Miss Brodie's utterances. Sandy's motivations for betraying Miss Brodie are not psychologically motivated or justified at any length. Nevertheless, for all that Miss Brodie's status is challenged and her stupidity highlighted, or her shocking selfishness emphasized, her glamour and charisma remain indomitable. The novel ends with an almost awestruck, affectionate attestation of her influence and power, as seen from Sandy's perspective, an influence diminished and placed in a historical tense: "There was a Miss Jean Brodie in her prime."[51] The girls, now women, visit Sandy when she is a nun – more for the sake of something novel to do than out of genuine feeling – and without their "head," this "body" decomposes into its disparate parts.

Fellow Survivors: The Girls of Slender Means

The Girls of Slender Means was published hard on the heels of *The Prime of Miss Jean Brodie.* The "girls" of the title, however, are not connected to a central authority, as in the previous work. Instead, they are organized hierarchically according to their physical position in the women's hostel, the May of Teck Club. Those housed on the lower floors are undifferentiated; those at the top are the elite. The narrative moves back and forth between the days at the end of the war, more specifically VE day and VJ day, and a future timeline when Jane Wright, one of the girls who has become a "woman's columnist," telephones former inhabitants of the club to tell them about the death of Nicholas Farringdon, whom they all vaguely remember. For one reason or another, these calls are always interrupted and cut off. Back in 1945, states the narrator, "few people alive at the time were more delightful, more ingenious, more movingly lovely, and, as it might happen, more savage, than the girls of slender means."[52]

Of course, Spark is just as interested in this savagery as she is in the loveliness. As she notes in "The Desegregation of Art," we "should know ourselves better by now than to be under the illusion that we are all essentially aspiring, affectionate and loving creatures. We do have these qualities, but we are aggressive, too."[53] The particular savagery of the girls of slender means takes the form of selfishness during the days of rationing and austerity. The novel builds up to a vision of selfishness that sparks a religious conversion in Nicholas Farringdon, although no one else seems affected in the least. Rather than camaraderie, as one might expect from the title, the girls are fellow survivors who use each other mercilessly for their own ends.

The May of Teck Club is a Victorian house, formerly a private residence, turned into a hostel for the "pecuniary convenience and social protection of ladies of slender means below the age of thirty years, who are obliged to reside apart from their families in order to follow an occupation in London."[54] On the first floor, in a former ballroom, is the dormitory. The room is separated by curtains into cubicles, and the youngest members of the club, girls between the ages of eighteen and twenty, stay here, sharing jokes and repeating phrases in a way that approximates the "collective euphony of the birds in the park."[55] In keeping with the principles of an ensemble novel, in which the group takes priority over the person, the narrator does not accord the women on the ground floor any individuality. As with the villainous Mrs Hogg in *The Comforters*, God knows where they go in their privacy, if, in fact, they have any.

On the floor above them are shared bedrooms, occupied by women in transit as well as two elderly spinsters, Collie and Jarvie, who share a room to save money for their old age. They argue loudly in the bathroom, which allows everyone else in the house to know the exact contours of their disagreements.[56] Their "hostile fellowship" could define several of the relationships between the girls in the May of Teck Club.[57] On the floor above them are the virgins and celibates, including another elderly spinster, Greggie, and a "mad girl" named Pauline Fox. Joanna Childe, a clergyman's daughter and student of elocution, lives on this floor as well. At the top of the house, the fourth floor, are the "most attractive, sophisticated and lively girls." Four are beautiful and slim, especially Selina Redwood; the other, Jane Wright, is known for her "brain work" and has the cachet of working in the publishing world. All these women are thrown together by circumstance – penury, war, professional ambition – rather than friendship.

The failure of friendship among the women extends to a failure of ethical obligation and duty to care for each other. Much of the plot depends on thinness as a prerequisite for survival. Selina realizes that a bathroom window, seven inches wide by fourteen inches long, offers access to the roof. Only a few of the girls are thin enough to squeeze through. Of course, Selina has no problem. Anne Baberton, only slightly less thin, needs to cover her naked body with margarine or soap before squeezing through the window to sunbathe, and Selina pre-emptively tells her that she will not be sharing her soap (this during a time of strict rationing). Anne responds harshly:

> "I don't want your bloody soap. Just don't ask for the taffeta, that's all."
>
> By this she meant a Schiaparelli taffeta evening dress which had been given to her by a fabulously rich aunt, after one wearing. This marvellous dress, which caused a stir wherever it went, was shared by all the top floor on special occasions, excluding Jane whom it did not fit. For lending it out Anne got various returns, such as free clothing coupons or a half-used piece of soap.[58]

Friends might be expected to operate within a gift economy, to share what little they have freely. The characters in this world instead operate within a bartering economy: no soap, no dress. Jane overhears these "haggling bouts."[59] Rather than generosity or impulsive kindness among the girls, self-interest reigns.

Nicholas Farringdon visits the May of Teck Club and wants to return after forming a poetic image of the hostel and the women who live there; he takes out Jane Wright and asks her question after question about the club: "Jane pondered as to what she could barter for this information which he seemed to want."[60] Realizing Nicholas's ulterior motive, Jane tries to get as much out of him as she can. Selina does the same when, after having sex with him, she prompts him to give her his clothing coupons. In this wartime world, nothing comes for free, and the girls' savagery derives from their impoverishment.

The novel culminates in an instance of such deep spiritual impoverishment that it prompts Nicholas to convert to Catholicism. He witnesses an "action of savagery so extreme that it forced him involuntarily to make an entirely unaccustomed gesture, the signing of the cross upon himself."[61] The action itself is not all that remarkable. An unexploded bomb detonates in the back yard of the hostel, trapping a number of girls upstairs. Selina is able to get out, but then goes back inside. Rather than returning to help the imperilled girls, she takes something that is not hers. Nicholas sees her "carrying something fairly long and limp and evidently light in weight, enfolding it carefully in her arms." It is the Schiaparelli dress, the coat-hanger dangling from it "like a headless neck and shoulders."[62] Feline Selina values the dress above all else, even above human life, which is lost when the top floor of the house collapses and Joanna Childe dies.

Just as Miss Brodie fails to turn her set into a group of friends, the women in the May of Teck Club never achieve any friendly feeling toward each other. It becomes clear in the narrative present that Jane is only calling her former acquaintances because she wants to gauge their reactions to the death of Farringdon and mine their memories for a future story she plans to write. In fact, the word "friend" scarcely figures in the novel at all, except in relation to boyfriends or people outside the hostel. Spark's ensemble novels test the likelihood of trust overcoming treachery, or collective interest overcoming self-interest. Usually the test fails, as in *The Girls of Slender Means*. If friendship is a matter of goodwill and mutual affection, Spark's ensemble novels prove, if anything, that there is no place for true friendship to thrive in the novelistic milieu.

Fellow Cross-Dressers: The Abbess of Crewe

A reviewer in the *New York Times* observed: "The short dirk in the hands of Muriel Spark has always been a deadly weapon, and never more so than in *The Abbess of Crewe*."[63] This very slim and "deadly" novel is set in an English Benedictine convent.[64] The narrative moves between a time when Abbess Alexandra has bugged the convent with listening devices with the help of her henchwomen, Sisters Walburga, Mildred, and the stupid Winifride, and the time before the election for abbess, when Alexandra is challenged by another nun for the top position. Widely construed as a satire on the Watergate scandal, with Richard Nixon costumed as Alexandra and Richard Kissinger cast as globetrotting Sister Gertrude, this novel returns to the problem of authoritarianism, as in *The Prime of Miss Jean Brodie*, with a vertical structure between a group and its head.[65]

The Abbess of Crewe brings out the extremes of surveillance, intrusion, and interference in a hilarious and unnerving way. With categorical certainty, Abbess Alexandra asserts, "The Ancient Rule obtains when I say it does. The Jesuits are Jesuitry when I say it is so."[66] She is very much like Miss Brodie, careful to keep her set in line, although she is more perverse, in that she uses religious language and elected authority to justify her unilateral rules. There is a strict hierarchy within the convent, as in *The Girls of Slender Means*: "The nuns, high nuns, low nuns, choir nuns, novices and nobodies, fifty in all, follow two by two in hierarchical order, the Prioress and the Novice Mistress at the heels of the Abbess and at the end of the faceless line the meek novices."[67] The "novices and nobodies" and the "faceless line" underscore, with a jolt, how insignificant most of these women are within the "hierarchical order," and how merciless the narrator is in her descriptions of them.

No one is what they seem or just what they are in *The Abbess of Crewe*: it is a world where everyone performs an alternate identity by cross-dressing. Abbess Alexandra recites British poetry under her breath rather than religious verses; Sister Felicity wants to set up a "love nest" for sex in the convent, "right in the heart of England,"[68] if she is elected abbess; Sister Walburga has already had multiple lovers. The Sisters wear religious habits but are not nuns for any religious reasons. Ultimately, all of them are in drag; by reading allegorically, we cannot help but see that underneath their habits and female genders all of these nuns are American men in suits. The plot includes a break-in, a cover-up, an investigation, an exposure. The whole convent is bugged. Within the Watergate parody, Walburga and Mildred resemble Nixon's advisers, John Ehrlichman and H.R. Haldeman; Sister Winifrede stands in for the scapegoat, John Dean. Although Sister Gertrude resembles Henry Kissinger, Secretary of State under Nixon, she also stands in for Deep Throat: the other Sisters often ask her if she has bronchitis or a cold. Spark is very playful about this narrative transvestism. Sister Walburga notes how Gertrude "should have been a man," and the Abbess notes that she is indeed "[b]ursting with male hormones."[69] Sister Winifrede herself is described as "tall and handsome as a transvested butler."[70]

Political intrigue with false identities creates another fictional climate where friendship cannot take root. Spark replaces friends with allies, enemies, henchmen, and conspirators. The herd of nuns, like the youngest girls at the May of Teck Club, are undifferentiated and hardly acknowledged. They are the "nobodies" and the "faceless line," comprised of nuns who barely have an existence and who fail to notice what is going on around them. During meals, one of the nuns regularly reads aloud to the group from the Rule of St Benedict. At one point, a senior sister reads and switches to the lines: "To obey the commands of the Abbess in everything, even though she herself should unfortunately act otherwise, remembering the Lord's command: 'Practise and observe what they tell you, but not what they do.' – Gospel of St Matthew, 23."[71] No one comments, although all the nuns raise water to their lips. The same sister opens another book and quietly starts to read:

> *In recording, the tape is drawn at constant speed through the airgap of an electromagnet energized by the audio-frequency current derived from a microphone.*
>
> *Here endeth the reading. Deo gratias.*
>
> "Amen," responds the refectory of nuns.[72]

The undiscerning – one might say stupid – nuns also fail to notice or care when a recitation of religious texts alternates with excerpts from Machiavelli. They very docilely eat the food served to them, including "a cat-food by the name of Mew, bought cheaply and in bulk," and "rice and meat-balls, these being made up out of a tinned food for dogs which contains some very wholesome ingredients, quite good enough for them."[73] The narrator reveals her uncompromising judgment, further damning them by insisting that a "less edifying crowd of human life it would be difficult to find."[74]

Spark is merciless in her assessments of characters, even persecutorial. The greatest crime that a character can commit is to be stupid. Every character is positioned on a spectrum of stupidity, not just for their lack of intelligence but also for their dullness, lack of wit, obtuseness, failures of moral discernment, or figurative blindness. While there is an etymological connection, according to the *Oxford English Dictionary*, between stupidity and speechlessness, for Spark stupid characters can be the most inarticulate, but they can also be the most loquacious. Delineating stupidity from intelligence is part of the narrator's task. There is the obvious dim-wittedness that Winifrede exhibits: she constantly forgets that the convent is bugged everywhere, and she reveals information that Alexandra must deny for the record. When Sister Mildred whispers angrily that "[n]othing must be said in the hall," Winifrede, "aghast at her mistake," says loudly, "I forgot you've just bugged the hall."[75]

Rather than sympathy, such as Mary Macgregor elicits when she is killed off pitilessly in *The Prime of Miss Jean Brodie*, the reader is invited to feel derision and intolerance, even if deriding Winifrede's stupidity creates a moral dilemma about who is in the right and who is in the wrong. Her stupidity can be condemned, but her thoughtless contribution to the bugging cannot be condoned. After a botched break-in, the Abbess needs to pay off two Jesuit seminarians for their silence; Winifrede arranges the drop-off at a women's restroom in Selfridge's. One of the Jesuits dresses as a woman to pick up the bag of money, and Winifrede is chastised because this act of cross-dressing might have led to an arrest. As the Abbess notes, "He could have been arrested as a transvestite."[76] When they later need to arrange another drop-off, Winifrede is told to come up with a better plan. Ever the buffoon, she arranges a drop-off in the men's bathroom at the British Museum and dresses as a man in a suit. She is accused of being a "poof" and arrested for transvestism, and on the way to the police station confesses everything.[77]

We are meant to view Winifrede with contempt and to side with Alexandra in this novel, which is uncomfortable given the latter's views. For instance, she hints that she would like to segregate the abbey, as they did "back in the day," with separate entrances for those of noble birth and for the lower bourgeoisie. Because of the Watergate scandal, we know that the Abbess is heading toward exposure and disgrace, even though her fall is never made explicit. Sister Gertrude, the "Deep Throat" figure, betrays her. The eloquent Alexandra's failure to predict who her betrayer will be is a wilful form of stupidity, as it is with Miss Brodie, because it rejects the obvious. The stupidity of Winifrede and Alexandra is part of a larger farce, a generalized folly that Spark gaily and darkly satirizes. More than an inhibitor of friendship, stupidity can be viewed as the diametric opposite of friendship. To call someone stupid relies on an inherently cruel judgment; it is also isolating, degrading, and final.

Such a foreclosure of possibility could not be further from the creative possibilities and freedom offered by genuine friendship. The targets of Spark's satire are consistently naivety and sentimentality: she relishes dismantling idealistic views of friendship, religion, piety, authority, and intelligence. An attentive reader of the Bible, Spark certainly would have agreed with this statement in Ecclesiastes 1:15: "the number of fools is infinite."

Imagined Friendship

In *A Far Cry from Kensington*, the central and lovable character, Mrs Hawkins, offers advice to aspiring authors. She tells them to imagine that they are writing "a letter to a friend." This is a "dear and close friend, real – or better – invented in your mind like a fixation."

> Write privately, not publicly; without fear or timidity, right to the end of the letter, as if it was never going to be published, so that your true friend will read it over and over, and then want more enchanting letters from you. Now, you are not writing about the relationship between your friend and yourself; you take that for granted. You are only confiding an experience that you think only he will enjoy reading. What you have to say will come out more spóntaneously and honestly than if you are thinking of numerous readers.

The letter should make the imagined friend "smile or laugh or cry, or anything you like so long as you know it will interest."[78] Writing with the public in mind will have the effect of putting the writer (and reader) off. Mrs Hawkins claims that this method has proved successful in at least two cases with first novels and in other cases with short stories. Friendship of the kind described by Mrs Hawkins rarely exists in Spark's fictional universe. Yet it does exist as the imaginative precondition of writing. It can exist fully in an imaginary, ideal state, creating a sense of privacy, interest, and intimacy that is liberating for the writer. Friendship undergirds her fictional worlds, creating that buoyancy which, along with her ruthlessness, forms part of Spark's hallmark style. Just as she uses authoritarian narrative structures to poke holes in authoritarianism, she uses intimacy to expose intrusions upon intimacy.

Spark was very much aware of the milieu in which she was writing, and the demands placed upon artists of the twentieth century. With evidence on all sides of inflated egos and blatant abuses of power, and of aggression within us all, she argues that neither sentiment nor protest is sufficient in literature – they have reached a "point of exhaustion."[79] The only efficient weapon is ridicule; Hitler and Mussolini, she is convinced, would never have had a chance if they were greeted by crowds overcome with helpless laughter at their antics. The art of ridicule, she writes, "can penetrate to the marrow. It can leave a salutary scar. It is unnerving. It can paralyse its object."[80] It deflates pretension and disarms stupidity. Not only that, but "given the world we have," the "only effective art of our particular time is the satirical, the harsh and witty, the ironic and derisive."[81]

Friendship rests on a foundation of sentiment: it conjures images of clasped hands, genuine smiles, true camaraderie. Spark embraced such sentiment in her work to the extent that it was invisible and prior to the act of writing. Beyond that, she approached her fictional worlds with a blade at the ready, wanting, like all satirists, both to stab and to entertain. Spark very rarely represents true friends in her fiction, yet by addressing the reader as a dear friend, she fashions readers who will side with her satirical mission – those who will join in her derisive laughter at those who are stupid, obtuse, and absurd. We are the friends who will keep reading and keep coming back for more, soothed and horrified, amused and unsettled. And ideally, we will also become more finely attuned to – and thus better able to defend ourselves against – the "ridiculous oppressions of our time."[82]

NOTES

1 Muriel Spark, "The Desegregation of Art," in *The Informed Air: Essays by Muriel Spark*, ed. Penelope Jardine (New York: New Directions, 2014), 81.

2 Ibid., 80.

3 Ibid.

4 Ian Rankin, in "Living in the Memory: A Celebration of the Great Writers who Died in the Past Decade," *Guardian Review*, 31 January 2009.

5 Michiko Kakutani, "Her Serene Tyranny, A Mistress of Mayhem," *New York Times*, 15 May 1997.

6 A 1970 review of *The Driver's Seat* in *The Independent* described its "complexity which magnifies the impact of its spare length many times over."

7 According to Martin Stannard, Graham Greene along with Evelyn Waugh provided "plaudits for the dust jacket" of *Memento Mori*. Greene wrote, "This funny and macabre book has delighted me as much as any novel that I have read since the war." Martin Stannard, *Muriel Spark: The Biography* (London: Weidenfeld and Nicolson, 2009), 209.

8 John Updike, "Topnotch Witcheries," review of *The Abbess of Crewe*, by Muriel Spark in the *New Yorker*, 6 January 1975.

9 John Lanchester, introduction to *The Driver's Seat*, by Muriel Spark (London: Penguin, 2006), n.p.

10 In many ways, *The Mandelbaum Gate* is an outlier in Spark's oeuvre. It is longer; it has a different tone; it explores the tenuous but meaningful connections between individuals from different walks of life; and it gave Spark more trouble than her other novels.

11 Summarizing various reviews, Randall Stevenson states, "even when not explicitly the novel's subject, issues of authority, authorship and the control of worlds, fictional or real, inescapably figure among the interests of her [Spark's] writing" (100). He quotes Valerie Shaw's assertion that "all of Spark's fiction certainly displays a fascination with authority of diverse kinds and forms," as well as Malcolm Bradbury, who called Spark "high-handed" both "with her readers and her characters" (101). Other reviewers make similar points. Michiko Kakutani, reviewing *Reality and Dreams*, refers to the "serenely tyrannical creator" and suggests that Spark's usually "poised authorial manner" becomes "peremptory and pinched." In Charles McGrath's opinion, "Spark loved to play God, loftily manipulating her characters' fates, and she was less the benign and loving God of traditional Catholic theology than Calvin's cruel jokester, who would allow you to think you were saved only to surprise you at the end." See Randall Stevenson, "The Postwar Contexts of Spark's Writing," in *The Edinburgh Companion to Muriel Spark*, ed. Michael Gardiner and Willy Maley (Edinburgh: Edinburgh University Press, 2010), 100; Kakutani, "Her Serene Tyranny"; Charles McGrath, "Muriel Spark, Playing God," *New Yorker*, 22 April 2010.

12 Spark, *Informed Air*, 265–71. In *The Only Problem*, Harvey Gotham is writing a monograph on *The Book of Job*. In an essay also entitled "The Only Problem,"

Spark states, "I could never quite leave the Book of Job alone, and it would not leave me alone." Spark, *Informed Air*, 273.

13 Spark, *Informed Air*, 268.

14 "Now when Job's three friends heard of all this evil that was come upon him, they came every one from his own place; Eliphaz the Temanite, and Bildad the Shuhite, and Zophar the Naamathite: for they had made an appointment together to come to mourn with him and to comfort him" (Job 2:11).

15 Spark, *Informed Air*, 270.

16 Spark, *The Comforters* (New York: New Directions, 1957), 43.

17 Ibid.

18 Ibid., 48.

19 Ibid., 97–8.

20 Ibid., 57.

21 Ibid., 69.

22 Allan Hepburn, *A Grain of Faith: Religion in Mid-Century British Literature* (Oxford: Oxford University Press, 2018), 138.

23 Spark, *Comforters*, 144.

24 Ibid., 169.

25 Ibid., 146. Hepburn writes about Hogg's intrusion on others' privacy. Hepburn, *A Grain of Faith*, 139–41.

26 Spark, *Comforters*, 164.

27 Ibid., 207.

28 Spark, *Loitering with Intent* (New York: New Directions, 1981), 93.

29 Hepburn, *Grain of Faith*, 141.

30 Spark, *Comforters*, 213.

31 Hepburn, *Grain of Faith*, 136.

32 Updike, "Topnotch Witcheries."

33 Spark regarded *The Prime of Miss Jean Brodie* as her "milch cow" because it "generated a small fortune" for her over the years. Stannard, *Muriel Spark*, 325.

34 Matthew Wickman, "Spark, Modernism and Postmodernism," in *The Edinburgh Companion to Muriel Spark*, ed. Michael Gardiner and Willy Maley (Edinburgh: Edinburgh University Press, 2010), 68.

35 Spark, *The Prime of Miss Jean Brodie*, in *The Prime of Miss Jean Brodie, The Girls of Slender Means, The Driver's Seat, The Only Problem* (New York: Knopf, 2004), 5–6.

36 Ibid., 12.

37 Ibid.

38 Ibid.

39 Ibid., 29–30.

40 Ibid., 28.

41 Ibid., 29.

42 Ibid.

43 David Hayman quoted in John Somer, "The Self-Reflexive Arranger in the Initial Style of Joyce's *Ulysses*," *James Joyce Quarterly* 31, no. 2 (1994): 65–6.

44 Ibid., 66.

45 The novel generates soundscapes similar to those of T.S. Eliot in *The Waste Land* or of Woolf in *Between the Acts*. Spark was fascinated by Eliot's poetry and plays throughout her career.

46 Spark, *Prime*, 120.

47 Marilyn Reizbaum, "The Stranger Spark," in *The Edinburgh Companion to Muriel Spark*, ed. Michael Gardiner and Willy Maley (Edinburgh: Edinburgh University Press, 2010), 42.

48 Spark, *Prime*, 122.

49 Ibid., 118–19.

50 Paddy Lyons, "Muriel Spark's Break with Romanticism," in *The Edinburgh Companion to Muriel Spark*, ed. Michael Gardiner and Willy Maley (Edinburgh: Edinburgh University Press, 2010), 90.

51 Spark, *Prime*, 125.

52 Spark, *The Girls of Slender Means* (New York: New Directions, 1963), 9.

53 Ibid., 82.

54 Ibid., 9.

55 Ibid., 28.

56 Ibid., 77.

57 Ibid., 104.

58 Ibid., 34–5.

59 Ibid., 35.

60 Ibid., 65.

61 Ibid., 60.

62 Ibid., 125.

63 Herbert Mitgang, "Two, Well, Short Fictions," *New York Times*, 26 November 1974.

64 We might compare *The Abbess of Crewe* with Sylvia Townsend Warner's *The*

Corner That Held Them (1948), which is also set in a convent. The nuns in Warner's novel do form a community, although one not rooted in spirituality. There is political intrigue and gossip and murder, but there is also at least one friendship.

65 Stannard, *Muriel Spark*, 408–9.

66 Spark, *The Abbess of Crewe* (New York: New Directions, 1995), 9.

67 Ibid., 12.

68 Ibid., 40.

69 Ibid., 24.

70 Ibid., 15.

71 The actual lines read: "The scribes and the Pharisees sit in Moses' seat: All therefore whatsoever they bid you observe, that observe and do; but do not ye after their works: for they say, and do not" (Matthew 23:2–3).

72 Spark, *Abbess*, 15.

73 Ibid., 37, 76.

74 Ibid., 50.

75 Ibid., 36.

76 Ibid., 97.

77 Ibid., 101–2.

78 Spark, *A Far Cry from Kensington* (New York: New Directions, 1988), 84–5.

79 Spark, *Informed Air*, 81–2.

80 Ibid., 81.

81 Ibid.

82 Ibid., 82.

Part Four
Contemporary Friendships

10

Critical Distance, Reparative Proximity: Changing Representations of Queer Friendship

ROBERT L. CASERIO

Prefatory: Attachments, Alignments, Sex

One might begin thinking about friendship's representation in fiction in terms of what Rita Felski calls "*solicitations* of affect" in readers.[1] Perhaps a fiction about friendship would solicit readers to practice, in faithful acts of attention, thoughts and feelings that replicate the text's version of friendly attachment. Such a replication would be grouped by Felski with what she labels *alignment*: "the directive force of narrative, description, and point of view ... whose perspective we are invited to adopt."[2] Felski sees such invitations as always present: the attaching effects of alignment are available from any artwork, regardless of subject matter. But alignments can also include detaching directives and effects. Felski thinks that attaching and detaching alignments are constantly intermingled in the responses that artworks invite. Yet what if there are artworks and eras of cultural history that resist such intermingling and alter the possibilities of alignment? If we are invited to adopt only some possibilities rather than others, how might an acceptance of that invitation change fictional portrayals of friendship and readers' expectations about attachment and detachment in response to what they read?

In the ensuing pages, I adumbrate the appearance of that possible change in two works: Hanya Yanagihara's *A Little Life* (2015), whose protagonist is a gay man permanently traumatized by sexual abuse in his youth; and Matthew Lopez's novelistic drama *The Inheritance* (2019), whose title page announces that it is "inspired" by E.M. Forster's novel *Howards End*. As a character in Lopez's play, Forster muses, "What does it mean now to be a gay man?"[3] Both Yanagihara's and Lopez's texts seek an answer to that question. In doing so, they unwind, I argue, the interminglings of alignment noted by Felski. They represent unqualified attachment as essential to friendship, and supremely valuable. For these authors, unqualified attachment – regardless of the conflict-laden content at issue – is also essential to a reader's investment in imaginative work.

To illustrate this contention, I contrast *A Little Life* and *The Inheritance* with two mid-century novels, James Baldwin's *Another Country* (1962) and Mary McCarthy's *The Group* (1963). In Baldwin's and McCarthy's narratives, friendship and queer experience complicate the meanings of "alignment" and "attachment": the referents of those terms are intermingled with their opposites and diversely evaluated, although the weight of affirmative evaluation falls on the side of detachment. Yanagihara and Lopez look askance at the complexity and the value of detachment. Sex is at the root of their mistrust. The sexual horrors that victimize Yanagihara's queer protagonist corrode all evocations of *eros* in the novel; the abused protagonist's husband happily resigns himself to a sexless marriage because he rates friendship higher than sexual and marital ties. Lopez duplicates Yanagihara's model; his leading figure, resolutely monogamous, willingly enters a *mariage blanc* as a heightened form of friendship, more pressing than sexual intimacy.

For queer writing to enlist readers' capacity for an attaching alignment with suspicion of sex constitutes a surprising turn against twentieth-century gay and lesbian traditions. Perhaps the change is only an arbitrary result of my choice of texts rather than anything larger in scale; but I hope that the readings to follow suggest a cogent motivation. As a final prefatory observation, I venture a sample of possible contextual causations to frame my proposed historical difference between contemporary and mid-century fiction.

One context is the impact on friendship of AIDS, which in Lopez's play matters centrally, and which is present-by-absence in Yanagihara's novel, where sexual abuse is the equivalent of the viral scourge. Tom Roach's *Friendship as a Way of Life* offers a contextual account of friendship under the shadow of AIDS. Roach argues that Foucault's meditations on friendship in 1981 advanced a compelling new formation of what that word can mean. "Foucault's model of friendship," Roach states, "involve[s] *critical distance* [between or among intimates], a deflection of commonality, and a refusal of transcendence."[4] Friendship thereby provides "a micro-model for alternative communal and political forms."[5] According to Roach, the AIDS plague instantiated this micro-model, especially among AIDS patients and their caregivers who worked within a buddy system developed by the Gay Men's Health Crisis in the early years of the pandemic. It was the co-presence of mortal finitude and death among patients and buddies – among the dying and the still living – that brought those involvements into the experience of friendship.

Critical distance also matters to readers' alignments with Baldwin's and McCarthy's novels. To a certain degree, the picture of friendship that I derive from these earlier writers matches Roach's observations. But two caveats about the AIDS context must be registered. First, the characteristics of friendship that Roach claims as "a way of life" are laid out prior to AIDS and prior to Foucault in Maurice Blanchot's 1971 essay "Friendship." Because Blanchot belongs to the era of Baldwin and McCarthy, his concept of friendship, as well as his way of reading friendship, means that "shared estrangement" pre-dates the AIDS pandemic. *Another Country* or *The Group* brings me to the second caveat, which pertains to the anti-erotic conception of sexuality in Lopez's and Yanagihara's texts. Baldwin and McCarthy do not look askance at sex or its many varieties. Neither, one assumes, does Roach. Yet Roach's devotion to Foucault's critiques of sexuality makes it necessary for him, in the name of "friendship as a 'post-homosexual' practice," to declare "Foucault's friend only comes to be when the sexological category of 'homosexual' is overcome."[6] Must the homosexual be overcome for friendship to come to be? If so, does this post-homosexual friendship explain the turn against *eros* that marks Lopez's and Yanagihara's works?

That turn has another possible component: an involvement with "attachment" that seems less derived from art than from psychiatric discourses of "attachment theory" and "traumatology." Attachment theory, whose chief proponent is the British analyst John Bowlby, emphasizes, according to Oliver Davis and Tim Dean in *Hatred of Sex*, the origins of "intrapsychic conflict" not, as with Freud, in "the inescapable human condition," but in a child's "first attachment relationship" to a principal caregiver.[7] Any failure in this first attachment is adjudged the cause of lifelong difficulties, especially in sexual development. Those difficulties, attachment theory stresses, shape sexual practices as hazardous, and tend to alienate persons from "models of happy intimacy"[8] that hark back to infantile safety. Therapy repairs a patient's capacity for attachment.

"Traumatology" further elaborates attachment theory. In their summary of Judith Herman's *Trauma and Recovery*, Davis and Dean identify trauma, whose paradigm is childhood sexual abuse, as a generator of "personality fragments," in contrast to a healthy, single-minded identity. Traumatology theorizes attachment types as measures of "a determining total psychological identity affecting all ... experience"; it defines "good parenting" as a commitment to "life-long positive effects" that are antithetical to all varieties of abuse; and it conflates emotional "security with safety" from what might otherwise be understood as ordinary adult conflict.[9] These tenets of psychiatric discourse, I propose, throw a special contextual light on Yanagihara's and Lopez's versions of friendship, in particular their ways of inviting readers' attaching alignments with their fictions. But I turn first to Baldwin's instance of the value of critical distance for novels and for their readers.

Critical Distance 1: Another Country

"We're *all* bastards. That's why we need our friends."[10] So says a principal character in *Another Country*. The statement typifies an edginess characteristic of many assertions in Baldwin's novel. A reader is invited to agree with this remark while also taking up an interrogative distance from it. Given the six friends on whom the narrative centres, does the generalization hold up? Provoked to reflect, a reader waits to see.

During the wait, if a reader comes to feel closer to Baldwin's characters and what they say, Baldwin unsettles that sense of intimacy. The characters themselves experience personal relations in ways that make it difficult to tell friendship apart from alienation, especially when love or sexual love takes over. In the initial event of the novel, Leona, a white woman from the South, is picked up by Rufus, an African American from New York. Rufus, sensing that Leona is a person with a story, feels wary of her because, he thinks, "all stories were trouble."[11] Rufus's friend Vivaldo, an aspiring novelist, utters a complementary remark: "He was tired – tired of Rufus' story, tired of attending, tired of friendship ... He was tired of the troubles of real people. He wanted to get back to the people he was inventing, whose troubles he could bear."[12] If that is all a reader of *Another Country* can bear, then such a reader will feel close to its characters only because they and their troubles are fictive. Because of the gravity of the social and sexual dilemmas in the novel, one cannot take Vivaldo's retreat as a measure of the truth of Baldwin's invention.

Yet Baldwin's truth, whether it be about friendship, race, sex, or novelistic art, is not easy to get near. I propose "critical distance" as the name of a novelistic effect that prevents readers from easily identifying with any novel's characters and events, or with its generalizing assertions. My use of "critical distance" converges with Roach's, but my use also signifies a detaching aspect of fiction inherent in Felski's "alignments." *Another Country* demands a reader's close attention, yet the paradoxical effect of that demand is a sharpening of the reader's exercise of speculative removal – an ability to remain disinterested as well as interested, in a state of suspension about an artwork's or a fictional character's unsettled meanings. Baldwin's novel elicits such a state, as does *The Group*.

A contrasting novelistic effect, in Yanagihara's and Lopez's texts, I name "reparative proximity": an alignment by writers and readers with attachments to characters in fiction that model friendship as a builder of "safe spaces." Expecting to be unwavering friends of a novel's protagonists, reparative-minded readers contribute to the creation of those "safe spaces." Those spaces are allied with a generalized aim to repair real-life hurt and abuse, whether sexual, social, or other. Compared to meanings aligned with "critical distance," meanings for readers who are attached to safe spaces are clear-cut and settled.[13]

Surely, it will be said, racism constituted a supreme abuse for Baldwin, and his fiction seeks out and constitutes spaces of refuge from it. But that rebuttal will not suffice. The distancing phenomenon is always present. I would say that we cannot get in touch adequately, and certainly not fully, with what is going on in *Another Country*. Racism, to be sure, explains why friends in the novel are "equal in misery, confusion, and despair."[14] After Rufus dies by suicide in the wake of his tortured love-hate relation with Leona, his sister Ida says repeatedly to her Italian American lover Vivaldo and the other white protagonists that their unhappiness results from the racism they are forged by, and for which all whites must pay. The lesson is absorbed by Cass, the white middle-class wife and mother who befriends Ida. When Vivaldo says to Cass that Black and white in America are not distinct identities because the same things happen to both, she responds that things "didn't happen to you *because* you were white. They just happened. But what happens up [in Harlem] happens *because* they are colored. And that makes a difference."[15]

Nowadays, impatient to repair the harms of racism, we would contradict Cass's idea that what happens to whiteness just happens. We would underline her racial contrast in the way the external narrator does, taking a critical distance from Cass. The narrator says that Vivaldo hangs out in Harlem as a proud badge of difference from his white roots, but that his whiteness doesn't "just happen." He comes to Harlem because he is "a poor white boy in trouble and it was not in the least original of him to come running" to Black people.[16] His "badge of difference" is mere escapism.

This assertive judgment seems intended for a reader's immediate assent, not for questioning from an additional disinterested distance. Yet the narrative is made up of many moments not intended to cement a reader's arrival at fixed significance or judgment, not even about racism. Baldwin is able to move a reader's alignments to a distance from the very motivations that *Another Country* depends on. In Rufus's relation to Leona, the sadomasochistic and misogynistic elements belong to a tumult of forces that exceeds conventional causal understanding. When a white television producer accuses Vivaldo of possessiveness toward Ida that he would never feel about a white girlfriend, Vivaldo wonders if the man is right, then he "realized that he would never know, there would never be any way to know."[17] Ida, who seems most to know the external narrator's causal assertions about race, can be also surprisingly dislocated from them. Although hatred of whites determines her, she is also determined by attachment to Vivaldo. "If any *one* white person gets through to you," she tells Cass, "it kind of destroys – your single-mindedness. They say that love and hate are very close together. Well, that's a fact."[18] In such moments, of which there are many, *Another Country* transcends intelligible intersections among friendships, racial antagonisms, and *eros*.

Racism and anti-racism, love and hate co-habit in Baldwin's friendships; so do sex and *agape*. Baldwin's friends have sex – with each other, with others – but they mostly are surprised by their sexual enactments. How astonished Vivaldo and Eric are when, after they make love to each other, they each say, "I must have loved you for a very long time," but "I didn't *know* I knew."[19] If one judges by Eric's sexual relations with Yves, Rufus, and Vivaldo, Eric is gay; his adultery with Cass is a passing episode. But no less than his relation with Cass, Eric's gay loves always confront him with an inherent alienating distance. He might well be claimed as an instance of "post-homosexual" practice, if it were not that his homosexual practice endures, even when he is past it. Eric assumes that Yves will exit his life, just as Rufus did, just as Vivaldo will. But distance marks Eric too: a distance from his friends, himself, and the reader.

Baldwin represents distance as a mark of Eric's value. Eric is a stage and screen actor. A view of his elusive character is afforded by a film close-up of his face, which reveals

> a glimpse of who Eric really was ... It was the face of a man, a tormented man. Yet, in precisely the way that great music depends, ultimately, on great silence, this masculinity was defined, and made powerful, by something which was not masculine. But it was not feminine, either, and ... resisted the word *androgynous* ... There was great force in the face, and great gentleness. But, as most women are not gentle, nor most men strong, it was a face which suggested resonantly, in the depths, the truth about our natures.[20]

Turning unfriendly, the narrator does not disclose this truth; nor does the narrator ask the reader to enlist a reparative proximity that will heal the gap. Eric himself expresses the limits of disclosure, whether of his identity or the causes of his personal and social afflictions. "One is never what one seems," he tells Vivaldo, "yet, what one seems to be is ... almost exactly what one *is.*"[21]

As for the causes of being versus seeming, Eric tries to assign them to homophobia without success. "I wanted to believe that, somewhere, for some people, life and love are easier – than they are for me, than they are. Maybe it was easier to call myself a faggot and blame my sorrow on that."[22] Mockingly blaming his sorrow on homophobia, identifying and not identifying with "himself," Eric knows that explanatory blame is friendly to storytelling. Blame is too easy for *Another Country* to make exclusive use of, even though Baldwin keeps it strongly on his textual surface. The capacity to sustain self-distancing and self-division that Baldwin assigns to Eric would seem to make him, from the perspective of traumatology, an icon of unhealthy "personality fragments," dangerously far from "normal" single-mindedness. Yet Eric's distance from the latter is for Baldwin the manifest sign of his strength. Baldwin's reader is invited to share that distance.

Less immediately on the novel's surface there is something to attend to that involves the nexus of friends in a self-reflexive drama about art, novelistic art especially. How Baldwin's and my other chosen texts project ideas about their constitutive genres is essential to the ways they direct readers' attaching and detaching alignments. One moment in which Baldwin's self-reflexive aspect is in play begins when Eric wonders if sexual repression is at the root of American disorder and violence; he doubts that it is. Vivaldo thinks that the cause of national chaos is "grim privacy," a radically anomic state inhabited by all Americans. "What order could prevail against so grim a privacy?" Vivaldo and the narrator wonder in unison. "And yet, without order, of what value was the mystery?" they continue, without identifying what the mystery is. Perhaps the mystery is what Vivaldo has just envisioned: "he was briefly and horribly, in a region where there were no definitions of any kind, neither of color, nor of male and female."[23] That would seem to be a reparative region free from the defining deformations identical with American chaos; Eric's face might signal that freedom. But a freedom from definitions – if that is the mystery – can only lead to violence, Vivaldo thinks. "When people no longer knew that a mystery could only be approached through form,"[24] they become saturated by violence, and addicted to it.

Form is clearly the antithesis of chaos. The form nearest Baldwin and the reader is the novel. In *Another Country*, that form is an all-powerful agent, whose surprising effects include a detaching, distancing attitude toward itself. Cass's husband Richard is another aspiring novelist. His novel works destructively: his absorption in writing alienates his wife, leads her to Eric, and brings his marriage to dissolution. Richard's novel inspires additional treachery: through Richard's publishing connections, Ida, a budding jazz vocal artist, comes into the ken of a white television producer with whom she betrays Vivaldo. In turn, because Vivaldo thinks Richard's fiction is a sell-out, unlike what Vivaldo hopes his own novel to be, the two men's intimacy comes to an end.

Novels, it seems, are fatal to friendship. Other arts are affected by Baldwin's stiff-arming of his own métier. Baldwin sets the last rendezvous of Eric and Cass in the Museum of Modern Art, where the abstract paintings they walk past renew a reader's vision of grim privacy: the art is said to "stretch adoringly in on itself, reaching back into unspeakable chaos."[25] Given Baldwin's identification of novels and mid-century American art with destructive force and chaos, it is a wonder that he writes fiction. Friendship as shared estrangement perhaps marks the relation of Baldwin's art to life. But if Rufus's and Ida's distinguished jazz musicianship is legible not only on its own terms but also as a metaphor for novelistic art, then art can mitigate chaos. The destructiveness of Richard's novel-writing is counter-balanced by the tenderness it provokes between Cass and Eric, as well as between Vivaldo and Eric. Having metafictively estranged his own novel from himself, Baldwin ends with a re-attaching gesture. In the last pages of *Another Country*, Vivaldo happily discovers a long-searched-for detail for his novel so that his book finds a resolution at the same time Baldwin's text ends. But the reader is not given the detail.

If only, *Another Country* seems to say, novelistic art exemplified the independence, intelligence, and mysterious truth of Baldwin's non-novelist, Eric. Of course, it takes a novel to invent Eric and to suggest, through him, an idea of fiction that is critically distant from unexamined assumptions about the form, including assumptions about its reliability as a diagnosis of historical conflicts and about its reliability as a prescription for the resolution of conflicts. Baldwin risks soliciting that distance, I surmise, because he does not expect readers to be solely identified with a story, nor to find in fiction a safe space wherein insoluble phenomena appear to be resolved. Closeness of identification can obstruct a reader's open-minded probing of the complexities of artifice and of whatever artworks are about.[26] *Another Country* is "about" race, sex, identity, and art. It invites readers to analyze closely its representation of those topics, and yet to allow them to remain inexhaustible. At present, are readers willing to tolerate what does not immediately present itself, in art or in life, as a clear-cut problem that can be repaired by a clear-cut solution?

Reparative Proximity 1: The Inheritance

In *The Inheritance* the meaning of present-day gay male life is a clear-cut problem. Because E.M. Forster has served as an inspiration and a *point de repère* for gay men for a century – long before the posthumous publication of *Maurice* in 1971 – Lopez's decision to take up this novelist and his novel for the stage is canny.

Lopez's play parallels the plot of *Howards End*, with some transpositions of straight into gay characters, or male into female. The protagonist Eric, for example, stands in for Margaret Schlegel. When Forster is introduced as a character at the rise of the curtain, Eric's friends, who familiarly call Forster "Morgan," invoke *Howards End* with a list of nouns that express its virtues. The friends say that the novel offers "guidance," "compassion," "wisdom," "humanity," "honesty," "comfort," and, especially, help with "self-discovery."[27] Although one friend contends that too much time between now and *Howards End* makes the text useless for self-discovery, Morgan responds, "Hearts still love, don't they? And break?"[28] In other words, on a sentimental or emotional basis at the very least, gay past and gay present can be intimate friends.

As an intertext for the play, Forster's novel promises the comfort of a nurturing attachment that accepts breaks only in order to overcome them. Forster is interpellated, for queer tradition, as a safe and saving space. What reader, even one who has closely read *Howards End*, would seek detachment from a reading that assigns so many virtues to the content and effect of Forster's novel? If traumatic breaks – between cultural past and cultural present, and among gay men – are under consideration, repairing them apparently requires intense attachment to this version of "Morgan" and to Eric, who becomes Morgan's latter-day emanation. This invitation to close alignment with *The Inheritance* exemplifies what I mean by an artwork's solicitation of an audience's or a reader's reparative proximity.

To be guided by that alignment would be to assume that a celebrated novel is authoritative because it endorses "healing" messages. No questions are in play about what purposes novels or dramas serve – other than for inspiration. Baldwin corrosively submits his chosen genre to a questioning critical distance. Lopez, in contrast, does not self-consciously explore novelistic or dramatic form, or their intermingling. Instead, he attaches his drama to a narrative genre to insure the solidarity of novel and theatre with moral and psychological elevation. When Leo, a nineteen-year-old sex worker, reads *Howards End* on Fire Island, he finds "his life forever changed."[29] One of the play's onstage commentators says that Forster's characters "hummed with a human truth – Leo felt their vibrations."[30] In particular, he vibrates to "self-discovery."

Within four years, with Eric's help, he renounces sex work, overcomes homelessness and suicidal thoughts, surmounts HIV infection, and discovers himself by writing a novel called *The Inheritance.*

What *is* self-discovery, and how does a novel or drama enable it? Different representational eras provide contrastive answers. Baldwin's Eric says, "one never is what one seems – never."[31] Discovery of his identity is baffled; his self is a struggle without an issue. That baffling has a possible good effect: it subverts racism insofar as racism is rooted in narcissistically secured selfhood or possession of others' selves. Nevertheless, incurable distance subtending life's relationships, even its most intimate ones, is an ontological given in Baldwin. In *The Inheritance* distance is equated with psychological imbalance and lack of close caring, which demand therapeutic reversal. Morgan says that "if we are to learn what we mean to each other, we must learn what we mean to ourselves."[32] This platitude suggests alignment with the kind of single-minded self that traumatology assigns to "normality." Morgan asserts that he was never afforded the chance to be at one with his authentic self; hence, he could not be close to others. "So many of us," Morgan muses, "were never given a healthy example of what it means to be homosexual … No one ever taught us how to be. How to love, how to accept love … Sometimes we caused each other great pain."[33]

As historical fact, what Morgan says is untrue. The Edwardians number many examples of "healthy" homosexuality. As for how novels or plays by Morgan's contemporaries enabled such healthiness, if those enablements were not then as plentiful as they are now, the cause might be that artworks in the modernist era were not universally expected to prevent "great pain" or to promote well-being. Closer perhaps to Forster's time than to ours, Baldwin's characters do not go to doctors to be relieved of historical and emotional duress. They fight out the conflicts of their cultural moment through sex and art, from which they derive unsecured pain and pleasure. *Another Country* aligns its readers with a like insecurity.

At the other end of the spectrum, Lopez's gay friendships model safety and security from unruly desire, bodily disease, and mental illness. In *The Inheritance* the archetype of healthy homosexual friendship is Walter Poole. An intermediate between Morgan and Eric, Walter redeems his originally shamed gay existence. In the 1970s, he was the closeted lover of a closeted family man,

Henry Wilcox. During the darkest days of the AIDS pandemic, Walter broke with Henry after bravely deciding, despite Henry's disgust, to devote an upstate country house – a new Howards End – to the sheltering and care of dying AIDS patients. Thirty years later, Walter meets Eric when Eric needs healing from heartbreak caused by someone who did not know "how to love." This friendship opens the way for Eric, after Walter's death, to marry Henry and inherit Walter's house, which Eric will revive as a place of restoration for, among others, Leo.

One must be on closely friendly terms with one's self to feel the therapeutic advantage of friendship, at least as Lopez represents it. Eric parts company from his first love and from Henry because they refuse to know themselves. The first lover is Toby, a budding playwright. He and Eric separate because of Toby's lust for a young actor whom the couple have befriended. Sex with friends is not acceptable to Eric: this is not *Another Country*. Worse for Eric than Toby's philandering is Toby's playscript, which Eric declares is a flight from authenticity. The drama is not based on Toby's autobiography, which a formal protocol emphasizing reparative proximity seems to require: a close attachment of author to text, and thereby of audience and readers to author. To avoid imposing too much distantiating detachment on the audience, at the start of the play Morgan announces "truth is something Toby has spent his life running from."[34] Henry also runs from the truth. He asks Eric to start off their marriage as a *mariage blanc*, even as he hires Leo for sex on the side. The revelation of this deceit initiates Eric's reparative vocation at Howards End, where gay men will arrive, Eric says, to thrive, not to die, and to receive their due of social justice. Eric insists that Leo's homelessness and illness are Henry's ethical responsibility: "You don't get to take full advantage of a desperate young person when it suits you and then turn your back on him when it becomes inconvenient."[35] Indeed, Henry has acted with the same compartmentalizing meanness toward Eric that he acted toward Leo and, previously, toward Walter.

Unfortunately, while Eric can help Leo and rebuke Henry for his trespass, neither his medicating spirit nor social justice can save Toby, whose conduct has included abuse of Leo's psyche and body. Neither can Toby be saved by a belated turn to self-discovery when he decides to write another play, this time a reparatively close autobiographical one, about his traumatized queer boyhood. Perhaps because Toby's reformation cannot be counted on, an ultimate choice is demanded of him in an oracular utterance by one of his friends. "Heal and seek truth, dignity, and fulfilment," the friend's voice commands. "Heal and build a life that is real. Or burn it all … Heal or burn."[36] Alas, Toby cannot accept healing because, as his ghost posthumously explains, "healing was too hard."[37]

Toby's belated approach to authentic self-discovery is insufficient; it requires that he attach himself to external help in the safe space of Howards End. Like Toby, an audience or reader brooking detachment from such a therapeutic model of repair apparently faces a clear-cut opposition: heal or burn. The opposition easily maps onto attachment theory and traumatology, which Davis and Dean identify with "a reduction of nuanced adult social experience into melodramatic oppositions between good and bad caregiving."[38] Of course, melodrama in the realms of fiction is a respectable and politically progressive genre. In *The Inheritance*, however, the melodramatic mode reductively diminishes an extensive canvas of gay adult social experience. Nor, despite its evocation of the AIDS era, does the play illustrate the buddy system's intermingling of friendship with estrangement. Lopez's melodrama forcibly divides one from the other.

Authentic self-discovery versus inauthenticity, sexual licence versus celibacy or monogamy, abusive predators versus abused victims – these oppositions in *The Inheritance* simplify complex matters. Baldwin's Rufus dies by suicide because alternatives such as "heal or burn" are suspended in *Another Country*, where healing and figurative burning can be conjoined, just as will and willlessness, or lovers and friends, can be one and the same. Lopez's desire to build a bridge of friendship between the gay past and present sorts badly with his characterization of Toby, who is a caricature of the immoralist outlaw in gay literary tradition (Oscar Wilde or André Gide rather than Forster). To evoke that tradition as wilfully suicidal argues a condemnation of the past, not a "dignified" fulfillment of it. Thus the playwright himself burns a gay literary inheritance. If Morgan, Eric, Walter, and Leo constitute the ideal gay friends, not to mention the meaning of queerness now, they are more than a little puritanical, and they conform, certainly in comparison with Toby and Henry, to an antithesis between asexuality and libertinism. Inasmuch as Lopez echoes that structure, he does not ask his audience to question the simplifying thrust of his play; nor does the play ask its audience or his readers to expect a critical working-through of definitions for "dignity" and "fulfillment." Although these words are heard often enough in real life, do we know what *they* mean? Artworks might be expected to do more than piously repeat them.

Reparative Proximity 2: A Little Life

In response to the limitless psychosexual crippling that Yanagihara's protagonist Jude St Francis has experienced, a preternaturally close-knit group of his friends endows him with their permanent care over the course of forty years. The friends are as much Yanagihara's subjects as Jude is. His trauma makes him yearn to kill himself; but the friends' reparative proximity keeps him alive and succeeds for decades, although not ultimately. Still, a sympathetic reader should not think that unwavering commitments among friends are pointless. When Jude was an undergraduate, he rebuffed his friends' curiosity about his troubles. Mistakenly, Jude's closest college friend, Willem, thinks "Proof of friendship [with Jude] lay in keeping your distance."[39] But in Yanagihara's novel, friendship mixing with distance – shared estrangement – is purely harmful, nearly fatal. Unremitting friendly attachment is everything. "I know *my* life's meaningful," Willem avers in maturity, "because … I'm a good friend."[40] By the time Willem makes this comment, he has long been an international movie star, and he has become Jude's husband, although he has ceased to require marital sex out of respect for Jude's enduring sexual trauma. Neither fame nor marital status is important when compared to friendship, which is the fount of Willem's patient love of Jude and the best therapy that he can provide his spouse.

Therapeutic friendship must stay close to its object. Yanagihara's narrative structure solicits a reader's attachment in the mode of reparative proximity. The friends who watch every move of Jude's, and who are always in suspense about the facts of his tortured life, are the reader's doubles. The friends do not want anything to stand in the way of nearness to the mutilated protagonist – if anything does, how can they aid Jude, or keep him alive? – so they incite Yanagihara's readers, Jude's other friends, not to want a narrative medium whose temporal unfolding and whose withheld secrets about Jude obstruct their relation to him. But the narrative piles up hundreds of pages before the history of Jude's abuse comes out. Do these pages not provoke a reader's critical distance: a suspense of attachment to the story and its protagonist, and a disinterested assessment of the authorial artifice that is at work? I do not think so. The longer Yanagihara's medium obscures Jude's history, the more it stimulates readers' impatience and the more it stirs readers' outrage that Jude's life has been deprived of fulfillment by a dreadfulness inherent in human sexuality and extending itself into a person's entire life. "Not having sex: it was one of the best things about being an adult," Jude thinks.[41] This sentiment simultaneously matches attachment theory's cautions against the dangers of sex and testifies to the traumatizing failure of caregiving that is "conducive to attachment."[42]

To show better how Yanagihara co-implicates sex, friendship, fiction, and reading in the cause of reparative proximity, I must offer a summary of *A Little Life*. Jude begins life as a racialized baby – Black or possibly Indigenous, no one knows for sure – abandoned in a dumpster at a monastery. The monks, besides raising him, abuse him physically and sexually. Brother Luke, more delicate than his confrères, grooms the boy first to escape, and then to become his lover. For years the fugitive pair live in motels across the country. To finance their expenses Luke prostitutes Jude to pederasts who spring up plentifully along the road. To alleviate the boy's shame, disgust, and guilt over coercive sex, Luke instructs Jude on how to cleanse his conscience by cutting himself with razors. Bloodletting becomes a lifelong practice; it turns Jude's arms and legs into a mass of scar tissue and ultimately leads to amputation of his lower legs. But that is later. The police, catching up with Luke, send Jude to an orphanage, where he is sexually abused. He runs away, hitching rides with truckers who demand sexual favours. Then Jude is picked up by a doctor, who locks him in a basement, and beats and rapes him. When Jude escapes, the doctor runs him down with his car, permanently injuring Jude's spine and legs. At long last, Jude is rescued by a female social worker. It so happens that, in the monastery and in the intervals between his coerced sex work, Jude has learned mathematics, several foreign languages, and many other subjects. He is brilliant. Adversity cannot prevent him from excelling.

The social worker steers Jude toward an elite college, where he meets his three lifelong friends, one of whom is Willem. Willem has lost a brother to cerebral palsy, so family history makes him prone to attach himself to disabled Jude. Another predisposition to attachment affects one of Jude's law school professors, Harold. Harold and his wife have lost their only son to severe illness; consequently, they want to adopt Jude, who consents to this unusual request even though he is an adult. Jude next becomes a dazzlingly successful corporate lawyer. Meanwhile, he is racked by pain and a guilt-ridden need to mutilate himself. He hides that mutilation as much as possible. Fortunately, another friend, a doctor, knows what Jude is doing, and for decades makes himself available for round-the-clock medical repair.

A hopeful prospect dawns when Jude finds a lover, but the lover turns out a sadist, and all but kills Jude by throwing him down a flight of stairs. Jude attempts suicide; the friends rescue him. Willem bravely risks losing film stardom by coming out as gay and moving in with Jude. Willem loves Jude because Willem's "work, his very life, was one of disguises and charades ... But to Jude, he wasn't an actor: he was his friend, and that identity supplanted everything else."[43] It supplants sex, because Willem realizes that Jude loathes it, although Jude will not disclose why. When Jude finally tells his story, Willem "stayed, unquestioningly, out of love, out of loyalty."[44] Building an upstate house as a safe space for themselves and friends, the couple becomes happy. Unfortunately, chance too is an abusive predator: Willem is killed in an automobile accident. Traumatized and victimized by sex and misfortune from first to last, Jude again prepares to kill himself.

Confronting this string of calamities, a reader might find an identification of the friends with agents of therapy as unpersuasive. Nevertheless, if *A Little Life* does provoke a mutual mirroring of characters and readers, then in imitation of Jude's friends, and in therapy-motivated response to the traumas that constitute Jude's experience, readers might well look for sources of repair for Jude's case. Outside the novel – from the list of supposed virtues available in *Howards End* and by extension in *The Inheritance* – readers might want to prescribe the keys to recovery. Inside the novel Willem and the other friends live up to those standards of "guidance," "compassion," and so forth, almost as symbols of them, without any critical authorial questioning.

Readers reaching for a reparative Forsterian inspiration would be assuming Yanagihara's novel to be reality-based and plausibly true. Certainly, it is not a specimen of a non-realistic genre. At every turn, however, the novel strains plausibility. The monastic origins of Jude's tale, the abyss of mental horror from which bleeding Jude cannot escape, the cosmic sadism that adds Willem's death to Jude's injuries, and the unqualifiedly devoted friends suggest that the novel is a gothic melodrama offering a battle between diabolical evil and angelic good.[45] Yanagihara precedes Lopez in a contemporary disjoining of elements in friendship and fiction that intermingle opposites.

An adjunct to gothic melodrama are *A Little Life*'s frequent historical anachronisms, which separate the four friends from temporal specificities. Yanagihara seems fully conscious of the pressure her weird elements put on realism. She makes Jude say that his life prior to the advent of his friends "became more improbable by the year."[46] Jude's doctor tells Willem that Jude "wants you to tell him that his life, as inconceivable as it is, is still a life … Do you know what I mean?"[47] I think he means that this novel still represents "life," inconceivable as its events might be. Given the metafictive play, Yanagihara suggests a self-reflexive meditation on fiction. If so, her novel, in the same manner as Baldwin's, is invested in a critical distance effect. Yanagihara apparently wants readers not to assume the closeness of novels to life but rather to think about the difference made to life and ordinary language by the artifice of fiction.

Yet Yanagihara toys with metafictive possibilities as if literary tradition exacted them from her without her full engagement. She does not take them to heart because they imply a detaching effect on readers that deviates from her primary objectives, namely rendering the bodily immediacy of trauma, and valuing as reparative the proximity to suffering that is exemplified by Jude's friends. The bodily immediacy – the eternal present of Jude's scarring – pushes away traditional novelistic realism's careful registration of historical times and places. One of Jude's friends, JB, is an artist. He might be read as a projection of Yanagihara because he paints scenes from the life that Yanagihara narrates. But JB portrays his friends, her characters, under the general title "Seconds, Minutes, Hours, Days." Every picture he paints documents its subjects according to *specified moments* of past time. Realism in Yanagihara, however, is reassigned to an ahistorical dimension. Ordinary historical circumstance does not endure as sexual abuse does. For example, after Willem's death, in a scene at the Whitney Museum during a retrospective of JB's work, Yanagihara undermines JB's realism. JB secretly loves Jude. When he plants a passionate kiss on Jude's lips, Jude takes it as a betrayal of Willem's memory, and faints. Is this event to be read as an authorial notice that no representational realism, such as JB's, can come close to, or repair, the actuality of violation?

If the museum scene is a critical distance effect, Yanagihara does not develop it. She wants her reader to feel her art more than think about it. Her melodramatic contrivances sort with a vision of life that Davis and Dean call "traumatological": it "divides the world into abuser-predators and survivor-victims, simplifying social reality into … the melodramatic play of opposites."[48] Even Jude's friends, as delegates for attached readers, become survivor-victims of the monks and their kind, because the friends cannot escape their reparative vocation, hence cannot escape an indirect abuse of their own lives by the predators. But the friends' constraint does not mean they share anything with their opposite numbers, in the way that friendship is intermingled with estrangement, or with other unfriendly phenomena, in Baldwin, Blanchot, Foucault, or Roach. Nor are Jude's friends ever, or rarely ever, of two minds about Jude's inability to love himself or to reward their pains. Single-minded attachment to him is their heroism.

But "single-minded" is an insufficiently "feeling" term for what Jude and his friends and their readers are invited to be aligned with. Characteristically, Yanagihara heightens her normally efficient sentences at explosive or repulsive moments so that closeness to violent and violating sensation will absorb reader-response. Jude is described as "so lonely that he sometimes feels it physically, a sodden clump of dirty laundry pressing against his chest. He cannot unlearn the feeling."[49] For the reader to continue learning the feeling seems Yanagihara's aim, as a way of inspiring reparative reaction. Because Jude's self-cutting distorts his body, he thinks he resembles a particularly deformed client he was once subjected to. "He doesn't want someone [who looks at him] to have to stand before the toilet retching, as he had done after [servicing that deformed client], scooping handfuls of liquid soap into his mouth, gagging at the taste" (347). The reader might well retch in sympathetic attachment to Jude.

At the Whitney exhibition Jude sees a picture of himself telling a story to Willem. He "feels his breath abandon him; it feels as if his heart is made of something oozing and cold, like ground meat, and it is being squeezed inside a fist so that chunks of it are falling, plopping to the ground near his feet."[50] For a reader's response to distance itself critically from this – for example, to assess the writing by suggesting the sloppy repetition of the word "ground," and the banal rhyme of "meat" and "feet" – would put the reader out of alignment with Jude and his friends. Trauma matters, not style, not genre. After Jude's death, his adoptive parents discover a written document that Jude has hidden among their books. This narrative reveals to them for the first time the entire history that the reader already knows. Jude's parents are overwhelmed; but faithful readers as they are, despite all apparently impassable distance, his father thinks that he, the friends, dead Jude, and dead Willem too, are "closer" than might appear.[51] Closeness models the ideal reader of *A Little Life*: a close reader who is an empathetic reader-friend, not an analytically distanced one.[52]

Critical Distance 2: The Group

Authorial joy in analysis permeates Mary McCarthy's treatment of the Vassar graduates, who are all classmates and who compose the circle of friends in *The Group*. One analytic mainstay for McCarthy is free indirect discourse. Yanagihara also uses the device, but she does not foreground its ability to combine fidelity with freedom from its source. In contrast, McCarthy exploits the device's combination of distance and nearness. Her free indirect discourse tends to emphasize an external narrator who is at a remove – often a critical remove – from the discursive origin, even as the sentences mimic that origin. In the following example, free indirect discourse renders a description by one classmate of another classmate's lover. The other classmate is Polly; her lover is a publisher who charges a Communist Party member (the novel takes place in the 1930s) with the seduction of the publisher's wife. "Up to now, he [the publisher] had been pretty pink himself but never a party member, and he had brought several important authors who were Communist sympathizers to the firm, but now the Communists were turning a cold shoulder to him because he wanted to divorce his wife and name this other man, which they called a 'splitting tactic' or something."[53]

Gossipy offhandedness indicates a dubious imprecision in the speaker and even in the external narrator's reporting. A sudden uncertainty about reliability offers the reader an occasion for reflective detachment from the narrative's immediacy. A "splitting tactic" is indeed at work – a novelistic one. To dramatize this split self-reflexively, McCarthy writes it large in the communication style of group member Helena Davison: "Her mother's habit of underlining or stressing her words had undergone an odd mutation in … Helena. Where Mrs Davison stressed and emphasized, Helena inserted *her* words carefully between inverted commas, so that clauses, phrases, and even proper names … had the sound of ironical quotations."[54] Free indirect discourse can sound like ironical quotation. McCarthy exploits that sound, and produces an additional splitting: "While everything Mrs Davison said seemed to carry with it a guarantee of authority, everything Helena said seemed subject to the profoundest doubt."[55] Straddling authority and doubt, even in a single sentence, narrative rhetoric shapes one's reading of *The Group* into a form of critical distance. Irony undoes melodramatic antitheses, and makes it possible for estrangement and attachment – among McCarthy's characters and among a reader's alignments – to be compatible despite their differences.

McCarthy's splitting tactic is motivated by a desire to oppose the rigidities inherent in generalizing ideologies, especially in systematic discourse that impacts partisanships, personal trauma, sex, and, of course, friendship. Norine, an arch-leftist classmate, illustrates the simplifying partisanship from which *The Group* alienates us as we read. Norine's "emotions" and intellectual claims, the narrator reports, "had a topical resonance, even when she touched on the intimate"; in her living quarters "nothing had been admitted that did not make a 'relevant' statement.'"[56] Although McCarthy registers her hostility to Norine's relevance-addiction, McCarthy nevertheless does not make her text an authoritative criticism of 1930s American leftism.[57] Priss, a young wife and mother, impels McCarthy's close sympathy, because her generous attachment to the New Deal is derided by her mean-spirited husband. He is a careerist pediatrician who terrorizes his wife with demands that she breastfeed rather than bottle-feed their infant, because breastfeeding is natural – for him. Yet McCarthy also renders Priss from a critical distance. "Finally we are going to have a scientific picture of the child,"[58] Priss enthuses about her husband's destructive work, which is the very same science that harrows her.

By referring to the trauma of Priss's maternity, I have medicalized it and suggested a need for a therapeutic solution to her misery. Although McCarthy does not underestimate Priss's pain or the emotional suffering of any of her characters, she tends to satirize therapy, especially psychiatry. Opposing attitudes toward therapy emerge by juxtaposing *The Group* with *The Inheritance* and *A Little Life*. Polly's classmate Kay, whose wedding sets the narrative in motion and whose death, apparently by suicide, is its penultimate event, becomes a victim of psychiatric treatment when her husband manipulates medical protocols so that he can confine her temporarily in a hospital ward. Meanwhile, Polly's publisher-lover Gus undergoes psychoanalytic therapy, with immobilizing consequences for him and with maddening consequences for her. Polly cannot tell which aspects of Gus's therapy are revelatory and reparative, and which are not. She imagines that she herself embodies every "charted neurosis."[59] At the same time, she views "this alarming picture with humorous fascination,"[60] even though she worries that the fascination is another sign of her illness.

Humorous fascination, alternating with melancholy, is another example of McCarthy's critical distance effect. It is humorous that a psychiatry-hating psychiatrist frees Polly from her mental labyrinths, and then marries her. McCarthy seems to hate psychiatry as much as he does. But he wants to become an independent researcher into the causes of "mental illness": he remains committed to the medical discipline he has rejected. His author does not suggest that his commitment disqualifies him as a model of behaviour. What McCarthy criticizes in one part of her textual weave, she endorses in another. Her reader must befriend that flexibility.

That flexibility, I would say, suggests an intellectual courage in the writer and the writer's hoped-for reader, not an incitement to impatience with distance effects. Impatience when it comes to the fictional treatment of sex seems on the rise nowadays. *The Inheritance* envisions a support-group-like gay community as superior to *eros*. *A Little Life* contains no explicit representations of sexual acts, except those that cry out for curative relief from disgust and guilt. In tandem with demands in attachment theory for "sexual safety,"[61] Lopez and Yanagihara invite audiences or readers to see the justice of a newly acceptable restraint upon desire. Why brook contradictory, self-distancing points of view when community identity and reparative proximity are the most needful solutions to current gay problems, if not essential to what it means to be gay in the contemporary moment? Even shared estrangement, it appears, is no longer attractive.

Unlike Lopez's and Yanagihara's, McCarthy's views remain buoyantly multiple. Her representation of Dottie Renfrew's willing loss of virginity is another of mid-century American writing's great things. It holds the reader close to it, perhaps in the service of partisanship with women's sexual liberation; it expresses sadness at Dottie's subsequent retreat from unregulated sexual pleasure, typified by the admirable libertine whom she asks to "seduce" her. Yet the worst character of all, Kay's actor-playwright husband, is excoriated for his libertinage. Evaluative and representational perspectives in McCarthy are to be read case by case. The lesbian finale of *The Group* is the ultimate illustration of what I have been meaning. Lakey, an art historian and the originator of the group (she is, like McCarthy, its author), is absent in Europe until late in the novel. When she returns to the US, she brings her lesbian lover, the Baroness, in tow. Lakey's classmates do not know how to take this development because Lakey and her partner do not conform to their assumptions about grouping.

Does a group of women suggest a closely uniform identity? Do lesbians constitute a uniform identity, with unvarying attributes, emotions, and claims, along the lines of Norine's "relevant statements"? To the surprise of Polly and Helena, Lakey and the Baroness enjoy the company of the Vassar classmates who are not lesbians; they also adore their classmates' children. After Kay's funeral, Lakey, who has always despised Kay's lying husband, has a showdown with him. This showdown resolves the text with a queer triumph. The widower tries to impress upon Lakey that he is suicidal (one of his frequent put-ons), and he pressures her: did she not once sleep with Kay? Did she not "corrupt the whole group"? Lakey does not answer, and, by her maintenance of a silent distance, subtly manipulates him "at last to be truthful ... he revealed a hatred of 'abnormality.'"[62] Lakey's critical distance brings the truth forward; simultaneously, the narrative takes its distance from "abnormality" by placing it inside quotation marks and thus marking its questionable meaning.

There is affinity between McCarthy and Baldwin in their attachment to a doubleness of perspective that is characteristic of critical distance. Baldwin's framing visions of race and sex are paramount for him, but no less paramount are the individual relations that he shows moving beyond those frameworks. What is communal is fissured by what is individual and vice versa. Ideologies in both novelists' works depend upon groupings – historical, sociological, sexual, psychological – and upon close friendships. But a group or a friendship is not more solidly definable than Eric's self in *Another Country*, or than McCarthy's narrative form in *The Group*. In McCarthy's novel, narrative is deliberately disjunctive; friends have limited knowledge of each other, even though they assume otherwise.

A group or a friendship is not the closely unified, unqualified companionability suggested by Lopez and Yanagihara. Indeed, Lopez and Yanagihara want to repair or therapeutize the novelistic effects that McCarthy and Baldwin rely on. For those mid-century novelists, meanings, like friendships, intermingle with their opposites while remaining separate. McCarthy and Baldwin align readers by turns with that intermingling and with that detachment. It would be a mistake to think that the strategies in *Another Country* and *The Group* and their effects on readers require a cure, or that the best way to approach those fictions is to judge them now in the light of reparative proximity.

NOTES

1 Rita Felski, *Hooked: Art and Attachment* (Chicago: University of Chicago Press, 2020), 29.

2 Ibid., 94–5.

3 Matthew Lopez, *The Inheritance* (London: Faber, 2020), 83.

4 Tom Roach, *Friendship as a Way of Life: Foucault, AIDS, and the Politics of Shared Estrangement* (Albany: SUNY Press, 2012), 95; emphasis added.

5 Ibid., 95.

6 Ibid., 63.

7 Oliver Davis and Tim Dean, *Hatred of Sex* (Lincoln: University of Nebraska Press, 2022), 99.

8 Ibid., 89.

9 Ibid., 116–17.

10 James Baldwin, *Early Novels and Stories*, ed. Toni Morrison (New York: Library of America, 1998), 410. In this and subsequent quotations, italics are Baldwin's.

11 Ibid., 376.

12 Ibid., 429.

13 I use "reparative proximity" in a far different sense from Sedgwick's powerful plea for "reparative cultural practices" (128). In 2003 and before, Sedgwick sought repair from literary criticism's over-reliance on "strong theory" (133). Therapeutic versions of repair have become a new strong theory. Among those versions I include the alignments that accompany what I call "reparative proximity." Eve Kosofsky Sedgwick, "Paranoid Reading and Reparative Reading, Or,

You're So Paranoid, You Probably Think This Essay Is About You," in *Touching Feeling: Affect, Pedagogy, Performativity* (Durham: Duke University Press, 2003), 123–51.

14 Baldwin, *Novels and Stories*, 635.

15 Ibid., 466.

16 Ibid., 484.

17 Ibid., 511.

18 Ibid., 680.

19 Ibid., 713.

20 Ibid., 661–2.

21 Ibid., 664. Freeburg argues that love in Baldwin's novel is "crucial to identity-making" (181), and that it is generally reparative and redemptive. Christopher Freeburg, "Baldwin and the Occasion of Love," in *The Cambridge Companion to James Baldwin*, ed. Michele Elam (Cambridge: Cambridge University Press, 2015), 180–93.

22 Baldwin, *Novels and Stories*, 668.

23 Ibid., 636.

24 Ibid.

25 Ibid., 729.

26 Levine implicitly argues for such open-minded "reading practice" because it must "address the extraordinary density of forms that is a fact of our … daily experience" (22). Caroline Levine, *Forms: Whole, Rhythm, Hierarchy, Network* (Princeton: Princeton University Press, 2015).

27 Lopez, *Inheritance*, 9.

28 Ibid.

29 Ibid., 200.

30 Ibid., 201.

31 Baldwin, *Novels and Stories*, 664.

32 Lopez, *Inheritance*, 143.

33 Ibid., 219–20.

34 Ibid., 38.

35 Ibid., 260.

36 Ibid., 265.

37 Ibid., 286.

38 Davis and Dean, *Hatred of Sex*, 108.

39 Hanya Yanagihara, *A Little Life* (New York: Anchor, 2016), 84.

40 Ibid., 779.

41 Ibid., 346.

42 Davis and Dean, *Hatred of Sex*, 104.

43 Yanagihara, *A Little Life*, 495.

44 Ibid., 586.

45 According to Peter Brooks, melodrama and the gothic novel "nourish one another" (17). My assessment of *A Little Life* ranges me alongside Daniel Mendelsohn, whose controversial review of the novel focused on the ethical and aesthetic gratuitousness of its cruelty. Daniel Mendelsohn, "A Striptease among Pals," review of *A Little Life*, by Hanya Yanagihara, *New York Review of Books*, 3 December 2015.

46 Yanagihara, *A Little Life*, 635.

47 Ibid., 639.

48 Davis and Dean, *Hatred of Sex*, 137, 138.

49 Yanagihara, *A Little Life*, 346.

50 Ibid., 770.

51 Ibid., 814.

52 Herring and I equally oppose the impact of "modern therapeutic ideals" (136) as they are presented in *A Little Life*. Yet Herring's strong reading of Yanagihara is antithetical to mine. He sees her novel as critical of the supposed health of rigidly committed attachments. I might be better persuaded if the novel's writing were distinguished, and without the novel's dependence on bathos. Scott Herring, "Never Better: Queer Commitment Phobia in Hanya Yanagihara's *A Little Life*," in *Long Term: Essays on Queer Commitment*, ed. Scott Herring and Lee Wallace (Durham: Duke University Press, 2021), 134–54.

53 Mary McCarthy, *The Group* (1963; New York: Houghton Mifflin Harcourt, 1982), 270.

54 Ibid., 139.

55 Ibid.

56 Ibid., 162.

57 In 1963, Norman Mailer attacked *The Group* in *New York Review of Books* because he thought McCarthy had betrayed the radical political hopes of the 1930s. For a corrective view, see Justin Mitchell, "Norman Mailer and 'The Mary McCarthy Case' Revisited," *Post45*, no. 4 (2020), post45.org/2020/01/norman-mailer-and-the-mary-mccarthy-case-revisited/.

58 McCarthy, *Group*, 441.

59 Ibid., 337.
60 Ibid.
61 Davis and Dean, *Hatred of Sex*, 93.
62 McCarthy, *Group*, 486.

11

The European Generation X Novel

BARRY MCCREA

Knausgaard or Ferrante?

The epigraph to Virginie Despentes's (born 1969) *Vernon Subutex* is taken from one of Horace's odes: *Non omnis moriar*, "I will not entirely die."[1] The relevance of the epigraph to the three-volume novel that follows is not immediately clear. The novel recounts the adventures of the eponymous Vernon, who back in the 1990s owned a record store called "Revolver." Now in the 2010s, his business long displaced by streaming services, Vernon finds himself scraping by on state benefits and hustling for lodgings, drugs, and money in an increasingly expensive and hostile Paris. The epigraph retrospectively draws our attention to what the novel truly – and seemingly incidentally – evokes: the cultural soup of the late 1980s and 1990s in which Vernon and his friends were cooked. Like the kind of business Vernon used to run, that world is long vanished. Despentes, in the long and often hilarious digressions and flashbacks that characterize the novel, brings that vanished world back to life. The epigraph is a guide to her achievement: less the portrait of an individual psychology and more the rendering in artistic form of a collective, generational experience that might otherwise go unrecorded. To record it, however, is not simply a matter of content: different times require or create different aesthetic forms and the novel's whole shape and narrative system have been wrought for, or by, the times that it recounts.

"The great poet in writing himself, writes his time," says T.S. Eliot with reference to Shakespeare and Dante.[2] For Eliot, whose own work, of course, reveals some unexamined and sometimes unappetizing aspects of the political and cultural climate that surrounded him, this idea was fundamental. When writing about the poetry of his hero John Donne, Eliot states, "what appears at one time a curious personal point of view may at another time appear rather the precise concentration of feeling diffused in the air about him."[3] No matter how much writers try to seal themselves off from the present – by reclusion, migration, the inward training of attention, or the imitation of Old Masters – the spirit of their age will always find a crack through which to leak onto the page and alter the form of the work of art. It is perhaps when writers do not harbour ambitions to capture a historical moment or represent a zeitgeist that they are most convinced they are plumbing lonely, private depths, and the economic and cultural winds that blow around the world outside the writer's room exert their most interesting effects on a literary work.

In a critique of Amitav Ghosh's call for novels depicting climate change, Kate Marshall suggests that social, political, and environmental circumstances might most meaningfully manifest themselves in novels when the writer is not deliberately setting out to address them: "An alternative beginning of the project [of depicting climate change in fiction] would be to make a stronger case for the literature of the twentieth and twenty-first centuries whose response to systematic change may not be overt but rather subtly and insistently present, and to look not only for the primary genres of climate fiction but rather their hybrid traces in novels not otherwise considered within that frame."[4] In other words, we should not look at what novels talk about but at how they work, what kind of narrative fuel they draw down from the real world in order to keep their plot engines running.

Critics have identified in the novels of the Irish author Sally Rooney (born 1991) something specific to her generation, that cohort born between the early 1980s and mid-1990s, known as "millennials." In fact, Rooney has been called the "first great millennial author."[5] Outside the English-speaking world, other millennial writers have produced novels that resemble Rooney's. What promises to be a more radical and exciting leap in novelistic form, however, is beginning to emerge, belatedly and, it seems, spontaneously, on the European continent, among the generation of writers preceding Rooney's. A set of striking structural affinities can be identified across a great number of novels written in the past decade or so by writers from various continental countries who were born between the late 1960s and early 1980s. "Generation X" is a demographic squeezed between, and often overshadowed by, baby boomers and millennials. Douglas Coupland coined the term in his novel of the same name to designate the children of the baby boomers whose economic prospects were poorer than those of their parents. Where the boomers were enthusiastic insiders in the social order, propelled by ambition, sincerity, and optimism, Generation X is characterized, in Coupland's account, by disaffection, detachment, and irony.

Coupland's novel diagnoses a particularly North American predicament. Both the historical background – Watergate, crack, yuppies, Reaganomics – and the cultural references are from 1970s and 1980s US and Canada. In Western Europe, those of the post-boomer generation came of age with the fall of the Berlin Wall, the anti-globalization protests in Genoa, Interrail passes, and U2. They are the first generation to grow up with the European Union as an established pole of identity and belonging. It is also a generation that has often seen itself excluded from academic, political, and cultural institutions, with the casualization of labour and intellectual work in particular. In general, this generation has an exceptionally high level of education but a low expectation of socio-economic advancement. It is a cohort in which long-term professional precarity is extremely common. Coupland invents the word "McJobs" to describe their mode of employment.

While there have been some individual European writers born in the 1970s who have achieved recognition and success, this collective experience seemed, until recently, not to have coalesced into an identifiable literary mode. There are signs now that in Western Europe this is changing: a highly distinctive form of the Gen X novel is emerging. Its structural system and narrative orientation are in striking accord with contemporary political, economic, and ecological concerns, even when – maybe especially when – they are not explicitly addressed in the plot. The combination of educational achievement and economic precarity characteristic of European Gen X (notably though by no means exclusively in Italy) might seem to lend itself perfectly to the picaresque. But the emergent Gen X novelistic typology cleaves instead to techniques proper to classical epic: high, formal literary language; long digressions, cut-aways, and extended metaphors that undermine or even usurp the chronological progression of the plot; the evocation of a shared cultural world, its habits and rituals; an emphasis on comradeship rather than family as the sustaining, structuring model of human connection.

Some of these devices are present in Coupland's *Generation X*, but in a very different form. It is as though the sardonic pop-culture references, which characterize the dialogue in Coupland's novel, have been turned inside out: the emphasis on knowingness and on a shared cultural pool is there, but the irony has become an epic yearning, and the referential field now stretches far beyond 1980s television, not only forward to the twenty-first century but also in the other direction, all the way back to the classical tradition.

While this European Gen X mode seems not to have been adopted thus far by novelists in the English-speaking world, its distinctiveness has registered itself in anglophone literary tastes. In 2015, Joshua Rothman published an article in the *New Yorker* entitled "Knausgaard or Ferrante?"[6] Deliberately echoing George Steiner's 1959 essay, *Tolstoy or Dostoevsky*, Rothman compares two serial novels then enjoying a popular success in the English-speaking world unheard of for literary fiction in translation: Karl Ove Knausgaard's six-volume *Min Kamp* (*My Struggle*)[7] and Elena Ferrante's four-volume *L'amica geniale* (*My Brilliant Friend*). (In Italian the title refers both to the first volume and to the whole series; in English, the four volumes are collectively referred to as *The Neapolitan Novels*.) *My Struggle* and *My Brilliant Friend* have a good deal in common: a rootedness in European history and literature; serial form; an insistent focus on articulate, introspective writer-protagonists fascinated by their own story; an interest in parental conflict and trans-generational change.

As Rothman argues, the two books also "embody opposed values."[8] Rothman maps out a set of polarities, some of them concrete aspects of their setting, "snow over sun, anger over awkwardness, herring over prosciutto, women over men, the north over the south, 1955 over 1985," and others more abstract, "spirituality or materiality; the unseen or what's right in front of you; the unknowable world or the world as it is."[9] From a structural point of view, the difference between the two writers in what we might term "narrative orientation" is keyed to another binary not on Rothman's list – the generational sensibility of the baby boomers (Ferrante) and that of Generation X (Knausgaard). This fundamentally different disposition to narrative time, the fictional shaping of the human life, the lasting form of relationships, is most readily identified through the vastly different structural role of friendship in the two novelists. Rothman considers Ferrante the novelist of friendship and Knausgaard the novelist of solitude. In fact, although the theme is signalled much more overtly in Ferrante's series, Knausgaard's often gloomy, self-involved narrative is, in a quieter way, thoroughly built upon and sustained by friendship, through childhood companions who disappear and reappear, and through the memory of shared escapades and experiences.

The simultaneous success of Ferrante and Knausgaard in the 2010s is proof that at junctures of social and economic transition (or perhaps any given historical moment) different artistic modes coexist and conflict with each other. The comparison between the two writers, especially in their treatment of friendship, shows, moreover, how the form of the novel is inseparably connected to economic life. The radically different approach to narrative and time that distinguishes Ferrante from Knausgaard gives force to the contention that the novel is the genre of the middle classes, and as the destiny of the middle classes changes, the form of the novel changes with it.

Class, Friendship, and the Novel

The novel is the literary form that classically narrates economic mobility and with it, a parallel process of psychological and cultural development. Friendship – in the sense of disinterested bonds maintained over long periods of time – is a key device through which these transformations can be measured. Patricia Highsmith's *The Talented Mr Ripley* offers an instructive if dark version of this process, the plot proceeding according to a narrative logic of zero-sum success: for one of the two friends to thrive, the other must be obliterated.

This aspect is at the forefront of the action in *The Talented Mr Ripley* – the intertwining of the concepts of friendship and social mobility is the overt plot of the novel. In a novel like Dickens's (1812–1870) *Great Expectations*, its presence is much more subtle. Pip's rise in social and economic status, from rural blacksmith's apprentice to London man-about-town, is dramatically triggered by a mysterious inheritance. His change in class, however, is quietly preceded by something that has nothing to do with Magwitch or Miss Havisham or Jaggers: his acquisition of literacy. Pip's learning to read the newspaper is what first sets him apart from the labouring class into which he is born. From that early point, long before Pip receives any money, the plot of the novel has already begun its slide down the inexorable slope of middle-class *Bildung*. By the end of the novel, the feudal magic will turn out to be a red herring, and Pip's living ultimately will be made through clerking and trade rather than fantastical bequests. The power of bourgeois values is, in a way, one of the novel's final revelations.

This aspect of the novel's socio-economic meaning is underscored by a discreet subplot, which otherwise has very little import to the action: Pip's friendship with Herbert Pocket. Friendship in the excitable Freudian universe of *Great Expectations* is generally an unstable phenomenon, always at risk of spilling over into other kinds of relations – erotic, genetic, mercenary, juridical. Pip's quiet, dispassionate friendship with Herbert is the most constant and most consistently sustained human connection in the novel. Its unobtrusive but key role as a same-generation affinity is perhaps suggested in the wording of the opening passage, when Pip imagines that his dead brothers "had all been born on their backs with their hands in their trousers-pockets, and had never taken them out in this state of existence."[10] It is the only relationship to last fully intact from Pip's introduction to Satis House through to his childless middle age.

Other characters appear and disappear, like spirits showering luck, shame, desire, and suffering upon the protagonist with each entrance and exit, psychoanalytical manifestations who remain largely unchanged and untouched by time. The slow, steady, undramatic evolution of the friendship with Herbert, by contrast, is what actually gives the measure of Pip's changing circumstances and personality, and it is Herbert who provides Pip with the means to achieve a long-term livelihood. Herbert trains Pip as a bourgeois and teaches him middle-class manners, as when he advises that "in London it is not the custom to put the knife in the mouth."[11] Pip's dashed dreams of aristocratic love and enrichment, along with the counter-plot of his lifelong friendship with Herbert, take place against the backdrop of a general swelling of the ranks of the English middle classes and spread of bourgeois culture in the mid- and late nineteenth century. More than any other character in the novel, Herbert is the one responsible for the embourgeoisement of Pip's personality and tastes. In this, we might conclude that Herbert represents the regime of the novel, that he is a representative of its key Victorian values of progress and improvement.

In twentieth-century, continental Western Europe, the most rapid and far-reaching expansion of the middle classes took place in the decades following the Second World War. This period of economic development, social progress, and cultural change is known in Germany as the *Wirtschaftswunder*, in Italy as *il miracolo economico*, and in France as *les trente glorieuses*, with reference to the thirty "glorious" years of growth and material improvement between 1950 and 1980. From the point of view of the novel, the most important aspect of the postwar European boom is something ineffable in the air: an unquestioned expectation of improvement in one's social or economic circumstances, the assumption that one would, or at least could, become both richer and more cultured than one's parents. Formal education, widely available to an advanced level for the first time after the war, was an engine for both economic advancement and self-cultivation. The European postwar boom, like the industrial and commercial expansion in Victorian England, thus offered a socio-economic framework perfectly suited to the novel, a unified timeline in which cultural and financial enrichment are nicely bound together in a future- and growth-oriented temporality.

It is hard to imagine a more symptomatic novel of the European postwar boom than Ferrante's *Bildungsroman*, published between 2011 and 2014. The friendship plot that structures the novel deals with two girls from the same deprived neighbourhood of Naples. In parallel trajectories, they make their way from the 1950s to the twenty-first century. The savage logic of friendship in *The Talented Mr. Ripley* is present in a concealed, subliminal form in Ferrante's serial novel: one friend makes a rapid, dazzling escape from their semi-literate, dialect-speaking slum into the literary and academic circles of the prosperous, Italian-speaking *haute bourgeoisie* of the north; the other remains trapped in Naples, in poverty, dialect, and organized crime. Both are naturally "brilliant." Nonetheless, the success of the protagonist is gauged by the failure of her friend.

The initial chapters are focused on the girls' grades at school, with detailed comparisons of their relative abilities, their strengths, their weaknesses, the results they achieve in exams, the favour they find or fail to find with their teachers. Part of Ferrante's immense talent as a storyteller is to make these dramas of childhood seem urgent and real, especially, in the earlier volumes, the question of whether or not the girls will stay on in school. It feels intrinsic to the logic of the novel from the outset that only one of them will be allowed to remain and complete her education: this is not a friendship of similarity, but of exemplary contrast. The narrator, Elena, nicknamed Lenù, remains in school. She goes to the *liceo classico* in the city centre, then wins a scholarship to university in Pisa. With these accomplishments in hand, she becomes something of a player in national, Italian-speaking culture, by working first as a journalist, and then as a novelist. She is the one who tells the story. Lila, left behind in a Neapolitan life of manual and precarious employment, has a life history only accessible to us at one remove, through Lenù's account of events.

The order of events in the novel is strictly chronological, often keyed to school, examinations, diplomas, ranks in state institutions. A linguistic trajectory closely tracks this socio-economic plot. In the first volume, learning to speak Italian in school is the first sign of the two girls distancing themselves from the proletarian sphere of their parents. They are gradually initiated into Italian, which they learn as a school subject along with reading, writing, Latin, history, geography, and mathematics. Dialect in Ferrante's novel represents the life-world that has to be left behind to enter the middle classes, to become someone whose voice is intelligible to readers of novels. Yet Neapolitan barely appears in the book at all. All four volumes, including all of the childhood dialogue, are rendered in unremarkable, plain standard Italian.

This "dubbing" of the dialect conversations has the effect of highlighting the radically retrospective quality of the narrative. Since it is written in Italian – the mastery of which is the great goal of the narrator from the start – the novel's very existence is predicated on the narrator's having left behind both of these worlds, childhood and the proletariat, on her growing richer and more refined as she grows older. The novel has no interest in recreating the lost linguistic universe of childhood, nor in giving readers a taste of the idiomatic colour of Lila and Lenù's shared past. There is no need to: the book can draw all the energy it requires from the progress of the plot. Narrative momentum comes from the breathless dash into ever more exalted social, cultural, and economic domains. Indeed, the book is sustained by the unmistakable and exhilarating sense that we are always headed in a *direction*. This innate sense of forward, directed movement moving in a direction, foundational to the expectations and rhythm of the boomer *Bildungsroman*, is precisely what the Gen X novel is going to have to build a meaningful narrative world without.

The purpose of friendship in Ferrante's novel is not to explore psychological dynamics but rather to frame socio-economic possibilities. Lila, the friend who does not rise in status, also learns Latin, Italian, history, literature, and philosophy, but her education does not permit her to alter her social class or substantially improve her economic conditions. Lila's failure to rise in society not only highlights Lenù's dizzying upwards trajectory, it also, in a sense, narrativizes it. The contrast between the two girls' lives, increasingly pronounced as the novel goes on, is an encapsulation of the capitalist, boom-time logic of the world shaping their fates: competition, rivalry, getting ahead. The ambiguity of the novel's title – which of them is really the brilliant friend? – suggests that this question is at the heart of the story's meaning.

European Generation X Epic

The form of Ferrante's project, with its frame of a contrastive friendship, seems to derive from the socio-economic context of the *miracolo economico*, which it narrates, rather than that of the decade (the 2010s) in which it was written. At the time of the novel's composition, the economic miracle is long over; boom has been replaced by crisis and austerity. Mass schooling is still there, of course, and much more widely available than ever, but it is no longer so tightly bound to the promise of *improvement*. Italians born after the mid-1960s can in no way take the possibility of economic or social advancement as a given.

As with all artistic grammars, however, the boomer novel is both a product of a specific historical moment, and an aesthetic framework, which is available, at any time, for a writer to employ. One does not have to be writing about boom time to use a boomer narrative template. The millennial novel seems in some respects to double down on the boomer template of protagonists born in benighted provinces. Marked out by individual talent, they excel in school and are thereby granted entry into glittering cultural and literary worlds. Rooney is not alone in – apparently anachronistically – employing this form. The autobiographical novel *En finir avec Eddy Bellegueule*,[12] by the French writer Édouard Louis (born 1992), is an example of millennial form in the French tradition of autofiction. The novel recounts the narrator's escape from poverty and ignorance in small-town Picardy for a brighter destiny elsewhere. School and university are the key agents of this change, although, as in Ferrante's and Rooney's novels, native "brilliance" is given most of the credit. The narrator briefly mentions the Picard dialect spoken around him during his impoverished youth, but, as with Neapolitan in Ferrante, it does not make its way into the novel, which is all in a fairly plain, standard French. On the way up, the protagonist or author has erased all traces of dialect.

En finir avec Eddy Bellegueule is fuelled by the same forward momentum as appears in *L'amica geniale* and Sally Rooney's *Normal People*, in which age, social status, and cultural capital all grow in concert. The narrative has no need for temporal tricks, extended metaphors, linguistic colour, or experimentation. The rapid movement of the plot – cliff-hangers, desires, expectations, promises, rewards – is enough to keep the momentum of the story going. In Louis's novel, while there is no opposite-number friend, as there is in Ferrante's or Rooney's texts, the cameo parts played by classmates and contemporaries all appear under the sign of rivalry, exemplars of failure to escape or to improve. Their function in the narrative is largely, like the ugly sisters in "Cinderella," to highlight the narrator's glorious ascent. (In one scene, school bullies go from spitting on him in corridors to cheering him ecstatically for his local theatre performance in a play he wrote himself.)

As the title of *Conversations with Friends* suggests, friendship is much more explicitly central to the work of Sally Rooney.[13] In Rooney's novels, as in Ferrante's and Louis's, friendship is not really a theme or a concept to be explored. It is rather a structural device to give expression to the question of winning and losing that animates the plots. Rooney's prose is straightforward and unadorned. It does not go in for lyrical flights or colourful metaphor. Although there are inventive and surprising jumps in time, in general these move only forward, and the narrative eschews temporally complicating flashbacks, parentheses, or digressions.

As with Picard patois in *En finir avec Eddy Bellegueule* and Neapolitan in *L'amica geniale*, the vernacular energy of Rooney's Irish settings, whether Dublin or the west of Ireland, is almost entirely absent in the prose, other than in an occasional turn of phrase. The novels are driven by a plot dynamic of growth, purpose, and promise. The question of winning that propels the plot informs the text at every level, even in minor scenes. Characters are forever "winning" or "losing" conversations, debates, games of pool; the comparison of results in school and university exams is a matter of constant, serious discussion. The title *My Brilliant Friend* would have worked just as well for *Normal People*: at the end, there is only room for one of the two brilliant friends to "make it." *Normal People* ends with Connell being accepted to study creative writing at NYU, thus entering, like Pip or Lenù or Édouard Louis, the class of persons who speak the language of the novel.

In these novels, there is plenty of discussion about economics and politics among the characters. In Ferrante's serial novel, characters become left-wing militants, Communist journalists, members of parliament. In Rooney's, long exchanges, both in conversation and via email, are given over to Marxist critiques of late capitalism. In each case, however, politics is confined to the realm of thematic content. From a structural point of view, the underlying narrative model is one of growth, expansion, and development. Rooney, Ferrante, and Louis, each in their own way, use friendship to frame all aspects of life as competition – who is the prettiest, smartest, most successful, who does best in an exam, who picks the wrong husbands, who moves to New York or Pisa, who gets left behind in the sticks.

Millennial novelists' use of the boomer form is on the face of it a puzzling phenomenon. The glittering world of well-off academics and writers, which seems to be implicitly promised to the winner-protagonists of Sally Rooney and Édouard Louis, no longer exists in the early twenty-first century as it did for Ferrante's protagonists in the 1960s and 1970s. Louis and Rooney seem to cling to a form that is at odds with the actual circumstances of their contemporaries. (While Rooney's childhood took place during Ireland's belated economic boom of 1995–2008, her college years took place in the subsequent, devastating crash.)

Unlike Ferrante, whose plot arc brings its characters from childhood in the 1950s to old age in the 2000s, these millennial novels, naturally, leave off while their protagonists are still young. Both *Normal People* and *En finir avec Eddy Bellegueule* end with a protagonist receiving an acceptance letter that will bring them into artistic institutions: creative writing in New York for Connell in *Normal People*, a theatre program in Amiens for Eddy. "A way to distance myself even more from the village," Eddy the narrator explains.[14] We do not know anything of their lives after this moment of glorious promise; unlike Ferrante's these are not narratives of adult achievement. The boomer mode may be a useful template to capture the feeling of youthful promise and potential, the feeling that the world consists of plentiful and varied opportunities.

For Gen X novelists in their forties and fifties, however, this narrative template cannot possibly work. The promises that bubbled around their own youth in the 1990s have long fizzled out. As they finished formal education, Gen-Xers have had a much harder time than their boomer parents in converting their education into institutional power and recognition, economic wealth, or cultural capital. For the Italian generation that followed the boomers, the fate of Lila is more resonant than that of Lenù. Lenù sees herself and her friends move seamlessly from brilliant educations in their youth to an adulthood in which they occupy the key positions in the cultural, intellectual, and political life of modern Italy. Lila, equally brilliant in school, does not get to transform this talent into economic security or adult institutional recognition. Her head is full of Latin and history and maths, but her working life and her circle of acquaintance are characterized by precarious employment and ephemeral money-making schemes.

Gen X Expectations

In Italy, even more starkly than in other western countries, Generation X has been denied the institutional and economic rewards of adulthood. The stable employment on offer in the 1970s and 1980s has dwindled. It has become particularly difficult to make a living through intellectual or artistic pursuits. So many of those who entered the labour market in the 1990s or early 2000s have spent their lives in sporadic, uncertain jobs that they are known collectively as the *precariato*, the precariat. Intellectual, journalistic, and creative industries in Italy are now dominated by casual, limited-contract workers and freelancers rather than a mass institutionalized milieu. They expect to earn less money than their parents. Instead of acquiring property, they expect to sell off whatever they inherit. Instead of rising up through the socio-economic ranks as their parents did, they see themselves, slowly, inexorably, dropping down. They have had unfettered access to education, free and ample, from elementary school through university. They grew up in the same middle-class culture of the boomers. They feel an instinctive belonging to the middle-class world and its tastes in cinema, literature, food, and music. In their experience, there is a separation between cultural refinement and economic expectation, a peculiar combination that is beginning to produce a peculiar new form of the novel.

It is not a question of money – or at least not only of money – but of expectations. For writers formed in the milieu of the Gen X *precariato* – whether or not they have experienced precarity themselves – the novel as a vehicle of expression has had to unmoor its narrative engines from advancement and ambition, other than of a purely artistic nature. Their novels are also informed by the collective experience of belonging to a generation that has failed to become embedded within official institutions, never collectively acquiring the authority to speak that institutional recognition brings with it. As they move out of their forties and into their fifties, Gen X writers are realizing that their time might never come, "adulthood" will never arrive, their life experience risks going unrecorded.

Without necessarily being aware of each other's works, Gen X writers from several Western European countries show striking similarities in narrative technique and innovation. Even when they take an ostensibly personal or intimate form, these novels record a collective experience rather than an individual one. While Ferrante, Louis, and Rooney all place value on individual originality and emphasize the specialness of their protagonists (in this sense the title *Normal People* is in part ironic), the Gen X novelists deliberately focus on people who are typical rather than exceptional. Gen X novels strive to give a sense of their narrators and protagonists as products of their culture and society rather than producers of it, as being inside with their peers rather than standing out or against. The narrative impulse is the search for meaning and adventure *outside* the framework of growth, advancement, originality, or winning.

The narrative role of friendship in their narrative system is thus to highlight sameness and similarity. Instead of illuminating potential differences in life outcomes, friendship in the European Gen X novel evokes commonality of experience, both shared references and predicaments. This use of friendship to emphasize intragenerational similarities and solidarity is one of the narrative devices that ensures the Gen X novel in Europe is not a genre of disenchantment or bitterness but, counterintuitively, life-filled and humorous; it is a genre of epic re-enchantment. The forward-tumbling, highly directional narratives of promise, progression, ascent, and improvement that characterize

Ferrante's, Rooney's, and Louis's novels are replaced in Gen X fiction not with sorrow, stasis, disappointment, or chaos but rather with other forms of order and other types of movement – lateral, retrospective, parenthetical.

One very short but highly representative example in which many of the key features are present is the novella *Anni luce* (*Light Years*)[15] by Andrea Pomella (born 1973). This work is "about" friendship in the sense that it ostensibly recounts the japes of a narrator and his best friend heading to Paris on an Interrail trip in the early 1990s. The two protagonists find alcohol unaffordably expensive when they arrive in Paris. They calculate that it would be cheaper to take the train back to Rome, stock up on whisky in a train station kiosk, and return to Paris to resume their adventure. This minor, humorous incident sets the model for the whole of the novella. In a pattern common to many European Gen X novels, as the plot of *Anni luce* proceeds, objects or people or ideas encountered by the characters provoke, by a form of free association, philosophical digressions, detailed flashbacks, or extended metaphors that suspend or postpone forward chronological movement.

Every part of the boys' journey is interrupted in some way or other, each interruption producing reflections and even mini-essays on topics from Kurt Cobain to Giacomo Leopardi to Ezra Pound. Eric Auerbach identifies an analogous technique – what Goethe and Schiller call the "retarding element" – at work in Homeric epic. Auerbach cites the moment toward the end of the *Odyssey* when Odysseus' nurse recognizes him by a scar on his leg, and the narrative is interrupted for more than seventy lines to give the backstory of this childhood injury. For Auerbach, this feature –the opposite, he says, of suspense – is a key component in Homer's narrative system, contributing in important ways to the overall meaning of the epic: "The excursus upon the origin of Odysseus' scar is not basically different from the many passages in which a newly introduced character, or even a newly appearing object or implement, though it be in the thick of a battle, is described as to its nature and origin."[16] Auerbach's analysis of this aspect of Homeric method is illuminating for our understanding of the similar narrative technique employed across Gen X precariate novels: in both cases, the "retarding element," the "going back and forth" by means of episodes, runs counter to any tensional or suspenseful striving toward a goal.[17]

Pomella's Interrailing characters are not contrasts or polarities – they are companions, parallels, typical products of the same cultural world. The point of the novella's digressions is to value dwelling over movement, being over becoming. The whisky-buying interlude could stand as a figure for the Gen X narrative mode itself, an anti-boomer approach to the novel, which eschews arrival and promise in favour of digression and parenthesis, a narrative that chooses to linger – in times, in places, on things experienced or held or known in common. The form that friendship takes in Euro Gen X novels – emphasizing comradeship and common experience over individual distinctiveness – thus has the effect of producing another key epic effect, the evocation of a "nation," in the sense of the creation of a mythology that defines a cultural community, bound, in this instance, by generational similarity.

All of these epic tropes are fundamental to Knausgaard's *My Struggle*. In the first volume, published in English as *A Death in the Family*, the narrator's wandering thoughts about his father's death prompt a recollection of illicitly buying beer with his friend for a New Year's Eve party when they were sixteen. If this were a Joycean stream of consciousness, the memory would flare up as a quick association; instead, the trivial flashback becomes an adventure that lasts for a hundred pages and involves hiding bags in bushes, being forced to accept an unwanted ride from a passing uncle, having to sneak back to retrieve the concealed cans, and so on. The memory does not simply interrupt the narrative, it usurps it completely. In Knausgaard's novel, every time the "plot," such as it is, begins to move forward in time, it is knocked off course. A birthday party attended by one of his children, an encounter with an old acquaintance, a book he sees on a shelf – any of these events or objects can send the narrative spiralling off in a new direction. We never know at which part of his life it will land, his teenage years, university, elementary school, the day of writing, his first marriage some decades before. While the tone of *My Struggle* is apparently self-centred, this insistence on non-chronology and digressions ends up having the paradoxical effect of effacing the narrating psychology and showing instead the broad cultural framework – the time, place, and set of tastes – in which the narrator's sensibility was produced. (Knausgaard, like many of his fellow European Gen X novelists, frequently alludes to Stefan Zweig's *The World of Yesterday*.)

Why epic? The picaresque after all is ready-made as a narrative genre for temporary workers who move from job to job. It would have seemed the obvious choice of a narrative model for a generation characterized by unstable employment and a sense of being at the periphery of their own institutions. The purpose of the Gen X novels, however, is not to record an individual's journey through precarity but rather to compensate for it, to imaginatively transform it by staking a claim for a generation's experience as a full, authentic, unique, even noble form of life. As a literary project, it is about restoring dignity to their world by making a claim for its coherence and wholeness. Thus, instead of a forward-oriented trajectory toward a moment of "arrival," the narrative energy comes from shared language, references, ideas, metaphorical colour – not from plot. These novels insist on the significance of lives that do not lead anywhere notable; they offer recuperation but not promise or direction.

Friendship and the Gen X Novel

Emanuele Trevi's *Due vite* (*Two Lives*),[18] which won the Premio Strega in 2021, is a kind of autofictional epic of friendship. The lives in the title refer to Rocco and Pia, two deceased friends of the narrator. Trevi's novel, indeed, could have been called *My Brilliant Friends*, or even *Normal People*, but brilliance for Trevi does not mean the potential for worldly success, and there would be no irony in the adjective "normal." Rocco's and Pia's lives are implicitly set in relation to each other, and alongside the narrator's life, but the result is utterly divorced from a logic of winning or losing, improving or failing to improve, succeeding or being disappointed. Trevi offers this story of friendship as a portrait of a generation and apparently unremarkable lives treated as marvels.

Pomella's *Anni luce* and Trevi's *Due vite* are very short works, but, as befits an epic mode, the European Gen X novel reaches its fullest expression in much longer, encyclopedic projects. Paolo Zanotti (1971–2012) may be one of the earliest inventors of the Euro Gen X style. Zanotti, who studied comparative literature in Pisa at the Scuola Normale Superiore di Pisa in the 1990s, was firmly embedded throughout his short adult life in the milieu of the Italian academic *precariato*. He published only one novel – the dystopian *Bambini Bonsai* (*Bonsai Babies*), set in a post–climate apocalypse landscape resembling the city of Genoa – before his premature death.[19] In the intervening decade, several novels and collections of short stories have been published posthumously.

Throughout Zanotti's oeuvre, the same preoccupations recur: groups of childhood friends who form a collective protagonist; banal provincial life elevated to the level of epic adventure; careful attention to specific, time-bound cultural contexts. The horizontal community of intragenerational friends in

Zanotti's work inevitably eclipses the vertical relationships between different generations, and his plots are frequently built around more or less futile quests whose importance is overtaken by digressions and explorations of cultural epiphenomena. Whereas vernacular speech in the novels of Ferrante, Louis, and Rooney is scrubbed out of the novelistic world, Zanotti's final published work (though one of the earliest to be written), *Trovate Ortensia* (*Find Ortensia*),[20] includes a detailed glossary of the slang spoken by young Pisans in the 1990s.

The Paris-based Milanese poet Andrea Inglese (born 1967), who turned to the novel form only in his late forties, signals the key themes of the Euro Gen X novel in his titles: *Parigi è un desiderio* (*Paris Is a Desire*)[21] and *La vita adulta* (*Adult Life*).[22] In both cases, the titles indicate unreachable shores for the *precariato*. In *Parigi è un desiderio*, Inglese's protagonist physically arrives in Paris, but not to "Paris," the symbolic, Balzacian destination of novelistic ambition. His life in Paris, rather than an ascension to glory and success, turns into a comic, almost slapstick narrative of youthful escapades, temporary academic contracts, sideline nixers, short-term apartment leases, and other kinds of ephemerality. The title of the second novel wistfully encodes the sense that adulthood itself has become as much a Shangri-La as a romantic notion of a literary life in Paris. Out of this predicament of stasis and disillusion, Inglese forges what might be called the epic of the *vieux garçon* and his friends. In both of Inglese's novels, the disappointing progress of the ambition-narrative finds itself overwhelmed by long flashbacks, digressions, conjectures, or short essays provoked by this or that object, encounter, or trivial event. The flow and excitement of the narrative do not finally come from movement toward the future but from this archaeological exploration, digging down into the cultural context the narrators share with their friends, and from cultural allusions, extended metaphors, and a high, extremely refined prose style.

The great epic of the Gen X *vieux garçon*, in which intragenerational friendship is *the* central plot device, may be Despentes' *Vernon Subutex*. When the novel opens in 2014, the protagonist has long been put out of business by the internet and music streaming. His social and romantic world has gradually shrunk, his finances have been increasingly precarious, and now he finds himself evicted from his apartment. He embarks on a kind of loser's odyssey, knocking on the doors of long-lost friends and former bandmates in search of loans, cocaine, and couches to sleep on. A piece of clothing Vernon glimpses in a friend's apartment, the name of an old acquaintance showing up on a

Facebook thread, a song playing in the background – any of these things can send the narrative looping back to the early 1990s with an exhaustive, intimate account of the characters and their history. Some of them have become successful; some of them have been bitterly disappointed by life; some of them inhabit a zone between success and disappointment. Regardless of what they are, these "outcomes" are incidental to the meaning of the book. Instead of outcomes, Despentes' epic offers a sense of late 1980s and early 1990s culture that the characters shared, a whole universe for which the novel stakes a claim to coherence, nobility, and significance.

Taken together, these texts from Norway, Italy, and France show unmistakable signs of constituting a distinct new form of the novel that clearly originates in the collective experience of Europeans born in the long 1970s. However, if some high-profile millennial writers have found that the boomer mode of narrative friendship is the form that works for their own novels of youthful promise, there are also boomer-aged writers who have adopted the Gen X style for their narratives of retrospective maturity. The earlier novels of Annie Ernaux (born 1940) are perfect exemplars of boomer narratives. The opening line of *La place* (*A Man's Place*)[23] highlights the importance of formal education to the story of socio-economic ascent that is going to follow: "I took my practical test for the CAPES examination at a *lycée* in Lyon."[24] *La place* is set in a working-class milieu in the provincial town of Yvetot. A mid-century French education sends the protagonist to school, then to university, then to literary fame. The novel gives a succinct account of the logic of postwar boomer bourgeois *Bildung*: "My mother served potatoes and milk from morning to night so that I could sit in a lecture theatre and listen to someone talking about Plato."[25] The narrative rhythm, from the first sentence to the last, is set by social and cultural improvement.

Ernaux's approach to narrative undergoes a complete change in her 2008 novel *Les années* (*The Years*). Like Knausgaard, Despentes, or the Gen X Italians, *Les années* deconstructs the whole idea of direction as meaning. Instead, it gives us a series of images, phrases, food, dialect-words, and other ephemera from the 1940s to the present, but in no chronological order. The boom of the *trente glorieuses* happens in the background, but the novel resists its providential directionality. In *Les années*, in other words, boomer content is narrated in Gen X form. Indeed, there are some scenes in *Les années* that have near counterparts in Knausgaard's *My Struggle*. In both *Les années* and

Boyhood Island, the third volume of *My Struggle*, narrators stare at photos of their younger selves and declare that they are simply looking at a different person. This statement, of course, runs counter to the idea, encapsulated in Ernaux's earlier work, of progressive *Bildung*, the gradual production of an original self.

The formal orientation of the Euro Gen X novel suggests a suspicion of growth and productivity as inherently positive values. The Gen X novel spends a great deal of time describing repetitive, non-enriching labour: in Knausgaard, cleaning out his late father's house; in Despentes, finding a bench to sleep on for the night; in Pomella, sourcing affordable whisky. Like the lives of the protagonists narrated by Despentes, Trevi, Pomella, and others, these tasks do not lead anywhere, nor are they redeemed through profit or reward. Instead of novels of destiny, we have novels of habits; instead of plots that move forward, we have narratives that dig down; instead of growth and development, we have recuperation and recycling. Epic digressions, as Auerbach argues, force the reader to dwell at length outside the action. This may be a narrative strategy on the part of a generation that has been refused a clear role as actors in social institutions. Along with its refusal of originality as a value, its emphasis on learning as an end in itself, and its harnessing of friendship as a narrative engine of solidarity and commonality rather than competition, the Gen X novel models a new narrative form for an era that seeks meaning outside growing and winning.

NOTES

1 Virginie Despentes, *Vernon Subutex*, 3 vols (Paris: Grasset, 2015–17).

2 T.S. Eliot, *Selected Essays* (New York: Harcourt, Brace, 1932), 117.

3 Ibid., 251.

4 Kate Marshall, "The Readers of the Future Have Become Shitty Literary Critics," review of *The Great Derangement*, by Amitav Ghosh, *Boundary2*, 26 February 2018, www.boundary2.org/2018/02/kate-marshall-the-readers-of-the-future-have-become-shitty-literary-critics/.

5 Ellen Barry, "Greeted as the First Great Millennial Author, and Wary of the Attention," profile of Sally Rooney, *New York Times*, 31 August 2018, www.nytimes.com/2018/08/31/world/europe/sally-rooney-ireland.html.

6 Joshua Rothman, "Knausgaard or Ferrante?," *New Yorker*, 15 March 2015, www.newyorker.com/culture/cultural-comment/knausgaard-or-ferrante.

7 Karl Ove Knausgaard, *Min Kamp* (Oslo: Oktober, 2009–11); Karl Ove Knausgaard, *My Struggle*, trans. Don Bartlett (London: Harvill Secker, 2012–18).
8 Elena Ferrante, *L'amica geniale* (Rome: Edizioni e/o, 2011–2014). Elena Ferrante, *The Neapolitan Novels*, trans. Ann Goldstein (New York: Europa Editions, 2012–2015).
9 Rothman, "Knausgaard or Ferrante?"
10 Charles Dickens, *Great Expectations*, introduction and notes by David Trotter (1861; London: Penguin, 2003), 3.
11 Ibid., 179.
12 Édouard Louis, *En finir avec Eddy Bellegueule* (Paris: Éditions du Seuil, 2014); Édouard Louis, *The End of Eddy*, trans. Michael Lucey (London: Harvill Secker, 2017).
13 Sally Rooney, *Conversations with Friends* (London: Faber and Faber, 2017).
14 Louis, *Eddy Bellegueule*, 204. My translation: "Façon de m'éloigner plus encore du village."
15 Andrea Pomella, *Anni luce* (Turin: ADD Editore, 2018).
16 Erich Auerbach, *Mimesis: The Representation of Reality in Western Literature* (Princeton: Princeton University Press, 2003), 5.
17 Ibid.
18 Emanuele Trevi, *Due vite* (Milan: Neri Pozza, 2020).
19 Paolo Zanotti, *Bambini Bonsai* (Milan: Ponte alle Grazie, 2010).
20 Paolo Zanotti, *Trovate Ortensia* (Milan: Ponte alle Grazie, 2021).
21 Andrea Inglese, *Parigi è un desiderio* (Milan: Ponte alle Grazie, 2016).
22 Andrea Inglese, *La vita adulta* (Milan: Ponte alle Grazie, 2021).
23 Annie Ernaux, *La place* (Paris: Gallimard, 1983), 11; Annie Ernaux, *A Man's Place*, trans. Tanya Leslie (New York: Four Walls, 1992).
24 Ibid. My translation: "J'ai passé les épreuves pratiques du Capes dans un lycée de Lyon."
25 Annie Ernaux, *Une femme* (Paris: Gallimard, 1990), 66; Annie Ernaux, *A Woman's Story*, trans. Tanya Leslie (New York: Seven Stories, 2003). My translation: "Ma mère … servait des pommes de terre et du lait du matin au soir pour que je sois assise dans un amphi à écouter parler de Platon."

Afterword

Friendship: A Coda

MARIA DIBATTISTA

Friendship, if one heeds the testimony of the essays in this volume, the writings they consult, and indeed the unsolicited promptings of one's own heart, occupies a unique but somewhat insecure place in the annals of human relationships. Aristotle believed that friendship was necessary to human life itself, a cognate and manifestation of the will to live, "for without friends no one would desire to live, though he had all other goods."[1] He considered friendship not only a supreme good but an inducement to self-refinement, hence its reputation, which he helped burnish, for encouraging *arete*, excellence in character, in intellectual as well as moral endeavours.

Yet being both necessary and, in its most disinterested form, noble and ennobling does not account for why and how *particular* people become close friends. Montaigne held that the truest friendship resisted explanation. After canvassing, as was his habit, the moral legends and axioms of classical tradition, the lore of cultures other than his own, and more familiar, contemporary manners and ways of feeling, including and especially his own, Montaigne confessed that there was no way to explain why his cherished friendship with Étienne de la Boétie was a friendship with this good and lovable man and not another perhaps equally good and lovable. "If you press me to tell you why I loved him," he writes in one of his most quoted – and touching – apothegms, "I feel that this cannot be expressed, except by answering: Because it was he, because it was I."[2] Uncharacteristically at a loss to answer a question he himself has posed, Montaigne can only volunteer that friendship, at least his friendship, cannot be comprehended except in its own self-evident terms. It appears that genuine friendship can only be rendered through tautology – it is what it is. What may remain ineffable but is, however, implicit in the unavoidable tautologies of friendship is the acknowledgment, hence the implied ethics, of difference. Lurking in the proposition that we are friends because I am I and he is he is a moral invitation to affirm and cherish the friend as inalienably Other.

Emerson responded to this invitation with his customary vehemence. Asserting that he is "equally balked by antagonism and by compliance," Emerson pleads, almost importunes, that his friend must "not cease an instant to be himself. The only joy I have in his being mine, is that the not mine is mine."[3] Friendship as a transcendental, yet unmistakably personal, relation reflects and is sustained by the clear difference between what is me and mine and what is not me and not mine. Emerson gives an existentially robust construction to the classical idealization and valorization of the friend as another self. For him the true friend does not directly mirror but ramifies his identity in the prism of absolute but not alienating difference.

Still, where there is difference there is distance. In Emerson's mapping, this distance encompasses the ample space between antagonism, where serious rivals, "frenemies," and declared adversaries tend to congregate, and compliance, where differences dissolve or are annulled in a concord that is negotiated or conceded rather than mutually felt. The movements that occur within these emotional and moral outposts can range from the most intimate nods of shared and often secret understanding – the knowing winks or half smiles – to the most sublime acts of fealty and devotion, of which, as the Gospel of St John tells us, there is no greater instance than laying down one's life for one's friends (KJV 15:33). The fate as well as quality of friendships hinge on such gestures, on the sincerity but also the constancy of the feelings they visibly express. For though we may know what a friend has been to us in the past and is to us now, we can never, with any real certainty, predict what a friend might become or might eventually be capable of.

Montaigne, as if to acknowledge this uncertainty, professes the ultimately reasonless, but not baseless grounds of his love for La Boétie, a formulation that would seem neither to admit nor require further comment, in the middle rather than at the end of his essay, where it would enjoy the prestige of a final word on the matter. Friendship, even in its purest form, unalloyed by self-interest or the more negligible, if pleasurable forms of sociality, is still and always susceptible to alteration or complication, to narrative development – or deterioration – as the case, happy or lamentable, may be. The "harmony of wills"[4] that for Montaigne marks and seals genuine friendship commits those bonded in friendship to a shared future, to joint exchanges and endeavours whose character and import are bound to change over time. Happiness may have no history, but even the most frictionless friendship does.

The novel, as the essays in this volume convincingly attest, is the literary genre most invested in exploring this history. Unlike the epic and romance, whose plots, characters, and conventions it shamelessly borrowed, relentlessly if affectionately parodied, and ultimately transformed into a new fictional idiom, the novel was fascinated by persons and their relations for their own sake. It proved to be a genre inordinately hospitable to relationships that were equal in strength, durability, and emotional value to the bonds forged in the family, wedlock, or service to the state, relationships that discounted and were able to surmount blatant differences in sex, class, cultural background, economic circumstance, ethnicity, race, and even – if we credit the testimony of J.R. Ackerley's memoir *My Dog Tulip* and its fictional descendent, Sigrid Nunez's *The Friend* – species. Restless to establish its own imaginative claims on reality, the novel reached its present cultural ascendancy by venturing into a wider, more unsettled terrain of sociability, so eager was it to discover and, when inspired, to invent potentially liberatory relationships that defy, and on occasion transform, traditional categories of association.

Don Quixote, in the mistaken belief that he was restoring a defunct rather than inaugurating a literally novel tradition, owes much of his repute as the founder of a new narrative order to his being the first to rush, pell-mell, into this territory. He does not go unaccompanied. After his disastrous first sally, which he rashly pursued on his own, he decides to take on, as stipulated by the chivalric code he has pledged himself to honour, a helper. What he acquires, however, indeed we might say what he makes, is a friend. It is a friendship born of and responding to the social and economic dislocations, but also the hopes, most of them valiantly utopian, of modernity. Sancho Panza, recruited as a squire but regularly overrunning the parameters of his occupational and narrative function, is obligingly receptive to Quixote's vision of a revived Golden Age, especially since it includes the offer of an island to govern. René Girard interprets this receptivity as a paradigmatic instance of external mediation, or desire according to the Other.

For Girard the social and intellectual distance that separates Sancho, the desiring subject, from the mediator, Don Quixote, being spiritual rather than physical, is insuperable: "The valet never desires what his master desires. Sancho covets the food left by the monks, the purse of gold found on the road, and other objects which Don Quixote willingly lets him have. As for the imaginary island it is from Don Quixote himself that Sancho is counting on receiving it, as the faithful vassal holds everything in the name of his lord."[5] Yes, but when provided the chance to govern an island, even for a day and as a joke, he proves a surprisingly sage ruler and judge. There is, then, perhaps another way to think about their relatively untroubled and increasingly affectionate partnership. We might begin by noting that the first thing we learn about Sancho is, though "he is not much in the way of brains," he is "a good man (hombre de bien) – if that title can be given to someone so poor."[6] That "if" suggests a moral egalitarianism that the novel will explore as a plausible social and, ultimately, human possibility. As the novel progresses, and with it their friendship, Sancho, the "hombre de bien," closes what Girard insists is the insuperable spiritual gap between him and his master.

Despite disagreements about tactics and the considerable, even daunting social and intellectual distance between them, they morally unite through the "concurrence" of their desires for what is unattainable but not inconceivable: a world in which cruelty and injustice are confounded by the superior forces of goodwill and in which there is plenty to eat for everyone. In the unlikely pairing of a wizened, impoverished hidalgo whose wits have been turned by too much reading and a wily, paunchy peasant whose appetites are keen but capable of moral refinement, friendship enters the western imagination to challenge sexual love, social ambition, and the romance of power as subjects for narrative and not just philosophical investigation.

These narrative incursions into the psychological and social domains unique to what we have been calling the friendship plot are undertaken in allegiance with, but more often in veiled competition with, the novel of manners and the *Bildungsroman*, narratives also but differently invested in chronicling how feeling finds the social forms that fulfill or, in more distressing scenarios, inhibit, distort, or potentially extinguish it. The reciprocal esteem and shared aspirations, but also divisions, dissensions, and outright betrayals, that preoccupy characters who regard friendship as the defining good of their lives sometimes coincide, but more often are overshadowed by the erotic intrigues, emotional feints, social manoeuvrings, and negotiations that propel the novel of manners, a form disposed to privilege the marriage over the friendship plot. For those novelistic characters anxious about their social fate, which includes primary and secondary characters alike, friendship is either valued or distrusted, in extreme instances revoked depending on whether it serves to strengthen or weaken the sturdier bonds and collective interests of family, clan and, when in play, the state.[7]

Friendship conceived and experienced as an adventure in intimacy presents an opportunity (for soul-enlarging rapport with another) but also a problem for the *Bildungsroman* protagonist, whose maturing individuality may be compromised by friendship, which can divert time and moral energy away from the purposeful labour of self-cultivation. The problem is compounded in the *Künstlerroman*, in which the solicitude of friends, however well-meaning, and the social pressure, or personal inclination, to please may interfere with the development of the artist's independence of vision and judgment.

Thus Proust is guarded and Joyce mistrustful before overtures of friendship. Proust, a declared apostate ("athée de l'amitié"),[8] warns against the seductive pleasures and comforts of friendship, especially when emanating from a character as appealing as Robert de Saint-Loup, whose kindness is allied with and informed by intelligence. The first commandment of Proust's artistic creed is that the artist shall not worship the meretricious gods of society, but devote himself religiously to the solitary rites of art. "An artist if he is to be absolutely true to the life of the spirit," the narrator writes after visiting the studio of the painter Elstir, "must be alone, and not squander his ego, even upon his disciples."[9] Friendship interferes with the artist's duty to live in the presence of reality and "extract … the element of truth that it contained."[10] This truth only can be found, indeed only exists, within, never outside and beyond oneself.

For Stephen Dedalus, Joyce's bemused portrait of himself as a gifted, if prickly, forgivably callow young man, friendship is less a temptation than an ordeal to be endured, a test of his artistic mettle. *Non serviam* is the defiant battle cry Stephen hurls against the powers of family, state, and religion that would trammel his imagination and thwart his intention to create "the uncreated conscience of [his] race."[11] In *A Portrait of the Artist as a Young Man*, Cranly, Stephen's closest friend and interlocutor (Stephen assigns him the mythico-Biblical role of precursor), asks Stephen if he really understands that his unyielding spiritual pride in his artistic calling condemns him to a terrible loneliness: "Alone, quite alone. You have no fear of that. And you know what that word means? Not only to be separate from all others but to have not even one friend."[12] Stephen's response, like his commitment, is total and heroic: "I will take the risk."

In *Ulysses* Joyce confronts another, less heroic but bigger risk in the person and friendship of Buck Mulligan. Joyce reimagines the plight of Telemachus, the son whose birthright is threatened by suitors ravenous for his mother's hand and father's goods, as a struggle between two friends for artistic control of Stephen's will, his words, his maturing artistic project, and even his money. Stephen's odyssey is as much a movement away from Mulligan, the usurper masquerading as friend, as it is toward Leopold Bloom, in whom the dispossessed son might find the father, invoked in the final line of *Portrait*, "to stand [him] now and ever in good stead."[13]

The novel has been enriched by the psychological complexities, the social heterodoxies and emotional éclat of the friendship plot, which is frequently more candid than the novel of manners or of education in impressing upon us what Elizabeth Bowen identified as the "fatal distinction between kinship and affinity."[14] The fatality of this distinction, plotted as distressing, often disastrous collisions between family allegiances and elective affinities, has spurred the novel to elaborate a richly diverse and sophisticated typology of friendship to rival that of the most intricate kinship system. Many of these types are studied in this volume: the friend as soulmate, helper, mentor, and guide; as *ficelle* or translator who assists in the task of understanding an obscured or baffling reality, of rendering foreign ways and unfamiliar tongues into a comprehensible language of respect and affection. The friend can even be kin, the sister or brother in whom the innate sympathy and affections of a shared childhood are subsumed and reorganized into the extra-familial economy of friendship. It is a gift economy in which exchanges of love and ideas, advice and material support are not mandated by a sense of familial obligation but offered – we speak ideally here of course – simply because he is he and I am I.

Ideal, but not impossible of realization. The promise of affection and loyalty freely given has inspired the novel to invent the occasions and devise the means for expanding the meaning but also the kinds of friendship that might fulfill that promise. In his last novel, E.M. Forster lamented, "Century after century of carnal embracement and we're still no nearer to understanding one another."[15] He experimented with the friendship plot, testing the patience – and imagination – of the "dear reader" idly seeking more variations on what had by then become the standard amatory coquetries, dalliances, estrangements, and reconciliations of the marriage plot by positing, with great care and tact, the unlikely affinity between an elderly English woman and a young Muslim doctor, recently widowed and looking for romance. The experiment was undertaken to test whether a friendship that so unexpectedly transcended national, ethnic, religious, and sexual differences, as well as the disparities of age, could last. It could not, not there, not then.

But perhaps here and now it might. Such is the hope offered by the spectacular success of Elena Ferrante's *Neapolitan Novels* of (brilliant) female friendship or Sally Rooney's *Normal People*, novels in which the unique pleasures and rewards, but also the challenges and travails of friendship alternately abet and compete with the marriage and *Bildungsroman* plots. Such novels announce a resurgent interest in friendship as both a touchstone of what we most desire and indeed, according to Aristotle, what we most need in our life and an emotional adventure fraught with risk – rivalry, betrayal, all the more sinister for being disguised and donning the cloak of goodwill. Friendship is predicated on the moral good of difference, which it can cherish, exploit, or despoil. Philosophers may analyze and promote that moral good, but it remains the primary burden of the novel to chronicle its social fate, even as it is busy incubating new emotional and social formations to ensure its future.

NOTES

1 Aristotle, *Nichomachean Ethics*, trans. David Ross (Oxford: Oxford University Press, 2020), 192.

2 Michel de Montaigne, "Of Friendship," *The Complete Works of Montaigne*, trans. Donald Frame (Stanford: Stanford University Press, 1958), 139. Alexander Nehamas observes that in the first edition, Montaigne had been more polite

than forthcoming in writing: "If you press me to tell why I loved him, I feel that this cannot be expressed." "I understand him to be saying here," Nehamas writes, "that his love could not be expressed in general terms – 'considerations' – since he still thought that sonnets might give an accurate picture of his friend. But when, in the Bordeaux Manuscript, he excises the poems and abandons that effort as well, he expands the original sentence with what has become the most moving statement about friendship ever made." Alexander Nehamas, *On Friendship* (New York: Basic Books, 2016), 119.

3 Ralph Waldo Emerson, "Friendship," in *Emerson: Essays and Lectures* (New York: Library of America, 1983), 350.

4 Montaigne, "Of Friendship," 137.

5 René Girard, *Deceit, Desire and the Novel*, trans. Yvonne Freccero (Baltimore: Johns Hopkins University Press, 1976), 9.

6 Miguel de Cervantes, *Don Quixote*, trans. Edith Grossman (New York: Ecco, 2003), 55.

7 Thoreau, with typical antinomian verve, contends that a harmony of wills is also possible for friendship, if it is noble, and statecraft, if it is just and wise. He assures us that "we cannot have too many friends; the virtue which we appreciate we to some extent appropriate, so that thus we are made at last more fit for every relation of life." He concludes, "A base Friendship is of a narrowing and exclusive tendency, but a noble one is not exclusive; its very superfluity and dispersed love is the humanity which sweetens society, and sympathizes with foreign nations; for though its foundations are private, it is, in effect, a public affair and a public advantage, and the Friend, more than the father of a family, deserves well of the state." Henry David Thoreau, *A Week on the Concord and Merrimack Rivers* (New York: Library of America, 1985), 225.

8 Marcel Proust, *Marcel Proust et Jacques Rivière: Correspondance (1914–1922)*, ed. Philip Kolb (Paris: Pion, 1955), 67. Proust's attitude is much more ambiguous, even tortured, when this confession of apostasy is seen in its full context: "Notez du reste que si théoriquement je suis un athée de l'amitié, je la pratique avec beaucoup plus de ferveur que tant d'apôtres de l'amitié." My translation: "Moreover, if theoretically I am an apostate of friendship, I practise it with much more fervour than many apostles of friendship." For an excellent discussion of the disparity between Proust's faith and practice of friendship, see Duncan Large, "Proust on Nietzsche: The Question of Friendship," *Modern Language Review* 88, no. 3 (1993): 624.

9 Marcel Proust, *Within a Budding Grove*, trans. C.K. Moncrieff and Terence Kilmartin (New York: Random House, 1981), 923.

10 Ibid.

11 James Joyce, *A Portrait of the Artist as a Young Man* (1916; Oxford: Oxford University Press, 2000), 213.

12 Ibid., 208. Richard Ellmann, remarking that in life, as against fiction, Joyce found "a certain relish for the violent breaking of friendships," notes that "a favorite word in his early work is 'sunder.'" Ellmann, "A Portrait of the Artist as Friend," *The Kenyon Review* 18, no. 1 (1956): 66.

13 Joyce, *Portrait*, 208.

14 Elizabeth Bowen, *Friends and Relations* (1931; New York: Avon, 1980), 91.

15 E.M. Forster, *A Passage to India* (1924; Mineola: Dover, 2020), 99.

Contributors

ROBERT L. CASERIO, emeritus professor of English, comparative literature, and women's, gender, and sexuality studies at the Pennsylvania State University, is co-editor of *The Cambridge History of the English Novel* and the editor of *The Cambridge Companion to the Twentieth Century English Novel*. His most recent book, *The Cambridge Introduction to British Fiction, 1900–1950*, appeared in 2019.

MARIA DIBATTISTA is the Charles Barnwell Straut Class of 1923 Professor of English at Princeton University. Her books include *Fast-Talking Dames* (2003), *Imagining Virginia Woolf* (2008), and *Novel Characters: A Genealogy* (2010). She is co-editor of *The Cambridge Companion to Autobiography* (2014) and *Modernism and Autobiography* (2014). Her latest book, *At Home in the World: Women Writers and Public Life, from Austen to the Present* (2017), co-authored with Deborah Nord, is a study of women's political writings.

JAY DICKSON is professor of English and humanities at Reed College in Portland, Oregon. He is the author of many essays on modernism and literary culture, including most recently in *Mansfield Studies*, *The Bloomsbury Handbook to Katherine Mansfield*, and the *James Joyce Quarterly*.

BRIAN GINGRICH is assistant professor of instruction in the Department of English at the University of Texas at Austin. He is the author of *The Pace of*

Fiction: Narrative Movement and the Novel (2021), as well as several essays on modernism, the novel, and transnationality. An affiliate of the International Network for Comparative Humanities, he studies film and fiction across the Atlantic and the globe.

JONATHAN GREENBERG, professor of English at Montclair State University, is the author of *Modernism, Satire, and the Novel* (2011) and *The Cambridge Introduction to Satire* (2019), both from Cambridge University Press. His essays on modern and contemporary literature have appeared in *Daedalus*, *Modern Fiction Studies*, *Modernism / modernity*, PMLA, and other journals. With Nathan Waddell, he edited *Brave New World: Contexts and Legacies* (2016). He is also an Emmy Award–winning writer for children's television and co-author, with Mo Rocca, of the New York Times bestseller *Mobituaries: Great Lives Worth Reliving* (2019).

ALLAN HEPBURN is James McGill Professor of Twentieth-Century Literature at McGill University. He is the author of *Intrigue: Espionage and Culture* (2005), *Enchanted Objects: Visual Art in Contemporary Literature* (2010), and *A Grain of Faith: Religion in Mid-Century British Literature* (2018). He has edited seven books, including *Around 1945: Literature, Citizenship, Rights* (2016) and *Diplomacy and the Modern Novel: France, Britain, and the Mission of Literature* (2020). He co-edits the Oxford Mid-Century Studies series at Oxford University Press and the Hugh MacLennan Poetry Series at McGill-Queen's University Press.

BARRY MCCREA is the author of three books: a novel, *The First Verse*, winner of the Ferro-Grumley prize for fiction, and two academic books, most recently, *Languages of the Night*, which won the 2016 René Wellek Prize for an outstanding book in the discipline of comparative literature. He holds the Keough Family Chair at the University of Notre Dame, where he teaches modern literature on its campuses in Indiana, Rome, and Dublin.

DEBORAH EPSTEIN NORD is professor emerita of English at Princeton University. She is the author of *The Apprenticeship of Beatrice Webb* (1985), *Walking the Victorian Streets: Women, Representation, and the City* (1995), and *Gypsies and the British Imagination, 1807–1930* (2006). With Maria DiBattista, she co-authored *At Home in the World: Women Writers and Public Life, from Austen to the Present* (2017). She also edited John Ruskin's *Sesame and Lilies* (2002). Her current work engages the relationship between nineteenth-century fiction and the visual arts.

ERWIN ROSINBERG is an associate teaching professor at Emory University, where he teaches courses on British modernism, novel theory and history, and environmental literature. He has published on D.H. Lawrence's *Women in Love* in *Modern Fiction Studies*, and he is working on a project about representations of the British countryside in twentieth-century fiction.

JACQUELINE SHIN is associate professor of English at Towson University in Baltimore, Maryland. She has published articles on Elizabeth Bowen, Graham Greene, and Sylvia Townsend Warner. Her essay on Virginia Woolf and film appeared in *The Oxford Handbook of Virginia Woolf* (2021). Her current book project explores the distanced aesthetics of five twentieth-century female authors, including Muriel Spark, and a number of contemporary filmmakers who have adapted novels into film.

LISA STERNLIEB is an associate professor of English and Jewish Studies at Penn State University. She is the author of *The Female Narrator in the British Novel: Hidden Agendas* (2002). She is currently revising a manuscript on the pleasures of neo-Victorian literature.

EMILY O. WITTMAN is professor of English at the University of Alabama. Her monographs include *The New Midlife Self-Writing* (2021), *Interwar Itineraries: Authenticity in Anglophone and French Travel Writing* (2022), and *Translation and Modernism* (2023). She is a translator of the French philosopher Félix Guattari and a co-editor of *Modernism and Autobiography* and *The Cambridge Companion to Autobiography*.

Index

the baneberry disaster

a generation of atomic fallout

Larry C. Johns, with Alan R. Johns

UNIVERSITY OF NEVADA PRESS *Reno & Las Vegas*

University of Nevada Press | Reno, Nevada 89557 USA
www.unpress.nevada.edu

Cover photograph courtesy of National Nuclear Security Administration Field Office

LIBRARY OF CONGRESS CATALOGING-IN-PUBLICATION DATA
Names: Johns, Larry Charles, 1944– author. | Johns, Alan R., author.
Title: The Baneberry disaster : a generation of atomic fallout / Larry C. Johns & Alan R. Johns.
Description: Reno : University of Nevada Press, [2017] | Includes index.
Identifiers: LCCN 2017005507 (print) | LCCN 2017006203 (e-book) | ISBN 978-1-943859-45-0 (pbk. : alk. paper) | ISBN 978-0-87417-638-4 (e-book)
Subjects: LCSH: Baneberry Nuclear Test, Nev., 1970—Trials, litigation, etc. | Nuclear weapons—Testing—Law and legislation—United States. | Wrongful death—United States. | Roberts, Harley. | Nunamaker, Bill. | LCGFT: Trial and arbitral proceedings.
Classification: LCC KF224.B257 J64 2017 (print) | LCC KF224.B257 (e-book) | DDC 344.7304/633—dc23
LC record available at https://lccn.loc.gov/2017005507

The paper used in this book meets the requirements of American National Standard for Information Sciences—Permanence of Paper for Printed Library Materials, ANSI/NISO Z39.48-1992 (R2002).

FIRST PRINTING

Manufactured in the United States of America

In memory of our parents,

Ray and Helen Johns,

whose motto was,

"To the valiant heart, nothing is impossible,"

and

Shields Warren, 1898–1980, Father of Radiation Pathology,

Alice Stewart, 1906–2002, Mother of Radiation Epidemiology.

Contents

Preface

The Baneberry Disaster is a true story about two men, Harley Roberts and Bill Nunamaker, who died of leukemia after they were contaminated on December 18, 1970, by radiation from a failed nuclear test code-named *Baneberry*. Their contamination and deaths resulted in lawsuits brought by their widows against the Atomic Energy Commission (AEC). Their case was tried in 1979 before a federal judge in Las Vegas, Nevada, the hometown of the AEC's continental atomic testing program. The twelve-week-long trial ended in April 1979, but it took the federal judge four years to write a two-sentence decision in favor of the AEC. It took another thirteen years before the Baneberry litigation finally ended in the Ninth Circuit Court of Appeals in April 1996.

By April 1996, when the final appeal was argued in the Ninth Circuit, both widows and the federal judge were dead. Ninth Circuit Chief Judge James R. Browning, who had heard all prior appeals, commented when the case was called, "Ah, Roberts and Nunamaker. It's like visiting an old friend."

Had the widows' claims against the AEC been tried to a jury of ordinary citizens in Las Vegas in 1979, instead of this federal judge, justice would have been swift. The jurors would have begun their deliberations in early April 1979. If they decided the AEC was responsible for the deaths of the two men, they would have awarded the widows monetary damages. Had the jury decided against them, the widows would have left the courtroom with nothing, and the lawsuit would have ended.

Southern Nevada is the setting for the events described here. Everyone is now familiar with Las Vegas, but few know that it was not even on the map until the early 1900s. Since its establishment by the railroad in 1905, Las Vegas has become globally significant as the Divorce Capital of the World, the Gambling Capital of the World, the Entertainment Capital of the World, and the Mob Capital of the World.

On December 18, 1950, when southern Nevada was selected as the Atomic Energy Commission's continental test site, the population of Las Vegas was only 24,000, and 95 percent of the barren state of Nevada was owned by the federal government. The Test Site was ostensibly selected because its remote location could be easily secured and activities kept secret. Given the AEC's history, however, it seems that southern Nevada was suitable for another reason: the AEC could easily beguile and bully, if necessary, the patriotic populace, the politicians, and the local press.

When the AEC came to test atomic bombs in 1951, the State of Nevada had already foreshadowed its role in the atomic testing program through its namesake, the battleship *Nevada*. Although it received less acclaim than other warships, the *Nevada* was, at one time, a source of pride to Nevadans.

On December 7, 1941, the bulk of the U.S. Navy was peacefully anchored at Pearl Harbor, Hawaii. Battleship Row included eight American battleships: the *Nevada, Arizona, Tennessee, West Virginia, Maryland, Oklahoma,* and *California,* with the *Pennsylvania* in dry-dock. The *Nevada* was the big sister and oldest of the armada, commissioned over twenty-five years earlier.

When the Japanese struck at 7:55 AM, it was the *Nevada* that singly distinguished herself and her crew. She maintained her composure throughout the chaos, even concluding her band's playing of "The Star-Spangled Banner" after the attack began. It was the *Nevada* that got underway, without the assistance of tugboats, and fought her way from the channel through the Japanese strafing, torpedoes, and bombs. She could have gone out to sea, but was ordered to beach herself inside the harbor. Although damaged, she remained seaworthy and rejoined the fleet after modernization.

The *Nevada* performed honorably throughout the Second World War in two oceans. She was the flagship for the Normandy invasion and when she shifted to the Pacific Theater was known as the Sweetheart of the Marine Corps. At Iwo Jima, her big guns blasted away at the impenetrable bunkers and fired directly into the mouths of enemy caves.

In an ironic twist of fate—possibly a harbinger of things to come for the State of Nevada—when the war was over, the illustrious *Nevada* was selected as the target ship in the first Pacific A-bomb test. It was expected her career would end in a bikini lagoon on July 1, 1946. The *Nevada* was painted with a red bull's eye, and the bombardier designated to drop the bomb boasted that he could hit the target. Despite its critical position, however, the *Nevada* confounded experts by sustaining only minimal damage.

Twenty-four days later, the *Nevada* was again positioned for test *Baker*, the first underwater test. As with most of the ships that survived the Bikini atomic experiments, the highly contaminated Nevada became the object of target practice. And so it was, after hours of shelling its hull, the U.S. Navy accomplished what no enemy could. It sank the battleship *Nevada*.

But now with full-throated bragging rights, Nevadans embraced the A-bomb testing program as the state's contribution to the nation and commitment to its motto: "All for Our Country."

ABOUT THE STORY

The idea for this book originated in 1979 after the conclusion of the *Baneberry* trial, when drafts of memorable events were prepared by myself and Larry. Yet the story could not be told until the lawsuit ended in 1996. By then, the trial transcripts and boxes of records had been packed away in storerooms and closets. In 2008, Larry ran across the original drafts and material and realized that the only way to purge his soul of *Baneberry* was to relive the events and tell the story. His goal was to complete the book by December 2010 to coincide with the fortieth anniversary of the Baneberry test and a month before the sixtieth anniversary of the first atomic test in Nevada in January 1951. But like the *Baneberry* case itself, telling the story took longer than expected.

— Alan R. Johns

Acknowledgments

The *Baneberry* case would not have been possible without the support of my wife, Mary, who supported the cause and shouldered the burden of raising our four children, Charles, Laura, Julianna, and Jason, who grew up with *Baneberry*.

Alan bore the burden of *Baneberry* equally, and his wife Loretta and their three children, Tris, Greg, and Brian shared the adventure.

Without Bill Cleghorn there would have been no *Baneberry* lawsuit, and without Paul Duckworth's help in preparing the lawsuit, we might not have been introduced to Dr. Shields Warren, who never faltered in his conviction that his opinion in the Roberts's case was correct. With Dr. Stewart, Dr. Gofman, Dr. Morgan, Dr. Tamplin, and Dr. Bertell on our team, it seemed inconceivable that justice would not be done.

The manuscript would not have been finished without encouragement and editorial advice from Mary D. Wammack, who worked as a legal assistant on both the *Baneberry* and *Prescott* cases and earned a doctorate in history with a focus on nuclear policy.

During the twenty-five years the *Baneberry* and *Prescott* cases were in court, we met countless Test Site workers, atomic veterans, downwinders, and others. Bennie Levy worked tirelessly on behalf of the workers and Janet Gordon for the downwinders. Dale Haralson, who tried the *Allen* case and headed our team in the *Prescott* case, passed away in December 2015. Dale and so many others are not here to thank for their contributions, including thousands of Nevada Test Site (NTS) workers who made the nuclear testing program possible.

the baneberry disaster

Introduction

In 1950, Las Vegas had one high school, Las Vegas High, only a handful of elementary schools, and Fifth Street Grammar School for fifth through eighth grades. On December 18, 1950, the Las Vegas Bombing and Gunnery Range, a vast government reserve in south-central Nevada, was selected to test atomic bombs. On January 11, 1951, the Atomic Energy Commission issued a press release, warning that A-bomb tests would begin soon, but there would be no public announcement of the time of specific tests.[1]

On January 27, 1951, the first A-bomb was dropped from an airplane on Frenchman Flat at the Nevada Proving Grounds.[2] The two-inch headline, "VEGANS ATOM-IZED," described the reactions of people throughout the Las Vegas valley who saw the predawn flash or heard doors and windows rattling in their homes nearly seventy miles south of the blast.[3]

The first few tests were unannounced. But in the fall of 1951, when the AEC did begin announcing upcoming tests, witnessing an A-bomb blast was an initiation into the atomic age. We perched on the roof of our home on North 12th Street to watch the flash of light over the Sheep Range north of town and wait for the rumbling as the sound waves traveled south to Las Vegas.

The A-bomb tests seventy miles away were intriguing but impersonal, until the AEC began civil defense training to prepare Las Vegans for atomic warfare. At North Ninth Street School, where my mother taught second grade, my twin sister Linda and I, and older brother Ron, participated in "Bert the Turtle, Duck and Cover" exercises, crouching under our desks or lying face down on the playground, shielding our eyes and wrapping our arms around our heads.

Soon after testing began, the AEC became part of our community. Anyone who lived in Las Vegas during the 1950s had a family member, neighbor, or acquaintance who worked at the Test Site or attended school with kids whose fathers worked there. Most Las Vegans participated in, or lined up on Fremont

Street to watch, one or more of the three Helldorado parades that proceeded up Fremont Street to the Union Pacific Depot on Main Street. Floats celebrating the atomic bomb were featured in the Sunday Beauty Parade, the last of the three parades.[4]

In May 1953, the Las Vegas High School yearbook, the *Wildcat Echo*, displayed an A-bomb blast on its cover.[5] Las Vegas High students were taken out to the football field to watch the flash and mushroom cloud rise over the mountains north of town. Each test series was publicized in the local newspapers. A-bomb tests became so commonplace we paid little attention.

From January 1951 through October 31, 1958, a hundred atomic bombs were exploded in the atmosphere at NTS. In addition, nearly two dozen nuclear devices were detonated in tunnels on Rainier Mesa or in shafts drilled hundreds of feet below Yucca Flat.[6]

There were a few incidents involving atomic testing at NTS that most Las Vegans recall. On May 19, 1953, fallout from an A-bomb test dropped radiation on St. George, Utah. The event was reported in the local newspapers, but there was no television coverage; our first television station began broadcasting in August 1953. The AEC assured us that radiation levels in St. George were not harmful and we believed them.[7]

In the spring of 1955, the AEC began civil defense experiments at NTS to measure the blast effects of an atomic bomb. A fabricated home was constructed at NTS with furniture, appliances, and mannequins of adults and children. The devastation was described in the newspapers and sparked interest in building bomb shelters.[8]

In the fall of 1956, Utah sheep owners, who claimed their sheep were exposed to lethal levels of radiation from aboveground tests in 1953, took their case to trial in Salt Lake City, Utah. On October 23, 1956, the federal judge ruled against them.[9]

In early November 1956, Dwight Eisenhower was re-elected president amidst concerns from noted scientists that fallout from atmospheric tests was polluting the atmosphere and would cause an epidemic of cancers. In 1958, President Eisenhower and Soviet Premier Khrushchev signed a moratorium suspending nuclear testing. The last NTS nuclear test before the moratorium was on October 30, 1958.

Although testing was suspended in 1958 and thousands of displaced NTS workers sought other employment, Las Vegas continued to grow. By 1960, the population was 72,000—three times its population in 1950. Las Vegas had two high schools and one under construction. North Las Vegas had its own high school, Rancho High.

On the evening of January 17, 1961, three days before John Kennedy was sworn in as our new president, Dwight Eisenhower's farewell address to the nation was televised. It was a perplexing speech to a high school student interested in politics, who had participated in the Sun Youth Forum and who would attend Boys State at the University of Nevada in Reno a few months later. Eisenhower's warning about the "military-industrial complex" made little sense to a conservative Republican teenager who had grown up in Las Vegas during the 1950s.

Those who lived through the tranquil 1950s and the turbulent 1960s that followed have vivid memories of the Cuban Missile Crisis, the assassination of President Kennedy, the Vietnam War, the Civil Rights Movement, and the Haight-Ashbury "hippie" counterculture. Fortunately, college, law school, and romance were a wonderful distraction, until I returned to Las Vegas in the fall of 1968, to practice law and start a family. Nuclear testing at the remote Test Site was of little interest, nor could I imagine it would be.

On December 18, 1970, exactly twenty years after NTS was selected as the continental testing site, an underground nuclear test, code named *Baneberry*, was detonated 912 feet below Yucca Flat. Baneberry, the 666th United States nuclear test, would change my life and the lives of many others.[10]

I learned much from the Baneberry lawsuit about physics, geology, radiation, cytogenetics, and leukemia, especially the horror of leukemia to those afflicted with it and their families. As Alan and I traveled the long Baneberry journey, I learned something I had not expected, something William Pitt warned about in 1770: "Unlimited power is apt to corrupt the minds of those who possess it...where law ends so tyranny begins." I think that is what President Eisenhower was trying to warn us about in his farewell address in 1961.

The Baneberry case was a small piece of a puzzle put together in the 1980s by the actions of individual citizens, courageous scientists, "dreaded" lawyers, a judge in Utah, a jury in Oklahoma City, members of the press, and representatives of the people. When the mosaic was finally pieced together, a frightening picture of an American tragedy was on display for all to see and, hopefully, all to remember.

Baneberry, in retrospect, was perhaps an impossible quest for justice, a dream, at times an un-ending nightmare, but a fascinating, enlightening, disillusioning, and life-altering experience.

NOTES

1. *Las Vegas Review-Journal*, January 11, 1951.
2. The Nevada Proving Grounds was renamed the Nevada Test Site in the mid-1950s.

3. *Las Vegas Review-Journal*, January 28, 1951. Nearly every day from January 28, 1951, through February 6, 1951, banner headlines and photos of the predawn blasts were on the front page of the *Review-Journal*.

4. Ibid., May 18, 1953.

5. We had three copies of *The Wildcat Echo*. My older brother Alan and older sister Judy attended LVHS in 1953; my father taught American history at LVHS.

6. *United States Nuclear Tests July 1945 through September 1992*, DOE/NV-209, REV 15, December 2000.

7. *Las Vegas Review-Journal*, May 19, 1953; *Las Vegas Sun*, May 19, 1953.

8. Ibid., May 6, 1955.

9. Bulloch v. United States, 145 F. Supp. 824 (1956).

10. *United States Nuclear Tests*, 62–63.

[1]

To the Dark Tower

January 16, 1979

"All rise. The United States District Court for the District of Nevada is now in session. The Honorable Roger D. Foley presiding."

The judge ascended the bench, sat down, and banged the gavel. "You may be seated." He looked down at Alan and me and then over at the lawyers seated at the government's table. "This is the time set for the trial of the consolidated cases of *Dorothy Roberts versus the United States of America* and *Louise Nunamaker versus the United States of America*. Are the parties ready to proceed?"[1]

Dorothy Roberts and Louise Nunamaker looked forlorn and frightened as they heard their names echo across the vaulted courtroom that morning. They glanced nervously at each other and then over at the two young lawyers seated next to them at the plaintiff's table. Dorothy and Louise were the widows of two men who died of leukemia in 1974, less than four years after the men were contaminated by radiation when underground nuclear test Baneberry vented on December 18, 1970.

When we came to court that morning, we had been involved with Baneberry for over eight years but still did not know who gave it that ominous name: Baneberry, a poisonous berry. The root word of Baneberry is *bane*, which is universally defined as a cause of death or ruin, or a deadly poison. The nearly ten-kiloton Baneberry nuclear device, the size of the Hiroshima bomb, was buried 912 feet below the surface at the Nevada Test Site. The blast was supposed to be totally contained to prevent the release of radiation into the atmosphere. In fact, any release would violate the 1963 Nuclear Test Ban Treaty.

But Baneberry did not take orders from the United States of America and did not give a damn about international treaties. Within minutes after it exploded, it ripped a hole to the surface and pumped nearly 7 million curies of radiation up a column of dust and gas into a huge hammerhead-shaped cloud. The radioactive cloud hovered over the test basin three miles east of a base camp in Area 12 where hundreds of workers watched in awe. Had the AEC cleared the workers out of Area 12 before the test, as in four previous underground tests that week, Dorothy and Louise would not have been in the courtroom that morning. Baneberry, the final test that week and the last test of the year, was scheduled for Friday. The AEC decided to take a chance and left 900 workers in Area 12.

For ten minutes, the black column of radioactive dust and gas continued to feed the ever-expanding Baneberry cloud. Then, suddenly, a large part of the column plummeted to the ground a couple miles south of the Area 12 Camp and began moving up the hill toward the camp.[2] When the test manager in charge of the Baneberry test could no longer ignore Baneberry's movement to engulf the hapless workers, a small band of security guards was mustered to race to the camp to try to evacuate them before they were contaminated.

Dorothy's husband, Harley Roberts, was one of those guards. He and the Baneberry cloud spent nearly an hour together in Area 12 Camp as he rushed the workers out. Harley received the highest radiation dose of the eighty-six men exposed to the Baneberry cloud that day.[3]

Louise's husband, Bill Nunamaker, was one of the men who did not get out before the Baneberry cloud settled on his body and he inhaled its radioactive gas. Bill Nunamaker's radiation dose was only a tenth of that of Harley Roberts's but high enough to require multiple showers to scrub the radiation off his skin and swab out his nasal passages with Q-tips. Yet both men died of acute myeloid leukemia less than four years after their rendezvous with the Baneberry cloud. Their widows suffered through their long and agonizing deaths, watching the bone marrow cancer suck the life out of the men they loved.

The years after Louise buried her husband were hard, but the toll was much worse on Dorothy. She was only fifty-two when she took Harley back home for burial in Bicknell, Indiana, in April 1974. Baneberry took her husband and their life savings. She was left to battle her disabling diabetes with only $178.00 a month in Social Security benefits to pay medical bills, monthly expenses, and a $16,000 hospital bill for Harley's last illness. And, in 1977, things got worse for Dorothy. The IRS threatened to seize her small mobile home for nonpayment of $1,500 in back taxes Harley Roberts owed. Harley and other security guards had taken a deduction for travel pay to the Test Site, which the IRS disallowed.[4]

When Dorothy and Louise came to the office at 8:15 the morning of the trial, neither had slept, worrying about how they would handle their appearance in court and dreading interviews with the reporters they knew would be waiting on the front steps of the federal courthouse.

To avoid the media, we were dropped off near the back courthouse entrance and raced inside to the elevators. But as we waited for the ding of the elevator, a reporter spotted us and bolted over in time to snap a photograph of Dorothy, Louise, and Alan.[5] When the elevator doors opened, we scurried inside to avoid an interview.

We entered the courtroom, escorted our clients through the swinging bar of the court, and seated them at the plaintiffs' counsel table. On our side of the courtroom, our secretary, Kathy Trout, came in and sat in the front row right behind us.

At the government's table, several attorneys were already seated. Bill Elliott was nearest to us. He was from the Justice Department in Washington, D.C. and lead trial counsel for the government. He scowled a sort of acknowledgment as he glanced our way through narrow slits wrapped in folds that hung over his eyelids. When Elliott first joined the defense team in 1977, we tried to be cordial, particularly Alan, who got along with nearly everybody. But during the trial, Elliott's arrogant attitude and contempt for "the Baneberry widows" surfaced in a newspaper article. A reporter asked him how much the government intended to spend to defend the case. "As much as it takes to win," he boasted.[6]

Seated next to him was John Thorndal, head of the local private law firm prospering from the hundreds of thousands of dollars in legal fees it had racked up to carry out Mr. Elliott's pledge.[7] Well over a dozen lawyers and staff from Thorndal's firm, the U.S. Attorney's office, and the local office of the Atomic Energy Commission milled around in several rows on the government's side of the courtroom.

Every nerve pulsed in the pit of my stomach as I sat there. I felt like a sprinter in the starting blocks waiting for the gun. It had all come down to this. The fate of the women made widows by Baneberry was now in the hands of one frail, elderly federal judge, who would hear the evidence and ultimately decide some of the most complex scientific issues of the age. At stake was the United States' thirty-five-year love affair with the atomic bomb and the credibility of the Atomic Energy Commission, which had assured Nevadans and all Americans that its atomic testing program caused harm to no one.

The Baneberry test was headline news in both Las Vegas newspapers on Saturday, December 19, 1970, the day after it erupted.[8] But at the time, it was of no interest to Alan and me. We were furnishing our law office and preparing to open for business on January 2, 1971. Little did we know that a few months later Baneberry would disrupt our fledgling legal practice and become a dominant part of our lives for the next twenty-five years.

This is my story about Baneberry and how it beguiled my brother Alan and me into embarking on a quest to hold the Atomic Energy Commission responsible for the deaths of Harley Roberts and Bill Nunamaker. Baneberry was an alluring and irresistible challenge for two young lawyers who had grown up in Las Vegas with memories of the town before the AEC came in 1951 and who believed that the AEC could be held accountable, like anyone else, under what we thought was the best and fairest judicial system the world had ever known.

NOTES

1. *Baneberry Collection*, MS 19, Special Collections, UNLV Libraries, University of Nevada–Las Vegas. The Trial Transcript, hereinafter "TR" is 5,404 pages in length. Unless quoted, the trial testimony is summarized.

2. Films and videotapes of the Baneberry vent were classified. We had to file motions to compel their release. In 1975 the court allowed us to view the films and videotapes at the AEC building. But we were subject to a protective order that precluded us from copying or reproducing the films or communicating information to anyone about them. On October 6, 1977, the AEC released to the press a black-and-white photo of the Baneberry vent cloud (*Las Vegas Review-Journal*, October 6, 1977). In the photo the portion of the Baneberry cloud that plunged to the ground is on the left or west side and looks like a wolf's head. Rainier Mesa, where Area 12 Camp and the tunnel complexes were located, is behind and left of the column. On March 8, 1979, the government showed selected portions of the films at trial (*Las Vegas Review-Journal*, March 9, 1979).

3. *Baneberry Collection*, EX 66. References are to trial exhibits. EX 66 is the *Baneberry Summary Report*. Figure 1 tabulated the exposures of the eighty-six men exposed at Baneberry but did not identify them. On June 27, 1977, after we filed multiple motions to compel the government to produce the radiation readings for the eighty-six men, the court ordered the government to supply a list of each man exposed and his radiation dose. EX 91 disclosed Roberts's and Nunamaker's radiation doses.

4. *Las Vegas Review-Journal*, May 22, 1977.

5. Ibid., January 17, 1979.

6. *Los Angeles Herald Examiner*, March 11, 1979.

7. *Las Vegas Sun*, May 25, 1979. In hearings before the House Oversight and Investigations Subcommittee in May 1979, William Shaffer, deputy assistant attorney general, testified, "the government spent more than $500,000 in 46 days of [the Baneberry] trial."

8. *Las Vegas Sun*, December 19, 1970; *Las Vegas Review-Journal*, December 19, 1970.

[2]

Thar She Blows

December 18, 1970

AT 6:45 AM, HARLEY ROBERTS pulled next to the trailer at security station BJY and slammed the door of his pickup truck. He stepped briskly over fresh patches of snow left from an overnight dusting and walked up to the trailer. As he opened the door, he heard his brother-in-law, Ernie Dyer, in a heated argument with the shift captain. Ernie's face was bright red. "Orders are orders, Dyer," the captain shouted. "Calm down. There's nothing you can do about it."[1]

Harley walked over and stood next to Ernie. The two men were quite a contrast. Ernie Dyer was nearly six feet, 170 pounds, bald, with penetrating blue-gray eyes. Harley was five nine, 145 pounds, with thinning brown hair and sparkling blue eyes. Ernie was assertive with a shrill, cocky, somewhat sarcastic voice. Harley was laid back, and his voice was jocular with a deep, nasal tone.

They were both fifth-generation Hoosiers whose great-great-grandfathers settled in western Indiana before the mid-1850s. Both came to Las Vegas in the 1960s to join the security force at the Nevada Test Site. Ernie came first. He and Harley's sister, Dixie, were living in Phoenix in April 1961, when he saw an ad in the newspaper for a security job at NTS. He drove to Las Vegas for an interview, passed the physical exam, and was hired immediately. Dyer was one of five in the first security training class; Bill Cleghorn was one of the others. Dyer and Cleghorn came to NTS in May 1961 to help secure the site for the resumption of nuclear testing that had been suspended since October 30, 1958.[2]

The Test Site was the home of the most amazing man-made spectacle the world had ever seen. Tens of thousands of soldiers and civilians had been part of the nation's grand nuclear experiment. The broad test basin was littered with concrete foundations sprouting twisted metal, residue of fifty atomic bombs detonated on steel towers as high as 700 feet above the desert floor. Trenches where tens of thousands of soldiers huddled waiting for the shock wave from the blasts were still visible, although sagebrush and Russian thistle had conquered much of the landscape. The huge tunnel portals on the Rainier Mountain Range were closed, but the rails and rail cars still waited for crews to return to cut drifts deeper and deeper.

On September 1, 1961, the Soviets detonated the first nuclear device since the October 31, 1958, moratorium. On September 15, 1961, President Kennedy responded with the United States' first underground nuclear test, *Antler*, detonated in a reopened tunnel in the Rainier Range.[3] The nuclear arms race was on again.

But tunnel tests were not enough to satisfy the hunger for experimentation. The largest drill rigs in the country were hauled onto the Test Site to drill shafts over seven feet in diameter and up to 1,000 feet below the desert floor to emplace nuclear devices.[4]

Reopening the Test Site for underground tests in tunnels and shafts required the expertise of geologists, hydrogeologists, physicists, geophysicists, and other scientists, if the multikiloton blasts were to be completely contained. The excavation workforce needed engineers, muckers, miners, drillers, heavy equipment operators, laborers, plumbers, teamsters, and various support personnel. The Test Site was transformed from an atmospheric laboratory into a catacomb as thousands of workers descended on the site to dig, dump, and detonate a nuclear device in every crack and cranny that could be carved quickly and filled with a nuclear device.

Harley and Dorothy Roberts had stayed in close contact with the Dyers after Ernie went to work at the Test Site in 1961. When Ernie and Dixie came to Indiana for Christmas in 1961, Ernie bragged to Harley about his new job with good union wages and a pension. He tried to talk Harley into moving to Las Vegas to join him at the site. But Harley was not interested. He liked his small-town lifestyle. He fished and camped with his wife and son, played golf with a group of friends, and competed on a town basketball team. Other than a short stint in the military and his job at a defense plant in Detroit during the war, he had lived his entire life in western Indiana.

Over the next four years, the Dyers frequently returned to Indiana. They were persistent and wanted the Robertses to join them in Las Vegas. By the fall of 1965, Harley was ready for a change. His mother and sister had now followed the Dyers to Las Vegas. He had operated his own small service station, worked as a route-man delivering soda pop, and for the past couple years had run an insurance agency. Yet despite a lifetime of hard work, he had not saved much for retirement. At forty-five, he was still in excellent physical condition. He figured he could work at the Test Site until he was sixty-five. In twenty years, he and Dorothy could move back to Indiana with some savings, a company pension, and Social Security benefits.

Harley applied for a security job at the Test Site. In the fall of 1965, he came to Las Vegas for an interview and passed his physical exam. On New Year's Day 1966, Harley, Dorothy, and their fifteen-year-old son, Randy, drove into Las Vegas.

When Harley reported to security station BJY shortly before 7:00 AM on December 18, 1970, he had been working at the Test Site for nearly five years. He was a good sounding board for his more vocal brother-in-law; this morning was no different. Ernie walked Harley to the other end of the trailer to get away from the captain.

"What's got you so pissed off?" Harley half whispered.

"Does it show?" Ernie scowled and without waiting for a reply related the events during the long night. "I got here at six last evening and asked the captain when we were going to sweep Area 12. You know what he said? 'Ernie, they're leaving Area 12 open for this shot.' I couldn't believe it. How could they possibly leave nearly 1,000 workers only a few miles from the shot point? If the damned thing blew, it would dump radiation on them before they could clear out.

"I asked him to call headquarters to make sure. He said he had already confirmed the orders and was not going to call and question them. I kept bugging him until he finally called. He put the blame on me, said the night shift sergeant was demanding that he confirm that they weren't going to evacuate Area 12 for this test. He put the phone close to my ear so I could hear the chief tell him the orders were correct and were going to be carried out.

"Harley, you know we swept Area 12 for four previous shots this week. This shot is a lot closer to Area 12 Camp than any of the others."

"Yeah," Harley affirmed.

"That's what I told the captain. He blew me off; reminded me that none of the prior tests vented, so why should we worry about this one."

"I guess he's got a point," Harley noted.

"Yeah. Anyway, I let it go. We went out to sweep east from the guard station outside Area 12 Camp up through Areas 8 and 15 and then south to the station here at BJY. After we finished around midnight, me and the captain went at it again. I flat told him it was crazy to leave Area 12 open and demanded he call and try to get the orders changed. He was getting pretty hot and wouldn't call. So, I pointed out we only had the two guards posted near Area 12 Camp. If it vented, there was no way in hell they could move a thousand workers out of there.

"He wouldn't budge, so I tried another angle. I asked him to call headquarters to see if we could put sixteen guards up at Area 12 Camp just in case. He knew I wouldn't shut up until he called. So, he finally called and got the same bullshit response. I asked him to try to get permission to put eight men up there. He asked, but they told him to drop it. We went out and finished our second sweep at around three. At six o'clock, we cleared the arming party to go up and activate the device. I've been bitching ever since."

Ernie sighed and continued. "You know everybody had a bad feeling about this Baneberry test all along. They had problems drilling the hole; a lot more than any test anybody can remember. They had to postpone the damn thing several times. It just doesn't make sense to cram all these tests into the last week of the year and end with this one."

When Ernie finished, the rest of the day-shift guards had checked in at the security trailer at BJY. Dyer told them to stand by for shift change.

From the north window of the trailer, the Baneberry site, where the nuclear device had been lowered 912 feet down the hole, was in plain view nine miles away. As the sun crested above the eastern mountain range, the broad test basin, patched with fresh snow, sparkled in the bright winter sun. The Rainier Range to the northwest also had a light blanket of snow. Carved deep into the mountains were the massive tunnel complexes filled with hundreds of workers nearing the end of their shift. The tunnel portals were not visible, but Area 12 Camp, perched on a plateau at the base of the range, was in plain view, as the roofs of its metal buildings reflected the sun.

Area 12 Camp was built to provide housing and facilities for the thousands of workers who poured shift after shift in and out of the tunnels. There were over 300 rental trailers for temporary housing. In addition, the camp had a cafeteria, movie theater, recreation hall, library, baseball field, tennis and basketball courts, and a fire station.

A quarter mile east of Area 12 Camp, two security guards were posted in a shack on Rainier Mesa Road. Bob Yager and George Holly had worked all night ahead of the countdown. They had a clear view of the Baneberry site down the hill three miles away.

Tom Hayes, a radiation safety monitor, or "Rad-Safe monitor," employed by Reynolds Electrical and Engineering Company, REECo, sat in his pickup truck at the same location. A few minutes prior to shot time, Hayes put on his protective gear, rubber boots, rubber gloves, full-body coveralls with orange vest, and hood. He also had a facemask with air filters to avoid inhaling any radioactive dust and rolls of masking tape to seal the seams of his gear to prevent any skin contact with radioactive material.

At the Area 12 cafeteria, hundreds of day-shift workers were finishing breakfast and preparing to board buses up to the tunnel portals to relieve the night crew. Bill Nunamaker, shop foreman at T Tunnel, was sipping a final cup of coffee. He had driven nearly a hundred miles from Las Vegas that morning.

The main entrance to the cafeteria faced southeast, with a view of the Baneberry site and the entire test basin below. The basin was pockmarked with craters from hundreds of underground tests; the largest was the mammoth 1962 *Sedan* crater nearly 1,300 feet in diameter and 300 feet deep. It was a landscape like none other on earth. But the high-desert vegetation had already reclaimed much of the cratered ground.[5]

Behind the Area 12 cafeteria, atop a pole fifteen feet above the surface, sat a radiation detection device. Hardwired to the operation control center, CP-1, nineteen miles south, it was the only permanent radiation-measuring device in the one-square mile Area 12 Camp.

Dyer and Roberts moved over to the window at 7:25 AM to listen to the countdown. Nine miles south of BJY, Frank Cluff, the Baneberry test manager, and his advisory panel were at the control point, CP-1. They were seated around a conference table talking and staring at screens displaying images of the Baneberry site transmitted from closed-circuit cameras around surface ground zero.

Cluff and his panel had met for a readiness briefing at 2:30 PM the day prior to Baneberry. At that meeting, orders were given to clear all personnel from areas one quarter mile east of Area 12 Camp, where security guards George Holly and Robert Yager were posted. But Area 12 Camp and the tunnel complexes in Area 12 were left open. At that meeting, fallout predictions were discussed if Baneberry were to vent. One panel member, V. Urban commented, "If Fred's Folly were to erupt tomorrow, I will try to guess." He went on to make predictions about where the vent cloud might move.[6]

When the panel met again for a final briefing at 5:15 AM on December 18, 1970, all areas one-quarter mile east of Area 12 Camp had been swept during the night. But no one reported that Sergeant Dyer had repeatedly called to challenge the decision to leave Area 12 Camp open or that he had requested permission to place a guard force near Area 12 Camp in case Baneberry vented. Cluff and his panel were confident that Baneberry posed no "apparent threat to either personnel or the Test Ban Treaty" and directed the device be armed at 6:00 AM.[7]

When the countdown reached zero, Dyer and Roberts looked north out the trailer window and saw a cloud of dust rise over the Baneberry site as the chimney above the vaporized cavity 900 feet below the surface transmitted the force of the explosion to the surface. From their guard shack, Yager and Holly looked three miles down the hill at the Baneberry site and saw a circular plume of dust swirl around ground zero. Seconds later, their building shuddered. Workers in the tunnels also felt the shock wave pass through the rock under their feet and waited for the all clear. In the Area 12 cafeteria, the dayshift crews felt the ground move and knew it was time to get ready for the eight o'clock shift change.

At CP-1, the test manager and his advisors watched the screens blur as the cameras around ground zero bounced up and down from the force of the underground blast and then stabilized, recording a 200-foot-diameter circle of dust leap a hundred feet into the air. The test manager's primary duty was to assure that the underground test was completely contained. If he failed and the test vented radiation into the atmosphere, it was his responsibility to make sure the workers were evacuated to avoid radiation exposure.

Two minutes after the shot, the captain chided Dyer, "See, I told you Dyer, nothing to worry about." Dyer and Roberts walked away from the window. There was a collective sigh of relief all over the Test Site. The scientists in charge of the test began preparing to drive up to the Baneberry site to collect data from instruments housed in trailers stationed on a grid several hundred yards south of surface ground zero.

A minute later, the test basin silence was shattered by a thunderous sound as a column of dust and smoke shot a thousand feet above the Baneberry site and kept climbing. At the control point, the images on the screens bounced again, as the cameras shook from the force of the eruption. After a few seconds, the cameras began to stabilize, showing black smoke pouring from a 300-foot-long fissure. To the film crew aboard a helicopter circling the site at about 10,000 feet, fire seemed to erupt the full length of the 300-foot crevice.[8]

Deep below the surface, the core of the Baneberry nuclear device exploded in the wet clay deposit in which it had been placed, producing a super-heated, gas-filled cauldron and isotopes measuring in millions of curies. Roiling and churning against the walls of the spherical cavity, the radioactive stew of pressurized gas probed the substrata until it found a weak point. A fault line tangent to the cavity provided a seam and pathway upward. The pressurized gas ripped open the seam and followed the crack several hundred feet upward, then blew open a 300-foot-long crevice to the surface, spewing gas and charred dust high into the atmosphere.

In the trailer at station BJY, everyone ran to the north window to watch the enormous column climb 8,000 feet above the desert floor and then top out in a huge hammerhead-shaped cloud. Most of the men in the trailer that morning came to NTS in the 1960s and had only seen pictures of the spectacular A-bomb blasts in the 1950s. Baneberry, with its black column and distorted billowing top, resembled the surface tests, although it was detonated far below ground.

In the Area 12 cafeteria, someone yelled and hundreds ran outside to watch the column rise and billow. As they stared, the column and cloud cast a massive shadow over the test basin just south. For most, it was their first glimpse of an atomic test, and they were riveted by the spectacle, paralyzed, waiting for orders. The explosion had not been contained. Now the test manager had to try to figure out where the radiation released into the atmosphere would go. He ran outside the trailer and watched helplessly as the radioactive cloud nearly eighteen miles north of his trailer swelled.

Test Manager Frank Cluff was a meteorologist, uniquely qualified to gauge the movement of the Baneberry cloud. There were wind instruments and radiation detection devices scattered across the site to help him make the right decision. The first radiation measurement came from a device 1,000 feet west of surface ground zero. It maxed out at 1,000 R or 100,000 mR and probably registered 10,000 R or more. But 1,000 R was enough to kill anyone exposed to that dose. Fortunately, the nearest people were the two security guards and the Rad-Safe monitor three miles west near Area 12 Camp. But trailers on a grid nearby were filled with instruments to collect data from the test. The intense gamma radiation penetrated them and fried equipment and data.

The test manager waited. Five minutes after the venting, an instrument on a thirty-foot tower 1,500 feet west of ground zero reported surface winds heading southwesterly. But at that point, the rising cloud was 8,000 feet above the ground. The test manager was not concerned.

At 7:40 AM, while the column was still feeding the ever-expanding cloud at its top, a large chunk of the column plummeted several thousand feet to the valley floor. A photographer aboard a helicopter circling the site filmed the collapse and the cloud of radioactive dust that settled over the basin. Within minutes, the falling dust cloud formed two arms that looked like huge black snakes and began slithering up the mesa toward Area 12 Camp.

At 7:43 AM, the 800-foot chimney of rock and dirt collapsed into the spherical Baneberry cavity, producing a dust cloud and crater several hundred feet in diameter and seventy-five feet deep. Normally, the cratering of a device seals off any further radioactive release from the cavern below. But Baneberry defied the norm. Nine hundred feet below the surface, pockets of compressed radioactive gas continued belching radiation to the surface. This lasted for the next twenty-four hours until the last bubble was depleted.

The test manager was transfixed as he received reports of the progress of the swirling surface cloud hovering in the basin south of Area 12 Camp. At 7:45 AM Rad-Safe monitor Troy Ellis and four other monitors were on Stockade Wash Road at the head of a caravan of thirty-five to forty-five cars and three buses proceeding east to Area 12. Ellis called to tell his supervisors that the cloud was heading straight toward Area 12 Camp and asked permission to set up a roadblock to intercept all vehicles heading east into Area 12. He was told the cloud was not going to Area 12 Camp. Along with nearly two hundred other workers, he drove on into Area 12.

Just after part of the column plunged to the desert floor, Yager and Holly called to report that the cloud was moving up the hill toward them and asked permission to move west to the Area 12 Camp entrance. The request was denied. Although not a meteorologist or one those "critters that are supposed to chase winds," Yager knew why the radioactive dust cloud was moving up the hill toward his location. Having spent a lifetime in the outdoors fishing and camping, he knew that as the sun began to warm the desert basin, the surface winds were going to head uphill "like the dickens." It was a phenomenon well known to firefighters. He stood on the plateau and watched the cloud climb toward him.[9]

At 7:35 AM, Walter Adkins sat in his bus in the parking lot outside the Area 12 cafeteria as Bill Nunamaker and others boarded for the ride up to T Tunnel. When the bus arrived at T Tunnel at 7:50 AM, Nunamaker went to his shop just inside the portal.

On any other morning, Adkins would have driven his bus back down to Area 12 Camp. But the T Tunnel supervisor could see the Baneberry cloud approaching and instructed Adkins to stand by. Adkins turned his bus around facing downhill and got a first-hand view of the cloud as it moved up the canyon toward him.

At station BJY, Dyer was tired and frustrated. He had pleaded with his supervisor to evacuate Area 12 and had worked nearly fourteen hours when *Baneberry* vented. At 7:43, he and the others watched a large chunk of the column fall to the ground blocking their view of Area 12 Camp, sealing off the direct route from BJY into Area 12.

By 7:47 AM, the test manager's last hope that the surface winds would turn away from Area 12 Camp was dashed. The wind instrument recorded surface winds moving westerly toward Area 12 Camp. The test manager needed a miracle to stop the cloud from blanketing the camp.

Rad-Safe monitor Tom Hayes, at the same location as Yager and Holly, called his supervisor at 7:50 and asked permission to move a quarter-mile west on Rainier Mesa Road to the entrance to Area 12 Camp. His request was denied. Hayes watched the grayish-tan wall of fine ash particles move toward his position and called again at 8:00 AM. He was told to hold fast until the readings were above background. While Hayes was on the phone, his Geiger counter began to click as it picked up the first readings. When the instrument pegged out on its lower scale, 20 mR gamma, he switched to the higher scale, 20–200 mR gamma, as the readings rose to 50 mR.[10]

At CP-1, the test manager had ignored calls from the Rad-Safe monitors and reports from crews aboard helicopters that the cloud was moving toward Area 12 Camp. But he could not ignore the radiation readings Hayes reported from his station on the road a quarter mile south of Area 12 Camp. For five minutes Cluff hesitated. But at 8:05 AM, when no doubt remained that the Area 12 Camp was Baneberry's target, test manager Cluff gave the order to conduct an emergency evacuation to remove the 900 workers trapped in Area 12 Camp and the nearby tunnel complexes.

On December 10, 1970, the *Test Manager's Operation Plan for Baneberry*, signed by Frank Cluff, outlined all pre- and post-Baneberry activities. Item 18 was directed to Reynolds Electrical and Engineering Company (REECo), the prime contractor at NTS that employed all Rad-Safe monitors. It stated: "No.18. — H-30 min. [7:00 AM] — REECo Rad/safe will provide standby teams of monitors to be used in an emergency situation as directed by the TM."[11]

Even earlier than the test manager's Baneberry Plan, on April 1, 1969, the AEC adopted *Chapter 0544 EMERGENCIES IN AEC OPERATIONS*. Its stated objective was "to provide maximum practical protection of AEC and AEC contractor personnel."[12] It required that emergency plans be prepared and periodically tested. REECo was to prepare "written emergency plans for the evacuation of personnel in Area 12 Camp" and designate an "Area 12 Camp coordinator to carry out the evacuation."[13]

At 8:05 AM on December 18, 1970, when the test manager finally gave the order to start the evacuation of Area 12 Camp, there was no evacuation plan for Area 12 Camp and no designated Area 12 Camp evacuation coordinator. More important, REECo did not have teams of Rad-Safe monitors standing by thirty minutes before shot time to conduct an emergency evacuation.[14]

Without any of the above, Cluff gave the order to evacuate Area 12 to AEC security chief Chan Griffin, who directed Wackenhut Services Inc. (WSI), the security contractor at NTS, to implement the order immediately. Sergeant Ernie Dyer, the highest-ranking WSI field officer in the forward area, was ordered to gather as many men as possible and carry out the evacuation.

The only emergency warning device in the one-square mile Area 12 Camp was a siren at the fire station. But the firemen on duty did not turn it on. In fact, it was not activated until 8:40 AM, after Dyer arrived and demanded that it be turned on.

Even without orders, the workers in Area 12 Camp saw the looming cloud and realized they had to get out fast. The Area 12 cafeteria chief knew what to do. He shut down the registers, closed the cafeteria, and told everyone to get the hell out of the camp. Guards Holly and Yager, stationed at the entrance to the camp, blocked the route east and funneled the fleeing workers west onto Stockade Wash Road away from the cloud.

When the order to evacuate was conveyed to the T Tunnel supervisor, the workers raced out of the portal and boarded buses or jumped into their vehicles and headed down the canyon and into Area 12 Camp. Walter Adkins's bus was full, as he headed into the oncoming cloud. Fine grayish particles fell like snowflakes, covering the bus. Some of the passengers tried to seal the windows by sticking paper in the cracks. When they arrived in Area 12 Camp, the cloud had already settled there. They carpooled in private vehicles and headed out.

When Dyer received the order just after 8:05 AM, he left one man at station BJY and mustered thirteen security guards to assist him. Because the cloud blocked the ten-mile direct road into Area 12 Camp, Dyer and his men took a circuitous twenty-five-mile route, driving seventy miles per hour on icy roads and arriving in Area 12 Camp at around 8:30 AM.

When Dyer passed Rad-Safe monitor Hayes's location at 8:30, Hayes's Geiger counter had maxed out at 200 mR gamma. He switched to a Pic6A instrument that fluctuated wildly between 500 and 800 mR gamma. Hayes assumed the instrument was saturated by high readings in the cloud and called for another Rad-Safe monitor to come by and take readings. Rad-Safe monitor Ron Perry arrived at 9:00 AM and recorded a reading of 1,500 mR gamma.[15]

As mentioned, the only radiation device in Area 12 Camp was the probe atop a fifteen-foot pole behind the cafeteria, hard–wired to the control point. Like Hayes's Geiger counter, it was designed to measure only gamma radiation. Handwritten notes taken down at CP-1, showed that gamma readings reached a maximum of 700 mR at around 9:00 AM.

It was cold that December morning, and all the security guards wore standard uniforms of heavy flight jackets with an imitation fur collar that collected radioactive particles from the cloud. And since the guards were not expected to enter a radiation field, they did not wear hats or gloves to prevent the swirling radioactive particles in the cloud from collecting in their hair and sticking to faces and hands. Jack Cupples, one of guards who evacuated Area 12 Camp that morning, tied a handkerchief around his face, bandana style, to try to reduce the amount of radiation he drew into his mouth and nose.

At his command post on the main road below the Area 12 cafeteria, Dyer took charge. He ordered the guards to fan out over the one-square-mile camp and clear personnel from all buildings. Harley Roberts and one other guard were ordered to clear all personnel in trailers on the far eastern end of the camp.

Roberts left his truck at the command post and sprinted a quarter mile down the hill to Rainier Street. In the grayish fog-like haze, he raced from trailer to trailer beating on doors ordering the occupants out. Passing the window of one of the trailers he saw his face reflected. It was ghostly white with an almost ashen hue from the dust that covered his entire face. At another trailer window, he caught a fleeting image that haunted him for his remaining days. His head appeared to be x-rayed against the glass panel. Absent hair, skin, and flesh, only the skull stared back at him.

Roberts cleared over seventy-five trailers in about forty-five minutes. Breathing rapidly, he sucked the radioactive gas and dust deep into his lungs and was assaulted from every angle by the penetrating gamma rays. At 9:15 AM, he raced back up the hill and reported to Sergeant Dyer that all trailers in his sector were clear. He was the last man to report. The other guards had completed their assignments ten minutes earlier and left the camp.

After Dyer set up his command post and ordered the guards to begin the evacuation, he went down to the fire station to find out why the emergency siren was not sounding the evacuation warning. The firemen curtly told him they had not received any orders and would have to check with their chief. Dyer demanded they get the chief on the phone. They were defiant, so Dyer called AEC security. Minutes later, the fire chief ordered his men to "turn on the damned siren." By the time the siren went off, the evacuation was already well underway.

When Roberts reported back to Dyer at 9:15 AM, he was ordered to head west on Stockade Wash Road and then up G Tunnel Road to make sure all personnel in G Tunnel were out. Dyer headed back down to the fire station and told the firemen to leave. They again refused until they got orders. After the earlier episode and over fifteen hours on the job, Dyer's patience was spent. Though tempted to order the firemen out at gunpoint, he called AEC security again. A minute later the order came. The firemen shut off the evacuation siren and left in a huff.

By the time the evacuation was complete, the Baneberry cloud had passed over Area 12 Camp. The metal roofs no longer sparkled in the bright morning sun. Everything was covered with ash and dust. Dyer pulled out of Area 12 Camp at 8:30 AM. Ordering the security guard and Hayes to precede him, Dyer's pickup truck was last in a line of over 400 vehicles winding west up Stockade Wash Road to Area 17 Camp. He remained at the end of the convoy until all vehicles had reached the Area 17 checkpoint.

NOTES

1. Based on personal interviews with Harley Roberts and Ernest Dyer.

2. *United States Nuclear Tests, July 1945 through September 1992*, DOE/NV-209-REV 15, December 2000, 16–23. *Antler*, the first shot after testing resumed on September 15, 1961, blew out the tunnel portal and released radiation offsite, as did tunnel tests *Feather, Platte*, and *Des Moines*.

3. *United States Nuclear Tests, July 1945 through September 1992*, DOE/NV-209-REV 15, December 2000, 16–17.

4. Ibid., 16–26. *Operation Nougat* consisted of forty-four underground tests beginning with *Antler* on September 15, 1961, and ending with *Sacramento* on June 30, 1962. The next test at NTS was *Sedan*, the first of the *Plowshare* tests designed to determine the feasibility of using nuclear blasts to dig a canal across Central America.

5. *United States Nuclear Tests, July 1945 through September 1992*, DOE/NV-209-REV 15, December 2000, 24–25. The crater from the 104-kiloton *Sedan* underground nuclear test, 320 feet deep and 1,280 feet in diameter, released radiation off-site, as did crater or surface tests *Johnnie Boy, Small Boy*, and *Little Feller II*.

6. *Baneberry Collection*, EX 2. Test Evaluation Panel Readiness Briefing Notes, p. 3. Urban's Report, EX 27, projected the fallout pattern and dosage estimates for offsite populations but did not consider the possibility that workers in Area 12, just three miles from surface ground zero, might be exposed to the radioactive cloud.

7. *Baneberry Collection*, EX 3, Readiness Briefing Notes, 5:15 AM.

8. We did not see films of the Baneberry venting until 1975, after we filed multiple motions to compel their release. On October 6, 1977, the AEC released a photo of the Baneberry vent showing the huge hammerhead-shaped cloud. *Las Vegas Review-Journal*, October 6, 1977.

9. *Baneberry Collection*, TR.

10. The Geiger counters Hayes and all Rad-Safe monitors carried on December 18, 1970, measured only penetrating gamma radiation, not Beta particles present in the cloud.

11. *Baneberry Collection*, EX 9.

12. Ibid., EX 5.

13. Ibid., EX 7.

14. Ibid., EX 49. A list of all REECo radiological safety personnel on duty the day of Baneberry disclosed that there were 109 personnel, including fifty-nine Rad-Safe monitors in the field. But only one, Tom Hayes, was posted near Area 12 camp at shot time.

15. A standard chest x-ray delivers a gamma dose of about 30 mR.

[3]

The Luck of the Draw

AT 9:25 AM, ROBERTS LEFT DYER and drove out of the camp. As he left, the last remnant of the Baneberry vent cloud was moving up and over the Rainier Range. It was as if Harley Roberts had been Baneberry's primary target, and when he left it had no reason to linger.

Following orders, Roberts drove several miles up Stockade Wash Road and turned right to check out G Tunnel. A half mile up the narrow canyon, he met a security guard who told him all personnel were out of G Tunnel. Roberts turned around and followed him back to Stockade Wash Road and joined the long line of vehicles heading west up the mountain road. At the top of the hill, Rad-Safe monitors were stopping everyone to take readings with their Geiger counters. Roberts waited his turn.

As monitor Troy Ellis ran his instrument over Roberts's pickup truck, still coated with a layer of ash and dust, Roberts rolled down his window and heard the Geiger counter clicking wildly.

"Better have you step out and move away from the truck, so I can take a reading on you," Ellis ordered.

Roberts got out and Ellis motioned him over to the side of the road. Ellis held his Geiger counter thirty inches from Roberts's upper body and turned on the instrument. It whirred frantically as the needle hit the right side of the dial on the instrument. Ellis switched to the highest scale. It whirred again to pure static as the needle pegged at its maximum reading of 200 mR gamma.

"Man. You're hot as hell," Ellis exclaimed. "You need to be decontaminated as soon as possible. Get in your truck and proceed past the convoy and report to Area 17 Camp. I'll call ahead so they'll be looking for you."

Ellis had been monitoring evacuees for over an hour. All other security guards involved in the evacuation, except Dyer, had already passed his checkpoint. None had readings nearly as high as Roberts. Ellis called his supervisor, gave him Roberts's name and badge number, and told him the readings pegged his instrument and that Roberts needed to be deconned as soon as possible.

Harley figured he was hot. He had been in the cloud for nearly an hour. But so were the other guards who helped evacuate the camp. He assumed they were about as hot as he was. He jumped in his truck, sped past the long line of cars, and pulled into Area 17 Camp. He walked up to the security trailer, cracked the door, and told the captain, "Better stay away from me. A Rad-Safe guy said I'm hot as hell and need to be deconned."

The captain in charge at Area 17 Camp was not involved in the evacuation of Area 12. His job was to organize the convoy of vehicles and move them to the decontamination facility at CP-2 for monitoring. He seemed unconcerned by Harley's comment and waved him off. Roberts closed the door and walked over to join several other security guards standing nearby.

After about ten minutes, the captain opened the door, rushed over to where Harley and other guards were standing, and said he just got orders to post a guard at Dead Horse Flats to close off incoming traffic from the north. He picked Roberts to post the blockade and said he would get a Rad-Safe man to join him. Roberts did not remind the captain that a Rad-Safe monitor had told him he was "hot as hell" and should be decontaminated. He obeyed the order.

Roberts was teamed up with Rad-Safe monitor Willie Virgil, who had recently completed his training. Virgil grabbed his equipment and jumped in Roberts's pickup. They left Area 17 at around 9:50 and took the road up through the canyon into Area 19 to Dead Horse Flats. Radio reception was poor. Roberts drove around for several minutes to find a spot with fair reception. He parked his vehicle in the middle of the road and called headquarters to report that the roadblock was in place.

After they settled in for what they knew would be a long day, Roberts told Virgil about the evacuation of the camp and that a monitor on Stockade Wash Road told him he was hot as hell. When Virgil heard this, he said he should take some readings of Roberts and his vehicle. Roberts got out of the truck and Virgil told him to move twenty to thirty feet away from the vehicle. There, Virgil turned on his Geiger counter and held it chest high about thirty inches from Roberts. It made the same sound Harley had heard hour earlier. Virgil told Roberts he was registering around 300 mR gamma, and his vehicle was reading around 90 mR gamma. But Virgil seemed unconcerned about Roberts's readings and did not ask to use his radio to report them to his supervisor.

For the next six hours Roberts and Virgil sat in the truck. Virgil told Roberts he reported for duty that morning at 8:00 AM and watched the cloud moving toward Area 12 Camp. He and two other monitors spent fifteen minutes hunting for instruments and were stationed on Stockade Wash Road, several miles west of Area 12 Camp. Virgil was never in the cloud that passed over Area 12 Camp and was not exposed to any radiation.[1]

At around 10:00 AM, ten minutes after Roberts left Area 17 Camp, Dyer pulled in next to the security trailer. He opened the door and confronted the captain in charge. He demanded to know what the orders were for his guards. Dyer had worked seventeen straight hours. He was tired and angry. His men had carried out an evacuation that should have been done by Rad-Safe personnel. The captain called headquarters and spoke to WSI Captain Tackett. Dyer and his security force were given top priority and were directed to proceed immediately to CP-2 for decontamination. "Damn right," Dyer said angrily. "We got the dirty work no one else would do. They better take care of us."

Dyer stormed out and rounded up eleven of the guards who helped him evacuate Area 12 Camp. Two were missing, Harley Roberts and Carl Peterson. Dyer told his men to get in their trucks and follow him down to the CP for decontamination. With sirens blaring, they passed the convoy slowly snaking its way down Pahute Mesa Road. Dyer got on the phone and called Captain Tackett to see if he had any information about Roberts and Peterson. Ten minutes later, Tackett called to tell him that Peterson had been located and was behind them on the way to CP-2. But no one knew where Roberts was.

The REECo Rad-Safe decontamination pad was situated at CP-2, near CP-1, where the test manager and his advisors were located. When Dyer and his men arrived, the Rad-Safe monitors were waiting. They ordered the guards to remove their clothing, wrote down readings of their clothing, and placed them in plastic bags marked with each guard's name. The film in their identification credential was removed and placed in a box for processing. Then the guards themselves were monitored. All readings far exceeded the 25 mR gamma reading for required decontamination. They were told to swab out their nasal passages with a Q-tip. A Geiger counter was run over the Q-tips and the readings recorded for each.

Then they were ordered into the showers. When the showers were turned on, ice-cold water streamed out. The guards complained but were told the boiler was broken and they would have to take cold showers. Hair thick with ash and dust, faces chalky, and nasal passages encrusted with radioactive particulate, they entered the cold showers and soaped, scrubbed, and swabbed and gargled to wash out noses and mouths.

After ten minutes, the guards emerged and wrapped themselves in towels to get warm. The Rad-Safe monitors ran the instruments over them and placed the Geiger counters on their necks to see if radioactive iodine was concentrating in the thyroid glands. The readings were still far in excess of 25 mR. They were told the radiation levels were still too high and ordered back to the showers.

While Dyer and the guards were showering, their pickup trucks were being monitored in the yard. All vehicles were impounded and kept at CP-2 for over a month to scrub the exterior and vacuum and wash down the interior to bring the radiation back to safe levels.

After Dyer completed his first shower, he refused to reenter the showers until he called headquarters to find out where his missing guard was. He called Tackett and asked where the hell Roberts was. Tackett said they were still looking for him. Dyer commented scornfully that Roberts could not have just disappeared and the captain better get on the horn and find him. Tackett promised he would and to send him in for decontamination.

Dyer rejoined the other guards for his second shower. The guards went through the same showering and monitoring process multiple times. Several guards joked that Carl Stevens, one of the palest guards on the force, was turning blue from the ice-cold water. Finally, after additional showers, the monitors said they could not bring the radiation levels down any further. They dried off, put on paper coveralls and booties, then boarded a bus and were transported twenty-five miles to Mercury Medical for more monitoring and decontamination.

Meanwhile, the great convoy began arriving at CP-2. Most of the 900 workers in Area 12 had gotten out before the cloud settled there. Those who did not were only in the cloud for a few minutes before leaving. But eighty-five men, including Dyer's security crew, had readings above 25 mR gamma when they arrived at the decon pad and also had to take cold showers and swabs.

Walter Adkins, the bus driver who drove from T Tunnel down the canyon directly into the cloud and Area 12 Camp, took several showers before he was released. Bill Nunamaker, T Tunnel shop foreman and on Adkins's bus, also took several showers before he was released in a paper suit. His vehicle was impounded for a month. After Nunamaker was released from the decon pad, he carpooled to town. When he got home, dressed in paper coveralls and booties, he told his wife, Louise, he was "right in the middle of it."

As soon as Dyer and his men arrived at Mercury Medical, Dyer called Tackett to find out if Roberts had been found. Tackett said he was still looking. Dyer threatened to contact the AEC manager directly, if Tackett did not find him. Dyer and his men took several warm showers at Mercury Medical and were monitored for radiation levels. When they finished, it was nearly 4:00 PM. Dyer called Tackett again, but Roberts was still missing. Dyer and his men were told they needed more testing and would be bused to Las Vegas for a whole-body scan. At 4:15 PM, just before boarding, Dyer again called Tackett. Roberts had been located up at Dead Horse Flats, and someone was being sent to relieve him.

Ernie Dyer called his wife, Dixie, in Las Vegas and told her he was heading to town for more tests, and Harley would not be far behind. Dorothy Roberts, who was with Dixie, finally got word about Harley. It had been an agonizing day for her. She heard about the Test Site blast from a neighbor midmorning and drove over to Dixie's house to wait for news about Harley and Ernie.

By 5:30 PM, all guards involved in the evacuation of Area 12, except Roberts, were in Las Vegas at the U.S. Public Heath building, and by 7:00 PM they were home. Dyer was exhausted after his twenty-four-hour shift.

While Dorothy waited anxiously for news about Harley, he was manning his post at Dead Horse Flats. At 3:30 PM, he received word on his radio that relief was on its way, but the relief was for Rad-Safe monitor Virgil. At 4:00 PM, Bill Earnest, a long-time Rad-Safe monitor, arrived in his Rad-Safe vehicle. Virgil told Earnest he thought his Geiger counter was saturated and inoperable and asked Earnest to survey Roberts.

Earnest knew his instrument had just been calibrated and was accurate. Following standard procedure, he had Harley step away from his vehicle and remove his jacket. He moved his instrument up and down Harley's body. When it pegged on the lower scale, he switched to the highest scale. The readings for Roberts were still above the maximum 200 mR gamma at thirty inches from his lower legs. Earnest moved the instrument thirty inches from the upper body, and the clicking was much more intense.

Earnest was primarily interested in the upper-body readings, because it was in Roberts's breathing zone. He took separate readings of the jacket with the fur collar and compared them to the body readings. Based upon his training and experience, he estimated Roberts's gamma readings were around 1 R or 1,000 mR, the equivalent of thirty-three chest x-rays.

Earnest called in the readings and informed his superiors that Roberts should be relieved immediately for decontamination. Earnest turned his truck over to Virgil, who drove down to CP-2, and got in Roberts's truck. They waited nearly an hour for relief to arrive.

Harley Roberts arrived at CP-2 at around 6:00 PM. Only one Rad-Safe monitor was still at the decon pad, and he was getting ready to leave. It was Troy Ellis, who had monitored Roberts at 9:30 AM that morning on Stockade Wash Road. Ellis was surprised to see Roberts and asked him where the hell he'd been all day, reminding him he told him he was hot as hell when he checked him earlier. Roberts explained that he told the captain at 17 Camp he was hot but was ordered up to Dead Horse Flats and had just been relieved.

Ellis made him remove his jacket and clothing, took readings, said they were still very high, and placed them in a plastic bag marked with Roberts's name and identification number. He placed the Geiger counter to Roberts's neck for a thyroid reading. The needle immediately pegged the right side of the scale. Readings of his hair were even higher. Ellis swabbed the inside of Harley's nose, wrote the down the readings, and put the swabs and the written readings in another plastic bag.

Roberts was the eighty-sixth man ordered into the showers that day. When the blast of cold water hit him, he complained, but Ellis told him everyone had taken cold showers that day. Roberts soaped and scrubbed face, hands, and body and swabbed out his nasal passages. He was in the shower ten to fifteen minutes. After his first shower, readings were again taken, recorded, and placed in a plastic bag.

After his third shower, his readings had come down, but his hands were still over 50 mR gamma and the nose swipes recorded readings of 100 mR gamma.

Ellis wrote down all of Roberts's readings at CP-1 and filled out forms that were turned over to his supervisors. Those forms and readings disappeared.[2] Ellis gave Roberts a paper suit and rubber booties and told him he was going to personally drive him down to the Mercury Medical facility for further decontamination. On the way, Ellis described the Baneberry operation as mass confusion and said he was glad it was over.

At Mercury, Roberts was monitored again and sent in for a warm shower. It felt so good he did not want to get out. His radiation readings were recorded, and he was told to bend over a brick-like structure so they could check his thyroid level. When he was released, he was told his hands were still reading over 25 mR gamma, and there was nothing more they could do. He was given a pair of rubber gloves to wear to bed that night and some paper coveralls.

Before Roberts was discharged from Mercury Medical around 10:30 PM, he called Wackenhut. The normally mild-mannered Roberts had had enough. He demanded they find him some cloth coveralls. It was cold, and he was not going to wear a damned paper suit to bed. He was picked up fifteen minutes later and driven to the barracks. When he hit the bunk, he was exhausted.

Except for Harley Roberts, all eighty-six men deconned that day joined their families in Las Vegas that night. The drinkers drank a little more than usual. The lovers were a little more arduous, the thinkers a little more contemplative. In bars and bedrooms, the events of the day were relived. Every version was different, but all conversations ended with the same questions: what went wrong, and why?

Those questions were also consuming the AEC's top command and the scientists who planned Baneberry, all part of the atomic oligarchy. One thing was certain. There was no way the vent cloud could be squeezed back into that underground cavern. As the sun set early that December day on the eve of the winter solstice, the radioactive cloud was moving relentlessly across eastern Nevada, Utah, and into the U.S. heartland on its way to Canada and into the air stream to circle the globe.

International treaties were violated. Millions of dollars of equipment were hopelessly contaminated. Workers at NTS were exposed to radiation at levels they did not understand. Some wondered whether they had been injured and might develop cancer or some other illness.

But this was the least of the AEC's concerns. It had already moved into damage-control mode. Before the venting had abated, REECo contacted its radiation consultants. The AEC was mustering a force of its own, rounding up scientists to sit on a panel to evaluate the cause of the vent, assess the radiation doses, dispel any claim of injury or damage, and assure the public and the media that everything was okay.

As the diffusing Baneberry cloud distributed radiation across the country, the radioactive particles and gas it dumped on Area 12 was bombarding the lungs, blood, and organs of the men who participated in the day of the bane. Baneberry-day ended at midnight on December 18, 1970. But the cataclysmic struggle between radiation and living tissue in the bodies of the men exposed had just begun.

NOTES

1. *Baneberry Collection*, EX 91.
2. Ibid., TR; *Las Vegas Sun*, January 25, 1979.

[4]

The Bulldog

April 1971

When we opened our law office in January 1971, the practice of law was a noble profession we were honored to join. There were fewer than 150 members of the Clark County Bar Association, and we knew most of them.

Mike Hines, a long-time lawyer and one of Alan's first bosses, hosted a party at his ranch each year to welcome the new members. It was the event of the year, where the new lawyers were introduced to the judges and the leading members of the bar. Considering the amount of alcohol consumed, it is amazing that those who attended Mike's parties could navigate their way home after the affair. But those were the days before Mothers Against Drunk Driving, so the miscreants could quietly negotiate their citations with the judges who attended the same party.

In mid-April 1971, a call came into our office. The caller asked to speak with either Alan or me. Alan was in court, so I took the call.

"This is Bill Cleghorn," the caller announced. "I was referred to you guys by your former boss, DA George Franklin. He said you were good lawyers and might be able to handle this case."

"Well, that was nice of George," I responded, wondering why George, now in private practice, had not taken the case himself. "What's your case about?"

"You probably read about the Baneberry underground test that blew out last December and exposed all those workers at the Test Site to radiation. I'm president of the Independent Guard Association of Nevada, the union for the guards. Our guys had to go in and evacuate all the personnel in the base camp and got the highest radiation doses. They made a written request on the AEC to give them information about their radiation readings but were ignored. We're considering filing a lawsuit.

"I don't know what you guys know about it, but Baneberry was a mess. Everybody out there knew it. Anyway, would you be interested in handling the case? We're going to interview some other lawyers. So, if you're not interested say so," Cleghorn ended.

"I'll talk to my partner," I responded. "But I think we'd be willing to meet to discuss the matter. Do you want to make an appointment?"

At precisely 10:00 AM the next morning, Bill Cleghorn arrived. He was ushered into my office, where Alan and I were waiting. Bill was around 6' 4", over 200 pounds, and in good physical condition; the type of security guard the AEC needed to protect its nuclear weapons testing program.

Bill opened his briefcase, pulled out a manila file, and launched into a discussion about the Baneberry event. Fourteen guards were exposed to radiation, all were decontaminated that day, and all but one went to the U.S Public Health facility for additional tests. The guards wrote to the AEC requesting their radiation doses, but the AEC did not respond.

We asked Bill if the guards gave written statements. He said they did, but their statements were taken and classified, and the guards weren't allowed to make copies.

Bill handed us two articles in our local newspapers about the Baneberry venting.[1] He also gave us an article with an AP photo of the Baneberry cloud rising over a mountain range east of the Test Site with the headline: "600 Flee Nuclear Spill."[2] But the most interesting news story he supplied was by Colin McKinlay, *Los Angeles Times* staff writer, headlined: "Nevada Nuclear Blast Goes Wild, 500 Workers Evacuated." In the article, McKinlay interviewed an AEC spokesperson, who stated, "Exposure levels are not estimated at being above permissible dosage levels.... We don't know how much gamma radiation they got or what they inhaled or got internally."[3]

Baneberry released more radiation into the atmosphere than any test since the resumption of underground testing in September 1961. Bill knew this to be a fact, because he came to the Test Site in June 1961. He also mentioned that President Nixon had suspended nuclear testing until an investigation was completed. An official report was to be issued by the AEC in a few weeks.

When Bill Cleghorn asked if we were interested in the case, Alan and I looked at each other and one of us responded that we would consider it. Bill said he would get back to us. After he left, we discussed the matter but did not expect to hear from him again.

Nearly a month went by. Then, on May 13, 1971, Cleghorn called to tell us the AEC was going to hold a press conference the following day to announce the results of their investigation. He said he could not attend, but one of the guards would pick up whatever material they handed out and drop off a copy at our office.

At around 4:30 PM on May 14, 1971, copies of the *Baneberry Summary Report* and *AEC Press Release, May 14, 1971* were delivered to the office.[4] The press release assured the public that there was no hazard to anyone exposed to the radioactive Baneberry vent cloud and announced that testing would resume at the Test Site.

The *Baneberry Summary Report*, a sixteen-page stapled document with a bright yellow cover, stated that the vent was an accident that could not have been anticipated. Significantly, it confirmed that two Test Site security guards received the highest radiation doses and included Figure 1, which graphed the radiation doses of the eighty-six men exposed. There were four categories, Beta, Gamma, Lens of the Eye, and Thyroid Dose, but names and individual doses were not given.[5]

On May 19, 1971, five days later, we saw an article by James Barrows, *Sun* staff writer: "AEC Ignored Advice of Five Scientists." Barrows reported that five scientists were against the Baneberry test and that it was improperly planned and engineered. He focused on the radiation readings of two security guards who got "exposure to the lens of the eye almost equal to the exposure limit."[6]

In late May 1971, we agreed to handle an estate matter with the prospect of our first good fee and hoped that Cleghorn had found other lawyers to take the case. But in mid-June he called and came in. Cleghorn was out of patience. Requests for radiation records had been ignored by the AEC. He wanted us to file a lawsuit to force the AEC to produce the records. We suggested he make a formal request as president of the Independent Guard Association of Nevada (IGAN).

On June 20, 1971, *Feature* magazine in the *Las Vegas Sun* displayed photographs of failed, leaking underground nuclear tests at NTS prior to Baneberry and questioned the AEC's claim that it did not anticipate that the Baneberry test might vent.[7]

On June 21, 1971, Cleghorn, as president of IGAN, made a written request upon the U.S. Public Health Service for radiation readings of all security guards sent there for testing on Baneberry-day, December 18, 1970.[8]

NOTES

1. *Las Vegas Sun*, December 19, 1970; *Las Vegas Review-Journal*, December 19, 1970.
2. *Unknown*, December 19, 1970, copy in author's possession.
3. *Los Angeles Times*, December 19, 1970.
4. Summary report: *Baneberry Collection*, EX 66. Press release: *Baneberry Collection*, EX 65.
5. Ibid., EX 66.
6. *Las Vegas Sun*, May 19, 1971.
7. *Las Vegas Sun*, *Scene Feature Magazine*, June 20, 1971, with photos of vents of Platte, Eagle, Des Moines, and Eel.
8. William Cleghorn to U.S. Public Health Service, June 21, 1971. Copy in author's possession.

[5]

The Georgiadis Curse

October–December 1971

After sending the letter to U.S. Public Health Service, Bill Cleghorn called us several times to report there had been no response. By early October, he insisted we meet to discuss what could be done to get the radiation records.

When we met, Bill ranted about the mistreatment of the security guards and wanted us to file a lawsuit against the AEC. The Independent Guard Association of Nevada would bring the case on behalf of the fourteen security guards. In his view, as president of IGAN, he had a duty to protest the AEC's use of security guards to enter a radiation zone to evacuate the camp. At the very least, a lawsuit would force the government to produce the radiation records for his men.

When he finished, we explained that the union, by itself, could not file the lawsuit he wanted to bring. It could demand information on behalf of individual members, which it had. Only the individual guards exposed to radiation could file a lawsuit against the Atomic Energy Commission. But before they could bring a suit against the AEC, each had to fill out a federal tort claim stating the basis for his claim and demand a monetary amount as damage.

We told Bill we had not met any of the guards and had no idea how they felt about the matter. Cleghorn assured us he had talked to all of them, and they wanted to pursue it. But his assurances were not enough. We had to meet with each to make sure they wanted us to file a claim in their behalf. Bill understood and said he would contact them to make an appointment with us.

Although we had met with Bill several times, the subject of our legal fees had never been discussed. Bill asked what kind of a retainer we would need to file a lawsuit. We told him we would have to meet with the guards and then decide whether to proceed with the case. At that point, we would discuss legal fees, but we also made it clear that we were not willing to underwrite the costs and expenses of litigation against the government. Cleghorn said he would get the union to pay the costs.

Over two weeks passed. We assumed the union board was not willing to pay costs and the individual guards had lost interest in pursuing the case. But we learned Bill Cleghorn was determined that something be done and had a strong ally in Ernie Dyer, the sergeant in charge of the Area 12 Camp evacuation.

In early November, Cleghorn called and asked us to prepare a retainer agreement to cover our court costs. He was confident the executive board would approve it and the guards would call our office to make appointments to meet with us.

Over the next week, Alan and I discussed whether we should get involved in a lawsuit against the AEC. The *Baneberry Summary Report* claimed the vent was an unforeseeable accident, but news articles questioned the AEC's claim that it was unexpected. Further, the AEC's refusal to provide radiation records for the guards shrouded Baneberry in mystery. We wanted to know more and could not let it go. And within a few days, guards began calling to set up appointments.

Over the next few weeks, we met with thirteen of the fourteen guards; the fourteenth man was not interested in pursuing the matter. The guards were a very patriotic group of men, most with prior military service. They wanted us to proceed, but some were hesitant to talk about their activities at the Test Site or their specific activities at Baneberry. They had taken an oath not to disclose any information about the Test Site, and their written reports about their activities at Baneberry were classified. Some were concerned they might be prosecuted for divulging classified information.

All guards confirmed that when they joined the guard force, they had a two-week orientation, which did not include a discussion of radiation or its health effects. Their job was to secure and control access to areas where radiation was present, and they were not supposed to enter a radiation zone. Only Rad-Safe monitors, scientists, and personnel with clearance were authorized to pass through their checkpoints.

They all knew that radiation can cause cancer, and a few were concerned for their future health. But nearly a year had passed since Baneberry, and all were in good shape.

We explained that each guard had to file a tort claim against the AEC alleging they were negligently exposed to radiation at Baneberry and asking for damages for injuries they might sustain in the future. All thirteen guards agreed to submit a tort claim and file suit, if necessary, to get their radiation readings.

Ernie Dyer's interview was the longest. He was not reluctant to tell us about his battle with the captain all night before the test, his fight with the firemen, and his efforts to locate Harley Roberts. Nearly a year after the event, he was still angry and critical of the AEC, REECo, and his own Wackenhut superiors for exposing the guards to radiation and leaving Harley at a remote post all day.

Our meeting with Harley Roberts was the most memorable. He was not angry like his brother-in-law and seemed unworried about his radiation exposure. He had a good memory of the events and took us through his activities that day, from his discussion with Ernie when he first arrived at BJY, his graphic description of clearing out the trailers in the camp, the monitors' comments about his readings, to his decon procedures and release at Mercury Medical at 11:00 PM wearing rubber gloves. He mentioned he had diarrhea for several days following Baneberry but thought it was just the flu.

We asked about his life prior to the Test Site. He spoke fondly of living in Indiana and said that although he was only five feet ten he loved basketball and was a good player for his size. He played on town basketball teams until he was forty-five. Hoosiers, he explained, love basketball as much as Texans love football. He was also a good golfer and had won quite a few trophies. Camping and fishing were his favorite family activities back home.

The move to Las Vegas was a big change. He worked four twelve-hour shifts at the Test Site every week, checking badges and clearing out areas before shots. Unless he was called in, he avoided overtime. He spent two of his three days off playing golf or fishing and camping at Lake Mead. He came to the Test Site for the pay and intended to return to Indiana as soon as he retired.

We asked about his health prior to Baneberry. He said he never went to doctors in Indiana. Other than the annual physical exam required by Wackenhut and an occasional sinus flare-up after he came to the desert, he had not seen any doctors. He did not have as much energy as he used to, but was fifty-one and probably slowing down a little.

Harley knew he got more radiation than most of the other guards and there was a chance he might develop cancer sometime in the future. When asked if he wanted to file a claim and, if necessary, a lawsuit, he did not hesitate. If nothing else came out of it, he wanted to find out what radiation he received and why they sent the guards into that mess.

After talking to all thirteen guards, we knew Harley had received the highest radiation dose in all categories. His diarrhea after Baneberry raised questions whether his dose was higher than reported in the *Baneberry Summary*

Report, since diarrhea is a classic sign of high radiation exposure. But it could indeed have been the flu, as he assumed.

Cleghorn called the office in late November and asked us to send a retainer agreement for the union to sign. We wrote up a simple one-page agreement covering costs and mailed it to Cleghorn. On December 3, 1971, he dropped the signed document off at the office and wanted to know what was next.

Now there was no turning back. "Here's another fine mess you've gotten me into," Alan would chide me repeatedly over the years, as if the decision to take the case was entirely my own. Baneberry had beguiled us both and continued to lure us further and further into its web.

In December 1971, we filed federal tort claims for thirteen of the Wackenhut security guards involved in the evacuation of Area 12. For twelve of the thirteen, we asked for $250,000 in monetary damages each. But Harley Roberts's claim was for $500,000, because the AEC did not decontaminate him promptly, which in our view increased his radiation dose and risk of developing cancer.

The tort claims were served on the United States Attorney in Las Vegas, the legal representative of the United States and the AEC. We did not think the AEC would respond to the claims and we would have to file a lawsuit. But we did assume the federal judge, at the very least, would force the government to disclose the radiation records of the thirteen security guards.

December 1971 marked the first anniversary of Baneberry and the end of our first year of private practice. Divorces tend to slow down around the Christmas holiday; but one memorable client that year was Mr. Georgiadis. He had left his wife in Greece and come to Las Vegas to take a job on the strip. Now he wanted a divorce and brought in rental slips at a local motel, confirming his six-week residence prior to filing. We filed his divorce complaint and had his wife served with the complaint in Greece. We sent along a letter and power of attorney for Mrs. Georgiadis to sign, authorizing an attorney to appear for her in court and not contest the divorce.

But Mrs. Georgiadis refused to sign. Instead, she wrote us a letter. It was a stinging rebuke of her husband who had promised to send her money so she could join him in Las Vegas. For assisting her husband to commit this perfidious act, she devoted an entire paragraph to invective against us. She said she was placing a Greek curse upon us. At the time, we found her letter somewhat amusing, particularly the curse. We had never heard of a Greek curse and had no idea how long one lasted. But coming as it did as we were preparing and filing the Baneberry case, we have wondered over the years whether Baneberry was the curse and Mrs. Georgiadis the priestess who delivered it.

[6]

The King Can Do No Wrong

THE UNITED STATES had six months to respond to the tort claims we filed in December 1971. If it ignored them as we anticipated, we then had to file an action under the Federal Tort Claims Act (FTCA) by December 1972.

The Federal Tort Claims Act was enacted in 1946.[1] Although it had been under consideration by Congress for nearly thirty years, the event that seems to have precipitated its passage was when a B-25 bomber, flying in dense fog during World War II, crashed into the north side of the Empire State Building. Although it was unintentional and the United States could not be sued, Congress offered money to the victims. Most accepted, but some rejected the offer and filed suit against the government. When the Tort Claims Act was passed in 1946, it provided a retroactive remedy for the crash victims.

For the first time, U.S. citizens could sue the United States for damages caused by negligent acts of government employees. Its passage ended the immunity our founders inherited from the English Common Law doctrine, "the king can do no wrong," firmly settled in England by the 1200s, when Henry de Bracton explained: "Our lord the king cannot be summoned or receive a command from anyone," citing a judgment of the King's Court in 1234."[2] Over 500 years later, Alexander Hamilton, in *Federalist No. 81*, restated de Bracton's rationale for the doctrine: "It is inherent in the nature of sovereignty not to be amenable to the suit of an individual without its consent."[3]

On its face, the FTCA appeared to open the courts of the land for suits against the government in a nation that prided itself on the sovereignty of the people and the concept of "justice for all." But the right to sue came with draconian limitations and defenses available only to the government.

First, suits can only be tried in the United States federal courts, before a judge appointed by the president with the advice and consent of the Senate. Federal judges serve for life and can only be removed by impeachment in the House of Representatives and trial and conviction by the Senate. At first blush, it might seem a federal judge appointed for life would be immune from politics and all other influences. But of course, we were not naïve. We knew that a judicial appointment is a highly political matter. A United States senator makes the recommendation from the home state to the president, who then formally nominates the judge. Approval requires a majority vote of the Senate. But the nominations were rarely challenged. The FTCA is an explicit statement that the federal government does not trust the state courts or its judges to preside over suits brought by citizens against the United States government.

Second, trial by jury, the most sacred right our colonial ancestors brought from England to the American colonies and embodied in the Seventh Amendment to the United States Constitution, is expressly denied. Instead, a federally appointed judge decides all facts and law in a trial against the government. The denial of the right to trial by a jury of ordinary citizens was obviously very significant to the government.

When Congress passed the FTCA, it recognized that the federal judges who would decide cases involving government conduct had been nominated and would render their decisions mindful of their political affiliation and their pension benefits. Federal judges sit in a federal courthouse, which is an enclave with its own federal marshals in charge of security and access to the building. The federal judges derive their authority directly from the federal government in Washington and are not answerable to the people in the state where they hold court. Their decisions are reviewed by federal appeals courts and are not subject to scrutiny or review by the state judiciary. The prestige, power, and celebrity of their office come from the United States government and endure for life, including all attendant retirement benefits.

By contrast, a jury of ordinary U.S. citizens represents a cross-section of the community in which they live. They take an oath to "well and truly" hear the evidence and decide the truth of the matter. They do so in virtual anonymity, without celebrity, without opportunity for gain, for a short period time, and for minimal compensation. A verdict by a jury in a civil case in federal court requires a unanimous decision by at least six jurors (and frequently more) based upon their collective conscience. For over a thousand years, the jury has stood as the most incorruptible and impartial system devised by man to determine the facts and arrive at the truth.[4] Congress was unwilling to trust ordinary citizens to judge the U.S. government's behavior.

Other rights taken for granted by parties in ordinary lawsuits were denied or severely limited by the act. One defense is not available to any other defendant. The federal government granted itself "immunity" from liability for acts or conduct carried out by government employees in the "exercise of their discretionary authority." This term was not defined in the act. Over the next fifty years, federal trial and appellate judges wrestled with its meaning and redefined the term.

Whatever the intent of the act at the time of passage, practically everything a government official or bureaucrat does is pursuant to some authority, directive, rule, or regulation. Most of their duties are within the ambit of their limited discretion somewhere down the links of the command chain.

Carried to its logical conclusion, the sovereign immunity defense, interposed to protect the government, allows government officials to do almost anything under the umbrella of a chain of command that runs straight up to the president of the United States. The only notable exceptions are intentional or criminal conduct or garden-variety negligent conduct like an auto accident caused by a postal worker for which the government employee could be sued directly.

Our research led us to *Dalehite v. United States*, the first U.S. Supreme Court case to test the new act. It involved the Texas City Disaster of April 1947. A ship loaded with fertilizer blew up in the harbor at Texas City, Texas, killing over 500 people, injuring 5,000, and nearly leveling the city.[5]

Henry Dalehite's successors filed suit under the FTCA alleging that the government "shipped or permitted shipment to a congested area without warning" of a potentially highly explosive substance, ammonium nitrate, the same explosive Timothy McVeigh loaded into his rented Ryder truck and parked outside the Murrah Federal Building in Oklahoma City in 1995. Although no specific acts of government negligence were alleged, the government had overseen the entire fertilizer export plan, which included this shipment on its way to Europe.

The district judge found in favor of Dalehite's heirs and others and awarded damages of $75,000 for each victim. The government appealed and the circuit court reversed the award. The case was then appealed to the Supreme Court, where six justices acknowledged that "acts of subordinates carrying out operations of government in accordance with official directions cannot be actionable" and that executive- or cabinet-level decisions are not subject to question by anyone, including a federal judge. The Supreme Court, by a majority, found that the "decisions held culpable [by the trial judge] were all responsibly made at a planning level rather than operational level and involved considerations more or less important to the practicability of the Government's fertilizer program."

Three Supreme Court justices dissented. They would have held the government liable, commenting about the FTCA, "Surely a statute so long debated was meant to embrace more than traffic accidents. If not, the ancient and discredited doctrine that 'The King can do no wrong' has not been uprooted; it has merely been amended to read, 'The King can do only little wrongs.'"

The next case we studied was *Bulloch v. United States*, the ill-fated sheep case decided by a federal judge in Utah in October 1956.[6] Members of the Bulloch family and other Utah sheep owners claimed their sheep were exposed to lethal radiation from the 1953 atmospheric tests at the Nevada Test Site. They lost their FTCA lawsuit because the federal judge found they had not been able to show that the sheep deaths were caused by radiation from atmospheric testing. Because the judge found the Bulloch plaintiffs had not presented evidence to support their damage claims, he did not decide whether the government had acted negligently in exposing the sheep to radiation from atomic tests. We could only wonder whether the judge had taken the easy road to avoid the "sovereign immunity" issue.

These two decisions were not encouraging. In one, where death and destruction were catastrophic and caused by an explosion, the case was thrown out based upon the sovereign immunity defense. In the other, the judge took the government's side, ruling that the fallout from an A-bomb test in 1953 did not cause any harm. We knew we had to overcome both defenses to win.

We had read *Bleak House* and were amused by Dickens's stirring admonition to "suffer any wrong rather than enter the English Court of Chancery."[7] But it was a novel, a piece of fiction about conditions in nineteenth-century England. Still, as we reviewed the law dealing with the Federal Tort Claims Act, we realized there were a dozen reasons "to suffer any wrong rather than enter" the federal court system to test again the FTCA, and almost no good reason to retest the AEC's atomic program, particularly in Las Vegas.

We pressed on with great trepidation. Fortunately, none of our clients at that point was suffering any acute effects from radiation at Baneberry. But it was too early to be sure there would be no long-term effects, and there was plenty of evidence of government negligence.

Our review of Baneberry and the post-shot exposure of the guards to the Baneberry cloud involved decisions and directives made by AEC officials before and after the test vented. The decision to fire the test came from the top, but the order was carried out by countless underlings down the chain of command. The direct order to Dyer to muster the guards to evacuate Area 12 that morning came from his Wackenhut supervisor Captain Tackett. But that order came from the top AEC security officer at the control point.

The order directing Harley Roberts to the remote Dead Horse Flats station was issued by a Wackenhut captain after Harley told him he was "hot as hell."

But the order to decontaminate all the guards involved in the evacuation came from the command center and filtered down the chain to Wackenhut. The failure to locate and decontaminate Roberts, in compliance with that order, was an extension and violation of that order.

Monitoring and recording the radiation exposure the guards received was the responsibility of the AEC test manager. But the procedures for monitoring and determining the doses were carried out by REECo Rad-Safe monitors and technicians who were not government employees.

Since every nuclear test had to be preapproved by the president, we expected the government would argue that the entire testing program—top to bottom—was a discretionary decision, and the government was therefore entitled to claim sovereign immunity from suit.

In late 1971, when the claims were filed, we reviewed the facts and decided—or as Alan would later claim, I decided without any strenuous protest from him—to test again the sovereign immunity defense. The claims were filed, and the ball was in the government's court.

While the government reviewed the claims, we began an intense investigation to understand the inner workings of the Nevada Test Site. Prior to Baneberry, we knew almost nothing about the 1,350-square-mile reserve or the interrelationship between the nearly 10,000 employees who carried out the day-to-day work and the scientists who planned the hundreds of different tests.

We learned that REECo became the prime contractor at the Test Site in 1952 and employed most of the workers, directly or through subcontracts, including nearly 300 radiological safety personnel. The Radiation Safety division of REECo was responsible for issuing the film badges worn by all persons allowed access to the site and employed the Rad-Safe monitors and technicians to measure radiation levels all around the Test Site. Finally, they collected all film badges worn at the Test Site and filled out forms recording radiation exposures. Rad-Safe monitors had specialized training and were equipped with full-body protective clothing and respirators that they were required to wear when entering radiation zones.

After eighteen years of radiation monitoring at the Nevada Test Site and with about 300 fully trained and equipped employees, we were perplexed that Rad-Safe monitors had not been mustered and ordered to enter the radiation cloud to conduct the evacuation of Area 12.[8] The appearance of suited up Rad-Safe monitors with hoods and respirators would have left no doubt in the minds of the workers in Area 12 that the radioactive cloud was dangerous. But on the morning of December 18, 1970, there was only one monitor near Area 12 camp at 8 AM. Fully outfitted in his Rad-Safe protective gear and facemask, he hailed the guards and waved them on into Area 12 Camp but never entered the camp or took a reading there the entire time the guards were conducting the evacuation.

The more perplexing question was why one contractor, REECo, which employed directly or through subcontractors most of the 10,000 workers at the Test Site, was also in charge of radiation monitoring and in exclusive control of all instruments used to determine radiation exposures of the workers. Was it likely that one division of REECo would condemn the conduct of another division?

Further investigation revealed that the vast Nevada Test Site was divided into thirty separate areas and that two scientific laboratories designed and carried out nearly all nuclear tests there since testing began in 1951.[9] Los Alamos Scientific Laboratory (LASL), a division of the University of California headquartered in Los Alamos, New Mexico, conducted most of the early tests at the Nevada Test Site. In 1952, Nobel physicist Ernest O. Lawrence set up a separate laboratory, the Lawrence Radiation Laboratory, later Lawrence Livermore Laboratory (LLL) at the University of California, Berkeley. The labs were rivals and competed for federal dollars.

We had no idea why the scientists in both divisions of the University of California could not collaborate and consolidate their efforts, nor any idea what either of them had accomplished in the over 500 atmospheric and underground tests conducted at the Nevada Test Site over the preceding twenty years. All we knew was that the Baneberry test was in Area 8 and Area 8 was LLL territory.

The physicists at LLL who designed the Baneberry test, reputedly top scientists in the field, were employees of the University of California, not government employees. But the test was approved by the AEC and the president. Moreover, as employees of the University of California, we would have to join LLL, a subdivision of the State of California, and face the Eleventh Amendment to the U.S. Constitution, which bars suits by citizens of one state against one of the United States.[10]

We learned that another AEC contractor, Fenix & Scisson, oversaw the design and drilling of the eighty-six-inch diameter Baneberry emplacement hole. These drilling experts should have known about the geology of the formation where the Baneberry device was placed. As a private contractor, they were not immune from suit under the FTCA.

We had enough evidence to support filing suit against the contractors for their negligent acts related to the Baneberry test without naming the Atomic

Energy Commission. On February 2, 1972, we filed suit in the U.S. District Court of Nevada on behalf of each of the thirteen guards, and at Cleghorn's request, also named the Independent Guard Association of Nevada as a plaintiff. We named as defendants Reynolds Electrical and Engineering Company, Wackenhut Services, Inc., Fenix & Scisson, and Forest Tackett, the Wackenhut captain who failed to locate Roberts. We served the defendants and waited for their response.

Since we had never been to the Test Site and were unfamiliar with the sciences related to atomic testing and radiation effects, we hired Ronan & Associates, a consulting firm, to investigate the Baneberry case. In late April 1972, they gave us a report and bill for $1,350. They also delivered two thick publications: *Radiological Health Handbook*, revised edition, January 1970, and *Public Safety and Underground Nuclear Detonations*, June 1971, by Samuel Glasstone.[11]

We forwarded the bill and report to Cleghorn and plunged into our reading. Over two weeks later, Cleghorn told us the union board was grumbling about the $1,350, but he would get them to pay it.

In June 1972, we were flooded with legal documents filed in court in response to the complaint. We knew that once the defendants mustered their lawyers, the case would explode. Faced with all the costs and expenses and countless hours dealing with the legal issues, it was time we took a serious look at the Baneberry lawsuit. We reviewed the documents and the applicable law and by the end of the month had decided we could not pursue the case.

While in the process of drafting a letter to the union and the individual guards to inform them of our decision, Harley Roberts called.

"Larry," he began, "I've been feeling pretty bad for the past few months."

"What's the problem?"

"I just feel tired all the time. I mentioned it to one of the guards, and he recommended I make an appointment to see Dr. Chauncey Smith. He's Chief of Medicine at Loma Linda University."

"Have you seen any local doctors?"

"No. I guess you know I don't like to go to doctors. But Dr. Smith comes highly recommended."

"It's probably a good idea."

"I'm going to have to do something. Dorothy's worried. She can tell I don't seem to have much energy. Oh, I manage to get to work all right. But, I've been taking more sick days lately and I avoid overtime whenever possible."

"Have you told anybody at Wackenhut that you're not feeling good?" Larry asked.

"No. But I'm getting concerned. We work long hours and I work solo a lot of times at some of the checkpoints. If I get caught sleeping, it's automatic discharge."

"Have you made an appointment to see Dr. Smith?"

"Not yet. I thought I better let you know. I'm going to schedule it during my vacation in July. That way the company won't know anything about it," he ended.

A couple weeks later, Harley called and said he had an appointment with Dr. Smith at Loma Linda Hospital on July 20, 1972. He was there for five days and met Dr. Smith and several specialists. When he got back to Las Vegas, he made an appointment to see us but did not want Dorothy present. We met on July 27 and had him sign a medical authorization so we could get copies of his Loma Linda records.

Harley looked pale. He said they did lots of blood tests and described how they stuck a big needle into his hipbone for a bone marrow study. It was quite painful. Dr. Smith told him he had something called "leukopenia" and that the bone marrow test showed it was abnormal. He mentioned to Dr. Smith that he had been exposed to radiation at the Test Site in December 1970. Dr. Smith made a note of it and told him to make an appointment to return in August for a recheck of his blood.

We sent the medical release to Loma Linda Hospital in July but did not get the records until early September. By that time, Harley had returned for a follow-up visit on August 25th.

The medical records of the June hospitalization disclosed much more than the doctors had told Harley. The bone marrow test showed he was missing a chromosome. Dr. Irvin Kuhn, the hematologist, concluded, "One should bear in mind the possible preleukemia state and therefore I would recommend repeat blood studies every month for four to six months or more unless the etiology [cause of the disease] is found."[12]

Preleukemia is the phase of the leukemic process preceding manifestation. On September 15, 1972, Harley called with good news. He got a letter from Dr. Smith reporting that his August blood test results were normal. But in September the results turned negative again. Christmas at the Roberts home was filled with apprehension, as Harley braced himself for the next round of blood tests.

We never finished the letter we were drafting in June. We could not drop Harley's case while he was fighting for his life. Baneberry was drawing us deeper and deeper into its web.

NOTES

1. Federal Tort Claims Act, Public Law 601, §28 U.S.C. 1346(b)(1946) governs federal tort claims actions. Collectively, hereinafter referred to as FTCA.

2. Sir Frederick Pollock and Frederic William Maitland, *The History of English Law*, Vol. I, Legal Classics Library, (1982). Henry de Bracton's *Summa*, published between 1250 and 1258, "is the crown and flower of English Medieval jurisprudence." In it, he cites over 500 decisions. Regarding the notion that the "king can do no wrong," it was never established law. In fact, "the king can do wrong; he can break the law; he is below the law, though he is below no man and below no court of law" (514–16).

3. *The Federalist*, Legal Classics Library (1983, 318): "This is the general sense and general practice of mankind; and the exemption, as one of the attributes of sovereignty, is now enjoyed by the government of every state in the union."

4. Pollock and Maitland, *The History of English Law*, Vol. I, Legal Classics Library (1982, 140–41): "We must look to the Frankish *inquisitio*, the prerogative rights of the Frankish kings.... He [the king] orders that a group of men, the best and most trustworthy men of a district, be sworn to declare what lands, what rights, he has or ought to have in their district. He uses this procedure for many different purposes. He uses it in his litigation:—he will rely on the verdict of the neighbors instead of battle or the ordeal.... The procedure which he employs in support of his own rights he can and does grant as a favour to others.... All this we see in the Frankish empire of the ninth century; we see it in the Neustria which the Normans are invading.... Yet on the whole we may say that, but for the conquest of England, it would have perished and long ago have become a matter for the antiquary."

5. Dalehite v. United States, 346 U.S. 15 (1953).

6. Bulloch v. United States, 145 F. Supp. 824 (D. Utah 1956).

7. Charles Dickens 1853, *Bleak House*. Complete Works, Centennial Edition, 1967. Vol. I, p. 3. London: Heron Books. A more complete quotation: "This is the Court of Chancery;... which gives to monied might the means abundantly of wearying out the right; which so exhausts finances, patience, courage, hope; so overthrows the brain and breaks that heart; that there is not an honorable man among the practitioners who would not give—who does not often give—the warning, 'Suffer any wrong that can be done rather than come here!'"

8. We did not learn until years later, as we prepared the case for trial, that the Test Manager's Baneberry Plan required that REECo have teams of monitors standing by thirty minutes prior to shot time or that the AEC required REECo to prepare specific written emergency plans for Area 12 Camp.

9. Sandia Laboratories in New Mexico was involved in some tests.

10. U.S. Constitution, amendment XI. "The Judicial power of the United States shall not be construed to extend to any suit in law or equity, commenced or prosecuted against one of the United States by Citizens of another State, or by the Citizens or Subjects of any Foreign State."

11. Bureau of Radiological Health, U.S. Department of Health, Education, and Welfare, *Radiological Health Handbook*, revised edition, January 1970. Washington, D.C.
Samuel Glasstone, *Public Safety and Underground Nuclear Detonations*, June 1971, TID-25708. Atomic Energy Commission: Washington, D.C.

12. *Baneberry Collection*, EX 110.

[7]

We're Here to Help You

January 1973–February 1974

By early April 1973, Harley Roberts was struggling to work his four twelve-hour shifts each week. He called Dr. Smith, and he and Dorothy drove to Loma Linda on April 17. Dr. Smith ran blood tests and was amazed Harley could continue working. He filled out a total disability form for Harley to submit.

We met with Harley after he returned from Loma Linda. He was nearly in tears explaining his financial condition. He was a proud man who knew they would have to depend upon Dorothy's income. She took daily insulin injections and worked as a change girl at the nearby Safeway store.

Harley was born in 1920 and grew up during the Depression. He knew hard times, but this was worse. He and Dorothy thought about selling their home and moving back to Indiana but decided they needed to stay close to Dr. Smith for medical treatment. They also wanted to be near Harley's mother and sister in Las Vegas. Their son Randy was in the Marine Corps.

Harley was soon largely housebound except for Saturday night card games with the Dyers and occasional fishing trips to Lake Mead. He had not been able to play golf for nearly a year, and his disease had progressed to the point that B-12 injections and blood transfusions were all that kept him going.

By June 1973, Dr. Kuhn classified Harley's condition as preleukemic. When we told Harley, he knew what that meant. Leukemia was a death sentence. We learned that the AEC's Oak Ridge Hospital was a leading research facility in radiation-related cancers and leukemias and asked Harley if he would be willing to go there if the government would pay the expenses. Harley was desperate and eager to try anything. We contacted government counsel to inquire whether the AEC would consider sending Harley to Oak Ridge for a comprehensive examination and recommendation for supportive treatment.

After negotiating for several weeks, the AEC agreed to pay Harley's expenses for the trip and evaluation by their doctors. Harley asked if they would pay Dorothy's expenses. We made the proposal, but the AEC refused. In mid-August Dorothy drove Harley to the airport. He was admitted to Oak Ridge Hospital on August 16, 1973, and discharged on September 1, 1973. The Oak Ridge doctors knew Harley had filed a lawsuit against the AEC. He saw many physicians, and each asked him about his radiation exposure at Baneberry. Harley said he felt like he was the enemy.

We made requests upon government counsel for the records of Harley's hospitalization at Oak Ridge, but the records were not produced until nearly two months after he was released. Even then, they were not produced to us but were sent to Dr. Smith at Loma Linda, who sent us copies. When we examined the records, we noted references to oral communications between the AEC and the AEC doctors at Oak Ridge regarding Harley Roberts's radiation readings and readings of urine samples after his exposure at Baneberry.

The Oak Ridge doctor who reviewed the thyroid readings sent by the AEC acknowledged that the bioassay (urine sample) results "were unclear because... [they] did not know exactly what [iodine radioisotope] was measured." To us, this statement confirmed that Harley's internal exposure from inhalation of radioactive gases was the unknown element and possibly the most significant component of his radiation dose.

The reports varied wildly regarding Harley's dose from exposure to the Baneberry cloud on December 18, 1970. An extensive handwritten report by one physician ignored all documented radiation readings for Roberts. He stated that Roberts received a "brief estimated 10–15 millirem [mR] exposure" and referred to the "exposure in question," implying that Roberts may not have been exposed to radiation at all. Another physician referred to exposure to "100 Rods of radiation" (100 *Rads* or 100,000 mR) for which there was no support in any of the records that came from Loma Linda or anywhere else.

From our review of the Oak Ridge record, it was unclear what radiation dose the Oak Ridge doctors relied upon for their analyses. But the bone marrow studies they performed showed that of twenty bone marrow cells examined eighteen contained only forty-five of the forty-six chromosomes. The head physician at Oak Ridge, Dr. Gould Andrews, prepared a summary concluding that although radiation could not be ruled out, he felt the dose was too low to have caused the condition.

In late January 1974, the government lawyers called and told us it was imperative they take Harley Roberts's deposition as soon as possible. We assumed the doctors at Oak Ridge had told them Harley's condition was grave and he might not have long to live. Harley's deposition was set for February 20, 1974.

On February 20, we met Harley in the lobby of the AEC building. He was so pale we wondered how he had managed to drive unaided from his home.

Alan, Harley, and I were seated on one side of a long conference table with government lawyers aligned on the other side. Harley was sworn in and answered a series of general questions about his background, education, and life before coming to the Test Site.

When the government lawyer finally got around to asking about his health before and after Baneberry, Harley began to bristle. He looked the lawyer in the face and said he was in great shape before Baneberry. When asked what health problems he attributed to his exposure to radiation at Baneberry, Harley looked puzzled, as if he did not know where to begin. He said he was short of breath because he did not have any oxygen in his blood, was down to around 127 pounds, and felt like he was not really living. He had only been sick two days in his life before Baneberry and that was when he had diphtheria as a child. He never had any sign of fatigue until after Baneberry and proudly stated that he played basketball regularly until he was forty-five years old.

When asked whether he had ever been exposed to any toxic substances or chemicals before Baneberry, he said he had not. He was out in the wide-open spaces in Indiana most of his life and wished he had stayed there.

When the government lawyer asked if he was worried about his health, Harley's countenance went from astonishment to anger. He glared at the government lawyer and nearly broke down. After a short pause, he began speaking in almost a whisper. He was sure it was just a matter of time. He probably had a year or two, maybe not even that long; he did not know. The lawyer was reluctant to follow up, but Harley did. He said he could not do anything anymore. He still drove the car a little and had driven himself to the AEC building this morning, but when he got out of the car and the wind hit him in the face, he thought he was never going to breathe again. He said he nearly passed out in the hall. The room fell silent. Now it was the government lawyer who did not know what to say.

When the deposition ended, we asked Harley if he was okay to drive home. Harley said he thought he was and told us he was relieved he had finally gotten to tell his story about Baneberry and explain how it had ruined his life. He was irritated by the questions and referred to the government lawyer as a "smart-ass jerk."

A week later Harley called. He was feeling terrible. He had just gotten off the phone with Dr. Smith, who told him to drive down immediately and check in that evening through the emergency department at Loma Linda. Dr. Smith would instruct the ER physicians to admit him. Harley and Dorothy left town right after he hung up.

[8]

A Ray of Hope

HARLEY'S EMERGENCY TRIP to Loma Linda so soon after his deposition was unexpected. The Oak Ridge doctors would not support his case and offered no suggestions for treatment. We needed a radiation expert willing to get involved in a lawsuit against the AEC.

We called Paul Duckworth, our consultant, and told him Harley was back in the hospital and asked him to see if he could get the name of a medical expert to review Harley's case. Paul called back a few days later and gave us the name and telephone number of Shields Warren, a doctor in Boston. Paul said he got Dr. Warren's name from Robley Evans, a well-known physicist, who had studied radiation effects. Paul called Dr. Evans and asked him if he could look over Roberts's radiation information and records. Evans disclosed that he had served as a consultant for REECo since the mid-1960s and had been hired by REECo to investigate Baneberry shortly after it vented. He supplied Dr. Warren's telephone number as one who might be willing to consult on the matter.

We had no background information on Dr. Shields Warren but knew we had to find an expert. We called the number Paul Duckworth gave us and asked the woman who answered whether Dr. Shields Warren was available. She asked the purpose of the call and we explained that Robley Evans had suggested we call Dr. Warren to see if he would be willing to consult on a case involving a Test Site worker exposed to radiation.

"I'll see if he's available," she said and put us on hold. We all but held our breath while we waited to see whether Dr. Warren would accept the call. When we called, we expected Shields Warren to be qualified but had no idea we would be talking with one of the founding fathers of radiation pathology and probably the leading expert in the world on the effects of radiation from atomic testing.

"Hello, this is Shields Warren," a voice responded with a pronounced stutter. "I understand Robley Evans recommended me to you."

"Yes, Dr. Warren. I'm Larry Johns and my brother Alan Johns is also on the line. We are attorneys in Las Vegas, Nevada, who represent a Test Site worker exposed to radiation in December 1970. Dr. Robley Evans is consulting for the AEC in a court case here in Las Vegas involving the radiation exposure. He gave us your name."

"I've known Robley Evans since the 1930s. He's not a medical doctor, but has done a lot of work in radiation measurements. Can you summarize what the case is about?"

"Yes. We represent thirteen Nevada Test Site security guards exposed to radiation when the Baneberry test vented in December 1970. They were ordered into the radioactive cloud to evacuate workers from a base camp. Harley Roberts, the security guard who had the highest reported radiation readings that day, is at Loma Linda Hospital. His diagnosis is acute myelogenous leukemia, and he isn't expected to live much longer."

"What information do you have about Mr. Roberts's radiation exposure on December 18, 1970?"

"The only information we have is from a report the AEC put out in May 1971, five months after Baneberry. It states that a security guard received a gamma dose around 1.00 rem, a beta dose around 4.5 rem, and a thyroid dose around 3.75 rem. We are certain those are the readings for Harley Roberts, since he was in the radiation cloud for nearly an hour and was not brought in for decontamination until eight hours later. Mr. Roberts testified at his deposition that he was monitored shortly after he left the base camp and the radiation monitor told him he was hot as hell. After he was decontaminated around 10:00 PM that night, his hands were still reading 25 mR, and he was issued rubber gloves and told to wear them overnight due to the readings on his hands."

"Both the gamma and beta readings were undoubtedly recorded on Roberts's film badge," Dr. Warren explained. "I was director of Biology and Medicine when the Atomic Energy Commission was created in 1947. In that position, I oversaw health and safety at all the AEC's facilities, including the Nevada Test Site when it opened. In fact, I watched the first aboveground test in Nevada in January 1951."

When Dr. Warren mentioned his connection with the AEC, we were deflated, expecting a polite decline to review a case against an agency he had worked for. But to our surprise he launched into a long explanation, more like a lecture on all aspects of radiation. We were spellbound as we listened and scribbled notes on our legal tablets, trying to absorb the information.

"The film badge is generally a reliable instrument that records the gamma rays and beta radiation that was in the radioactive cloud. Gamma rays have the same penetrating energy as x-rays and would reach all the internal organs of the body. Most would penetrate through the cortex of the bones into the bone marrow, where the leukocytes or white cells are formed. Myeloid leukemia originates in the bone marrow and is derived from the Greek word *mye* which means "bone," and leukemia from the Greek work *leukos* which means "white" and refers to the white cells that fight off infection.

"The external gamma and beta readings recorded on Roberts's film badge are only part of the picture. Roberts would have been inhaling radioactive gases while in the Baneberry cloud. His thyroid readings confirm that he inhaled radioactive iodine present in the cloud that concentrated over time in his thyroid gland. Based upon many years of experience, I believe I could make a rough estimate of his external and internal bone marrow dose from the various sources, but it would be helpful if you could provide additional information. I also need all of his medical records both before and after his exposure to radiation in December 1970," Dr. Warren told us.

"We have records of annual physical examinations by the Test Site doctors from 1966, when he joined the force, that show he was in good health prior to the test. For several days after his exposure, he complained of diarrhea and mild fatigue, which he thought at the time was the flu. In July 1972, he went to Loma Linda University and was diagnosed with anemia. The doctors ordered bone marrow studies, which showed that he was missing a chromosome in the C group."

"That is extremely interesting," Dr. Warren interrupted. "Radiation has been known to cause chromosome mutations since the early 1900s. Dr. Boveri, the German embryologist, was the first to publish studies suggesting such a relationship.

"I assume you are aware that in the late 1920s Dr. Hermann Muller performed experiments for which he was later awarded the Nobel Prize demonstrating that fruit flies subjected to radiation showed chromosome mutations and deletions. It has been generally accepted since that time that radiation can cause an abnormal number of chromosomes in the daughter cells.

"The fact that Mr. Roberts was exposed to radiation in December 1970 and tests a year and a half later showed that he was missing one of the C chromosomes in his bone marrow stem cells is evidence that his radiation exposure may have caused the chromosomal mutation. There is evidence that the absence of a C chromosome is a precursor of myeloid leukemia. Once the missing

C chromosome is found, the patient progresses to leukemia within a few years, as appears to have been the case here. Roberts's exposure to radiation at Baneberry in 1970 may have caused his condition."

When we heard this, we were thrilled and tempted to comment, but Dr. Warren continued.

"I have been interested in radiation effects since medical school. I began my own studies of radiation effects and published many papers on the subject in the 1930s. After the bombs were dropped on Hiroshima and Nagasaki, I was commissioned to organize a team of Navy doctors and hospital corpsmen to travel to Japan and work with the Japanese doctors to study the survivors at Nagasaki. We were later joined by a team of Army doctors, headed by Dr. Stafford Warren, and expanded our studies and worked with Japanese doctors in Hiroshima.

"Within a year and a half, there was pretty clear evidence that leukemia would develop and by 1950 there had been a significant increase in leukemia among the Japanese survivors. The study of the survivors of the atomic bombings confirmed my prediction that there would be a sharp increase in leukemia that peaked around four to six years after the bombings."

As stellar as Dr. Warren's qualifications were, we knew that Harley had been examined by doctors at the AEC's Oak Ridge Hospital and were concerned that once he learned that the AEC's doctors had examined Harley, he might be reluctant to challenge their findings.

"Mr. Roberts was sent to Oak Ridge Hospital last August," we interjected. "The doctors there confirmed the missing C chromosome and diagnosed his condition as preleukemia. Dr. Gould Andrews's summary does not rule out the possibility that the Baneberry exposure could have caused his condition but suggests that his radiation dose, as reported, was probably too low."

"Well," Dr. Warren responded, "Dr. Andrews and the AEC doctors at Oak Ridge would certainly have been looking to accurately diagnose the disease and should have understood the significance of the chromosome deletion. I would want to have all of their records to review."

"Obviously, we would not expect you to offer any opinions without reviewing all of the records," I interjected. "But we are planning to visit Mr. Roberts in the next few weeks. May we tell him that we have been in contact with you and that you are willing to consult on the case? It should be encouraging for him to know that you are interested in the matter."

"Certainly," Dr. Warren responded. "You may tell him that I am reviewing it. I have studied many patients with leukemia, and the last stage is very difficult for the patient and the family. I would request that when you visit him you ask his doctors to perform an autopsy, and prepare slides of his bone marrow, since it is very important that a correct diagnosis be made. As a pathologist, I would consider an autopsy imperative."

"We will see him soon," we said, "and will talk to his doctors and explain the need for an autopsy. May we mention your name and tell them that the request came from you?"

"Yes, and I would also request that following the autopsy, the bone marrow slides be sent to my laboratory here for my own review. Although I would have no reason to doubt the findings, I would be more comfortable in giving my own opinion based upon my review of the slides."

"We very much appreciate your willingness to review this matter. If you require a consultation fee, please let us know."

"I would be willing to review the records for $500. Please assemble the dose records, medical records, and other information and send it here to me. I will not have a chance to review this matter now, so unless there is some urgency, we may want to wait until after the autopsy has been performed, so I can review the slides."

"We'll send all the records we have and make sure the autopsy slides are sent to you."

"Very well. I will wait for the records. I will be on vacation for two weeks, but should be available in late April, if you have any questions."

"Thank you for agreeing to consult on this matter," we ended.

"Not at all. Goodbye," he said.

Dr. Warren had been gracious and utterly unembarrassed by a pronounced stutter, which produced delays during the phone call. But his mild impairment allowed him to make a much more deliberate explanation of each point and made it easier for us to take notes and understand the complex medical issues.

We were ecstatic that an expert of the caliber of Dr. Warren was willing to review the case. His summary of his qualifications, particularly his involvement with the Japanese survivors and former position with the Atomic Energy Commission, could leave no doubt that we had found the perfect expert to review the case.

In early March 1974, we made plans to visit Harley at the hospital in Loma Linda.

[9]

The Ides of March, 1974

I WAS NOT LOOKING FORWARD to driving over to Loma Linda Hospital to see Harley. Alan and I agreed we could not both go, so I volunteered. There's an old saying that a lawyer should not get emotionally involved in his client's case. It is a fine-sounding legal axiom I probably heard in law school from some old professor cautioning his students to remain detached and totally objective about their clients' cases. But it was too late for trite legal crap. Harley was a warm, friendly, down-to-earth sort of guy. He was unpretentious and humble, except about Hoosier basketball, which he boasted was the best in the country.

Alan and I got to know Harley well in the years after he came in for his initial interview in November 1971. We shared his anxious moments and saw his depression deepen as his health steadily declined. He was not a man who expected a lot out of life, but neither had he planned on dying and leaving his wife Dorothy alone and nearly destitute.

It had been less than a month since Harley went over to the AEC building to tell his story about Baneberry in the deposition. Now he was back at Loma Linda. We had practically memorized his medical records. His diagnosis on admission a few weeks earlier was cold and impersonal but laid out his story. "The patient is a 53-year old Caucasian male, with a myeloproliferative disorder and history of exposure to radiation at the Nevada Test Site. Diagnosis: acute granulocytic leukemia." His medical records detailed the progression of his disease from the first faint hint of general fatigue to full-blown leukemia. They were punctuated by mysterious medical terms such as "blood dyscrasia," "sideroblastic anemia," "myeloproliferative disorder," "leucopenia," "pancytopenia," and "hypodiploidy," words that were now part of our vocabulary.

After talking to Dr. Warren in late February, we knew that Harley's leukemia had just about run its deadly course. There had been many other hospitalizations, and he had rebounded. But not this time. Dr. Warren had insisted on an autopsy, and we knew what that meant. I had to face Harley and wondered how I would react if he asked me about his condition. Did I have an ethical duty to tell him he was dying? Could I conceal from him that Dr. Warren wanted to make sure an autopsy was performed? Should I tell Harley the next chapter in preparing his case for trial against the AEC was an autopsy of his remains?

As I passed the Las Vegas J. C. Penney, I remembered how store-window mannequins were taken out to the Test Site and placed in fabricated homes during the 1950s atmospheric tests. We were excited when the AEC told us the tests were intended to replicate blast effects on a typical American family. Later, we learned that the scientists were trying to reconstruct the Japanese radiation doses at Hiroshima and Nagasaki. Those mannequins were an expendable sacrifice for the atomic testing program. Harley was not.

I pulled into Paul Duckworth's driveway a little past 6:00 AM. We had hired Paul to assist us in investigating the Baneberry case because of his engineering background and his years working at the Test Site for Livermore (LLL), the lab running the Baneberry test. Paul was watching from the window and quickly jumped in to avoid a cold March breeze.

"Are you ready for this?" I asked.

"Not particularly."

At 9:00 AM, we took the Loma Linda exit and stopped for breakfast at the first restaurant. It was balmy and misty, the coastal fog still not burned off by the morning sun.

Loma Linda University Hospital was majestic, compared to the small curbside hospitals in Las Vegas. The Veterans Hospital down the street was equally impressive, another stark contrast to Las Vegas, which had only a small outpatient clinic for the thousands of southern Nevada veterans who had to travel to California or other states for serious medical care.

The cancer ward was a large room with a circular nurses station. Stacks of monitors were feeding information from each of a dozen or more patient rooms on the perimeter. We checked in at the nurses station and asked to see Harley Roberts. The nurse in charge issued us paper masks, explaining that infection was the greatest danger facing terminal leukemia patients. She pointed to a room. A clipboard and chart hung on the door with Harley's full name in bold black ink.

Harley was lying on a small hospital bed, upper body elevated and head propped up with pillows. The yellow walls and yellow glow coming through the small curtained window contrasted with the stark and sterile white bed linens in which a pallid, emaciated face swam. There were tubes and wires everywhere: a plastic oxygen tube was stuck into Harley's nose, a tube ran to a urine bag hanging by the bed, tubes came from under the sheets to dangling IV bottles, and wires ran between the machines and monitors. The stillness was broken only by the slight hum of the oxygen machine, as the flickering monitors silently registered vital information transmitted to the nurses station.

Harley was asleep. Overcome by the sight of his ghastly visage peeping out from the sheets, I debated whether to wake him or return a little later. But it was too late. Harley's eyes cracked open, and he greeted me with his familiar wry smile.

"Hello, Larry," he spoke almost in a whisper, but with that resonant, nasal tone so recognizable to those who knew him.

"Hey, how are you doing?" I asked.

"Well, I'll tell you," he half chuckled, gasped, and then turned deadly serious, "I feel like hell…I can't get my breath." It was a long minute before he could continue. "I don't have the strength…to even get out of bed. If I could, I'd pull out these damn tubes…and get it over with."

I could not find words to respond. Harley was gasping and desperate, and I felt helpless as I watched him struggle. Fortunately, Paul Duckworth changed the subject.

"I'm Paul Duckworth. I've been working on the Baneberry case with Larry and Alan. I worked for LLL out at the Test Site for many years."

"Oh, sure. I recognize you." Harley paused to get his breath. "You came through my checkpoint…You probably don't remember me. But you know… we check badges and log people…so we remember just about everybody."

"I'm sure you checked me lots of times. I left before Baneberry. I couldn't take the AEC's cavalier attitude about health and safety. Baneberry is just one more example of their incompetence."

"Nobody can believe the bastards…won't just admit they screwed up," Harley interjected. "Everybody at the site knew…Baneberry was a mistake."

His voice filled with despair and anger, Paul replied, "I think it was obvious long before they fired it with all the drilling problems they had. I wrote the AEC shortly after the blowout. I asked them to tell the truth about the vent. They never responded, of course. They just don't seem to care. Anyway, I've got a lead on a couple of geologists from the University of Kansas. I hope they will agree to investigate it. It looks like the AEC is going to fight every step of the way."

Finally, able to rejoin the discussion, I tried to lift Harley's spirits. "Harley, we've spoken about your case with Dr. Shields Warren. He's an expert in radiation effects at Harvard University. He thinks we may be able to make a case for you and has asked us to send him all your medical records, including the ones from Oak Ridge. Without him, we'd have a tough time showing that your condition was caused by Baneberry. Of course, he hasn't completed his investigation, so it's too soon to say for sure."

"You know," Harley followed up in a bewildered tone, "I still can't understand…why the AEC agreed to send me to their…hospital in Oak Ridge last year…if they didn't damn well know they caused this."

"We felt the same way at the time, Harley," I replied. "We thought they were concerned about you and wanted to help. Those Oak Ridge doctors get their funding from the AEC and aren't going to bite the hand that feeds them. It was probably a mistake to send you there. It looks like all they really wanted was to get you to their hand-picked doctors to try to figure out a way to cover their asses."

Harley sighed, "I wouldn't care…if they had come up…with some kind of treatment for this. I guess all I got…was an expense-paid trip to Tennessee."

It seemed like a long time before Harley broke the silence again, pleading, "Fellas, I can't take much more of this. I'm just hanging on for Dorothy's sake… She doesn't seem to realize…how bad I am…and I just can't bring myself to tell her." Harley turned away to conceal the tears he was fighting.

"You've got to hang on. You can't let them win," I said.

"Larry…let's not kid ourselves. I'm not gonna be around much longer… They give me transfusions…but, it only helps for a short time." His voice trailed away as he turned to the wall.

And again, silence. Neither Paul nor I knew how to respond to Harley's matter-of-fact statement that his life was ebbing away. But Harley was not done.

He abruptly turned to face us again and angrily said, "The AEC doesn't give a damn about me…Dorothy's diabetes is really bad…We can't even afford for her…to come stay with me."

Then, with what little strength he could muster, he propped himself up on his left arm, tubes sticking out from under the sheet, clenched his fist, and looked me in the eye. "Larry…you got to make the bastards pay for this. They know they caused this…They can't kill people and get away with it."

"Harley, you know we'll do everything we can," I said.

"If their smart-ass lawyers…had to go through just fifteen minutes of this," he tapered off and then suddenly snapped, "by God…I'd give anything to trade places with them…just for one day…then I could die in peace."

His outburst was interrupted by the nurse who had noticed his vital signs spiking erratically and decided the visit had to end. She said she had to check Harley and we would have to leave for a while. Harley held out his bony hand. I grasped it warmly and was struck by how cold and lifeless his once strong and calloused hand had become. For just a moment, I cradled Harley's frail hand in both of mine. And then, trying not to show our relief, Paul and I headed for the door.

Turning back, I said, "Well, Harley, we'll see you later. We just wanted to see how you were doing and bring you up to date. We're going to see your hematologist, Dr. Kuhn, and tell him we've talked to Dr. Warren. We'll see you in Vegas after you get released."

"Thanks for coming," he said. Then raising his head from the pillow, Harley looked me straight in the eye one more time and spoke with all the strength he could muster, "Don't forget, Larry…you got to make the bastards pay."

Harley's last will and testament, "you got to make the bastards pay," was not written on gilded parchment, subscribed and sworn by witnesses before a notary public. But it was Harley's dying command. Over the next twenty-two years, as Harley's Baneberry case wended through the federal court system in the longest roller-coaster ride in the history of the District of Nevada, my darkest moments were inspired by Harley's grim and determined plea.

We pushed open the double doors, discarded the paper masks, and headed to the information desk on the first floor to find Dr. Kuhn. Neither Paul nor I spoke. We were both struck dumb by Harley's unburdening of emotions that had wracked his soul in the years since Baneberry. No team of government lawyers or high-paid government doctors could deter this Indiana farm boy from the plain, unvarnished truth. He knew Baneberry had poisoned him, and he knew the AEC knew it too.

We entered the Hematology Department, approached the desk, and asked if Dr. Kuhn was available. Several minutes later, Dr. Kuhn came out. He was fit and trim and looked younger than I had expected from our phone conversations over the past year. After exchanging introductions, he ushered us down a hall past logging stations and into a small office.

"Have you seen Harley?" he asked.

"Yes. He's very discouraged. He said he just wants it over," I responded.

"He's suffering terribly, physically and mentally," Dr. Kuhn said. "His type of leukemia, we call it acute granulocytic or myelogenous leukemia, they are the same, alters the white cells, the ones that attack infection. His bone marrow is manufacturing white cells but they are nearly all abnormal, replacing the few normal cells he has left. We've given him transfusions, but that's about all we can do. Without the transfusions, he would have been gone long ago."

"Have you had a chance to review the records from Oak Ridge?" Paul asked.

"Yes, and I'm pleased they confirmed my finding that he has a missing a C chromosome. To me that's significant and the most unusual feature of his case. Otherwise, I can't see that they have come up with anything new. I mean, they call it preleukemia, but of course that simply means they know it's progressing toward frank leukemia. I'm really not qualified to discuss whether his leukemia is the result of his exposure to radiation at the Test Site, although it could not be ruled out."

"We've spoken to Dr. Shields Warren," I said. "He's a radiation pathologist at Harvard. He told us it looks like Harley's exposure at Baneberry could be the cause, but that is merely his preliminary view, and he wants all of the medical records."

"Well," Dr. Kuhn noted, "everyone knows of Shields Warren's work. If he's considering the case, I doubt you would need any opinion from me."

"Well, we would be interested in your observations, nevertheless. You may be asked your views at some point, in any case."

"I'm afraid I can't be of much help either way," Dr. Kuhn explained. "As a clinical hematologist, I diagnose and treat blood disorders, including leukemia. Harley's type of leukemia is unique in my experience because he has this missing C chromosome. I believe very little has been published about leukemia cases involving missing chromosomes."

It was time to let Dr. Kuhn know that Dr. Warren had wanted an autopsy. "Dr. Warren is grateful that you discovered the chromosome abnormality right at the beginning. He told me that your initial findings are very important in the case and many specialists might not have done the detailed investigation and followup you did. He did ask me to make sure that an autopsy is performed and that slides of the bone marrow are taken so that he can review them. He wants to make sure that acute myeloid leukemia is the cause of death, since it is the first type of leukemia that ordinarily shows up after one is exposed to radiation. He will probably call you with the information about where to send the slides."

"That's fine. I'll inform Mrs. Roberts of the necessity for an autopsy immediately after his death. Tell Dr. Warren I'll be waiting for his call. In the meantime, we'll try to make Harley as comfortable as possible. He's constantly fighting respiratory infections. Once it gets him, it will likely progress rapidly to pneumonia, which he will not be able to fight," Dr. Kuhn explained.

"Thank you, doctor, for your time," I said, sensing that he was anxious to get on with his work. "I hope we can call you if we need any information."

"Sure." Dr. Kuhn walked us out to the hall, shook hands, and returned to the lab.

Paul and I left the hospital and headed back to Las Vegas. Neither of us felt like talking. I was haunted by Harley's emaciated, pallid form wrapped in the bed sheet. A light rain began to fall as we entered the freeway, but through the whine of the tires on wet asphalt and the cadence of the windshield wipers, I kept hearing Harley's final words, "Make the bastards pay."

APRIL 17, 1974

In early April, it was evident that Harley had indeed developed pneumonia. He declined rapidly. Thankfully, his son Randy was granted an early discharge from the Marines in late March to be with his parents during his dad's final days. Randy knew how much his mother depended on Harley. Taking daily insulin injections placed an added burden on her. Randy drove his mother and grandmother to Loma Linda on Dorothy's days off and whenever Dorothy could be spared from her work.

By the 10th, Dorothy, Randy, and Harley's eighty-year-old mother were at the hospital every day, keeping vigil. By mid-April Randy knew the end was near. Harley was sleeping most of the time, but Dorothy kept hoping he would get better. Harley's mother was facing one of the most difficult things a parent can face, the death of a child. But she bore her suffering silently and did what she could to help Dorothy.

On April 17, after a very difficult night, Dorothy clung to Harley's bed, refusing to leave. By late afternoon, her legs were so swollen and she was so exhausted the hospital staff was threatening to hospitalize her if she did not follow their advice. Randy finally persuaded her to lie down on the cushioned sofa in the hallway and take a nap.

Dorothy collapsed and slept. Randy stayed beside Harley, watching the monitors falter and flatline. Randy found his mother sound asleep on the hallway sofa and gently touched her shoulder. At first, she thought she must be dreaming. But somehow, she responded to the urgency of his touch. She finally opened her eyes and saw Randy stooping over her, his own eyes misty and his voice breaking as he told her. "Mom, he's gone." And she knew what he meant more from his face than the words he spoke. Harley had been more than a father to Randy; he had been a friend and companion.

As soon as Dorothy realized her Harley was gone, panic and shock grabbed her. She rose, burst through the door, and staggered toward his room with desperation, as if she could somehow stave off death or at least arrive in time to say goodbye. She had had no opportunity for a final farewell, unwilling as she had been to admit the gravity of his condition. But when she reached the bedside and saw the expression on the nurse's face, the truth hit her like a hammer. She went numb...passive. So complete was her retreat from reality that she could recall almost nothing of the event or what followed over the next several weeks.

She signed the consent for an autopsy and arrangements were made. The bone marrow slides sent to Dr. Warren confirmed the Loma Linda pathologist's diagnosis. Harley died of acute myelogenous leukemia, the type of leukemia long known to be caused by radiation exposure.

Arrangements were made for his body to be flown back home to Indiana to Harley's beloved Bicknell for burial. Harley Roberts, like the Baneberry vent cloud, passed over Nevada and into the American heartland. His nightmare was finally over.

[10]

Cracking the Shell of Secrecy

In early May 1974, Dr. Warren called to report that he had reviewed the autopsy slides from Loma Linda. They confirmed that Harley Roberts died of acute myelogenous leukemia. But his next words were quite unexpected.

"I thought I should let you know that I have reviewed all of Mr. Roberts's medical records and his film badge readings, and it's beginning to look fairly certain that the radiation from Baneberry caused Roberts's C chromosome deletion, which in turn led to his leukemia and death."

Dr. Warren spoke in his very deliberate manner, leaving little doubt in our minds that, if anything, he had understated his conviction that radiation from Baneberry was the most probable cause of Harley's death. But he would need more information about Harley's radiation dose before he would prepare a written opinion.

We told him we were scheduling the depositions of the Rad-Safe monitors who took readings of Roberts and would send copies. This could take several months. Dr. Warren said he looked forward to receiving the additional information.

Dr. Warren's call was exhilarating. When we filed the lawsuit in February 1972, it was primarily to protest the AEC's casual attitude in ordering the security guards into a radiation zone but also to force it to produce the guards' radiation exposure records. We had not anticipated that any of the guards would develop health problems.

With Dr. Warren firmly on our side and with newfound enthusiasm, we were determined to find the truth about the cause of the Baneberry vent and pursue the Roberts case to its conclusion, no matter how long, difficult, or costly.

When Dr. Warren called, the AEC's explanation about the cause of the December 1970 Baneberry vent was unraveling. In late 1973, we took the depositions of Baneberry Test Manager Cluff and the scientists who selected the

Baneberry site. We learned that the United States Geological Service (USGS) had investigated the cause of the vent and issued a report early in 1971. We also learned that in January 1971 the AEC had completed its investigation of Baneberry, prepared a comprehensive report, and had reviewed films of the vent.

We filed motions to produce the two reports and the films, but the government opposed our motion. The AEC claimed disclosure would compromise national security. We persisted and ultimately prevailed, despite opposition by government counsel, who summed up the government's disdain for us and the public: "This isn't a case where the public has a right to know what the scientists are doing, but this has to do with some highly technical classified information."[1]

We were dumbstruck by the arrogance and could not imagine how the records, reports, and primary data about the geology of the Baneberry site and the films could compromise national security. In our view, a geological formation laid down eons before the AEC began testing A-bombs at NTS could not be classified "secret." Geology, we thought, was an imperishable science, which even the AEC could not alter, distort, or conceal.

Ever since the AEC first came to town in 1951, they had let us know how fortunate we were to have such eminent scientists in our backward community. Now, twenty years later, they asked us to accept, without question, statements by the eminent scientists that either they did not fully investigate the Baneberry geology or did not understand the consequences of detonating a device in the geologic formation they selected.

Although we had long suspected, particularly our consultant Paul Duckworth, that the May 1971 *Baneberry Summary Report* was inaccurate, we were now convinced the AEC was engaged in a cover-up and would try to bury all contradictory information.

The court granted our motion to produce. We were provided a heavily redacted copy of *NVO-95*, the January 1971 *Baneberry Summary Report.*[2] We were also provided a copy of the USGS report issued in January 1971.[3] But we had to file additional motions before the court allowed us to view the films of the Baneberry vent.[4]

In June 1974, I traveled to Denver to take the depositions of the USGS geologists who had prepared the report. Their testimony established that the *Baneberry Summary Report* was false or very misleading in its conclusions about the geology of the Baneberry site and the cause of the venting.

Armed with *NVO-95* and the USGS report, Paul Duckworth contacted two geologists at the University of Kansas, in Lawrence. Ernest Angino was professor and chairman of the Department of Geology. His expertise was in geochemistry. He served as chief of the geochemistry section of the Kansas Geological Survey from 1965 to 1970. John Halepaska earned his doctorate in geoscience in 1970, after completing an MS degree in groundwater hydrology. He was chief of the groundwater section of the Kansas Geological Survey.

Both were eminently qualified to challenge the AEC's contention that the Baneberry vent was unexpected. Between 1969 and 1972, they headed up a study to determine the feasibility of burial of high-level nuclear waste in Kansas. Based upon their investigation, the Kansas Geological Survey recommended against the idea. This was significant, because they had opposed the AEC and beaten them.

Drs. Angino and Halepaska reviewed the geological information and concluded that the AEC's statement in the May 1971 *Baneberry Summary Report* that the "primary cause of the vent was an unexpected and abnormally high water content in the medium surrounding the detonation point" was unsupported by the evidence. They relied upon the USGS report that showed "water content of the clay medium at Baneberry was very high" and that another "nuclear test (*Stutz*), known to have been conducted in a similar clay medium, gave an unusually high seismic response similar to Baneberry." They pointed out that the USGS report revealed another deliberate omission in the *Baneberry Summary Report*.

> A large fault lies nearly tangent to the Baneberry shot point cavity [and that] the vent path was probably up this fault to its intersection with a tension fracture in the alluvium and thence up that pathway to the surface. Thus, the venting at Baneberry was probably related to a coincidence of structure [a fault], including fracture orientation, and water-bearing clay.

They pointed out that *NVO-95* also discredited the bastardized May 1971 *Baneberry Summary Report*. *NVO-95* contained over thirty charts and tables and acknowledged that there was "high montmorillonite clay content above and below the shot horizon." This "caused the much higher water content than is normally expected at this depth in Yucca Flat." It concluded, "The implications of geology with respect to containment are implicitly recognized by the Laboratories [LLL and LASL], but the explicit implications for this specific case were not fully considered by the entire testing community."

It took only a moment to decipher this cryptogram. The scientists at LLL recognized there was a high likelihood Baneberry would not be contained, but others in the testing community did not.

In late July 1975, we disclosed to government counsel the opinions of Drs. Angino and Halepaska. The government immediately scheduled their depositions. I traveled to Lawrence, Kansas, for Dr. Angino's deposition on September 3, 1975, and to Tampa, Florida, on September 4, 1975, for Dr. Halepaska's deposition.

After our two geologists were deposed, we were confident we could show that the AEC had deliberately misrepresented the geology of the Baneberry site when they issued the May 1971 *Baneberry Summary Report*. It had been a painful awakening. The AEC's decision to issue the May 1971 *Baneberry Summary Report*, with full knowledge that *NVO-95* and the USGS report contradicted it, amounted to a gross misrepresentation of the truth.

We began our investigation of Baneberry in early 1971, trusting an agency that had been part of our community for over twenty years. Over the next four years, as we investigated the Baneberry vent, we realized we were dealing with AEC officials and a platoon of government lawyers prepared to do whatever was necessary to protect the AEC's image and defeat our claims in court.

NOTES

1. *Las Vegas Sun*, September 6, 1975.

2. *Baneberry Collection*, EX 62, *Baneberry Summary Report, January 1971, NVO-95*. Unlike the fourteen-page May 14, 1971 *Baneberry Summary Report, NVO-95* was seventy-five pages with multiple tables and charts. The copy we were supplied with looked like Swiss cheese, with countless redactions.

3. *Baneberry Collection*, EX 36. *Results of the Exploration of the Baneberry Site, Early 1971*, USGS-474-145. The report was over 110 pages in length, including multiple figures, tables, and redactions.

4. We filed multiple motions to produce the films. On April 21, 1975, the court allowed us to view the films at the AEC offices but under a protective order, which precluded us from copying or reproducing the material or communicating to any person information about the films.

[11]

Tell That Lawyer to Go to Hell

Dr. Warren was a careful investigator who wanted as much information as we could obtain before he would give us his final opinion in the Roberts case. It took five months to complete the depositions of Rad-Safe monitors and others who collected the data on dosage.

We called in November 1974 to make sure Dr. Warren had received the information. He said he had but had not worked through the stack of documents. He believed he would be ready to discuss the case with us in early January and would have his secretary call to schedule a telephone conference.

The conference was held in mid-January. We listened to Dr. Warren for nearly an hour as he discussed Harley's medical records, Harley's deposition testimony, and the radiation records. He spoke to us as if we were his medical students and he was tutoring us on the science, as he walked us through every aspect of his analysis and opinion. In addition to the many hours he spent reviewing the material we supplied, he researched the medical and scientific literature. And we received not only Dr. Warren's opinion that Harley's radiation exposure at Baneberry caused his leukemia, but also an education in the field of radiation effects that explained why there could not have been any other cause. We understood why Dr. Warren was revered in the scientific community, considered by many as the father of radiation pathology.

He explained that radiation had long been recognized as a highly potent cause of chromosome abnormalities. Dr. Boveri conducted the first research in the field and established the point in the early 1900s. In the 1920s, Dr. Muller studied the effects of radiation on fruit fly chromosomes, which are very large and easily identifiable, unlike human chromosomes.

Harley's exposure to radiation at Baneberry was sufficient to cause his chromosome abnormality. But unlike Dr. Muller's experiments, which produced immediate chromosome damage clearly visible under the microscope, Harley's chromosome abnormality from radiation at Baneberry, although immediate, was not detected until July 1972, eighteen months later. The bone marrow sample taken at Loma Linda Hospital in July 1972 revealed that Roberts was missing a C chromosome in one of the six pairs of C chromosomes. It was later specifically identified as a C-7 chromosome.

Dr. Warren then quantified Roberts's radiation exposure and explained how it caused the C-7 deletion. The film badge Harley wore showed he had received a whole-body dose of 1,045 mR gamma radiation. This dose was sufficient to cause the chromosome deletion. But there were other measurements of Harley's gamma exposure taken by Rad-Safe monitors throughout the day. The gamma radiation in the Baneberry cloud penetrated his body from every angle during the nearly one hour he was in the Baneberry cloud. However, many studies have shown that only about 70 percent of gamma rays penetrate the cortex of the bone and reach the red bone marrow, where the blood-forming stem cells are produced. Therefore, the 1,045 mR gamma reading on his film badge would need to be reduced by roughly 30 percent to arrive at a whole-body bone marrow dose.

The film Roberts wore also recorded a beta dose of around 4,500 mR at the surface of the body. Unlike gamma rays, beta emitters that strike the surface of the body penetrate only about half a centimeter. Still, the beta emitters would add somewhat to Roberts's overall bone marrow dose, since a small percentage could penetrate the skin and the bone cortex to reach the red bone marrow in his skull, sternum, rib cage, spine, and pelvis where a large part of the red marrow is located.

In addition to the external radiation dose, Harley was inhaling radioactive gases in the Baneberry cloud the entire time he was in Area 12 Camp. While measurements were taken of radioactive iodine concentrated in his thyroid gland, there would have been many other radioactive gases present in the Baneberry cloud that were not measured. As Dr. Warren explained, these other radioactive substances in the cloud, like the iodine, would have been inhaled into the lungs and taken into the blood stream to circulate throughout the body, contacting all his cells, including the stem cells in the red bone marrow.

Dr. Warren said that he could not give any firm overall radiation dose to the red bone marrow, but most probably it was about 15 R or 15,000 mR, more than sufficient to cause damage to bone marrow stem cells.

All stem cells in Roberts's red bone marrow probably received radiation from Baneberry. But it was radiation to a single bone marrow stem cell in the process of cell division that caused the damage and initiated the leukemic process. Dr. Warren explained that Dr. Rudolf Virchow, the nineteenth-century German pathologist who is considered the father of pathology, first advanced

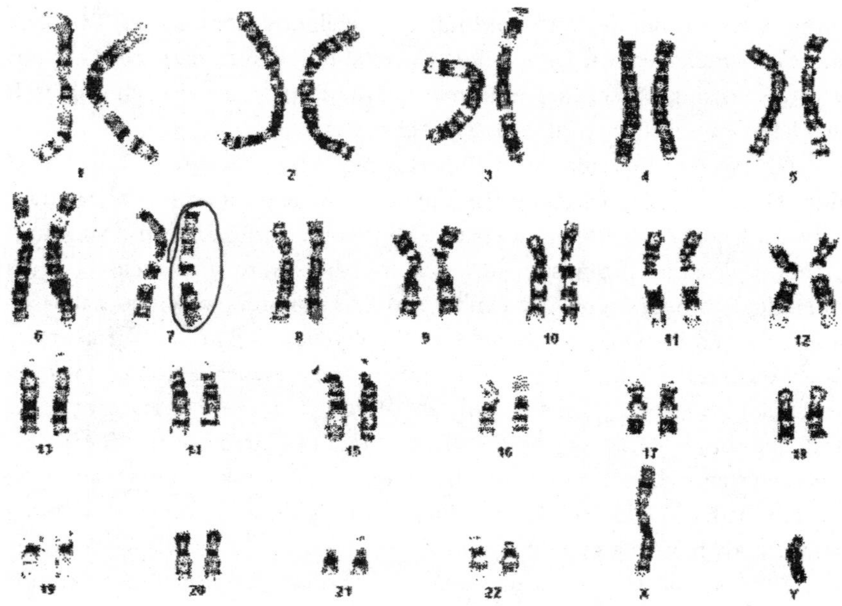

Representative copy of chromosome karyotype work. Harley Roberts had only one 7 chromosome after his Baneberry exposure. Courtesy of the author.

the theory that leukemia and cancer begin with the alteration of a single cell that multiplies and overpowers the normal cells. Dr. Virchow's theory has been generally accepted since that time.

The bone marrow cell damaged by radiation at Baneberry was in the process of dividing. The twenty-three pairs of human chromosomes in the bone marrow cells can only be viewed microscopically, when the cell is in the process of division. At that point, the chromosomes line up in pairs and are clearly visible and the chromosomes are most vulnerable to damage from radiation.

Dr. Warren assumed we had never seen a picture of the chromosomes in a human cell and had no more than an abstract notion how they are analyzed. He described the different chromosomes as looking like Chinese characters. When visible under the microscope, a photograph of the twenty-three pairs can be taken. For further analysis, each pair is cut from the photo and pasted on a board from chromosome 1 through chromosome 22. The final pair, chromosomes 23, are the sex chromosomes, X for female, and Y for male. The photograph is referred to as a karyotype. We didn't have a karyotype at the time he was explaining the matter, but his explanation certainly gave us a mental image of the violence radiation can do to a chromosome during cell division.

Dr. Warren explained that after the radiation destroyed the C-7 chromosome, one of the two daughter cells would have the missing C-7 chromosome. That abnormal cell has distinct advantages over the normal cell and would reproduce rapidly. Over time, it would overpower the normal cells. The rate of reproduction would be fast, because the bone marrow cells are among the most rapidly dividing cells in the body and in a constant state of division, replenishing all the blood cells that circulate throughout the body.

By July 1972, when a serrated needle was stuck into Harley's pelvic bone to draw out bone marrow cells for examination, the abnormal daughter cell produced on December 18, 1970, had proliferated to such an extent that many cells were detectable under the microscope. The growth rate of the abnormal bone marrow cells examined was consistent with the rate that would have been expected eighteen months after that first cell was altered by radiation from Baneberry.

Of course, the abnormal cells continued to increase and by February 1974, when Roberts was officially diagnosed with acute myeloid leukemia, 90 percent of his bone marrow cells contained the missing C chromosome. As expected in these cases, Roberts survived only two more months and died on April 17, 1974.

Dr. Warren explained that in 1974, there were only a few cases in the literature that described patients with a C-7 deletion. This was because it was not possible to clearly distinguish the C-7 cell until Dr. Caspersson, a Swedish physician, developed a new staining technique called banding for each of the twenty-three human chromosome pairs. Dr. Warren knew Dr. Caspersson and witnessed a demonstration of the new banding technique when he came to Boston in late 1972.

Although there are only a few cases in which the C-7 deletion has been found, they confirm that once it is detected in the bone marrow, the patient progresses to acute myeloid leukemia within a couple of years, followed by death within months. These cases, in Dr. Warren's view, established the connection between the course of Roberts's disease and death and his radiation exposure.

Dr. Warren then explained that in his opinion Harley's leukemia could not have any cause other than his Baneberry exposure. He reviewed with us Harley's medical history before and after Baneberry, which showed that REECo doctors gave him a physical examination when he joined the security force in 1966 and had annual physical examinations prior to Baneberry and one on February 18, 1971, a couple months after Baneberry. His blood studies were normal. He pointed out that the study done in February 1971 occurred so soon after Baneberry that it could not be expected to show any signs of a blood disorder.

In addition to the blood studies, which ruled out any blood disorder prior to Baneberry, Roberts's medical records showed that on December 18, 1970, he was in good physical condition for a man fifty years of age. On that day, he carried out rigorous duties, running from trailer to trailer for nearly an hour to evacuate workers.

Dr. Warren said he had carefully reviewed Harley's work history prior to Baneberry and saw nothing that could have caused a chromosome abnormality. He further explained that the C-7 deletion, once detected, takes no more than a year, two at the most, to cause anemia and other blood conditions. Therefore, it was very unlikely that Roberts had his C-7 deletion prior to Baneberry.

Summing up his analysis, he felt confident that Harley's exposure to radiation at Baneberry was the most probable cause of the chromosome deletion, which set in motion the progression to the anemia and the leukemia from which he died. As he put it, Baneberry left its fingerprint inside the body of Harley Roberts.

After Dr. Warren ended his explanation, he asked if we had any questions. We did not. In fact, Dr. Warren had anticipated all questions that could possibly bear on the relationship between Baneberry and Harley's death. By the time he finished, we were confident that no one could dispute his opinion in the case. Dr. Warren told us he would write up his opinion in the next week or so and mail it to us.

On January 30, 1975, Dr. Warren sent us a five-page, single-spaced letter, entitled *Analysis of Data and Opinion in the Case of Harley Roberts and Opinion of Shields Warren, M.D.* It set forth the basis of his opinion that Roberts's exposure to Baneberry on December 18, 1970, caused his C-7 deletion, which progressed to leukemia and death.[1]

A few days later, Dr. Warren called. His normal calm, professorial tone was replaced by disgust and anger. He said he had received a visit by a lawyer for New England Deaconess Hospital, where the Shields Warren Radiation Laboratory and his office were located. The hospital's counsel informed him that a lawyer from the Justice Department had contacted him after learning that Dr. Warren had given an opinion in a lawsuit against the AEC. The Justice Department lawyer advised hospital counsel that given the substantial funding his hospital received from the AEC, he considered it inappropriate for Dr. Warren to consult and serve as an expert in a lawsuit against the AEC. The Justice Department lawyer stated that Dr. Warren's involvement in a case against the AEC was a conflict of interest.

Dr. Warren reacted with outrage. In his view, the conflict of interest claim masked something more nefarious. In turn, he considered it a blatant effort to stifle his right to testify about a subject to which he had devoted his entire career. For a split second, we thought that the Roberts case had been dealt a serious blow, and we would need to find another expert. But Dr. Warren silenced our fears.

"I told the hospital's attorney to tell the government lawyer to go to hell," he said angrily, and described the government lawyer's tactics as "dirty pool." Dr. Warren assured us that he would testify in the case and no one could prevent him from doing so. His reassurance was not enough, however, to shake our rising panic that the government had nearly derailed our effort to pursue the Roberts case in court.

Until that moment, we had not appreciated the lengths to which the AEC and the Justice Department lawyers would go. It was sobering to learn that they immediately tried to bully Dr. Warren, one of their own. We realized we were dealing with a closed network of AEC-funded laboratories and hospitals and how difficult it might be to find other medical experts willing to testify against them.

TUCSON, ARIZONA, MARCH 1975

In late February, Dr. Warren called to tell us he would be in Tucson for two weeks in early March and invited us to meet with him to discuss the Roberts case. We were honored but a bit nervous that he might also have wanted to meet us to take the measure of the lawyers who had entangled him in the case. I had attended the University of Arizona and was anxious to meet the man who had so courageously defied the AEC and the Justice Department.

I arrived just before 10:00 AM at the Arizona Inn near the University of Arizona Medical School. Dr. Warren was dressed formally in a light gray suit and wore spectacles. He struck me as a proper Bostonian who had changed neither his dress nor his manner over the past fifty years as he worked tirelessly to reach the top of his field. After we shook hands, Dr. Warren explained that he came to Tucson every spring so he could break up the long, cold New England winter and swim in the unheated sixty-eight-degree swimming pool. He had allotted precisely two hours to go over the information and answer any questions.

We sat opposite each other at a small table stacked with all his records and files in the Roberts case. He handed me a copy of his single-spaced, twenty-page written résumé and told me that he had not updated it in the last couple of years. I quickly scanned through it and calculated that in addition to his education, honoraria, memberships, editorial boards, and professional societies, he had authored well over 400 papers and publications.

I had seen résumés of expert witnesses in other cases. Usually, they had one or two pages, including a few publications. But Dr. Warren's listing of his work was so overwhelming, I had to ask how he had managed to conduct so much research and publish so many articles. He looked at me and said matter-of-factly that he was one of those fortunate people who only require about four hours of sleep a night. This allowed him to start his work well before dawn and continue late into the night.

He must have sensed I was intrigued by the work in which he had been involved, some of which he had mentioned during our lengthy phone conversations. He began with a discussion of the Japanese survivors of the atomic bombings and the role he played in setting up the protocol for the studies. He described in some detail the conditions when he first arrived and the efforts to assist the Japanese doctors treating survivors suffering from acute radiation sickness, radiation burns, anemia, and other blood disorders. It was gruesome, but as a pathologist he had spent a lifetime dealing with disease and death.

Dr. Warren followed up with a discussion of the long-term studies of those who did survive and noted that he was primarily interested in blood studies to see whether they would develop leukemia.

Based upon the protocol he set up, he followed the group and documented the first case of leukemia that he considered to have been a direct result of the bombings. Relying upon that case and other records, he published the first paper predicting an outbreak of leukemia. He could not conceal how proud he was of his role in setting up the protocol and how important the studies were in tying together all the information about long-term radiation effects.

I imagined that the work in Japan must have been part of his standard introduction to his Harvard medical students over the years. It was fascinating for me to connect in a small way with his firsthand experiences after such horrible but momentous events. But in his descriptions, there was no hint of arrogance, just a genuine desire to educate me on the basics of radiation and its effects, using the most poignant and best-known example.

He must have sensed my awe. I wondered whether he was satisfied that he had placed his standing and reputation in the hands of the young lawyer opposite him and whether he felt I was capable of adequately presenting the Roberts case at trial.

He spoke about Harley Roberts with genuine compassion. He had, after all, seen firsthand the devastating effects of radiation that culminated in leukemia and an agonizing death. As Dr. Warren talked, I could not help comparing the approach of this sympathetic man to the Oak Ridge doctors whom Harley had described as cold and impersonal and treated him as the enemy. I was profoundly sorry that Harley was unable to meet him, for Dr. Warren's compassion might have made the suffering a little more bearable.

After commenting about the Justice Department lawyer's attempt to prevent him from expressing his opinion in this case, he mentioned that it was not the first time he had taken a principled stand and asserted his right to express his opinions about radiation risks. In the early 1950s, he related that he had a clash with the Department of Defense. It occurred when he was director of Biology and Medicine at the Nevada Test Site.

"I was in conflict with the military brass during that early period," he explained. "I was concerned that the soldiers were stationed in trenches too close to the atomic tests."

"How did they determine the dose the soldiers got?" I asked.

"That was part of the problem," he answered. "The military had their own radiation monitors who randomly issued film badges to the soldiers and were primarily interested in measuring gamma radiation. I was concerned about all the fission products produced in the explosion. This is the material sucked up into the fireball and then scattered over the area where the soldiers were ordered to march. There was no effort made to measure the radioactive gases and particles inhaled by the soldiers, and it would be impossible for me to determine the health risks to which they would be exposed. It is the same concern I have regarding Roberts's bone marrow dose from inhalation of gases in the Baneberry cloud.

"In the spring of 1952," he continued, "when the military resumed the series of aboveground tests and placed thousands of soldiers within a couple miles of ground zero, I again voiced my concerns and felt that they should not be placed closer than seven miles from the blasts. But the military's demand for active participation by the soldiers overrode my complaints. I registered my objections in writing and resigned my position effective July 1, 1952. I've never regretted that decision. I could not, in good conscience, continue as director and did not want to be held responsible for those soldiers."

It was nearly noon when he finished. He asked if I had any questions. Though I had reviewed his résumé quickly, I noted that it did not include any reference to testimony in lawsuits. In early 1974, that information was not required to be disclosed in a witness résumé. Today, court rules require an expert witness to produce a list of court cases in which he or she has given a deposition or testified at trial. I asked how often he had testified in court.

"Usually," he responded, "if I give an opinion, which I have on many occasions, that seems to end the matter. If my opinion supports the plaintiff, the case is usually settled. If my opinion supports the defense, the case is frequently dismissed. But, over the years, I have testified in court on a few occasions."

It was another matter-of-fact and credible statement befitting a man of his stature. I dared not inquire any further regarding the strength of his opinion in the Roberts case, but I could see why the government had wanted to remove him as our expert witness.

Within a week, government counsel sent a letter asking us to arrange a time for them to take Dr. Warren's deposition in Boston. His deposition was scheduled at the Shields Warren Laboratory at the New England Deaconess Hospital on June 9, 1975.

BOSTON, MASSACHUSETTS, JUNE 9, 1975

I arrived in Boston on Sunday night, June 8, and met with Dr. Warren early the next morning. The first thing he told me was that Robley Evans, the expert hired by the government, had called him late Friday afternoon, June 6, to discuss the Roberts case. Evans said the reason for calling was to tell Dr. Warren he was authorized by the government to disclose information regarding the breakdown of the various radioactive iodine isotopes produced by the Baneberry nuclear explosion. However, Evans conceded that there were no measurements of iodine or other radioactive gases taken in the Baneberry cloud during the time Roberts was present in Area 12 Camp.

Dr. Warren said he sensed that the real purpose of Evans's call was to try to persuade him that Roberts's bone marrow dose was too low to cause his leukemia and to determine whether Dr. Warren would change his opinion. He told Evans that the information regarding the iodine component was helpful but did not alter his opinion that the bone marrow dose was sufficient to cause the C-7 chromosome deletion and initiate the leukemia process. He had studied radiation-induced chromosome damage over many years and remained convinced that the radiation dose at Baneberry, even if less than he had originally thought, was sufficient to cause the C-7 deletion.

Dr. Warren explained to me that he understood Evans's point of view. But Evans was not a medical doctor and was unfamiliar with studies of radiation-induced chromosome abnormalities, which might account for his failure to understand what Dr. Warren considered the most important aspect of the case.

Dr. Warren showed me around the laboratory while we waited for the attorneys. At just before 10:00 AM, two government lawyers arrived with a court reporter in tow. The deposition lasted until 1:30 that afternoon.

The government lawyers were aware of Robley Evans's call to Dr. Warren and were hoping Dr. Warren had changed his opinion. But they learned that Dr. Warren had not been persuaded to accept Evans's estimated bone marrow dose. However, upon questioning, Dr. Warren did concede that his original estimate of 15 R or 15,000 mR was probably high, due largely to his not having been provided all the information, including a breakout of the radioactive iodine present in the cloud. He remained convinced that Roberts's bone marrow dose from external gamma radiation, combined with the internal dose from gas inhalation, was considerably higher than Evans's lower estimate of less than 1 Rem and "something under my first top estimate of 15 Rem." In either case, it would not change his opinion, because there was abundant evidence that radiation causes chromosome deletions, which was the bedrock upon which his opinion was based.[2]

Following the deposition, Dr. Warren took all three attorneys to lunch at the Harvard Club. Later that afternoon, he drove me to his home on Pilgrim Road in West Newton, where he had on display memorabilia and awards from his life-long study of radiation and contributions to other fields of medicine. He did not have time to discuss them all but did point with pride to an award from Hiroshima University and the Japanese government for his studies of the A-bomb survivors.

Dr. and Mrs. Warren then took me to dinner at a restaurant overlooking the Charles River. Near the end of dinner, the conversation came back to Baneberry. Between a thinking-out-loud comment and question, Dr. Warren wondered if another worker exposed at Baneberry might develop acute myeloid leukemia.

"Having one acute myeloid leukemia in the Baneberry group," he said, "is quite striking, but two cases would be truly remarkable." It was a curious thought that lingered with me on my flight back to Las Vegas. When I got to the office the next morning, I mentioned it to Alan.

NOTES

1. *Analysis of Data and Opinion in the Case of Harley Roberts and Opinion of Shields Warren, M.D.*, January 30, 1975. Copy in author's possession.
2. *Deposition of Shields Warren, M.D.* Copy in author's possession.

[12]

The Second Man

AFTER DR. WARREN made his observation about another possible leukemia in the Baneberry group, we asked Bill Cleghorn and Paul Duckworth whether they knew of any workers exposed at Baneberry who were having health problems. They checked around but did not find anyone.

Other than running an ad in the local newspaper, we knew of no way to find the names of the eighty-six workers. Today, attorneys solicit clients through television ads seeking persons exposed to asbestos or pharmaceuticals for the obvious purpose of filing lawsuits in their behalf. But in 1975, it was a violation of the canons of professional ethics to advertise or solicit clients for litigation.[1] "Barratry" is the term that prohibits lawyers from stirring up litigation in this way.

After the Justice Department tried to disqualify Dr. Warren from assisting us in the Baneberry case, we knew it would pounce on a chance to pursue disciplinary action against us before the Nevada Bar Association and seek to disqualify us from pursuing the case if we solicited other workers to join the lawsuit.

From July 1975 through the end of the year, we had no further information to pursue Dr. Warren's speculation that there might indeed be another leukemia. We assumed Harley's leukemia was the only one. But in January 1976, a call came into the office.

"Larry, Bill McGimsey is on the phone," the secretary told me over the intercom.

Bill and I had been friends since grade school. We and another grade school friend, Bill Steele, were roommates at the University of Arizona. Bill McGimsey and I passed the Nevada bar in 1968 and were sworn in in October.

"Hello, Bill, what's up?" I asked.

"I have a lady in my office who drove down from Indian Springs to talk about a real estate matter. She told me her husband worked out at the Test Site and was involved in the big blowout in 1970. I assume she's referring to

Baneberry and told her you and Alan filed a lawsuit against the government over that test."

"Is her husband with her?" I asked.

"No. She said he died of leukemia."

"Really? I'd like to ask her a couple questions."

"I'll hand her the phone."

"Hello. This is Louise Nunamaker."

"Hello. This is Larry Johns. Bill said your husband worked out at the Test Site. Was he in the Baneberry test in 1970?"

"Yes. He was there. He came home in paper coveralls that evening."

"Bill said your husband died of leukemia. When did he die?"

"It was December 10, 1974. I'll never forget that date and how much he suffered during the last few months."

"Mrs. Nunamaker, I don't know whether you are aware that we filed a lawsuit for a security guard who was in the Baneberry test. He died of leukemia in April 1974."

"No. I've been in a state of shock ever since he died. I've been living up at Indian Springs and hadn't heard anything in the news about a lawsuit. Could I make an appointment to meet with you? I'd like to find out whether I have a case against the government over my husband's death."

She was only in town for the day, so we met with Louise Nunamaker early that afternoon. She told us her husband died of leukemia and produced a death certificate she kept in her purse. William Nunamaker died on December 10, 1974 of acute myelomonocytic leukemia, Naegeli type.

Louise was positive Bill was in the Baneberry test. She said he took a lot of showers, came home that day wearing a ridiculous paper suit and told her, "Mother, I was right in the middle of it." They kept all his clothing and even the car, which wasn't returned for nearly a month. He went on working for the next four years. Then he "just fell apart," she said, wiping away tears with the tissue she had been clutching.

When we told her about Harley Roberts and the lawsuit his widow Dorothy was pursuing, she asked us to file suit over her husband's death and wanted us to know about her husband and their life together.

We knew from the death certificate that Bill Nunamaker was born in Nebraska in 1913. She did not talk about his life before she met him during World War II. She knew he enlisted in the Navy right after Pearl Harbor and served in the Pacific during the war. They met in 1943, while he was on leave, and married right after the war ended. Bill was an operating engineer, and they moved around a lot. He worked all over the northwestern United States before he came to Las Vegas to take a job at the Test Site. Everybody liked him. He did not talk about his job, but she knew he worked in the tunnels and was promoted to shop foreman. He drove to work every day, because he did not like to leave her alone at night. They had four children, all grown and living on their own. It had been very hard for her without him.

After we met with Louise, we called Dr. Warren and told him there was another leukemia, an acute myelomonocytic leukemia, Naegeli type. He explained that Nunamaker's leukemia was essentially the same as Roberts's. I then asked him how he had known or suspected that there might be another acute myeloid leukemia in the Baneberry group. He said that of course he did not know there would be another leukemia when he made the comment, but since acute myeloid leukemia is the first cancer one would expect to see in a group of people exposed to radiation and Roberts had already been diagnosed with the disease, if there was going to be another acute myeloid leukemia, it would most probably show up in the first four to five years after Baneberry. That was the case with the Japanese.

On February 23, 1976, we again met with Louise. She now insisted we file a lawsuit against the government. We prepared the tort claim form, which she signed, and a two-page "Request for Release of Radiation Data and Medical Reports." They were served upon Mahlon Gates, manager of the Energy Research and Development Agency (ERDA) in Las Vegas.[2]

ERDA did not send the radiation exposure information or the medical records Louise requested. We obtained an autopsy report for William Nunamaker and other medical records and sent them to Dr. Warren for his review.

On November 15, 1976, Dr. Warren wrote us, indicating that although the time from the Baneberry radiation exposure to development of acute myeloid leukemia was compatible with exposure and the onset of Nunamaker's leukemia, he did not think the radiation dose was sufficient to induce the disease. His preliminary conclusion was that it was a spontaneous case of leukemia in the group of men exposed at Baneberry. But he agreed to continue his investigation of the Nunamaker case.[3]

NOTES

1. Attorney advertising was not allowed until the U.S. Supreme Court struck down the Arizona Bar Association's prohibition of advertising in 1977, Bates v. State Bar of Arizona, 433 U.S. 350 (1977).

2. In 1974, Congress passed the *Energy Research and Development Act*. ERDA succeeded the Atomic Energy Commission. In 1977 Congress enacted the *Department of Energy Act*. The DOE succeeded ERDA.

3. Shields Warren to Larry Johns, November 15, 1976. Copy in author's possession.

[13]

A Hobson's Choice

BY THE END OF OCTOBER 1975, we had taken over twenty-five depositions to prepare for trial: Frank Cluff, the Baneberry test manager; Drs. Weart and Brownlee, the scientists who signed the *Baneberry Summary Report*; Dr. Lawrence Germain, an LLL scientist who sat on Cluff's Test Evaluation Panel; Chan Griffin, AEC Security Chief; Richard McArthur, the LLL geologist who selected the Baneberry site; four USGS geologists who authored the USGS report; five Rad-Safe monitors who took radiation readings on the day of Baneberry; Captain Forest Tackett, WSI chief; and a dozen others.

The government also took over twenty-five depositions: Harley Roberts and the other security guards exposed at Baneberry; Paul Duckworth our consultant; Dr. Warren our medical expert; Drs. Angino and Halepaska, our geologist experts; and others.

We had forced the government to disgorge the "secret" documents that discredited the AEC's May 1971 *Baneberry Summary Report* and had viewed films of the Baneberry vent that showed the radioactive cloud blanketing Area 12 Camp. Most important, Dr. Shields Warren was prepared to testify at trial in support of the Roberts case.

The court closed further discovery on December 30, 1975.[1] We expected the case would be set for trial in the spring of 1976. But discovery did not close. On January 30, 1976, the court filed Amended Standing Order No. 24, which required the parties to attend a settlement conference to "fully and fairly" discuss settlement of the case.[2]

Discovery was extended to March 31, then to April 30, and then to June 18, 1976. With discovery set to close on June 18, 1976, we sent defense counsel a letter offering to settle Dorothy Roberts's case for $500,000, the amount Harley Roberts requested in the tort claim he filed in December 1971.[3] The offer was based entirely upon Dr. Warren's opinion supporting Roberts's case. The government had not challenged Dr. Warren's opinion. In fact, Dr. Gould Andrews, who reviewed Roberts's medical records at Oak Ridge Hospital, reported that he "could not rule out radiation as the cause, although he felt the radiation dose was too low."[4]

Dorothy's offer was high, but we were authorized to reduce it by half if the government was willing to negotiate. We received no oral or written response to our settlement offer until April 28, 1977. During the ten months from June 4, 1976, to April 28, 1977, we were bogged down with motions, discovery disputes, hearings, extensions, and court orders, capped off by an order setting a pretrial conference before the court on February 7, 1977, then reset for March 14, 1977.[5]

On February 10, 1977, Alan and I met with John Thorndal and Bill Elliott to discuss trial witnesses and exhibits. We met again on March 2, 1977. During the meetings, we brought up the Roberts settlement offer but got no encouraging response. When we pointed out they had not identified an expert to counter Dr. Warren, they said they would disclose a radiation expert from Oak Ridge. On March 3, 1977, we sent a letter stating we would object to their adding expert witnesses as untimely, since the trial was set to begin on May 1, 1977.[6]

On March 9, 1977, the proposed pretrial order was lodged with the court.[7] In it, the government identified Dr. Clarence Lushbaugh, an Oak Ridge doctor, to counter Dr. Warren. On March 14, 1977, we filed a motion to strike Dr. Lushbaugh from the government's witness list as untimely, but when we attended the pretrial conference that day, the judge reopened discovery through June 17, 1977, to allow us to take Dr. Lushbaugh's deposition.[8]

On April 6, 1977, as we made final preparations for trial, an article appeared on the front page of the *Las Vegas Review-Journal*: "A-blast, then Leukemia." The article began, "Paul Cooper is dying of leukemia. His doctors say it's because he stood unprotected about 3,000 yards from a nuclear test blast in the Nevada desert nearly 20 years ago."[9]

We saw the news article about Paul Cooper. Dorothy and Louise also saw it and called us. They were saddened that another person exposed to radiation at NTS was dying of leukemia but believed the story would strengthen their claims. We were not so sure.

On April 28, 1977, the government responded to our June 4, 1976 offer to settle Dorothy's case. In the letter, Assistant Attorney General Barbara Babcock, by David Anderson, Chief of Litigation Division, offered to settle Dorothy Roberts's case for $75,000.00. She offered each of the other claimants $250.00 and gave us until May 10, 1977, to accept or the offer would be deemed rejected.[10]

The timing of the government's offer puzzled us. It came just three weeks after the headline news story about Paul Cooper. We called government counsel to discuss the $75,000 offer and inquired whether there was any room to negotiate a higher settlement. We also suggested that any settlement include the Nunamaker case. We were told they would convey our message to Washington.

After speaking with counsel, we called Dorothy, told her of the $75,000.00 offer, and asked her to meet us as soon as possible. Dorothy and her son Randy came in the following day. They were aware of our earlier $500,000 offer and could not understand why the government had offered so little for Harley's life. When Dorothy learned that Louise Nunamaker had been offered nothing, she looked puzzled but said she did not know much about Louise's case.

After telling Dorothy we had spoken to counsel about negotiating a higher settlement, we told her if she did not accept the offer by May 10, it would expire. We could see Dorothy was overwhelmed by the situation and was looking to Alan and me for advice. We could have taken the burden off her shoulders. We could have told her we were unwilling to spend more money and time and she must settle for whatever we could get. But we believed the ultimate decision was hers.

Dorothy asked the question every client asks when a settlement offer is made: "If I accept the $75,000.00 offer, how much will be left for me after all expenses are paid?"

We had never discussed with Dorothy the arrangement we made with the guard union in December 1971. The union agreed to pay all costs, but after they paid the $1,350 Ronan & Associates invoice in 1972, the board reneged and refused to pay further costs. We did not tell Dorothy and Randy that the costs we had paid already exceeded $40,000, and the costs would mount rapidly as we prepared for trial.

The thousands of hours we had devoted to the case over the past six years were incalculable. We had not kept records. We told Dorothy if she accepted the $75,000.00 offer, we would settle our costs for $20,000 and our fees for $20,000, which would leave her with $35,000.00.

Dorothy was not surprised by the cost figure and said we were being generous accepting only $20,000 for all the work we put into the case. She seemed genuinely sorry that we would all be left with so little if she accepted the $75,000. We reassured her we would be satisfied with $40,000, but the ultimate decision was hers.

She asked about our chances if we went to trial. We told her what she already knew: her case was based entirely upon the standing and opinion of Dr. Warren. The government would not have offered $75,000.00 had they not realized he was a formidable witness. But the government had also recently disclosed a doctor from Oak Ridge to counter Dr. Warren. We thought we had a strong case but could not predict the outcome if we went to trial and reminded her again that we had to respond in less than two weeks.

We could see the anguish in her eyes. It was tempting to take the settlement and end the ordeal. She looked at Randy and commented that it would make her life a little easier but only for a short while. After a very long moment, she said she was sorry, but she just could not take the offer. Harley's life was worth a lot more than $75,000, and she had suffered too much to accept so little. As tears welled in her eyes, she said, "I'd give anything if I could talk to Harley. I just don't believe he would want me to sell out so cheaply."

I had never mentioned to Dorothy the last words Harley spoke to me at Loma Linda in March 1974: "Make the bastards pay." Now, three years after Harley's deathbed plea, Dorothy delivered the same message with as much passion.

After our meeting, we called Dr. Warren. He understood her refusal and thought the government would too and would offer more. We also discussed the publicity about Paul Cooper's claim against the VA. Dr. Warren was aware of it. He found it interesting but offered no comment about the merits of Cooper's claim.

Next, we met with Louise Nunamaker. If Dorothy had agreed to settle for $75,000, it would have been a very unpleasant meeting. We would have explained to Louise that the Roberts case was much stronger than hers because of Dr. Warren's opinion. We had no expert to support her case and would not have been willing to expend additional time and money to pursue her lawsuit. Our involvement with Baneberry would have ended in May 1977.

Louise was furious when told the government had offered Dorothy $75,000 but nothing for her. She calmed down when we explained that Dorothy had rejected the offer. We told her we hoped the government would be willing to negotiate a higher settlement for Dorothy and offer to settle her case, but the deadline was May 10. We waited but heard nothing from government counsel. On May 10, 1977, the $75,000 offer expired.

Dorothy was disappointed and bitter. Unable to settle the case and faced with an IRS lien on her mobile home, on May 15, 1977, she wrote a letter to President Carter asking for his help. A few days later, a reporter came to her home to interview her. The interview appeared on Sunday, May 22. In it, she described her nightmare, the IRS's threat to take her mobile home, that "she had lost faith in her government," and "couldn't take much more of it." She said she had written to President Carter asking for his help and commented about Paul Cooper, the soldier exposed to radiation in 1957, which "caused the leukemia that is killing him."[11]

Although we knew it was probably futile, on May 24, two days after Dorothy's story appeared in the *Las Vegas Review-Journal*, we sent Bill Elliott a letter offering to settle the Roberts case for $225,000.[12] In the letter, we took a different tack from relying upon Dr. Warren. We referred to the October 30, 1973 decision by Judge Foley awarding Mrs. McGarry $185,000.00 and her adult daughter $40,000.00. Mrs. McGarry sued the AEC for the death of her husband, Thomas McGarry, a REECo employee electrocuted at the Test Site on December 10, 1969.[13]

Our reference to *McGarry* was a not-so-subtle reminder that Judge Foley had found the AEC liable for the death of an NTS worker. The Ninth Circuit Court of Appeals had affirmed his decision in December 1976.[14] We knew *McGarry* was on appeal to the U.S. Supreme Court but thought it would be decided soon.[15]

By the end of May 1977, any hope of settling the Baneberry case was over, and, by July, the Baneberry case expanded to include Louise Nunamaker's case. Publicity about Paul Cooper and other veterans exposed to radiation at NTS, was, as we had feared, a two-edged sword. The April 1977 article about Paul Cooper was the catalyst for the $75,000.00 offer to Dorothy. But in our view, extensive publicity about Cooper and other atomic veterans dashed any hope for a fair settlement of Dorothy Roberts's case. In fact, the amount offered was punitive, since the government knew we would have to absorb our costs and time, leaving Dorothy with very little.

The Cooper case elevated the investigation into the health effects from NTS radiation from a parochial concern in southern Nevada to an issue of national concern.

We did, however, make one final effort to settle Dorothy's case and Louise's as well. On March 17, 1978, we sent two letters to Bill Elliot. The first offered to settle Roberts for $200,000, which included $25,000 for her son Randy. One basis for our offer was that Dr. Akio A. Awa, a Japanese cytogeneticist who reviewed comments in Dr. Lushbaugh's deposition, stated that Lushbaugh had misinterpreted his findings. Another basis referenced recent investigations challenging the AEC's claim that low-level radiation was harmless. We ended the letter with a calculation of Dorothy's economic damages based on Harley's life work expectancy.[16]

In the second letter, Louise Nunamaker offered to settle her case for $125,000, based upon a calculation of Bill Nunamaker's work-life expectancy.[17] We received no response to either letter.

NOTES

1. DS 202. The docket sheet prepared by the U.S. District Court clerk in Roberts v. United States of America, CV-S-1766-RDF, is a chronological record and summary of all documents and court orders, beginning with the filing of the complaint on February 2, 1972: (1)—2/2/72—filed Complaint. The order closing discovery is DS 202. A copy of the docket sheet is in author's possession. Copy in author's possession.

2. DS 211.

3. Larry Johns to John Thorndal, June 4, 1976. We also offered to settle the claims of the other security guards for $25,000.00 each. Copy in author's possession.

4. *Baneberry Collection*, EX 73.

5. DS 230–270.

6. Alan Johns to John Thorndal, March 3, 1977. Copy in author's possession.

7. The proposed pretrial order was lodged, not filed, and has no docket sheet number but is noted on March 9, 1977.

8. DS 264; DS 265.

9. *Las Vegas Review-Journal*, April 6, 1977. Paul Cooper's battle with the VA began in 1976, and was extensively covered. *Salt Lake Tribune*, *Parade*, June 19, 1977; *Las Vegas Review-Journal*, July 17, 1977, *Las Vegas Review-Journal*, August 10, 1977.

10. Barbara Allen Babcock to Larry Johns, April 28, 1977. Copy in author's possession. David Anderson was chief litigation counsel for the government in Baneberry until he was promoted. He was replaced by Bill Elliott.

11. *Las Vegas Review-Journal*, May 22, 1977.

12. Larry Johns to William Elliott, May 24, 1977. Copy in author's possession.

13. McGarry v. United States, 370 F. Supp. 525 (1973).

14. McGarry v. United States, 549 F.2d 587 (1976).

15. On October 31, 1977, the U.S. Supreme Court rejected the government's appeal. The *Review-Journal* headlined the decision: "Government Liable for Test Site Death." *Las Vegas Review-Journal*, October 31, 1977.

16. Larry Johns to Bill Elliott, March 17, 1978. Copy in author's possession.

17. Larry Johns to Bill Elliott, March 17, 1978. Copy in author's possession.

[14]

GI Joe and the Smoky Vets

IN EARLY 1976, PAUL COOPER, a resident of Idaho, went to see his family doctor complaining of weakness and fatigue. He was referred to specialists in Salt Lake City, Utah, who diagnosed his leukemia. When Paul told them that he was among a large group of young soldiers exposed to radiation during aboveground bomb test *Smoky* at NTS in August 1957, they helped him fill out a claim with the Veterans Administration and attributed his leukemia to his exposure to radiation at the Test Site. The VA denied his claim.

Paul Cooper refiled the claim and began searching for other veterans who had participated in Smoky. It was not long before another veteran, Donald Coe, from Kentucky, came forward. He also had been diagnosed with leukemia. Coe filed a VA claim seeking disability benefits.

By the end of 1976, Cooper and Coe were pursuing benefits, supported by doctors who believed their leukemias were caused by Smoky, a 44-kiloton blast at the Test Site on August 31, 1957, part of the twenty-nine-shot *Plumbob* series conducted between May and October of that year. Dr. Glyn Caldwell, an epidemiologist at the Centers for Disease Control (CDC) in Atlanta, became interested and initiated a study of the soldiers exposed at test Smoky.

After the headline story about Paul Cooper appeared in our local newspaper on April 6, 1977, we called Dr. Caldwell in Atlanta and explained that we represented workers exposed to radiation at the Baneberry test in December 1970 and two had died of acute myeloid leukemia in 1974. We mentioned that Dr. Shields Warren had given an opinion that the acute myeloid leukemia of one of the workers was caused by his exposure to radiation at Baneberry and inquired whether Dr. Caldwell could study the group of men exposed at Baneberry. Dr. Caldwell asked us to send more information for him to review.

On May 4, 1977, we sent Dr. Caldwell a letter with some information and Dr. Warren's deposition and again inquired whether he could perform a study of the Baneberry group.[1]

Dr. Caldwell wrote back on May 31, 1977, indicating he could perform an epidemiological study of the men exposed at Baneberry if we were able to provide the date of birth, race, sex, date of death (if deceased), radiation dose, and any illness (especially leukemia and cancer) for the men exposed.[2]

On June 9, 1977, in reliance upon Dr. Caldwell's letter, we filed a Request for Production of the names, ages, sex, race, and radiation doses of the workers exposed in Area 12 on the day of Baneberry.[3]

On June 19, Dr. Caldwell's study of the Smoky vets was the subject of a multipage insert in the *Salt Lake Tribune, Parade Magazine*, including a full-page color photo of an atomic test with a group of veterans in the foreground.[4]

Paul Cooper's claim was again front-page news in Las Vegas on July 17, 1977. The *Las Vegas Review-Journal* carried a photo of Paul Cooper and his wife with an article in which Cooper described his exposure to the radioactive cloud at test Smoky.[5]

Within days after the story appeared, Dr. Caldwell telephoned. He said he had been contacted by an attorney from the Justice Department who told him "it was inappropriate for me [Larry Johns] to ask and for the center [Dr. Caldwell and the CDC] to agree to conduct a study" of the Baneberry workers. Of course, we were reminded of the Justice Department call to counsel for the New England Deaconess Hospital, two years before, stating that it was inappropriate for Dr. Warren to support the Roberts litigation because the hospital received funds from the AEC.

On July 25, 1977, an aide to Congressman Tim Lee Carter of Kentucky contacted us to inquire about the Baneberry case. Congressman Carter was spearheading the congressional investigation of the Smoky vets, including his constituent Donald Coe. I wrote to James Santini, our Nevada congressman, to inform him that Congressman Tim Lee Carter's office had contacted us to inquire about the Baneberry case. I also related that Dr. Caldwell had told me that a Justice Department lawyer had admonished him that the CDC could not investigate the Baneberry group. Finally, I commented that I could see no distinction between the CDC's investigation of the Smoky veterans, who had filed claims for veteran's benefits, and our litigation against the government on behalf of the men exposed at Baneberry, who also were seeking compensation.[6]

On July 26, I wrote to Dr. Caldwell to memorialize what he had told me about the call from the Justice Department, to advise him of Tim Lee Carter's call to us, and to tell him I hoped "that Congress doesn't get a communication from the Justice Department that it is 'inappropriate' for them to look into this matter because of pending litigation."[7]

On August 10, 1977, the *Las Vegas Review-Journal* carried a banner story from the *Washington Post* about test Smoky and Dr. Caldwell's CDC study. The article, after referencing Cooper and Coe, noted that the CDC "recently turned up two additional ex-servicemen with leukemia who say they, too, were at Smoky."[8]

On September 2, Congressman Santini wrote us and attached a letter dated August 25, 1977, from Dr. Foege with the CDC, quashing our request to have Dr. Caldwell study the Baneberry group because it would be "inappropriate."[9]

Although Dr. Caldwell was unable to conduct a study of the Baneberry group, his study of Cooper, Coe, and the others exposed at Smoky was not squelched by the Justice Department. And Paul Cooper and the CDC study of the atomic veterans continued to receive front-page coverage in our local newspapers and likely spawned claims and lawsuits by others.

On November 30, 1977, Pat Broudy's struggle to gain benefits for the death of her husband, Major Charles A. Broudy, was on the front page of the *Las Vegas Review-Journal.* Pat filed a lawsuit in federal district court in Los Angeles alleging that her husband's death on October 27, 1977, from cancer of the lymph nodes was caused by his exposure to radiation at the Nevada Test Site and at Bikini Atoll.[10]

Paul Cooper's story was again on the front page of the *Las Vegas Review-Journal* on February 5, 1978. The article, "VA quietly awarded radiation claims," disclosed that the VA had awarded disability benefits to ten veterans exposed to radiation from atomic tests in the Pacific or at the NTS who developed leukemia or other cancers. VA representatives acknowledged that exposure to low-level radiation was not a determining factor and "not that important." It discussed Dr. Caldwell's study of the Smoky vets pointing out that eight leukemias had been found, and that the "VA Appeals Board granted him [Paul Cooper] 100 percent disability." It reported that Donald Coe's appeal was pending before the appeal board and there was a congressional investigation of the atomic veterans' claims by the House Commerce Subcommittee on Health and Environment.[11] Five days later, we learned of Paul Cooper's death from acute myeloid leukemia.[12]

The CDC study of the Smoky vets and the congressional investigations were relentless and continued despite setbacks by veterans who filed suits against the United States under the Federal Tort Claims Act for injuries they said were caused by exposure to atomic radiation. Their FTCA claims were barred by the Feres doctrine, which precluded service members who sustained injuries while on active duty to filing claims with the Department of Veterans Affairs.[13]

By September 2, 1980, Dr. Glyn Caldwell had confirmed that nine of the 3,233 men exposed to the Smoky test had contracted leukemia, three times higher than expected and statistically significant.[14] Although Dr. Caldwell was disqualified from performing the study of our Baneberry group, he did provide the name and telephone number of Dr. Alice Stewart, an epidemiologist in Great Britain.

NOTES

1. Larry Johns to Glyn Caldwell, May 4, 1977. The letter and attachments cannot be located, but is referenced in Dr. Caldwell's letter response and in the August 25, 1977 letter from the CDC to James D. Santini.
2. Glyn Caldwell to Larry Johns, May 31, 1977. Copy in author's possession.
3. DS 297.
4. *Salt Lake Tribune*, June 19, 1977, *Parade Magazine* insert. The article mentioned Paul Cooper and Donald Coe, a resident of Kentucky, and urged veterans exposed at Smoky to contact Dr. Caldwell at the CDC.
5. *Las Vegas Review-Journal*, July 17, 1977.
6. Larry Johns to James Santini, July 25, 1977. Copy in author's possession. I did not have Dr. Warren's permission to disclose the call from the Justice Department after he agreed to assist us and would not have involved him in the controversy, although we kept Dr. Warren informed of our efforts to persuade the CDC to study the Baneberry group.
7. Larry Johns to Glyn Caldwell, July 26, 1977. Copy in author's possession.
8. *Las Vegas Review-Journal*, August 10, 1977, p. 3.
9. James Santini to Larry Johns, September 2, 1977, with Dr. Foege's August 25, 1977 letter attached. Copy in author's possession.
10. *Las Vegas Review-Journal*, November 30, 1977.
11. Ibid., February 5, 1978.
12. Ibid., February 10, 1978.
13. Feres v. United States, 340 U.S. 135 (1950).
14. *Las Vegas Review-Journal*, September 2, 1980.

[15]

Dr. Alice Stewart, Éminence Grise[1]

We telephoned Dr. Alice Stewart in Birmingham, England, in early September 1977, told her about the Baneberry case and that we had contacted Dr. Caldwell to study our Baneberry group, similar to his Smoky investigation. She seemed flattered that Dr. Caldwell had recommended her and asked for detailed information about the Baneberry group. We told her eighty-six men had been exposed to the radioactive cloud and two died of acute myeloid leukemia within four years. We mentioned that Dr. Shields Warren had given an opinion in support of one of our clients and thought it highly unlikely that two cases of acute myeloid leukemia would occur by chance in the group exposed.

Dr. Stewart knew of Dr. Warren's standing and role in the A-bomb studies and seemed quite surprised that we had someone of his caliber supporting our case. She was willing to review the material but was very busy. However, she said that she would be at the University of Pittsburgh in early December and suggested we meet there to go over the information. She and her colleague, Dr. George Kneale, a mathematician, were to attend a weeklong conference with Dr. Tom Mancuso. Dr. Mancuso had asked them to review an ongoing study of workers exposed to plutonium over the period from 1944 to 1974 at the AEC's Hanford Works, in Washington state. I agreed to send a letter with some of the information and the two death certificates, and meet her in Pittsburgh.

On December 4, 1977, I left Las Vegas and five hours later descended through heavy cloud cover to land in Pittsburgh around 5:00 PM. I took a cab to a motel near the university and called the number Dr. Stewart had given me. Dr. Mancuso answered, and when I asked to speak to Dr. Alice Stewart, he handed her the telephone.

Dr. Stewart said they were still at Dr. Mancuso's office working into the evening and insisted that I come right over to meet her. I grabbed my briefcase with Baneberry records and walked about four blocks to the lobby of the building that housed the Department of Epidemiology.

A tall, slender, very fit lady in her late 60s with a crop of short gray hair was waiting just inside the glass doors. After introducing herself and giving me a brisk British handshake, she said she wanted to speak with me before she took me in to meet George Kneale. He was a brilliant Oxford-trained mathematician, she explained, but a bit odd and rather asocial. She was much older than George and had somewhat taken him under her wing. Additionally, she cautioned me not to be offended if he did not talk much. On occasion, he would not speak at all.

I was apprehensive when she led me into the room and approached the desk where Dr. Kneale was seated staring down intently at a pile of documents. He looked to be in his mid-thirties and a bit out of shape. Given Dr. Stewart's comments, I was pleasantly surprised that this eccentric mathematician greeted me warmly and joined in our discussion about the Baneberry test. He asked some pointed questions about the workers and offered some statistical information about the incidence of leukemia in men of early to middle age. He also volunteered statistics about cancer incidence among the workers in the Hanford study, which they were in Pittsburgh to review with Dr. Mancuso.

When we met again the following morning, Dr. Stewart apologized that she had not thought to bring her curriculum vitae or any sort of résumé and felt she ought to introduce herself by giving me a summary of her education and work experience.

She mentioned that both of her parents were physicians who had lived into their midnineties, her mother among a small group of pioneering female physicians. Dr. Stewart got her medical degree at Cambridge in 1930 and was certified in hematology, the branch of medicine that studies blood diseases, including leukemia. During World War II she was invited to Oxford, where she served as First Assistant in Hematology. After the war, she shifted her practice to the new field of social medicine, referred to as epidemiology in the United States. She spent the next few years studying workers exposed to tetrachloride, coal miners in South Wales suffering with pneumoconiosis, and tuberculosis in workers in the shoe-making factories.

Her interest in radiation effects began in 1955. By that time, the studies of the Japanese survivors, initiated by Dr. Warren, had been published in reports by the Atomic Bomb Casualty Commission. The studies confirmed that radiation had caused an epidemic of leukemia, which peaked four to six years after the bombs.

By 1955, doctors in Britain noticed a general increase of leukemia, with the most dramatic among three-year-old children. This strange occurrence was inexplicable, since prior to that time leukemia was almost an unknown disease among them. She began collecting medical records on leukemia and cancer patients for the prior three years, 1953 through 1955. This was rather easy because medical records were well maintained in Britain following the creation of the National Health Service after the war.

When she analyzed the records, she discovered that children who had been exposed in utero to a single diagnostic x-ray were developing leukemia at a much higher rate than those whose mothers had not been x-rayed.

Dr. Stewart said she took the information to the Medical Research Council to get support and funding for a larger study, but they considered the project too ambitious and too costly. So, she decided to conduct the study on her own. By early 1956, the first results of her work were published confirming that fetal exposure to a single x-ray caused cancer and leukemia at a significantly increased rate.

This phenomenon was eminently sensible, since the cells in the developing fetus are undergoing cell division at an astronomical rate. Bone marrow cells are the most radiosensitive in an adult body and even more so in a developing fetus. The womb, which shields the fetus from external forces, cannot protect it from x-rays.

Dr. Stewart expected that her findings would be controversial, since they challenged the long-held belief that there was a threshold dose below which no harmful effects occurred. At the time, it was assumed that a single x-ray, which delivers a dose of about 25 mR gamma to the cells of the fetus, was too low to have any effect. Indeed, her findings were initially dismissed by physicians and the nuclear industry in Britain and in the United States. But she persisted, publishing, republishing, and expanding her study and responding to her critics. Her report, the *Oxford Survey of Childhood Cancer*, is now accepted by the scientific community as a classic study in the field of radiation effects.

Dr. Stewart and I then went over the information I brought regarding the odd phenomenon of the occurrence of two leukemias in the Baneberry group. But it was not sufficient for her to conduct an epidemiological study. She needed the same basic information about the eighty-six men exposed to radiation from the Baneberry vent that Dr. Caldwell had requested: name; age; sex; date of birth; current medical history, if known, or death certificate; and the radiation dose of each of the individuals who required decontamination. With that data, she could perform an epidemiological study of the Baneberry group. She told me my assignment was to demand this vital information from the government. If I needed her assistance, she would supply a statement.

A little over a month after I returned to Las Vegas, journalist Walter Pincus wrote a lengthy story, carried nationally, about Dr. Mancuso's study of the

Hanford workers and his collaboration with Alice Stewart and George Kneale. Mancuso had been hired by the AEC in 1974 to refute a Washington State Public Health Service study that found an excess of cancer deaths among workers exposed to low-level radiation at the Hanford Works. When his initial findings confirmed the results of the prior study, his contract was terminated. But he persisted and with assistance from Stewart and Kneale, published the results in December 1977. They showed an excess of cancers. The article, headlined "Does low-level radiation cause cancer?" in the *Las Vegas Review-Journal,* discussed the Baneberry case and Dr. Shields Warren's anticipated testimony that low-level radiation could have caused leukemia.[2]

As mandated by Dr. Stewart, I requested the information and renewed our earlier motion to compel relying upon an affidavit from Dr. Stewart. On June 27, 1978, the court finally buckled, ordering the government to produce the name, date of birth, social security number, and radiation dose of all eighty-six men exposed at Baneberry. Even so, we did not receive the information until July 27, 1978.[3]

By then, we were in the final stages of trial preparation with a pretrial order due on September 29, and a pretrial conference in November 1978. From July through early November, we could only track down fifty-six of the workers, but it was sufficient for Dr. Stewart's study.

In October, counsel exchanged witness lists and proposed issues of fact. We offered as an issue of fact: "There is no safe level of radiation exposure." This set off a firestorm. On October 20, John Thorndal and Bill Elliott objected strenuously, claiming it raised a new issue in the case.[4] On October 23, we responded, pointing out that the government sought to include a finding that "any individual exposed to less than 5 Rem per year is without a remedy regardless of cause and effect."[5]

On November 9, 1978, Bill Elliott called late in the afternoon to inform us that Dorothy Roberts had contacted the DOE seeking cost data the government spent to defend her lawsuit. He was agitated and concerned "that the information might bring adverse publicity upon the government." He also told us "although Dorothy Roberts is entitled to the information," if she decides to "publicize it, the government might seek a gag order to prevent you from disclosing it."[6]

On November 10, I wrote Dorothy telling her what Mr. Elliott had told us the prior day. In the letter, I explained that I doubted that any publicity about the government's defense expenses would influence the judge and understood her frustration that the government had spent so much money trying to "defeat her claim where she can scarcely afford to eat." Dorothy was incensed to learn that the government "would fly all over the world to take the depositions of our experts, Stewart, Bertell, and Tamplin, at the taxpayers' expense," while she was "unable to send a representative." I explained that, as her attorney, I could not seek publicity or encourage her to do so, but "you have pursued this independently and may continue to do so." Finally, I told her I was not familiar with the criteria for a gag order but in my view, she was entitled to "exercise her First Amendment right regardless of this litigation."[7]

The DOE did not respond to Dorothy's oral request for information about the amount of money they had spent trying to defeat her lawsuit, and she did not pursue it. We assumed the time and expenses of the salaried Justice Department lawyers, U.S. Attorney lawyers, and DOE lawyers and their staffs was substantial but not broken down. But the legal fees and costs paid to the private law firm headed by John Thorndal over the years since the Baneberry lawsuit was filed in 1972, would be accessible, and, based upon the legal time we had spent and the costs we had paid, had to approach a half million dollars or more before we began the trial.

We did not raise the matter of the government's expenses nor did Dorothy after she called the DOE in November 1978. But Bill Elliott did on March 11, 1979, two months into the trial, when he told a reporter the government "would spend whatever it takes to win."[8]

On December 6, I sent Bill Elliott a letter regarding final trial preparation issues. In it, I referenced Elliott's request to informally discuss the Nunamaker case with Dr. Warren and explained that Dr. Warren was not disposed to informal discussions, pointing out that we "have received no opinions from your experts nor do I expect any prior to their testimony as was the case with Dr. Lushbaugh."[9] But Dr. Warren did speak with them and kept notes of the conversation.[10]

Dr. Alice Stewart was deposed in London, England, on December 5, 1978; Dr. Arthur Tamplin in Washington, D.C, on December 14, 1978; and Dr. Rosalie Bertell in Buffalo, New York, on December 15, 1978. We were unable to attend any of the depositions but knew the essence of their opinions and were confident government counsel could not persuade them to alter them, just as with Dr. Warren's deposition nearly four years earlier.

With the addition of Dr. Alice Stewart and her medical opinion and statistical analysis in support of the Roberts and Nunamaker cases, Baneberry was ready for trial. But other radiation claims, arising long after our investigation began in early 1971, attracted national attention and dwarfed our Baneberry case.

During 1978, people who lived downwind of the 1950s atmospheric tests were gathering information about the cancers and leukemias they witnessed among family members and had contacted attorneys to pursue claims against the government. Some called Alan and me, but in 1978 we were overwhelmed with Baneberry and unable to consider assisting them. In 1977, we met with MacArthur Wright, an attorney from St. George, Utah. In 1978, Dale Haralson, an attorney from Tucson, came to our office to discuss our case and told us he had been contacted to represent persons living downwind from the 1950s aboveground tests. We also spoke by telephone with Stewart Udall, Secretary of the Interior under presidents Kennedy and Johnson and now a Phoenix attorney. He had met many southern Utah residents who wanted him to file claims.

In late 1978, as we prepared for the Baneberry trial, stories about cancers and leukemias among the downwinders had gained national attention and were covered in Las Vegas. On November 28, the *Las Vegas Review-Journal* ran a banner headline, "Utah fallout probe ordered by Carter."[11] On December 1, the headline in the *Las Vegas Sun* read, "Utah Governor Seeks AEC files on fallout."[12] On December 9, the *Las Vegas Review-Journal* said, "NTS picked prior to fallout study."[13] And the *Las Vegas Review-Journal*, December 9, declared, "Truman rushed Nevada testing."[14]

On December 17, the first of a series of five articles appeared in the Sunday *Las Vegas Sun*: "St. George and the nuclear dragon." It depicted a dragon spewing poison on the fearful residents of St. George, Utah. The first article featured several persons who died of leukemia and cancer, including a young Nevada boy, Martin "Butch" Bardoli, exposed to fallout from the 1951 and 1953 atomic blasts who died of leukemia in 1956 at the age of seven.[15]

The next four articles in the series were published between December 18 and December 21, 1978.[16] The series contrasted the AEC's reassurances that fallout from the atomic testing at NTS was harmless, with stories from families exposed to radioactive fallout who lost loved ones to leukemia and cancer. They had trusted the AEC, but now believed that it had deliberately concealed the dangers.

The December 19, 1978, article stated, "Scientists at Oak Ridge have demonstrated that a single particle of radiation can damage the nucleus of a cell." A few paragraphs later, it added, "In 1959 a Joint Committee for the AEC reported that the 'best assumption that can be made at present concerning the relationship of biological effects of radiation dose is to assume that any dose, however small, produces some biological effect and can be harmful.'"[17] The fourth installment on December 20, "Feds downplayed radiation danger," discussed the public relations efforts of the AEC to "keep the public on their side."

All this publicity was a prelude to an article that appeared in the *Las Vegas Sun* on December 22: "Udall files 100 nuclear test claims." These were the first claims filed on behalf of the downwinders against the Department of Energy under the FTCA. The team of lawyers pursuing the claims was Stewart Udall, Dale Haralson, and MacArthur Wright.

On December 28, Nevada governor Mike O'Callaghan joined Utah governor Scott Matheson "ordering an examination of the effects of atmospheric testing at the Nevada Test Site during the 1950s and 1960s."[18] On February 15, 1979, newly elected Nevada governor Robert List joined former Nevada governors, Charles Russell, Grant Sawyer, and Paul Laxalt in calling for the probe.[19]

On January 9, 1979, the *Las Vegas Review–Journal* reported: "Fallout-leukemia link report found." It disclosed that a 1965 report by U.S. Public Health officer Dr. Weiss had been shelved by the AEC. Dr. Weiss had reported twenty-eight leukemia deaths in one year in southern Utah, and that there was only "a 2 percent chance that so many leukemias would be recorded in southern Utah in one year among a population of 21,000."[20]

Based upon the national interest in the plight of the downwinders and calls from the president, governors of Utah and Nevada, and representatives of downwinders in Congress, including our Nevada congressman James Santini, the Committee on Interstate and Foreign Commerce and its Subcommittee on Oversight and Investigations, began collecting evidence to investigate the issue.[21]

As we were preparing for trial, the legal team headed by Gerry Spence, nationally acclaimed trial attorney, was preparing *Silkwood v. Kerr-McGee* for trial before a jury in Oklahoma City, Oklahoma. The Silkwood trial opened on March 8, 1979,[22] and resulted in an $11.5 million jury verdict in favor of Karen Silkwood's heirs on May 18, 1979.[23]

NOTES

1. Dr. Stewart was quite a cynic. I nicknamed her *éminence grise*, a reference to Voltaire.

2. *Las Vegas Review-Journal*, January 18, 1978.

3. DS 351. In that order, the judge consolidated for trial the Roberts and Nunamaker cases.

4. John Thorndal to Larry Johns, October 20, 1978. Copy in author's possession.

5. Larry Johns to John Thorndal, October 23, 1978. Copy in author's possession. In the letter, we explained that we had no intention of agreeing to the government's position and would call Drs. Warren, Stewart, Tamplin, and Bertell to challenge it.

6. Larry Johns to Dorothy Roberts, November 10, 1978. Copy in author's possession. Elliott's statements are reported in the letter sent to Dorothy Roberts.

7. Ibid, November 10, 1978.

8. *Los Angeles Herald Examiner*, March 11, 1979.

9. Larry Johns to Bill Elliott, December 6, 1978. Copy in author's possession.

10. Following Dr. Warren's death in 1980, his secretary called to ask if I would like his personal files on the Baneberry case. They were sent to me and included notes of that conversation. Copy in author's possession.

11. *Las Vegas Review-Journal*, November 28, 1978.

12. *Las Vegas Sun*, December 1, 1978.

13. *Las Vegas Review-Journal, Trailblazer Edition*, December 9, 1978.

14. *Las Vegas Review-Journal, Final Edition*, December 9, 1978.

15. *Las Vegas Sun*, December 17, 1978.

16. Ibid., December 18–21, 1978.

17. Ibid., December 19, 1978.

18. *Las Vegas Review-Journal*, December 28, 1978.

19. *Las Vegas Sun*, February 15, 1979; *Las Vegas Valley Times*, February 15, 1979.

20. *Las Vegas Review-Journal*, January 9, 1979.

21. *Las Vegas Sun*, February 27, 1979. This article reported the official launch of the investigation and noted that Nevada congressman James Santini had called for the probe "to get the facts on the table and find out where the truth lies." In March 1979, newly elected Nevada governor List joined Utah governor Matheson in pursuing the probe (*Las Vegas Review-Journal*, March 10, 1979). On March 22, 1979, Governor List appointed a panel to study "The effects of aboveground nuke tests" (*Las Vegas Sun*, March 22, 1979). The results of the Subcommittee's investigation were published in the *Forgotten Guinea Pigs Report*, August 1980. It called for a legislative solution to assess radiation claims and provide compensation, citing several reasons: "(1) the existing legal remedy under the FTCA offers no degree of certainty or predictability regarding questions of causation which are unique to radiation claims; (2) nuclear radiation victims should not bear any further burden, particularly in terms of time and expense…; (3) the government must accept responsibility, whether legal or moral, for the injuries sustained by individuals as a result of the government's operation of the nuclear weapons testing program; and (4) a legislative remedy would provide the most adequate and expeditious means by which the government can accept such responsibility."

22. *Las Vegas Sun*, March 8, 1979: "Nuclear Facility Negligence Trial Opens."

23. *Las Vegas Sun*, May 18, 1979; *Las Vegas Review–Journal*, May 18, 1979.

Downtown Las Vegas before 1950, looking east down Fremont Street, with Union Pacific Depot in foreground and Pioneer Club. Photo courtesy of the Union Pacific Railroad Museum.

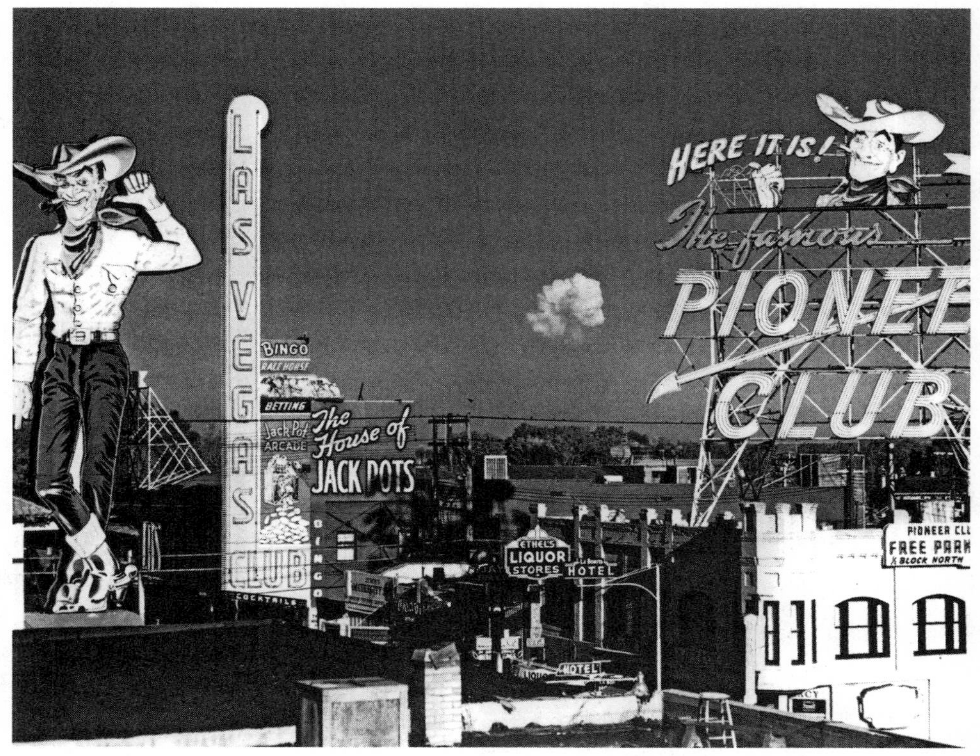

Downtown Las Vegas showing A-bomb cloud, looking north with Pioneer Club, Vegas Vic, and the Las Vegas Club. The A-bomb cloud is from test "Dog" detonated at NTS on November 1, 1951. Photo courtesy of the Las Vegas Convention and Visitors Authority.

Desert Rock atomic veterans at test "Dog" detonated at NTS on November 1, 1951. Photo courtesy of National Nuclear Security Administration Nevada Field Office, Nuclear Testing Archive.

The Baneberry vent. We viewed films of the venting in 1975, of which this is a single frame. Our viewing was under a protective order, and we were directed not to copy the films or disclose any information about them. The photo was released to the press and published in newspapers on October 6, 1977. Photo courtesy of National Nuclear Security Administration Nevada Field Office.

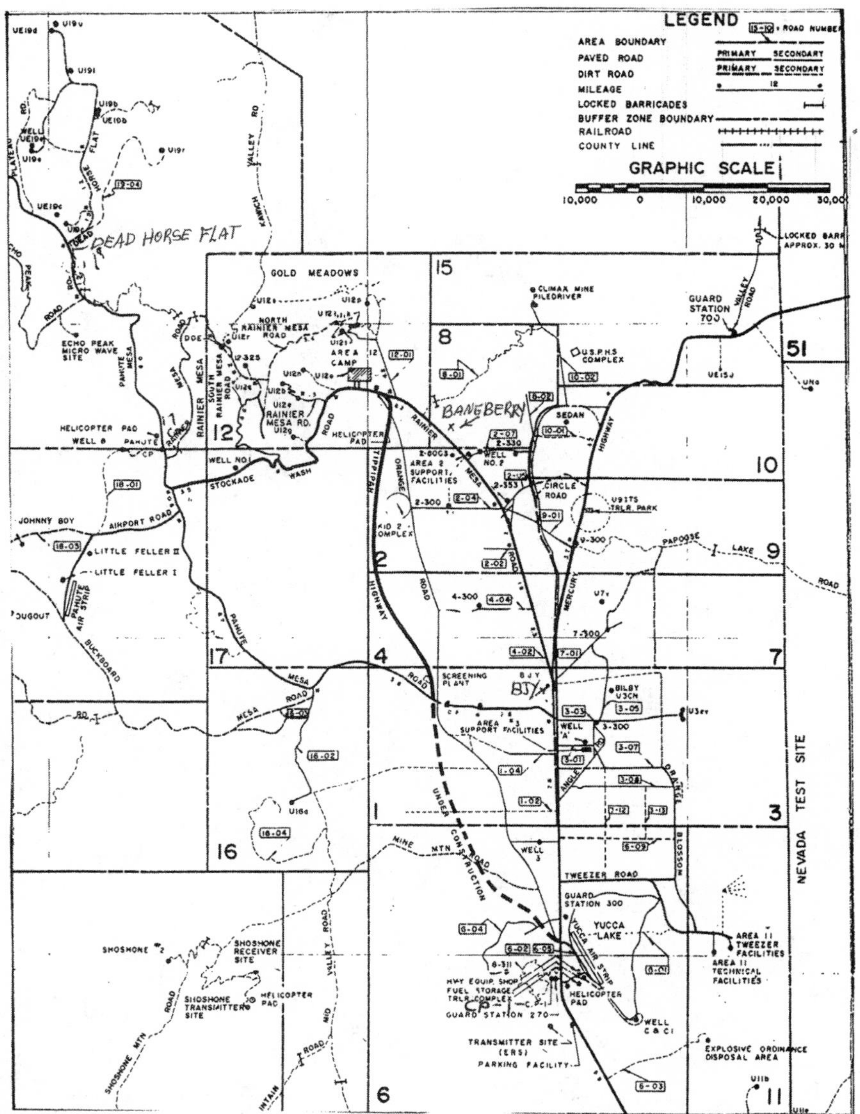

Map of Nevada Test Site. Courtesy of the author.

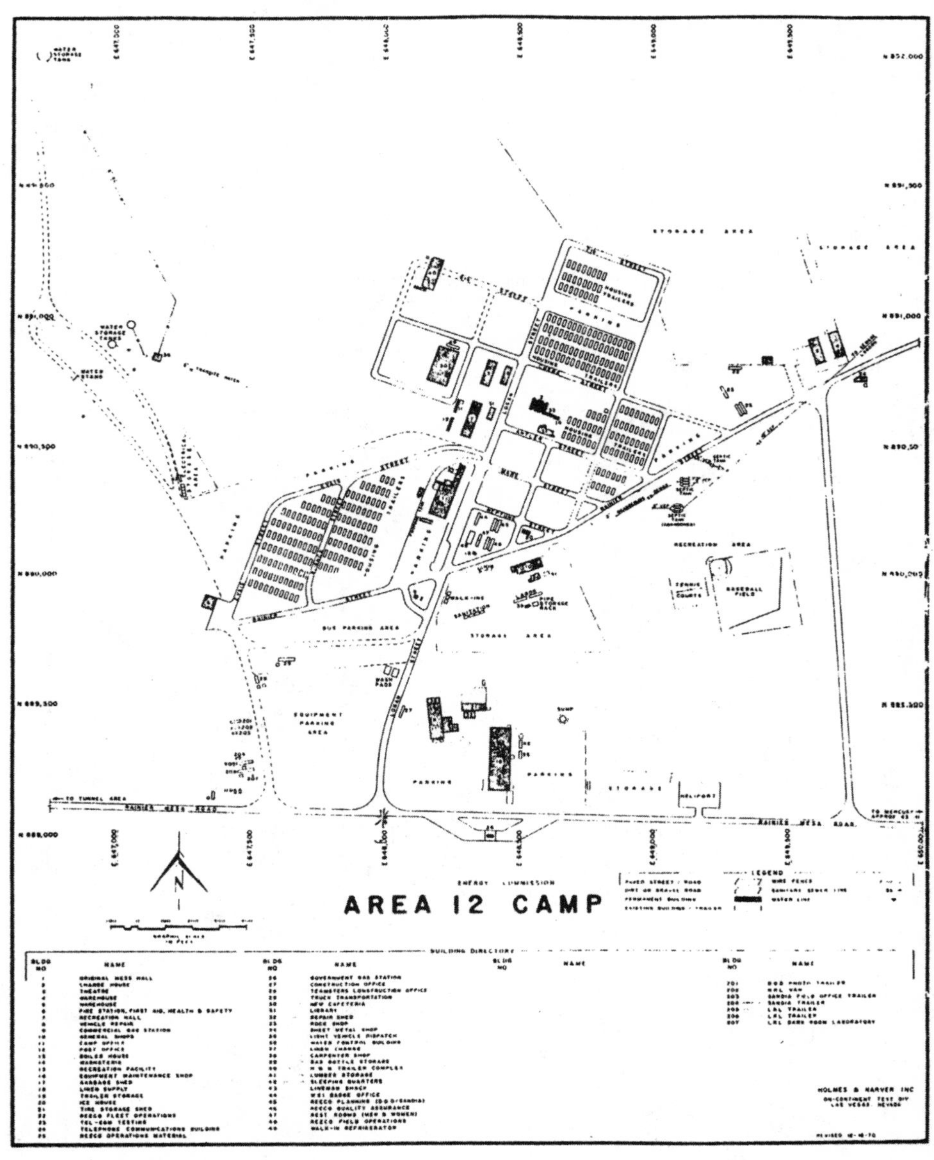

Map of Area 12 Camp. Courtesy of the author.

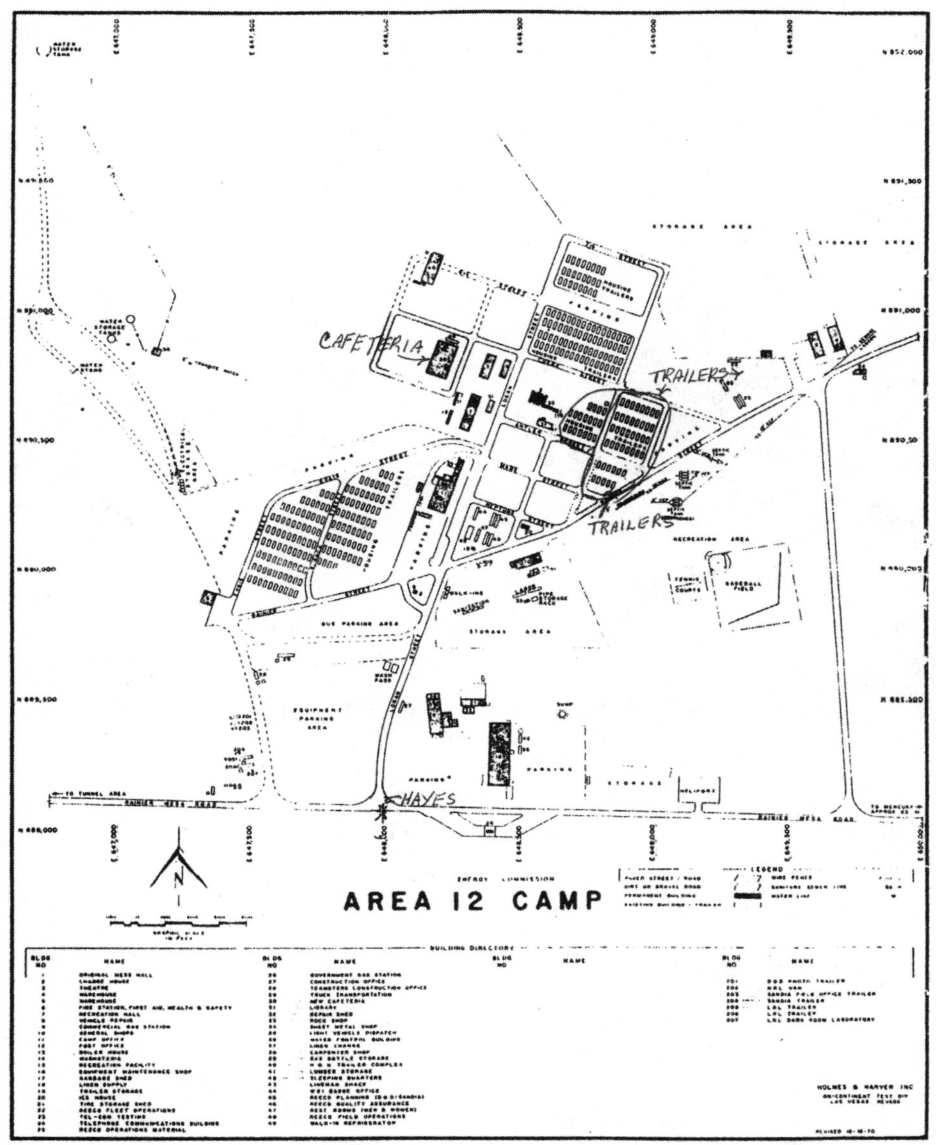

Trial exhibit 21. Map of Area 12 Camp with notations. Courtesy of the author.

Trial exhibit E-11: Baneberry surface cloud of radioactive dust in the basin just below Area 12 Camp at about 7:50 AM. Courtesy of the author.

Louise Nunamaker, Dorothy Roberts, and Alan Johns standing in front of the elevator on January 16, 1979. Courtesy of Randy Tunnell, photographer.

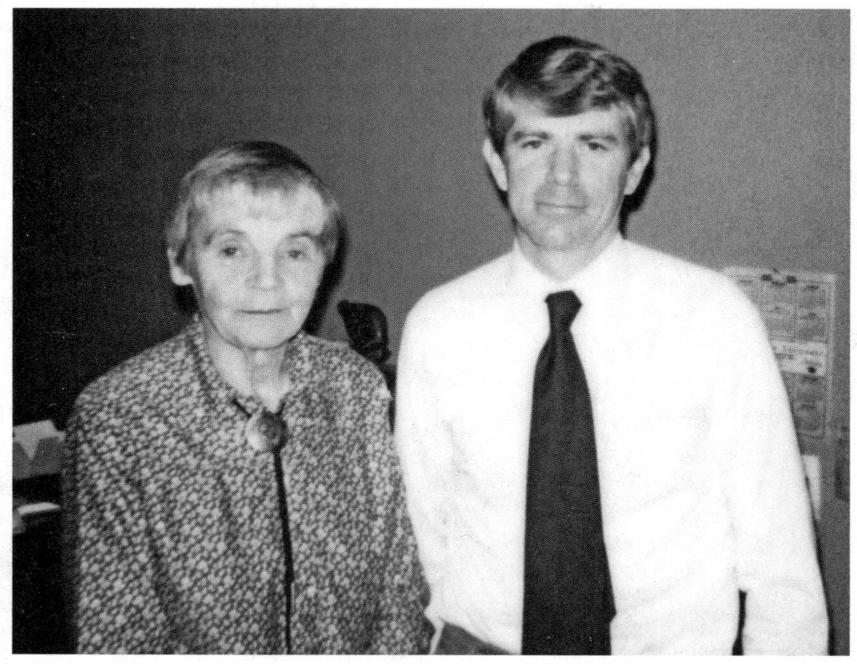

Dr. Alice Stewart and Larry Johns. Courtesy of the author.

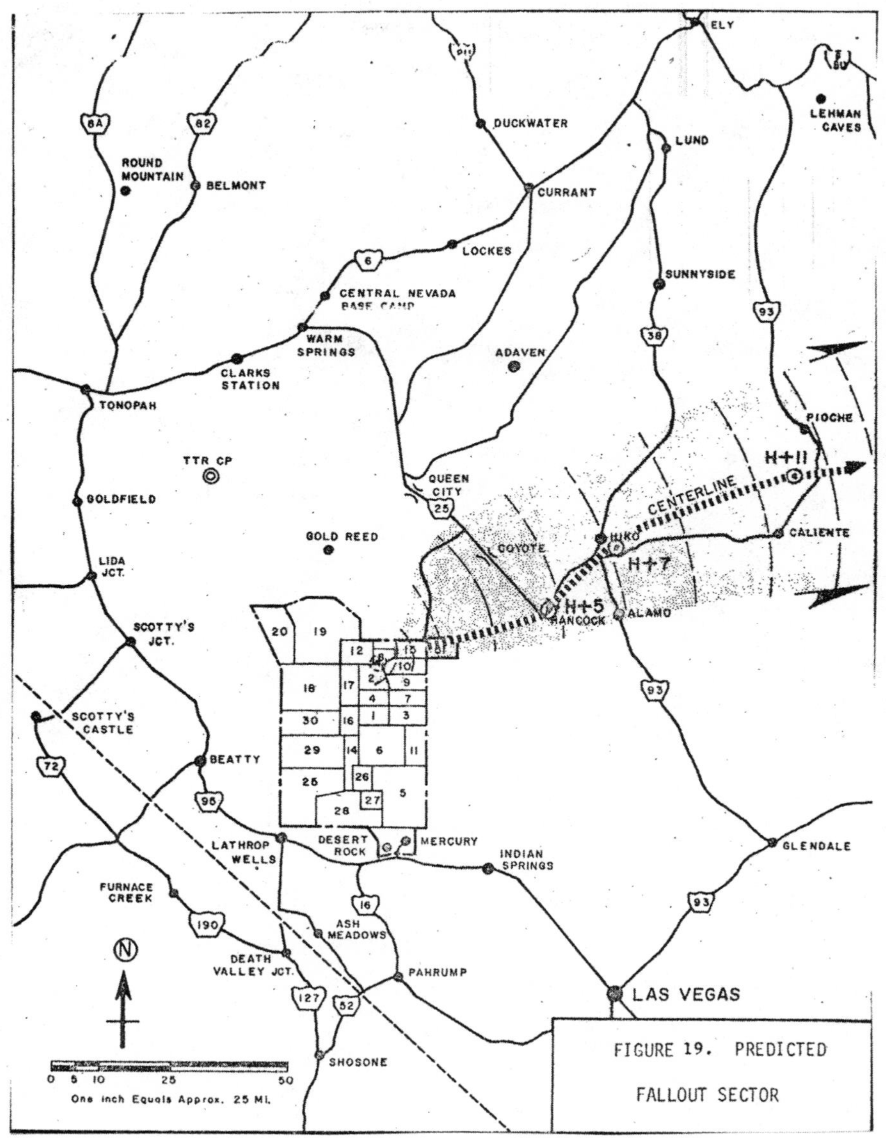

Trail exhibit 62. Map of entire Nevada Testing Site, the location of the Baneberry site, and the predicted path of fallout. Courtesy of the author.

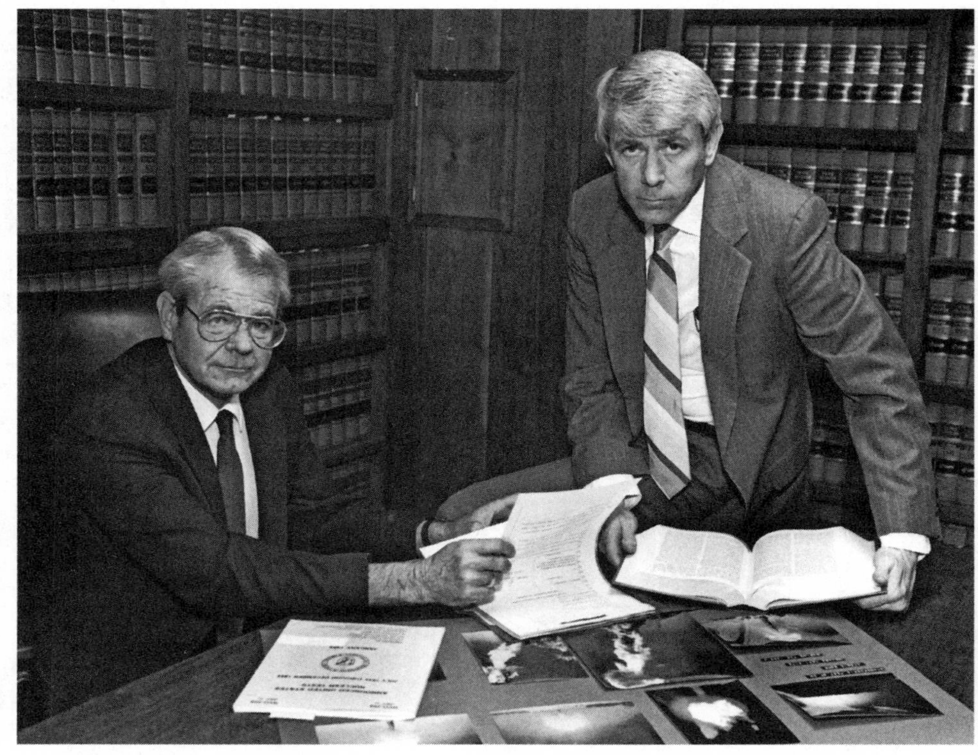

New York Times photo of Alan and Larry Johns, December 12, 1989, after we had been involved in the Baneberry case for nearly nineteen years. Courtesy of the author.

Harley Roberts. Government counsel objected to the introduction of this photo, which Dorothy brought to court. Courtesy of the author.

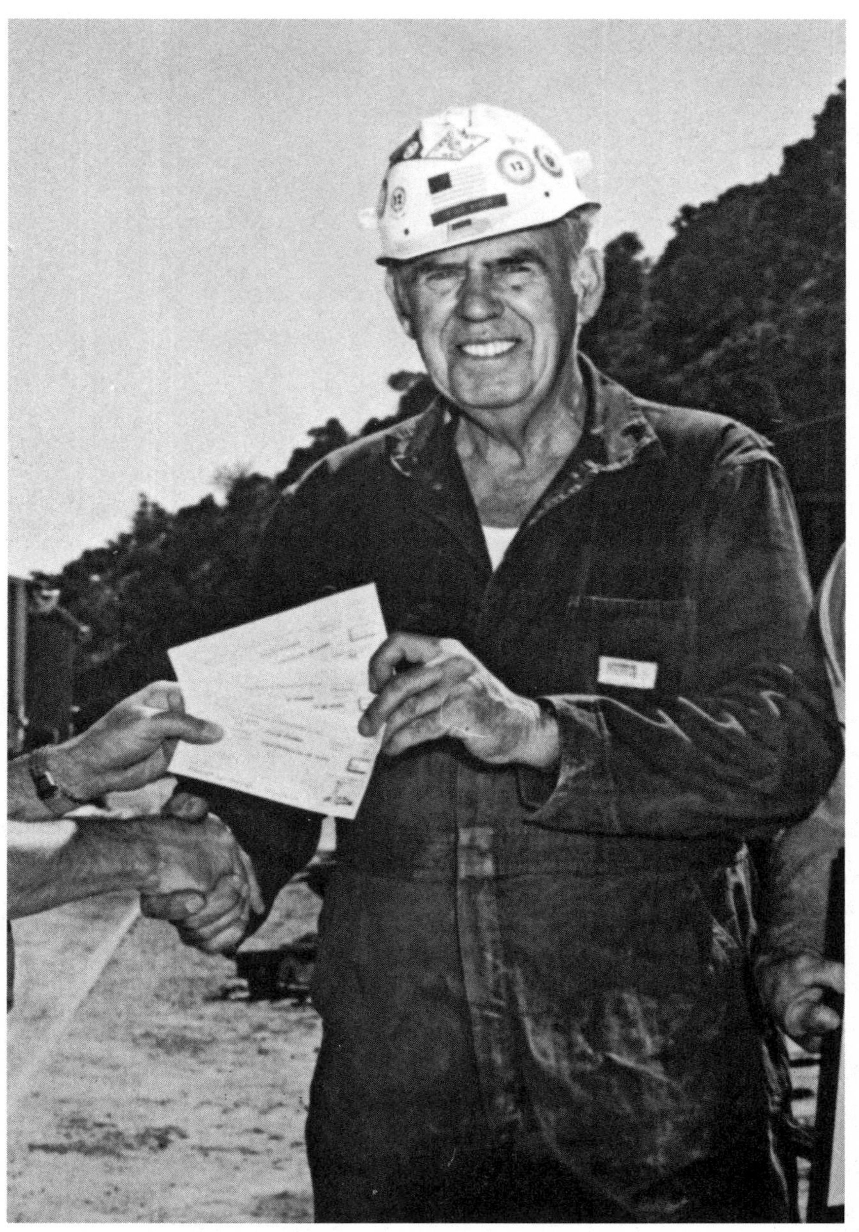

William Nunamaker. Courtesy of the author.

[16]

Was It Really an Accident?

On January 15, 1979, we made our final preparations, gathered our exhibits, and spent the day reviewing for the trial set to begin the next morning. That night, a rare snowfall covered the Las Vegas Valley, reminiscent of the snowfall that had blanketed the Test Site the night before the Baneberry test nine years earlier.

At 9:15 AM on January 16, Dorothy, Louise, Alan, and I were driven from our office four blocks up the street to the back entrance of the federal courthouse. We took the elevator up to the third floor and entered the large courtroom of federal Judge Roger D. Foley. The Judge was from an established and influential Democratic family. He followed his father Roger T. Foley, who was appointed to the federal bench in Nevada and was on senior status when President Kennedy nominated Foley's son for the position in 1962. Roger D. Foley was elected district attorney for Clark County in the early 1950s and then was Nevada attorney general for three years prior to his appointment to the federal bench.

As Judge Foley ascended the bench, his slight build and frail appearance made him appear much older than his sixty-two years. After announcing the case, he asked if the plaintiffs were ready to proceed. Alan stood up and formally introduced Dorothy Roberts and Louise Nunamaker to the judge. He then stepped to the podium to give the opening statement.

"We are going to prove that the defendant, the United States Government, through agents or instrumentalities that are directly responsible to it or in many instances owe their entire existence to the federal government, was guilty of not one, two, three, or four, but in fact in this particular case, at least twenty separate acts of negligence, individually or together—interrelated—that contributed to the exposure and ultimate deaths of these individuals."

The judge seemed shocked as he interjected, "Twenty acts of negligence by the United States?"[1]

Alan appeared unfazed by the court's seeming incredulity that the United States could commit so many negligent acts in one case and went on to chronicle the twenty links in the chain of negligence. He started with decisions regarding placement of the device in a clay formation the AEC knew was water saturated and would cause the device to behave as if it were much more powerful, buried closer to the surface, and likely to vent. The AEC knew, or should have known, that there were fault lines adjacent to the detonation point. This weakness in the substrata contributed to the venting of the explosion.

Alan pointed out that since the government had steadfastly refused to disclose the purpose of the test, it might have planned for a vent. The judge was surprised by this remark and admitted he had not considered that possibility. Alan followed up the judge's comment, acknowledging that unless all the still-classified material was produced, we could not prove that it was deliberately vented. But it was not necessary to show deliberate conduct for us to prevail. All we needed to show was negligent conduct on the part of the government.

This led to a discussion of the curious name for the test. Alan pointed out that the root word of Baneberry is *bane,* which is universally defined as a cause of death or ruin, or a deadly poison. Whether by accident or design, Baneberry would be forever associated with the release of a poisonous cloud of radiation and linked to the deaths of Harley Roberts and William Nunamaker.

Alan then outlined another series of negligent acts that occurred during the drilling of the Baneberry emplacement hole. The drill hole caved in frequently, because workers were drilling through a montmorillonite clay deposit. They tried to rectify this weakness by pumping enormous amounts of cement into the hole to stabilize it and then redrill through the concrete. There were further problems. Over a hundred thousand gallons of water were used to drill the hole, which added more water to the already saturated montmorillonite clay medium. The drilling problems, caving, cementing, and redrilling to create a stable hole, were well known to everyone at the site. Workers referred to Baneberry as a "bad hole." All the drilling complications caused several delays beyond the initial test date. Ultimately, to avoid further postponement, the AEC decided to shave seventy feet off the planned depth of the shaft and scheduled the test for Friday, December 18, 1970, the last test of the year.

The judge interrupted and asked Alan whether it was his position that the government should have abandoned the hole and started drilling somewhere else. Alan stated emphatically that it was our position that the hole should never have been drilled in a water-saturated clay medium near a fault in the first place. But given all the drilling problems, he ended, "Yes, your honor, prudence dictated that they should have abandoned the hole and started over."

Judge Foley was curious that the shot was detonated at a shallower depth than originally planned. He asked if it was our position that detonating at a shallower depth caused the test to vent. Alan acknowledged that we could not prove that this factor by itself caused the vent. But it was certainly another example of conduct that might have been a link in the chain of negligent acts.

After outlining the negligence related to drilling the Baneberry shaft, Alan shifted to a discussion of wind conditions on the morning of December 18, 1970. He explained that the test manager and his panel knew or should have known that wind direction and speed were critical factors in determining whether to proceed. The test manager was negligent in proceeding with the test that morning, with the wind direction at around 7:30 AM shifting and unpredictable. The judge understood the importance of planning tests when wind direction is steady, stating that he himself had witnessed an aboveground test at News Nob in the early 1950s and was aware that such tests were usually detonated when it was known that winds would carry the mushroom cloud easterly into Utah, rather than south into Las Vegas.

The judge asked Alan how many tests had vented since underground testing had begun. Alan stated we knew of around twenty-seven. I could not help noticing that this disclosure caused a stir at the government lawyers' table and among AEC representatives seated in the first few rows behind them. Some raced out of the courtroom to the public phones in the hall to confirm or dispute this number. But when they returned to the courtroom, none stepped up to question the number. Alan ignored the disturbance, pointing out that such a large number of vents should have caused the AEC to take the possibility of a Baneberry vent seriously and to plan accordingly.

Alan pursued the point, explaining that the government should have known that if the test vented, it imperiled the Area 12 base camp, which was only a little over three miles from the detonation point. The government, he continued, was clearly negligent in failing to evacuate the 900 workers in Area 12 prior to the shot as they had done previously for shots that were farther away from Area 12 than Baneberry. The AEC was also negligent in failing to abide by its own rules that required a written evacuation plan for Area 12 in an emergency exactly as in Baneberry. In fact, there was no plan at the time of Baneberry.

After Baneberry vented, the AEC was negligent in failing to order the immediate evacuation of Area 12. Instead, the test manager waited over thirty minutes to give the order. As Alan explained, the delay was inexcusable, because eyewitnesses from all over the Test Site reported to the control center that the cloud was moving toward Area 12 Camp within ten to fifteen minutes after it vented.

When the order to evacuate finally came, Alan told the court, it was implemented in a manner fraught with a series of negligent acts. Rad-Safe monitors, trained and properly equipped to enter the radiation zone, should have been ordered to conduct the evacuation. Harley Roberts and the other guards had neither the training nor the equipment to manage an evacuation safely and should not have been ordered to conduct it. They had no training in radiation safety and were provided no protective equipment or respirators to minimize exposure to the radioactive cloud.

Alan emphasized numerous negligent acts that were specific to Harley Roberts, which substantially increased the extent of his radiation exposure. After Roberts completed his duties in evacuating workers from Area 12 Camp, a Rad-Safe monitor took his readings, called them in to headquarters, and told them Roberts needed to be sent in for decontamination immediately. Instead of ensuring Roberts was decontaminated, he was sent to a remote outpost at Dead Horse Flats and left there all day, accumulating additional radiation from his contaminated clothing and vehicle.

Negligent acts regarding William Nunamaker included the decision to allow him and the entire day crew to be sent up to T Tunnel for the 8:00 AM shift change, after Baneberry vented and when it was obviously heading straight toward Area 12. Had the order to evacuate Area 12 been given as soon as Baneberry vented, Nunamaker would have been out of the Area 12 Camp before the radioactive cloud arrived.

In summing up the long list of such acts, Alan stated that negligence or incompetence on the part of the government existed before, during, and after the Baneberry event. In fact, he noted, it was hard to find anything that was done right. Baneberry was a classic example of Murphy's Law, or the law of interminable bungling.

Further negligent conduct included the failure of the government to accurately measure and determine the precise amount of radiation Roberts and all others received at Baneberry. This violation of duty made it more difficult for medical experts to assess the cause of both Roberts's and Nunamaker's leukemias.

Alan pointed out that neither Roberts nor Nunamaker should have been exposed to any radiation at Baneberry. "Radiation isn't just a harmless necessity," he explained. When inhaled or absorbed into the body, it can alter cells. In this case, it altered the bone marrow stem cells, which are the most susceptible cells to radiation damage in the body. These altered bone marrow cells went on to cause acute myeloid leukemia and the deaths of both Roberts and Nunamaker.

When Alan restated that *any* amount of radiation can be harmful, which is why radiation exposure should be kept as low as possible, the judge asked if it was his position that there is no such thing as a safe level. The judge brought up this point, noting that he had skin cancer some years ago and was treated with radiation therapy following surgery, a practice he said he did not think was current.

Alan answered by restating that radiation penetrates and alters cells. In Harley Roberts's case, Dr. Shields Warren, whose career was devoted to the history of radiation medicine and radiation pathology, would explain to the court how radiation at Baneberry caused Roberts's leukemia. Alan then identified Dr. Alice Stewart, the British physician and epidemiologist, as our first witness. She would testify that both leukemias were the result of radiation the two men received at Baneberry. He identified two other experts who would discuss the harmful effects of radiation and add support to our case. Dr. Arthur Tamplin, a biophysicist, would discuss his studies of radiation effects. Dr. Rosalie Bertell, a biostatistician, would discuss her involvement in studying the effects of radiation and that it had been shown to cause leukemia and cancer.

Before sitting down, Alan informed the court that Dorothy Roberts was a diabetic and asked the court's permission for her to be excused at around 11:30 AM each morning to give herself an injection in the restroom.

Bill Elliot, lead counsel for the government, then rose and walked ponderously up to the podium. He wore a dark blue suit that fit tightly around his shoulders and barely buttoned at the front over his large frame. He exuded confidence, almost contempt, as he tried to counter Alan's catalogue of multiple acts of negligence.

Setting the tone for the AEC's ultimate defense of the negligence case against it, he said, "The context in this case is an accident occurring in an experiment with nuclear energy, which was conducted in the national defense." We scribbled the gist of the comment on our note pads, reflecting that it was AEC code for their standard position: the AEC is above reproach; our conduct cannot be questioned.

Elliot then discussed geology, sticking firmly to discredited statements in the May 1971 press release that asserted that the geology of the Baneberry site was unknown and poorly understood when the site was selected. In a brash but not unexpected move, he admonished the judge that he must be careful not to exceed his authority to review the AEC's conduct. "The Court clearly may not, and indeed must not, through an act of hindsight, superimpose the inventions or knowledge of the present on conduct occurring in the past," he said, and demanded that the court "create a time warp which will allow it to go back in time and place itself in a position of knowing nothing which occurred after December 18, 1970. Only in that way," he warned Judge Foley, "can a judgment be made of whether the Defendant acted in a non-negligent manner."

The admonition was prelude to introducing the two men directly responsible for not knowing or understanding what the other was doing. One would contend he did not realize the implications of detonating the device in the Baneberry geological formation, even though they fit his own specific criteria and objectives. The other would claim he did not study or understand the geology of the Baneberry site when he selected it to meet the specifications for the test laid out by his counterpart. It was, we thought, a masterful display of finger pointing by which both sought to escape responsibility.

The first government expert to be called was Phillip Coyle, Test Director for Baneberry. Defense counsel assured the court that Mr. Coyle would explain the scientific criteria for the test, or "experiment," as he called it. The Test Director was looking for a site that would produce a seismic velocity, which we understood to mean that the device would transmit sound waves through the subsurface strata at the requisite speed.

The second man, Richard McArthur, was the geologist who searched the Test Site and located the Baneberry site. It was his job to select a geological formation that would guarantee the seismic velocity criteria required by Test Director Coyle.

Judge Foley clearly understood this important issue. He bluntly asked Bill Elliott whether the water content in the clay medium and the presence of the fault were known prior to the detonation. This prompted Elliott to try to redefine "known" to mean "fully understood." But this ruse was unsatisfactory. When pressed further about the Baneberry fault, Elliott had to admit that a fault was "inferred" to be present but claimed that it was inferred to be farther away from the detonation point than it actually was.

Elliott conceded what Alan had stated in his opening: the venting was caused by the combination of these two geological conditions. But he also felt compelled to comment on Alan's statement that there had been twenty-seven vents prior to Baneberry. He conceded he could not dispute it but tried to downplay the number by describing the different types of vents and the various devices used to monitor radiation releases.

He then concluded his opening statement with a general discussion of radiation, asserting that neither of these two leukemias was caused by radiation from Baneberry and identified some of the medical experts who would testify for the defendant. Anticipating Dr. Warren's testimony about the C-7 deletion and its significance in the Roberts case, he perfunctorily stated that the defendant would call Dr. Janet Rowley, a cytogeneticist, who would testify that radiation from Baneberry did not cause Roberts' C-7 chromosome deletion or his leukemia.

When Bill Elliott finished, the judge asked us to call our first witness. Dr. Alice Stewart took the stand and the oath. She stated her current position was Senior Research Fellow in the Department of Social Medicine and subdepartment of Cancer Epidemiology at Birmingham University in England. She explained that she came to Birmingham four years earlier from Oxford, where she had served many years as head of the Department of Social Medicine.

After outlining her education, training, and expertise, she offered her opinion that both Harley Roberts and William Nunamaker died from acute myeloid leukemia and that the most likely cause was their exposure to radiation at Baneberry. Then she began to explain the bases for her opinion.

First, the bone marrow is the most radiosensitive tissue in the human body and myeloid leukemia is a cancer of the bone marrow. This is generally known and has been conclusively established in numerous studies, including the atomic bomb survivor studies and her Oxford survey of childhood leukemia.

Second, persons fifty years of age and older are more sensitive to damage from radiation than younger people. This susceptibility is part of the aging process. Both Harley Roberts and William Nunamaker were over fifty at the time of Baneberry. Roberts turned fifty in 1970 and Nunamaker was fifty-seven.

Third, both men had chromosome abnormalities, and everybody who had studied radiation effects agreed that the immediate effect of radiation exposure is chromosome damage. Roberts's chromosome abnormality, a deletion of C-7, was detected about eighteen months after Baneberry. Nunamaker's chromosome abnormality, chromosome breakage, was detected when he was hospitalized in September 1974.

Fourth, the latency period, the length of time from their exposure to radiation on December 18, 1970, to the diagnosis of their acute myeloid leukemias, was quite compatible with the latency period in numerous studies. Those studies included the Japanese atomic bomb survivors and Dr. Stewart's study of children who were exposed to x-rays in the womb. Following their common exposure to radiation on December 18, 1970, Roberts's latency period was three years and three months and Nunamaker's three years and nine months.

Finally, all parties agreed that both men were exposed to radiation at Baneberry, although there was debate about the full extent of their specific radiation doses. Dr. Stewart noted that her fetal studies confirmed that a single x-ray was sufficient to alter the highly sensitive bone marrow cells and thus the doses Roberts and Nunamaker received were sufficient to initiate the leukemic process.

After she had finished outlining all the clinical bases for her opinion, she discussed epidemiology. She explained that epidemiology is the branch of medicine that studies an increased incidence of a disease—an epidemic—over the number of cases that would have been expected. Epidemiological studies have produced the evidence that now forms a basis for analyzing the causes of disease in general. The epidemiological studies of persons exposed to radiation, such as the A-bomb survivors, established that radiation caused an excess of leukemia and cancer, although there was dispute about the level of radiation required to produce that excess. The A-bomb survivor studies, her Oxford Survey, and others confirmed that leukemia is the first cancer that will show up in a group of persons exposed to radiation.

Dr. Stewart performed an epidemiological study of the eighty-six men at Baneberry who were exposed to radiation doses considered to be high enough to require decontamination procedures. Relying upon the information provided by the government, she had traced fifty-nine of the eighty-six workers.

Based upon her qualifications as one of the leading epidemiologists in the world, she presented statistical evidence that the odds of two persons in that group dying of leukemia during the eight-year period from 1971 through 1978 was three in 100,000. Statistically, there should have been only .023 leukemias in that group over that period. The statistics showed that these two leukemias could not have been a chance occurrence. The most probable explanation for this epidemic, or increased incidence of leukemia, was the radiation from Baneberry.

When Dr. Stewart ended her direct testimony late that afternoon, we had presented clinical and statistical evidence that Roberts's and Nunamaker's leukemias were caused by their exposure to radiation from the Baneberry vent cloud.

The court recessed until the next morning. Dorothy and Louise sat through Dr. Stewart's testimony and followed her explanations closely. After court, we all returned to the office. Dorothy and Louise both knew they were at the beginning of a long ordeal. But Dr. Stewart's compassion and concern was evident, and meeting and thanking her for her help and support boosted their spirits more than anything Alan or I could possibly have done.

NOTES

1. *Baneberry Collection*, TR.

[17]

Murphy's Law

THE SECOND DAY of trial began with government counsel's cross-examination of Dr. Stewart. With the tenacity of an English bulldog, she stuck to her clinical opinion that both leukemias were the result of Baneberry. In her view, there was simply no other explanation for the occurrence of these two unique leukemias, a type known for decades to be radiation caused. But she did concede, reluctantly, that if one of the two leukemias did occur purely by chance, she would be forced to acknowledge that Mr. Nunamaker's leukemia would likely be the chance occurrence, since he received a smaller dose of radiation than Roberts. While it arguably hurt the Nunamaker case, it seemed to strengthen the likelihood that Roberts's leukemia was caused by Baneberry.

When Dr. Stewart was excused, we called Frank Cluff, the test manager for Baneberry. In the opening statement, Alan had confidently criticized many of Cluff's acts. My job was to ask questions that would show the decisions he made the night before the test and on the day of Baneberry were not prudent, thus needlessly exposing both of our clients to radiation.

I began my questioning by asking about his education and background. He had a master's degree in meteorology from the University of Utah and after college worked for what was then called the U.S. Weather Bureau. Because of his work, he knew meteorologists involved with the Nevada tests who were responsible for mapping the fallout patterns from the aboveground bomb tests. In 1957, he went to work for the AEC and joined a group that predicted the fallout trajectories. He explained that the objective throughout the 1950s was to ensure that the radioactive fallout passed easterly into southern Utah and away from populated areas such as Las Vegas or California.

Mr. Cluff retired a few years after Baneberry and had not reviewed any of the documents or exhibits in preparation for his trial testimony. Since he had no background in geology or physics and thus the complex scientific issues underlying to the site selection and reasons for the vent, I did not waste time asking him about them.

As test manager, Cluff was responsible for the safe conduct of the Baneberry test and specifically to assure the safety of the Test Site workforce and the off-site civilian population as well. To show that the decisions he made after Baneberry vented were unsupported, I showed Mr. Cluff the Test Manager's Operation Plan for Baneberry, which he admitted was the blueprint for the test.[1] It included detailed plans for the preshot evacuation or "sweeping" all personnel who were within the designated test area. At meetings the day before and early on the morning of the test, there had been discussions regarding which areas should be swept. Mr. Cluff acknowledged that the ultimate decision was his.

I asked Cluff if he thought it was prudent to leave Area 12 open when there were nearly a thousand workers just a little over three miles from the Baneberry test. As the basis for his decision to leave the workers near the test, he relied on preshot readings from weather stations around the Test Site taken over a twelve-hour period ending around 5:15 AM the morning of the test. Those readings predicted decreasing surface wind speeds that would be very light or nearly calm by around 7:30. I asked him whether readings hours before were reliable in predicting surface wind direction at the time of the test. I was surprised when he admitted that they were not and that the last forecast a few minutes prior to the test predicted a wind change at shot time that would carry any fallout southwest of surface ground zero. This shift in the surface wind trajectory would move the radioactive cloud into the basin just south of Area 12 Camp instead of northwest, away from the camp, as the earlier predictions had indicated.

When I asked about surface wind readings after the venting, his testimony was even more surprising. By 7:38 AM, just five minutes after the venting, the weather station nearest ground zero reported southwesterly surface winds, exactly as the last reading prior to the shot predicted. Two minutes after that reading, a large section of the cloud collapsed to the desert floor south of Area 12 Camp and began swirling around. By 7:47 AM, surface wind readings were blowing due west toward Area 12 Camp. Readings from this same station at 7:52, 7:57, and 8:01 AM confirmed that the surface winds were now blowing directly toward Area 12 Camp.

When I finished my questioning about the wind direction, everyone in the courtroom knew that Mr. Cluff had ignored the surface wind predictions just prior to the test and inexplicably refused to accept postshot readings confirming those predictions. Given those readings, there was simply no reason for Mr. Cluff to wait until 8:05 AM to order the evacuation of Area 12. Or was there?

We presented evidence explaining the dilemma he faced after the shot vented: his own written Test Manager's Plan, AEC Policies and Procedures,[2] and a written requirement that there be an Emergency Evacuation Plan for Area 12 Camp and a designated Area 12 Camp coordinator to carry it out.[3] When confronted with these documents that governed the emergency presented by the Baneberry vent, Mr. Cluff appeared flummoxed. All he could do was accept responsibility for the failure to implement any of the required procedures. For example, when I asked him to identify the designated Area 12 Camp coordinator on the day of Baneberry, he shrugged, responding that he assumed there was such a person but had no idea who that person was. When asked to identify the organization charged with responsibility for the evacuation, all he could say was that he "was not sure of the organization that would aid [in the evacuation] but I keep thinking it was part of the Teamsters."

Cluff's ignorance of the emergency evacuation policies was even more surprising because Area 12 Camp was the largest forward area facility on the Test Site. And judging by the feeble way he ended his responses, he must have known that he had failed to carry out his duties as Test Manager. The most he could offer was a vague recollection of an evacuation plan.

As I reached the end of my examination, I sensed by Mr. Cluff's frustration that he thought he could excuse his lapse of memory by relying upon the passage of time, his retirement since the event, and his age. But there was also, I suspected, some resentment on his part that he had been made the scapegoat for the entire Baneberry test, designated to take full responsibility for the venting and the lawsuit that arose out of it.

Government counsel tried to rehabilitate Mr. Cluff. They stressed his credentials as a meteorologist and discussed the years he worked in the field. From our perspective, they failed. Virtually every decision he made before and after the venting was either wrong or too late to avoid the exposure of eighty-six persons to radiation from the vent cloud. And he failed spectacularly in the field where he had the most expertise—wind conditions at the Nevada Test Site.

When Cluff stepped down, we called witnesses to show that we had established, out of his mouth, the elements of negligence. They were called to highlight Cluff's negligence and discredit his statements. Among them was Chan Griffin, the top AEC security officer at Mr. Cluff's side on the day of Baneberry. He testified unhesitatingly that there was no evacuation plan for Area 12 Camp on the morning of the Baneberry Test.

The Test Manager's Plan for Baneberry required REECo to have teams of monitors standing by at thirty minutes before shot time to conduct an emergency evacuation. But there were no teams of monitors. Tom Hayes was the only REECo Rad-Safe monitor anywhere near Area 12 Camp. He stood near his truck, a quarter mile east of the entrance to Area 12 Camp and three miles from the Baneberry site, at the same location as security guards Yager and Holly.

Hayes recounted his activities after the vent. He called the control point at 8:00 AM, as the grayish-tan radioactive cloud caused his Geiger counter to jump to 50 mR and then watched it engulf the Area 12 Camp. Other than Rad-Safe monitor Perry, who, at Hayes's request, came by his station at 9:00 AM to double-check Hayes's readings, no other Rad-Safe monitor was in the radiation cloud that morning.[4] And none of the Rad-Safe monitors assisted in the evacuation of Area 12 Camp. When Hayes was asked who had responsibility for conducting the emergency evacuation of Area 12 Camp on the morning of Baneberry, he said he "didn't know and wouldn't hazard a guess."

To leave no doubt that Cluff and his panel were negligent in failing to order an immediate evacuation of Area 12 Camp, we called Holly and Yager, who saw the swirling surface cloud coming up the hill toward them and called to ask permission to move their station. Bob Yager explained why he knew they would be engulfed by the cloud: as the sun began to warm the desert test basin, the surface winds were going to head uphill "like the dickens."

We called Rad-Safe monitor Troy Ellis, who had led a caravan of thirty-five to forty-five cars and three buses into Area 12 that morning. At 7:45 AM, he called to warn that the cloud was approaching the camp and tried to block ingress. But he was ignored, and hundreds of workers flooded into the camp, only to be ordered out later.

To show that REECo, not the security force, was required to evacuate persons in a radiation zone, we called Jack Cupples. He had worked security for the AEC beginning in 1948 at Los Alamos, New Mexico, and came to work as a security guard for Wackenhut Services at the Nevada Test Site in 1965. In all that time, he had never received any training in radiation or radiation safety. He was astounded to learn that Area 12 Camp would be left open for the Baneberry test, because it had been evacuated for four previous tests that week, each farther from the camp than Baneberry. He told the judge he was positive Baneberry was the closest shot there had ever been to human beings or any personnel at all.

When asked if he had ever been ordered into a radiation zone before, Cupples was adamant that in all the years he had worked security for the AEC he had never been asked to enter a contaminated area. That was not part of their job.

Over the next few days, we called other witnesses who had warned their supervisors at the control point that Area 12 was in danger. By the end of the first week of the trial, we had established that the test manager had failed to contain Baneberry, failed to evacuate Area 12 Camp prior to the test, and failed to order the evacuation immediately after the venting, leaving 900 workers in Area 12 trapped by the vent cloud. We had established that fourteen untrained and unequipped Wackenhut security guards were ordered to enter Area 12 to get the workers out. It was time to call Sergeant Ernie Dyer, the man in charge of the evacuation and brother-in-law of Harley Roberts.

We knew Ernie was the one witness who could put the entire day of Baneberry in perspective to reinforce the multiple acts of government negligence previous witnesses had already shown. He had lived the Baneberry nightmare from the time he reported to work at 6:00 PM on December 17 until late the following day. He had tried to locate Harley throughout the day of the vent and then helped Harley and Dorothy as Harley slowly died.

Dyer testified that he joined the guard force in 1961 and had a one-week training course. It did not include any instruction in radiation or radiation safety. If radiation was present in any area, their job was to keep people out of harm's way. They were posted outside the radiation zone and allowed only those persons trained in radiation safety and fully equipped with protective gear to enter. There were hundreds of REECo Rad-Safe monitors at the Test Site who were qualified, equipped, and trained to enter radiation zones as part of their duties.

Dyer also related his futile efforts to get Area 12 Camp evacuated before the shot and efforts to post a force of security guards near Area 12 Camp if Baneberry vented.

NOTES

1. *Baneberry Collection*, EX 9.
2. Ibid., EX 5.
3. Ibid., EX 6.
4. Ibid., EX 91. Perry's brief trip to Hayes's station, where he recorded radiation readings of 1,500 mR gamma, resulted in his contamination. See EX 91, list of 86 men decontaminated at CP-2.

[18]

To the Rescue

When Mr. Cluff gave the order to evacuate Area 12 at 8:05 AM, he did not know what radiation levels the Wackenhut security guards would encounter when they reached Area 12 Camp to begin the evacuation. But although he knew the security guards had no protective equipment or respirators, he took no steps to muster Rad-Safe monitors to accompany them into the Area 12 Camp for readings to be taken and reported to him.

Given Cluff's uncertainty about the radiation levels at the camp, Dyer and his men could not know the peril they faced. They figured the Baneberry cloud must be dangerous. Otherwise, he and his men would not have been ordered to circle around the cloud to try to get to the camp ahead of it. But the Baneberry cloud would not be outflanked. It climbed up the hill and waited at the entrance to greet Dyer and his men when they arrived.

Dyer gave a complete picture of the evacuation that had become his responsibility. His testimony highlighted the irony that Dyer, who had spent all night trying to talk sense into the big shots at the control point, turned out to be the man Cluff placed in command of the evacuation. After testifying about his night-shift efforts to get clearance to sweep Area 12, Dyer talked about his vigil as he waited for the countdown and then watched Baneberry blow a hole in the test manager's assumption it would stay underground.

Within a minute after the order to evacuate was relayed from AEC security Chief Chan Griffin to WSI Captain Tackett and then to Dyer, he began mustering the guards to evacuate all personnel in Area 12. He got on the radio and gathered a force of eight whose pickup trucks fell in behind him and climbed up onto the Pahute Mesa Ridge. Traveling at speeds up to seventy miles per hour over icy roads, Dyer thought about his efforts to get Area 12 swept the night before the test. He was still angry, but too tired to complain. Besides, every minute counted now.

As Dyer drew within ten miles west of the camp, evacuees passed him heading west. Dyer would later learn these early evacuees were on the move due to the foresight of the Area 12 cafeteria chef, who closed the cash registers, ordered everyone out, told them to leave the camp, and locked the door.

At 8:25 AM, Dyer reached the blockade where monitor Hayes and security guards Yager and Holly were posted. As he turned left on Logan Road and drove a quarter mile to set up his station near the Area 12 cafeteria, the cloud was blanketing the entire camp. He parked his vehicle and sized up the situation. He ordered the guards to fan out to cover the one-square-mile Area 12 Camp. Harley Roberts was sent to clear the trailers in the easternmost sector, farthest from the Area 12 cafeteria.

Dyer described his confrontation with the firemen at the fire station and the ten-minute delay before the siren was turned on. He testified that Roberts was the last of his guards to report back and recounted his second confrontation at the fire station. Dyer was that last man out of the evacuated camp and when he met Hayes at his post outside the camp, ordered him out and then took his place at the end of several hundred cars heading west.

According to Dyer, it took less than an hour for the guards to evacuate over 900 people from Area 12 Camp and the tunnel complexes in Area 12. Dyer and all the witnesses confirmed that there were no Rad-Safe monitors anywhere in the entire Area 12 Camp.

After Dyer described the evacuation, he discussed his efforts to locate Harley Roberts and made a point of the fact that Captain Tackett, who gave him the order to evacuate, was the focus of his repeated demands that Roberts be located and sent in for decontamination.

Dyer and other guards testified about the cold showers at CP-2. But Dyer was far more concerned about his brother-in-law and the failure of Tackett and the AEC security chief to find him. Nine years after the event, Dyer's anger had not subsided. He refused to accept their excuses and considered their unconcern regarding Roberts the worst blunder of the day. Dyer felt personally responsible for Roberts and wondered whether the failure to locate and decontaminate him contributed to his death.

Harley was not present to testify about his activities that day, but Alan and I read his deposition into the record. I played Harley and Alan played the government lawyer who examined him at the AEC building five years earlier. Reading the words Harley spoke was a poor substitute for the sound of his voice, the expression on his face, and the feelings he expressed on February 20, 1974. We remembered how pale his face had been that day.

In the deposition, Harley described the incident on Stockade Wash Road where the monitor took measurements and told him he was "hot as hell." He remembered arriving at 17 Camp, telling the captain he was contaminated and how the captain came out of the command post and selected him to go up to Dead Horse Flats. He talked about the readings taken by Rad-Safe monitor Virgil at Dead Horse Flats after they set up the blockade and Bill Earnest's measurements taken late in the afternoon. Finally, he described the decontamination procedures and showers he had to take at the CP-2 decon facility and at Mercury Medical later that night and the gloves he was told to wear to bed because his hands were still reading 25 mR.

Bill Nunamaker died over a year before we first met Louise. He could not testify about his activities and never filled out a report as Harley and the guards had done. Only one witness recalled seeing Bill Nunamaker that morning. We called Walter Adkins, the bus driver. He transported Nunamaker and others up to T Tunnel for the 8:00 AM shift change and stood by because it was obvious the radiation cloud was heading up canyon toward the tunnel.

When the evacuation order came, Nunamaker and others jumped back into Adkins's bus and rode down canyon directly into the Baneberry cloud. Adkins described how some of the workers stuffed paper into the cracks around the windows to keep the radioactive dust from seeping in. He said when they arrived in Area 12 Camp the guards were starting the evacuation. He did not see Nunamaker after he got off the bus there. Adkins was covered with radioactive fallout and had to take showers at CP-2 to clean it off.

On the day of Baneberry, Dyer and his men knew little about radiation or the amount they received while in the cloud. But they knew they were exposed to enough radiation to require showers and decontamination at CP-2 and the medical facility at Mercury. And they figured their radiation doses were of concern to the AEC or they would not have been bused to the Public Health facility in Las Vegas for further tests.

They also knew that Harley Roberts had been in the same radioactive cloud, was not decontaminated until later that day, and had died of leukemia. They were strong men and none wanted to appear unduly concerned that they would develop cancer, but they realized they could develop cancer in the future.

[19]

The Fault Is in Ourselves

Armed with the USGS report, *NVO-95*, the opinions of our two geologists, and admissions by government experts, we put on our case to show that the AEC knew or should have known that there was a high probability that Baneberry would vent.

In his opening statement, Alan had planted the seeds of doubt, implying that the AEC may have planned for Baneberry to vent. We knew we could not get the government to admit it, but we intended to show that the AEC's decision to proceed with Baneberry was a reckless display of incompetence, since the scientific evidence pointed to a high probability it would vent.

We intended to prove that the *Baneberry Summary Report* distributed to a trusting populace at a press conference in Las Vegas in May 1971 was filled with statements the AEC knew at the time were false or at best grossly misleading. We called our two geology experts, Drs. Angino and Halepaska, to prove our position.

Dr. Angino was called to establish that the sixteen-page, May 1971, *Baneberry Summary Report* contained statements about the geology of the Baneberry site that were not supported by evidence in the possession of the AEC at the time the report was issued.[1] Referring to the January 1971 USGS report, Dr. Angino pointed out that the geologists who investigated the cause of the Baneberry vent reviewed the geological information available prior to and during the drilling of the 980-foot shaft into which the device was placed.[2] It was clear that the nuclear device was placed in a 98 percent water-saturated montmorillonite clay deposit extending about 200 feet above the shot point. This evidence established that the statement in the *Baneberry Summary Report* that the "primary cause of the vent was an unexpected and abnormally high water content in the medium surrounding the detonation point" was not true.

Based upon the USGS report, Dr. Angino testified that it was known, or should have been known, that there was a fault close to the shot point. The

USGS report included a drawing of the fault, named the Baneberry Fault, to illustrate its location 130 feet from the shot point. Dr. Angino reviewed the same material the USGS relied upon and concluded the fault was there prior to the shot, and its presence would have been known to those who selected the Baneberry site.

Dr. Halepaska was specially trained in groundwater hydrology and had drilled several hundred holes in montmorillonite clay. Having served as chief of the groundwater section of the Kansas Geological Survey at the time it investigated and recommended against the burial of high-level nuclear waste in Kansas, he was uniquely qualified to support the conclusion of both the USGS and Dr. Angino that the Baneberry device was detonated in a water-saturated montmorillonite clay medium. He based his opinion on drill logs during the drilling of the hole. It was his opinion that those who drilled the hole must have known this. Dr. Angino also confirmed that all the geological data showed that a fault was present adjacent to the Baneberry shot point.

The cause of the vent was clear, and it was also clear that on May 14, 1971, the AEC had handed out the *Baneberry Summary Report* and issued a press release containing information they knew was false, then compounded their duplicity by trying to avoid disclosure of *NVO-95* and the USGS report.

Although the twin falsehoods about the geology of the site were exposed, the AEC still hoped it could exonerate itself by claiming no one could have anticipated the increased force, or enhanced coupling, of the ten-kiloton device. To knock out this last defense, we called two scientists.

First, Dr. Robert Brownlee, a member of Frank Cluff's Test Evaluation Panel that reviewed the geologic information before Baneberry and approved the test. Dr. Brownlee also sat on the five-member panel that authored *NVO-95*. In testimony, he answered my question about the effects of detonation in a water-saturated medium.

> A: [DR. ROBERT BROWNLEE] I think it is fair to say that those of us who have been involved with containment for many years have always recognized that a medium which is saturated with water behaves quite differently in a nuclear explosion to a medium which is very porous, where the pores are filled with air.
>
> I first did calculations on the subject of water coupling for nuclear events in 1956, so it is something that…
>
> Q: [LARRY JOHNS] Is there any kind of ratio or formula or whatever—in other words, let me suggest to you that—I have heard it increases the coupling anywhere from two to five times in a [water] saturated medium. Do you agree with those general figures?

> A: Yes, and I think that covers most of the range; actually, I don't know why you stopped with two. It can couple depending upon the circumstances from one, which means no coupling right on up to fifty [times due to the water-saturated medium]. We will be conservative.

Second, Dr. Wendell Weart, Dr. Brownlee's colleague on the *NVO-95* panel but not involved in the Baneberry site selection, confirmed that detonating in a water-saturated medium would substantially enhance the force of the device. In fact, he stated that had he been consulted prior to the shot, he would not have endorsed detonation.

Through the evidence at trial, we had exposed the AEC's deception in publishing its May 1971 *Baneberry Summary Report* and its efforts to cover up that deception by invoking national security. Had a jury of ordinary citizens listened to this evidence, we thought they would have been as shocked and disillusioned as Alan and I to learn the truth about the Baneberry venting. It might have so tarnished the AEC's image in the eyes of jurors that they would be skeptical of the AEC witnesses called to discuss our clients' radiation doses and to offer opinions as to whether those doses caused their leukemias.

The judge must have understood the significance of what we had shown, but we had no way of knowing whether it would raise questions for him regarding the veracity of the government witnesses who would come to testify for the defense.

NOTES

1. *Baneberry Collection*, EX 66.
2. Ibid., EX 37.

[20]

No Harm, No Foul

ONCE WE HAD ESTABLISHED the government's negligence in exposing Roberts and Nunamaker to radiation, we then sought to show how that negligence also caused their leukemias. Dr. Alice Stewart had carefully reviewed the medical records and work histories of each man prior to Baneberry and found nothing other than radiation at Baneberry to account for their leukemias.

Medical records and work histories are cold and impersonal. We wanted to present evidence supporting Dr. Stewart's assessment to show them as strong, healthy, hardworking husbands and fathers before Baneberry.

Our first witness was Harley Roberts himself. He answered questions from government lawyers about previous employment and denied that he had been exposed to pesticides or any other toxic substances prior to Baneberry. Dorothy Roberts listened stoically to Harley's words, and though someone else read them, she heard his voice and understood his thoughts and feelings as only she could. She sat motionless as she heard Harley describe his activities on the day of Baneberry. But when he began to describe their life back in Indiana, his jobs as insurance agent, filling station operator, and route man and their weekend camping and fishing with son Randy, it brought back all the happy memories of life before they came to the Test Site. When he began to describe his failing health and hospitalizations after Baneberry and then told the government lawyer he knew he did not have much time left, Dorothy relived a flood of painful memories of his last agonizing months. She bowed her head and wept quietly.

The negligence phase of the trial was cold, scientific, and impersonal. But the lives of these two men, their suffering, and their deaths were deeply personal. Harley could speak through his deposition, but Bill Nunamaker could not. The only way we could bring them back to life to speak about their lives was through the testimony of their wives, families, coworkers, and friends.

We wanted to show that Harley and Bill, dedicated family men, were needlessly exposed to radiation at Baneberry and had suffered and died as a result. But as we began to present evidence to show the consequences of the government's negligence upon our clients, we would have preferred having a jury decide the case, denied us in this FTCA action.

It became clear the strategy of the government lawyers was to depersonalize and dehumanize Harley and Bill and to make the trial an abstract discussion of radiation and leukemia. Any testimony about the lives and agonizing deaths of Harley Roberts and William Nunamaker was, to the government, an uncomfortable reminder of the human consequence of their blunders.

We knew the AEC had carefully planned to minimize the amount of its radiation exposures and then claim that Baneberry could not have caused harm to anyone. Baneberry would be portrayed as just another day at the Test Site. Yes, the venting and the radiation cloud were the result of an unfortunate miscalculation and, yes, all the decontamination measures gave the appearance that the workers were in danger. But no, the radiation caused no harm. It was a classic "no harm, no foul" defense.

Dorothy Roberts and Louise Nunamaker saw the trial through a different lens. Day after day they listened to testimony about complex scientific issues and activities at the Test Site on the day of Baneberry. For them, the trial was not an exercise in geology, wind direction, radiation exposure, nor was it about someone else's illness. It was about the men who had shared their lives and the loneliness their deaths had brought.

Dorothy Roberts testified next. After introducing her, I showed her an eight-by-ten photograph of her husband and asked her to identify it. Government counsel objected. "It doesn't matter whether an individual is handsome or not handsome or what he looks like. It is simply irrelevant." When the government lawyer cut her off with his objection, Dorothy looked perplexed and hurt, trying to understand why a photograph of her husband, who had lived through Baneberry, testified about it in a deposition read in court and, in her mind, died from Baneberry, was irrelevant to the case and of no consequence to the government.

The court asked the purpose of the photo, and I explained it was simply to identify Harley Roberts. I was surprised the judge had asked the purpose of offering the photo, since a photograph of the deceased is routinely admitted into evidence in a wrongful death case and this trial was all about the death of Harley Roberts. The judge overruled the objection. But the objection by counsel and the judge's question were troubling.

Had the case been tried before a jury, we thought the men and women in the jury box would have wanted to see a photograph of Harley Roberts to put a face to the man whose testimony was read in court. They would have wanted to see the central figure on the day of Baneberry, whose death was the reason they had been called to jury duty. Had government counsel raised the same objection in their presence, we suspected the jurors might have been as shocked as we were, wondering why the government did not want them to see the treasured photo of Harley Roberts, which his widow had brought to court.

Dorothy then gave her description of their life together. She met Harley before the war in 1941. He was inducted into the Army after Pearl Harbor. At boot camp, the top bunk fell and hit him, and it was discovered he had no sense of smell. He was given a medical discharge and went to work at a defense plant in Detroit, where she was also working. They were married on October 21, 1944. Harley was working as a deliveryman for a creamery when she met him in 1941 and returned to that job when they married in late 1944. He owned a filling station for a short time, delivered pop for RC Cola over the years, and had an insurance agency before they moved to Las Vegas in early 1966. She discovered she had diabetes when she miscarried her first child and had been self-administering insulin injections ever since. She and Harley had only one surviving child, a son, James Randall Roberts, born in 1949. She miscarried a little girl several years later.

She spoke with pride about Harley's physical condition before Baneberry. He was healthy and very active. He played basketball on town teams in Bicknell, Indiana. He won many golf trophies. She played golf herself, and she and Harley frequently played together back in Indiana. Harley liked to take his family camping, fishing, and boating. After they moved to Las Vegas, Harley played basketball at the YMCA with their son Randy and golfed with friends nearly every weekend on his days off. The fishing was not as good as in Indiana, but they went out to Lake Mead camping twice a month when the weather allowed.

During the years they lived in Bicknell, Harley never had a doctor. He had minor surgery in the early 1950s at a hospital in nearby Vincennes for a hydrocele, a swelling in his scrotum. A year or so after they moved to Las Vegas, Harley began complaining about his sinuses. He went with Dorothy to see the doctor who was treating her diabetes. The doctor told him all he could do for his sinus problem was wash out his nasal passages with salt water.

Dorothy heard about the Baneberry blowout from a neighbor late in the afternoon. She did not see Harley until the following day. When he came home around noon, all he said was "I guess you heard about the excitement we have had." He did not talk about it, because he did not want to worry her. Dorothy said she never knew he had leukemia. Harley never told her and neither did anyone else. Even though he was in the hospital several times and was at Loma Linda for five weeks before he died, she never believed he was going to die. She was asleep on a sofa outside the cancer ward when her son, Randy, knelt and whispered to her, "Mom, he's gone."

When I asked Dorothy to describe how Harley's illness and death had affected her, the government lawyer objected. "Her physical condition or needs are not relevant. She could be a millionaire or could be very poor. It makes no difference." The judge appeared unconcerned and took the government's side. She was only allowed to testify that she was a brittle diabetic, the type of diabetes that is hard to control.

When I asked Dorothy about her financial condition after Harley's death, the government lawyer objected again. Dorothy's impoverished situation during Harley's long illness and following his death were of no concern to the government. The judge acknowledged that the loss of her husband's earnings was a measure of economic damages but would not allow her to go into the matter. He made it clear that he wanted us to move quickly into the figures for loss of income: tax returns, pay stubs, and employment records.

Dorothy could not provide that information. We had hired an economist to discuss the loss of income. But she could testify about the unpaid hospital bill at Loma Linda for the final six weeks of Harley's life and identified receipts for payment of Harley's funeral and burial costs in Bicknell, Indiana. They totaled around $12,000.00.

I ended by asking her if she felt her claim for $500,000, the amount stated in the federal tort claim, was reasonable. She replied, "Well, really there is no figure that would be reasonable because it wouldn't bring him back, and I have lost so much. No amount of money in the world."

After Dorothy stepped down from the witness stand, we called Dixie Dyer, Harley's younger sister. Her testimony lasted less than fifteen minutes. She was very close to both Harley and Dorothy and described her brother as very active and in excellent health before Baneberry. After Baneberry, he tired easily and needed a Bird Machine to help him breathe. A family member bought the machine because Harley could not afford it. In late 1972 or early 1973, she and Harley went out to Lake Mead to fish. She packed up the fishing gear and had to help him back to the car. It was his last fishing trip.

Dixie loaned Harley her compact car for trips to Loma Linda hospital, because his pickup truck used too much gas. When he could no longer drive himself to Loma Linda, she drove him there on a couple of occasions. After

Harley died, Dorothy was alone and dependent upon neighbors and family to take her everywhere. Dixie took Dorothy to the emergency room on a couple of occasions when she went into a diabetic coma.

As we listened to Harley's widow and sister testify, the reason the Federal Tort Claims Act protects the government from a trial by a jury became even more apparent. Without a jury, the government's legal team could avoid dealing with the human consequences of its negligent conduct. And, reluctantly, Alan and I realized we should have expected the treatment Dorothy and Louise would receive during this trial before a federal judge who seemed as willing as government counsel to avoid dealing with the messy human costs.

After Bill Elliott took over as chief counsel for the government, he jokingly or sarcastically referred to Dorothy and Louise as the Baneberry widows and the press picked up that characterization. In our minds, it was a denigrating label that stripped Dorothy and Louise of their identity as loving wives whose suffering was immense and unknowable to anyone but them.

But through the testimony of Dorothy and Dixie we had at least reinforced Dr. Stewart's opinion that there was simply nothing other than Baneberry to explain Harley's leukemia. We needed our strongest witness to persuade the judge that Baneberry caused the death of Harley Roberts and to personalize the profound effect of his death upon his widow.

[21]

Occam's Razor

Dorothy Roberts knew her case depended almost entirely upon the testimony of Dr. Shields Warren. She had rejected the government's settlement offer, and we agreed to try her case on the strength of Dr. Warren's opinion and to honor Harley's last request.

Dr. Stewart testified as our first witness in order to accommodate her travel plans in the United States. This was not our preference. Ideally, we would have had Dr. Stewart and Dr. Warren testify back-to-back as our two chief causation witnesses. It would have been a fascinating display with two of the world's leading figures in the field of radiation complementing each other's testimony: one male, one female; one a pioneering pathologist in the study of radiation effects; one a hematologist and pioneer in radiation epidemiology. Dr. Warren was eighty and Dr. Stewart seventy-two. Each stood at the pinnacle of outstanding medical careers.

As we worked through the negligence part of the case, we stayed in close contact with Dr. Warren. We wanted him to testify as one of our final witnesses to close our case on a strong note. By late January, he called and told us he had other commitments and had to plan his testimony in Las Vegas accordingly. He could block a couple of days during the week of February 5 to fly to Las Vegas.

By court order, we were required to disclose to government counsel a list of witnesses we intended to call at least forty-eight hours in advance of their testimony. On Friday afternoon, February 3, 1978, we disclosed that Dr. Warren would testify the following Tuesday and made travel arrangements for his arrival Monday afternoon.

On Monday morning at around 7:00 AM, Dr. Warren called the office. He was agitated. He said Robley Evans, the government's radiation dose expert, had called him at his home Sunday evening. Evans said he had been told Warren would be coming to testify on Tuesday. Evans seemed surprised and was calling to confirm that Warren was going to testify and that he had not changed his opinion supporting the Roberts case. Warren was taken aback by the call. It reminded him of the Justice Department lawyer's effort to pressure him into withdrawing his support of the Roberts case and again Dr. Evans's call prior to his deposition in 1975. We could tell he was displeased. He said he told Dr. Evans that he had not changed his opinion in the Roberts case and had indeed arranged to fly to Las Vegas.

This call by Dr. Evans was a chilling reminder of the government's high-handed tactics. But we also realized that the government was worried about Dr. Warren's opinion.

Dr. Warren arrived the day before he was scheduled to testify. We met briefly after court, but there was no need to go over his opinion. He had testified in court many times.

He took the oath at around 9:30 AM on February 7, 1979, and identified his curriculum vitae, which included his education, his life work, all his honorary degrees and awards, and listed over 450 scientific papers authored over fifty-five years of medical practice. We could have spent half a day chronicling his work in the field of radiation effects. We needed to establish his preeminent position as the leading radiation pathologist in the world.

After earning his MD degree from Harvard Medical School in 1923, he served a two-year residency in pathology at Boston City Hospital and then became an instructor in pathology at Harvard. Except for an interruption while on active duty with the Navy during World War II, he taught pathology at Harvard continuously until 1967, when he became professor emeritus. He explained that his office was in the Shields Warren Radiation Laboratory at the New England Deaconess Hospital in Boston. The lab named in his honor was the headquarters and primary research unit for the Department of Radiology for Harvard Medical School.

He held certifications in anatomical, clinical, and forensic pathology, the last a special qualification awarded to pathologists who offer opinions in court cases or worker's compensation hearings about the cause of disease and death, just as he was doing in the Baneberry matter.

Radiation pathology is a subspecialty. His interest in radiation effects began during his residence training in 1923 when he performed autopsies on patients treated with radiation to study the cause of death. At that time, there were only a few pathologists in the world studying radiation effects. A leading medical researcher in this new field, he published his findings and documented virtually all known effects of radiation on all systems of the body in 1940 in the *Archives of Pathology*—before the Manhattan Project began development of the atomic bomb.

With the dropping of the A-bombs in August 1945, radiation effects on humans became a matter of tremendous importance. Dr. Warren, serving as Commander in the Navy Medical Corps, was selected by the Department of the Navy to lead a team of naval doctors to study the effects of radiation on blast survivors. His team waited at Okinawa for the signing of the treaty aboard the USS *Missouri* then flew immediately to Sasebo, the port city where the survivors of Nagasaki were being treated in hospitals, just over a month after the blast.

Dr. Warren and his team of physicians were not allowed to treat the Japanese victims, but they assisted and offered advice to their Japanese colleagues. He kept careful records and set up the standards used to study the short-term and long-term effects of radiation. His study, begun in 1945, was carried on until assigned by the National Academy of Sciences (NAS) to the Atomic Bomb Casualty Commission (ABCC) formed in 1950. Dr. Warren was appointed the first director of Biology and Medicine for the AEC when President Truman formed it in 1947. In his position, as medical director and as a member of the NAS committee involved in setting up the ABCC, he supervised the transfer of the data and information. It was also his responsibility to see that the AEC properly funded the project.

Dr. Warren began his study of the effects of radiation on chromosomes in the early 1930s. The first detailed work with chromosomes began with Theodor Boveri in 1905 and continued into the 1920s. It had been known since 1907, when Dr. Boveri published his first papers, that a cell in the stage of division is especially sensitive to radiation. Dr. Warren's own studies confirmed that radiation produces abnormalities that show up in the daughter cells. In the late 1920s, Dr. Hermann Muller performed his studies of the effects of radiation on fruit fly chromosomes. His work earned him a Nobel Prize.

Dr. Warren's active laboratory studies continued until he took emeritus status 1967. Over many years, he had technicians and graduate students working on chromosome studies. Those studies confirmed that radiation to the bone marrow produces chromosomal abnormalities.

Dr. Warren discussed the honors and awards he had received over his long career. At the top were the two highest honors the Defendant AEC could bestow: the Albert Einstein Medal and the Enrico Fermi Award. He considered these two awards as having the same standing in his scientific field as the Nobel Prize. He was also elected a member of the prestigious National Academy of Sciences, the only witness in the Baneberry trial upon whom that honor had been bestowed.

Dr. Warren understood the various types of radiation produced by nuclear fission and the radiation to which Harley Roberts was exposed at Baneberry.

When he was overseeing the AEC's health division from 1947 until July 1, 1952, some of the world's leading experts advised him in setting standards.

His study of the long-term effects of x-rays and gamma radiation was heightened by his concern for older physicians exposed to radiation while diagnosing or treating their patients before safety measures were introduced. Using all the information he had gathered over the years, Dr. Warren laid down the criteria for the pathologic and diagnostic effects of radiation.

Dr. Warren knew that Harley Roberts's film badge recorded external gamma of slightly more than 1 R or 1,045 mR, a dose he considered more than sufficient to cause chromosome deletion. He was also aware that Harley Roberts was in the radioactive Baneberry cloud for nearly an hour that morning, but was not decontaminated until late evening. Over strong objection from government counsel, Dr. Warren, formerly the highest health and safety official in the AEC, testified that the failure to decontaminate Roberts immediately after he was irradiated in the camp was clearly a "poor practice."

When we asked whether he had formed an opinion as to whether Harley Roberts's exposure to radiation on December 18, 1970, was sufficient to have caused the chromosome abnormality that resulted in his leukemia and subsequent death, he stated that it did cause the leukemia and supported his opinion in a series of well-reasoned segments.

First, he admitted the difficulty of determining a direct cause-and-effect between a radiation dose less than 25 R (25,000 mR), say in the range of 1 or 2 R (1,000–2,000 mR), which he felt might be the case here. Therefore, one must consider many factors.

Primary among these other factors was the certainty that a dose of 1 R (1,000 mR) or somewhat less can cause chromosomal damage. This had been demonstrated over and over. In fact, it was the general assumption of geneticists that some of the chromosome abnormalities in the human gene pool are due to accumulated natural background radiation. Humans accumulate natural background radiation over a lifetime in extremely small doses, primarily gamma rays from interstellar space.

He was emphatic that there was no known threshold dose of radiation below which it *did not* cause chromosome damage. To illustrate the point, he approached the easel and drew a graph depicting a linear hypothesis, which is generally accepted by the vast majority of the scientific community. Accordingly, as the radiation dose decreased, there would be fewer and fewer cancer cases. But until one reaches the zero point, there would be the probability of another case or two in addition to the spontaneously occurring cases.

Dr. Warren stated unequivocally that any amount of ionizing radiation had deleterious effects, which is why radiation standards required that human exposures be kept as low as possible. His testimony underlined why Frank Cluff had noted that his primary duty was to contain the device to avoid exposing personnel to radiation.

Throughout his examination, Dr. Warren stated that Roberts's gamma dose per his film badge was in the range of 1 R and that dose was probably delivered to all the cells of his body in a short period. There is a significant difference between the 1 R gamma bone marrow dose Roberts received at Baneberry over an hour, and a 1 R Gamma dose delivered over a long period from accumulated background radiation.

As he explained, "The whole reason man and other life forms have been able to survive in this environment is that they have the ability to repair a whole range of injuries. And the rate at which the injury occurs, therefore, is a very important thing."

The next area dealt with the dose of radiation to the bone marrow, where the blood-forming stem cells of the body are manufactured. Dr. Warren explained that there are two kinds of marrow: the red marrow is the blood-forming marrow, while the yellow marrow is fat containing, which accounts for its color. The red marrow is located primarily in the flat bones of the ribs, sternum, pelvic girdle, skull, and vertebrae. The long bones in the legs, arms, and hands contain the yellow marrow that has nothing to do with the formation of the blood elements. In this case, gamma rays penetrated all cells of the body, including those in the red bone marrow.

To illustrate the penetrating power of external radiation to reach red bone marrow, Dr. Warren placed his hand on his own ribs and skull and with a wry smile noted that the bone marrow in the flat bones of his ribs, sternum, and skull are covered by a thin layer of skin. Based upon his anatomical illustration, and although Dr. Warren recognized that beta radiation can only penetrate about half a centimeter of human tissue, his demonstration showed that the external radiation, including a small amount of external beta radiation could reach the red bone marrow.

Finally, he maintained that the bone marrow gamma dose recorded on the film badge—1 R or a little less, in his view—did not consider the internal bone marrow dose Roberts received from inhaling radioactive iodine and other radionuclides present in the cloud that would have entered his lungs and then the blood stream. Because there were no readings taken of the radionuclides present in the Baneberry cloud in Area 12 Camp, Dr. Warren would not speculate or quantify the additional bone dose Roberts received. Instead, he accepted the bone marrow dose proffered by Evans and simply stated his opinion: "This is one of those cases involving low-level radiation which everyone assumes will occur so long as the linear theory applies and can be demonstrated by examining all of the clinical evidence."

And that is what Dr. Warren did. He explained that Roberts's leukemia was a two-step process. The external gamma rays probably reached all the cells of his body, but damaged only one of the bone marrow stem cells. In this case, the damage resulted in the loss of a chromosome in the C group, a group of six chromosomes (C-6 through C-11) that contain the genes involved in forming blood cells. The missing C chromosome, detected in July 1972, was not clearly identified as a missing C-7 chromosome until late 1973, after Dr. Caspersson developed his banding technique that made it possible to clearly distinguish each of the twenty-three pairs of chromosomes, including C-6 to C-11.

Roberts's C-7 chromosome deletion occurred instantly or with the speed of an average chemical reaction in the body. It would have been apparent in the first cell division, when one of the daughter cells was missing the C-7 chromosome. Bone marrow stem cells, which are found in the red marrow, are among the most rapidly dividing cells in the body, because they are required to produce all blood cells. By July 1972, eighteen months after Baneberry, the abnormal bone marrow cell with its missing C-7 chromosome had multiplied and overpowered the normal cells. They were detected in the bone marrow test and clearly seen under the microscope.

The C-7 deletion is a rare chromosome abnormality. When Dr. Warren came to testify, there were only thirteen reported cases in the medical literature. In all thirteen, it was seen in patients who had a blood disease that caused them to seek medical help. And in all cases, there was a clear connection between the C-7 deletion and blood abnormalities.

The second stage of Roberts's disease was the development of acute myeloid leukemia. In every case where the C-7 deletion has been detected, the patient develops acute myeloid leukemia within two years and dies within two or three months after diagnosis. Dr. Warren noted that Roberts followed this trajectory exactly.

Dr. Warren then carefully reviewed Harley Roberts's medical records before Baneberry. In the summer of 1969, a year and half before Baneberry, he had his annual physical examination, required by his employer Wackenhut. He was in good physical condition. His blood study was normal and showed no signs of any disorder.

He was exposed to radiation at Baneberry on December 18, 1970. He went to Loma Linda University in July 1972, complaining of chest congestion and fatigue. Blood tests revealed an abnormality, which caused Dr. Kuhn, his hematologist, to study his bone marrow. The study revealed either the process of recovery from an injury to the bone marrow or the presence of a blood disorder. Dr. Kuhn was extremely alert and did additional studies, discovering that Roberts was missing a chromosome in the C group. Roberts was followed continuously as his condition progressed. He was diagnosed with leukemia at Loma Linda in February 1974, during his final hospitalization, and died there on April 17, 1974.

Dr. Warren concluded that the time from Baneberry in December 1970 to July 1972, when the C-7 deletion was detected, was a reasonable period to permit the bone marrow cells damaged by radiation at Baneberry to grow and become the predominant abnormality.

Dr. Warren discussed the latency period, the time between radiation exposure and diagnosis of leukemia, for a radiation-induced leukemia. He noted that the first case among the Japanese survivors where a probable relationship existed was about fifteen months after the explosion. The survivors were studied extensively: leukemia incidence rose in the first few years and peaked approximately five to seven years after the bombing and had been dropping off ever since. Also, there was a higher proportion of cases of acute myeloid leukemia than any other. Roberts had acute myeloid leukemia.

Dr. Warren also reviewed Harley Roberts's occupational and medical history prior to Baneberry. He indicated there was no evidence that he was exposed to any agent in his prior employment that could have caused the C-7 deletion.

When government counsel cross-examined Dr. Warren, he pointed out that Roberts had operated a filling station for about a year around 1960. Dr. Warren found nothing in that work experience that could have caused a C-7 deletion detected twelve years later.

Government counsel then asked Dr. Warren to identify any scientific studies showing that radiation in the range of 1 R had caused C-7 chromosome deletions. Dr. Warren explained that this was a very recently discovered syndrome. The researchers who reported this rare condition had not carefully studied or reported on the patients' prior exposure to radiation, so it was an open point whether radiation was the cause. Not content with this answer, counsel was determined to press the issue further and got an answer he did not want.

Dr. Warren referred to Dr. Alice Stewart's pioneering study as evidence to support his opinion. He explained that she studied a very large number of cancer cases in children exposed to radiation in the womb and that an increased number of them developed cancer and leukemia. The Court remembered

Dr. Stewart's testimony and wanted to be sure Dr. Warren agreed with her findings. Dr. Warren not only endorsed her findings, he pointed out that while the practice of subjecting pregnant women to x-rays was common in the 1950s, due to Dr. Stewart's work, it was now, fortunately, very rare.

Government counsel knew that Dr. Warren had spoken on several occasions with Dr. Robley Evans who was present in the courtroom while Dr. Warren testified. Counsel asked Dr. Warren whether he agreed with Dr. Evans's calculation that Roberts's bone marrow dose was less than .5 R gamma. Dr. Warren acknowledged that he was aware that Evans had arrived at bone marrow dose less than half the gamma dose reported on Roberts's film badge but would not back down from his opinion that the dose was in the range of 1 R and sufficient to cause the C-7 chromosome deletion. He also pointed out that Dr. Evans was not a medical doctor nor had he studied radiation effects on chromosomes as he had done over his lifetime.

Before Dr. Warren ended his testimony, he made sure the judge understood his opinion that Roberts's overall bone marrow dose was not limited to the external gamma dose of around 1,045 mR on his film badge. He explained again that there was an additional bone marrow dose from inhalation that was not included in Robley Evans's calculations, since Evans only considered the radioactive iodine that concentrated in Robert's thyroid gland. To emphasize the point, Dr. Warren looked directly at the judge and said, "I might say that there will have been other substances than iodines in the cloud, of course. One has, what one might term the ashes in an atomic explosion, a quite wide range of radioactive isotopes." But Dr. Warren knew that no measurements were taken of the cloud to identify the other isotopes and went no further. He stood on his reputation and his opinion that a radiation dose of 1 R or slightly less was sufficient to cause Roberts's C-7 deletion and leukemia.

We did not ask Dr. Warren about the Nunamaker case. But the government lawyers did. During cross-examination, Dr. Warren was asked if he had formed any opinion in the Nunamaker case. We objected to the question, but the judge allowed Dr. Warren to express his opinion. We knew that he could not support Nunamaker's case. He said that he had been unable to arrive at a firm opinion in that case because he found a number of conflicting pieces of evidence.

On one hand, Nunamaker did have several chromosome abnormalities, particularly ring chromosomes found in a large number of his bone marrow stem cells in September 1974. Ring chromosomes are formed when a break occurs in one of the arms of the chromosome, which loops around and attaches to the other, forming a circle or ring. Radiation is the most widely recognized cause of ring chromosomes. This was evidence that the radiation Nunamaker received at Baneberry could have caused the ring chromosomes identified in September 1974.

On the other hand, Nunamaker's external gamma exposure was about one tenth of the 1 R gamma dose he testified was sufficient to cause the C-7 deletion in Roberts's case. Because of these conflicting issues and Dr. Warren's reliance upon the C-7 deletion as the cause of Roberts's leukemia, he was unable to arrive at a firm opinion that Nunamaker's leukemia was caused by his exposure to Baneberry.

Court ended at around 4:45 PM. Dr. Warren, Alan, and I were driven back to the office. Dorothy rode with Louise and arrived a few minutes after us. When Louise came through the back door, she was understandably upset with Dr. Warren and confronted him. Angry and tearful, she could not understand why he had not testified for her, even though she knew he had not been able to support her case. Dr. Warren was as gracious as possible under the circumstances. He told her he was sorry he could not give a firm opinion in her favor.

Dorothy watched with embarrassment. She had wanted to talk to Dr. Warren after court and express her gratitude, but under the circumstances could not. She asked us discretely for Dr. Warren's address so she could send him a letter. We never saw her letter, but Dr. Warren told us it was a very nice letter of appreciation. Dr. Warren left immediately and was driven to the Golden Nugget and later that evening took a cab to the airport to catch a red-eye back to Boston for an early morning board meeting.

After he left, we tried to calm Louise, explaining that her case was supported by Dr. Alice Stewart and her family physician, Dr. Russell Miller, who had also agreed to testify. We also told her that Dr. Arthur Tamplin and Dr. Rosalie Bertell had called the office and were ready to testify the following day. Each would support both cases. This seemed to placate her.

Before Alan and I went home, we called Dr. Tamplin and Dr. Bertell and arranged to meet them early the following morning to coordinate their trial testimony. We expected their testimony would help the judge understand that low-level radiation was harmful, as Drs. Warren and Stewart had already stated, but we knew that in the person of Dr. Shields Warren we had brought into a Nevada courtroom an unparalleled medical doctor and scientist in the field of radiation effects who was feared by the AEC, its team of lawyers, and the experts we knew they would call to challenge him.

It was obvious to us that the judge was impressed by Dr. Warren and the logic he applied to set forth each premise of the syllogism upon which his opinion was based. We could not imagine how any objective person could fail to find in favor of Dorothy Roberts. Dr. Warren's testimony was particularly satisfying to us, knowing that he had withstood a justice department lawyer who tried to disqualify him and had not backed down when Robley Evans subtly tried to dissuade him from testifying. The government's tactics were, in Dr. Warren's view, "dirty pool," but he was a man of impeccable integrity. He would not have allowed us to bring up those matters, and we dared not do so.

[22]

Nickeling and Diming Them to Death

DR. WARREN'S TESTIMONY was the high point of our case. While he was concluding his testimony, our next two experts had flown in and were waiting to testify the next day.

Dr. Arthur Tamplin earned his PhD in biophysics at UC Berkeley and worked at LLL from 1963 until the early 1970s. He was there at the time the LLL scientists planned and fired the Baneberry test. Dr. Tamplin was a charter member and group leader of LLL's biomedical division, working under Dr. John Gofman, the lab's director of Biology and Medicine.

Dr. Tamplin's group was commissioned by the AEC to determine the amount of radiation released into the atmosphere and the types of radiation and doses received by people living downwind from tests at the Nevada Test Site between January 27, 1951, and October 31, 1958, when the test moratorium went into effect. The purpose of the study was to assess the long-term health effects on people exposed to radiation from the tests. It included other studies, classified, suggesting that radioactive iodine from those tests had caused injury to children in southern Utah.

Tamplin's group completed their analysis and concluded that the radiation doses were much higher than earlier crude estimates, particularly to the thyroid glands of the exposed children. Thus, the biological effects on the downwind population were much more serious than the AEC had expected. The findings were not well received, because they challenged the AEC's position that no harm from atmospheric testing had befallen downwind populations.

The AEC withdrew funding for Dr. Tamplin's studies soon after the AEC learned the results. But in 1977, Dr. Tamplin published the results in an article entitled "The Biological Effects of Radiation: Ten Times Worse than Estimated." Referencing his own studies and those of numerous other scientists, Dr. Tamplin showed that radiation doses at levels previously thought to be harmless had, in fact, caused cancers among the downwind population.

Dr. Tamplin educated the judge about the types of radiation produced by an atomic blast and described how they affect the tissues and cells of the human body, including damage to human chromosomes. Dr. Tamplin corroborated Dr. Warren's statement that there was no threshold dose below which radiation had no harmful effects and embraced the linear theory Dr. Warren graphed, which posited that radiation affects human tissue at doses all the way down to zero. To support Louise Nunamaker's case, he stated that the biological data would indicate that a dose as low as .1 R is enough to cause leukemia.

Rosalie Bertell, PhD, followed Dr. Tamplin. Her doctorate in mathematics was earned under a special biometry program established by the National Institutes of Health to train mathematicians in the study of biology and medicine. She continued her training under a postdoctoral grant from Roswell Park Memorial Institute, the world's first cancer research institute.

At Roswell Park, Dr. Bertell was deeply involved in a study of 16 million people in the states of New York, Minnesota, and Maryland. Every confirmed leukemia case in that population base was included in the study, which became known as the Tri-State Survey. Extensive interviews of the leukemia patients and reviews of their medical records were carried out, based upon guidelines established after Dr. Bertell and others met with Dr. Alice Stewart. They consulted Dr. Stewart because her Oxford Survey was recognized as the gold standard for an epidemiological study of this nature.

Over 3,000 leukemia cases were identified in the Tri-State Survey, broken down into five distinct categories, one of which was acute myeloid leukemia, the type from which both Roberts and Nunamaker died. Dr. Bertell testified that the findings of the survey confirmed Dr. Warren's statement that a linear "no threshold" relationship exists between myeloid leukemia and radiation down to the lowest reported amount of exposure. The "increase [was] across the board" and "this was true at the smallest dose they could measure, which was about 5 millirad [5 mR]."

Dr. Bertell, a mathematician and epidemiologist, calculated the probability that acute myeloid leukemias in Roberts and Nunamaker occurred purely by chance. Her independent tabulation agreed with Dr. Alice Stewart's, showing that the odds of two leukemias occurring purely by chance among the group of eighty-six men exposed to radiation at Baneberry were 3 in 10,000.

Neither Dr. Tamplin nor Dr. Bertell was a medical doctor and neither was allowed to offer a medical opinion that the Roberts or Nunamaker leukemias were caused by Baneberry. But they had confirmed Dr. Warren's testimony that there was no safe or threshold dose.

We had promised Louise Nunamaker that Dr. Russell Miller would testify in support of her case. Dr. Miller had practiced medicine in Las Vegas for many years and treated Bill Nunamaker until his death in December 1974. He consulted specialists to diagnose and treat Bill's leukemia and ordered an autopsy to confirm that he died of the disease. Based upon the autopsy, Dr. Miller confirmed that Nunamaker's final diagnosis fell under the general category of acute myeloid leukemia, although referred to as acute myelomonocytic leukemia, Naegeli type.

Dr. Miller testified to a reasonable degree of medical certainty that Bill Nunamaker's leukemia was caused by his radiation exposure at Baneberry. He stuck to his opinion despite efforts by government counsel to diminish his qualifications. "I can only tell you what has been published about the causes of leukemia. It is agreed that radiation causes leukemia," he stated. Dr. Miller also reviewed Nunamaker's work history prior to his employment at the Test Site and stated that he was unaware that Nunamaker was exposed to any agent, other than the radiation at Baneberry that could have caused his disease.

Dr. Miller lacked the standing of Dr. Warren, but Louise Nunamaker was pleased and relieved that he came to court. She beamed throughout his testimony.

After Dr. Miller finished, Louise took the stand. She was much more emotional than Dorothy and broke down frequently as she described her husband and their life together. She identified a picture of Bill in his Test Site work clothes and hardhat. It captured Louise's image of her husband. He was a big, almost bearlike figure, a man in charge, who protected the wife who adored him and worked hard to raise their four children.

We suspected the judge was no more interested in hearing about Louise's and Bill's life together than during Dorothy Roberts's testimony about Harley. But Louise was determined to tell her story and looked over frequently at the judge who responded with restrained courtesy. Bill was in the Navy during World War II, she told him with obvious pride. They met in 1943 and married as soon as the war ended. Bill was qualified to work in various kinds of construction and had worked all over the Pacific Northwest with his family in tow. They came to Las Vegas, where Bill took a job at the Test Site. Very experienced and liked by everyone, he was promoted to foreman and ran a shop in the tunnels.

Louise remembered the Baneberry blowout. She wanted the judge to know that when her husband walked through the door that evening wearing a paper coverall and booties, he told her, "I was right in the middle of it." When we asked about Bill's health before Baneberry, Louise described how strong and healthy the man in the photo was before his radiation exposure.

After Baneberry, Bill went right on working as hard as ever. Then he just fell apart. He went to Dr. Miller in September 1974 and entered the hospital for tests. Louise struggled through multiple crying spells, as she described the last few months of his life. It was "terrible, just terrible." She was in a state of shock when he died and did not think she'd ever recover. They were so happy until he got sick. When asked the basis for her $500,000 damage claim, she responded as Dorothy had. Nothing could ever bring him back.

When the government lawyers cross-examined Louise, they were careful to avoid questions that might evoke the emotions she had expressed about her life with Bill and her loss. Instead, they wanted to emphasize that Bill Nunamaker was an older worker. He was fifty-seven when he was exposed at Baneberry and sixty-one when he died in December 1974. They sought to emphasize that he was near the end of his working years when he passed away. To bring home the point, they asked Louise her age. She squirmed in the witness chair and seemed genuinely offended. She commented that she thought it was improper to ask a lady her age, then coyly looked over at the judge and said that if she was required to answer she would whisper the number to him. The judge acquiesced and she stood and leaned over the bench and told him. The government knew her age and that she was nearly two years older than Bill when they married. Louise was sixty-eight in February 1979 when she testified, but the record does not show it.

After Louise finished, we called family members to testify how close Bill and Louise were and how happy they had been until Bill developed leukemia. Their testimony was brief. We knew the judge wanted us to present the economic information about the income the two widows had lost when their husbands died.

Our final witness was Clarence Ray, an associate professor of economics at the University of Nevada, Las Vegas. He had calculated the economic loss from the men's deaths. It was a simple arithmetic calculation set out on two separate sheets. The calculation for Roberts included several assumptions. First, it assumed that if Roberts, age fifty-four at the time of his death, had worked until 1985 and age sixty-five, he would have earned $260,000. Second, it assumed that if he worked to age seventy, the economic loss was $367,000. Each calculation included interest that would accrue on income over the years.

Dr. Ray calculated Bill Nunamaker's loss using similar assumptions. First, it assumed that if Nunamaker, age sixty-one at the time of his death, had worked until sixty-five, he would have earned $98,000; and if he worked to age seventy, he would have earned $248,000. His figures also included interest that would accrue on income over the years.

The government lawyer began his cross-examination suggesting that the men might have retired before age sixty-five or could have been laid off or disabled and asked if he had considered that possibility. Dr. Ray indicated that he had not and their deaths in 1974 prevented our knowing whether they would have retired early. The government lawyer then challenged Dr. Ray's inclusion of subsistence pay each man had earned in his tabulation of annual income and insisted that Dr. Ray set up another column on the far right of his calculation sheet to reflect amounts counsel insisted should be deducted from Dr. Ray's figures.

In Dorothy Roberts's case, in addition to deducting subsistence pay reported on Harley's pay stubs, the government lawyer pointed out that she had received the proceeds of a $10,000 insurance policy. This should not be included, he insisted, since Harley's employer, Wackenhut, had paid the premiums for the policy and the AEC reimbursed Wackenhut for the premiums under its contract. Dorothy looked stunned.

There were other deductions government counsel insisted Dr. Ray include. But the final insult was when he demanded that Harley's annual income be reduced by 40 percent per year after his death, since he was dead and would not have consumed that amount of his annual income. Dr. Ray objected. He explained that even if he accepted the proposition that some amount should be deducted, the figure could not be more than 20 percent, since the standard expenses of any household include fixed items such as a mortgage, utilities, taxes, and others, and the widow ought to be allowed to remain in the family home.

As the lawyer added more and more deductions, the total income loss was chopped down substantially. After going over Harley's economic loss with Dr. Ray, the government lawyer went through the same procedure with Bill Nunamaker. As he was whittling away, I leaned over and whispered in Alan's ear that I was afraid when all the deductions were made, Dorothy and Louise might end up owing the government money for their husband's deaths.

The nit-picking on the part of the government was not lost on Dorothy Roberts. It affected her much more than Louise, because she had been left with so little when Harley died. She had listened patiently as Dr. Ray was directed to deduct amounts in the separate column. But when 40 percent of Harley's annual income and his subsistence pay were deducted for each year, the tactics seemed to her stingy and coldhearted. She had struggled through the last year of Harley's life, and when he died was forced to sell the house, the car, and virtually everything Harley had worked for his entire life. They had lived very modestly on his Test Site salary, putting away enough for retirement. After Harley's death, she returned to Indiana, intending to stay there.

Now the government lawyer demanded that she live on half of Harley's income and deduct the $10,000 life insurance money she used to bury Harley and buy a small house trailer so she could move back to Las Vegas to be near her son. She had gone from a nice home to a trailer, no car, and scarcely enough money to allow her to eat and pay for the diabetes treatment. Having downgraded her lifestyle well below the poverty level, she was dependent upon the charity of friends and family and even had to get Louise to pick her up each day to bring her to court. She had borne her humiliating circumstances with dignity, carried on the lawsuit for the past five years, and now was stunned that the government begrudged what she thought was fair.

Dorothy could not express her feelings in court as she listened to Dr. Ray and the government lawyer bicker about her. But after court ended that afternoon and we returned to the office, Dorothy, who rarely commented about the testimony and evidence, let loose emotions bottled up for years. She wanted us to know how disgusted she was about the way her government had treated Harley the day of Baneberry and how degraded she felt when the government lawyer sliced away at the numbers, as if Harley were nothing to the AEC and his life had no value.

After venting her emotions for several minutes, she said with contempt that she was surprised they did not demand that Dr. Ray deduct the amount she owed the IRS for the travel pay deduction Harley had taken on their tax returns. The IRS had been thwarted and embarrassed, she said, when they tried to take her trailer to pay the amount owed. But the way the lawyer was going, she kept expecting him to try to pry the money out of her one way or the other.

When Dorothy finished, Louise chimed in. She said she could not help feeling that that the government lawyer's whole purpose in attacking Dr. Ray was to make them look like a couple of greedy widows trying to get rich off the deaths of their husbands. She was hurt by the suggestion, pointing out that she had never talked to Dr. Ray and had not seen the numbers he offered until he came to court. To Dorothy and Louise, the government had spent far more money defending the case than the amounts they felt would be fair for the loss of their husbands.

After Dr. Ray gave the judge the numbers he had been seeking, we rested our case. Government counsel immediately raced to the podium and moved to dismiss our case, arguing that we had not established negligence on the part of the government or that radiation from Baneberry caused their deaths. The judge listened patiently but summarily denied the motion and recessed for the day. The government lawyer seemed surprised, as if he could not believe what he was hearing. Your honor, he protested, and continued arguing even as the judge stepped down from the bench to exit the courtroom. Both Alan and I were a bit amused, but were also struck by the thought that the government's lawyer acted as though he believed, or had been led to believe, the judge would dismiss the case and the government would not have to mount a defense.

When we left the courtroom that afternoon, we were elated that the government would have to participate in the trial. But when we returned to the office and listened to Dorothy and Louise describe how humiliated they felt by the government's attack upon Dr. Ray, we realized all over again that the government's plan was to depersonalize and dehumanize the two men who died and minimize and denigrate the widows' losses. The deaths of their husbands had deeply affected Dorothy and Louise and we thought would have impressed a jury as well. But now we were concerned that the government's strategy might have resonated with our federal judge.

[23]

Give 'Em the Old Razzle-Dazzle

In mid-February, the AEC began its defense. Since we had shown multiple acts of negligence on the part of the government, and Mr. Cluff had all but conceded that he violated his duty to avoid exposing our clients to radiation, we thought the government might abandon its defense of the negligence claim. But it did not give up gracefully. Instead, it tried to rehabilitate Mr. Cluff and even tried to justify its selection of the Baneberry site for the test. Neither, in our view, was successful.

To justify Test Manager Cluff's decision to leave Area 12 open for the Baneberry test and explain his inordinate delay in ordering the evacuation of Area 12, the government called a highly qualified meteorologist. Maps showing the location of all wind instruments operational on the day of Baneberry were spread out before him. He reviewed pages and pages of readings from each instrument at locations all over the Test Site.

Our heads were spinning as he went through the information and we wondered whether the judge could make sense of the data. If the purpose of calling the meteorologist was to show that the Nevada Test Site was one of the most carefully monitored places on earth, the government succeeded. The expert gave an elaborate explanation, meticulously pointing out how each of the stations had to be reviewed serially and at intervals to make projections of wind velocity and direction.

After he had lectured the court for the better part of an hour, it became apparent that his objective was to show that weathermen have one of the most difficult jobs any scientist could possibly have and that the court should feel sorry for Mr. Cluff and excuse his indecisiveness on the morning of Baneberry. But the judge was not taken in. After tedious explanations that never got to the issue, the judge finally called the lawyers up to the bench and commented, almost in a whisper so it would not be on the record or heard by the expert, that he was "sure the witness meant well" but wanted the government to get to the point and move on. Of course the point was that Cluff was befuddled and dawdled, and no amount of explanation by this expert could show anything else.

The government moved on. Lawyers tried to defend against the testimony of our geologist experts, Drs. Angino and Halepaska. Government employees wheeled into the courtroom a large, three-dimensional glass prism that purported to be a replica of the geology of the Baneberry site, depicting subsurface geologic formations, the shot point, and the vent path to the surface.

Although the government offered the display to assist the court in understanding the geology of the Baneberry site, we had never seen this two-by-four-foot wonder. When the court asked whether we objected, Alan and I were speechless. In fact, we were in awe, marveling at how much time and expense must have gone into preparing it. The judge allowed it into evidence with the caveat that it would not be marked or maintained as a trial exhibit but could be used by witnesses if it would help them explain the Baneberry geology.

The government wrapped up the defense of its decision to detonate Baneberry in the geologic medium displayed in the glass prism by calling to the stand Richard McArthur, the LLL geologist who selected the site. In his initial answers to questions from the government lawyer, McArthur was vague, suggesting that he did not truly realize the Baneberry device was placed in a water-saturated montmorillonite clay formation or that there was a fault nearby.

But the judge had heard the testimony of our geologists, Drs. Angino and Halepaska. He cut in and asked McArthur pointedly if he was aware of clay deposits at the site. McArthur tried to evade the question, but when the judge repeated the question, he conceded he was. Similarly, McArthur tried to downplay his awareness of the Baneberry fault and its nearness to the shot point. But that claim was difficult to make, since the government's own display, the impressive prism in the middle of the courtroom, clearly depicted the Baneberry fault and showed that it nearly intersected the shot point.

The AEC spent part of a day showing segments of the films of the Baneberry venting and movement of the cloud. We had seen the films four years earlier under a protective order that precluded us from describing what we saw. Prior to trial, we demanded that the films be shown in their entirety at trial, but the government had exclusive control of the films. They acquiesced partially, showing selected portions during their case, ostensibly to make it appear that the films supported the defense.

Some of the films shown were from cameras around surface ground zero that showed the massive eruption of dust and smoke from the 300-foot fissure. They were interesting, but the films taken by cameras in the helicopter circling

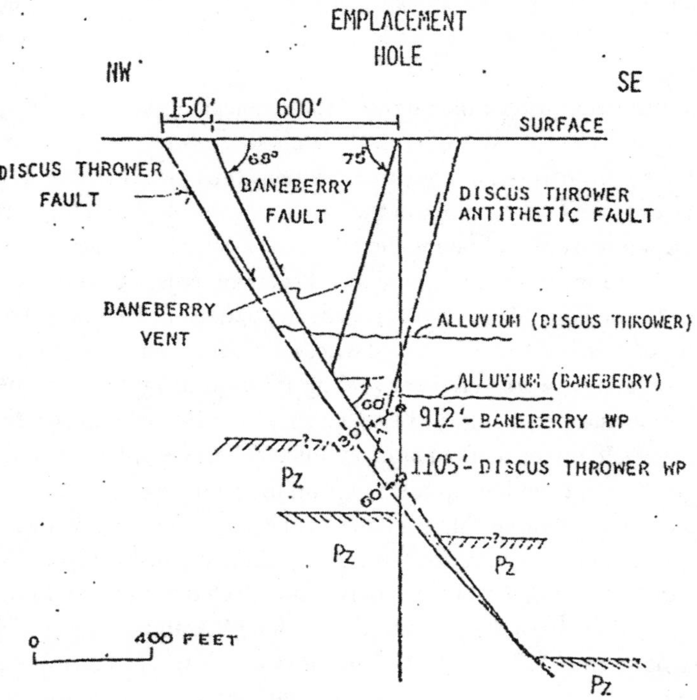

Figure 5.--Geometric comparison between the structure at Discus Thrower and Baneberry. WP, working point Pz, Paleozoic rocks.

Trial exhibit 37. Drawing of the Baneberry fault and vent path. Courtesy of the author.

the Baneberry site that morning were spectacular. They confirmed the testimony and evidence of the eyewitnesses we called in our case and established that the vent cloud covered the Area 12 Camp while Roberts was carrying out the evacuation and Nunamaker was in the camp.

But the expensive and elaborate glass model that explained what happened 912 feet below the surface, and the films of the Baneberry cloud, paled in comparison to what the government spent on the all-day trip to NTS the day after the films were shown. We were not consulted about the trip. The judge, however, perked up and seemed pleased that the government wanted to take him out to the Test Site. We dared not object.

It was an all-day affair with members of the press tagging along. The judge and all the lawyers were flown out to NTS in an Air Force helicopter. As we flew into Test Site air space, the helicopter dropped altitude. We were told we had to fly low to avoid allowing us to peer into the highly classified Air Force facility in Area 51, just over the ridge on the northeast end of the Test Site.

Dorothy and Louise drove up and met us. After landing, we boarded limousines and were taken to CP-1, where the test manager and his panel were stationed on the day of Baneberry. We peeked into the control center, where Cluff and his advisors sat around a table watching the monitors on a wall that relayed the feed from cameras around the shot point.

From CP-1, we went over to the decontamination facility at CP-2, where Roberts and eighty-five others took showers and turned in their film badges and clothes throughout the afternoon and evening of the test. Next, we went to station BJY, the trailer where Dyer spent the long night before the shot and where he and Roberts watched the vent the following morning. We then headed north about nine miles to the rim of the Baneberry crater and from there to the platform overlooking the massive Sedan Crater, one of the main attractions at the Test Site.

Around noon, we arrived at Area 12 cafeteria. Alan and I ate lunch with Dorothy and Louise. From the cafeteria entrance, we had a panoramic view of Yucca Flat and looked down the hill to the house trailers on the east end of the camp, where Harley spent nearly an hour clearing out personnel. After lunch, we were driven up to T Tunnel, where Bill Nunamaker's shop was located. Louise teared up when she saw where Bill worked all those years. We returned to Mercury Medical and were flown back to town.

The elaborate tour might have made some sense if we were in a jury trial. In that case, it could have assisted a panel of jurors from different backgrounds, with no knowledge of the Nevada Test Site, to understand and sort out the activities of Harley Roberts and Bill Nunamaker on the day of Baneberry.

In our case, the judge had been to the Test Site and the maps, drawings, and extensive testimony about the events that day could not have been confusing to him. More important, there was no dispute about the time of the events. To Alan and me, from the helicopter ride to the all-day luxury limousine tour, it seemed an obsequious AEC effort to impress the judge.

Soon after, the AEC took the judge on another trip. We spent an afternoon at the U.S. Public Health building next to the UNLV campus. The purpose was to inspect a whole-body counter. A news reporter captured the event, snapping a photograph of government counsel John Thorndal lying on the whole-body machine while Justice Department lawyer Bill Elliott stood on one side and the judge on the other.[1] The purpose of the trip was meaningless, since neither Harley Roberts nor William Nunamaker were sent to the building for whole-body counts. The measurements taken of others exposed at Baneberry late in the afternoon of December 18, 1970, simply confirmed that radioactive iodine was still present in their bodies over eight hours after Baneberry. Like the Test Site trip, we were not consulted in advance, but it was arranged for the judge, and he appeared flattered by the lavish attention.

These displays preceded calling to the stand Mahlon Gates, Test Manager for the Nevada Operations Office in Las Vegas, the highest-ranking DOE official to testify. He oversaw the NTS and all its Nevada operations. After retiring from the military with the rank of general, he assumed a civilian position with the AEC in Nevada in 1972, two years after the Baneberry event.

As near as we could determine, Gates was called to discuss the chain of command in 1970, from the AEC's Test Site operation in Nevada right up to the president. But this seemed redundant, since we had already introduced an elaborate exhibit that included the chain-of-command information.

During his testimony through government counsel, the judge and the general engaged in a lively discourse about atomic testing at the Test Site, but when it came time for me to cross-examine General Gates about Baneberry and the issues and activities that related to our lawsuit, government counsel objected. The General, counsel acknowledged, knew nothing about Baneberry and had no role in the decisions made by his predecessor or those at the Test Site under his predecessor's command. Why then, we wondered, was he called to testify in the first place, other than to impress upon the judge the importance to the government of his decision in the Baneberry case.

Through these actions, the government had underwritten Mr. Elliott's pledge to "spend as much as it takes to win." The judge was visibly pleased with all the attention he was given, and we had no way of countering the effect it seemed to have on him. All these measures, we thought, were calculated to distract him from the negligent acts related to Baneberry itself and to minimize Baneberry as a small, insignificant mistake in the grand scale of the AEC's thirty-year Nevada Test Site nuclear program.

NOTES

1. *Las Vegas Sun*, February 21, 1979.

[24]

Dr. Evans's Marvelous Cluster Theory

ALL THE GOVERNMENT'S razzle-dazzle was sandwiched between a host of witnesses and evidence on radiation, along with the government's methodology for calculating the bone marrow doses for Roberts and Nunamaker.

Dr. Robley Evans, hired by REECo right after Baneberry vented, had eight years to prepare the government's defense. He also knew what Dr. Warren had said, having sat through his trial testimony. The government had nickeled and dimed and denigrated the widows' claims. Now it employed a similar tactic to reduce Roberts's radiation dose to the lowest possible amount to make it seem inconsequential and harmless, in fact, so harmless there had actually been no need for Roberts or any of the workers to undergo the ice-cold showers and decontamination procedures the afternoon and evening of Baneberry.

The government opened the radiation part of its case by calling REECo Rad-Safe managers to the stand. They began with a rudimentary discussion of the structure of the atom, describing electrons whirling around the nucleus. Uranium, the core element in a uranium bomb, contains a massive nucleus of neutrons and protons and layers and layers of circling electrons. A nuclear explosion splits the uranium atom, producing an enormous number of radioactive substances that have various decay periods, depending on the half-life ascribed to each.

The witnesses then discussed the film badges worn by NTS workers. One brought a Geiger counter of the type used by the Rad-Safe monitors who took radiation readings in the field. Alan and I had learned about radiation and the instruments at the time we began our investigation of Baneberry in 1971. We found the testimony elementary and were perplexed that the government turned the courtroom into a classroom, going over the same basic information that Dr. Warren had already explained to the judge.

We sat through several days listening to REECo personnel. We surmised that it must have been important to the government that these REECo supervisors be allowed to testify, and they appeared proud to play a part in the trial. It was apparent that their sole purpose was to lay the groundwork for Dr. Robley Evans, the government's cleanup hitter, who sat through their testimony, frequently nodding his approval as they made their points.

After the Rad-Safe monitors had testified, Dr. Evans himself ascended the witness chair with as much aplomb as General Gates. His PhD was in physics from the California Institute of Technology with a subspecialty in mathematics. He taught physics at MIT from the 1930s until retiring in the early 1960s. He met Dr. Warren in the 1930s while Warren was teaching at Harvard.

We knew that Dr. Evans was hired in the early 1930s to reconstruct the doses of radiation delivered to the bones of young women who dipped their brushes in radium to illuminate watch dials. In the 1920s, health officials in New Jersey reported that the young women were suffering from bone cancers. The Radium Dial Company was forced to shut down its plant, and settlements were reached with the cancer victims.

Dr. Evans had served as a consultant to REECo since the mid-1960s, and was engaged by REECo immediately after the Baneberry event. He assisted REECo and the government throughout the eight years leading up to the trial, including preparation of Exhibit C-71, which REECo witnesses offered in evidence.[1] The exhibit, a sheet of graph paper with points depicting various radiation readings, included those taken from the darkened film in Roberts's badge, handwritten readings taken down at CP-1 from the Area 12 Camp probe, and readings of Roberts's clothing taken on December 21, 1971, three days after he was immersed in the cloud.[2]

Roberts's darkened film badge read 1,045 mR gamma. But Dr. Evans discredited that reading and revised it down to a maximum external gamma dose of 600 mR. Geiger counter readings of Roberts taken by field monitors were also discredited. Rad-Safe monitor Ellis took a reading on Stockade Wash Road at 9:45 AM. His Geiger counter maxed out on the 200 mR scale. Dr. Evans stated the reading was unreliable and called Ellis's comment that Roberts was "hot as hell" gross hyperbole.

Rad-Safe monitor Virgil's reading of 300 mR gamma at Dead Horse Flats at around 11:00 AM was also unreliable, since the needle on his instrument could only go as high as 200 mR gamma. Rad-Safe monitor Bill Earnest's reading at Dead Horse Flats at around 4:30 PM, when his instrument "pegged" at 200 mR gamma, was wrong, as was his estimate that Roberts's dose was probably around 1R gamma. It was growing dark, Dr. Evans opined, and Earnest must have misread his instrument or had the instrument on the lower scale, which peaked at 20 mR gamma.

Dr. Evans refused to accept any of Rad-Safe monitor Troy Ellis's readings when he took Roberts's measurements at the decontamination facility late that afternoon. Ellis's reading of over 200 mR gamma before Roberts entered the shower and his readings of 150 mR gamma after multiple showers could not be accurate, because Roberts's gamma readings should have decayed to much lower levels in the eight to nine hours after he left Area 12 Camp.

The 50 mR gamma reading of Roberts's hands when he arrived at the Mercury Medical facility, and the 25 mR gamma reading of his hands when he was released from Mercury Medical and issued rubber gloves to wear to bed also had to be discarded. His hands had been scrubbed multiple times; his readings should have dropped to imperceptible levels twelve or thirteen hours after he was in the Baneberry cloud.

If the readings of these monitors were given credence, they would not be consistent with the points on the graph upon which Dr. Evans relied in calculating Roberts's maximum external whole-body dose of 600 mR gamma.

The only Rad-Safe monitor who escaped criticism was Tom Hayes, whom the government recalled to the stand. Stationed on the road a quarter mile from Area 12 camp, Hayes never entered Area 12 Camp or took a single reading of Roberts on the day of Baneberry. In fact, Hayes did not take readings of any of the security force that evacuated the camp. The purpose in recalling him was to allow him to change the recorded readings he had taken at his station on the access road to Area 12 Camp. Hayes had testified that his Pic 6A device reached 800 mR gamma and stayed there during the hour he was at his station. Recalled to the stand, he claimed that his Pic6A reached 800 mR gamma between 8:25 AM and 8:45 AM and dropped significantly thereafter.

When we cross-examined Hayes, we pointed out that he had changed the report he prepared three days after Baneberry, and the testimony he gave at his deposition five years earlier.[3] He also ignored the report prepared by Ron Perry, who stopped by Hayes's station at 9:00 AM. All three clearly indicated that at 9:00 AM Hayes's Pic 6A instrument registered 800 mR gamma and Ron Perry's Cutie Pie instrument registered 1,500 mR gamma. When confronted with his own report, deposition testimony, and Ron Perry's report, Hayes looked puzzled and said he did not remember seeing Ron Perry that morning. But he admitted that a monitor stopped by and took readings at around 9:00 AM.

In our view, Dr. Evans's purpose in discrediting the readings taken by Rad-Safe monitors Ellis, Ernest, Virgil, and Perry, and the attempt to have Hayes reduce his readings, was to legitimize the readings from the only radiation instrument in the Area 12 Camp on the day of Baneberry: the probe at the cafeteria that peaked at 700 mR gamma at 8:40 AM.

Relying upon the probe, Dr. Evans reduced the gamma dose recorded on Roberts's film badge, concluding that Roberts's maximum exposure while in the Area 12 Camp was 300 mR. This left 745 mR of the 1,045 mR gamma dose recorded on Roberts's film still to be explained. Dr. Evans reduced that reading to 300 mR gamma, claiming the film was contaminated and that the fur collar on the jacket Roberts wore for eight hours was the source of the 300 mR gamma reading.

Having reduced the whole-body film badge reading to 600 mR gamma, Dr. Evans then calculated Roberts's total bone marrow dose. He multiplied each of the 300 mR gamma doses by 70 percent, as Dr. Warren explained should be done, since the cortex of the bone would block about 30 percent of the gamma rays that struck the exterior of the body. Dr. Evans's final calculation was that Roberts's bone marrow dose was exactly 210 mR (70 percent × 300 mR), while Roberts was immersed in the Baneberry cloud, and exactly 210 mR (70 percent x 300 mR) from the fur collar on his jacket. Evans had come up with an extraordinary mathematical coincidence of exactly 210 mR from immersion in the cloud in Area 12 Camp and exactly 210 mR during the eight hours Roberts wore his radiation-infused fur collar.

Dr. Evans had effusive praise for REECo and its Rad-Safe personnel, even though nearly all the monitors in the field did not know how to read their instruments, did not realize the instruments had more than one scale, or did not know how to calculate or extrapolate the readings on their instruments.

His only criticism was directed at Harley Roberts and his employer WSI, because Roberts was issued and wore a jacket with a fur collar that collected radioactive material that continued to bombard him after he left the camp, doubling his gamma dose. Dr. Evans did not see fit to criticize REECo, whose monitors stood on the sidelines fully suited up in protective gear waving Roberts and the other guards into the cloud with their offending fur collars. He also could not blame the AEC for ordering Roberts and the security guards into a radiation zone, without any training and without coveralls, booties, hoods, or respirators, standard-issue protective gear for Rad-Safe monitors.

Dr. Evans then reviewed Roberts's thyroid readings. He was present in court when Dr. Warren explained that Roberts inhaled radioactive iodine in the Baneberry cloud that passed from his lungs into his blood stream and collected in his thyroid gland. While Dr. Evans could not argue with Dr. Warren that Roberts had inhaled the iodine, he minimized the 3,680 mR dose to

Roberts's thyroid gland, opining that it added only 6 mR to his total bone marrow dose.

We were surprised at the remarkable mathematical precision of Dr. Evans's estimate of the bone marrow dose Roberts received and his certitude that it was exactly 426 mR. The judge appeared surprised as well, having listened attentively when Dr. Warren explained that in addition to the external gamma dose of around 1 R there would be some additional contribution from the 4,500 mR beta emitters and from inhalation. The judge interjected and referred to Dr. Warren's testimony on these matters on several occasions during Dr. Evans's testimony, but Dr. Evans stuck to his exact calculation.

After Dr. Evans arrived at his precise calculation of the bone marrow dose, the government lawyer tried to qualify him to offer an opinion regarding the cause of Roberts's acute myeloid leukemia. We objected on the basis that Dr. Evans, like our witnesses Dr. Arthur Tamplin and Dr. Rosalie Bertell, was not a medical doctor, and under well-established legal precedent not qualified to offer an opinion on the cause of anyone's leukemia. Government counsel argued vociferously that Dr. Evans should be allowed to offer an opinion on medical causation, but the judge sustained our objection.

Government counsel and Dr. Evans himself appeared crestfallen by the judge's ruling. But Dr. Evans was undaunted and shifted his testimony to a bizarre, nonmedical explanation to account for Roberts's leukemia and Nunamaker's as well. Dr. Evans called his alternative explanation the "theory of the clustering of rare events." Put another way, the occurrence of two simple events was a coincidence or an act of fate or God. He said he had written about his "cluster theory" but was unable to identify or pull out a single scientific publication by himself or anyone else that described the theory.

Dr. Evans asserted confidently that his cluster theory accounted for the occurrence of two acute myeloid leukemias in the group of eighty-six workers exposed at Baneberry. His explanation was as logically unsound as his bone marrow calculations were precise. He explained to the judge, "I will take a couple of examples from the newspapers, which I am sure you will remember, your Honor.

"There was a collision between two commercial airliners over the Grand Canyon some years ago, and the two airplanes involved were TWA and United. Not too long after those two, in Elizabeth, New Jersey, two commercial airliners collided, and it was again TWA and United. Now that is it. It hasn't happened since. In San Diego, last September, a commercial jet collided with a private plane, and there was a great deal of newspaper publicity, at least in

Arizona, about the tremendous loss of life, which I think was one of the greatest in the continental United States.

"But, it did not come to much public notice that on January 31st over San Diego, there was another midair collision. It was between two Navy jets, an F-4 Phantom and an A-4 Skyhawk collided over San Diego. So, rare events cluster."

Unsolicited, Dr. Evans offered another example: two sets of triplets were born at Michael Reese Hospital in Chicago in June, and two more sets of triplets were born at the same hospital in September of the same year. These two sets of triplets were among 3,800 births at Michael Reese that year.

We were taken aback by the examples Dr. Evans gave to explain his cluster theory. Alan and I huddled, whispering that his theory was akin to the notion that if one Hollywood movie star dies, another star's death will follow soon after.

As I approached the podium to begin my cross-examination, Dr. Evans leaned back in the witness chair and grinned condescendingly. I asked him if he was a medical doctor. He admitted he was not but went on to explain that he had vast knowledge of medical issues based upon his studies. I asked if he was an epidemiologist, like Dr. Stewart, and qualified to offer an opinion there. He conceded that he was not an epidemiologist and had not given an opinion in that field.

I then referred to the two plane crashes and asked whether he had performed any calculations of the probabilities of the occurrence of the two airline collisions. "There was no way to calculate that. There is no way of telling," he admitted. I then asked whether the Federal Aviation Administration had determined the cause of the collision over the Grand Canyon or the cause of the collision in Elizabeth, New Jersey. He admitted, "Of course there would be a cause," and went on to state that there was "a cause for the triplets born at Michael Reese Hospital," as well.

When I asked whether radiation is a known cause of leukemia, he conceded that it was and had been known to cause leukemia since the 1920s. When I asked his opinion of Dr. Shields Warren in the field of radiation pathology, he stated, "He is superb."

After this last response, the judge interjected, "Doctor, I am still troubled with the cluster effect. It strikes me as being unscientific and philosophical." This provoked Dr. Evans into another discussion of his cluster theory.

> As you get sensitive to it, you will notice it more and more. As you drive to and from your work, I don't know how far that is in your particular

> case, but it is a few miles—I know that once we would become aware of this, that if a dog was in the street while we were commuting to work. And it wouldn't be just one dog. If we saw one dog in front of us, very likely we were going to see another one that day but not the next day. Or it might be a child riding [running] in the street that day.

This response by Dr. Evans caused further inquiry by the court.

> THE COURT: With my untrained mind, I would explain that as a coincidence.
> DR. EVANS: Well, it is the same thing.
> THE COURT: You don't think that there is a relationship between the events, only that they do cluster?
> DR. EVANS: They do cluster.
> THE COURT: Do they cluster the more rare they are? Is there a ratio there?
> DR. EVANS: No, the fractional clustering is the same, regardless.

Dr. Evans had an interested audience of one and was not ready to give up an opportunity to continue the discussion. He asked and was granted permission to demonstrate his theory of the clustering of rare events. He explained that in his classes he would set a Geiger counter on his desk and the students would listen for a few minutes waiting to hear a "click-click-click-click-click" as gamma rays from space struck the instrument in rapid succession. He placed his Geiger counter on the judge's bench. The instrument was turned on and the entire courtroom sat breathlessly for what seemed an eternity, but probably around five minutes, waiting for the "click-click-click-click-click" Dr. Evans had foretold. Over the five-minute period, the silence was broken once or twice by a "click."

The experiment ended, but Dr. Evans persisted and wanted to give the judge another example. He asked permission to place a number of dimes on the judge's bench to demonstrate what he described as a periodic event, as opposed to a random one. The government lawyers seemed excited at this possibility and one after another fished in their pockets for dimes or other coins for the demonstration.

Judge Foley, however, had no patience for further demonstrations of the cluster theory. Visibly embarrassed, he declined the offer, thanked Dr. Evans for his testimony, and recessed the proceedings for the day.

Dr. Evans's professorial effort to convert nonsense to science was the humorous highlight of the trial. Certainly, it came at a stage where we sorely needed a bit of levity. We still wonder what the coin demonstration might have yielded and, in a way, wish Judge Foley had let him proceed. The irony was that the United States government had pledged to "spend as much as it takes" to defeat the claims of these two widows. Yet, with its top expert on the stand, the entire defense team was unable to come up with enough pocket change.

NOTES

1. *Baneberry Collection*, EX C-71.

2. Troy Ellis, the monitor at CP-2, took readings of Roberts's clothing when he checked in for decontamination around 5:30 PM on December 18, 1970. He wrote them down on a sheet of paper and placed them in the plastic bag with the clothing. He also wrote down Roberts's readings before and after he entered the showers, but the handwritten sheets with those readings disappeared. *Baneberry Collection*, TR: *Las Vegas Sun*, January 25, 1979.

3. *Baneberry Collection*, EX 16.

[25]

Emptying the AEC Laboratories

WHEN DR. EVANS ENDED his testimony, the government moved into the final phase of its defense. It called upon its own: men and women who were trained and had spent most of their professional careers in AEC-funded laboratories or affiliated hospitals. Three came from the AEC's Oak Ridge National Laboratory in Tennessee and its affiliated Oak Ridge Hospital, where Harley Roberts was sent in August 1973. Two came from the AEC's Brookhaven National Laboratory in New York. A final expert came from the Argonne National Laboratory's affiliated Franklin McLean Hospital in Chicago.

We were not surprised the government medical experts were all part of the AEC establishment and knew we would be unable to shake them from opinions that supported the AEC's threshold theory, the linchpin of the government's defense. As we began our cross-examinations, we stressed their relationship to the AEC and forced each to concede it supported most of their work. Some bristled at the implication that the relationship would influence their views. One even boasted that only 55 percent of his funding originated there.

Dr. Warren knew firsthand the importance of AEC funding and had laid the groundwork for this issue. He did so by emphasizing in his testimony that when he served as director of Biology and Medicine for the AEC from 1947 to 1952, one of his primary jobs was to assure adequate support for all the AEC's laboratories and hospital facilities, including the three laboratories mentioned here. He realized that his chief antagonist was Dr. Janet Rowley, the AEC's cytogeneticist, who worked at Franklin McLean Hospital.

When considering the testimony of a witness, particularly an expert witness, one must remember that his or her potential bias is as important as the testimony itself. In a jury trial, jurors are instructed before deliberations that, in assessing witness credibility, they may consider the witness's relationship or connection with a party to the lawsuit and whether that connection might influence testimony. If our case had been tried to a jury, we would have hammered the point that all the government's expert witnesses were biased in favor of the government because of their manifold professional relationship with the AEC. This was in contrast with our medical experts, Drs. Warren and Stewart, who were totally independent of both sides and had given opinions based upon the medical and scientific evidence. Drs. Tamplin and Bertell, who had conducted studies funded by the government, were ostracized when the results of their studies did not align with the AEC's position that low-level radiation did not cause adverse health effects.

The judge recognized why we questioned each of the government experts on this issue and, over objection by government counsel, allowed us to explore the matter with them. But he could not appreciate, as we did, the AEC's power over those dependent upon it for funding. Further, he did not know that the Justice Department had sought to disqualify Dr. Warren because his hospital received AEC funding. Nor would he, because Dr. Warren's principles precluded our mentioning or questioning him about a strategy he himself called "dirty pool."

The AEC's experts were, not unexpectedly, among those scientists who still clung to the threshold theory, some refusing to admit that a radiation dose less than 100 R—100 times the 1 R gamma dose recorded on Harley Roberts's film badge—could be shown to cause leukemia or cancer. Our only success was to get all of them, with one oddball exception, to agree with Dr. Warren that Roberts's acute myeloid leukemia arose within the time frame, or latency period, that one would expect if radiation from Baneberry were the cause. Most also admitted that Roberts's and Nunamaker's medical records contained no evidence of any blood abnormality, chromosome abnormality, or preleukemic condition prior to Baneberry. This admission from the government's experts contributed significantly to our case.

Since radiation at Baneberry stood out starkly as the only significant time-connected event that could have caused these two leukemias, the government realized it could not rely entirely upon the threshold theory. Government counsel knew that Drs. Warren, Stewart, Tamplin, and Bertell had all testified that there is no safe radiation dose and had presented studies challenging the threshold theory. From the government's perspective, some explanation other than Dr. Evans's cluster theory, which came across as unscientific and frankly ludicrous, had to be offered to account for the leukemias. It called upon Dr. Janet Rowley.

Shifting from general radiation effects to specific effects upon human chromosomes, Dr. Rowley, a cytogeneticist from McLean Hospital, argued that radiation from Baneberry did not cause Robert's C-7 chromosome deletion.

She began her testimony by explaining that her specialty, cytogenetics, is the field of medicine that deals with the study of chromosomes: the twenty-three pairs of rod-shaped particles found in the nucleus of the cell that contain all the human genes. The chromosomes are only visible during the brief interval when the cell divides. At that time, all forty-six chromosomes can be clearly seen under the microscope, as they line up to divide into two cells—referred to as daughter cells.

Dr. Rowley provided the court with an interesting history and overview of the advances in the field. Our knowledge of chromosomes in humans was so primitive that not until 1956 was the correct number of human chromosomes clearly determined. The first chromosome abnormality associated with a disease was discovered in 1959 by French physician Dr. Gerome Lejeune, who identified the extra chromosome, or trisomy, found in infants born with Down syndrome.

By the early 1960s, techniques for identifying each of the specific chromosomes had improved. But a banding technique to clearly identify each chromosome was not developed until 1972. This explained why, in July 1972, Dr. Kuhn at Loma Linda was unable to determine which C chromosome Roberts was missing in his bone marrow cells. In late 1973, however, using Dr. Caspersson's new Giemsa banding technique, the missing chromosome was identified as C-7.

The significance of Dr. Rowley's testimony was that prior to 1956 the type of detailed study performed on Roberts's chromosomes in 1974 was not possible. One could only wonder how many Japanese blast survivors who then died of acute myeloid leukemia within a few years also had the C-7 deletion, which Dr. Warren considered the hallmark and key to our case.

Dr. Rowley agreed with Dr. Warren that the C-7 deletion found in Roberts's bone marrow cells in June 1972 was the seminal finding and key to the causation of his leukemia and death. Dr. Warren had recognized the significance of the deletion in our first conversation with him in late February 1974 and confirmed it in his January 30, 1975, written opinion.

Dr. Rowley was hired by the AEC years later and issued her written opinion in February 1978—over four years after Dr. Warren had explained the importance of the C-7 deletion. In 1978, she stated she was "uncertain whether the radiation from Baneberry caused the C-7 deletion, but inclined to think not," because she felt his dose was too small and the interval from exposure to diagnosis of acute myeloid leukemia too short.[1]

When she came to testify at the trial a year later, her view had solidified. She was now convinced that the radiation dose was too low, embracing wholeheartedly the threshold theory, like the other government experts. But she had also modified her view regarding the latency period. At trial, she agreed with Dr. Warren that the latency period from Baneberry to the diagnosis of Roberts's leukemia was not too short for Baneberry to be the cause.

Dr. Rowley's complete agreement with Dr. Warren that the C-7 deletion initiated the blood disorder and caused Roberts's leukemia and death was a crucial concession. It demonstrated that in 1974 Dr. Warren was among the first in the field to recognize this significant finding, years ahead of his colleagues.

The only remaining issue was the cause of the missing C-7 chromosome identified in Roberts's bone marrow cells in July 1972. By 1979, when the trial began, there were only thirteen reported cases of patients with this rare C-7 deletion—not including the Roberts case. Dr. Warren had reviewed all thirteen cases published in the medical literature, several of which were Dr. Rowley's own cases. From his review, Warren concluded that radiation could not be ruled out as the cause in any of them, because the medical records in some of the cases did not include sufficient information on the patient's history to determine radiation exposure prior to the detection of the C-7 deletion. As Dr. Warren aptly put it, "You can't prove a negative."

Dr. Rowley claimed initially that radiation was not the cause of any of the C-7 deletions in the thirteen cases. But the judge, who remembered Dr. Warren's testimony, queried her on this point.

> THE COURT: I'm not clear in one area. What is the relationship in your experience between patients that were given radiation doses, such as you just described, and chromosome aberrations like the missing C-7? Is there a relationship?
>
> DR. ROWLEY: Well, we have too few patients to say that specifically, because only two of our patients had radiotherapy. And they had abnormalities of chromosome 7.

This admission by Dr. Rowley seemed to fully confirm Dr. Warren's testimony and debunk any suggestion that radiation was not a known cause of the C-7 deletion. Dr. Rowley must have realized that she had given ground on this very significant point. She then fell back upon the threshold theory to argue that Roberts's radiation dose was too low to have caused his C-7 deletion.

Next, she advanced another explanation for the deletion, relying upon a study by Dr. Felix Mitelman, a Swedish physician. Dr. Mitelman studied fifty-six people diagnosed with acute myeloid leukemia who had been exposed to solvents, insecticides, and petroleum products. His preliminary and tentative view was that such exposures might be related to their leukemias. Dr. Rowley claimed that Dr. Miltelman's study was evidence that Roberts's leukemia was more probably related to his exposure to petroleum products when he ran his filling station in Bicknell, Indiana, in 1960, or when he delivered soda pop and dairy products ten years prior to Baneberry.

Judge Foley interrupted and inquired whether the fifty-six people studied by Dr. Mitelman had been exposed to radiation. All Dr. Rowley could say was that per the study, anyone exposed to radiation was excluded. Our assumption was that the judge was somewhat skeptical that none of the fifty-six, mostly middle aged or older, had ever had an x-ray or other diagnostic procedure. We thought he must also have been influenced by Dr. Rowley's admission that two of her own cases were ones in which radiation was linked to the C-7 abnormality and would consider that evidence much more significant than the Mitelman report.

I thought Judge Foley's comments left Dr. Rowley vulnerable and asked her to abandon her opinion and reliance upon the report. But she dug in her heels and was adamant that Mitelman was solid evidence that Roberts's leukemia was more likely caused by his exposure to petroleum products. Her insistence forced me to go through the report and the specifics about the fifty-six study subjects. She stated that Dr. Mitelman classified twenty-three as having exposure to solvents, insecticides, or petroleum products; thirty-three had no apparent exposure. Only three of the fifty-six had a missing C-7 as their *only* chromosome abnormality, as Roberts had. Dr. Rowley further admitted that no patient who had been exposed to petroleum products had a C-7 deletion as the only chromosome abnormality.

I then focused upon the seven persons in the Mitelman study who were exposed to petroleum products. Since there was no information regarding the work history of the seven, Dr. Rowley could not explain specifically how they were exposed to petroleum products or the extent of their exposures. Of the seven, four were males twenty-three to forty-six years of age, none of whom had any chromosome abnormality at all. Only one of the seven had a C-7 deletion. He died at age thirty-two and had other chromosome abnormalities along with the C-7 deletion. Although Dr. Rowley had no specific information about this male, how he was exposed, or the extent and duration of his exposure, she remained resolute. For her, this single case in the Mitelman's study provided scientific support that Roberts's work a decade before Baneberry was the more likely cause of his C-7 deletion.

In his testimony, Dr. Warren had ruled out any relationship between Roberts's service station work ten years before Baneberry, because, as he pointed out, once the C-7 deletion occurs, it produces blood abnormalities within two to three years at most. Therefore, if the C-7 deletion occurred in the early 1960s, Roberts would have had blood abnormalities when he began at the Test Site in 1966 and certainly by 1970, when Baneberry occurred.

To emphasize Dr. Warren's testimony on this point, I asked Dr. Rowley how long, in her opinion, it took after the first C-7 deletion occurred to produce a blood abnormality. She hesitated and was unwilling to give any time frame, realizing that pinning herself down to an interval shorter than ten to twelve years would rule out her petroleum products theory.

I concluded my cross-examination by asking whether she felt the Mitelman study offered a sound basis for her opinion, since Dr. Mitelman acknowledged that his study was tentative and preliminary and had urged others to carefully review work histories to determine whether solvents, insecticides, and petroleum products were associated with chromosome abnormalities in patients diagnosed with acute myeloid leukemia. She conceded his study was preliminary and not conclusive but would not abandon her opinion.

In our view, Dr. Rowley had failed to counter Dr. Warren's testimony. In fact, her testimony confirmed his opinions. Judge Foley's questions to Dr. Rowley were significant, forcing her to admit that radiation in two of her own cases had caused C-7 abnormalities and challenging the relevance of the Mitelman study. We did not see how the judge could give any credence to Dr. Rowley's petroleum products theory as the cause of Roberts's C-7 deletion, where Dr. Mitelman himself had admitted that his findings were preliminary.

After the government's case ended, we believed Dr. Warren's careful analysis and opinion had withstood all the challenges of the AEC medical men and women. It boiled down to a matter of credibility, and Dr. Warren, unlike all the government witnesses, was not beholden to the AEC establishment.

Dr. Warren's opinion in the Roberts case was but a continuation of his life-long curiosity about radiation and, in this instance, his quest for the truth about its effects upon human chromosomes. The AEC invoked its threshold theory, and, when it became patently inadequate to deal with alteration of chromosomes in the process of cell division, shifted to Dr. Rowley's "petroleum products" theory in a feeble effort to explain away Roberts's C-7 deletion.

NOTES

1. Janet Rowley to Buford Allen, ERDA counsel, February 7, 1978, with attached *Analysis of Data, Opinion in the Case of Harley Roberts, and Comments on the Opinion of Shields Warren, M.D.* Copy in author's possession.

[26]

Not with a Bang But a Whimper

We concluded our case by calling Dr. John Gofman.[1] Dr. Gofman received his PhD in nuclear physical chemistry from UC Berkeley in 1943 and was deeply involved in the Manhattan Project. Among other duties, Robert Oppenheimer assigned him to utilize the cyclotron to produce 1.2 milligrams of plutonium. After World War II, he earned his medical degree at UC San Francisco in 1946. In 1947, he was appointed to the Division of Medical Physics, Department of Physics at Berkeley, became a full professor in 1954, and retired in 1973.

He taught the methodology and use of radioactive substances and the biological effects of radiation. In 1954, Ernest Lawrence, inventor of the cyclotron and founder of the Lawrence Radiation Laboratory (later LLL) appointed Dr. Gofman medical director, and in 1963 Gofman founded and became first director of the Biomedical Research Division there. The new position fulfilled a request from the AEC to LLL to conduct research into the health effects of radioiodine upon persons living downwind from atmospheric tests at NTS in 1962. This last résumé item refreshed the court regarding Dr. Tamplin's testimony about the study and its impact upon the AEC.

Dr. Gofman had reviewed Dr. Evans's calculations of the Roberts and Nunamaker bone marrow doses and found it "virtually impossible" that the doses could be so low," because

> they are based upon external gamma dose and they neglect totally the major source of exposure that these individuals would have had. Given the circumstances, I would estimate that the doses from this sort of blast, and I cannot give you exact dose simply because no one has given me the exact composition of the cloud and all of the radioactive substances in the cloud these men were exposed to, but, the external dose [Roberts] measured was 1 Rem, or take Robley Evans's

> four tenths (4/10) Rem to the bone marrow...and one tenth (1/10) for Mr. Nunamaker. It would be my opinion, based upon my work in this field, that the true dose must have been one hundred (100) times higher to the bone marrow of each of these individuals.

Dr. Gofman explained his statement by pointing out that the Baneberry cloud would have contained "short-life radionuclides in the first one to two hours when Roberts and Nunamaker were exposed to the cloud, and they would have decayed in the bodies of Mr. Roberts and Mr. Nunamaker, because they were not cleared from the site."

Dr. Gofman supported the opinion of Drs. Warren and Stewart that the radiation Roberts received caused his leukemia, even if he had to accept Dr. Evans's bone marrow dose, which he was convinced was wrong. He also supported Dr. Stewart's opinion that Nunamaker's leukemia was caused by Baneberry, in part because it was a statistical certainty, but also because there was no evidence of any medical problems prior to and for several years after his exposure until he was diagnosed in 1974 with leukemia.

Dr. Gofman reviewed the work history of each man. When asked about Dr. Rowley's opinion that Roberts's leukemia was caused by his exposure to petroleum products in 1960, he replied, "I find it rather absurd that the casual exposure to solvents and fumes in gasoline station operators could be regarded as a dominant cause of leukemia.... It is speculative; it is not science."

Finally, Dr. Gofman stated that there was no evidence to support the threshold theory upon which the government experts relied, and that the linear theory was accepted by most scientists in the field, supporting Drs. Warren, Stewart, Bertell, and Tamplin.

When the trial testimony ended, the denial of an opportunity to sum up the case was disappointing to me. Alan had given the opening statement, and we had agreed I would make the closing argument. Now there would be no final act in the Baneberry tragedy that had played out in the courtroom over the past three months. I would have no chance to say a final farewell to Harley Roberts and try to honor his deathbed request to "make the bastards pay."

Instead, the judge read in open court the posttrial schedule. The court reporter would prepare the transcript of the three-month trial, and we would then file briefs discussing nine separate issues.[2] After he gaveled the end of the trial and exited the courtroom, we glanced over at Mr. Elliott and Mr. Thorndal, packed our files, trial exhibits, and legal pads into briefcases and boxes and carted them out of the courtroom.

The end of a trial is a time for reflection and, regardless of the result, evokes a sense of relief. But the Baneberry trial ended like a funeral procession, Alan and I pallbearers carrying the Baneberry casket filled with records and documents to be placed in a crypt until a final decision was handed down.

When we got back to the office, we talked to Dorothy and Louise. Louise, the more vocal of the two, asked bluntly why Judge Foley, who listened to the same testimony they heard day after day, could not simply decide the case and end it. Surely, he understood the evidence. Why was it going to take a year or more for him to make up his mind? Dorothy nodded in agreement, and both looked straight into our eyes for answers.

We had none. All we could say was that Judge Foley was a federal judge with the power to do whatever he wanted. To console them, we pointed out that he recognized it was an important case and that we had presented strong evidence, or he would have ruled against us at the close of the trial. Neither Dorothy nor Louise seemed satisfied.

Alan and I were anxious to get home but lingered for half an hour reflecting on what Alan called "the fine mess" I had gotten him into. We talked about the financial drain the case had brought upon us and would continue to impose upon our small law practice. We were not looking forward to spending hundreds of hours reading thousands of pages of trial transcripts, combing through the trial exhibits, reliving the last three months, and preparing drafts of lengthy legal briefs. We had lost count of the costs and time already expended and were fatigued at the prospect of the additional time and expense required to push the Baneberry case to a conclusion.

As former prosecutors, we envied the salaried lawyers from the Justice Department, their extensive support staff, the U.S. Attorney's office, and the AEC's local office. But what galled us more was that John Thorndal and his private law firm, which had already made hundreds of thousands of dollars over the eight years leading up to the trial and untold thousands for the three-month trial, would now have a steady stream of income preparing legal briefs for Judge Foley and briefs if the case was appealed. Baneberry had been and would continue to be a boon to him and a bane to us.

NOTES

1. In early March 1979, Dr. Gofman testified as the chief medical causation expert for the plaintiffs in the Silkwood v. Kerr-McGee trial in Oklahoma City, Oklahoma.

2. *Las Vegas Review-Journal*, April 8, 1979.

[27]

Justice Delayed Is Justice Denied

WHILE WE HUNKERED DOWN in trial from January 16 through April 5, 1979, the AEC was being shellacked with adverse publicity about the effects of its nuclear testing program. The downwinders, whose first claims were filed with great fanfare by Stewart Udall on December 22, 1978, were headline news in Las Vegas on February 8, 1979: "Fallout to kill for 5,000 years." The article claimed the "government knew its atomic tests in Nevada would kill some people but lied to a public of 'guinea pigs' [who] will suffer the consequences for 5,000 years."[1]

On February 11, 1979, Stanley Jaffe, an army veteran exposed to radiation at the Test Site in 1953, won his appeal in the Third Circuit Court of Appeals. Jaffe's victory was followed by a March 5, 1979, story in the *Los Angeles Times*: "Pentagon disregard of A-test peril told." It reported that recently declassified documents disclosed that Dr. Shields Warren, AEC director of Biology and Medicine, had warned military officials about placing soldiers too close to A-bomb blasts.[2]

On February 15, 1979, the Bulloch family and other Utah sheep ranchers, who lost their case against the government in 1956, were again in the news. The *Las Vegas Review-Journal* reported, "Utah charges energy commission negligent." The article disclosed that 400 recently released documents showed their sheep were exposed to radioactive iodine doses 1,000 times the maximum allowable human dose, contributing to if not causing the deaths of the sheep, and that the government had refused to investigate.[3]

In late February, while the government was calling experts from its DOE-funded hospitals to challenge Dr. Warren's opinion in the Roberts case, the *Las Vegas Sun* headline read, "Feds to probe fallout of Nevada nuke tests." The House Oversight Subcommittee "would begin a full-scale investigation into all phases of health effects from radiation."[4]

On March 8, 1979, *Silkwood v. Kerr-McGee* opened in Oklahoma City. Dr. John Gofman was the first witness to testify. He told the jury about Karen Silkwood's exposure to plutonium while she worked at the Kerr-McGee plant.[5]

Just three days later, Bill Elliott crowed that the government would "spend whatever it takes to win [the Baneberry case]."[6] And on the same day, Drs. Gofman and Martell told the *Silkwood* jury that the plutonium Karen Silkwood ingested would have caused her to develop cancer.[7]

On March 24, 1979, as the government was winding down its defense of our case, Stewart Udall filed another hundred tort claims bringing to 547 the number of downwinders' claims.[8]

On March 28, 1979, after the government ended its case in Baneberry and we were in recess preparing our rebuttal, radioactive steam leaked from the Three Mile Island nuclear power plant.[9] By March 30, 1979, thousands were fleeing the area as 2.5 million curies of radioactive steam poured out of the Three Mile Island tower.[10]

The Baneberry trial ended on April 5, 1979, when the judge read the schedule of proceedings.[11] On April 8, 1979, our local press covered the nine issues he ordered us to brief.[12] But the *Baltimore Sun* focused on the precedential effect our case might have: "Nev. suit may set precedent for fallout claims."[13] Also, on April 8, 1979, members of both houses of Congress discussed the effect the Three Mile Island incident could have on the nation's nuclear power industry.[14]

News coverage about the effects of nuclear testing was not confined to U.S. citizens and military personnel. Earlier, we had learned of the trust fund set up for Marshall Islanders in an article that appeared in the *Las Vegas Review-Journal* on June 4, 1975. On March 27, 1978, Walter Pincus detailed the plight of the islanders. He recounted the latest chapter in the tragic tale of the natives exposed to fallout from the 1954 *Bravo* hydrogen bomb test: "Marshall Islands still affected by 1954 blast."[15]

On May 8, 1979, Dr. George Voelz, eminent radiation pathologist and chief of medical services at Los Alamos Scientific Laboratories (LASL), testified for defendant Kerr-McGee. He told the jury his autopsy on the remains of Karen Silkwood showed she only had 8.8 nanocuries of plutonium in her body, much less than the maximum lifetime safe exposure limit of 40. Dr. Voelz, called to counter Dr. Gofman's testimony, proclaimed that this small amount of plutonium in Karen's body "would have no adverse effect upon her health."[16]

On May 13, 1979, a *Las Vegas Sun* article, "They expect to talk until all survivors are dead," featured residents of St. George, Utah. It discussed recent congressional hearings in Salt Lake City and Las Vegas investigating the downwinders' claims.[17]

Except for coverage of the Baneberry case, the publicity from early 1978 through May 1979 was predominantly critical of the government, helping to create a nationwide concern that the AEC might have deliberately sacrificed U.S. citizens in the course of promoting its nuclear testing program.

But the bombshell came on May 18, 1979, when a jury in Oklahoma City arrived at a verdict in the *Silkwood* case. It found in favor of Karen Silkwood's three minor children and awarded them $10.5 million in damages against Kerr-McGee.[18] It was a stunning victory for the Silkwoods, their attorney Gerry Spence, and Dr. John Gofman, whose testimony the jurors found more persuasive than LASL's radiation expert, Dr. George Voelz.

In our minds, the *Silkwood* verdict, handed down by a jury of ordinary Oklahoma citizens, exemplified the stark difference between trial by jury and our trial before a federal judge under the FTCA. Two trials that involved exposure to radiation levels that government experts dismissed as too little to cause leukemia or cancer ended within a month of each other. Karen Silkwood's children were accorded speedy justice by a jury that rejected the opinions of the AEC scientists. But justice was not swift for Harley's widow and Bill's widow. They would wait another six years for the federal judge to enter judgment in their case.

Because the Baneberry trial did not end in April 1979, Alan and I could not extricate ourselves from the posttrial schedule Judge Foley imposed. But we did not foresee a six-year delay before judgment was entered or a seventeen-year delay before the case would end.

During those seventeen years, we became embroiled in litigation on behalf of 220 other NTS workers who believed, as we did, that they were just as entitled to seek compensation for their cancers as Roberts and Nunamaker, downwinders, uranium miners, atomic veterans, Karen Silkwood's heirs, Marshall Islanders, Rocky Flats workers,[19] Hanford workers,[20] and others.

When the trial ended in April 1979, we returned to the practice of law and had little time to think about Baneberry, until September 15, 1980, when the court reporter filed the last volume of the 5,404-page trial transcript. We scrambled to review the transcript and trial exhibits and filed our posttrial brief on November 28, 1980, then waited for the government to file theirs.

But the government did not file their posttrial brief as the court had scheduled. Instead, on January 30, 1981, it filed a motion for summary judgment, asking the court to dismiss Roberts's and Nunamaker's actions on the basis that the plaintiffs' exclusive remedy for their radiation-induced leukemias was to pursue a worker's compensation proceeding against their respective employers, WSI and REECo.[21]

In preparing our opposition to the motion, we contacted the Nevada Industrial Commission (NIC) and discovered that the AEC had made an agreement with it in June 1956, pursuant to which AEC contractors at NTS were not required to pay premiums into the state industrial fund to cover injuries or diseases caused by radiation exposure. Under the terms of the agreement, which we labeled a sweetheart contract, if a worker employed by an AEC contractor filed a claim for a radiation-related disease, the AEC would decide whether the claim had merit. If the AEC approved the claim, it agreed to reimburse the NIC for any benefits paid, if federal appropriations were available.

We realized instantly why the AEC had sent lawyers to Nevada in early 1956 to steamroll the NIC into signing the sweetheart contract on June 1, 1956. In 1956, the *Bulloch* case was nearing trial in Salt Lake City.[22] If Federal Judge A. Sherman Christensen found that the radiation that fell on sheep in the 1953 A-bomb tests had caused their lesions and deaths, it might occur to citizens in Utah and eastern Nevada, exposed to fallout from the same tests, or to Nevada Test Site workers, or soldiers at Camp Desert Rock, that they too might be in peril of developing cancer.

But in 1956, when *Bulloch* was tried, the AEC managed to silence scientists who disagreed with the experts they mustered to testify before Judge Christensen. The government won. When Judge Christensen learned, twenty-three years later, that the AEC had stifled all who might have testified against the government, he reopened the case on the basis that the government and its lawyers had perpetrated a fraud on the court.[23] But the government appealed his ruling to the Tenth Circuit Court and won again.[24]

The filing of the motion on January 30, 1981, was ironic in a way. Joe Carter, who worked as a laborer at NTS in the early 1950s, died of brain cancer in 1980. While we were investigating his medical history, we learned that Carter was one of four workers exposed to excessive radiation in a plutonium dispersal experiment on January 18, 1956.[25] Oral Epley, one of the four, died on February 1, 1956. On August 17, 1980, the circumstances of his death were on the front page of the *Las Vegas Sun*.[26] The article discussed my inquiry to LASL about Oral Epley's organs, which were sent to LASL for examination following his autopsy on February 1, 1956. It also mentioned assurances by Test Site supervisors, who visited Epley's family while he was in the hospital, that there was a $50,000 life insurance policy. But after Epley died, the $50,000 policy, like the organs sent to LASL, could not be found.[27] The rest of the story, not covered in the article, was that I called the mortuary in Oklahoma and spoke to the ninety-three-year-old mortician who received Epley's remains for burial. He told me he was contacted by someone from the government who directed him not to touch Epley's body because it was contaminated with radiation.

Judge Foley denied, for the second time, the government's motion to dismiss the Baneberry case based on the worker's compensation exclusive remedy defense. He also denied the government's identical motion filed in the companion *Prescott* case, which we filed in 1980.[28] The government appealed his decision in the Baneberry case and his decision in *Prescott*. In 1984, the Ninth Circuit Court of Appeals affirmed the rulings.[29]

We waited for the court to rule on Baneberry. On June 8, 1982, Judge Foley entered a six-page *Partial Decision—Negligence Issues*, setting forth the salient facts and finding, "Plaintiffs have proven by a preponderance of the evidence that employees of the United States were negligent in the manner in which persons were evacuated post-shot from Area 12 and in the manner in which persons who have been exposed to radiation were attempted to be decontaminated."

We would have been stunned if Judge Foley had ruled otherwise, since the evidence of Cluff's negligent conduct was overwhelming. Now, the only remaining issue was whether he would accept the opinion of Dr. Warren and find that the radiation Roberts received was sufficient to cause a C-7 deletion and leukemia. If he found for Roberts, he might also find in favor of Nunamaker.

After he handed down the ruling on negligence in June 1982, we believed the judge would want to make his final ruling before the downwinders' case, *Allen v. United States*, went to trial in Salt Lake City in September 1982. A ruling on Baneberry, filed eight years before *Allen*, could influence the *Allen* case and give Baneberry some precedential value.

But Judge Foley did not act. The *Allen* trial began before U.S. District Judge Bruce Jenkins. Dale Haralson, lead counsel for the downwinders brought to court twenty-four test cases: eight died of leukemia and sixteen others died or were diagnosed with various cancers. Press coverage of the trial was extensive in our newspapers through its conclusion in November 1982.

On January 20, 1983, four years after our trial began, Judge Foley issued a two-sentence ruling. He found that Roberts received 426 mR to his bone marrow and Nunamaker 100 mR to his bone marrow and ruled we had not presented evidence to support causation of the two leukemias. He directed the government lawyers to write the decision for him and to prepare the findings of fact.

In our view, it was a travesty. Judge Foley had a responsibility to measure the evidence presented at trial and render a reasoned decision based on that evidence. He had not only missed an opportunity to hand down a landmark decision that might have become a beacon for others who suffered because of AEC recklessness, he abdicated his responsibility as a jurist. In two sentences, he unceremoniously washed his hands of Baneberry and turned Roberts and Nunamaker over to government lawyers.

When we tried to explain Judge Foley's ruling to Dorothy and Louise, they could not understand why he had sat on the case for nearly four years and then insulted them with a piece of paper that said almost nothing. If the case was as simple as his ruling seemed, he should have had the guts to end it in April 1979. At least they would have been spared the misery of waiting. We were as shocked and baffled as they and could only conclude he had become so overwhelmed and weary of the burden of the Baneberry case that he simply took the safe course and ruled in favor of the United States government.

We knew what the government lawyers would do with carte blanche to write their own decision in the case. They would craft findings that absolved the AEC, slanted to portray the government and its agency as blameless. We knew they would make it appear as if Dorothy and Louise had needlessly put an innocent government agency, the AEC, through an expensive trial.

The government lawyers took a year to prepare the final document, which stretched Judge Foley's two-sentence ruling to proportions even we could not have imagined. It was eighty-eight pages long. And, as expected, it was a scathing and slanderous assault upon all our experts. It validated virtually every proposition, fact, and theory offered by the government and cleared the AEC of any wrongdoing or responsibility for Harley's or Bill's leukemias and deaths.

Dr. Warren earned a modicum of respect, more in the nature of a backhanded and condescending commentary. The government lawyers acknowledged his eminent qualification as a historic and revered figure upon whom the AEC had bestowed its highest awards. But they denigrated his well-reasoned opinions and made them appear as obsolete as their threshold theory truly was. The resurrected threshold theory became the centerpiece of their case and ultimate proof that no leukemia could possibly be caused by radiation that did not exceed their arbitrary exposure level of 100 R. Alan and I were relieved that Dr. Warren was no longer alive to review their comments and wondered whether they would have been so brazen if he were.

While discounting Dr. Warren's expertise, the government adopted wholesale Dr. Rowley's petroleum products theory. For the government lawyers, Dr. Rowley's reliance upon a single study by Dr. Felix Mitelman was incontrovertible proof that Roberts's C-7 deletion came from his earlier exposure to petroleum products. But one item that the government lawyers decided to omit was Dr. Evans's "cluster theory" as an explanation for the occurrence of these two leukemias. Even they must have recognized that no one, including the judge, gave any credence to such a bizarre argument.

On April 16, 1984, we filed our objections challenging most of the Findings of Fact and Conclusions of Law. And on May 4, we filed a motion to reopen the action or for a new trial. In support, we supplied an affidavit of Dr. Karl Z. Morgan, who, in January 1984 at our request, reviewed the trial testimony and trial exhibits that Dr. Robley Evans relied upon to calculate Roberts's bone marrow dose. In a comprehensive affidavit, Dr. Morgan attested that Dr. Evans had failed to consider the bone marrow dose Roberts received from inhaling radioactive isotopes present in the Baneberry cloud during the first one to two hours after the detonation.[30]

Dr. Morgan was the leading expert in the world on internal dose calculations. In 1947, he published the first paper showing how to calculate internal dose from radionuclides deposited in the body. Considered by many the father of health physics, he founded and served as president of the Health Physics Society, was editor of *Health Physics Journal*, and served as director of health Physics at Oak Ridge National Laboratory from 1943 until 1972. He was chairman of the Internal Dose Committee of the International and National Commissions on Radiation Protection (ICRP, NCRP) that set the standards and published the handbooks used to determine maximum permissible radiation doses.

Dr. Morgan identified twenty-eight radioactive isotopes that would have been in the Baneberry cloud in the first several hours after the device detonated. He calculated the dose each would have delivered to Roberts's bone marrow after it was taken into the lungs and irradiated the rib cage, where a substantial portion of the red bone morrow is located. He relied upon Dr. Evans's trial testimony and the King Tables in the leading internal dose handbook to calculate dosage. He concluded that Roberts's total bone marrow dose from inhalation of the twenty-eight radionuclides was 7,100 mR, which, when added to the bone marrow dose derived from external gamma readings on the film badge, showed total bone marrow dose at 7,830 mR.

Dr. Morgan's affidavit established that Dr. Warren had been right all along. Warren had stated that Roberts's bone marrow dose would have included inhaled radionuclides, "the ashes of the explosion, a quite wide range of radioactive isotopes." In fact, Dr. Morgan confirmed Dr. Warren's long-stated opinion that Roberts's "bone marrow dose was somewhere between Dr. Evans's low estimate of less than half a rem and my initial estimate of 15 rem."

Based upon Roberts's properly calculated bone marrow dose of 7.83 R (7,830 mR), Dr. Morgan calculated the probability of leukemia causation.

Relying upon the *BEIR III* report, he determined that the probability that Roberts's leukemia was caused by Baneberry ranged from a low of 38.3 percent to a high of 78.9 percent.[31]

Another basis for our motion was the discovery of an article published in the *Lancet*, by Dr. Felix Mitelman in December 1979, eight months after Dr. Rowley testified at trial. In the *Lancet* article, Dr. Mitelman now stated, "Furthermore, exposure to petroleum products seems to be associated with normal chromosomes, in contrast to exposure to chemical solvents and insecticides."[32] Dr. Mitelman repudiated Dr. Rowley's reliance upon an earlier paper that suggested a possible relationship between exposure to petroleum products and the C-7 deletion.[33]

We contended the court should reopen the action since Dr. Morgan had obliterated Dr. Evans's bone marrow dose calculations, and Dr. Rowley's petroleum products theory had been discredited by Dr. Mitelman, whose preliminary and narrow suggestion she had relied on entirely at trial.

On May 10, 1984, six days after we filed our motion, Judge Bruce Jenkins's 500-page Memorandum decision in *Allen* was released.[34] In stark contrast to Judge Foley, Judge Jenkins analyzed the facts presented by the lay and expert witnesses called to testify at his trial, included an elegant legal analysis of the arguments presented by counsel for the government and the plaintiffs, and found in favor of the heirs of eight persons who died of leukemia. He also found in favor of one woman who died of breast cancer and a young woman who survived, living with thyroid cancer. The judge awarded a total of nearly $2.5 million to the ten plaintiffs who prevailed.

The Jenkins decision was a thrilling victory for Dale Haralson, who led the team of lawyers for the plaintiffs and was a crushing defeat for the AEC. For over three decades, the AEC had insisted that not one single cancer or leukemia had been caused by radiation from its aboveground atomic testing program.

On June 1, 1984, we supplemented our motion to reopen, citing the *Allen* decision as compelling evidence that low-level radiation, which ranged from .36 rem to 3.7 rem, had been found by Judge Jenkins sufficient to cause the eight leukemias.[35]

In the government's opposition to our motion, it tried to defend Dr. Evans and Dr. Rowley. Dr. Evans supplied an affidavit in which he acknowledged that Dr. Morgan had "mechanically" tabulated the list of radionuclides present in the Baneberry explosion, but "fractionation" prevented those twenty-eight radionuclides from reaching the surface and entering the radioactive cloud. Somehow, unlike the radioactive iodine that was also present in the explosion and measured in Roberts's thyroid gland, these radionuclides were trapped below ground. However, Dr. Evans admitted that he could not support his "fractionation" position, because to do so would require actual measurements of the radioactive cloud in Area 12 Camp, and he knew none were taken.[36]

We filed a reply urging the court to reopen the case to allow Dr. Morgan to testify and to strike Dr. Rowley's petroleum products theory. Having waited over five years for the court's decision, we could see no reason why Judge Foley would deny us an opportunity to present evidence that would correct erroneous findings and could lead to a just decision in the case.[37]

On January 4, 1985, in a minute order and without explanation, the judge denied our motion.[38] We viewed this as a second act of abdication to the government. We could only conclude that the judge had resolved to stand by the government, despite clear evidence that Dr. Evans had not accurately calculated Roberts's bone marrow dose and that the petroleum products theory was as absurd as Dr. Evans's cluster theory. Instead, we hoped he would recognize Dr. Warren's opinion as credible and correct.

On January 5, 1985, six years after the Baneberry trial, Judge Foley adopted every proposed finding offered by the government, or as we would contend, rubber stamped the government's decision and entered judgment against Dorothy Roberts and Louise Nunamaker. We appealed the judgment and his denial of our motion to reopen.

On December 24, 1986, the three-member Ninth Circuit panel, headed by Chief Judge Browning, entered an Order of Limited Remand, sending the case back to Judge Foley directing him "to explain his reasons for denying Roberts's and Nunamaker's motion to reopen or grant a new trial to receive new evidence contained in three affidavits by Dr. Karl Z. Morgan and in recently published articles [Mitelman's paper] which Roberts sought to introduce."

On June 24, 1987, Judge Foley made findings and denied the motion to reopen. He ruled that Dr. Morgan could have been consulted and offered his opinion at trial or at some point earlier than his affidavits were offered. He also found that reopening the case would require considerable time and additional witnesses. Of interest to us, he observed that, since Dr. Morgan's testimony was offered to bolster Dr. Warren's testimony that Roberts's bone dose was sufficient to cause leukemia and Dr. Warren was deceased, the court would be denied the benefit of Dr. Warren's reassessment.

We appealed that ruling, and our appeal was reinstated in the Ninth Circuit in 1988. There was one final legal hurdle we had to overcome: the discretionary immunity defense that harkened back to *Dalehite v. United States* and the Texas City fertilizer explosion of April 1947.

By 1988, the Baneberry case and our companion Test Site case, *Prescott v. United States*, were the only FTCA radiation cases that had survived this defense. And if the government had its way, both cases would join all others: in *Allen v. United States* (downwinders), Judge Jenkins's decision had been reversed in the Tenth Circuit;[39] in *Begay v. United States* (uranium miners), the lower court's dismissal of the claims brought by uranium miners was affirmed in the Ninth Circuit;[40] in *Bulloch v. United States* (sheep case), the Tenth Circuit reversed Judge Christensen's ruling that reopened the case;[41] and in *Consolidated United States Atmospheric Testing*, the Ninth Circuit ended the atomic veterans' litigation for radiation related injuries.[42]

But despite the apparent odds, we won the legal battle in the Ninth Circuit. Our appeal in *Roberts and Nunamaker* was reinstated, and we soldiered on. We also defeated the governmental immunity defense in the Ninth Circuit in the companion case, *Prescott v. United States*.[43] The victory in *Prescott* allowed us to try six test cases. In 1994, we lost and did not appeal that decision.

By the time the discretionary immunity defense was swept aside by the Ninth Circuit in *Roberts and Nunamaker v. United States* and *Prescott v. United States*, the Radiation Exposure Compensation Act, RECA, had been signed into law. It offered compensation to eligible uranium miners, downwinders, and NTS workers who contracted leukemia and certain cancers—if they could demonstrate radiation exposure during aboveground tests in the 1950s or from radiation released into the atmosphere from the Plowshare tests in 1962.[44]

RECA was prefaced with an apology from the United States government for exposing its citizens to radiation. It was the last of a series of congressional efforts to provide compensation for those exposed to atmospheric radiation. The first effort began in 1979: "Bill aids nuke test victims,"[45] spawned by highly publicized investigations that began during the Baneberry trial and resulted in the publication of *The Forgotten Guinea Pigs Report, August 1980*, by the House Subcommittee on Oversight and Investigations.[46] The first proposals had only offered compensation to radiation victims living downwind from NTS.

In 1988, Congress enacted legislation to afford atomic veterans relief under the Radiation Exposure Veterans Compensations Act (REVCA). With the passage of REVCA and the Tenth Circuit's 1987 decision in *Allen* reversing Judge Jenkins's award, it was only a matter of time before Congress would act.

In 1990, the Radiation Exposure Compensation Act was signed into law. When it was passed, its sponsor, Senator Orrin Hatch, stated that he did not want it to be "a playground to benefit the lawyers," and it severely limited the fees attorneys hired to assist claimants could receive.[47] As of March 2015, 3,578 Test Site workers, 18,087 downwinders, and nearly 8,000 uranium miners or their widows and children have been awarded $2 billion in compensation for leukemias and cancers linked to the AEC nuclear testing program.

Many of our Test Site clients were eligible for benefits, and we handled a few claims for workers who fit the criteria, including Keith Prescott, who died of multiple myeloma, a cancer of the bone marrow. We also filed a claim on behalf of the daughters of Kenny Case, the Atomic Cowboy who appeared on the television show *What's My Line* in New York City in 1961. Kenny was an ardent supporter of the Test Site workers, led by Bennie Levy, as they pursued their lawsuit in federal court. At that time, Kenny was in excellent health and thought the radiation he received in the 1950s would have no long-term effects. He was wrong. In 1985, he died of leukemia. We assisted his five daughters in their claim, each receiving one-fifth of the $75,000 award.

In late 1982, just prior to issuing his two-sentence ruling in January 1983, Judge Foley took senior status and reduced his federal caseload, though he continued to handle *Roberts and Nunamaker* and the *Prescott* case.

In 1985, after the government wrote Judge Foley's decision and he had denied our motions to reopen the case, the federal building, where Dorothy and Louise had relived Baneberry in a fruitless search for justice, was named the Foley Federal Building to honor Judge Foley, his father, who preceded him on the federal bench, and the Foley family of attorneys.

Judge Roger D. Foley died in January 1996, before the final appeal of his ruling was heard in the Ninth Circuit Court. Near the end of his life, he realized that the Baneberry trial was the most significant legal case in which he had been involved, and one of the longest and most important in Nevada history. He arranged to deposit Baneberry trial material into the archival collections of the University of Nevada–Las Vegas. Alan and I were invited to the dedication ceremony. With considerable reluctance, we went with our wives, not to celebrate Judge Foley's decision in favor of the AEC, which we were convinced was wrong, but out of respect for Harley and Dorothy Roberts and Bill and Louise Nunamaker. By 1993, when we attended the dedication, Judge Foley's 1985 decision in favor of the AEC was of little consequence. It delayed but did not hold back the truth about the human consequences of the AEC atomic testing program.

During the Baneberry trial, a news reporter, aware of government lawyer Bill Elliott's pledge to "spend whatever it takes to win," asked Alan and me why we had pursued the case, knowing that it would require so much personal and financial sacrifice. Even now, it remains difficult to explain our commitment to Harley Roberts, our faith in Drs. Warren and Stewart, and our belief that the bane and curse of Baneberry might end favorably in a federal courthouse in our hometown. But the explanation may be no more complicated than Robert Browning's inspiring line,

> Ah, but a man's reach should exceed his grasp,
> Or what's a heaven for?

Sadly, and prophetically, Baneberry began and ended ever-faithful to its name. While it made sure that the widows of the two men who breathed its lethal radioactive gases received no compensation, it also played a part in awakening the public to the dangers of low-level radiation and helped to end the Nevada nuclear testing program. The AEC and its successor, the Department of Energy, left the Test Site a barren and toxic wasteland pockmarked from the Baneberry crater and countless others. A gravestone embossed with the odd-shaped Baneberry cloud should be erected at the National Atomic Testing Museum in Las Vegas engraved with the AEC's pledge as an immortal epitaph: "The government will spend whatever it takes to win."

And a memorial should be erected at the entrance to the Nevada Test Site to remind future generations of a tragic period in American history. As President Eisenhower warned the American people in his January 1961 farewell address, there are dire consequences when "a government contract becomes virtually a substitute for intellectual curiosity" and "public policy becomes the captive of the scientific-technological elite."

NOTES

1. *Las Vegas Review-Journal*, February 1, 1979. This was the first reference we can recall to the downwinders as "guinea pigs" and may have inspired *The Forgotten Guinea Pigs Report*, issued in 1980. Copy in author's possession.
2. At the meeting with Dr. Warren in Tucson in March 1975, he told me about his disagreement with the military and his resignation in June 1952, because he did not want responsibility for the health effects that might result.
3. The Bulloch family, lead plaintiffs, took the case to trial in federal court in Salt Lake City, Utah, in 1956 and lost. *Bullock v. United States*, 145 F. Supp. 824 (D. Utah 1956). See chapter 6.
4. *Las Vegas Sun*, February 27, 1979; *Las Vegas Review-Journal*, February 27, 1979.
5. *Las Vegas Sun*, March 8, 1979.
6. *Los Angeles Herald Examiner*, March 11, 1979.
7. *Las Vegas Sun*, March 11, 1979.
8. Ibid., March 24, 1979.
9. *Las Vegas Review-Journal*, March 28, 1979.
10. Ibid., March 31, 1979.
11. Ibid., April 6, 1979.
12. Ibid., April 8, 1979.

13. *Baltimore Sun*, April 8, 1979.

14. *Las Vegas Sun*, April 8, 1979.

15. *Las Vegas Review-Journal*, March 27, 1979. In 1981, the Marshall Islanders filed administrative claims seeking billions of dollars for injuries and deaths they claimed were caused by tests in the Pacific. *Las Vegas-Review Journal*, April 23, 1981.

16. *Las Vegas Sun*, May 8, 1979.

17. Ibid., May 13, 1979.

18. *Las Vegas Review-Journal*, May 18, 1979.

19. See *Krumbach v. Dow Chemical Co.*, 676 P.2d 1213 (Colo. App. 1983). Dr. Alice Stewart came to Las Vegas in 1980 and then Denver to testify that Leroy Krumbach's cancer was caused by his exposure to radiation at the Rocky Flats nuclear weapons plant in Colorado.

20. Dr. Thomas Mancuso's study of excess cancers among the Hanford workers swirled in controversy, even after, and perhaps because, Drs. Stewart and Kneale joined him early in 1978. See John Findlay and Bruce Hevly, *Atomic Frontier Days* (Seattle: University of Washington Press, 2011), for a comprehensive discussion of the history, politics, and billions of dollars spent to clean up Hanford.

21. DS 210. On July 23, 1976, the defendants filed the identical motion. On December 27, 1976, the motion was denied. DS 256. The defendants did not appeal that ruling. Defendants filed the identical motion in *Prescott v. United States*, the action we filed in 1980 on behalf of Keith Prescott and 220 other NTS workers who joined later. Judge Foley denied the motion. *Prescott v. United States*, 523 F. Supp. 918 (1981). The government appealed and the Ninth Circuit Court of Appeals affirmed his ruling. *Prescott v. United States*, 731 F.2d 1388 (9th Cir. 1984).

22. *Bulloch v. United States*, 145 F. Supp. 824 (D. Utah, October 26, 1956).

23. *Bulloch II*, 95 F.R.D. 123 (D. Utah 1982).

24. *Bulloch v. United States*, 763 F2d. 115 (10th Cir. 1985).

25. *United States Nuclear Tests*, July 1945 through September 1992, DOE/NV-209-REV 15, December 2000, pp. 6–7; *Las Vegas Sun*, January 19, 1956; *Las Vegas Review-Journal*, January 22, 1956. The January 18, 1956, test was the fourth and final test in "Operation Project 56, No. 4, Plutonium Dispersal in Area 11d.

26. *Las Vegas Sun*, August 17, 1980.

27. Ibid.

28. *Prescott v. United States*, 523 F. Supp. 918 (D. Nev. 1981).

29. *Prescott v. United States*, 731 F.2d. 1388 (9th Cir. 1984).

30. DS 520. Motion to Reopen Action or for a New Trial, May 4, 1984. Copy in author's possession.

31. *BEIR III, Biological Effects of Ionizing Radiation* (Washington, D.C.: National Academy Press, 1980).

32. *Lancet*, December 1, 1979, 1195.

33. *Baneberry* Collection, EX B-20; Felix Mitelman, "Relation among Occupational Exposure to Potential Mutagenic/Carcinogenic Agents, Clinical Findings, and Bone Marrow Chromosomes in Acute Nonlymphocytic [myelogenous] Leukemia," *Blood 52, no. 6* (1978): 1229–37.

34. *Allen v. United States*, 599 F. Supp. 247 (D. Utah 1984).

35. DS 522. Supplement to Motion. Copy in author's possession.

36. DS 526. Defendant's Response to Motion. Copy in author's possession.

37. DS 536. Reply in Support of Motion. Copy in author's possession.

38. DS 538. Minute Order denying motion to reopen or for new trial.
39. *Allen v. United States*, 816 F.2d 1417 (10th Cir. 1987).
40. *Begay v. United States*, 768 F.2d 1959 (9th Cir. 1985).
41. *Bulloch v. United States*, 763 D.2d 1115 (10th Cir. 1985).
42. *Consolidated United States Atmospheric Testing Litigation*, 820 F.2d 982 (9th Cir. 1987). Pat Broudy's case was consolidated with the others and dismissed.
43. *Prescott v. United States*, 973 F.2d 696 (9th Cir. 1992).
44. *Radiation Exposure Compensation Act*, 42 U.S.C. Sec. 2210.
45. *Las Vegas Sun*, September 25, 1979.
46. *The Forgotten Guinea Pigs Report, August 1980*, Subcommittee on Oversight and Investigations (Washington, D.C.: U.S. Government Printing Office). Copy in author's possession.
47. I have been unable to source the news article, but that statement is emblazoned in my memory.

Epilogue

THE TWENTY-FIVE-YEAR Baneberry odyssey ended in 1996, but the high and low points of the adventure are as fresh today as they were then.

The most exhilarating moment: Dr. Shields Warren's spell-binding explanation of the Roberts case, supported by Dr. Alice Stewart and Dr. John Gofman at trial, and his bone marrow dose estimate, vindicated posttrial by Dr. Karl Morgan's startling revelation that Dr. Evans had hoodwinked us all.

The most painful moment: watching Harley Roberts struggle to breathe, but determined to fight for justice with his last breath.

The most humorous: Dr. Evans's preposterous effort to sell his cluster theory to Judge Foley.

The most depressing: learning that Judge Foley had telescoped our eight years of preparation and forty-one-day trial into a two-sentence ruling, followed by a somber meeting with Dorothy and Louise.

The most insulting: a journalist questioning our motives for taking on our own government, which in turn was committed "to spend whatever it takes to win."

The irony of Baneberry is that two brothers, who held the AEC in high esteem when it came to town in 1951, became its enemy, unmasking a pattern of deception, cover-up, and intimidation we learned had been standard for decades prior to Baneberry.

On the Baneberry trail, we met many other atomic testing victims, whose stories and travails have been told, and told so well, by academics, historians, lawyers, and journalists.

In 1976, we learned about the mysterious death of Karen Silkwood. We followed the lawsuit closely and reveled in Gerry Spence's stunning victory in May 1979. The Silkwood story was told by Richard Rashke in 1981,[1] humorous anecdotes from the trial by Gerry Spence in 1982,[2] and made into a movie in 1983.[3]

In April 1982, on the eve of the downwinders' trial in Salt Lake City, Harvey Wasserman and Norman Solomon published a shocking exposé about persons exposed to atomic radiation beginning with U.S. soldiers who entered Japan in September 1945 and ending with the Three Mile Island meltdown in 1979.[4] It was the first of many books about radiation effects after our Baneberry trial ended and was highly publicized in Las Vegas.[5]

In 1978, we met Janet Gordon and other residents of southern Utah, who were collecting records of cancer deaths among people exposed to radiation from 1950s atomic tests.

The same year, we met MacArthur Wright, an attorney from St. George, Utah, and Dale Haralson, a lawyer from Tucson, Arizona. They were investigating cancer deaths among people living downwind from NTS. Haralson, Wright, and Stewart Udall filed federal tort claims for downwinders in December 1978.

In 1982, Dale Haralson led a team of lawyers who tried the *Allen* case in Salt Lake City. I was told there was not a dry eye in the courtroom when he ended his closing argument.

Dale Haralson's victory is embodied in Judge Bruce Jenkins's 500-page Memorandum Decision. The downwinders' story is told by Howard Ball, Phillip Fradkin, Richard L. Miller, and A. Constandina Titus.[6] Titus also chronicled Nevada's role in the atomic testing program from 1951 forward: the politics, legal issues, claims, court cases including Baneberry's role, and the early compensation efforts that led to REVCA and RECA.

In December 1978, we read of Martin "Butch" Bardoli, the Nevada boy who lived at the Twin Springs Ranch that borders the Test Site. Martin was exposed to radiation from the early 1950s aboveground tests and died of leukemia in 1956, at age 7.[7] His story was retold in greater detail on April 27, 1979, with a picture of little Martin and his classmates.[8] Martin Bardoli was very probably the first Nevadan to die of leukemia from atomic testing at the Nevada Test Site.[9] But he was not the last.

After Martin Bardoli's mother's complaints were derided,[10] and after Judge Christensen exonerated the AEC for the sheep deaths in October 1956,[11] there was little concern in Las Vegas about the health effects of atomic testing, until Baneberry vented in December 1971.

From July 1972 until April 1974, we watched Harley Roberts progress to the final stages of his leukemia and death. In 1976, we learned that Bill Nunamaker died of leukemia in December 1974.

In 1981, Gloria Gregerson, who watched the early 1950s radioactive clouds shower her home in Bunkerville, Nevada, called me from her hospital bed. Diagnosed with terminal leukemia at forty-one, she was told she was too old for a bone marrow transplant. Gloria was aware Dr. Alice Stewart was in Las Vegas and asked if I would bring her to visit. Dr. Stewart was delighted to meet Gloria, but nothing could be done. Gloria died a few months later.[12]

In 1985, Kenny Case, a Nevadan the AEC proudly dubbed the Atomic Cowboy, was dying of leukemia.[13] I visited him a few weeks before his death.

As Nevadans, Alan and I were primarily concerned with the plight of Nevada Test Site workers. We lost the court cases, but remain convinced of two things. First, Dr. Warren was correct in his conviction that Harley Roberts's bone marrow dose from radiation at Baneberry caused his death. Second, our lawsuits on behalf of Roberts, Nunamaker, Prescott, and 220 other NTS workers helped assure that Nevada Test Site workers were included in RECA when it passed in 1990.

The ultimate irony is that Harley Roberts, who gave his life for the cause, was not eligible for RECA benefits.

NOTES

1. Richard L. Rashke, *The Killing of Karen Silkwood* (Boston: Houghton Mifflin, 1982).

2. Gerry Spence, *Gunning for Justice* (New York: Doubleday, 1982).

3. *Silkwood*, directed by Mike Nichols (December 1983; Los Angeles, CA: 20th Century Fox).

4. Harvey Wasserman and Norman Solomon, *Killing Our Own* (New York: Delacorte Press, 1982).

5. *Las Vegas Sun*, *Las Vegas Sun Magazine*, April 25,1982, "Nuclear test coverups revealed in explosive book."

6. Howard Ball, *Justice Downwind* (New York: Oxford University Press, 1986). Phillip Fradkin, *Fallout* (Tucson: University of Arizona Press, 1989). Richard L. Miller, *Under the Cloud* (New York: Free Press, 1986). A. Constandina Titus, *Bombs in the Backyard* (Reno: University of Nevada Press, 1986; 2nd ed., 2001), Baneberry, 105.

7. *Las Vegas Sun*, December 17, 1978.

8. *Las Vegas Valley Times*, April 27, 1979.

9. Richard L. Miller, *Under the Cloud* (New York: Free Press, 1986), 147, 199–203.

10. Ibid.

11. *Bulloch v. United States*, 145 F. Supp. 824 (D. Utah 1956).

12. We would learn in the early 1980s that Utah children exposed to radiation from the early 1950s atomic tests also died of leukemia. Karlene Hafen died on November 17, 1956, age fourteen, three and one-half years after her home in St. George, Utah, was blanketed with fallout on May 19, 1953, from test *Harry*. Sheldon Nisson, who lived in Washington, Utah, near St. George, died of acute myelogenous leukemia on July 6, 1959, age thirteen, six years after he was exposed to radiation from Harry. See *Allen v. United States*, 597 F. Supp. 247 (D. Utah 1984)

13. Kenny Case, the Atomic Cowboy, is prominently featured at the National Atomic Testing Museum in Las Vegas, Nevada. But there is no mention of the fact that he died of leukemia.

Notes to Sources

The Baneberry story began as a memoir, recollections and ramblings about events that happened decades earlier. But Harley Roberts's and Bill Nunamaker's sacrifice required more. And Dr. Shields Warren, Dr. Alice Stewart, Dr. John Gofman, and Dr. Karl Morgan deserved a detailed and accurate rendition of the scientific and medical issues they presented so elegantly in the Baneberry lawsuit.

Therefore, I opened boxes and bins filled with musty news clippings, pleading files, the 5,400-page trial transcript, trial exhibits, posttrial briefs, posttrial motions, appellate briefs, correspondence files, and the pleadings and documents in *Prescott v. United States, Allen v. United States, Begay v. United States, Silkwood v. Kerr-McGee, Bulloch v. United States* (reopened), *Broudy v. United States*, and *Krumbach v. Dow Chemical.*

Our Baneberry correspondence files enabled me to back up statements about settlement discussions and trial preparation but also to refresh mental impressions of the events.

All documents filed with the court clerk in *Roberts and Nunamaker v. United States*, including nearly sixty depositions, are identified in the clerk's docket sheet. This was important, because we kept only a few depositions and discarded many documents filed in the case.

However, we did preserve the three posttrial motions to reopen the case in 1984, with Dr. Morgan's affidavits attached and Dr. Felix Mitelman's December 1979 publication that discredited Dr. Rowley's reliance upon his earlier paper.

After the Baneberry trial ended in 1979, I read publications by scholars and journalists about the history of nuclear testing and those exposed to radiation from nuclear tests: Wasserman and Solomon, Ball, Titus, Fradkin, and Miller. For Nevadans, Titus captured our unique role in the continental testing program.

The backstory—the politics behind the atomic testing program—came to light after the trial ended in 1979. It has been described by Wasserman and Solomon, Ball, Titus, Fradkin, and Miller, among others. In addition, I was given an in-depth tutorial into those matters by Mary D. Wammack, PhD, who shared with me her doctoral dissertation.[1]

In writing about Baneberry, I strived to tell the story as it unfolded and consciously avoided reliance upon source material collected by others after the Baneberry trial ended. My purpose was to place Baneberry in context and to focus on the bone marrow dose Harley Roberts received and the genesis of his leukemia as understood at the time.

Because Dr. Warren and others explained the scientific and medical issues involved in the case, I did not prepare a comprehensive glossary of terms.

The 5,404-page trial transcript and trial exhibits are housed in the *Baneberry Collection* at UNLV. In the possession of the author are: the trial transcript, trial exhibits, newspaper articles, pleadings, correspondence files, court decisions, posttrial motions, posttrial briefs, the clerk's docket sheet, and briefs filed in the Ninth Circuit Court of Appeals.

NOTES

1. Mary D. Wammack, "Atomic Governance: Militarism, Secrecy and Science in Post-War America, 1945–1958," PhD diss., Dept. of History, University of Nevada, Las Vegas, 2010.

Glossary and Characters

GLOSSARY

AEC: Atomic Energy Commission, created in 1946. In 1975, it was renamed the Energy Research and Development Agency (ERDA). In 1977, it was renamed the Department of Energy (DOE).

Area 12 Camp: Base camp in Area 12 where Harley Roberts and security guards carried out emergency evacuation of 900 Test Site workers after Baneberry vent (see NTS map and Area 12 Camp map).

Baneberry: AEC code name for the underground nuclear test detonated at NTS on December 18, 1970 (see NTS map).

Baneberry vent: Baneberry test released nearly 7 million curies of radiation into the atmosphere in a hammerhead-shaped cloud (see photos of vent cloud).

Beta radiation: Of the three common types of emissions from radioactive materials, beta particles have the medium penetrating power and can generally be stopped by a thin layer of metal or plastic.

BJY: WSI security trailer where Dyer, Roberts, and security force was located at 7:30 AM on December 18, 1970, when Baneberry was detonated (see NTS map).

CP-1: Operation control point where Baneberry Test Manager Frank Cluff and panel of advisors were located (see NTS map).

CP-2: REECo Rad-Safe decontamination facility where Harley Roberts and eighty-five other Test Site workers were decontaminated (see NTS map).

Gamma radiation: Extremely penetrating photon energy, produced by nuclear reactions. Gamma is higher wavelength than x-rays, and unlike alpha and beta radiation does not consist of particles. Gamma radiation, or rays, can be recorded on film badges and measured with Geiger counters.

Geiger counter: Portable instrument issued to Rad-Safe monitors to measure gamma rays.

IGAN: Independent Guard Association of Nevada, guard union that represented security guards employed by Wackenhut Services Inc. (WSI) at the Nevada Test Site.

LASL: Los Alamos Scientific Laboratory, designed and conducted the first nuclear test *Trinity* on July 16, 1945, as well as the first A-bomb test at NTS on January 27, 1951, and the majority of the 1,030 U.S. nuclear tests.

LLL: Lawrence Livermore Laboratory, founded by Nobel Laureate Ernest Lawrence in 1952 as Lawrence Radiation Laboratory (LRL). LLL Designed and detonated nearly one-half of the nuclear tests at NTS, including the Baneberry test.

NTS: Nevada Test Site, named Nevada Proving Grounds when atomic testing began in 1951, changed to NTS in 1955 (see map).

NVO-95: Sixty-four-page *Baneberry Summary Report,* issued January 1971. A sixteen-page edited version of *Baneberry Summary Report* was issued by the AEC on May 14, 1971.

REECo: Reynolds Electrical and Engineering Company, Inc. From 1952 through Baneberry, REECo employed directly or through subcontractors most NTS workers.

Rad-Safe: REECo Radiation Safety Division employed personnel who issued and recorded film badge readings, took radiation readings, and decontaminated the eighty-six men exposed to radiation released in Baneberry vent cloud.

USGS: United States Geological Survey, Department of the Interior, issued *USGS 474-14, Results of Exploration of the Baneberry Site, Early 1971.*

WSI: Wackenhut Services, Inc., employed security guards at NTS.

CHARACTERS

Alice Stewart, MD: British hematologist and epidemiologist who testified that exposure to radiation at Baneberry caused the deaths of Harley Roberts and Bill Nunamaker in 1974.

Bill Cleghorn: IGAN president who initiated the filing of the lawsuit on behalf of thirteen security guards exposed to radiation at Baneberry.

Bill Nunamaker: REECo employee exposed to radiation at Baneberry who died of leukemia in December 1974. In 1976, his widow, Louise Nunamaker, filed a lawsuit, consolidated and tried with Dorothy Roberts's case in 1979.

Ernie Dyer: WSI sergeant in charge of emergency evacuation of Area 12 after Baneberry vent and brother-in-law of Harley Roberts.

Frank Cluff: AEC test manager for Baneberry at CP-1.

Harley Roberts: WSI security guard exposed to radiation while carrying out emergency evacuation of Area 12 Camp. Filed a lawsuit in February 1972, and died in April 1974; his widow, Dorothy Roberts, brought the litigation to trial in 1979.

Janet Rowley, MD: Cytogeneticist at AEC's Mclean Hospital in Chicago, testified for the AEC that Harley Roberts's C-7 chromosome deletion was not caused by Baneberry but by exposure to petroleum products ten years prior to Baneberry.

John Gofman, MD, PhD: UC Berkeley professor of medicine (emeritus). As rebuttal witness, testified that leukemia deaths of Harley Roberts and Bill Nunamaker were caused by Baneberry, that Robley Evans's bone marrow did not include internal exposure, and that Janet Rowley's opinion that Roberts's leukemia was caused by exposure to petroleum products was not supported by scientific evidence.

Karl Morgan, PhD: Health physicist reviewed Robley Evans's bone marrow dose calculations and supplied posttrial affidavits that inhalation of radionuclides increased Roberts's bone marrow dose twenty times Evans's trial estimate.

Robley Evans, PhD: MIT physicist who had studied radiation effects and testified for the government. He performed calculations of Harley Roberts's bone marrow dose and offered his theory of "the clustering of rare events" as an explanation for the occurrence of two leukemias among eighty-six men exposed at Baneberry.

Roger D. Foley: U.S. district judge who presided over the Baneberry trial in 1979 and issued his judgment in 1985.

Shields Warren, MD: Harvard Professor of Medicine (emeritus). Testified at trial that Harley Roberts's exposure to radiation at Baneberry caused the deletion of chromosome C-7 that resulted in Roberts's leukemia and death in 1974.

About the Authors

LARRY C. JOHNS was born in Las Vegas, Nevada, on December 23, 1944, the youngest (along with his twin sister) of five children of Ray M. Johns and Helen H. Johns, longtime schoolteachers who retired from the Clark County School District in the 1970s. Larry attended elementary school, junior high, and Las Vegas High School, graduating in 1962. He attended college at North Texas University his freshman year, then transferred to the University of Arizona, where he completed his BA in 1966 (French/history) and Juris Doctor degree in 1968 at the College of Law.

He married Mary Pratt on June 4, 1966, in Tucson, Arizona. They have four children, Charles Johns, Laura (Johns) Bolhouse, Julianna (Johns) Cumiskey, Jason Johns, and seven grandchildren.

He returned to Las Vegas in 1968 and was admitted to practice law in Nevada in October 1968, Nevada Bar #1895. He served as Deputy District Attorney for Clark County, where he tried many felony cases. In 1971, he and co-author and brother, Alan Johns, formed a law partnership, Johns and Johns, Ltd. From 1971 to present, he and Alan tried hundreds of civil and criminal cases (primarily jury trials), as well as the *Baneberry* and *Prescott* cases. He has briefed and argued over two dozen cases in the Nevada Supreme Court and the Ninth Circuit Court of Appeals and filed Petitions for Certiorari in the United States Supreme Court.

From 1998 to the present, in addition to his private law practice, he has been appointed by the Clark County District Court to serve as an Arbitrator and Short Trial Judge in over a hundred civil cases.

He joined the Nevada Trial Lawyers Association and the Association of Trial Lawyers of America (ATLA) in 1975 and was active until 2002. In 1993, he was selected to membership in the Nevada American Inns of Court, Lloyd D. George Chapter, and remained active until 2005.

ALAN R. JOHNS

ALAN R. JOHNS was born in Dalton, Nebraska, on September 8, 1938. He came to Las Vegas with his parents, Ray and Helen Johns, his elder sister, Judy Johns, and younger brother, Ronald Johns, in August 1942. The primary author of the book, Larry C. Johns, and his twin sister, Linda, were born in Las Vegas.

After graduating from Las Vegas High School in 1956, Alan obtained his BA degree and Juris Doctor degree at the University of Colorado. He was admitted to practice law in Colorado in 1962 and in Nevada in 1963.

In 1963 Alan joined the Army Reserves, completed his basic training, and was honorably discharged in 1969. He married Loretta Jung on June 6, 1964 in Las Vegas, and they have three sons, Tristram Johns, Gregory Johns, and Brian Johns, and eight grandchildren.

Alan served in the Clark County District Attorney's office and was chief criminal deputy from 1963 to 1970. From 1974 through 1975 he served as Special Prosecutor for Clark County. He has practiced both criminal and civil law before all Nevada courts and administrative agencies, the U.S. District Court, Ninth Circuit Court of Appeals, and the U.S. Supreme Court. He has also served as an Arbitrator, Mediator, Judge Pro Tempore, and Supreme Court Settlement Judge.

Index